ASSAD

OR WE BURN
THE COUNTRY

ASSAD
OR WE BURN
THE COUNTRY

HOW ONE FAMILY'S LUST
FOR POWER DESTROYED SYRIA

SAM DAGHER

Little, Brown and Company
New York Boston London

Little, Brown and Company
Hachette Book Group
1290 Avenue of the Americas, New York, NY 10104
littlebrown.com

First Edition: May 2019

Little, Brown and Company is a division of Hachette Book Group, Inc. The Little, Brown name and logo are trademarks of Hachette Book Group, Inc.

The publisher is not responsible for websites (or their content) that are not owned by the publisher.

The Hachette Speakers Bureau provides a wide range of authors for speaking events. To find out more, go to hachettespeakersbureau.com or call (866) 376-6591.

ISBN 978-0-316-55672-9
Library of Congress Control Number: 2019936190

10 9 8 7 6 5 4 3 2 1

LSC-C

Printed in the United States of America

To the Syrians who rose up to demand freedom and dignity: Your heroism, sacrifice, and story will never be obscured by lies.

The youth o' mother heard freedom was at the gate, they came out to chant for it...

—Samih Choukair, *Ya Heif*

Contents

Contents

Syria

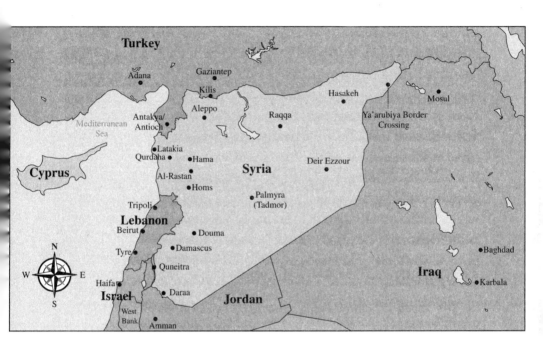

Damascus

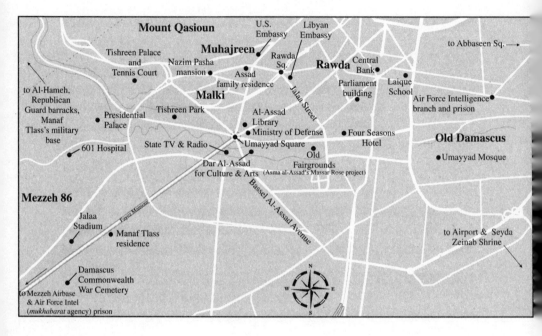

Mount Qasioun

U.S. Embassy

Libyan Embassy

Tishreen Palace and Tennis Court

Muhajreen

Nazim Pasha mansion

Rawda Sq.

Rawda

Central Bank

to Abbaseen Sq. →

Assad family residence

Parliament building

Laique School

to Al-Hameh, Republican Guard barracks, Manaf Tlass's military base

Malki

Jalaa Street

Air Force Intelligence branch and prison

Presidential Palace

Tishreen Park

Al-Assad Library

Ministry of Defense

Four Seasons Hotel

Old Damascus

601 Hospital

State TV & Radio

Umayyad Square

Old Fairgrounds
(Asma al-Assad's Massar Rose project)

Umayyad Mosque

Dar Al-Assad for Culture & Arts

Bassel Al-Assad Avenue

Mezzeh 86

Jalaa Stadium

Fayez Mansour

Manaf Tlass residence

to Airport & Seyda Zeinab Shrine

Damascus Commonwealth War Cemetery

to Mezzeh Airbase & Air Force Intel (mukhabarat agency) prison

N
W   E
S

Inside the Palace

Assad Family

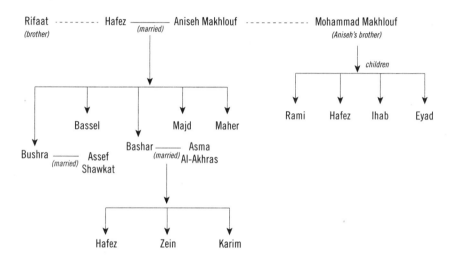

Mohammad Nasif Kheirbek, AKA Abu Wael
(longtime mukhabarat *chief and father-figure and mentor to Bashar al-Assad [He died in 2015])*

Tlass Family

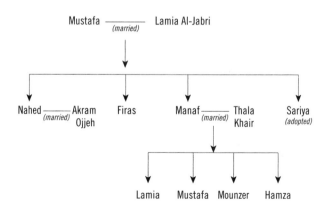

Outside the Palace

Mazen Darwish (Damascus human rights lawyer, activist, protest
   organizer, cofounder of local coordination committees/LCCs)
Yara Bader (journalist, activist, Mazen's wife)
Razan Zeitouneh (cofounder LCCs, Mazen's colleague)
Khaled al-Khani (painter, activist, protest organizer, 1982 Hama
   Massacre survivor)
Dr. Hikmat al-Khani (Khaled's father)
Sally Masalmeh (activist and youth leader in southern city of Daraa)
Fadi and Shaker (Sally's brothers)
Malek al-Jawabra (Sally's husband)

Introduction

The idea for this book was born during a trip from the Middle East to the United States toward the end of 2014, three months after I had been kicked out of Damascus by the Assad regime and put on its *mukhabarat* (secret police) watch list, without even being allowed to collect my belongings.

"Count your blessings, you're so lucky, you got away lightly," my Syrian friends kept saying. I could have disappeared in a *mukhabarat* prison, or worse, and the regime would have probably blamed it on "armed terrorist groups," they told me.

I had been the only Western reporter permanently based in Damascus. One year before my expulsion, I was detained by regime militiamen and briefly held in an underground *mukhabarat* prison, and I continued to face threats and intimidation after my release. Of course, what happened to me were mere inconveniences compared to what Syrians have had to endure under this regime. Perhaps I was simply lucky, or perhaps I was spared a much worse fate because I had been living and working legally inside Damascus, or maybe the regime reckoned that a spat over a US reporter was unnecessary at that particular moment in 2014 when America was fixated on Abu Bakr al-Baghdadi and the Islamic State (known as ISIS or, in Arabic, Daesh) and not on Bashar al-Assad and his war crimes. The regime and its patron Iran wanted to be Barack Obama's partners in the war on ISIS.

I had started reporting from Damascus in October 2012; earlier that year, two of my generation's best reporters, Marie Colvin and Anthony Shadid, had died while doing their job inside Syria. A Syrian *mukhabarat* chief would tell me two years later that the regime's targeting of the house where Marie was staying in a rebel-controlled section of the city of Homs was "justifiable" because she and other Western reporters had, as he put it, "embedded with the terrorists." It was in Homs that I witnessed, over almost two years, the aftermath of the pure terror unleashed by the Assads on a city that dared challenge their rule.

"They have even erased our names," said Abu Rami tearfully as we stood at the entrance of his apartment building in central Homs on the morning of June 18, 2014. A large burn mark and mangled wires were all that was left of the building's intercom, the work of looters who had ripped out the box and set the wires on fire to get at the copper. The flames had consumed the tenants' names that had been neatly handwritten in green next to each buzzer. The Arabic-letter equivalents of "B" and "R" were all that remained of Abu Rami's label.

Like vultures, the looters had meticulously stripped every apartment in Abu Rami's building, including his, down to its bare bones, taking the furniture, doors, windows, bathroom and kitchen fixtures, and even tiles. After being cleaned out, the apartments were set ablaze. Abu Rami's home library, evidently deemed worthless by the looters, was now a pile of ash. I followed Abu Rami to the balcony, where a few incinerated potted plants stood in the corner. We looked out onto an incredible scene.

Every building in the district had been subjected to the same systematic pillaging and arson. The entire street and neighborhood was awash in mounds of debris mixed in with the remains of people's lives—gutted teddy bears, crushed toys, abandoned school notebooks and photo albums, empty and battered suitcases, broken furniture. It was as if a hurricane had swept through central Homs, just a month after it reverted to Bashar al-Assad's control following a vicious three-year siege and bombing campaign intended to strangle communities that rebelled against him. Bashar made people choose between starving to death and surrendering to him, and when they had done one or the other, or fled the country altogether, he declared victory.

"Long Live Assad's Syria—Assad or We Burn the Country," was sprayed in big bold black letters on Abu Rami's building.

By the time this book comes out, the Assad family will have been in power for nearly half a century, outlasting eight US presidents starting with Richard Nixon.

Introduction

While the Islamic State's black-clad barbarian-like terrorists horrified people everywhere and dictated much of Western policy in Syria, the truth is that Bashar, a mild-mannered former eye doctor trained in the West and married to a glamorous British-born former investment banker, was the one chiefly responsible for the mayhem, destruction, and intense human suffering that consumed Syria and reverberated across the Middle East and world between 2011 and 2018. Bashar commanded and directed the army officers and soldiers, the *mukhabarat* bosses and agents, and the legions of militiamen doing most of the killing, and he was empowered by the extraordinary support he received from his allies and backers—Iran; the Lebanese militia, Hezbollah; and then, crucially, the Russian military.

When it comes to Syria, one often hears these arguments: *Everyone has blood on their hands. Bashar may be bad but ISIS is worse. There are no good guys in Syria.* Or more analytically: *This is a civil war that turned into a complex multilayered conflict and drew in regional and world powers.*

There are elements of truth in all these assertions, but there's one truth which can never be obscured: Bashar and his family, motivated by their quest to cling to power at any cost, were directly responsible for decisions and actions that turned the peaceful protests of the spring of 2011 into a devastating, years-long war and facilitated the rise and spread of ISIS—a truth buttressed by new evidence and details revealed in this book.

For the first time, I lay bare what went on in Bashar's innermost circle during the fateful period between March 18, 2011, when the first Syrian protesters were shot dead, and August 18, 2011, when President Obama said that Bashar must step down. I examine Bashar's decision to release Islamist militants from prison a few months into the popular uprising and deliberately abandon key outposts and regions on the Iraq–Syria border in early 2013 at the precise moment ISIS was emerging; through my hard-won access to regime insiders, I investigate the regime's rationale for using chemical weapons.

In the spring of 2016, I was in Geneva covering the UN-mediated peace talks between the Syrian regime and opposition (talks that Bashar skillfully turned into a charade and time-wasting exercise under the auspices of the Americans and Russians), when the UN envoy to Syria at the time, Staffan de Mistura, announced that the Syrian death toll had reached 400,000.[1]

The death meter has not stopped. Following de Mistura's report, tens of thousands more would suffocate to death, be incinerated, or get slashed to pieces from the airstrikes, incendiary rockets, ballistic missiles, cluster bombs, barrel bombs, chlorine bombs, and chemical weapons launched by either the Syrian regime or the Russian military. Not to mention those who would die because of lack of access to food and medicine due to sieges imposed principally by Bashar and his allies. Neither ISIS nor any of the rebel factions fighting Bashar possessed the Russian-made attack helicopters and fighter jets that rained death on civilians in opposition-held areas day after day and year after year under the watchful eyes of the international community and the pretext of "fighting terrorism." By early 2018, Russian President Vladimir Putin was boasting that he had already tested more than two hundred new weapons in Syria.[2]

Thousands more Syrians, mostly activists and protesters who resisted the regime peacefully, were hanged by sham military tribunals at the Saydnaya prison near Damascus,[3] exactly as Bashar's father, Hafez, had done at the Tadmor prison in the Homs desert four decades before. And just as in Hafez's era, the lives of many more Syrians were taken by medieval torture techniques in the *mukhabarat* secret prisons and dungeons located in the heart of Damascus's residential neighborhoods or at the notorious 601 Military Hospital, a five-minute drive from the palace where Bashar received successive UN envoys trying to negotiate peace in Syria. Photos of emaciated and numbered cadavers stacked at the hospital's hangar horrified the world, at least until the world's attention shifted to ISIS.[4] Ultimately, all those killed by ISIS terrorists in both Iraq and Syria represented a mere fraction of the Assad regime's victims.

Of course, the more than twelve million Syrians (about half the total population) who were either uprooted internally or had to flee the country altogether to neighboring states and beyond were not just escaping Bashar and his killing machine.[5] In fact, hundreds of thousands of them opted to stay under his regime's thumb in Assad-controlled areas, including the capital, Damascus, a reality I witnessed myself from 2012 until my expulsion in 2014. Bashar exploited the misery and desperation of average Syrians and used food rations doled out by UN humanitarian agencies based in his territories and operating according to his rules and restrictions as rewards to those who obeyed him and as weapons against those who defied him. Ironically, much of this food was paid for by the same foreign powers that were trying to topple him.

At the heart of this story are sons and daughters wrestling with their parents' choices and legacies.

From the moment that Bashar, an awkward and painfully shy second son, emerged as the substitute heir after the death of his eldest brother in the mid-1990s, he was on a quest to slay his inner demons and, in a way, the ghost of his still-omnipresent and powerful father, Hafez. Bashar set out to prove that he could be as cutthroat and ruthless as his father, if not more so, while also projecting youthfulness, reform, and dynamism. "There's no other way to govern our society except with the shoe over people's heads," a thirty-year-old Bashar told a private gathering in the summer of 1995, one year into his mentorship to inherit power from Hafez, as the regime's propagandists portrayed him as the "savior" who was going to fight corruption, reform the system, and usher Syria into the twenty-first century. The same script would be used by other ailing Middle Eastern despots to bequeath power to their sons.

At Bashar's side was Manaf Tlass, a handsome rising star in the Republican Guard force, who was among those enlisted by Hafez to assist and promote his heir. The Assad and Tlass children grew up together as practically one family, and the Tlass patriarch, Mustafa, was a pillar of the regime and, as Hafez often said, its gatekeeper. The fathers had been friends and lifetime companions from the time they were ambitious and scrappy twenty-something cadets in the early 1950s, as Syria and other Arab states grappled with their newly won independence from colonial powers. Manaf's father, Mustafa, accompanied Hafez every step of the way to the pinnacle of power and faithfully served him for fifty years. Together they wrote the manual for crushing all challenges to the regime, which they applied in the 1970s and '80s with horrific results. Mustafa was willing to kill to protect what he and Hafez had constructed, but was his son Manaf prepared to do the same? As the Arab Spring arrived in Syria in 2011, Manaf had to make decisions and choices that would forever alter his life.

Syria was at a crossroads. Outside the presidential palace walls we meet Mazen Darwish, a thirty-something human rights lawyer and free speech advocate, who had been agitating for real reform for nearly a decade. He saw the Arab Spring as the best chance to achieve what his own parents and an older generation of opposition leaders, jailed and persecuted for their non-conformist political beliefs, had long aspired to but could never attain under the Assads. The promise of the Spring also drew Khaled al-Khani, an artist who struggled for years to overcome the childhood trauma and deep family loss provoked by Hafez al-Assad's assault on his hometown of Hama in 1982. In conservative southern Syria, meanwhile, eighteen-year-old Sally Masalmeh, was captivated by the Arab Spring and, like so many of Syria's restless youth sensed an opportunity to find her voice and identity and free herself from the shackles of authoritarianism, the "voluntary servitude" often consented to by the older generation and "brutish masses," as the French humanist Étienne de La Boétie wrote in the sixteenth century.[6] Sally shrugged off her parents' warnings—"it will be just like Hama 1982," they kept saying—to embrace what she and other Syrian youth called the revolution.

How has this brutal dynasty survived for this long—from the moment Hafez seized absolute power in the fall of 1970 until Bashar appeared to emerge victorious by the end of 2018—and why has it gotten away with murder each time?

The Assad clan has embedded itself in the fabric of Syrian society and unscrupulously manipulated class and religion fissures to empower itself, effectively co-opting Syria's national identity. Syria became *Souriya al-Assad* ("Assad's Syria"). In much the same way and to the same ends, the Assads have been masterful in exploiting the divisions and bloody power struggles endemic throughout the Middle East. Further, both father and son relied on big lies to win the support of large segments of the Syrian population.

But all lies eventually wear off or are exposed. The Assads knew this. Deception was not enough. There had to be fear and terror maintained and applied by a sprawling and web-like internal security and intelligence apparatus, known as the *mukhabarat*, that monitored and controlled every facet of public and private life in Syria.

But another crucial constant emerges throughout this story: the Assads could not have survived if it were not for the way Western powers, democracies that profess to defend universal liberal values like human rights and freedom, have engaged with this turbulent and strategic corner of the world. Over the decades, the shortsighted and opportunistic bargains that Western powers have struck with almost all of the Middle East's despots and kleptocrats, not just the Assads, have never taken the interests of ordinary citizens into consideration.

After the Second World War, successive US administrations viewed the newly independent states of the Levant and Arabian Peninsula, including Syria, mainly through the prism of the Cold War struggle with the Soviet Union. Washington's priorities were to secure oil supplies and find a solution to the Arab-Israeli conflict. Few of the Middle East's rising tyrants knew how to exploit this broader geostrategic game better than Hafez al-Assad. By the mid-1970s, Hafez, who was busy enshrining a cultish dictatorship in Syria, received military aid and support from the Soviet Union at the same time that he was getting recognition and financial aid from the US and its rich Gulf Arab allies. There was an unspoken but well-understood quid pro quo with Washington: Hafez was free to do everything he needed to do to maintain his iron grip at home as long as he never waged war against Israel after 1973. Jimmy Carter later called Hafez a "strong and moderate" leader.

"Realpolitik" was cited by France when its president, François Mitterrand, flew to Damascus in the mid-1980s to meet with Hafez even though his own government and intelligence services had ample proof that the Assad regime was connected to terror attacks against French and Western interests in Lebanon and Europe. Terrorism was a "bargaining chip" for the Assads, noted one French official. After the collapse of the Berlin Wall in 1989, Hafez wasted no time in switching sides and joined the US-led coalition to confront Saddam Hussein, another regional despot propped up by the West and its oil-rich Arab allies in the struggle against Iran, before Hussein made the miscalculation of invading Kuwait. Hafez's reward was financial support from Gulf dynasties, free rein in Lebanon as it emerged from its civil war, and the space and resources to burnish his brutal regime's image and prepare for a transfer of power to his son.

Bill Clinton embraced Hafez and his regime in the hopes of going down in history as the US president who brokered comprehensive Arab-Israeli peace. All Hafez really cared about, though, was preserving his family's rule, winning respectability and recognition from the United States, and removing his regime from Washington's list of state sponsors of terrorism. "It seems to me he is poised and someone who is ready to assume his duties. I was very encouraged by his desire to follow in his father's footsteps," declared Clinton's last secretary of state, Madeleine Albright, as Bashar assumed power from Hafez in a coronation choreographed by Mustafa Tlass.[7] Bashar and his beautiful British-born wife, Asma, were feted as young Arab reformers.

For a time after the September 11 attacks, Bashar was a partner in Washington's global war on terror. Syria was one of the destinations of the Central Intelligence Agency's infamous rendition program during the George W. Bush administration. Bashar's calculus changed, however, as the United States prepared to invade neighboring Iraq and, along with France and other allies, sought to hem in the Syrians in Lebanon. The assassination of Lebanese leader Rafic Hariri was an "act of terrorism" for which Bashar's regime and its allies were responsible, announced the West in early 2005. But by then, America's need to get out of the Iraq War quagmire took precedence over accountability and justice. A bipartisan congressional report recommended engaging with Bashar once more to convince him to end his and his *mukhabarat*'s support for the Iraqi insurgency and shut down the pipeline of jihadists and suicide bombers flocking to Iraq through Syria to kill both Iraqis and American soldiers.

In the lead-up to the Obama administration, Bashar was no longer the Iran-backed villain and pariah but instead was once more the reformer supposedly doing his best to better his people's lot despite severe internal and external challenges and pressures. Nancy Pelosi, who at the time became the first female House Speaker, flew in for lunch with Bashar and Asma, while the stars of American and British TV news clamored to interview the Assad couple. Later John Kerry, who was at the time a US senator heading the powerful Foreign Relations Committee, told France's ambassador to Syria that Bashar was "a man we could do business with" because he had given his word that he would stop supporting insurgents and terrorist groups in Iraq.[8]

Even a few months into the 2011 Arab Spring revolts, the United States and its Western allies believed that Bashar did not necessarily have to step down like the dictators of Egypt, Libya, Tunisia, and Yemen, and that he could even be the one to implement the changes demanded by the people, underscoring how little they understood the Assad regime. From the onset, Bashar knew that the price of any real and meaningful concessions was going to be his own head. Facts revealed for the first time in this book show that Bashar's immediate impulse was to issue shoot-to-kill orders to his security forces in order to scare peaceful protesters off the streets.

Obama was absolutely right, of course, about not wanting to send US troops each time there was a crisis in the Middle East. But his approach to a fast-developing situation in Syria, that looked certain to have major life-and-death consequences for average Syrians and a wider impact on the whole world, was flawed from the start; one experienced Middle East analyst described it to me as a "catastrophic moral failure." I have no doubt that Obama and many members of his team were genuinely horrified by what Bashar was doing to his people and wanted to do everything they could to stop it, but at the same time, the 2003 invasion of Iraq and its consequences were still very much on the minds of Obama and ardent noninterventionists in his administration.

So the result was a middle-of-the-road approach in Syria that attempted to meld the twin goals of stopping Bashar's killing machine and making absolutely sure that the United States remained at arm's length from the whole conflict. For example, instead of taking concrete and bold actions to support the heroic protesters and activists who took to the streets, and the soldiers who defected rather than kill their fellow Syrians, the job was relegated to regional powers deemed to be US allies, like Qatar, Turkey, and Saudi Arabia. Qatar and Turkey, for their part, wanted to co-opt the change movements sweeping the Arab world and to empower their local Islamist protégés—and Syria was no exception. Saudi Arabia, at the same time, worked to stop Qatar and Turkey for an entirely different reason: the

Arab Spring was a direct threat to its own ruling family's legitimacy and grip on power, so the freedom movements had to be either controlled or smothered. Meanwhile, Bashar's patron and regional protector, Iran, was not just going to sit back and lose Syria, a crucial link in a line of Iranian power and influence extending from Tehran to Beirut via Baghdad and Damascus.

These poisonous regional conflicts and the West's reticence and caution gave Bashar and his backers ample time to decimate those resisting peacefully and to turn the standoff into an armed struggle fueled by sectarian extremists on both sides. Right in front of me, the Assad regime's henchmen mocked Obama's calls on Bashar to relinquish power and his warnings over chemical weapons use because they had calculated—correctly, it turned out—that these were merely words.

The complexity of the conflict became an excuse not to consider meaningful steps like a limited no-fly zone in parts of Syria, which, very early on, would have saved lives and stemmed the tide of refugees. The United States and its allies could comfort themselves with the notion that they were trying to do something, but it was the Russians and Chinese who were obstructing at the UN Security Council. Bashar dug in and was effectively given license to ratchet up his atrocities. The chemical-weapons attack of the summer of 2013 and Obama's vacillation in response were simply the culmination of an already failed and even cynical Western policy in Syria—practically an invitation by the West to Vladimir Putin to intervene further in Syria. It then became much easier for the West to rationalize its actions in Syria when choices were whittled down to either Bashar al-Assad or the barbarians of ISIS who were attacking Europe.

Understanding how the Syrian people have arrived at this moment has never been more crucial if the goal is to someday put an end to the scourge of terror and extremism and have real change and stability in the Middle East.

ASSAD

OR WE BURN
THE COUNTRY

1

You're Next, Doctor

Spring was beginning to return to Damascus on the February morning in 2011 that Bashar al-Assad played tennis with his friend and army general Manaf Tlass. The patchy grass lawns in nearby Tishreen Park had been seeded, and overgrown hedges had been given an overdue trim. The clay tennis court was nestled in a wooded grove within the Tishreen Palace compound, where the Assad family often hosted foreign guests.

A massive Syrian flag whipped in the wind some 300 feet above the court. Installed the previous July, the flag marked the tenth anniversary of Bashar's ascension to power as president. A large celebration had been held in the park at its unveiling; the prime minister spoke on the occasion and schoolchildren sang patriotic songs while waving heart-shaped cardboard cutouts of Bashar's face.[1]

As Bashar and Manaf began their match that day in February, Manaf sensed that his tennis partner was distracted and downbeat. The tall (over six feet), slender, and athletic Bashar, who had turned forty-five a few months earlier, normally relished physical activity as a reprieve from his often dull presidential duties. He was a fierce competitor and served hard as he fixed his blue eyes on opponents across the net. But today he seemed unfocused; something was not right, Manaf thought.

Manaf hit the ball with his racket, *thwack!*

Suddenly the flag looming overhead cracked violently in the wind, almost like a loud thunder snap. Rattled by the sound, Bashar dropped his racket.[2]

"Calm down, there's nothing to fear," Manaf said with a smile, trying

3

to put his friend at ease. Bashar laughed nervously and, in a moment, they returned to the game.

Bashar had much to fear that winter. In mid-January, a popular uprising toppled the head of a corrupt, entrenched regime in the North African state of Tunisia that for years had been backed by the West and the Arabian Peninsula's oil-rich dynasties. The Tunisian army broke from the ruler and sided with the people. More significant were the protests that engulfed the US-supported leader of Egypt, the long-ruling former army general who was grooming his son to inherit the presidency. Libya, sandwiched between Egypt and Tunisia, was also on the brink of revolt against the maniacal ex–army officer who held power. Saudi Arabia's monarchs, who had a long history of sponsoring strongmen across the region, looked on with trepidation as demonstrations gripped their poor southern neighbor Yemen and threatened fellow royals on the island of Bahrain, just across from their oil fields.

Arab regimes seemed stunned in disbelief as elation and a sense of liberation spread through the streets. It appeared nothing could stand in the face of the people's will. Comparisons were made to the fall of the Berlin Wall in 1989 and the revolutions that swept through the Communist-bloc countries of Eastern Europe afterward. The thinking was that, as in Eastern Europe, the Arab world's sclerotic regimes and merciless police states would collapse one by one like dominoes. The newfound and much-yearned-for *hurriyeh*, or freedom, would spread like the brilliant wildflowers that had just begun sprouting throughout the countryside near Damascus as winter drew to a close that year. It would be an Arab Spring.

Many were already betting that the Assad family, which had ruled for forty years, was next.

The family's ruthless guardians, however, saw matters differently. "It is impossible for Syria to witness anything of the sort...everything is under control...Syria is immune from the turmoil," was the unanimous conclusion in the written reports Bashar received from his multiple intelligence and security services.[3]

These assurances should have been enough to comfort Bashar and put his mind at ease. After all, these agencies and the myriad branches attached to them constituted the backbone of Syria's police state. Collectively known as the *mukhabarat*, they operated above any law and were responsible for watching the army, the government, every Syrian citizen—and each other. No detail of daily life eluded their scrutiny and control. It was as if America's CIA, FBI, and NSA worked nonstop to suppress any hint of criticism of the US president.

The mere mention of the *mukhabarat* horrified most Syrians. The common saying was that one could "disappear behind the sun" for doing anything that might upset the *mukhabarat*, a romantic euphemism for rotting in a prison cell with nobody knowing your whereabouts. The *mukhabarat* believed that the terror it had worked so hard for decades to instill in every Syrian's heart remained potent.[4] Even so, all the usual suspects were summoned one by one for a "cup of coffee" with senior *mukhabarat* officers who reminded them about the catastrophic consequences of rebellion.[5]

Meanwhile, the regime guardians bolstered their young leader with affirmation: Syrians adore you. Why should they protest? Your reformist and visionary leadership is miles ahead of the Arab world's restless youth. You have already implemented the Arab Spring's lofty ideals and slogans like "Bread, Freedom, and Social Justice." You are on the cusp of transforming Syria and the entire region. At forty-five, you have absolutely nothing in common with the Middle East's geriatric leaders who made peace with "our enemy" Israel and have been propped up for decades by America, Europe, and the petrodollars of Gulf Arab states.

The gist of the *mukhabarat* reports served as Bashar's talking points at the end of January 2011, when he was interviewed by American reporters from the *Wall Street Journal*.[6] The message was echoed by Bashar's articulate and stylish wife, Asma, a few weeks later when she hosted Harvard's Arab Alumni Association in Damascus. "Our identity must become that of a learning region…opening ourselves to new perspectives…adopting new skills," Asma told the accomplished Arabs.[7]

In those early months of 2011, when Arab masses were intoxicated with *thawra*, or revolution, and many Syrians secretly yearned to liberate themselves from the fear, humiliation, and deception they had been living under for almost half a century, the regime's greatest hope was that the narrative it worked years to construct, about Bashar and his leadership, his wife, and his vision, would shield it from the fever sweeping the region.

The narrative was something like this: Bashar was a genuinely nice guy. Educated, polite, modest, and even nerdy, he abandoned his career as an ophthalmologist and became his father's heir because he wanted to reform Syria and lead it into the twenty-first century. He was battling the system's corrupt and deep-rooted old guard. He was making great strides, but it was no easy task and he should be allowed more time. Complicating his mission were external factors like war and instability in neighboring Iraq and Lebanon, as well as conspiracies hatched by Syria's enemies, chiefly the United States and Israel. Syria's alliance with Iran and what the regime called "resistance movements," like the Lebanese militia Hezbollah, should make every Arab proud. Better ties with Turkey and rapprochement with the West and rich Gulf monarchies toward the end of the first decade of his rule were an extension of the maverick politics of his late father, Hafez al-Assad, "the builder of modern Syria."

The young leader's wife, Asma, was a bonus—two for the price of one. The pretty and intelligent British-born daughter of a Syrian surgeon had also abandoned a comfortable life in the West and a career in investment banking because she loved Bashar and shared his vision for a new Syria. While many focused on her designer outfits and stiletto heels, Asma worked hard on nurturing early-childhood learning, supporting rural women, and preserving cultural heritage.[8] The story was that Bashar and the first lady were on a quest to create an enlightened, empowered, and prosperous Syrian citizenry.

As proof of how modern and progressive the presidential couple were, their marriage transcended religious divides, he Alawite (a minority religion) and she Sunni (like the majority of Syrians)—not that this mattered in the secular Syria painted by the regime, of course. Showing that the couple also had the common touch was central to the narrative. They were pictured playing with their children at a Damascus park, biking and hiking in the countryside, and dining with the people at a traditional eatery. The president and his wife surrounded themselves with young friends, advisers and assistants who acted like them and shared their ethos and perspective.

Manaf Tlass and his wife, Thala Khair, were pivotal members of this cast of characters. Manaf, three years older than Bashar, was more than just a general in the Republican Guard, a kind of praetorian army unit charged with the president's security. The two men were close intimates, practically family. Manaf's father, Mustafa, the former defense minister, was the lifelong companion of Bashar's father, Hafez. They met as cadets in their twenties at the military academy and rose up together when their Baath Party seized power in 1963. Mustafa helped his friend neutralize all his party rivals and secure his power in a coup d'état in 1970 under the guise of reform. Mustafa served Hafez with unwavering loyalty until the elder Assad's death in 2000, and he was the chief kingmaker during the transfer of power to Bashar. The Assad and Tlass children had grown up together over the years. For a long time, Bashar addressed Manaf's parents *khaleh* and *ammou*—"aunt" and "uncle" in Arabic.[9]

Manaf was in the president's innermost circle and had direct access to him, even though he had not attained his father's status and had to contend with those—particularly Bashar's maternal cousins, the Makhloufs—who were intent on pushing the Tlasses out of this power orbit. Manaf, however, had something none of the other courtiers possessed: he and his wife, Thala, were strikingly charming and good-looking. With his boyish appearance, casual style, broad shoulders, shaggy salt-and-pepper hair, and frequent stubble, Manaf looked more like a movie star than an army general in a despotic Middle Eastern state.

Thala was beautiful, pedigreed, and interested in culture and education. She helped start one of the first model private primary schools, and the couple supported Syrian artists and collected their works. They led a busy and colorful social life, mingling with a young, hip crowd. Manaf was a movie buff, with encyclopedic knowledge of cinema and its techniques. In another life he could have been a film director.

One of the couple's favorite haunts was Marmar, a bar tucked in the alleyways of the charming historic center, which screened artsy foreign movies during the week and featured live performers and funky DJs on the weekend. The luncheons and parties Manaf and his wife hosted at their spectacular mountaintop retreat near Damascus were the talk of the town. Their friendship with Bashar and Asma meant Manaf and Thala were eagerly sought out by members of the Damascene upper crust and all those who wanted to get ahead or simply get things done in a country where navigating the layers of bureaucracy and the *mukhabarat*'s vagaries was no small feat.

In a way, Manaf and Thala's lifestyle and outlook accentuated and sustained the carefully constructed narrative of Bashar and his more open and youthful rule. Bashar knew this and endorsed it.

Bashar genuinely believed he was a reformer, but of course within the parameters and timetable set by him and his police state, and he wanted to believe the *mukhabarat*'s assurances about the power of the narrative, but experience had taught him to question their methods and motives. Bashar could not ignore the region's dramatic events and early signs in Syria itself. Everything pointed to trouble ahead for the regime.

Manaf saw his friend's confidence waver. On some days Bashar seemed untouched by the threat and confident of the regime's staying power, while on others he seemed to grow agitated and apprehensive. The insecurities Bashar worked all his life to suppress seemed to be resurging, Manaf observed. This was, after all, a man who on many occasions boasted to Manaf about his detachment, rationality, and coldness in tackling all matters, whether private or public.[10] To the world, Bashar appeared like a man who wore a steel armor shielding him from all human impulses. Manaf was one of the few who could see through this armor. They grew up together and remained close; Manaf witnessed Bashar's transformation from a painfully shy and tormented child and adolescent to the strong but reformist leader he craved to be.

The alarm sounded for Bashar and the region's autocrats after the eruption of massive protests in Egypt in late January 2011.[11] The world was transfixed by the sight of millions of Egyptians taking to the streets and occupying Cairo's central Tahrir Square. In the age of satellite TV channels and online social media, the slogans, defiance, and public outpouring of years of pent-up anger and frustration spread like wildfire, terrifying every Arab leader. What people might have spoken about behind closed doors was now in the open. The genie was out of the bottle. The floodgates had burst. If it could happen in *Masr*, or Egypt, then it could happen anywhere.

Many Syrians—aching to overcome decades of lies and terror—started dreaming of their own Tahrir Square in Damascus, a convergence point for millions. Citizens believing in an alternative to rule by one clan and party that controlled what they thought and spoke and how they viewed the world. People fed up with a state where rights, opportunities, and even human dignity depended on proximity to power and one's place in the system. Men and women who simply wanted to liberate themselves from the regime's shackles and find their own identities and voices.

Bit by bit, Syrians began testing how far they could go in fulfilling this dream.

It started in January 2011, with small gatherings in Damascus to express solidarity with protesters in Egypt and Tunisia. They were quickly put down, and the few who dared come out were beaten, insulted, and detained by regime forces and *shabiha*, or thugs.[12] A protest against one of the monopolies of Bashar's cousins followed on February 3, but it was crushed before it could even begin.[13]

On February 5, an anonymous call for a "Day of Rage" to protest against the regime, corruption, and Syria's perpetual state of emergency spread on Facebook but ultimately failed to bring people out into the streets.[14] Rumor had it that the *mukhabarat* itself issued the invitation to test how receptive Syrians actually were to such a call to action.[15] This seemed plausible to a citizenry nurtured on fearing the regime and force-fed its disinformation, conspiracy theories, and propaganda.

Then on February 17, 2011, an incredible scene played out in Al-Hariqa, Damascus's old commercial center. After sons of a textile merchant were insulted and beaten by policemen,[16] shopkeepers shuttered their stores and together with day laborers, many from impoverished rural areas, took to the streets chanting "Thieves, Thieves!" and "The Syrian people won't be humiliated."[17] The *mukhabarat* reports submitted to Bashar were wrong; Syrians were stirring.

Days after the Hariqa incident, a painter in his mid-thirties called Khaled al-Khani was among a few dozen people, mostly artists, actors, and creative types, who tried to protest outside the Libyan embassy in Damascus. They wanted to express solidarity with Libyans after Libya's dictator, Muammar Gaddafi, ordered loyalists to hunt down protesters, whom he called "germs," "rats," "teenagers on hallucinogenic pills," and "Islamist extremists."[18] Much of eastern Libya had fallen to rebels, and protests were spreading to the capital, Tripoli, prompting Gaddafi's crackdown. Militiamen brandishing machetes and machine guns began attacking protesters.[19]

In a rambling, defiant, and at times hysterical televised speech from his Tripoli compound, Gaddafi laid out in no uncertain terms what Arab leaders must do if they wished to overcome what he called a conspiracy by traitors and foreign enemies. Notwithstanding his cartoonish persona, Gaddafi's words were a precise roadmap for any dictator determined to stay in power at any cost: spread lies to sow confusion and manipulate the narrative, kill to illustrate the cost of defiance, and stoke paranoia to drive a wedge between people and make them fight each other. Keep the conflict going even if it means destroying the country: either the leader stays or the country burns.

"I have my rifle and I will fight to the last drop of my blood and with me the Libyan people," shouted Gaddafi, wearing traditional tribal robes and repeatedly raising a clenched fist and banging on the lectern in front of him.[20]

The following day, February 23, 2011, Khaled and a group of almost fifty friends and acquaintances, all of them captivated by the promise of the Arab Spring, converged at sundown on the Libyan embassy on Jala'a Street in the Abu Rummaneh neighborhood. Jala'a was a busy two-way street with embassies, banks, boutiques, and cafés on both sides and, as Bashar's diehard loyalists would say, proof of the leader's reformist and modernist vision. As the street ascended, Mount Qasioun came into focus. Over the years, slums had invaded the mountain's base like a marauding army. Thousands of lights twinkled on its slopes that evening.

As Khaled and the others congregated near the embassy, they were approached by a security officer.

"What are you doing here?" he asked.

"We want to protest, like yesterday," Khaled and others answered.

"Not allowed," he said.

"Why? It was okay yesterday," they persisted.

Indeed, the day before, the *mukhabarat* had allowed a small group including an actor whose mother was Libyan to hold a brief candlelight vigil outside the Libyan embassy, but they kept the gathering tightly hemmed in while plainclothes *mukhabarat* agents whipped out their phones to document all those present before ordering the protesters to disperse.[21]

"Yesterday the leadership gave its permission, today there's no permission, you must leave," declared the officer to Khaled and his friends.

"Well, call the leadership and see if they'll let us protest today, too," they pleaded.

As the back and forth continued, they spotted a group of armed men charging down from Rawda Square, where Jala'a ended as it rose toward Qasioun. This was, after all, the perimeter of Bashar's residence and office, and it was swarming with security personnel. Khaled and his group began running away, scattering in different directions. They were not giving up, though. They regrouped on a side street to plan their next move when they were approached by the same security officer with whom they had had the earlier discussion.

"The leadership said you could gather in the garden, provided you do not disturb people," announced the officer. This was a small garden square at the corner of Jala'a and another street, two blocks away from the Libyan embassy.

"The Libyan people have said it: 'Freedom is our quest, dignity is our demand,'" Khaled and a few dozen others chanted as they huddled in the small park on a winter night holding up candles and sheets of paper on which they hurriedly scrawled slogans.

"With our soul, with our blood, we sacrifice ourselves for you, O Syria!" they cried, purposefully omitting the president's name from the familiar chant.[22]

They recited lines from a poem by Tunisia's Abu al-Qasim al-Shabbi that became an anthem of the Arab uprisings that winter: "If, one day, the people wills to live, then fate must obey, darkness must dissipate and must the chain give way."[23]

As the protest grew louder and more animated it spilled out on Jala'a Street.

"I was standing there with Qasioun in front of me, chanting for the first time in my life, '*Hurriyeh, hurriyeh, hurriyeh*' ['Freedom, freedom, freedom']," recalls Khaled as his eyes well up. Khaled and his friends tried to move farther up Jala'a toward the Libyan embassy, but they were met by dozens of security force members in black fatigues wielding batons and shields. They looked like riot police. "They knew we were there to

11

challenge them and the regime and that our chants were in reality directed at Bashar," and not Gaddafi, said Khaled.

One of the black-clad men stepped forward. "If you do not turn back, I'll set my *shawaya* dogs loose on you," he said, referring to tribal folk from eastern Syria.[24] Over the years, the term became a derogatory way to describe gruff persons of darker skin tone.

Within seconds the blows were coming from everywhere. Khaled and the others were struck with batons, shields, and fists. Those who fell to the ground were kicked and trampled on.

Khaled managed to get up and run away, but others were not so lucky.

"People passed us by and saw us being pummeled," he recalled. "Nobody stopped to help."

This was to be expected in Damascus. Besides deep fear from the regime, there was economic self-interest. The capital's dominant bourgeois and merchant classes had benefited the most from rising living standards during the first decade of Bashar's rule, and many did not want to see these gains endangered by protests and instability. On the face of it, Khaled, too, had little reason to protest. He was making a name for himself as an artist. He had exhibitions in Syria and abroad, and his work was acquired by the city's rich and powerful. The president himself owned one of his paintings.

But Khaled had a deep well of anger from which to draw.

In 1982, when he was seven years old, Khaled's home, his neighborhood, and much of his native city of Hama were leveled to the ground by Bashar's father, Hafez. Manaf Tlass's father, Mustafa, the defense minister at the time, signed off on the massacre that occurred, sending regime opponents to the gallows. Khaled's father, Hikmat al-Khani, a well-respected ophthalmologist, was tortured to death by Hafez's forces simply because he had treated the wounded during the regime's assault on Hama.[25] Dr. Khani was among the nearly 10,000 who perished, according to the lowest estimate of the death toll.[26] Three of Khaled's cousins were among the thousands who remained missing.

Hafez justified the massacre at Hama as retribution against "terror-ists," members of a militant Islamist insurgent group. His message to all Syrians, especially non-Islamists who had peacefully challenged his regime during the same period, was unequivocal: This is what will happen to you if you ever think of rebelling again. It worked. Syrians were terrorized into submission for three decades.

Khaled had grown up internalizing the rage and trauma from witnessing the massacre, unleashing it only in his art—paintings filled with deformed, faceless figures and masses subsumed to an ancient and mythical godlike leader. "We should have rebelled the moment Hafez died and power passed to Bashar but we were too afraid," he said. "The Arab Spring was our best chance to try again."

But not everyone was ready to take the plunge.

The older generation, remembering Hama and its aftermath, was more fearful of the consequences of rebellion than Syria's youth. Although there were plenty of exceptions, members of minority groups like the Alawites, Christians, and Druze generally tended to see the current regime as their protector from the extremist tendencies they believed could emerge among the Sunni Muslim majority, which had long viewed the Assads and their Alawite sect as usurpers. After Hama, the regime enshrined the idea that Islamists were the agents of the nation's "imperialist, Zionist, and reactionary" enemies. A Christian from the Hama countryside—born fifteen years after the massacre and fourteen years old at the Arab Spring's start—grew up being told by his parents that the Hama massacre was necessary because it broke the Sunnis and supposedly made it safe for Christian women to venture into the city without being harassed for not wearing the veil.[27]

The biggest hurdle for those dreaming of change was transcending the socioeconomic, religious, and ethnic divisions that were exploited by the regime to protect itself while it pretended to be the defender of a secular and unified Syria.

There were of course those who truly loved Bashar and believed that Syria was on the right track at the start of his second decade in power, but the vast majority felt they had no choice but to accept the regime's gradual and piecemeal reforms because the alternative in their minds was the war and chaos that engulfed their neighbor to the east, Iraq, after the toppling of Saddam Hussein in 2003.

For those like Khaled and many other Syrians who believed that

13

change was long overdue and who could make the argument that the Arab Spring was a perfect opportunity, there was an even more basic issue to wrestle with that spring: How does a revolt even begin in a place like Syria, where the regime has for decades defined the national identity and imposed it on people? How do you rally Syrians around an alternative cause, message, and leader in a country where all expressions of opposition and dissent have been mercilessly crushed and where fear, lies, and mistrust have sustained the Assads' rule?

Channeling the yearning for freedom among many disaffected and aggrieved segments of Syrian society into a movement with a vision for change and a set of well-articulated demands was what preoccupied human rights lawyer Mazen Darwish day and night in those early weeks of 2011 as he watched the euphoria of revolution spread around him. Overthrowing Bashar was certainly not one of these demands, at least in the beginning.

In late February, Mazen and a friend and colleague, Razan Zeitouneh, reached out to a Kurdish political leader and arranged to meet for lunch in central Damascus.[28] They sat in a restaurant overlooking a giant bronze statue of Hafez al-Assad in a business suit, raising his hand over passersby like a deity offering a blessing.

"Lower your voice—he might hear us," whispered Mazen in jest.

As plates of hummus and tabbouleh were served, Mazen and Razan laid out their plan to the Kurdish leader Abdul-Hakim Bachar.

"Why don't we join you in the Nowruz celebrations and use it as an occasion to call for change and reform?" Mazen suggested.

Nowruz, the Kurdish new year and the official start of spring, would fall on March 21. As they had done in the past, Syria's Kurds were probably going to defy a regime ban on their celebrations and huge crowds would gather to light bonfires, picnic, sing, and dance. But beyond the merriment and festivities, every year the occasion has real political significance for the region's Kurds who are scattered across Iraq, Iran, Syria, and Turkey. It's a chance for them to come together and assert their identity and affirm their long-standing quest for independence—or, at the very least, more autonomy and rights in the states they reside. Syria's Kurds, subjected to decades of Arabization policies and frequently denied citizenship, were considered the most repressed in the region.

Mazen and Razan argued that the grievances of the Kurdish minority aligned with those of all Syrians. Since the ruling Baath Party took power in 1963 and established a state of emergency upheld ever since by the Assads, all Syrian people, regardless of religious sect or ethnicity, were subject to the *mukhabarat*'s power to detain, hold incommunicado, torture, and kill anyone deemed a threat to the regime. Perhaps the Kurds would want to join their advocacy for lifting severe restrictions on freedom of expression, for the release of thousands of prisoners of conscience, and for the legalization of political parties outside the Baath and its partners.

The Kurdish leader smiled as Mazen and Razan eloquently made the case for unified action, but he had an answer at the ready: "We bore the brunt in 2004 and now you want us to be on the forefront again. Find something other than Kurds to ignite your protests."

In 2004, four years into Bashar's rule, at least thirty-six people were killed and 160 wounded, mostly Kurds, when the regime violently quelled protests across northern Syria following deadly shootings by security forces at a soccer match. More than 2,000 Kurds were arrested.[29] Tensions persisted and several deadly incidents with Kurdish victims followed, including the last Nowruz celebration in 2010, when at least one person was shot dead by security forces.[30] The feeling among many Kurds was that the rest of Syria merely watched from the sidelines as they died.

But the rebuff by the Kurdish leader was not going to deter Mazen and his friends who have been advocating for human rights and freedom of expression in Syria for the past decade at great personal risk and against all odds. As for many, Mazen's commitment to the cause was deeply personal; his father had been forced into hiding after opposing Hafez al-Assad's coup in 1970, and his mother had been jailed for criticizing the regime. Mazen and other youthful activists believed this was their golden chance to achieve what had long eluded their parents, mentors and an entire generation of Assad regime opponents. Now, it seemed like the tide was beginning to turn all around them, and Syria would get swept up in the current soon enough. To Mazen, "it was not a matter of if but when in Syria."

The *mukhabarat*, bracing for the same inevitability, began arresting some university students suspected of starting protests and summoning known political opponents and activists like Mazen for lengthy interrogations about their intentions.[31]

"We were looking for any pretext to take to the streets, even something like celebrating the national day of the Republic of the Congo," said Mazen jokingly.

The first opening toward liberation for Mazen and his friends came on March 8, 2011, when, on the forty-eighth anniversary of the Baath's takeover of power in Syria, Bashar issued a decree pardoning certain categories of prisoners. It excluded most political prisoners, some languishing in cells and dungeons for decades. Immediately word spread that thirteen political prisoners in Adra prison near Damascus had gone on a hunger strike to be included in the pardons.[32]

Mazen and his associates decided to release a statement expressing solidarity with these prisoners and announced their own protest on March 16 in front of the Ministry of the Interior to demand the release of all prisoners of conscience. They signed it with their real names and posted it on Facebook. "We wanted to move our activity from the clandestine and secretive to the open," explained Mazen. "This is us and these are our real names and we are calling for a protest on a specific day and time regarding a Syrian matter — we the Syrian people."[33]

On March 16, nearly 300 people showed up in Marjeh Square — once the site of public executions when Syria was ruled by the French and, before them, the Ottomans. The streets were lined with cheap hotels, office buildings, and shops selling everything from cell phones to baklava. Usually visitors from the provinces idled in the square while children chased pigeons. But they were absent that day as the crowd formed and security forces ringed the interior ministry building just off the square.

The moment protesters began to wave posters of the prisoners and banners calling for their release, hundreds of security force members and pro-Bashar irregulars in civilian clothes poured out from surrounding buildings.[34] (They had been lying in wait in the stairwells all morning, Mazen later found out.) The regime enforcers charged toward the protesters, shouting with one voice: "With our soul, with our blood, we sacrifice ourselves for you, O Bashar!"[35]

Mazen and the other protesters tried to hold their ground and close ranks, chanting: "He who strikes his own people is a traitor!"

Within seconds, protesters were clubbed with batons, knocked to the ground, trampled on, and dragged on the pavement. Mazen watched in disbelief as Tayeb Tizini, a well-respected and elderly philosopher who was among the protesters, was hoisted up by two thugs and thrown against a lamppost again and again. Mazen and nearly two dozen other protesters were arrested and bundled into vans.

Two days later, Friday, March 18, Manaf Tlass strolled through Marjeh Square while on a morning walk, a near-daily routine. All seemed normal. There was more security than usual but otherwise nothing out of the ordinary.[36] Manaf lingered in the square for a few moments, then looked at his watch: it was well past ten o'clock. He decided to head back home to shower and change.

Later that day, Manaf and his wife, Thala, drove out to their weekend house in the mountains west of Damascus close to the Lebanese border. It was a simple stone house nestled on the flank of a six-thousand-foot mountain between the resort towns of Bloudan and Serghaya. Cars could not reach the crest, so visitors had to park three-quarters of the way and hike up to the house.[37] The Tlasses lived rather simply there: a family room, two bedrooms, and small kitchen powered by a private generator. Hand-woven Bedouin rugs covered the floor. The main attraction was the spectacular view from the outdoor terrace. Stretched out below were scenic valleys with farmhouses, streams, and apple orchards. One could see as far as the Lebanese city of Zahleh in the adjacent Beqaa Valley.

On this particular occasion, the Tlasses were hosting a lunch in honor of the Austrian manager of the Four Seasons hotel in Damascus, Martin Rhomberg, and his Mexican wife, Ana Luisa. It was intended as a farewell party for Rhomberg, who was being transferred elsewhere after three years in Damascus.[38] The hotel had been a joint venture between the Four Seasons chain and the Syrian state, one that Bashar hoped would send a message that Damascus was now open for business under his dynamic and reform-minded leadership.

ASSAD OR WE BURN THE COUNTRY

The guests started arriving at the Tlass weekend home, gathering on the terrace with their drinks. Given the warm, sunny weather, the Tlasses were planning a barbecue. Manaf, dressed in jeans and sporting a stylish army-green keffiyeh around his neck, held a glass of red wine in one hand and a Cuban cigar in the other as he chatted with his guests.

Talk before lunch drifted to the one question on everyone's mind: How will the Arab Spring affect Syria?

"I was ready with the standard response and our talking points: I did not think we would be affected, because our young president was already carrying out reforms," said Manaf.

His words proved to be false that same day.

Sixty miles south of Damascus in the city of Daraa, close to the Jordanian border, eighteen-year-old Sally Masalmeh was having breakfast at home with her parents and siblings. Since it was Friday, the beginning of the weekend, the whole family was gathered together to linger over plates of white cheese, olives, pickled eggplants, fried eggs, and hot bread—a typical Syrian breakfast.

As they moved to the living room to have tea after the meal, news from Al Jazeera, by then the Arab world's most popular satellite news channel, streamed in on the TV. Millions across the Arab world followed the channel's day-and-night live broadcasts of the cataclysmic events sweeping the region: Tunisia, Egypt, Libya, Yemen, and now potentially Syria.

"We are going to be next for sure," said Sally with a mischievous smile.

She was a thin girl with dark, almond-shaped eyes and sharp eyebrows that stood out below her colorful headscarf.

"Be quiet, they will arrest us all if you keep saying that," interjected her father. He was old enough to remember Hama.

Daraa was buzzing that day with talk of a possible protest planned after midday prayers by relatives of a group of teenage boys who had been arrested by security forces more than two weeks earlier for doing the unthinkable. Across school walls the boys had spray-painted: *"Jayeek el dor, ya daktor"*—"You are next, doctor," referring to Bashar.[39]

"It's going to be just like the other countries—twenty, thirty days maximum, and he'll pack up his bags and leave," Sally insisted. Bashar, she believed, would step down just like the presidents of Egypt and Tunisia.

18

"He's no Mubarak or Ben Ali, he'll kill all of you and he won't leave—mark my words," said her father as he got up to prepare to go to the mosque near the house, where he planned to pray. He wanted to avoid the central Omari mosque near where the protest might occur. Better to stay away from trouble.

After her father left, Sally helped her mother tidy up the house. Since the weather was nice, they were planning to go for a picnic when her father returned.

Suddenly, the sound of heavy gunfire filled Daraa.

As the sun started disappearing behind the mountains of Lebanon, some guests at the Tlass luncheon headed back to Damascus. It was getting chilly on the terrace. Manaf was tending to a few guests still lingering over dessert and coffee when his assistant pulled him aside with urgent news. There had been a protest in Daraa, he said, and it had turned violent and people had been killed.

Stunned, Manaf excused himself from the remaining guests and rushed to the base to try to piece together what had happened in Daraa. On Sunday morning he was still working to gather information when his cell phone rang. It was the president.[40]

"Hi, are you near a landline?" asked Bashar.

"Yes, I am at the base," said Manaf.

2

Embracing the Clouds

The journey of the Assads and Tlasses to the spring that forever changed them and their country began six decades earlier. It was fall 1952 when Hafez al-Assad and Mustafa Tlass first met at the military academy in the city of Homs.[1]

The budding Syrian republic that had recently gained its independence from France was eager to build its army officer corps and was calling for volunteers. It was a natural choice for poor, scrappy young men from the provinces like Hafez and Mustafa who were ambitious and politically minded. A ninth-grade education and an entrance exam were all it took to be admitted. Recruits were housed, fed, and paid a stipend.

Hafez had a baccalaureate, the equivalent of a high school degree, and was a bright student. He could have gone to university, but it would have been a burden on his large family. The Assads, like most inhabitants of the mountains of Syria's western coastal region, were Alawites—members of what was generally regarded as an offshoot of Shia Islam whose adherents were branded heretics by many mainstream Muslims and persecuted throughout history. (While the veneration of Shiite Imam Ali and their own desire to fit in has linked Alawites to Shiism, Alawites regard themselves as distinct culturally and historically from other sects; some of their beliefs have been traced to Christianity. But in general, secrecy and concealment shrouds Alawite faith and practices, something that has protected them but has also been used against them by their enemies.)

The Alawites and other minorities did, however, enjoy some measure of autonomy during the French mandate over Lebanon and Syria—states carved out from dominions of the collapsing Ottoman Empire at the end of the First World War. It was part of a French divide-and-conquer strategy predicated on preserving class and religious divisions and promoting regional separatist sentiments among local populations while keeping simmering nationalist fervor in check.[2]

Upon independence, Syrians sought to forge a modern state based on Western principles for a diverse nation whose constituents mistrusted one another and were swayed by long and deep-rooted traditions of feudalism and patronage. When Hafez and Mustafa entered the military academy a shift was underway, but most economic and political power was still in the hands of large landowners and urban elites who either belonged to the Sunni Muslim majority or were Christian.[3] Society's contrasts were breathtaking; many women in big cities dressed in the latest Parisian fashions, attended college, and worked in offices, while those in adjacent suburbs wore traditional attire and fetched drinking water in clay jars.

Mustafa was a Sunni, but like Hafez came from a rural and modest background. He was a farmer's son from Al-Rastan in the Homs countryside. Families worked the land and raised sheep, and, like all of Al-Rastan's women, Mustafa's mother did the laundry on the banks of the Orontes River which passed through the town.[4] During the Second World War, the Tlasses became so destitute that Mustafa's father sold their ancestral home and moved to a smaller place, where he also ran a bathhouse to survive.[5]

Mustafa failed his baccalaureate but found work as a physical education teacher in a village in southern Syria, with a meager salary and small room for accommodation.[6] Then he decided to enroll in the military academy, as becoming an officer was a path to better social standing for someone like Mustafa and possibly even a ticket to the pinnacle of power and glory. In the summer of 1952, just before Hafez and Mustafa went off to the academy, the entire Arab world was electrified by Gamal Abdel Nasser, the young lieutenant colonel who led fellow officers in deposing Egypt's Western-backed King Farouk. The officers promised to unify Arabs, recapture Palestine from the newly created Jewish state, and eradicate vestiges of the feudal and colonial past. Turning ambition and rabble-rousing rhetoric into reality was an altogether different matter, however.

21

Before the academy, Hafez and Mustafa were youth leaders in the Baath Party, which was formed a year after Syria's independence. The Baath was first and foremost an ideology—a curious fusion of European philosophies, socialism, Arab nationalism, and Islamic thought, whose theorists were Syrian graduates of the Sorbonne.[7] Its core doctrine was that Arabs must undergo transformation and unification beyond just geographic and political lines; they must shed imperial-era influences and return to their pure essence and virtues. This demanded a rebirth and resurgence, or *baath* in Arabic. These concepts, along with social equality and redistribution of wealth, appealed to those sidelined by their economic circumstances, like Mustafa, or by belonging to religious minorities, like Hafez. Arab identity was supposed to transcend all cleavages.

In January 1953, Hafez, Mustafa, and another dozen cadets were transferred from Homs to the northern city of Aleppo, where they became the first class admitted to a new air force academy established by the young Syrian state. It was not much. There was a runway, a couple of hangars, six training planes, an old barrack that housed the cadets' dorm, training officers' quarters, and a common mess hall, where the food was "not even fit for donkeys," according to Mustafa.[8]

Cadets risked expulsion if they broached the subject of politics, but Hafez, Mustafa and like-minded Baathists still found time in between pilot-training courses for animated political discussions. They voiced shared disdain for Adib al-Shishakli, a general nicknamed "the Arab Caesar," who ruled Syria after three successive coups in 1949 and allied himself to Britain, Saudi monarchs, and the United States. To Baathist cadets, Shishakli was "America's pet." Instead, they wanted "a leader who challenges and confronts."[9]

As they bonded over politics, Hafez and Mustafa found themselves drawn to each other by virtue of their different but rather complementary personalities. Hafez was a very serious, reserved, and hard-working young man determined to make something of himself. Mustafa, on the other hand, was handsome, gregarious, extroverted, and eager to talk about his romantic exploits. The dynamic of their relationship was clear from the start. Hafez was the leader, boss, and brains, and Mustafa his loyal, colorful, and funny sidekick—and the muscle when it was required.[10] They practiced ambushing their dormmates for sport; Mustafa would grab a fellow cadet from behind like a wrestler so that Hafez could knock him on the head with his large forehead.[11]

While Mustafa and Hafez were still at the academy, their Baath Party merged with the Arab Socialist Party, founded by a charismatic lawyer who incited Syrian farmers to revolt against their landlords. The new entity, the Arab Baath Socialist Party, participated in an uprising that overthrew the pro-American Shishakli.

Mustafa did not make the cut as a pilot. He was deemed too temperamental and heavy-handed during training flights, so he switched to tanks while Hafez graduated as a pilot officer.[12]

The newly minted officers were faced with a country that, barely a decade after gaining its independence, was reeling from a series of successive military coups, assassinations, and an internecine struggle in the army over the direction Syria should take and its place in the geopolitical map of the time. There were factions pushing for union with Nasser's Egypt. Their main opponents were those desiring unity with Iraq, ruled at the time by a king. These officers wanted Syria to be part of the so-called Baghdad Pact—a United States–backed organization that included Britain, Iraq, Pakistan, the shah's Iran, and Turkey—against Soviet encroachment in the oil-rich and strategic Middle East. Communists were also gaining strength in the army and wanted to see Syria firmly anchored in the Soviet camp.

As in ancient times, Syria was at the crossroads of civilizations and ideologies.

Hafez and Mustafa were mere lieutenants but were in the thick of all the army intrigue, and like most Baathist officers they believed that survival meant throwing their lot in with the Nasserites against the others, especially after Nasser's popularity surged following the 1956 Suez crisis.

In the fall of 1957, while Hafez was posted at the Mezzeh Airbase in Damascus, Mustafa was part of an army contingent sent to Aleppo as a show of force to dissuade Turkey from making an incursion into Syria. The Turks had amassed troops at the border at the behest of their

American allies who, with Britain, hoped to assassinate key Communist and Nasserite figures in Damascus in order to install a Western-friendly government.[13]

While posted in the north, Mustafa befriended Adnan Jabri, a young army engineer from a notable local landowning family. Adnan had recently returned to Syria with his American wife after studying in the United States. He introduced his sister Lamia to Mustafa, who became close with his family.

During the many lunches at the Jabri country home near Aleppo, Mustafa met the US consul Roy Atherton, a friend of the Jabris.[14] The United States was unsettled by the influence of the Soviet Union in northern Syria, and Atherton and others had been deployed to monitor the situation.[15] Connections to ambitious Baathists like Mustafa could be useful in the effort to confront the Communists and Nasserites, whom the Americans regarded as a more worrisome and formidable force in the nascent Syrian army and state. The American-British 1957 plot was not carried through, but Mustafa's acquaintance with Atherton later opened the door to crucial back channels in Washington as he and Hafez rose to the top. In Baath propaganda the Americans were supposed to be the enemy, but the power-hungry friends were ready to partner with the devil to get ahead.

Mustafa married Lamia in early 1958 after a short courtship. Their firstborn was a girl they named Nahed. Like becoming an army officer, marrying into the wealthy and landed Jabri family was a big step up for the poor young man from Al-Rastan.

Hafez opted for a similar match later in 1958, marrying Aniseh Makhlouf, an Alawite from one of his community's wealthier families. Initially the Makhloufs objected, scornful of Hafez's peasant background and membership to the Baath Party, whose pan-Arab ideals they rejected.[16]

But that same year Egypt and Syria unified under the leadership of Nasser—the first step toward broader Arab unity. Egypt became the Southern Region and Syria the Northern in what was called the United Arab Republic. The Baathists were among those pushing hardest for the union, thinking it would neutralize their opponents in Syria and turn them into equal partners with Nasser.[17] Their bet proved wrong almost immediately. Although Nasser appointed a Baathist as his deputy, his conditions for union were dissolution of all parties in Syria and exclusion of Syrian army officers from any role in political life. Nasser planned to rule with an iron fist and his position was significantly strengthened by the unprecedented outpouring of spontaneous popular support he received during multiple visits to Syria right after a unification referendum.[18]

"This is your people, Gamal!" screamed a headline on the front page of Syria's *Al Ayyam* newspaper above a photo of the hundreds of thousands who clogged central Damascus to get a glimpse of the leader turned icon for millions of Arabs.[19]

Baathist leaders were envious of Nasser, but for most Syrians he was the savior of a society feeling aimless and fragmented twelve years after independence.[20] The promise of stability, however, was fleeting. Through his local Syrian henchmen, Nasser brutally suppressed any whiff of criticism.[21] Sweeping nationalization and agrarian reform triggered the flight of the country's top industrialists and landowners, mainly to neighboring Lebanon. This powerful class began scheming to get Syria out of the union with Egypt.

Disillusionment and anger also set in among Baathists who felt cheated by Nasser. Baathist army officers seen as posing a threat to Nasser were transferred in 1959 to the provinces in Egypt, among them Hafez and Mustafa, who by then held the respective ranks of major and captain.[22] Both eventually moved to Cairo, where their wives joined them. In 1960 the Tlasses had their second child, a boy they named Firas. That same year Hafez's wife, Aniseh, gave birth to a daughter, Bushra. She, too, was their second born; their first baby girl had fallen ill and died upon their arrival in Egypt.[23]

In the spring of 1961, all indications were that the brief union with Egypt was going to unravel. Army officers, mostly from the Sunni majority and backed by wealthy families, plotted to grab power in Syria. These constituents were friendly to the United States and its allies. By then, Western powers were not only grappling with the Soviet-allied Nasser but also with a populist pro-communist Iraqi officer named Abdul-Karim Qasim, who toppled the monarchy in Syria's oil-rich neighbor state to the east. There was so much hatred for the pro-Western Iraqi monarchy and its government that a mob disinterred the deposed prime minister and crown prince and dragged their corpses through Baghdad's streets.[24]

As signs of the imminent undoing of the Egypt–Syria union mounted, Hafez joined a secret committee of Baathist officers in Cairo to assess their own chances of grabbing power. Initially the committee's core members were Hafez, two other Alawites like him, and two Ismailis, members of another minority group. These men felt they could trust one another because, beyond dissatisfaction with the Egypt union, they shared the grievances of religious minorities. The Sunni Mustafa Tlass and others were brought in later. In order not to raise suspicion, the co-conspirators met at each other's apartments under the pretext of social gatherings that included their wives.

At the end of September 1961, a group of Damascene army officers staged a coup in Syria and ended the union with Egypt. The Egyptians put all Syrian officers in Cairo under house arrest. Hafez was among those imprisoned for their suspected role in the coup even though he and other Baathists were at odds with the Damascene officers and ultimately wanted power for themselves.

Mustafa convinced the Egyptians to let him join the approximately fifty Syrian officers and their families eventually allowed to return to Syria. Mustafa brought his wife and children as well as Hafez's wife, who was three months pregnant, and their one-year-old daughter, Bushra, safely back to Syria. More than 600 people crammed into a small passenger boat that left Port Said on Egypt's Mediterranean coast for the Lebanese capital, Beirut. "We were herded into the ship as if we were sheep and goats," said Mustafa.[25]

Hafez, who was released later in exchange for Syrian-held Egyptian officers, was forever indebted to Mustafa for escorting his wife and baby girl all the way to the safety of the Alawite mountains. Back in Syria, the Baath's political leaders and party theorists were in full crisis mode: Do they endorse the new putschists even though they differed with them ideologically? Wasn't the Baath all about smashing frontiers between Arab states? Or do they cooperate with the Nasserites again to restore the union, forgetting how bitter and marginalized they were during that short-lived experience?

But Hafez and his circle of army officers knew exactly what they wanted. It was power for themselves, and the sooner the better.[26] They mounted a coup attempt in the spring of 1962, but things quickly went wrong as disagreements surfaced with a diehard Nasserite army faction.

Hafez escaped to Lebanon but was later returned to Syria and placed in jail alongside Mustafa and other comrades. Hafez was interrogated and then released after a few days, while Mustafa and lesser figures bore the brunt of the failed attempt.

That spring Hafez's first son, Bassel, was born. While Mustafa was in prison, his wife gave birth eight months later to a baby boy whom they named Manaf. In one of his letters to his wife from prison, Mustafa joked how Manaf was sent as help for his brother, Firas, to cope with their feisty and tough sister, Nahed, who was four by then.[27]

Hafez was cashiered from the army and given a civilian job in Latakia, but he continued to plot to capture power with his secret army committee.

In February 1963, Baathists in Iraq ousted Abdul-Karim Qassim, the populist leader who had toppled the monarchy a few years earlier. Exactly a month later, on March 8, 1963, Hafez and his comrades — with crucial aid from senior non-Baathist army officers with aligned goals — overthrew what they called "the secessionists," those who had precipitated Syria's separation from Egypt. Hafez and the others did not want to restore unity with Egypt, but appearing as if they were in favor of such a step would give them some measure of public support and legitimacy in the coup's aftermath.

Many more lies would follow.

The power grab was swift. Tanks rolled into Damascus and occupied key facilities, including army headquarters and state broadcasting in the central Umayyad Square, while Hafez personally headed the unit that subdued a critical airbase near the capital.[28] The Baathists declared their move a "revolution" and instituted martial law. A military council, formally known as the National Council for the Revolutionary Command and including Hafez and his comrades, ruled Syria through a government of their own creation.

Hafez was a step closer to the top.

"We were like wolves," said Mustafa, now commander of an army division stationed in Homs. "We turned each military base that we took over into a citadel of the Baath." Baathists seized most military bases and weapons depots to prevent countercoups by rival army factions.[29]

27

Within weeks the new junta began a purge in the army and all sectors of public life. Hundreds of officers and public servants were removed from their posts and replaced with loyal Baathists. Political parties, clubs, associations, and newspapers were shuttered under the guise of combatting enemies of the Syrian people, reactionaries, foreign agents, and opponents of Arab nationalism. An entire generation of political and community leaders was stripped of all civil rights. "Treason must be plucked out from its roots," declared the junta.[30]

More industrialists and businessmen fled Syria, fearing the worst.[31] The purge also provoked street protests and riots in Aleppo and Damascus between late April and early May 1963. Security forces were ordered in to control the situation, and calm was restored after some fifty protesters were shot dead.[32]

A second challenge came a few months later, when disaffected pro-Nasser army officers tried to carry out a rather clownish countercoup. They attacked the Ministry of Defense and state broadcasting buildings in central Damascus in broad daylight, triggering street battles with Baathists. Hafez, now a lieutenant colonel, was a prominent figure in the junta and the air force's de facto commander. He and his associates ordered the distribution of assault rifles to all party members. They were told to take to the street to defend their March 8 revolution.[33]

Mustafa telephoned Hafez to ask if he should return from Homs to help.

"They're just a bunch of mercenaries and we have crushed them already; stay where you are but be on high alert," Hafez told him.[34]

The Baathists prevailed, but hundreds of people were killed or wounded in the clashes, many of them bystanders caught in the crossfire. Those connected to the botched coup were hauled in front of a military tribunal and executed on the spot by a firing squad. Similar tribunals were set up all over the country, with Mustafa presiding over the one in Homs.[35]

These bloody events effectively institutionalized the mindset of vengeance and reprisal in the regime's fabric.[36] And with every challenge, the regime honed its skills and perfected its manual for dealing with threats to its power. Survival and self-preservation at any cost were Hafez's main objectives during all crises. Mustafa shared this thinking as he helped

Hafez navigate his way to the top. He was ready to kill for him. "We had to terrorize the revolution's enemies," boasted Mustafa.[37]

There was more unrest in February 1964, when students in Homs and the coastal region demonstrated against the one-year-old Baathist regime. Mustafa sent tanks to the streets and issued death sentences against student leaders, calling them "Zionist and colonial agents."

Two months later, Hafez and Mustafa were among those in the junta who took the hardest position against a more serious revolt in Hama. A firebrand Islamist preacher called Marwan Hadid had taken up arms and barricaded himself in a mosque along with his followers, mostly teenage boys. Hadid had been radicalized while studying in Egypt and had become disenchanted with what he saw as the passivity of his fellow Muslim Brothers in Syria in the face of "infidel" Baathists.[38] The Brotherhood, which saw Islam rather than Arabism as the unifying force, was at war with Nasser in Egypt, and Hadid wanted the Syrian branch to follow a similar path of violent confrontation.

Hama was mostly opposed to Hadid and his methods, but when the Baath regime shelled the mosque to rout Hadid out, the city's deeply conservative population revolted. Homs rose again in solidarity with Hama, while merchants in Damascus's central market called for a strike. The regime mobilized the army and members of a newly created paramilitary group known as the National Guard. Relying on shock troops and militias to act as a check on the army would be a recurring regime strategy going forward.

Mustafa was personally at the scene in Homs, ordering one of his armored vehicles to smash open the main door of the historic Khaled Ibn al-Walid mosque to flush out protesters who had barricaded themselves inside.[39] Not long thereafter, Mustafa presided over a military tribunal that sentenced Hadid and eight others to death. The regime hoped that the show trial would isolate and vilify all its opponents by casting them as fanatics like Hadid—a tactic to be deployed again in the future.[40]

The sentence was never carried out, however, and Hadid and his companions were released after Hama's notables and clergy intervened with the junta's figurehead president, General Amin al-Hafiz, a Sunni like them. The president was also backed by some in the junta who believed that the regime's actions in its first year in power—the purges, shooting of protesters, summary executions, and mosque shelling—were highly provocative and dangerous.

Hafez and Mustafa, however, were among those arguing for even more firmness. They believed letting Hama off so easily and reversing the death sentences was a grave mistake that could encourage further insurrection.[41] Regardless of the final outcome, the events of 1964 exposed the two major fault lines of religion and class that would underpin all future conflicts. Broadly, it was the conservative Sunni majority against the secular and, in its eyes, godless minority-led regime. Then there were the urban elites and prominent families against the humble countryside upstarts like the Assads and Tlasses who seized power.

The events also had a more immediate and consequential impact on the ruling military council. They ushered in a cycle of merciless culling in the council's ranks, an intrigue-filled succession war brutal enough for ancient courts. First to be taken out was the figurehead president, al-Hafiz, who felt that too much power was in the hands of Alawites like Hafez al-Assad and the army chief of staff, to the detriment of the Sunni majority. The president plotted with Baath Party founders to take power from the military committee. Hafez and Mustafa backed the army chief, Salah Jadid, a ruthless Marxist-influenced ideologue, who moved against the president and his co-conspirators when they tried to reshuffle the military command.

The president and his family surrendered on February 23, 1966, after a three-hour gun battle outside his official residence that left nearly fifty people dead.[42] Hafez and his youngest brother, Rifaat, a newly graduated officer with a streak of savagery who commanded a special strike force, were among those leading the assault against the president and his loyalists.[43] About 400 army officers and government functionaries, as well as one founding member of the ruling military council, were purged from their posts; some were tried and sentenced to death by hastily convened tribunals, while others went into exile overseas but, in some cases, were later tracked down and assassinated.[44]

✻   ✻   ✻

Internal party struggle culminated in a split of the Baath, initiated by its Iraqi branch. After Syria's military rulers got rid of their rivals in 1966, Jadid became de facto leader and appointed Hafez defense minister. Two Sunnis were appointed as figurehead president and prime minister.

There was barely time for the new government to settle in when, in June 1967, Israel captured the Golan Heights from Syria, Jerusalem and the West Bank from Jordan, and Sinai from Egypt during the Six-Day War. It was akin to a second *nakba*, or catastrophe, for Arab masses, the first being the creation of Israel in 1948.[45] Syria's military leaders fretted that the crushing defeat could cost them power.

As the defense minister, Hafez felt most vulnerable. He was determined to neutralize threats from wherever they came. When two banished ex-comrades returned to Syria, Hafez moved quickly to arrest them on suspicion that they might act against the weakened regime. Hafez called Mustafa and urged him to sentence them right away.

"I'll do it first thing tomorrow morning. It's 8:30 p.m. now," Mustafa responded.

"You have to do it this minute! You do not understand, the leadership is in real crisis, and there's panic that the regime may fall," Hafez insisted, stressing the impact of the Golan's loss.

Mustafa immediately put on his military uniform and drove to the army theater building in Damascus, where a tribunal was hastily convened. Mustafa, now a lieutenant colonel, presided over the five-officer court. Proceedings were filmed to show the public that losing the Golan had nothing to do with the regime's ineptitude or Hafez's possible treason, as many Syrians were beginning to murmur, but was the result of a conspiracy by Jordan's monarchy, the CIA, West Germany, and "enemies of the people" like the two disloyal Syrian officers, Salim Hatoum and Badr Juma'a, who were on trial.[46]

Hatoum, once a member of the ruling junta, was dazed and incoherent because of severe torture, but the lesser figure, Juma'a, confessed the explanation Mustafa was looking for: that they planned to topple the regime and put in place a government that was representative of all of Syria's political currents, including Baathists.

31

Mustafa adjourned for ten minutes and called Hafez to update him. He would issue the death sentence and carry it out instantly, and afterward he would deal with the formality of getting it approved by the junta's figurehead president.[47]

"Good job, and you won't be responsible for this on your own—I and all the comrades in the leadership are with you," Hafez assured him.

At three o'clock in the morning Mustafa sentenced his two former comrades to death by firing squad on charges of grand treason. Several reports emerged afterward that Mustafa had personally taken part in the torture and impalement of Hatoum and that Hatoum was already dead when he was dragged to the prison's shooting range.[48]

Hatoum's horrific execution did little to stem the disarray, recrimination, and backstabbing following what became known as the *naksa*, or setback, of 1967—Israel's swift defeat of Syria and other Arab states. To close ranks, Hafez installed Mustafa as army chief of staff. In the span of eight months, Mustafa had been promoted from lieutenant colonel to major general, a spectacular leap in rank and a long-due reward for absolute loyalty. Now the two friends worked to weaken and isolate Salah Jadid, Hafez's main competitor. They started purging figures in the army loyal to Jadid and then moved against his allies in the military committee, the core group of army officers that first conspired to carry out the 1963 coup.

Hafez signaled to crucial allies like the Soviet Union that he, not Jadid, was the winning horse and that they should strengthen him and supply him with advanced weapons in order to confront the United States and its allies in the region.

When Soviet defense minister Field Marshall Andrey Grechko visited Damascus in 1968, Hafez asked Mustafa to organize a dinner at his home for him and the Soviet guest. Mustafa's wife, Lamia, was part of the charm offensive, preparing *kibbeh* Aleppo style (patties of cracked wheat and meat stuffed with minced meat and pine nuts) for the Soviet commander.[49]

Mustafa later wooed Grechko by throwing him private parties with attractive teenage girls.[50] Soviet military aid to the Syrian army and especially the Hafez-controlled air force doubled from 1968 to 1970, the period of the final showdown between Hafez and Jadid.[51]

Jadid moved against Hafez and Mustafa at a Baath Party emergency national congress in late October 1970. During marathon sessions lasting almost two weeks, Hafez was held responsible for the shameful retreat in the 1967 war, accused of maintaining backchannels with "the imperialist West," and denounced as a defeatist who was going to ruin the party and gut its revolutionary ideology. For Jadid and his allies, the proof of Hafez's treasonous ties to the West lay in his refusal to mobilize the air force to help Palestinian guerrilla fighters in their battle against the US-backed King Hussein of Jordan during what became known as Black September in 1970. Jadid had sent tanks into Jordan to help the Palestinians and almost provoked war with the Jordanians.

Jadid proceeded to strip Hafez and Mustafa of their army ranks and positions, but Hafez had by then laid the groundwork to move against Jadid.[52] He had a lot to bolster his case. Syria's economy was in ruins after extensive nationalization. Central bank reserves stood at 50 million lira ($14 million), enough to cover state expenditures and civil servant salaries for a month or two at the most.[53] Hafez cast Jadid as scapegoat for the decision to confiscate private companies and property after the Baathists seized power in 1963, a move that resulted in capital flight to the tune of $1 billion during the ensuing two years.[54] Hafez argued that Jadid failed as party leader as well and that his foray into Jordan almost brought disaster.

Behind the scenes, Hafez gathered wide support by promising to ease Syria's isolation from its Arab neighbors (and, for that matter, most of the world), discard Jadid's unpopular Mao- and Trotsky-inspired revolutionary model, jumpstart the economy, loosen the regime's grip on society, and reclaim the Golan Heights. As the party congress came to a chaotic end, Hafez and Mustafa, in league with their loyalists in the army and intelligence services, began to execute the plan they had at the ready.

Jadid, the figurehead president, along with the prime minister and their allies, were rounded up one by one and taken to prison, where most remained until they died. As Hafez was finalizing his power grab, Muammar Gaddafi, a zealous young army officer who had seized power in Libya the previous year, arrived in Damascus. Hafez went to greet him at the airport and tasked Mustafa with broadcasting an announcement of the "Corrective Movement" to the people.[55]

"Your comrades have formed a temporary leadership out of a sense of responsibility to protect the party and the revolution," said Mustafa. "Your party is the party of workers, farmers, soldiers…the party of the poor and dispossessed."

A patriotic Baath song played at the end of his speech. *"From Qasioun, I look upon you my homeland and I see Damascus embracing the clouds…and the Baath sprinkling meteors over it!"* crooned a female vocalist.[56]

At the end of his visit, Gaddafi, who was twenty-eight years old at the time, told Syrian media he was "comforted" by Hafez's coup.[57]

A few days later at the Tlass residence in Damascus, the family's youngest member was getting dressed. Eight-year-old Manaf was a thin, quiet boy. He was different from his brother, Firas, two years his senior, who was chubby, outgoing, and constantly fighting with their sister and the eldest, Nahed. Nahed was tough but always kind to her younger brother Manaf.

The Tlasses moved from Homs in 1968 after Mustafa Tlass became the army's chief of staff while his friend Hafez al-Assad was still defense minister. They settled in an apartment on a quiet, leafy side street in the upscale Rawda neighborhood.

On that day in late November 1970, Manaf was escorted by one of his father's aides to the nearby office of Hafez al-Assad, now Syria's most powerful man. It was within walking distance, up Jala'a Street and past Rawda Square, in a nondescript bunker-like building.

Hafez wore a military uniform and sat behind his desk reviewing documents when Manaf was brought in. Hafez got up, smiled, and approached Manaf. He kissed him on both cheeks.

"My dear, this is Bassel. He's your age and you two go to the same school," said Hafez as he put an arm around his son, who was eight months older than Manaf and a grade higher. "Your dad and I are friends and the two of you must also become friends."

3

Creation and Punishment

The mustachioed army general and his men arrived at a pole with a flag at half-staff. The general grabbed the flag—red, white, and black with a hawk in the middle[1]—and displayed it to the crowd with a smile. Then, raising it to his lips, he kissed the fabric.[2]

"Hafez, Hafez, Hafez!" the crowd shouted wildly.

It was late June 1974 and Hafez al-Assad was in his early forties. He wore a khaki army uniform, a kepi, and black leather shoes; his epaulettes were decorated with a hawk, two stars, and two crossed swords. He was commander of the army, president of the republic, secretary-general of the ruling Baath Party, and now he was on his way to becoming a living legend—paramount leader, the nation's father, maker and giver of everything, and defender of the Arabs. There were other pretenders to this last title, including next door in Iraq where the equally ruthless Saddam Hussein aspired to similar grandeur under the mantle of a splinter wing of the Baath.

At Hafez's side that day in June was his faithful companion and defense minister Mustafa Tlass. Next to the men were two twelve-year-old boys in matching mop-top haircuts and khaki uniforms. Hafez's son Bassel and Mustafa's son Manaf were friends—exactly as Hafez had decreed.

An aide showered Hafez with flowers as he hoisted the flag amid frenzied cheering and clapping. Bassel carried a camera and snapped photos of his father and the euphoric scene.[3] Hafez and Mustafa stood shoulder to shoulder saluting the flag after it was raised. They had dreamed of this moment for two decades, having worked their way to the top with raw ambition, intrigue, and a trail of blood.

Hafez reached into his pocket and pulled out a folded piece of paper as the two boys looked on with anticipation. He began reading a speech.

"The people's will can never be subjugated... We must continue preparations to drive the enemy out of every inch of our occupied Arab land..." A nearby camera caught this made-for-TV moment. The ruling party said that more than 300 foreign journalists came to hear Hafez.[4]

"These masses will forever be the shining light of freedom... and dignity," Hafez added.

Party officials, soldiers, and average Syrians gathered together to watch history in the making. Peasant men in red-and-white-checkered headdresses and women in flower-patterned garb jostled to catch a glimpse of the leader. They had crammed into the back of dump trucks with their children for the journey to Quneitra, a largely demolished and dusty town on the edge of the rocky Golan Heights plateau southwest of Damascus.

As Hafez concluded his speech, Mustafa turned with a smile to his son and Bassel. "When you boys grow up and become officers, you too will fight Israel," he said proudly.[5]

That day in Quneitra was immortalized by the Syrian state as "Liberation Day" and Hafez became "Hero of Tishreen." Tales of the Syrian army's bravery under the great leader's command would be taught in schools and commemorated year after year.

"Our masses live the joy of liberation," pronounced the party's daily on its front page.[6]

It was more like the lie of liberation that the Assads would use to subjugate Syrians.

Less than a year earlier, Hafez made the decision on October 6, 1973, the month of *Tishreen al-Awal* in Syria, to join Egypt, then under the leadership of Anwar al-Sadat, in launching coordinated attacks against Israel in the Sinai Peninsula and the Golan Heights. The two leaders had divergent interests from the start. Sadat wanted closer ties with Washington and ultimately a deal with Israel to return the Sinai to Egypt. Sadat believed war or at least pretense of war was necessary to expedite such an outcome.[7] Hafez needed war for his own reasons. He had assured the army officers who backed him in the November 1970 coup that he would reclaim the

Golan and he intended to make good on that promise, in part to finally quiet those who blamed him for losing the territory to Israel in 1967.

War brought two crucial things that Hafez required to cement his grip on Syria: lots of weapons and military aid from the Soviet Union and cash from oil-rich Arab states to replenish state coffers and prop up the floundering economy. Hafez was also tempted to believe that war in 1973 could turn him into a hero of all Arabs like Sadat's tall and charismatic predecessor, the beloved icon Gamal Abdel-Nasser, who had died a few weeks before Hafez's 1970 coup.[8]

Assad and Nasser could not have been more different. Hafez was short and boxy-looking, with a protruding and expansive forehead, an aquiline nose with a somewhat bulbous tip, and unusually large ears. Public speaking was not his forte; he came across as cold and aloof. Hafez was in general conservative and risk-averse. He was a grand schemer who hated surprises and calculated every detail of all his moves.[9]

In what he hoped would be a Nasser-like moment, Hafez announced in a somber yet reassuring televised speech the start of war against Israel on his forty-third birthday in October 1973.[10] "You are today defending the honor of the Arab nation and protecting its dignity and existence," he told Syrians, invoking historic Muslim commanders and their conquests and triumphs. His friend Mustafa was deputy commander of the joint Egyptian–Syrian military council in charge of executing the war plans.

Israel was initially stunned by the two-pronged attack and suffered heavy losses. But a few days later Egyptian forces dug in after crossing the Suez Canal, which allowed the Israelis to concentrate on the Syrian front, mounting a counteroffensive that eventually threatened Damascus, a mere fifty miles north of the Golan. Toward the end of October 1973, a cease-fire was negotiated by the Americans and Soviets. This was followed by months of marathon meetings between US secretary of state Henry Kissinger and Hafez, who was portrayed as a crafty and intractable negotiator, prone to lecturing for hours on end.[11] Hafez insisted that he get back all the Golan even though his forces failed to recapture any territory during the war. The Israelis thought he was out of his mind. They fought hard for the Golan, an area of biblical and military significance and, most important, rich in water.

37

"He says his political survival is at stake," Kissinger cabled the White House after a four-hour session with Hafez in Damascus in May 1974.[12]

Finally, as a face-saving compromise, Hafez got Quneitra, a small town in the Golan's foothills, while Israel kept the rest of the territory.[13] In June 1974, Hafez signed a disengagement agreement that stationed UN troops for decades in a demilitarized zone between Israel and Syria. The Israelis dynamited buildings and infrastructure in Quneitra before handing it back to the Syrians.

In the middle of June 1974, Richard Nixon became the first US president to visit Damascus, holding talks with Hafez even as fallout from the Watergate scandal played out at home. Diplomatic ties between Damascus and Washington, severed seven years earlier, were restored, and there was a promise of US financial aid to Syria.[14]

The Americans concluded that Hafez was a dictator they could do business with, just like many others they were dealing with in Africa, the Middle East, and Latin America. Despite Syria's proclaimed socialism, alliance with the Soviet Union, and anti-West rhetoric, Hafez cared about one thing and one thing only: his own power. There was an unspoken but mutually understood quid pro quo with the Americans. Hafez was free to do whatever needed to be done to maintain his grip on Syria as long as he never again waged war against Israel, Washington's main regional ally.[15] Hafez's make-believe victories hardly bothered the Americans.

That year Hafez's propaganda machine celebrated his "Tishreen Epic" with a song that went like this: *Syria, my beloved, you have given me back my dignity, freedom, and identity; now I can truly call myself an Arab.*[16] Years later, many Arabs would realize that great harm was done to the Palestinian people from the way the Assads and other Middle Eastern dictators exploited the Arab-Israeli conflict over the years to safeguard their power.

When Hafez ousted his comrades-turned-enemies in November 1970 with the help of Mustafa and others, much of Syria was relieved. Hafez promised associates in the army and party, especially those from the Sunni majority, to reverse the anti-business and radical policies of his deposed rivals. He vowed rapprochement with the West and Sunni-led regional states. Merchants in cities like Damascus greeted Hafez's ascent with enthusiasm. They hoped he would be less dogmatic than his predecessor and bring stability and prosperity after years of coups and countercoups.[17]

"We asked God for deliverance, he sent us Assad," was the slogan adopted by Damascene merchants and clergymen.[18] Shortly after seizing power in 1970, Hafez and his generals went to pray at the Umayyad Mosque, a symbol of the glory of the dynasty that once ruled Muslims from Damascus. Merchants slaughtered sheep on Hafez's way to the mosque and blood washed the cobblestoned alleyways as the new leader smiled and waved at the crowds. *"Mansour inshallah!"* ("Victorious by the will of God!"), they shouted as he passed.[19] It was an affirmation of allegiance and goodwill for the new leader, the custom among Arabs and Muslims for centuries.

Hafez received overwhelming backing in a referendum in 1971 that made him president for seven years. Buoyed by popular support and hope for stability, he began the process of enshrining his family rule for life. A new constitution adopted in early 1973 effectively put executive, legislative, and judicial powers in the president's hands. Martial law and other repressive measures were maintained. Casting himself as hero and liberator after the October 1973 war, Hafez then set out to consolidate his grip on the Baath Party, turning it into a facade for his rule — a blend of military dictatorship, brutal police state, and feudal patronage.

Party membership grew dramatically, and it became a vehicle for expanding Hafez's reach across Syria and a platform for his glorification. The party's regional command, the equivalent of the Central Committee in communist states, was purged of those suspected of having less than absolute loyalty to Hafez.[20] Among the raft of decrees Hafez passed a month after he seized power was one creating the party's Revolutionary Youth Union "to prepare the young generation militarily."[21] Every corner of Syria down to the remotest hamlet had a chapter, and members had priority in college admission, government jobs, overseas scholarships, and military academy enrollment.

Inspired by what he saw during a visit to North Korea in the fall of 1974, Hafez ordered the creation of the Baath Vanguards Organization to indoctrinate children from grades one through six in schools and summer camps.[22] Schoolchildren wore khaki uniforms, learned military discipline and skills, and perfected a "Heil Hitler"–like salute performed each

39

morning in a ceremony before class. Later, the Syrian Scouts were suspended so as not to compete with the Vanguards.

The *mukhabarat*, a cornerstone of the police state, was modeled after East Germany's State Security apparatus, or Stasi, which implemented a wide-reaching and intricate system of citizen surveillance. Likewise, Hafez put in place a web of *mukhabarat* departments, sections, and branches to ensure that everyone was watching everyone else everywhere and that no attempt to oust him had any chance of succeeding. Syrians would have Hafez's eyes and ears inside their homes.

And like any dictator longing for immortality, Hafez needed colossal Soviet-like projects that his subjects could celebrate. Flush with financial assistance from oil-rich Arab states, the Soviet Union, and even, later, the United States, Hafez launched major infrastructure works, with nearly $1.5 billion earmarked for public investment in the 1971 five-year plan.[23] For decades, schoolchildren memorized that it was the nation's father, Hafez, who "subdued and tamed" the Euphrates River with the dams he built on it, starting in 1973.[24] In arts class, children went from drawing bucolic nature scenes to depicting the leader and his supposedly miraculous achievements. One student received high marks for cutting out Hafez's portrait in a magazine and pasting it over the sun in his drawing of spring.[25] Just like in the parades staged by fascists, schoolchildren took part in torchlight processions to commemorate key moments of the history and narrative created by Hafez. The veneration of Hafez became a core army doctrine.

"Our Leader Forever Hafez al-Assad!" would become the army's battle cry.

A cult of personality was constructed around Hafez, no different from that of his friends Nicolae Ceausescu of Romania and Kim Il-sung of North Korea. Shrines and statues in every town and city as well as an entire museum in Damascus built by North Korea were dedicated to Hafez and his purported Tishreen victory.

A central theme of regime agitprop was that an Assad-led Syria was a necessity for all Arabs because it was supposedly in the vanguard of perpetual resistance against the mortal enemy Israel and its Western imperialist backers. As such, any questioning of Hafez's authority was treasonous or even sacrilegious. It was a testament to the power of lies and fear. Many Syrians believed or wanted to believe that Hafez was destined to lift Syria from its backward and feudal past and propel it toward modernization. It meant that they were generally ready to accept the regime's lies about the Golan, the economy, the West, or any other matter. Then there was fear, fear so great it made people worship the object or person that terrified them, which bit by bit became the regime and Hafez himself.

Despite looking outside Syria for inspiration, Hafez forged his own unique identity and style as supreme leader by incorporating strong local family and clan traditions. Like a Levantine feudal lord or a Sicilian mafia boss, he ruled through a dozen or so handpicked figures underneath him. They included lifelong companions like Mustafa and other army and party chiefs and *mukhabarat* heads. Beyond their loyalty, they were chosen with sectarian, regional, and tribal criteria in mind. There was a sort of balancing act in the appointments. The importance of these individuals at any given moment was a function of their proximity to Hafez: those closest to the leader had the most power.[26] All owed Hafez the privileges and benefits they derived from the system, and they stayed in the game as long as they respected his rules. Ministers and members of parliament merely carried out orders of this regime apparatus and its head, Hafez al-Assad. Occasionally one of these functionaries made it to the inner circle.

Like a medieval king, Hafez decided what his lords got. In the mid-1970s he favored a Sunni businessman over his brother-in-law Mohammad Makhlouf in awarding a government contract to build Syria's first hotel chain.

As Hafez was busy consolidating his power, these early years were filled with happy memories for the Assad and Tlass children. Like most offspring of well-to-do Damascene families, they attended the Laïque school, established by France in the mid 1920s when Syria was still its protectorate. It was part of the *Mission Laïque Française*, or French Lay (Secular) Mission, a network of international schools set up as a counterweight to those run by Catholic orders. Young minds were supposed to be shaped by critical thinking, openness, and tolerance. But during the short-lived union with Nasser's Egypt and the subsequent Baathist power grab, Syria's

Laïque school was nationalized like other private institutions and businesses.[27] Much of the curriculum came under the Syrian state's influence, particularly subjects like history and civics. According to a former student from that period, "They wrote history as they saw fit and taught it to us — it was brainwashing."[28]

Bassel and Manaf were one grade apart but played together at recess and sometimes walked to school and back home together, trailed by presidential guards. During the October 1973 war, the boys were at school when Israeli American-made fighter jets swooped low over Damascus and dropped bombs on several targets. Sirens went off all over the city and schoolchildren ran home.[29]

Soon the boys were caught up in the thrill of war, seeing their dads as valiant warriors confronting the evil Israeli enemy as portrayed by the regime. They wanted to be like their fathers and were overjoyed when they accompanied them to Quneitra in June 1974 for the flag-raising ceremony. The following summer they went to the first children's military training camp on the banks of Barada River. They dangled from ropes, jumped through flaming hoops, rode horses, and posed with assault rifles. "Bassel was a real daredevil, he had a very strong personality even as a child," recalls Manaf.

The Assad and Tlass children, a total of eight by then, got together often at the Assad family home in Malki, a newish Damascus neighborhood mainly for well-to-do Sunni families. It was a square, two-story cement block house with an attached garden that was bequeathed to the state by a rich Saudi-Syrian doctor after Hafez took power.[30]

At the time, the Assads were probably the only Alawites in upscale Malki, but Hafez was determined to project ascetic tastes and manage his household with a certain degree of austerity and frugality. The furniture was basic and the kitchen counters were made of cheap pressed wood. The most ornate objects in the house were a pair of Chinese vases in the entryway. The family only had one maid, and Hafez's wife, Aniseh, cooked lunch on most days. At mealtime she fussed over her children and their friends to make sure they washed their hands first and had eaten enough. At the table, Hafez made small talk with his children's friends: "How was your day at school? What does your dad do?"[31]

*　　*　　*

At ten, Hafez's second son, Bashar, was thin, lanky, slightly stoop-backed, and shy. His posture made him seem as if he had a constant urge to go to the toilet.[32] He spoke with a pronounced lisp due to a deformity in his lower jaw. He was ignored by his father and oppressed by his older siblings, especially his sister, Bushra, an outgoing and bossy teenage girl.

"You have arrived! Do not make a mess," Bushra often shouted at Bashar and the few friends he brought to the house.[33] "Why are you making noise? Stay out of that room! Do not play with the ball there, dad is napping."

Bushra and Bassel were the favorite children in the Assad household. They had the nicest bedrooms. Bushra was usually chauffeured alone to Laïque. Bassel got his own car at an early age. Bashar, meanwhile, was driven to school with his two youngest brothers, Maher and Majd; the latter had a developmental disability.

At school, Bashar was quiet and aloof. He was nothing like his two raucous and troublemaking cousins, Duraid and Mudhar, who were in the same class.

"Bashar was nerdy but average academically, good at memorizing. He had lots of problems. He was moody and never able to make steady and close friends," recalled a classmate.[34] "He was your friend at the start of the year, and then after midterm break he pretended not to know you. The only reason we wanted to befriend him was because he was the president's son."

Teachers went out of their way to accommodate Bashar, and the school principal often made a point of chatting with him during his rounds on classes. "It was the most awkward moment for Bashar," said the classmate. "He would turn red. He did not want to be in the spotlight. He wanted the earth to swallow him."

On some occasions, especially during extracurricular activities, Bashar's shyness was so severe that he seemed to be crippled by it and was gripped by anxiety attacks. Classmates also remembered a mean streak. Unlike Bassel and his cousins, Bashar never seemed interested in helping anyone or sharing anything, not even a chocolate bar.[35]

Whereas Bassel was the natural leader and the one everyone deferred to, Bashar was an introvert and a loner. "Bashar was living in the shadow of his brother, in fact they were all living in Bassel's shadow," said Manaf.

Though a born leader, Bassel also had a rebellious and mischievous side. One time on the way back from school, Bassel wanted to play a trick on his guards. "Let's lose them," he told Manaf.[36] They managed to evade them and ended up at Manaf's home. The boys were very amused, but Bassel's mother was not pleased when the guards told her what had happened. She called the Tlass home a bit later and Manaf's mother assured her that the children had made it back safely.

Although Hafez al-Assad and Mustafa Tlass were intimate friends, their wives never grew close. Hafez's wife, Aniseh, was staid and withdrawn, made few public appearances, and tended to her children and husband like a typical Syrian housewife. There was talk in Damascene social circles that Hafez seriously considered marrying a second wife—someone perhaps more charming and extroverted—to help him woo Western leaders, with whom he wanted to forge better ties, particularly after Nixon's visit.[37]

Mustafa Tlass's wife, Lamia, was a loyal housewife, too, but loved to socialize, host parties, and tell jokes. She often went out of her way to enchant guests. On special occasions she traveled personally with her driver to neighboring Lebanon to shop for the best food ingredients not found in Damascus.[38]

Lamia learned very early on to live with her husband's womanizing, which became legendary. A family friend described Mustafa as a sex maniac who wanted to sleep with almost any woman he encountered.[39] "As my eyes were fixated on her beautiful breasts I noticed she was wearing a white and transparent nightgown that concealed nothing of God's creation," Mustafa wrote in his memoirs years later about a neighbor he fantasized about for days.[40] He was already married with three children.

Lamia may have realized that there were things she could not offer Mustafa but also, in any case, that she was always going to be his anchor and equal partner in what mattered to her the most: family, power, and status.

"Lamia was strong and in control; key decisions were in her hands," said the family friend.[41] "She could pick up the phone anytime and speak with Hafez, with whom she grew close. She called him Abu [father of] Bassel," a common form of address conveying respect and familiarity and which usually refers to a father's eldest son. Hafez respected Lamia, too, and sought her advice on certain matters. Lamia often baked Hafez his favorite chocolate cake.

Hafez's honeymoon period in power did not last long. From 1976 through the mid-1980s, he faced a series of external and internal challenges that rocked his regime's foundations. The regime's vulnerabilities, contradictions, and outright lies were exposed in the process, but Hafez also demonstrated his resiliency and just how far he was willing to go to retain power. The Assads never forgot the lessons learned from this trying and bloody period. And the Tlasses were by their side all the way.

In the summer of 1976, Hafez sent troops to neighboring Lebanon at the request of the Christian president, who feared takeover by a coalition of Muslim forces including Palestinian guerillas, Arab nationalists, and radical leftists. The pretext for the Syrian intervention was protecting Lebanon's sovereignty after the collapse of its army.[42] But Syria had always seen Lebanon as an integral part of its territory, artificially carved out by colonial powers, and it was eager for the chance to bring it back under its control. More important for Hafez, being in Lebanon gave him leverage over world powers like the United States trying to settle the broader Arab–Israeli conflict.

Before intervening in Lebanon, the Syrian regime had for years armed and supported the same forces threatening the Christian-dominated government. Syrian-backed Palestinians used Lebanon as a staging ground to attack Israel to the south.[43] When the principal Palestinian factions and their allies defied Hafez to pursue their own agendas, he backed their Christian-led enemies in hopes of currying favor with the West, which supported Lebanon's Christians and Israel.

Hafez's foray into Lebanon exemplified a core regime strategy: Fuel the menace and create the problem and then present yourself as the only one capable of ending it.[44]

The United States, meanwhile, hoped Hafez could rein in what it saw as Soviet-backed fanatics running amok in Lebanon. So Washington

45

pressured its ally Israel to exercise restraint toward the Syrian intervention.[45] Americans also provided Hafez with economic aid, totaling about $627.4 million by 1979, to counter communist influence and spur Syria to conclude a peace agreement with Israel.[46]

In 1978, Israel annexed southern Lebanon and signed a peace treaty with Egypt, thus isolating Hafez and potentially undermining all his leverage. More troubling for Hafez was the fact that some Lebanese Christian factions he previously supported were forging their own alliance with Israel, independent of him and his own agenda.[47] By then Lebanon was an arena for regional and international proxy wars. Atrocities were committed by all sides. Once more Hafez, for his part, turned against those who defied him.

Hafez's real crucible, though, was not in Lebanon but at home in Syria. It was a battle he waged with far less media attention and more brutal resolve.

In 1976, a militant wing of the Muslim Brotherhood party known as the *Tali'a al-Muqatila*, or Fighting Vanguard, launched a wave of assassinations and bombings targeting anyone associated with the regime, particularly members of the Assads' Alawite minority. Ostensibly, this was retaliation for the arrest of the group's leader Marwan Hadid (the Hama rebel from the 1960s) and his subsequent death in prison.[48] While some in the Brotherhood advocated confrontation with the regime, most opposed the violence and viewed the Vanguard as a dangerous renegade group.[49]

Separate from the Islamist militants' campaign, public discontent with the regime rose in 1977. Regime officials including Assad family members like Hafez's brother Rifaat and their business partners amassed fortunes and lived lavishly while average Syrians struggled with miserable wages, soaring consumer prices, and chronic food shortages. Corruption and outright banditry plagued all levels of government, especially in the provinces.[50]

There was also rising discomfort among the overwhelmingly Sunni population toward what they saw as a regime increasingly favoring and empowering Hafez's Alawite minority. Only token Sunnis known for their absolute loyalty, like Mustafa Tlass, were elevated to positions of power. New mostly Alawite settlements began to encroach on predominantly Sunni centers in Damascus and Homs as farmers flocked to the big cities for jobs in the security services and burgeoning bureaucracy. Sunnis also resented Hafez's initial support for Christians against Muslims in Lebanon.

In 1977, teachers and factory workers all over Syria threatened to go on strike because their salaries were being outpaced by inflation. In the summer of that year, no more than 5 percent of registered voters bothered to cast their ballots in elections organized by the regime for a new rubber-stamp legislature.[51] More troubling for Hafez was agitation by the influential professional associations and hints of cooperation between the Brotherhood and remnants of old enemies and rivals.[52]

One month after Hafez's term as president was renewed for another seven years, insurgents assassinated a senior Baath Party official and a relative of the Assads.[53] The Alawite community clamored for revenge. About 15,000 suspects were rounded up by the *mukhabarat*.[54] Hafez seized the opportunity and declared an all-out war against terrorism—a perfect pretext to crush political opponents while diverting attention from legitimate grievances.

War between Hafez and his opponents heated up in the summer of 1979 when a Fighting Vanguard militant, who later called himself the caliph (leader of all Muslims), led a bloody assault on the Aleppo Artillery School with the help of Sunni officers on the inside. During class, the main accomplice, a Sunni captain and Baath Party member, singled out Alawite cadets by name for execution. About eighty-three were killed and many more wounded.[55] The blatantly sectarian atrocity split the Muslim Brotherhood as well as the Vanguard itself over the tactics and pace of what it called its jihad, or sacred and God-mandated struggle, against the regime.[56] Hafez chose to wage war against the entire Brotherhood and anyone remotely associated with it.[57]

The Aleppo massacre exposed cracks in the army. Immediately after the killings, fighting broke out between Alawite and Sunni cadets at the Homs military academy. Mustafa personally went to the academy to restore order.[58] Hafez sent his brother Rifaat to deal with Aleppo. He was part of the inner circle and commanded a praetorian guard called Saraya al-Difa'a, the Defense Companies, made up almost entirely of Alawites. Rifaat's gruff persona and overt sectarianism helped rally fighters from the Assads' community. Unlike his older brother, Rifaat had an established reputation as a ruthless commander who also knew how to have fun; he had multiple wives and mistresses and a seemingly boundless sexual appetite, loved to flaunt his power and wealth, and often stayed up all night smoking, drinking, and gambling. He earned the admiration of thugs and had no trouble filling the ranks. Within a matter of hours after arriving in Aleppo, Rifaat and his fighters rounded up close to 6,000 people.[59]

Clashes and bombings engulfed the city and spread to Hama as violence flared in the capital and around the coastal city of Latakia. Many civilian detainees became scapegoats for the insurgency and were executed in sham trials.[60]

Toward the end of the summer of 1979, threats inched closer to the Assads and Tlasses—endangering their households and children.

In August 1979, Mahmoud Shahade, a neurosurgeon and army doctor close to Hafez, was gunned down in an ambush in central Damascus. Fear gripped the regime and new security measures were introduced.[61] The street passing by the Assad home was closed to the public, steel gates were erected, and more guards were posted on the perimeter. Similar measures were taken around the Tlass home.

Manaf and Bassel, who were in their late teens at the time, were under such tight security that they barely saw each other that summer and fall. Manaf was finishing high school, Bassel was about to start college, and fourteen-year-old Bashar was still at Laïque.

One afternoon, Bashar and his friends were strolling alone not far from home when Bassel spotted them as he drove by.[62] Bassel stopped his Mercedes in the middle of the street and got out.

"Where are your guards?" Bassel screamed at Bashar.

"Take this and DO NOT move from your place," shouted Bassel as he handed a stunned-looking Bashar a pistol. Minutes later presidential guards arrived at the scene.

Shortly after that incident, a driver for the interior minister's children, who were friendly with Bashar, suddenly disappeared amid talk he was arrested by the *mukhabarat* on suspicion of plotting to kill or kidnap Bashar.[63] Bashar's physics teacher at Laïque, suspected of being a secret Muslim Brotherhood member, disappeared, too.

The lesson for the Assad children was that their enemy could be hiding anywhere; they must never take any chances.

The Americans believed much of the opposition was homegrown despite assistance to the insurgents from neighboring rival Baathist state, Iraq. That same summer, Hafez had traveled to Baghdad to try to make peace with the Iraqis, but within weeks Saddam Hussein grabbed absolute power. In a chilling televised proceeding, Saddam smoked a cigar as he presided over a show trial for a group of comrades accused of plotting to assassinate him, allegedly on Hafez's orders. Hundreds were executed in the purge that followed.[64] It was a reminder to the Assads of just how ruthless they needed to be in order to stay in power.

At the end of 1979, Syria's Baath leadership gathered for a party congress in Damascus amid extraordinary security. Hafez spoke passionately about an American "Imperialist-Zionist" conspiracy in league with local enemies to topple him because he didn't make peace with Israel like Egypt's Sadat, who shocked Arabs that year by flying to Tel Aviv for a state visit.[65] "While we do not want to use force against anyone, it must be understood that we will use force and violence in the appropriate manner and…time if the misguided do not repent and continue their suspicious and questionable acts linked to Camp David," he said, referring to the Egyptian–Israeli peace treaty signed in 1978 at the presidential retreat near Washington.[66] (The Assads would blame the same conspiracies for another challenge to their rule three decades later.)

While Hafez spoke to his partisans about American conspiracies, Washington, on the contrary, was very eager for him to stay strong. A cable from the US embassy in Damascus that same year assessed Hafez's prospects in the face of internal challenges and concluded that any weakening in his position was detrimental to US interests, including Arab–Israeli peace and secure oil supplies. "We have grown accustomed to the leadership of President Al-Assad and the stability he represents," said the 1979 cable.[67] "While we have our differences with Assad, particularly in terms of tactics, many of his policies have worked to our advantage and in favor of stability in the area." The hope of getting Hafez to negotiate with Israel could be compromised "if he felt his domestic base was wobbly," added the cable.

49

During the same December 1979 party congress at which Hafez spoke, his brother Rifaat invoked Stalin's purges and Mao Zedong's campaign against state enemies and called for similar "national cleansing" in Syria. He proposed people's courts to banish "everyone who diverts from the patriotic path" to desert camps for rehabilitation, where they also toiled on greening projects.[68]

Hafez suspected that his brother wanted to upstage him by demonstrating to regime loyalists he was more uncompromising with their enemies than even the leader himself. So Hafez abruptly ended secret talks he was holding with elements of the Muslim Brotherhood and froze prisoner releases he had initiated to appease them.[69]

Then came the spring of 1980, when the Tlasses were reminded that their power and privileges were contingent upon total and absolute complicity with the Assads. They had to stand by the Assads even if that meant waging war against their coreligionists, the Sunnis, or the entire Syrian population for that matter.

In early March 1980, general strikes and anti-regime protests erupted in several cities and towns across Syria, most notably Aleppo, Deir Ezzour, Hama, Homs, and Idlib.[70] Damascus was minimally affected due to the intervention of a powerful Hafez ally, Badredeen al-Shallah, head of the city's chamber of commerce and scion of a Sunni merchant family.

Protest organizers included the Muslim Brotherhood, professional associations, labor unions, communists, socialists, and secularists. It was not just fanatics, as Hafez kept insisting, but a wide and varied front of diplomats, doctors, engineers, filmmakers, intellectuals, lawyers, students, workers, and everyone else who rejected his iron-fist rule and scorched-earth methods.

They demanded release of political prisoners, an end to martial law, restoration of civil liberties, and withdrawal of the army and regime militias from towns and cities. Some of Hafez's opponents went further, calling for an end to his rule.

Mustafa knew Hafez as someone with nerves of steel: "Not even tsunamis riled him."[71] The challenge to his authority in those early days of March 1980, however, shook Hafez to the core. He became hysterical.

This was a personal affront. Why were they rebelling against him? Did he not build factories and universities and give the masses opportunities? Did he not make them proud by turning their backward country into an entity to be reckoned with? Even US president Jimmy Carter called him a "strong and moderate" leader with "a great role to play because of his experience [and the] greatness of his country."[72]

As far as Hafez was concerned, the protests were completely unjustified and had to represent a grand conspiracy. The only option was to crush this challenge. He and his lieutenants took to their tasks efficiently and swiftly.

Mustafa Tlass hunkered down at the defense ministry to oversee deployment of army units to quell the protests. The first target was the picturesque northern town of Jisr al-Shughour, sitting at the crossroads between the epicenter of regime opposition in Aleppo and the Alawite minority's strongholds in western Syria. Rioters burned down the town's Baath Party office and raided an army barracks, seizing weapons and ammunition. Special forces arriving in helicopters surrounded the town and bombarded it until insurgents surrendered. Dozens were rounded up and executed in mop-up operations. An estimated 200 townspeople were killed within a few hours. More people were killed in similar operations in adjacent towns and villages.[73]

At the same time one of Hafez's trusted Alawite army generals was recalled from Lebanon and told to advance with his armored units on Aleppo.[74]

In Damascus, Hafez personally mobilized students, teachers, workers, and others. Loyalists underwent crash military training, were armed and instructed to crush their enemies. Almost no day went by in March 1980 when Hafez did not speak directly to the public, inciting them to action.

He told the confederation of artisans that those protesting against him were "enemies of the artisans" and CIA agents, and he called the United States the "mortal enemy of our people and its evolution."[75] The previous day he had told farmers that he was a peasant like them and urged them to do what they saw fit to defend the regime. "If you feel you need weapons, they are available and at your disposal," he said.[76] A few days later, he told newly armed high school and college students that their enemies were not just Islamists but everyone challenging the regime, including fellow students.[77] "You're now old enough to identify the homeland's enemies no matter what costume they wear…strike them without mercy," said Hafez.

Bassel wore a military uniform and accompanied his father to most events and rallies held in auditoriums all over Damascus. He was with his father when he cut a deal with Shallah, head of the Damascus chamber of commerce, to make sure the city's businesses and merchants did not strike.[78] It did not matter that Shallah, with his signature red fez cap and tailor-made three-piece suits, was a symbol of the elitists and reactionaries Hafez was railing against to farmers and laborers.

In effect, the Assads, Tlasses, and other regime families, who came from peasant backgrounds but accumulated great wealth and power, were now partnering with Damascus's business families to crush a popular uprising in the name of fighting elitists.

By early April, more than 30,000 soldiers including Rifaat's fighters encircled Aleppo's rebellious quarters. Artillery shells and rockets rained on residential areas, and then "cleansing operations" commenced—mass detentions, field executions, and looting when soldiers entered the neighborhoods. There is no exact count, but up to 2,000 people were estimated to have been killed and at least 8,000 detained in Aleppo alone between April and December 1980.[79]

At the start of the Aleppo assault, Hafez dissolved all professional associations; the *mukhabarat* took over their offices and arrested hundreds of members. Some were tortured to death in *mukhabarat* prisons, where techniques were given names like "tire," "flying carpet," and "black slave," the last one involving strapping a victim onto a device which when turned on inserted a heated metal skewer into the anus.[80]

Depriving the protest movement of its civilian leaders and peaceful activists was crucial for validating Hafez's lie that his only opponents were armed religious fanatics.[81]

The confrontation deepened and became more personal when Hafez survived an attempt on his life in the summer of 1980. He was at the presidential palace bidding farewell to a visiting African dictator when two grenades were tossed in Hafez's direction. He pushed one away with his foot while a bodyguard threw himself on the second one and died to protect him. Hafez suffered cuts on his chest and legs and was taken to the hospital.[82] The attacker fled and was never apprehended. The Muslim Brotherhood was blamed, and the next day a horrific reprisal took place. About 200 of Rifaat's men were flown to a notorious military prison. They were let into cells of suspected Muslim Brotherhood members and began executing inmates mostly by mowing them down with their machine guns; about 1,000 prisoners were killed in the massacre. The family was taking its revenge.[83]

The attempt on Hafez's life had a profound impact on his children, especially Bassel. "Bassel was nice and simple but he became aggressive, confrontational, and more complex," said Manaf. "Before the assassination attempt he did not act like the president's son, but after he became the president's son."[84]

Much of the country was filled with an atmosphere of terror that summer. A new law made membership to the Muslim Brotherhood punishable by death, but this, too, was simply a pretext for widening the regime's war on anyone daring to challenge it. Checkpoints were everywhere, and no day went by without raids by the *mukhabarat* and pro-Hafez militias to arrest suspected opponents, critics, or anyone perceived as such simply because of their birthplace, address, or appearance.[85]

That same summer of 1980, Manaf joined a military training camp organized by the Revolutionary Youth Union. It was a way for the Tlasses to demonstrate that all of their family, and not just Mustafa, was doing its part in rallying around Hafez and the regime.

"Bravo, well done!" Bassel told Manaf when he found out.[86]

Men and women trainees were taught how to storm buildings, parachute jump from planes, throw themselves from the back of a moving truck, and other bizarre and cruel skills like biting off a snake's head and strangling a puppy. "The universities are yours, the country is yours, everything is yours!" Hafez's brother Rifaat lectured Manaf and others at the camp as he pumped his fist in the air.

And they took it literally. Manaf and other high school and college students who completed similar training wore camouflage and carried pistols in class.[87]

After the training, Manaf started his freshman year at Damascus University's faculty of civil engineering, just like his friend Bassel.

A year later, September 1981, Manaf was with his father when they were stopped at a checkpoint by female soldiers, a unit of Rifaat's force known as the parachutists.

"Any veiled women in the car?" snapped one of them as she banged on the car's chassis.

"Shut up, this is the defense minister," protested Manaf before they were let through.

That day the parachutists arrived in buses in several Damascus neighborhoods including upscale Malki and Rawda, where the Assads and Tlasses lived. They stopped all veiled women, no matter their age, and made them take off their hijabs. Those who hesitated had them torn off. Some were insulted and beaten.

When Manaf and his father got home, they found several veiled women huddled in their building's entryway. They were hiding from the militiawomen; they thought the powerful Tlasses, Sunnis like them, could protect them.[88]

"Call Hafez al-Assad immediately, this should not happen, people should not be humiliated this way!" Manaf's mother, Lamia, ordered her husband as he walked in.

"If there's a plan to ban the veil in public, then people should be given some notice," Mustafa told Hafez.

Hafez had no knowledge of the order and later claimed that Rifaat's soldiers acted on their own because they were antagonized by the sight of veiled women. Two days later Hafez offered a mild rebuke of these actions during a speech in Damascus. It was a sign that he appreciated the zealotry of those defending his regime.

In fact, Hafez attended almost every graduation ceremony for the paramilitary forces headed by his brother, and it was always the same incitement. "You must look for traitors everywhere, in every corner, and you must pluck them out wherever they're found," said Hafez at one ceremony. "Have no mercy."[89]

Women in camouflage and berets, some with braids, raised their rifles with one arm, crying: "With blood we sacrifice for you, Hafez, with souls we sacrifice for you, Hafez."[90]

The myth that the regime's brutality and excesses during this period were the work of Hafez's brother Rifaat would spread later after a rupture between the siblings. In fact, Hafez was involved in every aspect of the terror campaign to crush the challenge to his rule. Rifaat was just a tool.

By 1981, Hafez had almost achieved what he wanted. He finished off the weakest of his opponents, such as the professionals, leftists, and students. Most were dead, rotting in jail, or exiled outside Syria. In many cases wives, children, and parents of fugitive opposition activists were arrested and tortured to pressure them to return.[91]

Now Hafez turned his attention to dealing a final blow to the Muslim Brotherhood, which by then was in total disarray; many of those previously advocating political activism and negotiations were compelled to move closer to the position of the extremists fighting the regime. Hama was the setting of the showdown.

In spring 1981, the city got a taste of the tragedy that befell it a year later. After insurgents ambushed security forces on Hama's outskirts, Hafez's forces moved into the city. Hundreds of men of all ages were arrested or executed on the streets.[92]

Later that year Damascus was hit by a series of massive explosions, including one in the vicinity of the Assad family residence and another not far from the children's school, the Laïque, which killed and wounded scores, mostly civilians and children, and appeared to target the nearby Baath Party headquarters.[93] Luckily the Assad children, including sixteen-year-old Bashar, had been transferred a few weeks before the bombing to another school closer to home. The regime blamed the Muslim Brotherhood, but subsequent reports suggested that the French secret service was involved, too, as retaliation for Syria's role in assassinating France's envoy to Lebanon earlier that year.[94]

In January 1982, the regime prepared a large-scale assault on Hama, the Muslim Brotherhood's last major foothold. Troops lay siege to the city and began their incursion in early February. A call for resistance was broadcast from mosques, and hundreds of civilians joined Islamist fighters to defend their city. It took the regime ten days to completely subdue the city and twenty days to carry out "cleansing operations." These involved house-to-house killing rampages and mass executions at public facilities, including factories that were turned into detention centers. Entire sections of the city were blown up and bulldozed. The militias and Alawite loyalists whom Hafez had trained, armed, and incited over the previous two years were set loose on predominantly Sunni Hama to kill, rape, and pillage. The death toll remains a source of controversy until this day, with groups like Amnesty International and Human Rights Watch putting it between 7,000 and 10,000, while regime opponents saying it's triple or quadruple that.[95]

There was also no precise figure of the number of people executed by the regime from the late 1970s until the early '80s. Mustafa Tlass said he signed so many death sentences that he eventually lost count. "At times in the 1980s, 150 death sentences a week were carried out by hanging in Damascus alone," he said.[96]

In many instances, Mustafa signed the sentences as a matter of bureaucratic routine after the hangings had already taken place, essentially providing official cover for mass murder.[97]

There was little reaction from Western governments, by then fixated on Lebanon and more concerned about threats posed by Middle Eastern terrorism in general than what a ruler like Hafez was doing to his own people. The fact that dictators like Hafez fueled and manipulated terrorism and fanaticism did not seem to matter.

"The situation in Hama does not seem to portend a general breakdown of law and order in Syria. The city is isolated and the recent uprising had largely been brought under control," began a terse five-line update on the situation in Hama in a memorandum to the director of the CIA on February 22, 1982, as Hafez's massacre was still underway.[98]

The Assad family ruled Syria uncontested for almost three decades after that.

4

Golden Knight

Mustafa Tlass was home playing backgammon with friends on a cold winter night in February 1984, exactly two years after the Hama massacre. The phone rang past midnight. It was Hafez al-Assad, who was convalescing after a heart attack. In his absence, the country's affairs were run by a six-man leadership committee including Mustafa, but still Hafez kept a watchful eye on the state.[1] He was calling about a matter that could not wait.

Hafez just learned that his brother Rifaat, who commanded a forty-thousand-strong paramilitary force equipped with tanks and attack helicopters, was plotting to take over the army and oust him from power.

Hafez instructed Mustafa to put on his uniform and head immediately to the defense ministry to mobilize army units and transfer them to key positions in and around the capital. Hafez hoped to nip the conspiracy in the bud and flush out those who might side with his brother.[2]

"Kill whoever disobeys you, even if it's my brother," Hafez directed his friend, without a hint of hesitation.[3] Manaf Tlass, now twenty-one years old, accompanied his father, carrying his own assault rifle and pistol. They braced themselves for the worst.[4]

Mustafa always obeyed Hafez's orders without question. In the sixties, late seventies, and early eighties, Mustafa by his own admission held hastily convened tribunals to execute regime opponents and quash any threat, whether it came from the army or the people. There was no doubt where he stood.

He remembered what Hafez had told party leaders in his presence after the 1970 coup: "Mustafa Tlass is a pillar of this regime — in fact, he's the regime's keeper."[5]

The fact that Mustafa and Hafez's brother Rifaat thoroughly loathed one another was going to make the job easier. Rifaat openly voiced contempt for Mustafa, called him Hafez's lapdog, ignored his orders as defense minister, and relished insulting him at every opportunity.[6]

Still, this was a delicate and perilous task for Mustafa; he was inserting himself in a feud between two equally strong-willed brothers. In 1980, at the height of the regime's war on its political opponents, Hafez sided with his brother against Mustafa in a dispute over a hugely inflated military fund allocation demanded by Rifaat. Mustafa became upset and went to Moscow briefly. Hafez called Manaf's mother, Lamia, and asked her to intervene as peacemaker.[7]

Four years later, Hafez was leaning on his devoted friend to confront his own brother.

Hafez dispatched two Alawite *mukhabarat* chiefs to support his defense minister in the dramatic face-off. The mission was going smoothly until Mustafa noticed that the special forces commander, Ali Haidar, was nowhere to be found. It seemed he was trying to hedge his bets, wait, and then support the Assad brother who emerged victorious in the showdown. Mustafa ordered Haidar's subordinate to move a special forces unit from its base on the northeast side of Damascus to the old fairgrounds in central Damascus near Umayyad Square. The buses that transported them from one end of the city to the other were masked as Iranian pilgrim coaches.[8] Special force officers disguised themselves as female pilgrims wearing black head-to-toe veils over their camouflage and hid their weapons under bus seats. Rifaat's men had set up checkpoints all over the city.

The ruse worked and proved to Haidar that his own men were ready to mutiny against him if he switched allegiance from the president to his brother.

The next day, Haidar came to Mustafa's office. Mustafa had his pistol on the desk. He told Haidar to call Rifaat right there and then. "Do not you know there's only one commander, and he's President Hafez al-Assad," Haidar told Rifaat.[9]

"Son of a bitch, you're giving me lessons in patriotism," shouted Rifaat and hung up.

After Hafez proved to his brother that the army backed him and a coup attempt would be suicide, he tried to console him with a symbolic government post.[10]

Rifaat rebuffed the offer and insisted on retaining command of his paramilitary force, the Defense Companies. In a show of defiance, Rifaat deployed some of his tank units in Damascus in early April 1984. This angered Hafez, and he personally went down to the streets to confront Rifaat's forces and order them back to their bases. He was accompanied by his eldest son, Bassel. There were extremely tense moments, with Rifaat repeatedly threatening to shell the defense ministry, but Hafez ultimately prevailed in what became a high-stakes game of wills.[11] The family standoff ended later that month when Rifaat accepted his brother's offer of $200 million and an honorary title in return for leaving Syria. Hafez got the money from his friend Muammar Gaddafi, the oil-rich Libyan dictator.[12]

It was as much a payoff as a token of appreciation from Hafez. Rifaat was the enforcer mobilized to mercilessly crush regime opponents in the 1970s and early '80s and preserve Hafez's absolute power in a campaign of state terror that killed or led to the disappearance of tens of thousands. Killing or arresting Rifaat would have been easy, but the repercussions in the family and Alawite community could be catastrophic for Hafez. When Alawite men and women joined Rifaat's forces they believed he was their savior, too; their very existence and power and privileges under the regime were in jeopardy. Hafez reckoned that moving violently against Rifaat could have destabilized the entire regime, so treating him generously was the best option.

As their fathers worked to shore up the regime's authority during the summer of 1984, Bassel and Manaf took their first outing in some time. After a morning spent shooting doves in the Damascus countryside, the two friends sat down for lunch.

Like most sons of rich and powerful Syrian regime officials, Bassel and Manaf were into fast cars, girls, and guns, but the events of the previous four years — the attempt on Hafez's life, the war to save the regime, and Rifaat's audacious bid — had had a profound impact on both of them. They were prompted to seriously ponder their future.

59

"What are your plans? Are you going into business?" Manaf asked Bassel, with a hint of sarcasm.[13]

They had talked about this for weeks, but nothing was settled one way or another. By this time Bassel had received his engineering degree and Manaf had one more year to get his.

"You're the son of Hafez al-Assad. You can't be a businessman or government employee," Manaf insisted. "The best thing is for us to go to the academy and become officers. Speak to your dad, and I'll do the same."

They went back to Damascus, and later that day Bassel called Manaf to tell him that his dad approved of him going to the academy to become a military engineer.

Bassel went to the Homs academy that fall and Manaf planned to follow him. But convincing his parents that this was the right path for him too was not so easy.

"Do not do it. I went through a lot with your dad," his mother, Lamia, pleaded with him. "You are better suited for civilian life, not the military."[14]

Manaf, meanwhile, clashed with his father, who did not want him to follow in his footsteps. "Mustafa felt his nice son could not survive the regime's cutthroat world," said a close family friend.[15]

In the end, Manaf defied his father. "I was close to Bassel and I came from a political family, so I wanted to go," Manaf said.[16]

"I was a good marksman, too," he added with a smile.[17]

Mustafa probably thought a business career for his son, alongside Manaf's older brother, Firas, was the best thing for Manaf and the family. By then twenty-four years old, Firas headed a company called MAS (an acronym for *Min Ajl Souriya*, "For Syria"), which had opened a cheese factory and meat-processing and canning plants and later started importing sugar, all thanks to lucrative army and government contracts secured with his father's help. There were plans to move into construction, and Manaf, with a civil engineering degree, would be well suited for that side of the business.

Then there was Mustafa's favorite child, Nahed, twenty-six and married to Akram Ojjeh, a Franco-Saudi billionaire of Damascene origin. Ojjeh was almost fifteen years older than her father, but he was one of the world's richest men. He had amassed a huge fortune from hefty commissions on the sale of arms and advanced military equipment, such as radars manufactured by French companies, to Saudi Arabia and other Middle Eastern autocracies. In gratitude for his services, the French had decorated him in the 1970s with one of their highest state orders, Commander of the Legion of Honor.[18]

Initially the Tlasses hoped that Nahed could marry Mansour, Ojjeh's son from an earlier marriage, but the match did not materialize. Instead, Ojjeh senior proposed to Nahed.

They married after lengthy deliberations in the Tlass family. Ojjeh's friends in Paris remembered Nahed when she first arrived as a timid and beautiful young girl bedecked in jewelry and gold bracelets. Nahed, though, was determined to be more than a pretty trophy wife. Ojjeh became a role model who taught her "about life" as she transformed herself into a charming and seductive Parisian socialite moving in power circles.[19]

Mustafa Tlass hoped that kinship with Ojjeh could also bring direct benefits to him and his family as well as his regime. Ojjeh was close to many political and business leaders around the world. The regime was battered and its resources were drained by the bloody war against internal enemies, the mess in Lebanon, and Washington's designation of Syria as a state sponsor of terrorism. (Syria has been on the US list since its creation in 1979.)

Mustafa and Hafez believed it was time to cut deals with the West, especially France, in the area that was of greatest concern to them: terrorism. In return, Syria would enjoy more political and economic cooperation, which would reward both the Assads and Tlasses. In November 1984, François Mitterrand — a friend of Ojjeh — became the first French head of state to visit Syria since it gained independence in 1946. In his press conference with Hafez in Damascus, Mitterrand denied accusations that Syria was connected to the assassination of the French ambassador to Lebanon in 1981, the bombing of a French base in Beirut two years later that killed fifty-eight soldiers, and a slew of assassinations and bombings in France and Europe, some targeting Hafez's exiled political opponents — allegations that had long hurt Syria's standing with Western powers. "There is nothing to prove that Syria was responsible. Since President

Assad has always asserted that this was not the case, I do not see why his word should be doubted," Mitterrand told reporters.[20]

Mitterrand's prime minister, Laurent Fabius, was furious over the visit because France possessed evidence that Hafez and his *mukhabarat* were connected to the ambassador's assassination and many other attacks on French interests.[21] Mitterrand overruled everyone and went to Syria anyway, hoping for some détente and cooperation with the Assads to stem the tide of violence being directed at France and other Western nations by a range of Middle Eastern radical groups.

"People understood it as realpolitik; there was no need to quarrel with a very dangerous country," said Michel Duclos, a French diplomat who later became ambassador to Syria.[22]

By the late 1970s, Hafez was convinced that the battle he was waging at home and the challenges he faced in Lebanon were all part of a conspiracy by his Arab and Western adversaries to corner him and force him to accept peace with Israel. Hafez sought retribution against these perceived enemies beyond Syria's borders. A special ops *mukhabarat* unit oversaw most assassinations and terror attacks and reported directly to Hafez.[23] His henchmen took out hostile journalists in Lebanon in 1980, and that same year they gunned down Salaheddin Bitar, cofounder of the Baath Party, who later broke ranks with the regime and organized an opposition front from Paris.[24] The following year they tried to assassinate the prime minister of Jordan, which hosted Syrian Muslim Brotherhood leaders, and a month later they killed the wife of a Brotherhood leader in Germany.[25]

Most regime attacks abroad, especially bombings in Europe, were conducted through proxies to allow for deniability, but several European intelligence services accused Syrian diplomats of smuggling bomb-making materials in privileged diplomatic suitcases.[26] The slain French ambassador Louis Delamare, who was seen as working at cross-purposes with Syria's agenda in Lebanon, was shot twelve times in 1981 by assailants from Sai'qa, a Palestinian militia founded by the Syrian regime.[27]

Lebanon's war became more complex and chaotic in 1982 as escalating tensions between Syria and Israel culminated in the latter's devastating invasion of Lebanon. American, French, Italian, and other foreign troops landed on Lebanon's shores to keep the peace.[28] Israel withdrew to the south and the Palestinian Liberation Organization leader Yasir Arafat was forced out of Lebanon,[29] but Hafez sought to retain and strengthen his position in Lebanon at any cost. He worked with Iran to train and support Lebanese Shiite Islamist militants and other extremists who attacked the West, seen as Israel's patron.

These Shiite militants, who later formed Hezbollah, were responsible for some of the deadliest and most heinous attacks against the United States in 1983. A suicide bomber driving a truck packed with the equivalent of 21,000 pounds of explosives leveled the American peacekeeping mission headquarters near the Beirut airport, killing 241 service personnel and wounding scores more. Earlier that year, more than sixty people were killed in a similar attack on the embassy.[30] No direct Syrian link emerged, but it was no secret that these extremists operated in Beirut and trained in Lebanon's Beqaa Valley in coordination with Syrian forces and *mukhabarat*.

"I bow my head—what do these Yankees really want? They cross great oceans with their ships and land on our beaches," Mustafa said a year after the attacks, praising the suicide bombers and tacitly acknowledging Syrian regime involvement. "We will kill until the invaders withdraw... The enemy must be killed, wherever he hides, and the ground beneath his feet must glow like hell..."[31]

The same Assad regime–linked terrorists later hijacked a US airliner in 1985 and kidnapped dozens of foreigners in Lebanon.[32]

"You have Arab-Israeli confrontation and America is siding with Israel, so it's normal for extremism to emerge," said Manaf, offering an argument often made across the Arab world to justify terrorism but also cynically and deceitfully used by the region's despots to protect and perpetuate their rule.[33]

Having ties to terrorists meant that the Assad regime could then offer its services to Western governments by passing on tips about planned attacks, convincing groups to forgo certain attacks, and helping negotiate hostage releases, all in return for concessions from these governments. "For the Syrian leadership, terrorism and intelligence are bargaining chips," said Duclos.[34]

By 1984, the French external intelligence service known by its acronym DGSE had extensive dealings with the Syrian regime, especially through Hafez's brother Rifaat.[35] Hafez later used intelligence sharing to pressure the French to grant Rifaat asylum in 1984 when he got rid of him.

The Americans, too, began to recognize the value and wisdom of working with the devil, cooperating with a regime they had labeled a state sponsor of terror.

"We respect traditional Syrian influence in Lebanon and expect it to continue," Republican Senator John Tower told Hafez in Damascus in February 1984 while praising the Syrian dictator's "tactical victory" in Lebanon.[36] Tower was accompanied by John McCain, a rising star in the House of Representatives and a former naval officer and war prisoner in Vietnam.

Hafez told the Americans he wanted "good and normal" relations.

With the regime secure at home and Western leaders coming to Damascus to meet with Hafez and seek his cooperation, Mustafa found time to dwell on his other passions: female celebrities and literary pretensions.

He established his own publishing house and promoted himself as a man of letters. His early works included a collection of poems titled *The Pillow of Sleeplessness*, dedicated to nineteen women he considered to be the world's most beautiful, among them Britain's Princess Diana and American *Playboy* model turned French pop singer Jeane Manson. "Manson inspired it, one day she sent me a pillow with her picture on it and a dedication. I took the pillow to bed, but could not sleep all night," Mustafa confided to German reporters.[37]

His publishing career was also marked by his fascist, anti-Semitic views. He penned the *The Matzoh of Zion*, about Damascene Jews allegedly killing Christians in the nineteenth century to use their blood in preparing unleavened bread, matzoh. A pro-Assad Lebanese Christian priest was believed to be the shadow author.

Mustafa relished being the regime's eccentric, brash, and larger-than-life persona. Critics called him a buffoon and a shameless sex maniac, and they joked that having him as defense minister for decades was Hafez's way of assuring Americans and Israelis after 1973 that Syria would never again wage war on the Jewish state. But one thing was certain: nobody in the regime ever dared speak or act like Mustafa.

He used the crudest profanities to attack regime enemies in public and was one of the few people his friend Hafez al-Assad felt at ease around and fully trusted.

On special occasions Mustafa loved to dress in his full military regalia, including cap, golden aiguillettes, and some three dozen army medals and decorations hanging from his neck or pinned to his chest. To relax he was often poolside at Damascus's Sheraton Hotel tanning, playing backgammon, and flirting with young women, according to many Damascenes who recalled seeing him there often, usually in tight, brightly colored swim trunks. He paid the pool membership of many young women.[38]

There also was a kindly and charitable side to him, friends said. He helped most petitioners who came from the provinces for an audience with him. In the 1980s, the Tlasses adopted a Palestinian baby girl who had reportedly lost her parents in the Lebanese civil war. She was named Sariya and raised as if she were Mustafa's own child.

By the 1980s Mustafa seemed ready for retirement, but there was still one crucial mission he had to undertake for Hafez: protect the regime from future threats and help to prolong the Assad family's rule.

Mustafa had no choice but to bow to his son Manaf's stubborn determination to go for a military career, like Bassel. The fathers decided that their sons would join a recently expanded army division called the Republican Guard.[39] After the many attempts to topple the regime, all military and security forces were scrutinized carefully. The Defense Companies, the notorious paramilitary force headed previously by Rifaat, was disbanded and replaced with elite divisions like the Republican Guard and others, which drew on the army's most competent and trustworthy elements.[40] Hafez's maternal cousins oversaw the unit in charge of his personal protection, and his son Bassel commanded a Guard brigade upon his graduation from the academy ahead of Manaf, while a relative of Hafez's wife was overall commander of the Guard.

By the early 1980s, the army and security forces had already been purged of hundreds of suspect Sunni officers to make room for more Alawites.[41] Standards were lowered at the academy to churn out more Alawite officers. "Many were unfit to be officers, but loyalty became the number-one criteria," said Manaf. Eighty percent of one batch of 3,000 officers graduating in 1983 were Alawites. "Welcome to the factory of Assad's cubs," read a huge sign at the academy's entrance.

Manaf would later criticize these moves and blame them for ultimately hurting the army, but at the same time he sought to justify his family's role in backing Hafez's quest to protect his rule by any means. In addition to their absolute loyalty, the Tlasses were also comforted by what they saw as strong support from the United States and its allies for the regime and its continuity. For the West, a stable and cooperative Assad regime was crucial for ending the war in Lebanon, protecting Israel, and combatting international terrorism.[42] Ultimately the Tlasses, too, benefited from the changes in the army. By the 1990s, they had their own annual quota of army officers filled by loyal kinsmen from their hometown Al-Rastan, which became known as "the second Qurdaha" after the Assads' hometown.[43]

After graduating from the academy, Manaf underwent additional training in the fall and winter of 1986 and joined the Republican Guard as a junior officer in early 1987. By then it was clear that his childhood friend Bassel was being readied to succeed his father as leader. Syria—a dictatorship masquerading as a democratic republic—was now going to be a dynastic dictatorship disguised as a republic.

"Whenever we asked Hafez if he was grooming Bassel, he would say the decision was up to the entire leadership and not just him, but he was certainly giving his son a lot of leeway and paving the way for him to the top," said Abdul-Halim Khaddam, Hafez's vice president.[44]

It was Hafez's shrewd tactic to come across as noncommittal in order to expose those in his regime opposed to Bassel.

With help from his father and handpicked mentors, Bassel set out first to assert his authority within the family, the Alawite community, the army, and the security forces. Everyone would have to fear him and recognize his strength. Then he needed to charm Syrians and win their admiration. Finally, he had to be exposed to the region, especially Syrian-occupied Lebanon, and the world.

The first order of business, though, was to burnish the regime's image, tarnished as it was by its association with international terrorism and the bloody crackdown on its own people. To that end, millions of dollars were spent in the fall of 1987 to build a giant new stadium in the coastal city of Latakia to host the tenth Mediterranean Games, held under the auspices of the International Olympic Committee.

At a grandiose opening ceremony lasting more than three hours, Hafez was greeted like a triumphant but aging Roman emperor. He delivered a speech as the masses feverishly chanted his name, and then the emperor's son Bassel, a handsome and rugged-looking young man of twenty-five years dressed in a tracksuit, spoke on behalf of Syrian athletes. "We want the [Mediterranean] Sea to be a sea of peace and friendship with seagulls, not warplanes of death and destruction, flying in its skies," Bassel said confidently as he looked up at his father seated in his special box.[45]

Athletes from fourteen countries including France, Italy, and Spain paraded in the vast stadium while local students and naval academy cadets put on colorful and carefully choreographed shows set to majestic symphonic music. A massive heart-shaped portrait of Hafez lit up the giant screen. There was also a performance of "Truly Welcome to Syria," an English song composed for the games.

In the actual games, Syria won the most medals, with Bassel getting two gold and one silver in equestrian competitions. From then on, he became the "golden knight" for the regime's propaganda machine. "Syrians have been accused of being terrorists, and of course any Syrian knows this is false, and all those that took part in the games, Arabs and non-Arabs, now know this is not true," Bassel told state television at the end of the games.[46]

Bassel was hardly just one of the athletes, as the regime sought to portray him. He bought the most expensive thoroughbreds, some costing over $200,000. He completely refurbished an old officers club and shooting range on the western outskirts of Damascus, turning it into his own equestrian club and rest house complete with an artificial lake, game room with billiard and Ping-Pong tables, swimming pools, and an English-style pub with leather armchairs.[47]

Bassel cruised around the city in the most expensive sports cars, such as a black Lamborghini Diablo. Regime children competed over who owned the latest and fastest model, and they all had guns in their cars. There were other toys, too.

"He kept taking off and landing in the garden all day—it drove us nuts!" said a neighbor of the Assads about the time Bassel showed off his newly acquired helicopter-piloting skills.

Bassel was quick-witted and "unbelievably" self-confident, said a childhood friend of the Assads and Tlasses who was among the regulars at the club.[48]

"Women were throwing themselves at him. He had real presence," said the friend.

Those who saw Bassel with his younger brother Bashar found it hard to imagine they shared the same parents. "He [Bashar] was so shy and bland you hardly noticed if he was around," said the friend who often spotted Bashar sitting quietly at the club's restaurant eating a sandwich. "Bashar had a real problem with his place in a family with very strong figures—paramount leader Hafez and Bassel, who later practically ruled Syria."

One of Bashar's high school friends, regularly invited to the club to swim and play Ping-Pong, witnessed the dynamic between the two brothers. "For us, Bassel was the scary monster. Everyone at the club became tense and nervous when he showed up," said Bashar's friend.

Bassel rebuked and even berated Bashar in front of his friends. It mortified Bashar and seemed cruel to others, but Bassel thought he had a duty to toughen up his brother. "You are hopeless. I wish you would get one thing, just one thing, right in your life," Bassel told Bashar once at the club, critiquing the way he played Ping-Pong.[49] Manaf, who often accompanied Bassel to the club, said Bashar would usually leave when his eldest brother arrived because everyone understood that "this was a place Bassel made for himself and his friends."[50]

Bassel developed a reputation as the enforcer of discipline, ready to strike against unruly behavior by his siblings and cousins, which he felt disgraced or embarrassed his father and family. He was presenting himself as a worthy inheritor of the role of *zaeem*, or chief—an established tradition in the paternalistic and male-dominated societies of the Levant and Middle East.

Bassel also clashed with his strong-willed, impulsive elder sister Bushra, who was already in her late twenties. Bushra felt she was more than qualified to be her father's heir, if it were not for the macho and conservative culture. She became interested in state affairs and sought to assert herself in other ways. She fell in love with a divorced army officer named Assef Shawkat, who was from a humble background. Her family did not approve, but Bushra was completely taken by the mustachioed and swarthy Assef, who was highly ambitious and already a rising star in a special *mukhabarat* unit. His relationship with Bushra became the talk of Damascus; even regime officials noticed how the lovers kept gazing at each other one time when Bushra accompanied her father to parliament. Assef was assigned to the president's security detail that day. Bassel strongly opposed his sister's involvement with Assef and had him arrested and thrown into prison. He was only released after Bushra pleaded with her father. Bassel then demoted Assef to a desk job in the army draft office, a clear act of punishment.[51]

Hafez was convinced that Bassel possessed the qualities of a natural leader and heir, but at the same time he was uncomfortable with his son's overt brashness toward even his family. This reminded him of his own brother Rifaat. Once, Manaf witnessed the intervention of Hafez and Bassel's grandmother Naisa to prevent a dispute between Bassel and some of his thuggish cousins from turning into a shootout on the streets of Latakia. Hafez wished his heir to tread more carefully and be more considered. He wanted Bassel to excel as a military commander but also to be more cerebral, politically minded, and calculating, a bit more like Hafez himself in his youth.

To Hafez, Bassel seemed like someone in a hurry to have it all right away. Hafez was aware of the discomfort that Bassel's meteoric rise was provoking among his army and *mukhabarat* chiefs who held prominent positions in the Alawite clans. There was no doubt in Hafez's mind that Bassel had to be his successor, but he wanted to do it the Hafez al-Assad way, step by step and stealthily.

For his own part, Bassel quickly realized the path to being a *zaeem* and eventual leader of the Syria of the Assads also required economic patronage and money, lots of it.

In the late 1980s, he began to develop his own business interests and formed a conglomerate of sorts that generated a fortune mainly from commissions, protection money, and kickbacks on a range of both lawful and illicit activities in Lebanon and Syria.[52]

Bassel kept this part of his life private, guarding it even from Manaf. It was a smart way of raising revenue behind his father's back, while at the same time securing the allegiance of those in his father's inner circle who were themselves amassing fabulous wealth. His message to these men was simple: I know exactly what you're doing and I have no problem with it as long as you play by my rules and I get my share.

Bassel identified the chief smugglers of cigarettes, currency, gold, ancient relics and treasures, medicine, and other goods and cut deals with them, sometimes in the unlikeliest settings. One evening Bassel's assistant was driving through Abu Rummaneh when he spotted Bassel in one of his sports cars parked outside the Badr mosque. He was not alone. In the front passenger seat was a cigarette- and currency-smuggling kingpin, who was also a clan leader from the Beqaa Valley across the border in Syrian-occupied Lebanon. Bassel noticed his assistant and waved at him to go.

Shortly thereafter, many of the Beqaa Valley's top hashish growers and drug dealers were brought under Bassel's protection. His assistant was among those ordered to issue them special Syrian security IDs so they could easily move through Syrian army and *mukhabarat* checkpoints in the area.[53]

Another big business was smuggling antiquities from Lebanon and Syria. Bassel often had first dibs on sites known to contain treasures like gold, jewelry, and statues. His assistants nurtured contacts with local tribal leaders who provided maps and lists of possible contents. Promising areas were sealed off by forces sent by Bassel's aides. Mustafa Tlass and others had a piece of the business, too.[54] Before leaving Syria, Bassel's uncle Rifaat seized priceless treasures buried in sites around the ancient Cherubim Monastery outside Damascus, where Aramaic and pagan Roman temples once stood.

By 1989, Bassel was on track to succeed his father. He began presenting himself as a political leader interested in world affairs, economic progress, reform, and technology—not just a tough guy who drove around in fast cars and always had pretty women at his side.

He tapped people who had studied abroad and returned to Syria to help him set up the Syrian Computer Society. The stated goal was to introduce Syrians to information technology, but naturally this would come under the regime's strict guidance and control. Other experts prepared feasibility studies on things like new industrial and free-trade zones. Manaf accompanied Bassel on most foreign trips and introduced him to a host of people deemed interesting and worldly.

"We spoke about corruption and Syria's image in the world. There were hints of 'things need to change' but nothing explicit," said Ammar Abd Rabbo, a Syrian photographer living in France, recalling a meeting with Bassel organized by Manaf. "I mentioned a book I was reading and he said he wanted to buy it. He came across as nice, charming, respectful, not like some sons of officials who were real thugs."[55]

There was a second meeting in Paris a year later. Abd Rabbo met Bassel and Manaf on a posh street off the Champs-Élysées. They visited a bookshop where Bassel bought lots of books on history and current affairs in English and French, most of them banned or unavailable in Syria. They lunched at a steakhouse, with most of the conversation revolving around the seismic political events in the world and the Middle East.

They spoke about the Gulf War and Hafez's decision to join the US-led international coalition to drive his longtime foe Saddam Hussein from Kuwait. They also spoke about the collapse of the Berlin Wall and the chain of events that eventually led to the unraveling of the Soviet Union, Syria's longtime patron, which came as a real shock to the Syrian regime and provoked an internal crisis. The Assad regime's debt to the Soviets had surpassed $10 billion.[56]

Hafez, though, wasted no time in shifting gears. He met for several hours with US president George H. W. Bush in Geneva to express his eagerness to mend fences with Washington and talk about everything, including the situation in Lebanon, peace with Israel, and terrorism charges.[57] In 1986, a British court had implicated the Syrian regime in an attempted bombing of an Israeli plane in London, which for a while triggered a diplomatic crisis and economic sanctions against Syria.[58]

The country's economy was in shambles by the end of the 1980s. Inflation soared by as much as 60 percent in 1987, while gross domestic product shrank by almost 10 percent in 1989.[59] A centrally planned system and a bloated public sector, combined with monopolies and mafia-like business networks benefiting regime leaders and their cronies, were wrecking the economy, especially as foreign aid dried up. "Syria was paralyzed, the country did not know which direction to take, there were not even annual budgets," said a Syrian journalist.[60]

The resumption of Saudi handouts could not have come sooner. One of the immediate rewards for Hafez's stance in the Gulf War was the return of generous financial aid from wealthy Gulf Arab states. The Saudis and their fellow Gulf monarchs greatly appreciated Hafez's solidarity with them and his decision to dispatch Syrian troops to take part in the US-led effort to dislodge Saddam's troops from Kuwait and thus defuse what they considered an existential threat to all the oil-rich dynasties. Previously, after he seized power in 1970, the Saudis had been among Hafez's most enthusiastic financial backers, but they pulled their support a decade later when Hafez pursued his own agenda in Lebanon and allied Syria with the Iranians against Saddam, whom the Saudis had generously backed and funded before he invaded Kuwait.

Hafez's maneuvering during the 1990 Gulf War not only helped him ease the bubbling discontent at home over the economy but also won him hegemony over Lebanon after the official end of the civil war there in late 1989 in a Saudi-mediated and US-blessed accord. The Syrians, a de facto occupation force, were entrusted to enforce peace.

More important for Hafez was securing the stability, financial resources, and international political support he needed in order to hand over power to Bassel at the right moment. If the make-believe victory over Israel in 1973 was the vehicle for turning Hafez into an absolute ruler, then the promise of reform and openness was what was going to help transfer the reins to Bassel. The regime took out a four-page ad in the *New York Times* promoting Syria's new "open door" policies toward foreign private investment.[61]

In late November 1993, Manaf, a rising officer in the Republican Guard, oversaw tank training maneuvers in the desert northeast of Damascus.

Bassel was watching. He was the real force in the army, negotiating foreign arms deals on behalf of his father even though his official rank was only major.[62] "Bassel was already the leader of everything," said Manaf.

It was a crucial moment for Manaf to prove himself and affirm his loyalty to the man who was about to inherit Syria, especially after doubts had emerged a few years back over Manaf's commitment to a military career. For a while Manaf was tormented and felt demeaned by the army's overt sectarianism and the jokes made about his father. Officially, Mustafa Tlass was Hafez al-Assad's deputy for military affairs and he was also the paramount leader's confidant and lifetime companion but still he was not "one of us" in the eyes of many powerful Alawites around Hafez.

Manaf's privileged and cushy upbringing had shielded him somewhat from Syria's realities.[63]

"Who do you think you are? You need to be more humble. You and your father work for us at the end of the day," Alawite officers, including those lower in rank than him, often told Manaf.[64] He thought about quitting the army but was ultimately dissuaded after a four-hour talk with his father.

"You must submit and learn to cajole and flatter. If you can't do that then you won't go far, perhaps no more than a brigade commander. I am still proud of you though," Mustafa told Manaf.[65] In the end Manaf stayed, with the thinking being that he would have an easier time as his childhood friend Bassel assumed more responsibilities and eventually took over from Hafez.

By 1993, Bassel's time was divided between his Republican Guard base and a private office high up on one of the flanks of Mount Qasioun overlooking Damascus. From there he ran the government and sent daily instructions to the prime minister, even though he still had no formal title. By then Bassel had amassed a personal fortune worth hundreds of millions of dollars, most of it held in Austrian bank accounts.[66]

Ahead of the first meeting between Hafez and US president Bill Clinton in Geneva in mid-January 1994, Bassel sounded out his network of advisers for tips on how the regime should plan the trip and what level of media access to allow. Hafez detested reporters—especially foreign ones who, from his point of view, were prone to ask annoying questions about human rights and regime links to terrorism while ignoring Syria's right to resist its "imperialist and Zionist enemies."

Bassel was not accompanying his father to Geneva but knew this was a crucial meeting, less for the substance — advancing peace talks with Israel, which could take years to achieve if ever — and more for the promise of improving bilateral ties with the United States and burnishing the regime's image. There was already great chemistry between Hafez and Clinton during their phone calls and correspondence over the past year, and the Assads wanted to capitalize on that and make sure nothing disturbed the developing warmth between the United States and Syria. Hardly anyone was talking about atrocities and human rights abuses committed over a bloody reign spanning a quarter of a century. Hafez thought Clinton was no different from his predecessors, and he believed that all US presidents cared mainly about the security of Israel and the Middle East's oil supplies, not how he treated his opponents at home. Furthermore, Clinton was eager to make history as the president who brought comprehensive Arab-Israeli peace to the region, and securing Hafez's buy-in was crucial to his plan.

On January 16, 1994, Hafez huddled with Clinton for nearly five hours.[67] During the press conference that followed, Clinton expressed admiration for Hafez's "legendary stamina." "I can tell you his reputation does not exceed the reality; he deserves every bit of it," said a beaming Clinton, amid laughter.

The next day, Hafez was in an extremely good mood on the flight home to Damascus. He was out of the woods and back in the game. All his plans were on track and everything was going to turn out okay, he thought. He was confident that he was not only stabilizing the regime and paving the way for Bassel's takeover but also shedding Syria's pariah status and transforming Syria into a partner in America's endeavors throughout the Middle East: rebuilding war-ravaged Lebanon, advancing Arab–Israeli peace, securing the oil-rich Gulf from the likes of Saddam, and even forging a détente of sorts with Iran's mullahs. All roads passed through Damascus.

Hafez thought he could convince the Americans to end Syria's designation as a state sponsor of terrorism for the sake of starting formal peace talks with Israel. During his meeting with Clinton, Hafez also brought up his crucial ally, the Islamic Republic of Iran. He told the US president he could not ignore Iran and that he should try to find ways to engage with it despite the deep hostility and enmity between the two countries. Clinton promised Hafez he would discuss Iran with him later over the telephone.[68]

Hafez had set out to build an alliance with Iran's clerics from the moment they seized power after the 1979 revolution. Syria was the only Arab state siding with Iran during its long and bloody war of attrition with Iraq in the 1980s. Hafez found the perfect match in Iran's supreme leader Ayatollah Khomeini and his clerical regime. Like Hafez and his Alawite-led regime, Iran's Shiite clergy had to contend with a region dominated by a hostile Sunni majority. Like him, they ruled through a blend of revolutionary dogma, terror, and pragmatism. For the Iranians Hafez was the master of Lebanon, where they set out patiently and slowly to build their first and most durable outpost among that country's downtrodden Shiites.

Five days after Hafez's meeting with Clinton, Bassel jumped into his Mercedes-Benz 500 E, a high-performance sedan dubbed a "wolf in sheep's clothing" when it came out. His maternal cousin Hafez Makhlouf, a rising *mukhabarat* officer, sat in the passenger seat. A guard was in the back seat. It was already a quarter past seven in the morning and they needed to be at the airport at eight to catch the Lufthansa flight to Frankfurt. Bassel was traveling for state and personal business.[69] At that moment in Germany, a trial was underway accusing the Assad regime of involvement in a bombing in Berlin in the early 1980s.[70]

Damascus Airport was only fifteen miles away, but he was very late and could miss the flight.

The speedometer exceeded 100 miles per hour as Bassel got on the airport road. A thick fog had rolled in that winter morning, and, by the time he realized that the road had reached a large roundabout ahead, the brakes could not slow the car in time. The car slammed into the roundabout's concrete edge, flipping and rolling over multiple times. The crash's impact was on Bassel's side. He did not have the seat belt on and his head smashed into the metal frame in between the windshield and the driver's door, killing him instantly. Hafez Makhlouf, who was wearing a seat belt, survived but suffered fractures. The bodyguard in the back crawled out through the shattered rear windshield. The Frankfurt flight was delayed for several hours because of poor visibility.

An hour later Manaf's phone rang. It was his mother, Lamia. "I have terrible news," she said.

Manaf had in his hands at that very moment an official letter promoting him to captain in the Republican Guard. It had been issued the day before.

"I felt my whole life flashing in front of me. He was my childhood friend, we had history together. I would be a lowlife if I said I was not devastated," said Manaf.

At around the same time, Adnan Makhlouf, commander of the Republican Guard, called Mustafa. There was a real crisis in the leadership over how to tell Hafez. The increasingly paranoid and conspiracy-minded leader could think his son's death was part of a coup attempt. It was decided that Hafez's longtime friend Mustafa, army chief of staff Hikmat Shihabi, and foreign minister Farouq al-Sharaa, who had just been with him in Geneva for the Clinton meeting, would go to the president's home. They arrived at about nine o'clock in the morning. Hafez was still in his pajamas. He had a robe over his nightclothes when he came into the living room to see them. He remained quiet when they broke the tragic news, but he looked shell-shocked and shattered. "God gives and God takes away," mumbled Hafez after a long silence.[71]

Hafez went to the hospital and brought his son's body back home. It was shrouded in a white sheet and placed inside a coffin. Hafez did not utter a word. He just locked himself in a room with the coffin and mourned over Bassel's body all night long, emerging only at daybreak.[72] Nobody slept that night, as a tearful Bushra consoled her grief-stricken mother, Aniseh. Maher and Majd stayed close by. They still could not fathom what had happened.

Bashar, who was studying ophthalmology in London, was summoned back immediately on a private jet. Unlike the others, he reacted with unusual calmness and hardly any visible emotion.

As the motorcade bearing Bassel's coffin made its way from the family home in Malki, across Umayyad Square and down the Mezzeh highway, throngs of women from a nearby Alawite slum lined the side of the road. The women wailed and waved posters of Bassel. Soldiers pushed them back as they tried to throw themselves in the convoy's path.

At the Mezzeh air base, the coffin was loaded onto the presidential plane. Hafez, accompanied by Mustafa and members of the leadership, waved from the plane's window to a sorrowful crowd gathered near the runway. They flew to the Assad hometown of Qurdaha in western Syria to bury Bassel.

Syria was plunged in official mourning for days as Quran readings were broadcast day and night from mosque loudspeakers all over the country. In official state media Bassel was eulogized as the "great martyr." "Syria was drowning in tears" and "hearts were bleeding" for the "beloved of the millions," "the golden knight," "the falling star."[73]

"At the age of thirty-two, at the peak of his youth and promise, he left life, his people, and his homeland," said a bespectacled and frail-looking Hafez in a televised speech mourning his son.[74]

What he probably did not know was that as he spoke there were tens of thousands of Syrians everywhere — in Aleppo, Damascus, and Hama — who were secretly celebrating Bassel's death as divine retribution.

5

To Whom the Horses after You, Bassel?

"You must stand by your dad," Manaf told Bashar when he arrived from London.

"Yes, I want to help him get over losing Bassel," Bashar assured him. The thin and over six-feet-tall Bashar seemed distracted. He wore a rumpled suit that was too big and a loosened tie.[1]

Bashar was twenty-eight and living in London, where he was finishing a residency in ophthalmology. He had grown up into a bookish, docile-looking, and shy young man who often felt awkward in public. Bashar had chosen a career in medicine. After completing compulsory army service as a medic and working at the military hospital in Damascus for a few years, in 1992 he headed to London, where a billionaire businessman of Syrian origin called Wafic Saïd asked the director of the prestigious Western Eye Hospital to accept him as a trainee.[2] Syria's ambassador to the United Kingdom solicited Saïd's help. Notwithstanding Saïd's intervention, Bashar worked hard. On many days he was first to show up and last to leave.

"He was a civilized person and a decent man. They loved him at the hospital," said Saïd. "We had lunch and he thanked me for my help. Sons of presidents in our part of the world do not do that sort of thing."

In London, Bashar kept to himself and hardly socialized with Syrian expatriates or anyone else.[3] The exception was the family of Mahmoud Maarouf, a businessman close to the Assads by virtue of his kinship to

Mohammad Nasif, an Alawite intelligence chief in Hafez's innermost circle and a guardian and godfather of sorts to the Assad children. The Syrian ambassador was assigned to attend to Bashar's every need. To protect his privacy, Bashar was sometimes introduced as Dr. Ayham from Damascus to the Syrians and Arabs he encountered casually through the Maaroufs.[4]

Bashar lived in a rented multilevel town house on a quiet street in affluent Belgravia. Two *mukhabarat* officers dispatched by Damascus lived with Bashar and occupied the lower floor. When not at the hospital or spending time with the Maaroufs, Bashar was at home studying. His guards got so bored that Bashar permitted them to venture out in the neighborhood. They became regulars at a casino in a nearby hotel.

Just before Bassel's death, Bashar was busy studying for a board exam to be licensed to work in the United Kingdom at the end of his hospital training. He wished to remain in London.[5]

Bashar was impressed with life in Britain and was beginning to flourish in his own way. He wanted to chart his own trajectory after Bassel was chosen to inherit their father's rule. He had always been shunned by his father and been in the shadow of his handsome and charismatic "golden knight" brother. Bassel was the family star, his father's favorite, the equestrian champion and daredevil army officer who parachuted from planes.

After Bassel's death, Bashar was forced into the spotlight. He was back in a family situation he had so happily escaped. From the moment he got off the plane in Damascus, he was expected to start behaving like the eldest son and to live up to their ideals of manhood and leadership that Bassel had so easily embodied.

Bassel's funeral in Qurdaha was an elaborate and massive event fit for a long-reigning leader. Egyptian president Hosni Mubarak, Lebanese prime minister Rafic Hariri, and Salman bin Abdulaziz, the Saudi defense minister who later became king, were among the dignitaries who came to Qurdaha to console Hafez.

Qurdaha was a backwater town in the hills overlooking Syria's Mediterranean coast, but at the time of Bassel's death a construction boom was underway as extended Assad family members and newly enriched regime officials broke ground on garish mansions and apartment buildings. Hafez built a grand mosque to honor his mother, Naisa, who died two years before Bassel. At the mosque's entrance, a large mural showed Hafez kissing the hand of Naisa, who wore a headscarf that barely concealed her hair, in the style of elderly Alawite village women. Qurdaha retained its provincial ways and ambience even after it was christened the Lion's Den (*assad* is "lion" in Arabic). On market day, farmers flocked to town to sell their crops. Old men with craggy faces hawked bags of dried tobacco leaves, butchers slaughtered sheep in the open air, and women wearing black went into the white domed shrine in the main square to say a prayer. It was one of a dozen *maqams*, or shrines, for Alawite holy men and miracle makers dotting the rolling hills around Qurdaha. There were several hundred such shrines across Alawite land in western Syria.

"I never imagined myself standing here in this grave moment, with my brother Bassel having departed our world," Bashar said timidly in his eulogy.[6] Bashar was clean-shaven except for a trimmed mustache. He had changed his suit and his necktie was properly knotted, but he still looked ill at ease. Hafez, trying to hold back his immense rage and grief, sat stone-faced in the front row at the service, watching his second son stumble through his speech while anxiously trying to keep the sheets of paper in front of him from being blown away by the wind.

No sooner had Bassel been buried than tensions flared in the Assad family and the Alawite community. Many knew that Hafez's health had already been in decline before Bassel's death, and they now wondered if Bashar was replacing Bassel as heir and whether he was up to the task. Some looked to his uncle Rifaat to assume the role of successor. He had helped Hafez lead the charge against regime opponents in the late 1970s and early '80s, after all. Rifaat was seen as a hardened and imposing leader, which appealed to average Syrians, especially the regime's core constituency, the Alawites. Who could be more deserving?

Rifaat was still living abroad per Hafez's payout, but the rupture was never total and tensions had eased between the brothers when Rifaat came back for their mother's funeral in 1992.

Rifaat was once again in Qurdaha when Bassel died. He believed this was his best chance to finally grab power. Unlike his aging and sick brother Hafez, Rifaat at fifty-seven looked fit and buoyant. His neatly trimmed beard, dyed hair, and expensive tailor-made suits gave him the air of a southern European aristocrat or an Arabian prince.

Within hours of the burial and after Hafez and his family had gone home to rest, Rifaat's supporters lifted him onto their shoulders and paraded him around Qurdaha's main square. "With our soul, with our blood we sacrifice ourselves for you, O Abu Duraid!" they cheered, referring to him as the father of Duraid, his eldest son. Part of the Assad clan was thus signaling in no uncertain terms that it wanted Rifaat anointed Hafez's heir. Manaf and other officers loyal to the president were in the square at that moment. Manaf pushed one of those holding Rifaat up. The chanting ended abruptly and scuffles broke out between the two sides. Guns were raised before the situation was defused.[7] It was an unequivocal show of Tlass family loyalty that did not go unnoticed by Hafez and Bashar.

Next morning, hundreds of Hafez loyalists showed up at his family house in Qurdaha. "With our soul, with our blood, we sacrifice ourselves for you, O Bashar!" they chanted. Bashar came out to greet them. A couple of men in the crowd lifted him up as the chanting for Bashar, Bassel, and Hafez turned more vigorous. Bashar was paraded around holding up a placard showing a smiling Bassel in formal equestrian attire.

"To whom the horses after you, Bassel?" said the caption underneath.[8]

It was another way of asking: Who's the heir after you, Bassel? The answer came quickly.

That week in Qurdaha, Hafez mourned the loss of his eldest son while holding court with Alawite clan and religious leaders to make the case for the second one. He argued that it was not only about safeguarding stability and their gains as a historically downtrodden minority but that, indeed, their very survival was at stake. Therefore, Bashar needed to assume power, because any rifts or struggles among Alawite clans could be catastrophic for the whole community. This would be a gift to their enemies.

In the back of everyone's mind were events of the 1970s and early, '80s, when Sunni extremists hunted down and assassinated Alawites on the streets and in the army. The Alawite leaders knew that many Sunnis in Syria still regarded them, albeit secretly, as uncouth heretics even after

Hafez secured a *fatwa*, or religious edict, pronouncing Alawites as a sub-sect of Shiite Islam. They all remembered stories passed from one generation to another about centuries of isolation in the mountains and oppression by Sunnis and feudal masters, who humiliated them with slurs like *kuffar* (infidels). In the end, few wanted to jeopardize the security attained under Hafez for the sake of a succession war.

Another factor in Bashar's favor was a belief by many of the superstitious and hermetic Alawites that Hafez and his progeny had a divine calling to elevate and protect the sect. The Assads had long cast themselves as protectors of Alawites and minorities in the Levant including Christians. (This idea was instrumental in mobilizing support for the regime at the start of the 2011 rebellion.)

It was decided that Bashar would give up his medical career and his dream of a quiet and orderly life in Britain. Within days of Bassel's burial, the regime began building on the idea that the purportedly impromptu rallies in Qurdaha, at which people chanted for Bashar, were proof that the masses, especially the youth, wanted him to bear Bassel's mantle of reform and modernization. "Bassel the role model and Bashar the hope," became the campaign's catchy slogan.[9] While Hafez's support was built on confronting Israel, striving to reclaim the Golan Heights, and uniting Arabs, in Bashar's case it would be the promise of ushering Syria into the twenty-first century while maintaining the regime's steady hand.

The first order of business, though, was to put Bashar on a fast track toward the highest military rank, a prerequisite for anyone at the Assad regime's helm. In a society ruled with the iron fist of the army and security services, military credentials were equated with manhood, leadership, and strength. In March 1994, less than two months after Bassel's death, Bashar joined an advanced officers' training program at the Homs military academy, even though he lacked the prerequisite qualifications.

Bashar's crash training as tank commander and his sleeping arrangements were all tailor-made for a dictator's son uncomfortable in a military setting.[10]

He graduated at the top of the class as staff captain in November of that year in a ceremony officiated by Mustafa and the army's top brass. Wearing his full military regalia, Mustafa looked proud as he handed Bashar an honors plaque. A few months after his stint at the academy,

Bashar was promoted to staff major. The elevated rank and honors for someone with little military experience and predisposition seemed unwarranted to most Syrian army commanders. "Bashar needed to take Bassel's place, so all rules were bent," said Manaf.

Hafez, meanwhile, quieted any objections to his son's appointment. When Ali Haidar, commander of the special forces, raised the idea that "it's not mandatory for Bashar to replace Bassel," he was swiftly arrested and confined to his village in the Alawite mountains for the rest of his life.[11]

Hafez enlisted a circle of trusted lieutenants to mentor and promote Bashar throughout this period, with Mustafa and his sons Firas and Manaf in the lead. Bassel's death left a void in Manaf's life and it was hard at first to develop the same rapport with Bashar, but transferring loyalty and friendship to the new heir was facilitated by the Tlass family's sense of duty to Hafez and his wishes. There was self-interest, too.

The Tlasses expected their already privileged position to be strengthened significantly. Manaf would one day succeed his father as defense minister, the businessman Firas would be among the main beneficiaries of economic liberalization, and even Nahed could be rewarded with a position like Syria's envoy to the Paris-based UNESCO.

Manaf accompanied Bashar almost everywhere he went; he barely had time for anything else. "Manaf was always on standby whenever Bashar needed him. We never saw him if Bashar was traveling. Manaf's job was to ensure that all was in order during these trips. He wanted to become the man Bashar could trust with everything," recalled a friend of Manaf.[12]

One of Bashar's key mentors was Mohammad Nasif, the Alawite *mukhabarat* chief and godfather-like figure to the Assad children.[13] Nasif hailed from the notable Kheirbek family and was better known as Abu Wael. A law degree and an interest in books earned him the nickname "the educated one" in *mukhabarat* circles. He was an imposing figure: wily, smart, and dapper, but also extremely ruthless. He headed a notorious *mukhabarat* branch in Damascus and personally oversaw the torture and killing of Hafez's opponents in the 1970s and '80s.[14] Hafez valued Abu Wael and his razor-sharp instincts. He tasked him with his children's welfare and security in addition to sensitive and high-priority briefs like relations with the United States, Iran, and its Lebanese militia, Hezbollah, as well as exiled opponents of Saddam Hussein. Hafez hosted many Iraqi dissidents, including Nouri al-Maliki, who would later become prime minister. Abu Wael was their overseer. Abu Wael was crucial in helping young Bashar gain self-confidence and grapple with the Assad regime's complex inner workings. The bonds forged between them were like those of father and son, particularly given Bashar's difficult relationship with his own father, who was often very exacting and critical. Bashar cherished the time he spent with Abu Wael away from Damascus.

In the family, Bashar could draw on support from his mother, Aniseh, who pushed him to be strong and close to his siblings and her relatives.[15] Bashar's youngest brother, Maher, was a rising star in the armed forces while his maternal cousins the Makhloufs were assuming prominent roles in the army, *mukhabarat*, and business, and were eager to demonstrate loyalty to Bashar. Bashar's new brother-in-law, Assef Shawkat—despised by Bassel and only able to marry Bushra after his death—was another important ally. Supporting Bashar in the face of detractors such as his wife, who like many in the wider Assad clan did not find Bashar fit to inherit power, was a way for Assef to ingratiate himself to the new heir and solidify his position in the family.

In the first few years after Bassel's death, the burden on Bashar to assert himself and prove his worthiness for leadership was immense. He had to inherit many of Bassel's previous roles. Like Bassel before him, Bashar was cast as Mr. Clean, brought in to fight corruption, drug smuggling, and all sorts of illicit activities in which the regime and Assad family itself were deeply involved.

And there was Lebanon, a de facto Syrian colony occupied by over 30,000 soldiers and *mukhabarat* agents, where Bassel had been increasingly involved. There was Bassel's computer society, his vast networks of friends, loyalists, and followers, and much more.

Compounding the pressure on Bashar was the way the regime turned Bassel, the "martyred golden knight," into a heroic, almost mythical figure. Murals and billboards of him on a galloping horse or in aviator sunglasses were everywhere. The school the Assad and Tlass children attended,

Laïque, was renamed in 1994 the Martyr Bassel al-Assad Institute. A museum paying tribute to Bassel opened there.[16]

The airport in Latakia, streets, hospitals, sports stadiums, and other facilities in every town and city in Syria were renamed after Bassel. Assessing Bashar in relation to both his brother Bassel and his father, Hafez, was inevitable. Bushra openly mocked Bashar within family circles. Whispers grew inside the regime that there was no hope of transforming Bashar into a leader like Bassel. "He will never be like him," said one of Bassel's ex-bodyguards, who was assigned to Bashar.[17]

One counterargument that Hafez himself promoted was that while Bashar lacked Bassel's militaristic and rugged traits, he was actually more like his father in his youth. They were said to be similar in their intelligence, shrewdness, cold-heartedness, and resolute character. Some of the slogans conceived by another Bashar mentor and *mukhabarat* officer and planted in newspaper articles and editorials in Lebanon and Syria included this: "Bashar the man of clarity and purity; Bashar the man of the present and the project for the future."[18]

The stress of meeting those high expectations weighed heavily on Bashar. For Bashar, the larger-than-life personas of his father, Hafez, and late brother, Bassel, were monsters he had to slay in order to prove himself. He was consumed by this inner struggle. "I want the world to forget Bassel and my dad—I can do it," he once confided to Manaf.

Around the first anniversary of Bassel's death in January 1995, the regime doubled down on the promotion of Bashar to quash any doubts about his suitability as future leader. The Tlasses, especially Mustafa and his eldest son Firas, hardly missed an opportunity to trumpet all the wonderful things that were about to happen in Syria under the new presumed heir. Ammar Abd Rabbo, the Franco-Syrian photographer who met Bassel a few times through Manaf, was among those contacted for a one-on-one with the "rising star," as Bashar was described to him.[19]

Abd Rabbo saw a polite, soft-spoken, and somewhat shy young man who was keenly interested in cameras and photography. A few days later there was a photo session at which Bashar quizzed Abd Rabbo about his techniques and what he sought to capture.

"To be honest, some of the photos I have seen of you show someone who is shy. Maybe I can do photos that change that," said Abd Rabbo.

"I like that," said Bashar.

Bashar's photo portraits accompanied a series of flattering articles that cast him as an honest and hardworking future leader attuned to the needs and aspirations of Syria's youthful population. "His decision to move into politics did not require much thinking…He is known for his modesty, discipline, precision in life, and energy for work that fills all his waking hours," marveled Ibrahim Hamidi, a Syrian reporter for a pan-Arab publication who was friendly with the Tlasses.[20] Hamidi spoke about Bashar's war on corruption, the team he assembled to receive citizen complaints and petitions, and his forays into "the Lebanese file."

Damascenes were intrigued by this tall, blue-eyed, polite and civilized, Damascus-born and -bred young man who came back from London. He began to crack down on the excesses of regime families, who were seen by city folk as vulgar peasants enriched at the state's expense. By Bashar's directives, regime officials and their families had to go through airport passport control like everyone else and could no longer be met by their drivers and entourages on the runway.[21]

Early 1995 brought a series of meetings in Beirut and Damascus between Bashar and Lebanon's key players, who had to demonstrate their fealty and loyalty to the new heir. The regime attached great economic, political, and national security significance to Lebanon and ran it like a province or colony of Syria. It was crucial for Bashar to begin involving himself in Lebanon's affairs the way Bassel had done before he died.

In 1989, Saudi Arabia brokered a peace deal that formally ended Lebanon's fifteen-year-old civil war. Saudis and other Arab monarchs had to live with Syria's role in Lebanon, especially after Hafez joined the US-led coalition to expel Saddam from Kuwait. For the United States and Europe, accepting Syria's presence in Lebanon was a fair price for cooperation with the Assad regime on combating international terrorism and keeping Syrians engaged in peace talks with Israel. Achieving comprehensive Middle East peace was a central objective of Bill Clinton's foreign policy. Hafez made it clear to Clinton that Syria and Lebanon were one when it came to any potential peace with Israel, and he was later angry with the Palestinian Liberation Organization for concluding the Oslo Accords with the Israelis in late 1993 and Jordan for signing its own treaty with Israel in 1994. Lebanon's deeply sectarian and feudal system, in which power was divvied up among leaders claiming to represent the country's religious mosaic, facilitated Syrian control. Many of these leaders were the same warlords who fueled Lebanon's civil war. After the war, they viewed the state and its resources as well as the economy as spoils they must battle over to enrich themselves and their families and to sustain their patronage networks.

Syria's resident *mukhabarat* chiefs were the Assad family's personal representatives and enforcers in Lebanon. They were arbiters in the frequent squabbles among the Lebanese and the ones sanctioning or blocking almost everything. Suitcases of cash, business partnerships, luxury gifts, cars, apartments, and even prostitutes were the price that many Lebanese politicians and businessmen had to pay in order to demonstrate absolute loyalty to the Syrian viceroys and gain their requisite approval and protection. Humiliation, imprisonment, or death was the fate of those who challenged Syrian authority. It was not unusual for some Lebanese to kiss the hands of Syrian officials as proof of their subservience.[22]

Conveniently for the Assad regime, Lebanon was the destination for hundreds of thousands of disgruntled and unemployed men from Syria's impoverished eastern and northern provinces, flocking to Lebanon as cheap labor. Lebanon's far more liberal economy and society also served as a conduit and outlet for the Syrian elite.

In Lebanon, one man had begun to dominate the political and economic scene. Rafic Hariri was a billionaire who rose from a humble background and made a spectacular fortune in construction in Saudi Arabia. He was given Saudi citizenship and became a protégé of the Saudi monarch. With Saudi support he set out to rebuild Lebanon after the civil war. He wanted to revive the glory of the capital, Beirut, as a commercial hub and playground for the rich—the Singapore or Monaco of the Middle East. Hariri's tastes and sensibilities in rebuilding Beirut mirrored those of his Saudi royal patrons, who were busy razing historical sites in the holy cities of Mecca and Medina to replace them with skyscrapers and shopping malls.[23] The vision was that prosperity and good times would heal the civil war's wounds—no need for national reconciliation or accountability for war crimes.

Hariri realized he could do little in Lebanon without Syrian consent and so began courting the Assads in the 1980s, well before his return to Lebanon from Saudi Arabia. Hariri undertook several projects in Syria, including the Tishreen Palace, one of the president's official residences, and a new exhibition center near Damascus Airport. In 1992, Hariri became Lebanon's prime minister only after being interviewed at length by Hafez. Once he had passed the test, Hariri sat down in Damascus with Hafez's vice president Abdul-Halim Khaddam to form his cabinet.[24] "Each time we agreed on a minister, I called Hafez to get his approval," said Khaddam.

By the time Bashar became the substitute heir in 1994, the regime was suspicious of Hariri and his growing power and prominence, and not just in Lebanon. Hariri was a Sunni Muslim like Syria's majority and had developed deep ties with Sunni regime figures like Khaddam and others. Average Syrian Sunnis, many of whom still bore a grudge against Hafez for his atrocities in the 1980s, also started to notice Hariri, who had commissioned a study on fixing the Syrian economy and spoke of a Marshall-like plan for the Levant.

Hariri went out of his way to please regime officials with generous cash handouts, gifts, and sweetheart business deals, and he also put his network of regional and international relationships at the service of the Syrians.[25] All of this did not quell the mistrust fueled by Lebanese rivals who felt threatened by Hariri and his agenda. There was a sense that Hariri was a free agent, powerful in his own right and eager to sever what was sometimes called Syrian guardianship over Lebanon. His friendship with leaders like France's Jacques Chirac added to the Assad regime's doubts. From the start there was no chemistry between Bashar and Hariri.

"Habibi, do not worry yourself about Lebanon, leave things to me," Hariri told Bashar during their first meeting in Beirut in 1995 as he sat on the edge of his office desk. (The Lebanese overuse the word *habibi*, my love, and in this context it's supposed to insinuate friendliness and warmth, but usually for ulterior motives.) Hariri often couched his swagger and confidence with affection.[26] As was his wont, Bashar kept calm during the meeting, but the interaction was enough to convince him that Hariri was someone he disliked and mistrusted.

When he returned to Damascus, Bashar recounted the story to Manaf and told him that he felt insulted by Hariri. Bashar read Hariri's protestations of affection as patronizing and not sufficiently deferential, as if Hariri did not take Bashar seriously as someone who was going to rule Syria and by extension Lebanon too, as far as the regime was concerned. Hariri was undoubtedly motivated by the desire to win some margin of independence for his government and Lebanon while assuring the regime that all dues would continue to be paid. Perhaps Hariri, who was fifty-one years old at the time, was also trying to be fatherly and helpful to the young heir. Bashar, however, did not want to be schooled by someone he considered a subordinate.

In the summer of 1995, Bashar invited friends and relatives for a weekend in Latakia, a coastal city and getaway spot for the Assads and regime elites. They stayed in a scenic bay north of the city, where the Assads had a mansion perched on a cliff with stunning views of the Mediterranean. Bashar seemed more assertive and confident, and brought a woman he was dating along for the trip.[27]

Manaf came with his wife, Thala Khair; they had already been married for five years. She was seventeen and he was twenty-eight when they wed; her father's only condition was that his daughter be allowed to complete her education. The Khairs were not rich but were well respected in Damascene society. Thala's grandfather was a member of the intelligentsia and a figure in the struggle against colonialism; he owned one of the first bookstores in Damascus. Her father tried to keep the bookstore open and also headed a musical association.[28] Manaf's marriage to Thala was typical for families of Assad regime officials who were eager to shed their humble countryside roots by having their children marry into prominent urban families. Thala's sister later married the son of an Alawite *mukhabarat* chief.

Bashar and some dozen of his guests biked on trails along the coast and lounged by the mansion's two pools.[29] Many were Bassel's friends, inherited by Bashar as part of the package of becoming Hafez's successor. Bashar, long on the sidelines, was now the center of attention and appeared to bask in it. Everybody was deferential and eager to please him. "He walked in like a prince, everyone stood up and then sat only after he was seated, and when he told a joke nobody laughed before him," recalled a guest.

Guests also got a peek into the mind of the young man about to inherit Syria.[30]

"One of the things you have to fix is education. Better educated people become better citizens," said another guest one evening as they all gathered around before dinner.

"Education is not enough. How do you explain the behavior of someone who studies in America and then returns to Syria to marry a veiled woman he has never dated or known?" said Bashar, who seemed to ignore that arranged marriages were the norm in Syria including among Christians.

"Education is not just about math and science," persisted the guest.

A back-and-forth ensued over how much exposure Syrians should have to historical and political narratives other than those formulated and disseminated by the regime.

Bashar concluded with this statement: "There's no other way to govern our society except with the shoe over people's heads."

Everyone understood that the heir was already well schooled in the regime's most important maxim: To stay in power you must maintain people's fear of the state and its tools of repression, notwithstanding your promises of reform and the margins of freedom you permit.

"Bashar started to change a bit. His interactions with the military and *mukhabarat* began to toughen him and mold his character; it was a new chapter in his life," said Manaf, who was forging closer personal ties to Bashar.[31]

Another change noticed by those around Bashar was his seemingly insatiable desire to have sex with as many women as he could. He sought out women who had previously had liaisons with Bassel.[32] It did not matter whether they were single or married. A friend from childhood remembered how Bashar had "blushed whenever the topic of girls and sex was brought up" while growing up. But now the new Bashar equated sex with power. For him it was not only a source of pleasure but something that seemed to help him feel strong and confident—an aggressive manifestation of a masculinity he had previously been hesitant to embrace. Three years into his new role, many thought Bashar was making progress in filling Bassel's shoes, even if he still seemed uneasy at public appearances.[33]

With his health deteriorating in the mid-1990s, Hafez made a concerted effort to clear the decks for Bashar. He tackled everything that might endanger his son's ascension to power. Hafez pardoned thousands of prisoners, including members of the banned Muslim Brotherhood. To dial down tensions with neighboring Turkey he expelled Abdullah Ocalan, a Kurdish separatist leader he had hosted and supported for years as Ocalan waged an insurgency against Ankara.

In 1998, Hafez stripped his brother of the symbolic title of vice president after Rifaat and his sons established a new political party along with a TV station and a magazine in Europe. Later that year, Hafez reshuffled senior officers in the army and security services; those who appeared resistant to Bashar's eventual takeover were sent into retirement or cast aside.

In summer 1998, Hafez traveled to France, one of his rare official visits to the West. For the regime, ties with France offered leverage for improving its image — from a dictatorship associated with terrorism and gross human rights violations to a state interested in making peace with Israel, contributing to Middle East stability, and embarking on reform after the demise of its Soviet and Eastern bloc allies. There was already significant collaboration between French and Syrian intelligence services that had foiled several terror attacks in France in the 1990s. Mustafa and his Paris-based daughter Nahed also fostered relationships across France's political spectrum, including with far-right groups, that were extremely useful to the regime.

Terrorism, Lebanon, and Syria's border with Israel were the bargaining chips that Hafez had used to secure his regime over the decades. Now he needed to call in favors to guarantee a smooth transition of power to his son. Both French president Chirac and his close friend Hariri, the Saudi-backed Lebanese billionaire turned politician, needed Syria to further their common agenda in Lebanon. In fact, the warmth between Chirac and Hafez was in part due to Hariri's efforts over the years.

"To secure his position, Hariri knew he needed to keep giving Hafez signs of his loyalty and usefulness outside Lebanon," explained Ghassan

Salamé, a Paris-based Lebanese academic who later became minister in one of Hariri's governments. Salamé was at the state dinner that Chirac gave in Hafez's honor at the Élysée Palace.[34] "He reminded me of my peasant father," said Salamé about his impressions of Hafez. "He looked frail and thin. His trousers were high up above his waist. I remember thinking to myself, 'This man is not in good shape.'"

During Hafez's visit, Syria signed bilateral agreements with France, and Hafez gave Chirac the impression that he was making a concession in Lebanon by giving him a say in naming the next Lebanese president, who must be Maronite Christian as per Lebanon's confessional political system. "He [Hafez] asked me to submit to him the names of five candidates [for the Lebanese presidency], and that he [Hafez] would choose one," said Chirac.[35]

All of this maneuvering had one objective for Hafez: winning Chirac and France over as an ally and supporter of his son Bashar. "Bashar is like your son and you must deal with him as such," Hafez told Chirac.[36]

After his France visit, Hafez gave Bashar the green light to begin acting like president. A more assertive Bashar, by then a colonel in the Republican Guard, gave his first interviews to local and Arab media outlets. Bashar's well-rehearsed answers made him sound scientific and detached, like an outside consultant diagnosing his country's woes; it would become a hallmark of his public pronouncements for many years.

"We think change must be controlled, meaning there has to be a precise goal and clear path so change does not lead to chaos," Bashar told a Saudi-owned weekly in a lengthy interview at his Damascus office, which had previously belonged to Bassel.[37] A photo of a thin and mustachioed Bashar made the magazine cover.

Bashar then traveled to Saudi Arabia and several other Arab countries where he met monarchs and heads of state,[38] meanwhile ramping up his anticorruption crusade at home, targeting business networks of certain regime officials and their children and associates. It was a perfect way for the Assads to get rid of people who had become a liability or posed a threat to the power transfer already well underway, unbeknownst to the average Syrian. What's more, a campaign to root out corruption was intended to endear Bashar to Syrians who blamed their economic ills and lack of progress on what regime propaganda called the avaricious old guard.

Following his decision to bequeath his rule to his eldest son, Bassel, Hafez bought the loyalty of key officials in his party, army, and security forces by allowing them and their children and protégés to move into the private sector in a bigger way than before. They soon amassed fabulous fortunes while the national economy went bust, as a private sector dominated by regime insiders and cronies was layered over a bloated and corrupt public sector. In the late 1990s, the country suffered a severe liquidity crisis, gross domestic product shrank, and unemployment reached nearly 20 percent.[39] It was a repeat of the economic woes of the 1980s. The only saving grace this time was an increase in oil exports from fields in northeastern provinces bordering Iraq as well as remittances of Syrians working abroad, most notably in Syrian-occupied Lebanon, which absorbed almost a million Syrian laborers.

"We want to get rid of all the rot, open up Syria and change mentalities," an enthusiastic Manaf kept telling Syrians at home and abroad during this period as he touted the promise of change embodied by Bashar.[40]

Naturally, Mustafa's proximity and unwavering loyalty to Hafez guaranteed that Tlass family business interests were untouched by Bashar's anticorruption crusade. But others in the Assad family's orbit were not so lucky. Mahmoud al-Zoubi, who had served as prime minister for the regime for thirteen years and had gotten along extremely well with the late Bassel, was charged with corruption and removed from his post and from the Baath Party. He then shot himself in the mouth rather than face a military tribunal, according to the official regime story.[41] Even if Zoubi was guilty as charged, it was inconceivable for him to be involved in any malfeasance without the knowledge and support of senior regime figures, including members of the Assad and Makhlouf families. Ministers, lawmakers, and judges served at the regime's pleasure.

In early November 1999, Bashar was hosted by Chirac for lunch at the Élysée Palace. It was a rare honor for a man who was not yet officially president of Syria. Bashar's reform vision and plans as well as Lebanon dominated the discussion. "Rafic [Hariri] organized it—he wanted to get back into Bashar's good graces," said Khaddam, Syria's vice president, who was close to Hariri.[42] When Bashar lunched with Chirac, Hariri had already resigned as prime minister after a dispute with the new president, Emile

Lahoud, an army general staunchly loyal to Bashar. Hariri was squeezed out amid corruption allegations, precisely the same way those deemed a threat to Bashar were eliminated or let go in Syria.

While in Paris, Bashar was reminded of what it was going to take to guard the power he was about to inherit from his father.

In retaliation for his uncle Rifaat and cousin Sumar's continued disloyalty, Bashar had ordered his brother-in-law, Assef Shawkat, to raid Rifaat's properties in and around Latakia and arrest dozens of his partisans. They also shut down a private port supposedly used by Rifaat and his associates for smuggling and other illicit activities.[43] The actions provoked clashes in which several people were killed and wounded, but ultimately forces loyal to Bashar and Hafez prevailed.

Tensions from the incident spilled over to the presidential palace in Damascus, where Bashar's younger brother, Maher, got into a heated argument with Assef, who was by then a senior officer in the *mukhabarat*'s Military Intelligence Directorate. Assef was working closely with Bashar on purging all potential threats in the army and the *mukhabarat*, especially officers suspected of secret loyalty to Rifaat.[44] Maher ordered Assef to stay out of the dispute with his uncle, but Assef insisted he was part of the family.[45] Assef already had three children, triplets, from his marriage to Bushra. Maher, who was carving out his turf within the power structure as Hafez's end seemed near, was also furious that one of his army loyalists was "whacked" by Assef in the Bashar-ordered purge, said Manaf.[46] The argument between Assef and Maher degenerated into shouting and insults and ended with Maher shooting Assef in the stomach. Assef was rushed to the hospital in Damascus and then flown to Paris for further surgery. He was recuperating at the Val-de-Grace military hospital in Paris even as Bashar lunched with Chirac at the Élysée Palace.[47]

It was a rite of passage for Bashar and a lesson that protecting his rule was at times a bloody business that might require taking out his own if necessary. Manaf saw the incident as a reminder of his parents' past warnings: securing his position in the Assad clan was no easy task, and like his father he, too, would be called upon to spill blood to defend the regime, despite the rosy talk of reform and a new era.

For Assef, this would not be his last perilous entanglement in the clan's machinations.

6

New King and Early Spring

Mustafa Tlass was first to break the heavy silence.

"We have to amend the constitution so Doctor Bashar can take over as president," he said. "The parliament speaker must convene an emergency session at once."[1]

He was among some dozen members of the leadership gathered in the living room of the Assad family's Damascus residence on the morning of June 10, 2000. As Mustafa spoke, the body of his lifetime friend Hafez al-Assad lay in the adjacent room. Hafez had died overnight, a few months before his seventieth birthday. For years he had battled heart disease, thrombosis, and other ailments; and dementia toward the end of his life.[2] The subject of Hafez's deteriorating health was officially taboo but hardly secret.

Mustafa had stood by Hafez's side for half a century. Together they eliminated rivals one by one until Hafez was able to seize absolute power. Once in power, they crushed every challenge to Hafez's rule, first by political opponents and armed insurgents and then by his own brother. Mustafa had seen his friend through the tragic death of his eldest son and heir, a heartbreak from which he'd never fully recover.

"Hafez slipped away bit by bit. He had trouble finishing his sentences. We felt he was already gone after Bassel's death," said Manaf.

Now Mustafa, who had turned sixty-eight a month before, had to carry out Hafez's last command: transfer the power for which we worked all our lives to Bashar. A year before his death, Hafez issued an exceptional decree to defer Mustafa's retirement and retain him as defense minister in order to shepherd the handover to Bashar.

There was much to take care of before Bashar could assume his father's place. The constitution needed to be amended to lower the president's minimum age to thirty-four from forty to accommodate Bashar. He needed to receive the army's highest rank of field marshal even though he was hardly a military man like his father and brother. A Baath Party congress needed to convene to install Bashar as party chief, and then, to provide some measure of public legitimacy, a plebiscite had to confirm Bashar as president. All of it needed to be done within a few weeks, but, more important than all the formalities, Mustafa had to ensure party leaders and the army followed the script and stayed in line.

After Hafez's death, Mustafa sensed grumbling by the likes of Vice President Abdul-Halim Khaddam, who was allied to the former army chief of staff, Hikmat Shihabi, one of several generals cast aside by Hafez to eliminate threats to Bashar's ascension.

"We have put the armed forces on high alert," Ali Aslan, Shihabi's successor, told the gathered regime apparatchiks.[3] Tanks were deployed on all roads leading to the Assad house and outside key military and security installations across the capital.

Bashar and his brother Maher, a senior army officer, were in the room as arrangements for the post-Hafez era were being worked out; so were their brother-in-law Assef Shawkat and maternal uncle Mohammad Makhlouf, already one of Syria's richest men.

Foreign minister Farouq al-Sharaa gently suggested that "Doctor Bashar's" age be verified before amending the constitution so that subsequent changes would not be necessary to correct potential errors. Bashar was turning thirty-five three months later, in September.[4]

"Godspeed," said Vice President Khaddam tersely when they finished discussing the succession plan. He had just returned to Damascus from his weekend beach home when he was urgently summoned to the Assad residence.[5] He was not given time to change the tracksuit he was wearing. Khaddam was told that all he had to do was rubber-stamp decisions by the family and leadership until Bashar officially took over later that summer. According to the constitution, Khaddam was supposed to rule as interim president for ninety days until a new leader was chosen by the Baath Party.

"There will be no transition. I am responsible for this matter. The power is for Bashar," Mustafa told Khaddam.[6]

Almost a year before Hafez's death, Bashar was already de facto leader. What came after were the technicalities of power transfer.[7] Still, Mustafa worried that any delay in installing Bashar as president could be exploited by Bashar's banished uncle and others who believed they were worthier of occupying Hafez's place. There were whispers before Hafez's death about a secret pact between Khaddam, a Sunni like the majority of Syrians, and generals from the Assads' Alawite community opposed to Bashar, whereby Khaddam would become figurehead president after Hafez's passing while they retained the real power. Months before his death, Hafez sent Ali Douba, one of the *mukhabarat* generals suspected of plotting with Khaddam, into retirement. Douba, Khaddam, and others, who had amassed massive fortunes over the years, got the message that they and their children could be ruined by corruption charges or even killed if they disrupted Bashar's takeover.[8]

"Bashar's father paved most of the way for him. My dad's job was orchestration: making sure there was no open dissent in the leadership, even if the chance was minimal. A power struggle could have led to a bloodbath," said Manaf.[9]

Besides wanting to be faithful to Hafez's wishes, Mustafa was also determined to preserve his family's long-standing function and position as the leading Sunni clan that propped up and, in a way, legitimized the rule of the minority Alawite Assads.

After the meeting at the Assad family house, Mustafa went straight to the Defense Ministry and summoned the army's top brass to his office. He laid out the succession plan that was to include Bashar's promotion to army commander. "Your support means that all your privileges will remain intact. Those who have any objections, please leave now through this door," said Mustafa pointing to a back door he often used.[10] Mustafa had posted soldiers outside the door and instructed them to kill anyone who came out. No one did.

In the end, it was a bloodless and silent coup to install Bashar; Mustafa later reveled in his "virtuoso performance."[11]

*　　*　　*

Not far from the Assad residence, the Hama native and painter Khaled al-Khani stepped out of the shower. He dried himself and went into the bedroom to get dressed. State TV was on in the background.

"The planet that illuminated the sky of Syria and the Arabs has been extinguished," said the presenter, who appeared to be trembling on the verge of breaking down in tears as he read from sheets in front of him.[12]

"Could the tyrant be dead?" thought Khaled as he stared at the screen in disbelief.[13]

He finished dressing. He put on a white shirt and sprayed on more cologne than usual. He went out to see a cousin living nearby. He had to be with someone. As he approached his cousin's place, Khaled encountered a crowd of soldiers and men in traditional tribal dress outside the office of Khaddam, the vice president.

"We sacrifice our soul and blood for you, Bashar!" they chanted, pumping their fists in the air. It got louder as more people joined in. Khaled walked into his relative's building with tears rolling down his cheeks. Any faint hope he had that Hafez's death might have spelled the end of the regime that had tortured and killed his father, destroyed his hometown, and, as he saw it, hijacked an entire nation for three decades was dashed with the crescendo of chants.

"God, Syria, and Bashar!"

The following day this and other chants drowned out all other sounds in Damascus as hundreds of thousands of regime loyalists took over the streets for Hafez's funeral. Bashar walked behind his father's coffin, which was draped in a Syrian flag and carried by eight Republican Guard officers. Tall, thin, and clean-shaven save for a small mustache, Bashar towered over everyone.[14] He wore a dark suit, white shirt, thickly knotted black tie, and sunglasses shielding his blue eyes. He showed no emotion. Bashar was flanked by his brother Maher and Mustafa Tlass, who wore his military uniform for the occasion. Dozens of regime officials walked behind them, including Manaf, who was by then in his late thirties and a colonel in the Republican Guard. He hardly left Bashar's side. The pallbearers were led by a military band and soldiers carrying giant wreaths as the cortege wound its way from the Assad residence down to Umayyad Square. There the coffin was put on a wagon towed by a military truck as Assad family members and regime officials got into black sedans.

The convoy headed to the People's Palace on the Mezzeh plateau over-looking the city, where the coffin rested on a pedestal draped in black cloth in a large marble hall. Hordes of people, including schoolchildren in black T-shirts, were planted along the route to the palace; they chanted the names of Bashar and Hafez on cue from armed soldiers and security officers.[15] Some women dressed in black fainted, ostensibly from grief, in front of the world's TV cameras. Every advertising billboard in Damascus was covered in black or replaced with giant posters of Hafez and verses from the Quran. Grieving was a duty in Syria and the regime's de facto colony, Lebanon.[16] The overzealous *mukhabarat* and their army of informants took careful note.

Still, many Syrians, including those who despised Hafez, felt loss and uncertainty when he died. For better or worse, he had been a force that loomed large in their lives for more than thirty years. "We were taught all our lives Hafez was immortal—and then he died," said a Damascus resi-dent. By the 1990s the cult of Hafez was so pervasive and overbearing that schoolchildren wrote phrases like "Yes! Hafez al-Assad our leader forever" on greeting cards they gave their moms on Mother's Day.[17]

There was also fear among many Syrians. They knew that Hafez had been ill and that this day would come sooner rather than later, but they worried about the impact of any possible power struggle on their lives. Many stayed home, bracing for the worst.

Delegations of Arab and world leaders and officials like Egypt's strongman Hosni Mubarak, France's Jacques Chirac, and US secretary of state Madeleine Albright arrived at the palace. They filed in one by one to view the coffin and pay their respects.[18] Dignitaries were then led to a large drawing room with arabesque chandeliers and fine wood furniture inlaid with mother-of-pearl to shake hands with Bashar.

"It seems to me he is poised and someone who is ready to assume his duties. I was very encouraged by his desire to follow in his father's foot-steps," declared Albright, dressed in a black outfit and hat, to reporters after a fifteen-minute audience with Bashar.[19] The Tlasses and others in the regime breathed a sigh of relief, interpreting Albright's comments as official US government benediction of Bashar and the Assads' uninterrupted reign.

Hafez's body was then flown to the Assads' hometown, Qurdaha, for entombment inside a grand mausoleum, where his son Bassel was previously buried.

Describing Bashar's demeanor during his father's funeral, Manaf recalled, "He was in full control, not a hint of emotion and not one tear. I was really puzzled—was it the birth of a leader or was this man devoid of any feeling?"[20]

A few weeks later, Bashar walked up the steps of parliament in downtown Damascus for the televised spectacle of taking the oath of office after he was made president. The alternating light and dark stones of the building were in the *Ablaq* style of Islamic architecture seen all over the city. The parliament building had been completely rebuilt after suffering heavy damage in the final days of the French mandate in 1945, when General Charles de Gaulle ordered air raids on Damascus to punish Syrians for refusing to grant France special privileges as part of their independence.[21]

"With our soul, with our blood, we sacrifice ourselves for you, O Bashar!" lawmakers chanted and clapped as Bashar entered their domed and wood-paneled chamber. Some pumped their fists in the air.[22] Despite the parliament building's storied history, lawmakers under the Assad regime had no real power or independence. Like the council of ministers, the judiciary, and other state symbols, they were simply part of the decor and facade of democracy. In truth, all those serving in parliament now did so at the whim of Bashar and his security apparatus.

After he was sworn in, Bashar delivered a speech intended to map his vision and strategy as new leader. Though it was a dry and at times theoretical discourse lasting an hour, Bashar spoke about concepts that seemed novel and exciting to most Syrians. "I find it very important to invite every citizen to participate in the journey of development and modernization if we're truly sincere and serious about attaining desired results in the shortest possible time," he declared, calling on all Syrians to present him with fresh ideas for change in all domains.[23] He spoke of critical thinking, tolerance for dissent and alternative viewpoints, accountability, transparency, and combatting corruption among other themes. In a blunt assessment (by Syrian regime standards), Bashar said Hafez's political leadership had been a "great success" but it came at the expense of the economy and education, which were left in shambles.

Bashar's underlying message was that these were his twin priorities, while political reform and Western-style democracy were off the agenda. "We must have our own particular democratic experience emanating from our history and culture… We can see the destructive experiments in front of us in far and near countries," he said. Bashar signaled that it was not going to be the *perestroika* ("restructuring") and *glasnost* ("openness") of the former Soviet Union and Eastern Europe, but rather something akin to *gaige kaifang*, China's model of economic reform.

"There were high hopes after the speech," said Manaf.[24] "He projected a reformist agenda to gain acceptance and popularity; he was eager to be seen as different from his father." Bashar craved genuine legitimacy.

Bashar sent all the right signals domestically and abroad. In an unequivocal message of support, Saudi Arabia's crown prince Abdullah flew to Damascus the day after Bashar was formally sworn in for talks with Syria's freshly minted youthful leader.[25] Four Saudi-backed businessmen, including Lebanon's Hariri and Wafic Saïd (the London-based financier who had helped Bashar get into the eye hospital), announced that they were establishing a company to invest in Syria with an initial capital fund of $100 million.[26] The oil-rich Saudis, who regarded themselves as leaders of the Arab and Muslim worlds, were worried about the rising influence of their rival Iran and were eager to bring Bashar under their wing as quickly as possible. Abdullah wanted to forge an alliance with Syria like the one the kingdom had with Egypt and Jordan.

French president Chirac, who was close to Hariri and the Saudis, also embraced Bashar, hoping Paris could play the leading role in opening up and reforming the moribund Syrian state and economy and ending Damascus's occupation of Lebanon while also boosting France's influence in the Levant and Mediterranean region.

"We cannot say Hafez al-Assad is a paragon of democracy and a symbol of human rights; simply, the interests of France in this region are of such importance that it is essential for our country to be present all the time," said Hervé de Charette, a former French foreign minister, in defending Chirac's presence at Hafez's funeral and his enthusiastic outreach to Bashar.[27]

This poignantly summed up the inconsistent way in which Western democracies have dealt with the Middle East's authoritarian regimes. All was forgiven and forgotten when it suited Western interests—and the reverse applied when those interests changed. As for the regimes, cries about the "imperialist, neocolonialist, and Zionist" West were amplified or muted depending on the situation at home and the level of threat to their rule. For many average citizens in Syria and other Arab states, the West was hypocritical, complicit with the regimes that oppressed them, or both.

That summer, Syrian-Israeli peace talks, mediated by the United States throughout the 1990s, hit an impasse despite Israel's unilateral withdrawal from southern Lebanon in May 2000 and a last-ditch attempt by Clinton to clinch a deal days before Hafez's death. Clinton's final term in office ended six months after Bashar took over.

High-stakes geopolitics and ambitious reforms had to wait as the young leader found himself a suitable wife. Apart from his sexual exploits, Bashar publicly had dated several women when he returned from London and was being groomed for power. But for one reason or another none was appropriate.

Word spread in regime circles that the country's most eligible bachelor was searching for a bride compatible with his image as the reformist and progressive president. She had to be open-minded and presentable at home and abroad. Bashar's father-figure mentor, Mohammad Nasif (known as Abu Wael), proposed a potential match: Asma al-Akhras, the beautiful twenty-five-year-old daughter of London-based Syrian cardiologist Fawaz al-Akhras.[28]

Abu Wael had known the family for more than a decade since he first went to London for a medical procedure. Akhras became a medical consultant and fixer for all senior Assad regime officials traveling to London to cure their ailments, while his wife, Sahar, worked as an administrator at the Syrian embassy. Their firstborn, Asma (Emma to her friends), was more British than Syrian. She barely spoke Arabic at all. She attended Queen's College, a prestigious girls school, and later studied computer science at King's College before starting a career in investment banking.

When he was in London, Bashar had met Asma and her parents through Abu Wael's relatives, the Maaroufs. She was nineteen at the time and caught his attention, but it went no further.

Asma worked at J.P. Morgan and was planning to get a master's degree in business to advance in banking when the connection with the shy and polite young man she had once briefly met was reestablished with his mentor's help. Asma's mother and her aunt, the widow of an interior minister under Hafez, saw the match as a golden opportunity and did everything to seal the deal with Abu Wael.[29]

A crash courtship of several weeks ensued between Bashar and Asma in the fall of 2000. Asma dropped everything, including her job and reportedly a boyfriend, too,[30] when she agreed to marry Bashar before the end of the year. It was a discreet ceremony in Damascus out of respect that it had not yet been a full year since Hafez's death.

Asma wore a simple white taffeta dress and a matching clip in her shoulder-length hair. She wore barely any makeup. Bashar was in a stylish gray suit and shirt with no tie.[31] They signaled that they were a tasteful and practical modern couple — nothing like the offspring of the region's autocrats, whose weddings were decadent spectacles costing millions of dollars. It was an image they would strive to project going forward.

Manaf and his wife, Thala, met Asma right after the wedding ceremony at a small gathering organized by Bashar at the Assad family residence.[32]

"She was nice but a bit stagy, and her Arabic was broken," said Manaf.

"He [Bashar] looked happy with her [Asma]."

Asma later glossed over the circumstances of her marriage to Bashar. "We have been friends for a very long time," Asma told a reporter in her flawless British accent. "I came to Syria every year since I was born. It is really through family friends who knew each other since childhood."[33] The story developed that they had been childhood friends all along but had kept their distance from one another, like children of all respectable Syrian families, until their formal courtship and marriage.

Many Syrians were enamored with their young president and his beautiful wife. They seemed to represent a clear break with the Hafez years. Unlike his father, Bashar chose to marry outside his Alawite sect. Asma's family was Sunni Muslim. She was a polished British-born girl but had roots in Homs, her father's hometown.

"People were really hopeful; he married a European-educated lady from a good family and was saying all the right things about change and reform," said a Damascus native who lived abroad but returned to Syria when Bashar took over. "People thought maybe the reign of the kingdom of fear was coming to an end."[34]

There was indeed a collective sigh of relief among many Syrians. The son was nothing like the father; the dark and repressive days of Hafez might be replaced with openness, change, and prosperity. The fall of 2000 felt to many like an early spring of rebirth and potential hope.

The first confirmation of this new feeling came from Syrian-controlled Lebanon. The Franco-Saudi embrace of Bashar resulted in the Syrian regime orchestrating through its Lebanese proxies parliamentary elections in early September 2000 that culminated in the return of Hariri as prime minister. It was what Hariri's patron Saudi Arabia wanted, and Bashar felt that pleasing the Saudis and their allies the French had to take precedence over his dislike for Hariri, at least in the short term. Saudi financial assistance to the Syrian regime in those early months of Bashar's rule was vital, given the miserable state of the economy. Saudi largesse included suitcases of $100 bills delivered regularly by private jet from Riyadh to Damascus.[35]

Then the unexpected happened inside Syria.

A group of former political prisoners, lawyers, poets, professors, and writers, among others, issued a statement demanding an end to martial law in place since 1963, the release of all political prisoners, and restoration of personal liberties and freedom of expression in all forms.[36] It became known as the Statement of the 99 for the number of its signatories. Almost twenty years after Hafez extinguished these diverse and nonconformist voices in the name of fighting Islamist insurgents, they spoke out again to test Bashar's seriousness in permitting criticism and opposing points of views, as outlined in his speech. It was like first light after a long somber night.

Still, it took intense deliberations to agree on what to ask for, with some calling for a restrained approach while others wanted to push the limits of what might be tolerated in the brutal police state they all knew so well. "The struggle was to gain some margin for alternative political activity, but under the regime's umbrella. Such a margin did not exist—it was forbidden," said Burhan Ghalyoun, a Paris-based professor and signatory to the statement.[37]

Among those emboldened by the promise of freedom in 2000 was the lawyer Mazen Darwish, then twenty-six. A human rights advocacy group he was secretly affiliated with announced resumption of its activities in Syria after being banned by Hafez in 1991 and forced to operate out of France.[38] Mazen was among those who started attending what Syrians called *muntadayat*, or debate salons. These were forums that sprang up informally in the living rooms of a handful of prominent Damascenes. There was usually a lecture about one aspect of reform, followed by discussion. "I was optimistic, like most Syrians. The mere idea of people gathering in a home and speaking openly was a leap for Syria," said Mazen about the period, eventually known as the Damascus Spring.

What followed, though, were choreographed reactions by Bashar and the regime, replicated when Mazen and others made similar demands for freedom a decade later.

Bashar never acknowledged the Statement of 99 but focused instead, in all his public discourse that fall, on lashing out at Israel after right-wing leader and former army general Ariel Sharon visited the Temple Mount in Jerusalem, touching off what became known as the Second Intifada.

Hoping to assuage those agitating for reform at home, Bashar pardoned about 600 prisoners, a quarter of them Lebanese, and ordered the closing of the Mezzeh prison in Damascus.[39] In tandem with this, the regime allowed parties allied to the Baath Party and part of its National Progressive Front to open offices across Syria and print their own newspapers. These parties served as window dressing to give the impression that Syria was being ruled by a diverse coalition and not just the Baath Party, the Assad regime's political facade.

But the reawakened real opposition upped the ante, issuing a statement in January 2001 signed by almost one thousand people under the banner of the Committees for the Revival of Civil Society that went much further than the Statement of 99. It called for comprehensive political and constitutional reforms to allow independent political parties, civil society organizations, and professional associations as well as a new election law putting the electoral process under the supervision of an independent judiciary.[40]

"These people are out of their minds, they are talking fantasies," Bashar told Manaf. "They are living on another planet."[41]

Some in Bashar's inner circle saw the latest statement more ominously: to them, it was a blatant coup attempt. Among them was Bashar's brother-in-law Assef Shawkat, who already had a reputation as a ferocious protector of the new king, Bashar.[42]

"These people must know their limits, they must be taught a lesson; we can't be complacent," Assef told Manaf about the Damascus Spring activists in a disdainful and menacing tone.[43]

Then began a public campaign to discredit and vilify those pushing for political reform and basic freedoms. The regime's minister of information told reporters that "civil society" was an "American term" and said that Western ideas were spreading like "spiderwebs" in Syria and other Arab countries. He called them the "modern weapons of neocolonialists" led by the United States.[44] The message was that Syrians advocating for civil liberties were agents of foreign powers and were therefore traitors.

At almost the same time, pro-regime thugs were blamed for a violent attack on a Damascus Spring figure after he opened a debate forum in Latakia, the heartland of the Assad family's Alawite sect.[45]

In February 2001, Bashar gave his first interview since becoming president. He declared that there was a misunderstanding of his inaugural speech and that his focus was "social and intellectual development," not political change.[46] He suggested that Syrian society was immature and ill-prepared for the kind of reforms and liberties being demanded, and said that those championing them were elitists who were either naïve about the consequences of their actions or were working for foreign powers to destabilize Syria.

On cue, security services banned the debate forums from convening without prior permission and license.

Mukhabarat chiefs, the Tlasses, and even Asma's uncle were among those mobilized to divide and co-opt the Damascus Spring's leading figures. Ghalyoun, the Sorbonne professor, was offered a post in a new cabinet that Bashar was planning to assemble. "This is a young and educated president, and he is looking for people like you to collaborate with," Asma's uncle told Ghalyoun over lunch in Paris.[47]

Ghalyoun declined the offer, and in the summer of 2001 he convinced his friend, businessman Riad Seif, to challenge the regime by reopening his debate forum. He told him he would come from Paris to give a lecture, and he warned Seif not to believe the *mukhabarat* chiefs who promised to license his political party if he kept a low profile.

Tensions were high in Damascus that summer. Riad al-Turk, a long-time regime opponent detained by Hafez in 1980 and then imprisoned for eighteen years, was rearrested after he spoke about the way Bashar had inherited power and how this had turned the regime into a "crossbreed between a presidential system and a monarchy."[48]

By then Seif, a fifty-five-year-old Damascene businessman turned law-maker and political activist, was disillusioned by attempts over the past decade to affect change from within the system. Before Bashar assumed power, Seif's efforts to expose regime corruption and mismanagement had been accompanied by the bankrupting of his German-licensed sportswear factory and the freezing of his business assets on what he said were trumped-up tax-evasion charges.[49] Seif was warned several times by power-ful regime figures that he was taking his role as parliamentarian too seriously. He thought that the start of Bashar's rule could be the best opportunity for change, and he enthusiastically embraced the promise of a new era under the young leader. Soon, though, Seif discovered he was wrong. In the spring of 2001, Seif committed a cardinal sin in the eyes of the regime: he raised questions in parliament about the cellular phone license awarded to Bashar's cousin Rami Makhlouf. Seif became a marked man.

On September 5, 2001, Ghalyoun arrived at Seif's home in the Damascus suburbs to deliver his talk. Several hundred people packed an auditorium and spilled out to the garden, where Seif set up loudspeakers. It was a large and animated crowd; many were excited to be challenging the regime's ban on forums. "Professor, have no fear, speak your mind. We came prepared to go to prison; I brought a change of clothes," said a man who stood up to address Ghalyoun while holding up a small suitcase.[50] There was loud laughter. The talk and discussion lasted past midnight.

Ghalyoun spoke about the urgency of deep and sweeping reforms and national reconciliation to heal wounds of the past fifty years.

There was never once any suggestion of toppling Bashar, however. In fact, Ghalyoun explicitly said that it made perfect sense for Bashar to lead the change process. Some in the audience pushed the envelope nevertheless. "Ten families run Syria and control everything. I'm happy to provide names," said Aref Dalila, an economist and leading Damascus Spring figure. The Tlasses were in the top five.

The next day and in the days that followed, the *mukhabarat* swept up Dalila, Seif, and several of the event's organizers and attendees. Ghalyoun, who worked and lived in France, was spared and flew back to Paris.

Mazen said Bashar was so worried about appearing to have broken the reform promises he made to French president Chirac that all those arrested were tried in civilian rather than military courts as had been the custom under Hafez. "Bashar wanted to present himself as a civilized man different from his dad; this is when he coined his famous phrase 'We have an independent judiciary and I do not interfere in their business,'" said Mazen.[51]

In fact, the regime's oppressive *mukhabarat* remained intimately involved in all proceedings, with the judiciary being just a front. Judges were instructed on the length of sentences to be handed out to each defendant. In one case Mazen took on as defense lawyer, the judge told him point-blank: "Look, there's nothing that can be done here, his three-year sentence was handed down to me by state security."

Bashar succeeded in giving the impression to many inside and outside Syria that perhaps he was willing to allow this early and brief political opening to continue, but he was overruled by the regime's uncompromising old guard and hawkish *mukhabarat* chiefs like his brother-in-law Assef. The truth, said Manaf, was that Bashar gave the green light to crush the Damascus Spring because he knew the grave threat it posed to the family rule he just inherited.[52]

As the outburst of freedom was extinguished in Damascus, nineteen men, mostly Saudis trained by Al-Qaeda, hijacked four passenger planes in the United States on September 11, 2001. Two struck the World Trade Center towers in New York, one hit the Pentagon outside Washington, DC, and another crashed into a field in Pennsylvania. Days later, President George W. Bush likened the war on terrorism to a "crusade," one that could last many years, and said that nations had the choice to stand with the United States or against it.[53] The world and particularly the Middle

East was never the same again. The US military campaign in Afghanistan was followed by the US-led invasion of Iraq and the toppling of Saddam Hussein's regime in the spring of 2003—a cataclysmic event that would have major repercussions for Iraq, Syria, and the rest of the region for many years. Neoconservatives associated with the Bush administration spoke about creative chaos and the need to redraw the map of the Middle East—in blood, if necessary.

At first the United States and the world saw a cooperative and conciliatory Bashar. In the aftermath of 9/11, Bashar sent President Bush a letter offering to share intelligence and collaborate on fighting terrorism. Hundreds of dossiers on Al-Qaeda operatives and their plans culled by the Syrian regime from its infiltration of cells in the Middle East and Europe were passed over to the CIA and FBI. These US agencies were allowed to establish intelligence gathering operations in Aleppo, close to the Turkish border. The Syrians also alerted the Americans about alleged Al-Qaeda plots like a plan to attack the US Navy in Bahrain.[54]

Several US officials, including CIA director George Tenet, credited Syrian cooperation with saving American lives. The Bush administration seemed eager to engage Bashar. Notably, Syria was omitted from the "axis of evil" designation that included Iran, Iraq, and North Korea, as Bashar received a stream of US officials at his palace in Damascus.

But Bashar was not going to stop there. He was young, ambitious, and out to prove that he could outsmart everyone and defy expectations of him as a weak and inexperienced son of a dictator. He thought that he could have it all and on his own terms; he could ultimately outdo his own father, chart his own path, and make his own history.

While he cooperated with the United States and its allies, he wanted them to understand that, like his father, he was going to be the master of his own house—they couldn't push him around and turn him into another one of their Middle Eastern lackeys. And further he was not going to give away something for free; they had to pay a price and make meaningful concessions. Bashar wanted the Americans to lift Syria's designation as a state sponsor of terrorism and commit not to threaten his rule in any way in the future.[55] Bashar and his regime saw the US war on terror as a unique opportunity that had to be fully exploited to their benefit, including financially.

Both before and after 9/11, Bashar kept resisting pressure from US officials to end a deal he had made with Saddam Hussein to siphon off Iraqi oil via Syria.

"I told Powell, 'No, you must pay us to shut the pipeline; I need to feed my people,'" a buoyant Bashar recounted to Manaf after a meeting with US secretary of state Colin Powell seven months before 9/11. Bashar was proud to show Manaf that he was standing up to a senior representative of the world's most powerful country.[56]

Iraq was under international sanctions stipulating it could only sell its oil through a United Nations–run and –monitored program to buy food, medicine, and other essentials for its people. One of the ways Saddam circumvented that, after he and the Assads repaired ties that had been frayed by decades of mutual hostility, was by pumping oil to Syria through an old pipeline. Powell pressed Bashar to put oil shipments from Iraq under the UN program. But that would be far less profitable for Bashar. The arrangement he had with Iraq gave Saddam cash outside the UN system and allowed Bashar to use cheap Iraqi oil for domestic consumption and then export Syria's own oil at market price.

After 9/11, Bashar felt the United States had no right to pester him about his deal with Saddam and that it should instead accept the arrangement as a small token of appreciation for his regime's contributions to the US war on terror.[57]

"Syria made about two billion dollars a year" from the Iraq oil deal, said Manaf.[58] But most profits went into the pockets of Assad family members, including Bashar's cousins and his brother-in-law Assef Shawkat.[59]

The Tlasses also had extensive dealings with Saddam. Manaf's brother, Firas, supplied goods and services to the Iraqis in return for what were called "oil vouchers." Firas also signed contracts with Baghdad to supply it with missile systems and other military gear, in violation of UN sanctions.[60]

Another arena where Bashar had leverage over the West was Lebanon.

After personally assuring the French and Saudis that he would do everything to support Lebanon's stability and sovereignty, Bashar then went out of his way to back and defend Iran's proxy Hezbollah and its declared right to maintain its private army and attack Israel even after the latter withdrew from southern Lebanon in May 2000.[61] The official excuse was a small strip of disputed land at the intersection of the Lebanese-Syrian border and the Israeli-occupied Golan Heights.

"For us, Israel is the source of terror," Bashar declared from Beirut in spring 2002,[62] while regime officials like Mustafa Tlass peddled conspiracy theories about 9/11, including a claim that Israel's intelligence agency, the Mossad, was behind the attacks.[63]

At the same time Bashar was cozying up to the Americans, he told his "axis of resistance" allies Iran, Hezbollah, and Palestinian groups Hamas and Islamic Jihad, also terrorists in Washington's eyes, that his support for them was unwavering and his cooperation with the West was merely tactical. They were, after all, his only guarantee should the United States turn on him in its quest to avenge 9/11 and remake the Middle East.

From the start, Bashar was captivated by Hezbollah, the fruit of nearly two decades of Iranian-Syrian collaboration. At Hafez's funeral in Qurdaha, after the official one in Damascus attended by Albright and Chirac, Bashar sat next to Hezbollah's charismatic black-turbaned leader, Hassan Nasrallah, as they watched a military parade by black-clad Hezbollah fighters with bandanas tied to their foreheads.[64] About 1,200 men from a Lebanon-based party, allied to both Hezbollah and the Assads and linked to terror attacks against Western interests, lined the streets of Qurdaha and raised their arms in a Hitlerian salute as Bashar's convoy passed by.[65]

Bashar believed that challenging and resisting what many in the Middle East saw as American and Western aggression and unfair support for Israel was the right and moral thing to do, but more crucially, he also thought that such a stance was going to make him a popular and beloved leader at home, in the region, and even around the world.

Bashar, however, had some way to go to realize this vision of himself and to feel fully at ease in the role bequeathed to him by his father.

In those early years of his rule, Bashar grappled with the same insecurities and fears that plagued him since childhood.[66] "He had tics and I felt he was not entirely confident, but he wanted to project proximity with his interlocutor and to impress me as somebody who thinks and listens," said Ghassan Salamé, the Paris-based professor who was culture minister in

Hariri's government in Lebanon between 2000 and 2003 and then joined the UN mission in Iraq after the US invasion. He met Bashar several times starting in 2001.[67] "I did not like the way he was very affirmative about very sophisticated matters," added Salamé. "He seemed to me the kind of person who lacked prudence and who could adopt certain ideas because someone told him or he read about them somewhere."

Bashar was obsessed with wanting to be seen as an intelligent and capable leader in his own right, not just the son of Hafez al-Assad. He boasted to Salamé his discussion with Pope John Paul II, when the pontiff visited Syria in May 2001, about the origins of Christianity.

While Bashar basked in the attention the world was giving him and his beautiful young wife, the patience of the Americans was wearing thin. Powell returned to Damascus in April 2002; this time the focus was on the need for Bashar to rein in Hezbollah in Lebanon, stop funneling Iranian military assistance to the group, and shut down training camps and offices of Palestinian militant groups in Syria. Hamas leader Khaled Meshaal had moved to Damascus the year before. Bashar made one concession: Hezbollah stopped border attacks against Israel for about five months.

In his interactions with US officials, Bashar wanted to leverage intelligence sharing on Al-Qaeda to win broader bilateral cooperation with Washington.[68] He wanted to cash in his collaboration, which by 2002 advanced beyond information. Like practically all Middle Eastern countries, Syria was part of the CIA's rendition program. One case involved Maher Arar, a Syrian engineer whose family fled Syria to Canada in 1987. He was arrested during a stopover in the United States based on flawed intelligence linking him to Al-Qaeda and then sent to Syria, where he was imprisoned and tortured for ten months before being released and returned to Canada.[69]

Less than a month after the fall of Saddam's regime, Powell was back in Damascus. His list of demands was longer. In addition to previous ones, Bashar had to support the new reality in Iraq and adopt the US-backed Mideast peace plan known as "the Roadmap." Powell also wanted to speak about Syria's chemical and biological weapons program. He was armed with intelligence reports indicating that Syria was stockpiling the nerve agent sarin and might have been working on the more toxic VX. Ultimately, Powell wanted to determine whether or not the swift collapse of Saddam's regime had changed Bashar's calculations.[70]

Bashar seemed more cooperative and conciliatory—but this, too, proved temporary.[71] He felt he had room to maneuver, given how unpopular the Iraq War was in the West as well as the rift between the Bush administration and key allies like France over the war. Working in his favor, too, was a lack of consensus in Washington on how to deal with him, how much pressure to apply to make him change his positions, and how far to go in cooperating with him without seeming to reward him for bad behavior. There were even suggestions by Donald Rumsfeld, the secretary of defense, that toppling Bashar by force might be an option.[72]

So Bashar decided to up the ante on multiple fronts. In the middle of the US campaign to overthrow Saddam in March 2003, he opened the border and sent busloads of volunteer fighters from all over the Arab world into Iraq, and he provided military assistance to the Iraqis. Syria's officially appointed top Islamic cleric, known as the mufti, issued a *fatwa*, or edict, calling for "martyrdom operations" against the "belligerent invaders."[73]

After Saddam's fall, Bashar's support shifted to the insurgency.

"He [Bashar] wanted to start a preemptive war against the Americans" in Iraq, said Manaf.[74]

Although Bashar was shocked by the Iraqi regime's precipitous collapse, Syria's ally Iran was ecstatic to see its longtime foe Saddam swept aside by the war-eager Bush. But like Syria, Iran felt threatened by the United States, which was already present on its eastern flank in Afghanistan. Tehran worried there were more regime change operations in the pipeline; Iran was, after all, part of Bush's famous "axis of evil." Iran wanted US troops to leave Iraq as soon as possible and by any means as it built its own presence and influence there.

Mazen Darwish, the human rights lawyer, tracked convoys of buses in late 2003 and early 2004 carrying fighters escorted by *mukhabarat* officers from Damascus to the Iraqi-Syrian border, a desert area with the same tribes straddling both sides.[75] That period coincided with an escalation in the gruesome and bloody attacks attributed to Al-Qaeda's emerging affiliate in Iraq.

In the beginning, not only people with Islamist leanings went to Iraq. There were also many secularists and leftists who wanted to fight "the imperialists coming to conquer Arab land." For Bashar, Iraq was the perfect outlet and distraction for those who had been agitating for change in Syria during the brief Damascus Spring.

Indeed, many of Khaled al-Khani's friends and acquaintances, especially those from his native Hama, the city destroyed by Hafez in 1982, took the jihad route to Iraq.

Khaled was part of a group of about forty Hamwis, as the city's natives are known, who got together regularly in the first months of Bashar's rule. Some saw an opportunity to launch an insurgency against the regime while Bashar seemed weak. Khaled was among those who opposed violence and spoke of the need to give the Damascus Spring movement a chance.[76] But as the hope for any opening at home dimmed, many of Khaled's Hamwi friends went to Iraq to fight the Americans.

While Mustafa practically crowned Bashar and Manaf did everything to remain close to the young leader, the Tlasses were troubled by developments in and outside the palace. They believed Bashar's challenge to the Americans in Iraq and his overt pivot to Iran and Hezbollah was reckless and highly provocative. "Bashar played on many red lines and even crossed them," said Manaf. "His dad gave him many cards but he burned them quickly. Hafez secretly developed strong ties with the Americans."[77]

The Tlasses also felt that despite everything they did to ensure Hafez's transfer of power to Bashar, they were being treated on a less equal footing than Bashar's cousins the Makhloufs and his wife, Asma, and her family.

The first cellular telephone licenses were awarded to two private operators in 2001. One went to SyriaTel, owned by Bashar's cousin Rami, and another to Areeba, owned by Najib and Taha Mikati, Bashar's allies in Lebanon and rivals of his nemesis, Hariri. Asma's family also had a stake in one of the concessions. Manaf's businessman brother was left out of these hugely lucrative contracts, and instead Manaf's wife, Thala, got a license that same year to open the first private school.[78]

Still, Manaf was determined to make the most of his friendship and proximity to Bashar. They played tennis regularly and socialized along with their wives. On the official level, Manaf was among those admitted to the Baath Party's central committee upon Hafez's death, and there was an expectation Bashar would promote him to Republican Guard general soon, paving the way for him to assume his father's posts in the party leadership council and defense ministry.

"Hafez al-Assad and Mustafa Tlass took the same road together and you and Manaf must continue their journey. This is Hafez al-Assad's wish. Promise me you'll honor it," Manaf's mother, Lamia, had told Bashar when he came to the Tlass home for lunch six months after he became president.[79] Lamia had prepared Bashar's favorite dishes, lamb kabob and a stew called *mloukhiyeh*.

"Yes of course," Bashar had assured Lamia.

To gain Bashar's trust, Manaf positioned himself as an intermediary between his friend at the palace and those still longing for reform and change even after the quashing of the Damascus Spring and arrest of its leading figures.

"Manaf kept telling us 'be patient, change is coming,'" said a member of Manaf and Thala's social circle.[80] As proof of change, Manaf pointed to the cell phone services, private schools, and the first ATMs, rolled out in 2001.

"Manaf was their mouth and ears: what they wanted to relay to us it was through Manaf, and he listened to our concerns and ideas and passed them on," said this person.

What Manaf told his network was one thing, though, and the reality he witnessed inside the palace was another.

Bashar loved telling Manaf that he wanted to bring in new blood and be different from his father by appointing people from outside the Baath Party. "He wanted to make a splash, but it was all cosmetic," said Manaf.[81] "When people he brought in clashed with the system, he pulled his support and left them hanging." The system being powerful Assad family members, the *mukhabarat*, and party apparatus.

For instance, Bashar appointed a somewhat independent-minded figure as editor-in-chief of a state-owned newspaper.[82] "Publish what you want," Bashar told the editor, Mahmoud Salameh. "There are no limits."

"Really, Mr. President?" said Salameh.

"Yes, whatever you want," said Bashar.

Salameh went as far as allowing figures in the short-lived Damascus Spring to write for the paper, *Al Thawra*. Inevitably, he clashed with the *mukhabarat* and was forced to resign.

"Salameh kept telling the *mukhabarat*, 'I swear to God, Dr. Bashar told me to publish whatever I want,'" said Manaf.

Salameh died shortly thereafter from a heart attack.

Bashar named Ghassan al-Rifai, a World Bank official, as minister of economy and trade as part of his 2001 cabinet. On paper, his job was to promote private investment by helping foreigners cut through Syria's bureaucratic maze. The reality, though, was that all decisions were made by Bashar and his family. Bashar told Saudi businessmen that they had to work with his cousin Rami to invest in Syria.

"Rifai was there for window-dressing—his ministry had no power whatsoever," said Bernard Pêcheur, a senior French civil servant.[83] Pêcheur was sent to Syria in 2004 by Chirac to help overhaul the country's public finance system and give the ministries of finance and economy real powers. Chirac sent other French experts to Syria, including teams to help Bashar fight corruption, reform the civil service, and establish a school along the lines of France's prestigious École Nationale d'Administration (ENA) to train Syrian civil servants. A French judge and prosecutor were dispatched, too, to advise on the very sensitive matter of judicial reform in a country where courts implemented regime and *mukhabarat* orders. There was even talk of the unthinkable: streamlining the *mukhabarat* and bringing it under the government's authority—for real and not just on paper. Chirac dangled a potential European Union–Syria partnership agreement as incentive.

"There was a gamble on the French side to try to promote a sort of *glasnost* and *perestroika* in Syria," said Pêcheur. "This was a paranoid, criminal, and evil regime, but it was an opportunity to try to get this country out of its rut." Pêcheur concluded that drastic measures were needed, given the fact that Syria had the symbols of a state, ministers and bureaucrats, but no real public administration—in the sense of a cadre of competent professionals loyal to the government but having a measure of independence from party and regime dictates.

"We will implement this report in full," Bashar assured Pêcheur with visible enthusiasm when he handed him his findings. Ultimately, the boldest change implemented was the creation of the position of cabinet secretary to coordinate among various ministries. As for another report, this one on judicial reform, it was tossed in the dustbin.

"I really do not want to talk about it!" snapped Bashar when a Syrian school friend he had brought in as economic adviser kept arguing for deeper reforms, including political ones. "Give them a finger and they'll want your arm. You can only deal with people with the shoe over their heads!"

The adviser, a graduate of France's ENA and the Massachusetts Institute of Technology, was mocked by many in the regime as *el frensawi*, "the French one."[84] He quit shortly after.

The line between Bashar's willful deceit and what seemed at times like his wishful thinking on reform became increasingly blurred.

One thing Bashar could tout as an early achievement was his British-born wife, Asma. Immediately after their marriage, she traveled around Syria to learn about "the issues" and people's "hopes and aspirations."[85] "I was able to spend the first couple of months wandering around, meeting other Syrian people. It was my crash course," Asma told a British reporter.

In the summer of 2001, Asma launched the first of many civil society initiatives: an NGO to help rural communities through micro-lending and development schemes. Asma was going to create the civil society and nongovernmental organizations that the Damascus Spring activists had been lobbying for before they were rounded up and thrown in jail.

Asma and her projects were in effect the beautiful and shiny wrapping paper around what remained a regime of lies and terror on the inside. This regime was going to reinvent itself with her help.

Asma was an instant hit as Syria's first couple hosted world leaders at home and traveled around the globe, sometimes with their firstborn baby, named Hafez after his grandfather. She dazzled the king and queen of Spain in Damascus in 2001. That same year she attended a state dinner at the Élysée Palace in a lace-embroidered top and long black skirt,[86] and the following year met the Queen of England in a Chanel suit.[87]

Fashion magazines could not get enough of Asma, but there were the occasional uncomfortable moments such as when Bashar, accompanied by a radiant Asma, was heckled as he got up to deliver a speech at city hall in Paris in June 2001. A member of the Paris city council stood up holding a sign: "Assad = Antisémite."[88] Bashar had previously described Israelis as more racist than Nazis,[89] and he suggested in the presence of Pope John Paul II that Jews were killing Arabs the same way they killed Jesus.[90]

Bashar loyalists in the audience quickly drowned out the French protester with their preferred mantra-like chant: "With our soul, with our blood, we sacrifice ourselves for you, O Bashar!"

On that same trip to France, Chirac decorated Bashar with the Legion of Honor medal.

But by the summer of 2004, both France and the United States were losing patience with Bashar and they began mulling ways to ratchet up the pressure. The Americans were angry over his support for the insurgency in Iraq, while the French were upset that he was blocking the initiatives of their man in Lebanon, Prime Minister Hariri, and insisting that the Lebanese constitution be amended so that Syria's chief Lebanese proxy, President Émile Lahoud, could remain in office after the end of his term. Bashar regularly called Hariri to Damascus to reprimand him for making moves without first consulting with him.

Relations between France and the United States were strained by Chirac's strong opposition to the war in Iraq, but the two allies seemed to find common cause on Syria. On the sidelines of D-Day commemorations in Normandy, France, in June 2004, Bush agreed with Chirac to start working on a UN Security Council resolution to demand the withdrawal of Syrian troops from Lebanon and disarming of Hezbollah, the militia backed by Iran and Syria.[91]

Bashar and his allies saw it as a declaration of war. He was enraged.

In late August, he summoned Hariri to Damascus. In a meeting lasting ten minutes, Bashar told Hariri he must obey his orders and carefully consider the consequences of challenging Damascus. "Are you with us or against us?" asked Bashar.[92]

Days later, the Security Council passed a resolution calling on all remaining foreign forces to leave Lebanon and all militias to disband and for fair elections to be held without foreign interference.

The next day Bashar's allies in Lebanon amended the constitution and extended the president's term in defiance of the United Nations. Hariri resigned in early October 2004 and was replaced by a stolid Hafez-era technocrat loyal to the Assads. International pressure on Bashar escalated.

"Do they want to plunge the entire region into the volcano? Have not we learned from 9/11 and Iraq? Has the world not learned its lesson?" said Bashar that same month, threatening violent consequences if pressure on him and his Lebanese allies persisted.[93] "When the volcano erupts, it will affect all countries, far and near, large and small."

Bashar was convinced that Hariri was conspiring against him and Hezbollah. "Hariri is an agent of America and France, he's sectarian and he is working against Syria," declared Bashar in a meeting with his officials in Damascus in early 2005.[94]

On February 1, 2005, Bashar sent his foreign minister to meet Hariri in Lebanon. An emotional Hariri spoke of decades of loyalty and service to the Assads and said he felt strangled by the *mukhabarat* reports transmitted to Bashar about him.[95] "I can't take it anymore," said Hariri. "I have been fighting these reports for four years."

On Valentine's Day 2005, a suicide bomber driving a truck packed with two tons of explosives rammed into Hariri's convoy on Beirut's waterfront, killing him and twenty-two others.[96] Thick plumes of black smoke shot up into the pristine blue winter sky.[97]

7

Hit Them Where It Hurts

D id you kill Hariri?" Manaf asked Bashar.

"No, of course not," said Bashar without flinching.

For weeks Manaf had been consumed by doubts as to whether the awkward boy he grew up with could turn into a brazen and cold-hearted killer. Manaf knew that Bashar thoroughly despised Hariri; Bashar often complained to him about how the billionaire politician was defying the Assads and doing what he pleased in Lebanon by bribing and co-opting senior Syrian *mukhabarat* officers. Manaf also knew that Bashar was determined to destroy Hariri. There were many unanswered questions.

At the same time, Manaf felt that persisting in his questioning of Bashar and probing too much into the Hariri killing was a dangerous thing to do.

His instincts were right. Eight months after Hariri's killing, Ghazi Kanaan, a *mukhabarat* chief who had ruled Lebanon as a fiefdom on behalf of the Assad family for two decades before he was recalled by Bashar, was found dead in his office in central Damascus.[1] The official government story was that he committed suicide with his pistol, but several regime insiders believed Kanaan was killed by the Assads because they suspected that he had information implicating them and Iran's Lebanese militia, Hezbollah, in Hariri's killing, and that he might share it with the Americans to clear his name.[2] Kanaan posed another potential danger to Bashar. He was a charismatic and powerful general who, at the behest of the Assads, had long-standing contacts with the Central Intelligence Agency and could have been a replacement for Bashar should the fallout from

Hariri's killing lead to efforts to oust him. Kanaan hailed from an influential Alawite clan that could rival the Assads. "Bashar became scared of him [Kanaan]," said Manaf.[3]

The US ambassador to Damascus had been recalled immediately after the Hariri assassination, which the Bush administration called a "heinous act of terrorism."[4]

Then came a UN Security Council resolution which established an international commission to investigate Hariri's killing, followed by a resolution compelling Syria to cooperate with the inquiry or face sanctions or possibly even military action.

A few weeks before his death, Kanaan had been among the Syrian officials interrogated in Damascus by the UN commission that, days later, issued a report detailing "converging evidence" of involvement by the Syrian intelligence services (*mukhabarat*) and their Lebanese associates in Hariri's killing.[5] A version of the report that was leaked before it was subsequently redacted and submitted to the Security Council had names of suspects, including Bashar's brother Maher, his brother-in-law Assef Shawkat, and Bashar's mentor and former speech writer, Bahjat Suleiman.[6]

For a while after the Hariri assassination, it seemed that the West, particularly France and the United States, was finally getting tough on the Assads and their allies. Washington even looked for ways to back and fund opposition figures in and out of Syria. They included regime opponents from the short-lived Damascus Spring and a subsequent umbrella group formed in the fall of 2005 called the Damascus Declaration. Khaddam, who remained in the post of vice president after Hafez's death, defected to his Paris mansion and began cooperating with the Americans and French.

"Hariri's death was a turning point and the biggest test of the first five years of his [Bashar's] rule. It was decisive," according to Manaf.

Bashar had to strategize his next moves carefully, and he looked back to the advice he had received from his mentors when he succeeded Hafez:

I. Time is on your side, so wait and let it play out because Syria, unlike France and the United States, has no real elections, parliament, and public opinion to contend with. Their leaders come and go, rise and fall, but you stay.

2. Maneuver, stall, mislead, and lie, but use force, extreme force, when necessary. Westerners will ultimately admire your toughness and perseverance. They love strong people and winners.

3. Make sure you have leverage and the right cards to play and hit them where it hurts. They will eventually come crawling on their knees to deal with you.

"If you intend to stay in power, you must make others afraid," Mustafa advised, a week after Hariri's death.[7] "We used weapons to assume power, and we wanted to hold onto it. Anyone who wants power will have to take it from us with weapons." Mustafa, now in his early seventies and retired from formal service in the regime, epitomized the old guard that Bashar looked to for guidance in this trying period.

As the West's pressure mounted, Bashar's partnership with Iran and Hezbollah strengthened. Together, they took on the United States and its allies, and the battlegrounds were Iraq, Lebanon, and the Palestinian-Israeli conflict. Iran was worried about encirclement by its US enemy, which moved into Afghanistan to the east and Iraq to the west under the guise of the war on terror and bringing democracy to the Middle East. With US troops bogged down in Afghanistan, Iran and its allies did everything to set Iraq ablaze while also going on the offensive in Lebanon and elsewhere to neutralize their adversaries' moves. Iran said it was siding with the region's oppressed people, supporting legitimate resistance movements, and standing up to Israel and "Zionism."

Iran's enemies, most notably Saudi Arabia, which had considered Hariri its man, said that Tehran wanted to destabilize the region by exporting its Islamic revolutionary ideology and militant brand of Shiite Islam. For Iran's turbaned clerical rulers, though, their efforts were ultimately about both confronting what they saw as US hostility that threatened their grip on power, and also projecting something akin to imperial might—influence and reach from Tehran to the eastern shores of the Mediterranean via Iraq and Syria. Religion was simply the cloak for these goals and ambitions. The proud descendants of the Persian Empire yearned to be a major power again.

In the immediate aftermath of Hariri's assassination in February 2005, a wave of demonstrations led by anti-Syrian-regime movements and parties broke out in Beirut and precipitated the withdrawal of Syrian soldiers and security forces from Lebanon. The Cedar Revolution or Independence Uprising, as it became known, was hardly the end of Lebanon's woes. The already dysfunctional country immediately became deeply polarized and lurched from one crisis to another. Lebanese political forces backed by Saudi Arabia, the United States, and others, and comprised mainly of Christians and Sunnis, moved to dismantle the Hezbollah militia, a virtual state-within-a-state backed by Iran and Syria and supported by most Lebanese Shiites and some Christians. A wave of bombings and assassinations targeted ardent critics of Hezbollah and the Assad regime as well as those connected to the Hariri investigation. The level of violence and retribution was reminiscent of the terror campaign unleashed by the drug baron Pablo Escobar against the Colombian state for going after him in the late 1980s.

Car bombs killed Gibran Tueni, publisher of Lebanon's most respected daily newspaper, *Annahar*, and Samir Kassir, an editorialist in the same paper who wrote eloquently about the short-lived Damascus Spring that followed Bashar's ascent to power in 2000. "What you can feel is that the Syrian intelligentsia was able to regain in record speed its ability to criticize and analyze despite having been in the freezer for decades...What you can feel is that when the fear barrier collapses, it does not get rebuilt easily," wrote Kassir in the summer of 2001.[8]

Facing mounting pressure to relinquish its weapons, Bashar's ally Hezbollah killed and kidnapped Israeli soldiers in the summer of 2006 in an operation it said was intended to compel Israel to free Hezbollah prisoners. Israel responded with a blistering campaign of airstrikes that escalated into a war lasting nearly a month. More than a thousand Lebanese were killed and more than 4,000 wounded, mostly civilians, while 43 civilians and 119 soldiers were killed on the Israeli side. An estimated one million Lebanese were displaced as sections of Beirut's southern suburbs and entire towns in southern Lebanon, all Hezbollah strongholds, were destroyed. Hezbollah fired thousands of rockets on northern Israel, with its chief, Nasrallah, boasting that his rockets could go beyond Haifa, some thirty miles from the Lebanese border.[9] "During the July 2006 war," said Manaf, "Bashar gave Nasrallah 20,000 rockets."[10] Nasrallah later said Bashar's rocket supplies played a decisive role in the war.[11]

The war ended in mid-August with a Security Council–imposed cease-fire to be monitored by UN forces stationed in southern Lebanon. Israel's failure to destroy Hezbollah, despite Israel's vastly superior army and US support, allowed Bashar, Hezbollah, and Iran to claim victory and tout their own narrative.

Hezbollah put up billboards everywhere, proclaiming "divine victory" and asserting that the war had been part of Bush's quest to redraw the Middle East's political map. "This is the new Middle East," read a Hezbollah poster affixed to a lamppost, one of few structures left standing in a southern Lebanon village leveled by Israeli bombing. "Made in the USA, Registered Trademark," said another propped atop a flattened building in Beirut's southern suburb.

The day after the ceasefire took effect in Lebanon, a defiant and triumphant Bashar weighed in from Damascus. He said it was he and his allies who were reshaping the Middle East by resisting America's "systematic aggression." "I am happy to be meeting you in the new Middle East, the way we understand it and desire it, even though the job isn't complete yet," said Bashar at a conference for the Syrian Journalists Union, a body controlled by his Baath Party.[12]

Bashar mocked as "half men" Arab leaders like a Saudi prince who chastised Hezbollah for provoking the war with its "foolhardy" actions. Bashar went on to present his own facts and theories. He said that Israel had started the war and its actions were premeditated; an extension of a US-led conspiracy to weaken his regime, assassinate Hariri and blame it on Syria, drive his forces out of Lebanon, dismantle Hezbollah, "subdue Arabs" by forcing them to accept peace with Israel, and divert attention from "the failure of the US occupation of Iraq." It was the same US conspiracy his father had railed against in December 1979.

Bashar spoke with disdain about all UN resolutions passed against his regime and Hezbollah, and he mocked European governments for sending him letters to express concern for the failing health of a Damascus Spring leader he jailed in 2001. "They are very worried about the health of this man—what nobility, what humanity, what grandeur," Bashar remarked sarcastically, barely containing a smile.

Bashar relished every moment of his speech; he was getting back at his tormentors and detractors, according to Manaf. Here was vengeance against all those who thought he was a soft and inexperienced leader who could be pushed around. Bashar believed that the 2006 war in Lebanon was as much his own victory as it was Hezbollah's. He outsmarted the Americans, the French, and their allies and taught them a lesson for driving him out of Lebanon and trying to isolate him. He regained leverage. He regarded Hezbollah's resilience as his personal achievement, too, on par with or even more important than his father's challenge to Israel in 1973. People would talk about *him* from now on and stop comparing him with his father. He was sick of hearing people tell him that Hafez would have handled matters this or that way.

"Hezbollah protected us, gave us back respect, and restored our standing," an ecstatic Bashar told Manaf after the devastating summer war.[13] In fact, Bashar's fascination with Hezbollah and its leader, Nasrallah, only intensified after the war. He commissioned a study of the lessons the Syrian army could learn from Hezbollah and wanted to create units resembling Hezbollah, which relied on asymmetric warfare.[14]

Manaf was unconvinced. "There's a difference between a militia and a national army like ours with its own doctrine," a skeptical Manaf, who was part of this army, told Bashar.

But Bashar's instincts were right. Only Iran, Hezbollah, and sectarian militias modeled after Hezbollah could ultimately protect him and his regime. Although Syria's army was one of the oldest and largest in the region and its generals ruled Syria following independence, Hafez neutralized the army and made it completely subservient to his agenda and power structure. This accelerated in the early 1980s after challenges to his rule. Members of his Alawite community were drafted in droves into the officer corps. Units like the Republican Guard and Fourth Division, organized on a sectarian basis and blindly loyal to the Assads, were favored over the rest of the force. Endemic corruption and lack of resources further eroded the army and its morale. Some derisively nicknamed the Syrian army *jaish abou-shahata*, "an army in plastic slippers."

A few weeks before the 2006 war in Lebanon, Bashar signed a mutual defense pact with the Iranians and formalized long-term military cooperation. After the war, the facilities and concessions Bashar gave Hezbollah and Iran were unprecedented.[15]

Syria became a hub for the shipment of weapons to Hezbollah, and operatives from the militia and Iran had unfettered access to the Scientific Studies and Research Center, where missiles and rockets were developed and tested and a biological and chemical warfare program was already in place. A senior officer in the Republican Guard, the unit in which Manaf was a commander, was tasked by Bashar to ensure that Hezbollah and the Iranians overcame all obstacles while operating in Syria. Bashar regularly met with the leader of Iran's overseas covert operations, Qasem Soleimani, and Hezbollah commander Imad Mughniyeh, who played a key role in the 2006 war and was on Washington's terrorist list for major attacks against the United States in the 1980s. "They kept telling Bashar how great he was and how he was becoming leader of the axis of resistance; they knew how to charm him and inflate his ego," remembered Manaf.

Naturally, Iran and Hezbollah had their own agenda and ultimately took over Syria's role in Lebanon after 2005. Through deadly violence, intimidation, and shrewd deal making, Hezbollah, with Iran behind it, became the most powerful force in Lebanon—a militia with a private army but also a political movement and crucial partner in the national government. It was a successful replica and extension of Iran's Islamic revolutionary model on the Mediterranean, but Tehran's ambition didn't stop in Lebanon. "Syria itself started changing, Bashar submitted to the Iranians and Hezbollah, he gave them most of his cards, he became their hostage," said Manaf.

That's not how Bashar saw it. As far as he was concerned, if the West and their Arab allies wanted stability in Lebanon and sought to open channels with Iran and even Hezbollah, then they had to come to Damascus first to meet him. And they did.

"What can they do about many issues in the Middle East that Syria is essential in solving them? Nothing. We are essential. They cannot isolate

Syria," Bashar told CNN's Christiane Amanpour during a 2005 interview in Damascus when she asked him if he was worried about fallout from Hariri's assassination.[16]

All roads went through Damascus, reckoned Bashar.

Iraq was another place where Bashar sought to gain leverage over the West. When the United States invaded Iraq, hundreds of former regime officials, including Saddam's sons and his lieutenants, crossed the border into Syria with large suitcases of cash. Saddam's sons, Uday and Qusay, stayed for a while at the Le Méridien Hotel in Latakia but then Bashar asked them to leave after he faced pressure from the United States to give them up.[17] They returned to northern Iraq and were later killed in a US raid in Mosul. But Bashar did permit several Saddam loyalists to establish bases in Syria in order to oversee and support the insurgency in Iraq.[18] A pro-insurgency TV station glorifying attacks on Americans later broadcast from Damascus.

Syria also became the main transit point for Arab fighters going to Iraq to join groups like Al-Qaeda's local affiliate, especially between 2004 and 2007. About 75 percent of suicide bombings in Iraq during a one-year period starting in August 2006 were carried out by foreigners coming through Syria.[19] In return for payment, Syrian *mukhabarat* officers facilitated the flow of men, cash, and materiel needed to sustain Al-Qaeda's Iraq branch.[20] Jihadist training camps opened in the Syrian desert near Iraq and a network of Muslim clerics in northern Syria and around Damascus, many working secretly for the *mukhabarat*, raised funds for Iraqi insurgents, preached violence against the United States and its allies to religious and impoverished Syrian youth, and helped them travel to Iraq.[21] "It was a chance for Bashar to get rid of Islamist fanatics at home," said Manaf.[22]

As America's Western coalition partners began to leave Iraq in the face of mounting violence, it was mainly the Bush administration and the US military that spoke out against the Syrian regime's role in supporting the insurgency and Al-Qaeda. Bashar and regime officials flat-out denied involvement but noted that it was impossible to control the Iraq–Syria border, which they claimed was as porous as the divide between the United States and Mexico. Occasionally they justified Iraq's insurgency as legitimate resistance against US occupation and a manifestation of the rage that this occupation provoked in Arab youth, including Syrians.

Bashar regularly offered his own explanation for suicide bombings and terrorism. "Terrorism today is a state of mind that on the one hand has to do with ignorance and on the other can be attributed to a feeling of desperation over the political situation... This appears to have been the background of this attack: a reaction to America's policies in Iraq, Palestine, and Afghanistan," he said in September 2006, referring to a foiled armed attack on the US embassy in Damascus in which the assailants and one Syrian guard were killed.[23] Bashar called the attackers "isolated young men from the Damascus suburbs" inspired by Al-Qaeda. Some in the regime said that the attack was orchestrated by Bashar's *mukhabarat* as a way of easing pressure from the Bush administration by reminding it of the regime's usefulness in combatting terrorism while also highlighting the perils of not cooperating with Syria. The regime called acts like these *rasayel*, "messages and signals," which it sent out from time to time.[24]

On top of the insurgency against the Americans and their allies, Iraq was embroiled in a Sunni–Shiite sectarian war that killed tens of thousands at its height between 2005 and 2007. Sunni rebels, ex-Saddam loyalists, and their supporters fought the Shiite-led government and its allied militias, backed by Iran. The collapse of Saddam's regime — a fraying and decrepit structure that nonetheless held the country's contradictory bits together — ushered in a revival of ethnic, sectarian, and tribal identity. These affiliations were people's best protection in the chaos that ensued.

While Bashar's support for the Sunni insurgency, also aided by Iran's enemies like Saudi Arabia, was at odds with Tehran's backing of Shiites, they proved in the end to be complementary.[25] Both Iran and Syria wanted to make sure that America was besieged on all fronts and would ultimately withdraw in humiliation; even some of Washington's regional allies had no interest in seeing democracy flourish in Iraq. Iraqi blood spilled for these agendas.

By the end of 2006, one of the main recommendations of the Iraq Study Group, a bipartisan panel tasked with assessing the situation in Iraq and finding a way out of the quagmire, was the need for the United States to "engage constructively" with Iran and Syria.[26] Punishing Bashar for Hariri's killing was no longer the top priority.

*　　*　　*

Six years into Bashar's rule, reminders of Hafez were still ever-present and continued to loom large for the young leader. The Tlasses wondered how "the eternal leader" would have handled the Hariri killing crisis and other challenges swirling around the regime.

In downtown Damascus, twin billboards of Hafez and Bashar side by side rose above the racetrack at the Tishreen Stadium. Both looked severe, but Hafez stared ahead coldly and intently while a youthful Bashar glanced oddly to the side. For those who knew Bashar well, this billboard represented the "old Bashar," someone who "never dared look you in the eyes"[27] — the nervous and shy young man who grappled with the Syria he inherited from his father.

But Bashar had remarkably changed in the last few years as he grew confident in his strength and the seeming limitlessness of his power. "He became someone who lied and looked you in the eyes. You knew he was lying but he dared you to call him out. He was not like that before," said a childhood friend.[28]

Bashar, though, remained an enigma to outsiders. Behind the mask of Bashar the reformist and urbane young leader was Bashar the remorseless and unscrupulous autocrat, who was ready to kill if necessary.

In the first five years of his rule, Bashar learned very quickly that to preserve the power he had inherited from his father he had to crush any aspirations for genuine political reform and all challenges to the system. At the start of the sixth year, Bashar began to consolidate power and put his own imprint on the country. In the process, the old guard — people from his father's era, like the Tlasses — gradually lost out to Bashar's immediate family and those with cultlike loyalty to him and his vision.

In the family, Bashar's youngest brother, Maher, was among those who amassed greater powers. Formally he was an officer in the army's Fourth Division, but he began overseeing all of the army's so-called elite units, dominated by members of the Assads' Alawite minority. They were the last line of defense should the rest of the army crumble. Maher started weighing in on Bashar's key strategic decisions and was among the few in the regime interacting with Hezbollah and facilitating its activities in Syria.[29] Maher fueled the perception of himself as a shadowy, mysterious, and ruthless leader, who, though rarely appearing in public, was the real power behind the throne. He saw himself more like tough Bassel than polished Bashar, a dynamic reminiscent of the one between Hafez and his brother Rifaat. Maher also moved into the economy, cultivating a network of businessmen in the cigarette market, media and advertising, and public works, as well as government contracts to supply computers to schools. Maher's business fronts later monopolized steel manufacturing.

"But really, the big stuff was Rami, Bashar's partner," Manaf recalled.[30] From the start, it was clear that Bashar's cousin Rami and the Makhloufs were going to play a central role in Bashar's plans for the economy. Short, balding, and baby-faced, Rami was four years younger than Bashar and had a degree in civil engineering. He was previously regarded as one of Bassel's loyal foot soldiers, but when Bassel died his allegiance transferred to Bashar.

"We are going to have economic liberalization but the family will take the lion share," Manaf declared to his friends. Rami's main cash cow became his control of Syria's largest telecommunications company, Syria-Tel. It was a concession that was supposed to revert to the state after the network was built. "But they found a way around it and he continued to keep most profits," said Manaf. The Makhloufs also operated duty-free shops at Syria's borders and airports, and both their real and front companies bid on every major government construction contract, so winning was assured.

The major transformation and entry into the big leagues, so to speak, came in late 2006, when the Assads and Makhloufs established their own business cartel, a private holding company called Cham ("Levant" in Arabic), in which some seventy businessmen, many from Syria's Sunni bourgeois and urban families, became partners. Through a complex network of new companies and joint ventures as well as offshore shells and fronts, Cham became involved in every sector of the economy, including aviation, banking, consumer products, manufacturing, oil and gas, real-estate development, retail, and tourism. The partners contributed initial capital of $350 million and launched projects worth $1.2 billion in the first year.[31] Bashar tapped Nabil al-Kuzbari, a Vienna-based Austro-Syrian tycoon nicknamed the "paper king" because of his sprawling global holdings in the paper industry, to be Cham's board chairman. Rami was vice chairman and held the real power. Kuzbari was someone both the Assads and Makhloufs trusted, having dealt with him for decades. He was close to Bassel when he branched out into business and amassed a huge fortune starting in the late 1980s, but Kuzbari repeatedly denied being one of the Assad family's money men.[32] "Cham Holding is the project of the country's future," declared Kuzbari in 2007. "It takes Syrian companies from the level of the individual and family and small foreign partnerships to a truly giant and purely Syrian company."[33]

Bashar sanctioned a similar but smaller holding company called Souriya ("Syria" in Arabic) that brought together younger businessmen from the same urban Sunni milieu. In effect, Bashar modernized and corporatized the mafia-like Hafez-era crony business networks which produced so much corruption by regime insiders that it drove the economy into the ground several times. Bashar believed that he could reconfigure and control this system in a way that would not only avoid past mistakes, but also generate real economic growth and prosperity. It would give the impression of reform while ensuring that he and his family were the prime beneficiaries. When it came to business and the economy, Bashar was thinking big—on a scale Hafez had never envisioned.

In another departure from his father, Bashar sought to draw in businessmen from Aleppo, Syria's largest city and traditional economic capital, who had been shunned by Hafez because of the city's role in the uprising against him. To help him with that task, Bashar turned to Suleiman Maarouf, the son of the family he had spent a lot of time with in London. Suleiman's father was Alawite like Bashar, but both his mother and wife came from prominent Aleppan Sunni families, and he also held British citizenship. He was seven years younger than Bashar and moved back to Syria shortly after Bassel's death, as Bashar was being readied to inherit power. Suleiman became a partner in the Cham and Souriya holdings and was the Assad family's front for investments in banking, car dealerships, e-commerce, publishing, media, and tourism. Suleiman imported Apple computers and devices, Bashar's favorites, and built a resort near the Assad family hometown called Mountain Breeze.[34]

As Syria looked primed for an economic boom, Syrian expatriates in

Europe and Arab Gulf countries flocked in for a piece of the action. Everyone was welcome—as long as they did not infringe on the oligarchs.

Bashar's logic was simple and practical. He wanted to secure his power by giving Syria's Sunni majority a real stake in the regime, albeit a financial one, not political. The hope was that wealth and employment opportunities generated by this partnership would energize the economy and trickle down to average Syrians—and, more important, buy loyalty. These economic networks spawned associations, charities, and media outlets dedicated to projecting Bashar and his wife, Asma, as reformists and beloved leaders. They were going to be the role models for their youthful citizens. It was the cult of Hafez adapted to the twenty-first century. The clearest manifestation was the *Menhebak* ("We Love You") campaign orchestrated by Rami and other businessmen around the May 2007 referendum to renew Bashar's term for another seven years.

If Bashar's cousin Rami became the poster child of the Assad regime's corrupt class, then his equally business-savvy wife, Asma, was going to be the embodiment of soft power. By 2007, Asma grouped her NGOs and civil society initiatives under the Syria Trust for Development, in effect another Assad family cartel, but one dedicated to showing Syrians and the world that the regime was evolving and listening to its people by taking the lead in bettering Syrian society through learning and culture.

More crucially, Asma had to do her part to demonstrate to the world that the Assads were not killers and sponsors of terrorism, as some Western governments charged. These were hateful lies, just look at Syria's first lady backing women "cycling for peace" from Aleppo to Jerusalem, countered the regime.[35]

Asma brought a regimented, rigorous, and at times aggressive approach to her work and life, as might be expected in the cutthroat world of London and New York investment banking but was largely unheard of in genteel Damascus, especially for women.[36] She usually woke up around five o'clock in the morning, worked out, had her first staff meeting around seven to go over the day's schedule, walked her children to school, and then went to her private office. She worked almost nonstop until 5:00

p.m., which was the start of family time. Her passion for her role and mission was real.[37]

"She reads reports in detail, has strategic and detailed commentary about everything, and knows where the organization is at all times. This is not somebody who just wants to keep up appearances," said Omar Abdelaziz Hallaj, an architect and urban development expert hired by Asma as chief executive officer of her Trust.

Like any astute businessperson, Asma knew that image, public relations, and marketing were crucial both at home and abroad. She adapted her message and look to the audience. In her interactions with the West, she always brought up her investment banking experience, how she planned to go to the Harvard Business School, and why she dropped everything to help Bashar transform Syria. She wore designer outfits and shoes, wanted to seduce and charm, and was adored by fashion magazines, but at the same time she complained that too much attention was given to her appearance and not enough to her ideas and work.

In her trips around Syria, she went out of her way to bond with the people she met by listening to them and their problems. She took off her shoes before entering homes and sat on the floor, as was the custom in rural areas. She played, colored, and laughed with children at the discovery centers attached to her Syria Trust. In meetings with government officials, she urged them to be creative and take initiative and risk.

But at times she seemed oblivious to how things really worked in a country and society that had been ruled by lies, fear, and terror for decades.

"Can you imagine, these people went to Apamea but none was able to write what they saw for themselves!" she complained to Franco-Syrian photographer Ammar Abd Rabbo, who was part of a media pool accompanying her on a visit to the ruins of Apamea, near the city of Hama, with an Italian archaeologist.[38] Syrian reporters on the trip asked Asma's staff to provide press releases or instructions on what to publish.

"You know it's more complicated than that. They must know what to write because any mistake can be very costly," the mild-mannered Abd Rabbo explained to Asma.

"You think so? Come on, I do not believe it," she replied.

It was perfectly understandable for someone born and bred in Britain not to be able to fathom these requests or fully appreciate what could happen to people who took too much initiative in the Assads' Syria. This is a country ruled from top to bottom by the reports, or *taqareer*, that the *mukhabarat* and its army of agents and informants write about everyone and everything. Their reach extends to every facet of public and private life. Most ministers and senior government officials have a *mukhabarat* agent watching over them. The *mukhabarat* accords extra attention and resources to media, publishing, and propaganda. *Mukhabarat* agents are on the staff of the Ministry of Information and major media outlets, they pen editorials and articles posing as independent writers or researchers, and they appear as pundits on TV shows.

Unlike Asma, Bashar knew precisely the kind of regime he had inherited, and he intended to be as ruthless as his father or more if that's what it took to preserve it. But, like his wife, he too was frustrated with the old way of doing things. He wanted to reshape the *mukhabarat* and his regime's organs of terror to better reflect the modern world, recent technological advances, and the persona he sought to cultivate. They had to be less crude and obvious and more calibrated and stealthy. They needed to prioritize threats and know when to act and when to back off and give people space. Power and strength must be projected differently.

This thinking was reflected in Bashar's obsession with his image and narrative. The last thing he wanted was to be a stereotypical dictator's son. He wanted everyone, including those closest to him, to see a dynamic, fit, and polished leader who shunned confrontation and threats and favored calm and logical discourse. He loved to use metaphors to make his points. He often told Westerners that he chose eye surgery as a profession because it involved little blood.

Even though Bashar put a premium on the advice of trusted family members and senior *mukhabarat* officers, he cast the net widely, soliciting as many opinions as possible and showing that he was trying to build consensus around any decision. There were long chats, "brainstorming sessions," and consultations with advisers, ministers, businessmen, and friends from all walks of life.[39]

Bashar hoped he'd be given the time to fully reshape his regime according to his vision, but he had to fight against fundamental contradictions in his own plan. He craved the rewards of engagement with the West but also fully embraced Iran, Hezbollah, and the so-called axis of resistance against the West. He was the moderate Muslim and protector of Christians and minorities but also the one who mobilized Islamist extremists when it suited him and his regime. He claimed to be the champion of reform, but it was he and his regime who decided for Syrians what this reform meant and how far it went. He urged his *mukhabarat* to be less intrusive but also expected them to crush any hint of threat to his power. He wanted to be seen as a legitimately elected and nonsectarian president for all Syrians but accepted the reality that his survival depended on his clan and sect—core elements of the system bequeathed to him by Hafez.

Even inside the family, Bashar could take nothing for granted and had to earn the right to be leader.

Bashar's feisty, strong-willed, and at times "hyperactive" sister Bushra, the eldest of the Assad siblings, always doubted his worthiness to be their father's successor.[40] When Bashar came to power, Bushra had an office at the presidential palace and weighed in on important government matters. Sometimes she challenged or tried to reverse Bashar's decisions. "You must do as I told you," she ordered a prime minister once.[41]

"But the president has given me different instructions," responded the puzzled official.

"Do as I told you. The president does not know what's best," persisted Bushra.

Bashar tried to rein in his sister, but tensions flared between her and his wife as Asma started to be in the spotlight because of the many overseas presidential trips and her NGO work at home. Neither Bushra nor her mother, Aniseh, who was determined to honor and perpetuate Hafez's legacy, warmed up to Asma. Bushra was enraged by references, especially in foreign media, to Asma as Syria's first lady; officially she was simply the president's wife. Bushra's thinking was that if her mother, the regime founder's wife, was never called first lady, then certainly the privilege shouldn't be accorded to Asma, seen by some in the family as an interloper.

The spat between the two women escalated to the point where rumors swirled at the palace that Bushra had insulted and slapped Asma, prompting Bashar's wife to leave Syria and return to her parents' home in London for a while.

"The dispute was ultimately settled in Asma's favor," said Manaf.

Bushra's husband, Assef Shawkat, meanwhile went out of his way to gain favor with Bashar from the moment he became heir after Bassel's death. Assef oversaw Bashar's dealings with Saddam Hussein and his lieutenants, before and after the US invasion of Iraq.[42] In 2005, Bashar named Assef to the most powerful post in the *mukhabarat* system, head of military intelligence, but Assef's boundless ambition, charisma, and large following in the *mukhabarat* and army eventually alarmed Bashar.

Assef's extensive ties with foreign intelligence agencies, particularly the French, were yet another worry for Bashar. For years Assef led efforts to infiltrate, co-opt, and exploit Islamist radical groups, including those linked to Al-Qaeda, to further the regime's agendas. It was in keeping with a long-established regime tradition of nurturing the beast and then presenting itself to the West as the only one capable of slaying it — but subject to preconditions.[43]

In the spring of 2008, after the regime was hit by major security breaches, Bashar demoted Assef to deputy defense minister, a symbolic post. In the fall of 2007 the Israelis had bombed a facility in the desert where they believed the regime was developing a nuclear weapons program with North Korea's help. The regime denied this.

Then came an even more serious and embarrassing blow to the regime in the heart of Damascus. Imad Mughniyeh, the senior Hezbollah commander, who regularly met Bashar and was the militia's point man in transferring weapons from Syria to Lebanon, was killed in early 2008 by a car bomb in what was regarded as one of the city's most secure neighborhoods. The CIA carried out the hit with help from the Israeli Mossad.[44] Mughniyeh was behind some of the deadliest attacks against the United States in the 1980s. He was supposed to be operating secretly in Damascus but blew his own cover. "Mughniyeh began having lots of affairs with women and became ostentatious, with a taste for luxury. He was at the Four Seasons Hotel just before he was killed and had a briefcase full of $100 bills stolen from him there," said Manaf.[45]

In the recrimination among the *mukhabarat* chiefs over the security breaches that allowed Mughniyeh's killing, Assef bore the brunt, facilitating Bashar's decision to remove him from his post and slash his powers.[46]

Disgraced, Assef left Damascus for his home on Syria's western coast while Bushra decided to move to the United Arab Emirates with their children. Asma had won.

"Bushra felt Bashar broke her husband," said Manaf.

For Manaf, Assef's fall from grace was yet another sign of Iran's rising power and tentacle-like reach within Bashar's inner circle. Besides their special relationship with Bashar, Iran and its proxy Hezbollah had patiently cultivated ties with several powerful regime figures, who conspired to push Assef aside.

At least Assef was spared the fate of the general who, up until the Mughniyeh killing, had been Bashar's point man in liaising with Hezbollah and procuring chemical and biological weapons. He was killed in mysterious circumstances.[47]

The Tlasses were not entirely shielded from the intrigue and crises roiling Bashar's family and inner circle, but they were determined to do everything they could to guard their status and privileges.

Manaf was Bashar's friend, but he was also close to the disgraced Assef and his family, which made him an enemy of Bashar's brother Maher and his cousins the Makhloufs, who always mistrusted the Tlasses' motives and wanted to sideline them, especially as the economic opening raised the stakes. Manaf's enemies portrayed him to Bashar and within the regime as a "lightweight," a "playboy," and a "pretty boy" who was more suited to womanizing and hobnobbing with the Damascene elite than dealing with serious military and security affairs. For a period, some of Manaf's own subordinates in the Republican Guard stopped obeying his orders. He had to ask Bashar to intervene to rectify the situation.[48] Bashar's cousin Rami also kept a watchful eye on Manaf's businessman brother, Firas, to ensure that his activities remained subordinated to his own agenda and interests. By then Firas had grown his businesses and branched out into cement manufacturing, construction, and real estate development.

The Tlasses realized they not only needed to keep reminding Bashar of their long history with the Assads but also had to prove to him their usefulness at home and abroad in the campaign to burnish his image and reestablish ties with the West following the rupture after Hariri's killing.

One year after her husband's retirement, Manaf's mother, Lamia, passed away from a cerebral hemorrhage. The increasingly eccentric Tlass family patriarch then published his memoirs in five thick volumes, tracing part of his half century journey with Hafez and offering his own telling of key events since Syria's independence, all of it peppered by his obsession with the female figure. The memoirs were no frivolous exercise, though—they were intended as a message to Bashar that the Tlasses were a pillar of the regime and as such they expected to not only maintain but also expand their privileges as he got rid of those he called the old guard and as his cousins the Makhloufs muscled in to grab more power. Parts of the memoirs were incredibly frank, with Mustafa admitting to having executed people deemed a threat to the regime and Hafez.

Then there were all the regime secrets the Tlasses were privy to. In one TV interview Mustafa claimed that one of Hafez's former generals was a CIA spy and that Hafez tolerated it because it was one of his channels to the Americans.[49] "You know, Bashar is practically my son and without me he would not have become president," Mustafa often boasted in private gatherings.[50]

The general who once sentenced thousands of people to death to protect Hafez's rule was settling into his role as the patriarch, gathering his children and grandchildren for a family lunch every week and indulging guests in viewings of his collection of medieval axes, drawings by Adolf Hitler, and his private den, a shrine for his wildest sexual fantasies.

Mustafa hoped to live long enough to see his son Manaf attain the same status that he enjoyed under Hafez. Manaf was promoted to brigadier general in the Republican Guard and held a senior position in the Baath Party, but there were no clear signals from Bashar that Manaf could be named defense minister, too, like his father.

But beyond the largely symbolic ministerial and party titles, Manaf and his wife, Thala, sought to fulfill a far more important function for Bashar. The Tlasses saw a great opportunity to regain some of their lost power in 2007, when the West and its regional allies once again did a

U-turn in Syria and resumed cooperation and engagement with the Assads. The charming and stylish Tlass couple were increasingly seen by both Syrians and foreigners as conduits to Bashar and a moderating influence on him, given the ruthlessness and greed of others in his entourage.

"In Bashar's strategy to charm the West and tell them he was ready to change, Manaf was a tool—but there was no need for a lot of manipulation. He and Thala were close to Bashar and Asma, and it came about naturally," said a Western diplomat posted in Damascus during this period.[51] "They were all part of the new Syria—a country opening to the world and young generation of beautiful people; it was exactly that."

Manaf did everything to maintain his friendship with Bashar. They continued to play tennis and had long chats in person or on the phone. Manaf was among those providing Bashar with input beyond what he was getting from his family and intelligence chiefs. Thala's interests overlapped with Asma's. Thala owned a private school and was into culture and the arts, and she was restoring an Ottoman-era house in the old city. The couples often met socially, but there was little chemistry between Thala and Asma. Thala had a much closer rapport with Bashar, who valued her perspective and advice on a range of topics.

Still, Thala was expected to play her part in public.

"She's an amazing woman," Thala effused about Asma to Diane Sawyer, the ABC News anchor who came to Damascus in early 2007 as Bashar sought a reboot with Washington. "Ever since she got here she got deep into things in every single sector. As much as she's working for women's rights, she's working on children's rights and culture."[52]

Asma, for her own part, told Sawyer that she was not ready yet for on-camera interviews, but they spent time together "at one of her private offices overlooking Damascus at sunset, where the pair sat for two hours, talking about Assad's country in the new century and her life."[53]

In his formal interview with Sawyer, Bashar said Syria was "the main player" in stabilizing Iraq and that he was ready to cooperate with the United States.[54] There was also a chance to show Americans a more intimate, down-to-earth side of Bashar as he joked and laughed with Sawyer about his iPod music library and secret passion for country singers like Faith Hill and Shania Twain.

Besides helping Bashar and Asma charm the West, Manaf and Thala also mixed with Syrians from varied backgrounds. There was a hip and progressive-thinking twenty-something crowd as well as members of the closest thing Syria still had to an intelligentsia under the Assads. Many advocated reforms and were critical of the regime—all of course within boundaries of their *mukhabarat*-run state and never crossing the redline: the person of Bashar al-Assad.

The message conveyed by the Tlass couple in interactions with these people, some of whom they considered friends, was always more or less the same: We agree things are bad and must change, but give it time, be patient; it's not so easy to dismantle a system like ours. As a token of his friendship, Manaf sometimes tried to assist those caught in the *mukhabarat*'s crosshairs—for example, helping someone get a reprieve from a travel ban. Syrians from the worlds of arts, business, and media mingled with foreigners at parties thrown by Manaf and Thala. When not hosting, the Tlasses were eagerly awaited guests.

"Manaf usually arrived at a social event like a Hollywood star, a bit late, open shirt, never a tie, and with a cigar. He drank red wine, chatted, laughed, and held everyone by the hand," recalled a Western diplomat in Damascus.[55] "He was the main attraction. Women were all over him and men were a bit jealous. Sometimes he was alone or with Thala. She's very smart and beautiful. She's the only one who could dim his light."

Foreign diplomats and companies looking to do business in Syria, especially the French, courted Manaf and his family, seeing them as indispensable for access to and influence over Bashar. The Tlass name and its place in Syria's political-business nexus was well established in French halls of power.

Upon the death of her billionaire arms-dealer husband in 1991, Manaf's sister Nahed became a young widow with an impressive inheritance, including the Parisian *hôtel particulier* where they lived, a palatial town house in one of the most exclusive sections of the sixteenth arrondissement.[56] The ballroom's exquisite interior was transposed from a Venetian palazzo, while the elegant salons and drawing rooms were bedecked with crystal chandeliers and masterpieces by Monet, Renoir, and Van Gogh.

It was in this sumptuous setting that Nahed hosted dinners where

French titans of finance and industry mixed with political leaders and media bosses. One French newspaper called her "Madame O," a sort of mysterious and exotic romantic-age character from the East charming her way to the top echelons of Parisian society and the circles of France's most powerful men to nurture connections beneficial to her and her Assad-allied family and the regime.[57] She had an affair with France's foreign minister Roland Dumas in the 1990s. They often flew to Damascus on her private jet for long weekends.[58] Among the gifts Dumas received from the Tlass family patriarch were four ancient mosaics from Syria's many archaeological sites.[59]

Nahed also dated Franz-Olivier Giesbert, a celebrated novelist and unofficial presidential adviser who became editor-in-chief of the *Le Figaro* daily. Dominique Strauss-Kahn, the disgraced former IMF managing director and onetime French presidential hopeful, was a member of a chess club bankrolled by Nahed. Dominique de Villepin celebrated his fiftieth birthday *chez* Nahed while he was foreign minister from 2002 to 2004. Nicolas Sarkozy, who became president in 2007, was a friend and a regular at Madame O's dinners.[60]

Thanks to her family and late husband, Nahed had the status of a Syrian diplomat, even down to the license plate of her yellow Rolls Royce. This meant that she did not pay taxes, but she did give generously to major French museums and institutions and, like her father, sought respectability and status by striving for degrees from prestigious universities.

The Tlasses wasted no time to exploit the returning warmth in Franco-Syrian relations in 2007 under Nahed's friend Sarkozy. French cement giant Lafarge bought a local plant in which Manaf's brother, Firas, was a partner. In addition to the money he received from the deal, Firas was granted a share in Lafarge's Syria operations.[61] Later Firas partnered with a company from the United Arab Emirates to build condominiums on land around Aleppo, Damascus, and Latakia that, like other regime-connected businessmen, he acquired for practically nothing.[62]

Manaf said he never abused his friendship with Bashar for personal gain, but several Syrian businessmen said that they gave Manaf expensive watches, envelopes of cash, shares in projects, and, on one occasion, new furniture for his office in return for favors like securing an audience with Bashar.[63] "This was how the entire regime operated. Manaf was no exception," said one businessman, adding that he and others were frequently invited to Manaf's private quarters for meetings over expensive wines and Cuban cigars. Manaf denied taking bribes, but admitted that cash envelopes were often sent to him, including by a Saudi prince once. Manaf said he rejected them all.[64]

But for sure Manaf enjoyed other perks.

He and Thala were the guests of honor at a banquet hosted in Damascus in 2008 by French oil giant Total, which wanted to conclude a partnership agreement with Syria to boost its presence and launch big projects.[65] Although Syria's oil production had been declining since 1995, the country still possessed significant but hard-to-extract oil and gas reserves that Total was eager to tap. Syria's location was also attractive to oil giants like Total who needed an outpost between Europe and the major production fields of Iraq and the Persian Gulf. Total wanted to renovate and expand pipelines connecting Iraq's fields with terminals on Syria's Mediterranean coast.

A preliminary memorandum of understanding for a long-term partnership between Total and the Syrian state was signed by Sarkozy during a visit to Damascus in September 2008. Total's existing license was also expanded to include new fields.[66]

Sarkozy's visit was a big deal for Bashar. It was the first trip to Damascus by the leader of a major Western power since late 2001, when Bashar had only been president for a little over a year. Even though Sarkozy only stayed one night and seemed distracted throughout his brief visit, Bashar made sure that the French president left with the right impressions. In keeping with his desire to be seen as a young and dynamic leader, Bashar drove Sarkozy in his own black Audi sedan for a lunch banquet at a trendy restaurant in the old city. After dessert of baklava and fruits, Bashar took Sarkozy up to the restaurant's rooftop to show him how church bell towers coexisted side by side with mosque minarets — proof that his was one of the Middle East's few secular regimes where Islam is moderate and minorities like Christians are protected and treated as equal citizens.[67]

Sarkozy stayed at the Four Seasons Hotel and insisted on going for a morning jog. The regime thought this was a perfect chance for Sarkozy to experience firsthand how safe and secure Syria was, thanks to Bashar's rule, even as war raged next door in Iraq.

And before Sarkozy hopped back on his jet to return to Paris, there was time for a quick quadrilateral summit and photo op in Damascus with Bashar, the emir of Qatar, Hamad bin Khalifa al-Thani, and Turkish leader Recep Tayyip Erdogan. Both the Qatari emir and Erdogan were pivotal in Bashar's renewed outreach to France and the West.[68]

The maverick emir, who had seized power from his father, was determined to use his little country's extraordinary wealth, mainly from natural gas, to become a major player in the Middle East and beyond. Qatar hosted one of the largest US airbases and it invested billions in the West, especially in France after Sarkozy came to power. The emir wanted to upstage the Gulf's traditional leader, Saudi Arabia, which was allied with Sarkozy's predecessor, Jacques Chirac, and had backed Bashar early on but dropped him after Hariri's assassination. Qatar's emir personally pleaded Bashar's case with Sarkozy, telling him the Syrian leader was serious about repairing ties and cooperating on a range of issues crucial to France, such as Lebanon and peace with Israel.

Starting in the fall of 2007, Sarkozy sent his chief of staff, Claude Guéant, and other senior advisers to meet with Bashar. To prove his goodwill to the French and their allies, Bashar made a couple of tactical concessions that he believed were ultimately not a big deal for his regime but would earn him significant short-term benefits. As Qatar committed to investing billions of dollars in Syria, Bashar leaned on his Lebanese allies in 2008 to back a Qatari initiative to end a nearly two-year-long political crisis in Lebanon marked by economic and political paralysis, bombings and assassinations, deadly clashes, and the takeover of central Beirut by Hezbollah and other pro-Bashar militias. To please the French, the Syrians signaled that they were ready to open an embassy in Lebanon and have normal diplomatic ties with a country they always considered part of their territory.

Once more, the Assad clan struck another one of its bargains with the West: we cease the terror in Lebanon but you stop hounding us over the Hariri killing and start treating us again with respect.

In another gesture to the West, Syria also began indirect talks with Israel, mediated by Turkey, over the Golan Heights. The Syrians said they would settle for nothing short of full return of the Golan, something the Israelis were probably never going to accept.

The immediate reward for Bashar was an invitation for him and Asma to Paris in July 2008 to attend the launch of the Union of the Mediterranean, an initiative led by Sarkozy to foster greater cooperation between the European Union and countries on the southern and eastern shores of the Mediterranean. The French also put back on the table the possibility of a trade agreement between the EU and Syria, initially proposed by Chirac but then frozen after Hariri's killing. Bashar and Asma were among heads of states and their spouses invited to watch the annual Bastille Day parade on the Champs Élysées.

Some French officials were incensed. How could Sarkozy include, on such a patriotic occasion, a head of a regime that they believed was responsible for killing the French ambassador and bombing the French barracks in Lebanon in the 1980s, and which was linked to acts of terror on French territory during the same period?

But Sarkozy, a showy and business-minded leader, felt this was old history and that his partnership with the Qataris, which extended into Bashar's rehabilitation, trumped these concerns. France's ambassador to Syria, Michel Duclos, said he and many colleagues at the foreign ministry had to reconcile themselves to the fact that Bashar was playing the same game as his father. The regime could not be circumvented and was an unavoidable interlocutor for France in the Middle East, a region whose stability was a matter of national security.[69]

And as Bashar met with Sarkozy in Paris, back in Damascus a daily newspaper owned by his cousin Rami Makhlouf printed a bold headline on its front page: "Full Admission by the French of Syria's Pivotal Role."[70]

8

Precious Interlocutor and Unavoidable Player

Two weeks before Christmas 2010, Asma and Bashar walked through the marble lobby at Le Bristol, a luxury hotel off the Champs Élysées in Paris. News agency photographers maneuvered around severe-looking Syrian presidential guards while well-wishers from France's Syrian community watched adoringly as the Assad couple made their way to a banquet room and took their place at the helm.

"You are the motherland's best ambassadors," Bashar told the carefully chosen expatriate Syrians gathered in the hotel.[1]

Earlier in the day Asma and Bashar had lunched at the Élysée Palace with Sarkozy and his wife, Carla Bruni, a glamorous singer and former model. During their whirlwind four-day stay in the French capital, the Assads effortlessly mixed business with pleasure. Besides talks with Sarkozy, Bashar met with influential French opinion makers and gave a prime-time TV interview. But the trip's star was Asma, who was by then commanding her own NGO conglomerate in Syria focused on development, culture, education, and more. She delivered a polished address at the Academie Diplomatique Internationale, a prestigious think tank, and held court at Le Bristol with the Louvre Museum's director and French government officials.

Asma was finalizing plans for a grand launch of her project to renovate the national museum and nearly thirty other smaller museums scattered across Syria, with French help. French archaeologists were also keen to explore two ancient cities believed to be buried under the desert sands in eastern Syria, potentially a more significant find than the more than four-thousand-year-old Palmyra.[2]

"You are a precious and indispensable interlocutor," gushed Frédéric Mitterrand, French culture minister, as he introduced Asma at the Academie Diplomatique.[3]

Asma spoke about cultural revival transforming Syria and providing hope and opportunity to its youth—those under twenty-five made up 60 percent of a population of about 22 million. "The very essence of the vision we are trying to promote," said Asma with her British accent, "is that this cultural heritage is at the heart of everything we are trying to do, not happening in parallel to economic development, education reform, and civil society expansion and participation. It's happening at the core of these facets."[4]

For the rest of their stay in Paris, Asma and Bashar were photographed strolling in Montparnasse, once the haunt of artists and intellectuals, having a cozy lunch at an art deco brasserie and catching a Monet exhibition at the Grand Palais. "Asma and Bashar al-Assad: Two Lovers in Paris," was the headline of an interview with Asma and a photo spread of her and Bashar in *Paris Match*.[5]

The couple seemed to be at the top of their game. They wanted to be linked to glamor, reform, modernity, and the twenty-first century, and not the brutality, repression, and terror that Syria and its regime were often associated with.

Their Parisian charm offensive was a bold and dramatic statement that worked to put distance between the reigning couple and past accusations of terrorism and murder. That winter in Paris, Asma and Bashar felt they finally turned the corner and were now admired and respected young leaders from a troubled region, trying to do their best despite difficult circumstances.

"I felt the keen desire of a man and woman to no longer be pariahs," said Claude Guéant, who was Sarkozy's chief of staff and personal envoy to Bashar between 2007 and 2010.[6] "They wanted to be recognized as ordinary heads of state."

* * *

Bashar savored every moment of being feted by a country that had tried to destroy his regime after Hariri's murder. But for him the real prize was not France or Europe but the United States, where a more momentous change of guard and opportunity occurred. A young senator named Barack Obama had become America's first black president. Obama regarded Iraq's invasion as a disastrous mistake and wanted to get out as quickly as possible. He wanted to make a clear break with Bush's policies, to change America's image as the world's sheriff and a cowboy who shoots first and asks questions later. Obama had priorities beyond Middle East regime change. The way Bashar and his allies saw it, Obama seemed like a realist, someone who was not going to hector them about reform and human rights but potentially accept that each country had its particular circumstances and situation.

Well before Obama's win in 2008, Bashar had made it clear to congressional delegations coming to Damascus that he was ready to turn the page with the United States after Bush. He played on deep divisions in the United States over the Iraq War and leveraged a bipartisan committee's conclusions that engaging with Bashar and the Iranians was crucial to winding down the war.

Bashar reminded US officials that he had shared intelligence with the Bush administration after 9/11 and had taken in alleged terrorists to torture as part of America's rendition program—but instead of gratitude he received orders and threats because of his position on Iraq and cooperation with "resistance movements" like Hezbollah and Hamas. "Syria wants a long-term dialogue, not one-two-three-four," Bashar told Speaker of the House and Democratic Party leader Nancy Pelosi during a visit to Damascus in the spring of 2007, referring to what he characterized as Bush's dictates.[7]

Bashar and Asma treated Pelosi and members of her congressional delegation to lunch *al fresco* in the Talisman's courtyard. It was an old house in Damascus's traditional Jewish quarter turned luxury boutique hotel; the courtyard's walls were painted deep red. Lunch was followed by a tour in the bustling old city and its famous souks. Bashar wanted to impress the visiting Americans, show them that Syria was stable and prospering under his rule, and that he had his own vision for reform and change. He wanted Western leaders to deal with him as an equal. He hated Bush's threats and Chirac's attempts to treat him like a son.[8] He wanted to pick up where Hafez had left off with Nixon and Kissinger in the 1970s and later with Clinton and Albright in the 1990s.

One immediate concession that Bashar wanted from the Americans was sanctions relief. They had been ratcheted up every year since 2004, when the first of the UN resolutions were passed against the regime over Lebanon. Several of Bashar's top *mukhabarat* chiefs and his cousins Rami and Hafez Makhlouf were hit with specific sanctions in 2007 and 2008.[9] US exports to Syria were banned except for food, medicine, and certain waivers. International companies in power generation and other vital sectors didn't want to deal with Syria, fearing they could get caught in violation of sanctions. Even Bashar's French-made presidential jet was grounded because it needed repair and spare parts that were covered by US sanctions.[10] For his July 2008 Paris trip, Qatar's emir sent him a plane that was only allowed to pick him up in Damascus, take him to Paris and return him home. The plane could not remain in Syria. Bashar felt humiliated.

Then, just before the US presidential elections in 2008, American special forces launched a raid inside Syria against an Al Qaeda-linked operative they said commanded one of the main networks responsible for ferrying foreign fighters to Iraq.[11] By then the United States had rallied Sunni tribes in the Iraqi border province of Anbar to its side with cash, government salaries, and promises of a say in the country's political future. Bashar responded by shutting the American school and the Embassy's Cultural Affairs Center. It was a rather muted reaction. Days later Obama won.

Bashar told the *Washington Post*'s David Ignatius that he was ready to work with the new US leader—provided there was an end to Bush's doctrine of "preemptive war" and no more regime change in the Middle East.[12]

Iraq was Obama's most pressing priority. He wanted to pull out as soon as possible; it was a campaign pledge he was eager to fulfill. Iraq's neighbors—particularly Iran and Syria—did the most to stoke the insurgency, and they were now crucial for keeping the peace after the departure of US troops. But the Saudis and Turks, who also backed sides in Iraq, especially the Sunnis, wanted to fill the void after US withdrawal and push back against Iran, which they felt had practically swallowed Iraq because of American missteps.

In January 2009, Obama appointed former senator George Mitchell as special Middle East envoy; he was expected in Syria. American diplomacy geared up for what it called reengaging with Syria. A cable from the embassy in Damascus at the end of January 2009 titled "Reengaging with Syria: The Middle East's Unavoidable Player" offered this advice: "Whatever principles Bashar evokes in his rhetoric, his ultimate goal is to preserve his regime, which for him requires preserving all existing options without forgoing new options. The only consistency in Syria's foreign policy is the…desire to play all sides off each other."[13]

Obama wasted no time in trying to secure Bashar's and, by extension, Iran's cooperation in Iraq. He dispatched John Kerry to Damascus in February 2009. The gentlemanly Kerry, a longtime senator and chairman of the Senate Foreign Relations Committee, already had one thing in common with Bashar: a towering presence. And to try to develop a personal rapport with Bashar, Kerry came with his wife, Teresa Heinz.

Kerry arrived in Damascus a month after a ceasefire in Gaza, where Israel had tried for more than three weeks to destroy what it said was the "infrastructure of terror" of Hamas, the group that controlled the densely populated coastal strip of Palestinian territory on Israel's western flank and was backed by Bashar and his ally, Iran.[14] As bodies of Palestinian civilians, including many children, piled up in mortuaries and their images were transmitted across the Arab world, much of public opinion swung behind Hamas and members of the so-called axis of resistance: Hezbollah, Iran, and the Syrian regime. The indirect talks between Syria and Israel collapsed, and Benjamin Netanyahu, who was set to be the next Israeli prime minister, vowed that Israel would never return the Golan to Syria.[15]

Kerry and Bashar met for more than two hours in the presence of their aides at the People's Palace on the Mezzeh plateau above Damascus. It was built in the last decade of Hafez's rule as a modern and deconstructed version of the historic citadels and fortresses found in cities across the Levant and southern Turkey. It was a vast white stone complex with imposing entrances and cold, cavernous white-marble hallways whose walls were occasionally enlivened by contemporary Syrian art. It was not Bashar's favorite setting. He felt more comfortable in his private study in a bungalow-like structure next to his family residence. But Kerry's visit was official business and he had to be as presidential as possible along with the requisite protocol.

Kerry spoke about how the approach of the Obama administration was going to be different and acknowledged that the United States needed to talk "respectfully and frankly with the parties in the Middle East." He noted "big changes" ahead in how the United States was going to be dealing with Iran, Syria, and the region as a whole.[16] Bashar offered nuanced views on the situation in Iraq and the dangers of breakup along sectarian and ethnic lines. He said that Syria's goal was not to see the United States "humiliated" in Iraq. Before the meeting with Kerry, Syria had sent signals of cooperation by announcing it had arrested 1,200 alleged Al-Qaeda fighters inside the country and shored up security at the Iraqi border.

Bashar and Kerry had a back-and-forth on credibility and trust. Kerry told him that the perception he got from regional leaders was that Bashar "says one thing and does another...or he says he'll do something and then does not do it."[17] Bashar conceded he had been uncooperative with Bush administration officials who came to him with a list of demands. "I was stubborn. I am like George Bush this way," mused Bashar.

Kerry asked Bashar how Hezbollah having 40,000 rockets and missiles aimed at Israel was going to be conducive to peace. Bashar argued that Hezbollah ultimately wanted peace, too, and that its chief, Nasrallah, was someone who could be trusted. "When he says something, he does it," said Bashar.[18]

Later, Bashar invited Kerry and his wife to his private residence to meet Asma. The Asma-Bashar charm offensive was in full swing.[19] The couples had dinner plans later that evening. Bashar casually asked Asma if she wanted to take her car or his. The four settled at a table next to a gurgling marble water fountain at Naranj, an upmarket Syrian-food restaurant in the old city. Waiters and waitresses in spotless white caftans served freshly baked pita bread and an assortment of appetizers.

At dinner, Bashar complained about a rise in the number of women wearing hijabs in Syria. "We want to be a secular country," he told Kerry.[20]

What Bashar probably didn't tell Kerry was that he, like his father before him, allowed mosques and Islamic schools and organizations to flourish so long as they stayed away from politics and remained under the *mukhabarat*'s watchful eyes. It was a way of gaining favor with large conservative segments of Syria's Sunni majority and ensuring their loyalty to the regime. It was Bashar himself who in 2006 had officially sanctioned a previously secretive women-only Sufi order that actively preached wearing the hijab even for young schoolgirls.

Bashar's complaints about the hijab echoed his double-dealing on almost everything. He denied that he was arming Hezbollah when he personally ordered the transfer of rockets and military hardware from Syria to Lebanon. He complained that he could not control the border with Iraq when it was he who instructed his *mukhabarat* to support insurgents and send suicide bombers to Iraq.[21] He denied possessing chemical and biological materials, even as a military research center under his direct control was actively working to weaponize these substances. He raved about his accomplished wife but continued to have extramarital affairs because it made him feel strong.

At the end of dinner with Kerry and Heinz, Bashar signaled to his friend and Republican Guard commander Manaf Tlass to come over and greet the American visitors. Manaf had been dining with Thala at a nearby table.

"I am happy that someone like you is by the president's [Bashar's] side," Kerry told Manaf.[22]

Toward the end of his stay in Damascus, Kerry met Michel Duclos, the French ambassador. Kerry, a fluent French speaker, said he believed he finally had a deal with Bashar on stopping the infiltration of foreign fighters to Iraq and sharing the identities of Al-Qaeda operatives. "This is a man we can do business with," an upbeat Kerry told Duclos. Kerry was totally beguiled by Asma and Bashar, observed Duclos.[23]

Still, Kerry and most other American and European officials knew the nature of the regime they were dealing with and the dangers it posed. They were engaged in a high-stakes strategy of trying to pull Bashar away from the Iranians and Hezbollah. This, they believed, would stabilize

Lebanon and Iraq and put Arab–Israeli peace talks back on a serious track. As for reform and change, they would come about as a result of an internal, organic, and gradual process once Bashar saw the benefits of engagement.

The underlying message to Bashar was that he could rest assured that the United States and its allies would do nothing to jeopardize his grip on power as long as he stopped using terrorism, murder, rocket supplies to Hezbollah, and a chemical-weapons program as bargaining chips.

"Bashar was like a reckless and stubborn kid carrying a crystal ball, and the Americans were gently and nicely trying to calm him down," said Manaf.

The consistent message that Western diplomats were hearing from Manaf and others in the regime was that Bashar was not wedded to Iran and Hezbollah—they were more like mistresses—and that he would break away from them if he saw concrete rewards of engagement, like the end of US sanctions. Manaf often painted to Westerners a picture of a Bashar surrounded by bad and nasty people like his cousins, *mukhabarat* chiefs, and Iranian and Hezbollah operatives, but that he could free himself from their clutches if he was supported and enabled by meaningful steps from the West.

In fairness, though, Bashar himself did not hide from the Americans and Europeans the importance he attached to his relationship with Iran. "Iran supported my cause when the US was against me, when France was against me…How can I say no?" he said to late US senator Arlen Specter at the end of 2008.[24]

Bashar often argued that no settlement of the Middle East's many problems was possible without the involvement of Iran and "resistance groups" like Hezbollah and Hamas.

A courtship of sorts between Bashar and the Americans followed Kerry's 2009 visit. There were tit-for-tat concessions and rewards, progress, and lots of promise, but also some setbacks, uncertainty, and a back-and-forth over whether each side was committed enough to making things better. In response to Kerry's prodding, the Syrians named their ambassador to Lebanon in March 2009, six months after their initial promise to the French.

They allowed the American Language Center in Damascus to reopen but kept the American school (The Damascus Community School) closed. The Syrian ambassador in Washington enjoyed more access to US officials, and some export restrictions to Syria were eased, though not as far as Bashar had hoped for.

Bashar often peppered the near-constant stream of US congressional delegations and officials who flocked to Damascus to see him with statements like "Every step has a meaning," "We need a road map for US–Syria relations," "I won't give it to you for free," "We have to build from an absence of trust,"[25] and "The media has not conveyed an accurate message — don't read the facts [about Syria], *see* them."

Then, in a clear snub to Washington, Bashar hosted Iranian president Mahmoud Ahmadinejad and Hezbollah chief Hassan Nasrallah in Damascus in February 2010, one week after Obama had nominated an American ambassador to Syria (something the regime constantly demanded). The Ahmadinejad-Nasrallah visit was billed as a summit, with a state dinner at the presidential palace. The militia leader, Nasrallah, had no official position in Lebanon, a country whose sovereignty Bashar had supposedly just recognized by appointing his ambassador to it, at Kerry's urging. Bashar went further by mocking a statement by US secretary of state Hillary Clinton the day before that Washington was asking Syria "to begin to move away from the relationship with Iran," and Hezbollah. "We must have understood Clinton wrong because of bad translation or our limited understanding, so we signed [an agreement with Iran] to cancel visas," a laughing Bashar told reporters.[26]

Openly hosting Ahmadinejad, known for his highly inflammatory anti-American rhetoric, and Nasrallah, head of a group classified as a terrorist organization by the United States, could have been Bashar's way of pressing Washington for more concessions.

Éric Chevallier, who had taken over the year before from Duclos as French ambassador to Syria, said that he interpreted the summit as perhaps the Iranians and Hezbollah trying to get Bashar back after his overtures to the Americans and Europeans. "This was exactly the triangle we were trying to break. We were worried but also feeling that if indeed they were trying to get him back then we were succeeding in some place," said Chevallier.[27]

The reengagement with Bashar, though, was narrowly focused on the respective agendas of the countries involved: America mainly wanted Bashar's help on Iraq and antiterrorism, while France's priorities were Lebanon and business in Syria.

For its part, the regime was prepared to engage Western officials on almost everything, including how to deal with Pakistan as the Syrian foreign minister once did, but was absolutely adamant about keeping off the table the issues that ultimately mattered the most to average Syrians: launching genuine and deep reforms, breaking the dreaded *mukhabarat* and its unlimited powers, and fighting the scourge of corruption.

In a sort of Jekyll-and-Hyde act, Bashar adopted a raft of new repressive measures at the same moment that he opened his arms to the Americans and French. On top of the long-standing state of emergency, the power to arrest without warrant, loosely worded "security provisions" in Syria's Penal Code, torture, and forced disappearance, Bashar added more tools to the *mukhabarat*'s arsenal. They included a law imposing strict controls on all print material, monitoring the Internet and censoring websites, having final say on licensing NGOs, and increased use of travel bans to punish activists and dissidents. The measures were applied arbitrarily and unpredictably to keep everyone in a state of constant fear and completely at the *mukhabarat*'s mercy.[28]

In 2009, as Kerry dined with Bashar and praised him as someone he could do business with, the *mukhabarat* shut down the office of human rights lawyer Mazen Darwish for daring to investigate the regime's brutal suppression of a riot at Saydnaya prison the year before, which had left at least seventy-five dead and fifty missing. Mazen found out that many Islamist prisoners felt betrayed by the regime, which rounded them up to please Washington and then started giving them harsh sentences, after having facilitated and encouraged their travel to Iraq to fight the Americans. One of Mazen's friends and colleagues, who was sent to Saydnaya in 2005 for criticizing Bashar, was beheaded during the chaos of the rioting.[29] Since 2008, Mazen himself had already been banned from traveling outside Syria, and his office had been closed once before, in 2006, after writing about the impact of Hariri's assassination on Syria.[30]

Then, in the summer of 2009, came an event that forever changed how Mazen and his colleagues viewed and waged their struggle for freedom. Protests erupted in Iran over the results of the presidential elections that handed the incumbent Ahmadinejad a second term. Hundreds of thousands of Iranians, mostly supporters of reformist candidate Mir-Hossein Mousavi, took to the streets in Tehran and other cities in what became known as the Green Movement. The Iranian regime's response was swift and brutal, with dozens killed and hundreds arrested over almost a six-month period.[31] With Iranian authorities banning traditional media outlets from covering the events, Iranians relied on social media, especially Twitter and YouTube, to get the news out.

"I thought so-called color revolutions were only possible in Europe, but what happened in Iran made me think it was also possible in our region ruled by police states and ideological and sectarian regimes," said Mazen. "Iran 2009 was hugely important for a segment of Syrian youth. We started saying to each other, 'Guys, hold on, we could do something like this, it's not only political parties and traditional opposition.'"

While Mazen thought the moment was right to launch a grassroots movement for change in Syria, Bashar had already dismissed any possibility for political reform in his lifetime. He called activists like Mazen naïve and impressionable. "It's like a young couple who want to get married because they think marriage is a great thing. They have strong emotions for one another, but then comes the reality shock," he said, days before his triumphant trip to Paris in July 2008.[32] It was a diplomatic version of what he often told Manaf in private: "You can only rule these people with the shoe."

But "these people" were changing, and the tight lid that Hafez had kept on them and the country was easing, at least when it came to daily life. People walked around with cell phones, Internet cafés sprang up, satellite dishes overtook TV antennas on rooftops, and tourism blossomed. Contact with the outside world and its influences was increasing, no matter the censorship and monitoring by the country's ever-present *mukhabarat*.

Still, Bashar never missed a chance to remind those asking for real change to consider Iraq's mayhem and appreciate what he was accomplishing in Syria. New jobs were created and private investment was rising. Bashar brought them the Internet, private banks and schools, malls, hotels, and restaurants. Syria was becoming a destination. World and regional powers were clamoring to engage the young leader. Discerning tourists and famous people were coming to Syria. In 2009, Asma and Bashar met Angelina Jolie and Brad Pitt in Damascus, and Manaf organized a tour of the country for one his favorite movie directors, Francis Ford Coppola.[33] If Syrians wanted civil society and NGOs, then there were Asma's many organizations. Religious associations? There were hundreds of state-sanctioned ones to choose from.

Change was indeed visible in big cities like Aleppo and Damascus. There were more cars, shops, and construction sites. The Agha Khan Foundation and the Germans were renovating old Aleppo, the oldest continuously inhabited city in the world. One could get lost all day in Aleppo's vaulted souks with merchants selling everything from spices and local soaps to cell phones and bridal gowns. Old homes converted into charming boutique hotels with evocative names were opening every few months. In your room, you would probably find one of the many new glossy English-language magazines. The July 2008 issue of a magazine called *Forward* had Asma and Michele Obama on the cover with this title: "What Michele Obama Can Learn from Asma al-Assad." In Damascus, the social scene and night life grew vibrant as new galleries, cafés, and rooftop bars opened throughout the city.

There were many Syrians who believed that their president and his wife were the best thing that ever happened to the country, and they made sure they told visitors this—but for the majority it was more making the best of the circumstances and forging ahead. Syrians in general were talented, resourceful, and incredibly adaptable, qualities that had nothing to do with Bashar and his regime.

"Two years in we realized nothing was going to change, but for Westerners they wanted to see what they wanted to see, not reality. They were saying Syria was opening up, but we would tell them this is an illusion, nothing has changed, we still have the *mukhabarat* on top of us and we have to pay bribes for everything," said a Damascene businesswoman, who was among those who benefited from Bashar's economic opening. "Experts came to fix this or that, the central bank, the government and so on—I cannot tell you how many experts came through—but the system remained the system."[34]

The painter Khaled al-Khani argued with his friends over whether what they were seeing was genuine and sustainable or an "optical illusion," as Khaled liked to call it.[35] "It was our daily discussion," said Khaled. "Many believed he had a vision and strategy—and they had a point, because something did change when he took over from Hafez. Things were changing on the surface, but in tandem there was massive mobilization through the 'We love you' campaign to penetrate and co-opt every segment of society: artists, actors, businessmen, and so on. The regime fully colonized society. You could say half of the Syrians worked for Rami Makhlouf, since he controlled half the economy."

The new class of superrich crony capitalists had so much money that they didn't know what to do with it. They even rushed to buy Khaled's abstract paintings, not recognizing that his works frequently depicted the violence and suffering inflicted by the regime. "They were fools, they just wanted to show themselves as patrons of the arts," he said.

Beyond the image proudly presented by the regime to the world, by late 2010 there were many signs of growing discontent in Syria. A perfect storm of old grievances and new conflicts seemed to be gathering around Bashar. Most alarming was the problem posed by his cousins and business partners the Makhloufs.

Fueled by seemingly insatiable greed, they wanted to muscle in on any lucrative business opportunity, from major infrastructure projects involving big foreign companies to retail franchises. Rami Makhlouf told foreign investors that their projects would be obstructed by Syria's notorious bureaucracy unless they worked through him.[36] By the end of 2010, Rami's companies controlled about 65 percent of the economy, according to an estimate by French ambassador Chevallier, who lunched with the magnate on occasion. Rami puffed on a Cuban cigar and did little to conceal his arrogance and pride. "He behaved like the king of the country," said Chevallier.[37]

Rami always made sure Chevallier understood this message: We're watching you and we know who you're meeting with. Rami's brother Hafez headed the Damascus branch of the General Intelligence Directorate, one of the *mukhabarat* apparatuses.

"We have the power and the money!" said Rami, banging his fist on a conference table during a meeting with some partners of Cham, the business cartel that he and Bashar had formed in late 2006. The partners were worried about the legality of a business decision that they were deliberating with Rami.

Another time, Bashar's planning minister, Abdallah al-Dardari, a polished economist from a prominent Damascene family who had been handpicked by Bashar to market his reforms to the West, tried to convince Rami that it was wiser and ultimately more profitable in the long run if he did not seek to monopolize everything. "If you let the cake grow, your own piece will become bigger," Dardari told him.

"I want the whole cake, Abdallah," Rami replied.[38]

Bashar tried to rein in Rami and the Makhloufs on a couple of occasions, but their sway over him went beyond kinship. The Makhloufs forged a strong alliance with his ambitious wife, Asma.

"Asma loved money, and they [Makhloufs] showered her with expensive gifts," said Manaf.[39] Asma's banking background meant that she shared Rami's business acumen, and having Rami and the Makhloufs on her side strengthened her position in the family after the acrimonious clash with Bashar's sister, Bushra.

With Bashar's recipe for economic liberalization came cancer-like corruption that plagued the entire state. The attitude of civil servants, *mukhabarat* officers, and almost everyone connected to the state became this: Why should the president's cousin, the big-shot businessmen, and regime officials be the only ones accumulating obscene fortunes? We deserve our cut—just crumbs compared to what these people are taking.

Discrepancies in income and living standards became staggering. Residents of the slums and rural areas around urban centers, what some called the "misery belts," watched the newly rich inside the cities get richer and flaunt their wealth. The rich were also frantically building malls and condominium projects on the city's outskirts, squeezing out the poor and marginalized even more. By 2009, almost 35 percent of Syria's population

of about 22 million was considered poor by the government's own defini-
tion of poverty, an increase from previous years.[40] This was hastened by a
severe drought in the country's northeast in 2006, which forced many
farmers to abandon their land and flock to the cities.

Compounding the poverty and misfortune in the north was a new
free-trade agreement that Bashar signed with Turkey. It made it harder for
textile factories to compete with cheaper Turkish imports. Some closed
and laid off workers. A fast-growing and more youthful and college-
educated population, coupled with Bashar's shift toward market-oriented
policies, made it harder for the state to keep fulfilling its traditional role as
the largest employer and provider of subsidized goods and services. By
2010, the real unemployment rate was estimated at 25 percent.[41]

"Hafez ruled Syria through a pact with the impoverished Sunni countryside. Sure, everyone was trampled on, but at least their basics were taken
care of," said Manaf.[42]

And even though urban Sunnis, especially families that were part of
the regime's business networks, benefited immensely, there were noneco-
nomic sources of disgruntlement among segments of this crucial population group. By 2010, Sunnis had been pushed down to the seventh rank in
terms of seniority in the army leadership, and this change had not gone
unnoticed. "He did not think appearances mattered. His father would
never have made this mistake," said Manaf.

There was also bubbling resentment among Sunnis over Bashar's
open-door policy toward Iran and Hezbollah since 2005. They were not
only his military and political partners, but they were also actively spreading Shiite faith in society, particularly in Damascus and remote, impoverished Sunni communities. Powerful Sunni clerics approached Western
diplomats and pleaded with them to mention it to Bashar.[43]

Conservative Sunni Muslims also felt that the regime was waging war
against them when, in 2010, it removed about 1,200 women from their
teaching posts for wearing the *niqab*, a head-to-toe black cover that only
reveals the eyes. The regime thought that its longtime pact with the Sunni
clerical establishment, which hinged mainly on allowing mosques and religious schools to proliferate in return for allegiance, was enough to maintain its sway over much of the Sunni community. But people were

increasingly exposed to other influences, mainly via satellite TV channels. Some saw the state-sponsored version of Islam ritualistic, unfulfilling, and too beholden to the regime. Syrians who traveled to Gulf Arab countries for work were affected by a harsh, puritanical, and overtly sectarian interpretation of Islam. And there were those who had gone to wage jihad in Iraq, often with help from the regime, only to return with a new militant take on Islam.

None of this was unique to Syria. Poverty, unemployment, injustice, corruption, and Islamic militancy infected all of the Arab world's autocracies. But the social trauma had deeper roots in Syria, and the lid maintained by the police state was much tighter—more like a pressure cooker.

In December 2010, as Bashar and Asma were wooing the French in Paris, Mazen met with some of his friends and colleagues. After the *mukhabarat* closed his office in Damascus, he rented a place on the city's outskirts where they frequently gathered. Since the 2009 protests in Iran, they had held several informal workshops on the use of social media applications like Facebook and Twitter and how to upload videos taken with a cell phone.[44] Some even set up accounts with fake names on these sites and were already posting writings critical of the regime. They were absolutely fascinated by the power of these tools in reaching wider audiences.

"What are you guys doing?" asked Mazen's wife, Yara, when she walked in that day.

"We are planning a revolution," said Mazen.

"What! If it's a secret, you really don't have to tell me. But don't tell me things like 'We are planning a revolution,'" said Yara, visibly annoyed.

"I'm not kidding—we're thinking how we could start a revolution," said Mazen calmly.

9

No More Fear after Today

A handful of young men rose up and began chanting *"Hurriyeh, hurriyeh, hurriyeh!"* ("Freedom, freedom, freedom!") and *"Selmiyeh, selmiyeh, selmiyeh!"* ("Peaceful, peaceful, peaceful!") the moment congregants were muttering their last prayers at the Hamza and Abbas mosque on the south side of Daraa city.[1] That was the designated signal to start the protest. It was Friday, March 18; spring was a few days away.

Others waiting anxiously outside the mosque joined in. These were words never spoken before in public, at least not in their lifetime. Many of the organizers were not particularly pious Muslims. They chose the mosque to kick off their protest for more practical reasons. Protests were forbidden in Syria, but mosques were one of the few places where large crowds could gather in public without immediately drawing the *mukhabarat*'s attention. Still, the dreaded security agencies kept a diligent and watchful eye on most mosques and vetted sermons delivered by clerics during the midday communal prayers on Fridays.

Security forces were posted outside several mosques in Daraa that Friday because the *mukhabarat* had information about a possible protest. One of the exceptions was the Hamza and Abbas mosque in the city's southernmost neighborhood, a poor and neglected area just a few miles from the Jordanian border. It was in this neighborhood, called Arbaeen, that a group of teenage boys sneaked out of their homes at night about a month earlier, armed with spray paint. There were five of them, the eldest about sixteen and the youngest about eleven or twelve.[2] They ran over to their local school. On the outer wall they sprayed graffiti: *"jayeek el door, ya daktor"*

161

("you are next, doctor") and *"ashaab yurid isqat an-nizam"* ("the people want to bring down the regime").

The slogan about bringing down the regime was the rallying cry of the popular revolts erupting across the Middle East in the early months of 2011 by which people, including in Daraa, were transfixed, thanks to nonstop coverage by the Arab world's main news channels, especially Al Jazeera. Egypt's Mubarak was forced to step down that month (February 2011), while Bahrain, Libya, and Yemen were already engulfed in protests. Syria, ruled by the Assad family for more than four decades, was expected to be next.

The boys thought nobody saw them. But these were tense times, and the *mukhabarat*'s "eyes," or informants, were awake everywhere. The following day, the five boys plus some twenty others not even involved in spraying the graffiti were swept up by security forces. Most were from the Abazeid clan. In tightly knit and tribal Daraa, seat of a largely rural province of more than one million people, each neighborhood was dominated by one or two big families.

Word spread later that the teenage boys had been transferred from Daraa to the regional *mukhabarat* headquarters in the adjacent province of Suwayda, which, unlike Sunni-majority Daraa, was dominated by the Druze minority. Even in deciding where to locate its organs of terror, the Assad regime carefully exploited religious and social cleavages. This was a horrible sign for the boys' families. They could languish in *mukhabarat* dungeons for months, possibly years. They could never come out. They were going to be tortured day and night until they confessed to crimes they never committed. Relatives inquiring about them could be arrested, too. All of this was common knowledge to most Syrians.

Abazeid male elders pleaded with local officials, including the governor, for the boys' release. But there was nothing an appointed functionary like a governor or prime minister could do in a country where real power was in the hands of the *mukhabarat* and the Assad clan. The elders finally secured an audience with the most powerful man in Daraa, Atef Najib—the head of the local branch of the Political Security Directorate, one of the four main agencies that make up the *mukhabarat*.[3] In addition to his powerful position, Najib was one of Bashar's maternal cousins; he was the son of Aniseh's sister, Fatmeh.

"No one in Daraa ever saw Atef Najib, let alone uttered his name. For some he was as mighty as God," said Ayman al-Aswad, a Daraa school-teacher and political activist who was following the case of the arrested boys.[4]

Najib, who was in his fifties, was known for his penchant for expensive suits and fine leather loafers. He had been one of Bassel al-Assad's acolytes before Bashar became the heir apparent. Najib worked for years in various *mukhabarat* branches in Damascus, including the department overseeing books and print media and another one responsible for hotels and night-clubs. He amassed a fortune from corrupt land and construction deals that became the talk of Damascus.[5]

"Forget you have children," a disdainful and mocking Najib told the group of fathers and elders who came to beg forgiveness for their sons' acts and plead their release.[6] "And if you want new children in their place, then send your wives over and we'll impregnate them for you."

This was the ultimate insult in a conservative and patriarchal society like Daraa. One of the elders felt so ashamed and dishonored by what he heard that he took off his red and white checkered tribal headdress and tossed it on the floor as the delegation left Najib's office, a gesture signify-ing injured pride.

There was another meeting between the elders and Suhail Ramadan, the *mukhabarat* chief in neighboring Suwayda, where the boys were held. Ramadan, for his part, supposedly hurled similar insults at them.[7] Although there were varying versions of what was said and done at these meetings with the *mukhabarat* officials, news of the purported affront to Daraa's honor and women spread like wildfire.[8]

It became popular, especially in subsequent media accounts of how Syr-ia's uprising began, to focus on the arrest of the boys who sprayed the graf-fiti and Najib's profanities as the reason why Daraa erupted in protest on March 18, 2011. This incident, though, was only part of the story. The arrests happened in mid-February, the meeting with Najib at the end of that month, and the protests more than two weeks later. The first cries out-side the Hamza and Abbas mosque were simply for dignity and freedom.

"The story of the kids was a trigger but not the real reason," said Aswad, a leftist and longtime regime opponent in Daraa, who had been fired in 2008 from his job as a math teacher because of his political views.

"The real reason was that we were gagged, trampled on, and subjugated for forty years."

In addition to grievances shared with all Syrians, Daraa had some of its own, too. Daraa bordered both Jordan and Israel, and draconian laws in place since the Hafez era—initially meant for Kurds living close to the Turkish border in the north—prohibited inhabitants of border provinces from selling or leasing land and building homes without permission from the *mukhabarat*. This law, however, became a vehicle for massive extortion by local *mukhabarat* agents and government officials, who were ready to overlook the law or break it—provided hefty bribes were paid in return.

Like many inhabitants of Syria's southern region known as Houran, Daraa's natives had flocked to oil-rich Gulf Arab countries in the 1980s and '90s to earn a living and improve their lot. After toiling abroad for decades, many returned to build retirement homes and farm their land—and had to contend with the *mukhabarat* and the bribes. "They drowned you in never-ending details and minutiae. You needed seventeen different approvals to open a shoe store," said Aswad.

Notwithstanding these resentments, over the years the regime built a sizable class of loyalists and cronies in Daraa who held senior posts in the Baath Party and government in Damascus and were granted concessions and privileges locally. These people were generally older tribal leaders and businessmen. The regime never imagined a rebellion could start in Daraa, or the "Baath's southern citadel and bastion," as it was called in propaganda. Hardly any attention, though, was paid to the youth, the impoverished, and those who were enraged about the wide gap between rich and poor and the practices of the police state and *mukhabarat*.

When protests erupted in Tunisia in December 2010, Aswad and other regime opponents in Daraa started meeting clandestinely. They were joined a few times by the Damascus-based Mazen Darwish and some of his colleagues.

"We used to say to each other, 'Let's go eat *mlaihi*,'" said Mazen, referring to a traditional Daraa dish of lamb and warm yoghurt on a bed of bulgur.[9] "As we ate we discussed how we could take advantage of what was happening around us. We wanted to have a civil and peaceful revolution against the regime. You want to call that a conspiracy? Sure."

Nobody spoke about Bashar's departure. The discussion was centered around the same issues that Mazen and his friends were talking about in Damascus: ending the state of emergency, releasing political prisoners, and freeing political life and media, among other things.

Aswad and some twenty other veteran opponents in Daraa, many of them elderly and previously imprisoned by the regime, tried to air these demands on March 15 in front of the city's main courthouse, but they backed off when they saw the number of heavily armed security force personnel swarming the area.

That same day, some 200 people, mostly young men and women, marched through the alleyways and souks of Damascus's old quarter chanting for freedom and dignity in response to a call to protest on Facebook.[10] The whole thing barely lasted thirty minutes before security forces and pro-regime thugs dispersed the crowd and arrested protesters. The following day, March 16, saw the demonstration for the release of political prisoners organized by Mazen and his colleagues outside the Ministry of the Interior in Damascus. A few activists came up from Daraa to take part and added their demand for the release of the boys who had sprayed the graffiti. Protesters were viciously attacked by pro-regime thugs and many were arrested.

On March 18, activists and regime opponents in Daraa were hesitating until the last minute about whether to protest or not after Friday prayers, given the heavy security presence in the city and the way Mazen and others had been violently dealt with in Damascus.

Aswad, who was not a particularly religious man and rarely prayed or went to a mosque, was home with some of his like-minded friends when his phone rang. It was a relative.

"Things have kicked off in Al-Balad!" said the excited relative and hung up.

Aswad understood that a protest had started in the city's old district, called Al-Balad.[11] He and the others got into their cars and drove toward the protest.

In other parts of the city, men were returning home from Friday prayers at their neighborhood mosques. (Women usually prayed at home and prepared lunch.)

Word of the protest was spreading, but it had not yet reached the home of eighteen-year-old Sally Masalmeh, who was among those eager for what many in the Arab world were calling *thawra*, or revolution, to come to Syria, too. Not far from Sally's home lived Malek al-Jawabra, a young man she did not know at the time but would meet a few years later in circumstances that neither of them could have ever imagined.

Malek, a twenty-one-year-old law student, was getting off his motorbike as his cousin Ahmad rushed toward him.[12]

"Do not you know what happened?" said an excited and breathless Ahmad.

"No," said Malek, alarmed.

"A protest left the Hamza and Abbas mosque and it has reached the Omari mosque," said Ahmad.

"Okay, let's go!" said Malek.

Malek restarted his motorbike and Ahmad hopped on behind him.

By the time they arrived, several hundred people were on the street outside the Omari mosque, a city landmark that was more than a thousand years old. It was built with the area's distinctive dark volcanic rocks and had a clock-tower-like minaret. More people kept arriving. There were a lot of teenagers and young men. They were the most fired up. There were also many fathers with their sons and a few elderly people in tribal dress, but not a lot. There were no women, but things would soon change.

It was more of an impromptu gathering than an organized protest, and even had a carnival-like air. People whistled, cheered, sang, and clapped. "*Hurriyeh, hurriyeh!*" ("Freedom, freedom!") they shouted. Malek and his cousin joined in.[13] There were no real political slogans or even articulate demands. Many people were there because they hoped this could pressure the *mukhabarat* to release the boys who had sprayed the graffiti.

There was one thing, though, that almost everyone present that day had in common: a sense of collective exhilaration and liberation. A people unshackled.

They were finally speaking out after being told all their lives to keep their mouths shut and mind their own business—otherwise they and their families could get into real trouble.

"*Ba'ad el youm ma fi khouf!*" ("No more fear after today!") they shouted that day in Daraa.[14] Nobody covered their faces. People held up their cell phones and took photographs and videos. It felt like emancipation after decades of servility.

"Young men, calm down, just write down your demands and we will read them," said a voice over a loudspeaker coming from inside the Omari.

One hour earlier, Bashar's cousin and *mukhabarat* chief, Atef Najib, had summoned the mosque's influential imam, Ahmad al-Sayasneh. He wanted the respected and well-liked cleric to pressure the crowds to go home. "Sheik Ahmad, all your demands will be met in a week, God willing, but we want you to calm people down," Najib told Sayasneh, adopting a conciliatory tone in total contrast to his earlier belligerence.[15]

"I have nothing to do with what's going on," said the blind, sixty-five-year-old cleric, who wore a white embroidered skullcap.

"No, they will listen to you," insisted Najib.

Sayasneh came back to the mosque and told protesters massed outside to hand him their demands so he could pass them on to local officials.[16]

"Liars, liars, liars!" was the crowds' answer to the call for calm. "Thieves, thieves, thieves!"

As the pleas for them to disperse persisted, the chants became more animated and bold.

"Down with Atef Najib! The people want to topple the governor! The people want to tear down corruption!"

The crowd kept swelling. By afternoon, there were several thousand people clogging the street in front of the Omari. They moved toward the provincial government headquarters on the north side of the city, a section called Al-Mahata. They hoped more people would join the protest as it made its way down the hill from the mosque toward Al-Mahata. The more-organized and politically minded in the crowd even thought they could present the governor with a set of written demands.

The crowd passed a metal archway with a portrait of Bashar in the middle.

Some looked up and began chanting: "The people want to bring down the regime!"

"No, no, no! The people want to *reform* the regime," shouted others in the crowd, hoping to drown them out.[17] There was a large contingent who advocated for more-measured change focused on ending corruption and releasing prisoners.

The chant grew louder and louder: "The people want to reform the regime!"

In the meantime, Najib called Damascus and the regional *mukhabarat* headquarters in Suwayda to send him reinforcements to deal with the protest. He had already mobilized all the forces at his disposal in Daraa, including regular police, military police, and civil defense.[18] The uniformed forces were divided into packs, each commanded by one of Najib's *mukhabarat* henchmen, all in plainclothes. Many wore tracksuits and sneakers and carried pistols.

As protesters came down the hill and reached an area called Al-Karak, they were met with a hail of tear gas cannisters fired by these forces. People responded by throwing rocks and stones at them. A couple of vehicles belonging to the security forces were quickly surrounded, and after their occupants had fled, the cars were smashed by angry protesters determined to press ahead.[19]

A cat-and-mouse game ensued, with protesters trying to go down the hill and security forces pushing them back up again. Some protesters were caught by security forces. These unlucky ones were beaten, trampled on, kicked, dragged on the pavement, and then bundled into *mukhabarat* vehicles parked at the bottom of the slope.[20] This only made protesters angrier and more defiant. Fire trucks tried to repulse the crowd by hosing people down, but that did not work either. By late afternoon the reinforcements that Najib had asked for reached Daraa, streaming in by helicopter and bus.[21]

"That's the big boss," said some Daraa residents as they spotted a swarm of helicopters touching down briefly inside the city's soccer stadium and then taking off again.[22] They thought that perhaps it was Bashar himself coming to Daraa to calm things down.

Shortly thereafter, masked gunmen in black began arriving at the scene of the standoff with protesters. They were members of an elite security force never previously seen in Daraa.

Some protesters started shouting *"Allahu akbar!"* ("God is greatest!") to try to give people courage and make them hold their ground. Others honked the horns of their motorbikes.[23] People burned tires and threw large rocks at the security forces to try to thwart them.

Malek and his friends and relatives watched from the side. The black-clad forces started shooting in the air. The barrage of gunfire lasted a few minutes. Many protesters scurried back up the hill. Others were determined to stand firm and even charged forward.[24]

Sharpshooters among the black uniformed forces were now perched on a hilltop overlooking the scene. There was more gunfire, this time more intense and sustained. Most of it was still into the air, but some of it was now being aimed directly at the crowd. Malek could see people being hit in their legs and arms.[25] Then he saw his relative Mahmoud al-Jawabra collapse to the ground. Another man standing nearby also fell. Mahmoud was hit in the neck. His T-shirt was soaked in blood. He was dead.

"One guy has DIED!" people began shouting as they frantically rushed up the hill toward the Omari mosque.[26]

A couple of people carried the bodies of Mahmoud and the other man, who was killed with a shot in the head.[27] They bundled them into cars and sped away. Malek fled on his motorbike with his cousin. People scattered as the black-uniformed forces chased them. There were more forces waiting for protesters on the hilltop next to the mosque. They were surrounded from all directions. The cars with the two dead men were stopped. Security personnel snatched the bodies and arrested everyone.

Malek and his cousin escaped, but two other relatives were arrested. Everyone found on the streets that day was swept up by security forces.

"They just killed people like that—impossible!" said Sally when the news reached her home.[28]

Her family, like many Daraa residents, did not know whether a protest was going to come out for sure that day. Yes, the situation was tense after the arrest of the boys, and yes, everybody was wondering when protests would start in Syria, like in other countries, but nobody thought people in Daraa could overcome their fears and take to the streets, just like that. And for people to be killed on the first day was also hard to fathom for Sally and others who were not yet born when Hafez crushed the rebellion against his regime.

Sally had a connection to the two slain young men. Mahmoud al-Jawabra's mother was related to Sally's mother. Sally casually met Mahmoud at a few family gatherings. His father had died when he and his siblings were very young. He was the eldest. He dropped out of school to support his family and later opened a small grocery store. He was a well-liked young man; many in Daraa knew him because he played for the local soccer team. The other man, Husam al-Ayash, was the brother of one of Sally's friends. He also came from a poor family. Like many in Daraa, he had gone recently to the Gulf to work and had come back to Daraa to get married before leaving again.[29]

"God help us all," said Sally's mother as the family gathered in the living room.

"We are not going to get off easy — it's going to be just like Hama," she added, referring to Hafez's siege and destruction of the rebellious city in central Syria in 1982. The older generation had never forgotten Hama.

The next day, elders from the tribes to which the Ayash and Jawabra families belonged went to meet with Bashar's cousin Najib. He was ready to hand over the bodies of the two dead men on this condition: They should be buried quickly and quietly without any elaborate funeral processions or protests.

Some of the elders were loyal to the regime and were eager for damage control. They did want to drag the names of their tribe and family further into the camp of those seen as agitating against the regime. They assured Najib that they would carry out his orders.

In the meantime, hundreds of people flocked to the homes of the two dead men. Elders arrived with the bodies and informed the grieving families of their deal with Najib.[30] Heated exchanges broke out at both homes. How could they make such an agreement with Najib? Younger members of both families saw the fallen men as martyrs. They were determined to hold a fitting funeral. At the Jawabra home the arguments turned into scuffles, with some young men destroying a traditional funeral tent set up outside the house, where condolences were to be received during the mourning period. They said that no condolences would be accepted before a proper funeral procession and burial.

Eventually the youth in both families prevailed over the tribal elders.

From the first moment, the struggle against the regime was a standoff between the younger generation that wanted to challenge and break free from fear and tyranny, and the older generation that still remembered Hafez and the heavy price he made Syrians pay for defiance.

The Ayash and Jawabra families agreed that the funeral processions bearing the coffins of the two young men would meet outside the Omari mosque, there they would merge and head toward the cemetery. The bodies were wrapped in blankets and placed in open coffins carried by relatives. Women ululated and threw rice grains and splashed rose water at the large procession as it passed by, rituals reserved for special occasions.

Sally stood on the balcony of her home facing the Omari. Many other women did the same. Some were on the street in front of their homes. Custom prevented them from going to the cemetery with the men, but they were eager to participate in their own way, too. Thousands of men joined the combined procession, and as their numbers swelled a massive anti-regime protest emerged.[31]

"We sacrifice our soul and blood for you, martyr," people chanted as they clapped and pumped their fists in the air.

"He who kills his own people is a traitor!"

Sally was determined to catch up with the procession as it headed toward the cemetery. She did not want to miss a thing. She told her mother that she was going to her aunt's house, which was near the cemetery, and ran out the door before her mother could stop her.

From the rooftop of her aunt's house Sally saw a sea of young men, children, and some elders moving toward the cemetery. They must have been in the tens of thousands.

"Revolution, revolution against tyranny and aggression!" they chanted in one voice.

That day—March 19, 2011—Republican Guard general Manaf Tlass was at his base in the mountains around Damascus. He had barely slept the night before as he and his aides tried to gather information about events in Daraa and decide what precautionary measures they needed to take in Damascus, which was a mere sixty miles away from the southern city.

What Manaf pieced together was that, on March 18, Atef Najib had called his cousin Hafez Makhlouf, who headed one of the *mukhabarat* branches in Damascus to let him know that he needed help to break the protest.[32] Hafez agreed with other *mukhabarat* chiefs, including Jamil Hassan, who commanded the Air Force Intelligence Directorate, to immediately assemble a strike force and fly it down to Daraa to deal with the protest. Manaf concluded that those who had opened fire on protesters must have belonged to this force.

The shoot-to-kill orders given were in keeping with Hafez Makhlouf's bloody tendencies and disdain for average Syrians. Hafez, who turned forty at the start of the uprising, was the second of the Makhlouf sons after the eldest, Rami. Unlike his business-mogul brother Rami, Hafez rarely appeared in public and most Syrians did not know what he looked like. He had miraculously survived the 1994 car accident that killed Bashar's older brother, Bassel. Hafez's slight-build, clean-cut appearance, and calm persona belied a murderous megalomaniac, according to those who interacted with him.

Following the death of the two protesters, Bashar and his brother, Maher, and their cousin Hafez decided on March 19 to dispatch more forces to Daraa, as well as two senior *mukhabarat* officers, Hisham Ekhtiyar and Rustum Ghazaleh, to establish a crisis cell there to deal with the situation. Ekhtiyar and Ghazaleh, a Daraa native, were given firm instructions to do whatever it took to restore order in Daraa and prevent the situation from escalating any further.[33] Bashar also sent civilians, including his deputy foreign minister and Daraa native Faisal al-Mekdad and another Baath Party apparatchik who was from Hama, to speak in a more conciliatory tone.

"His excellency [Bashar] considers Daraa to be in the forefront in its loyalty to the regime... He was shocked and so were we about what happened," Ghazaleh told the Daraa elders and officials he had summoned to the local Baath Party headquarters.[34]

The next day, March 20, Bashar called Manaf at the base. It was their first contact since the deaths in Daraa. Bashar decided to follow the advice of hard-liners like his brother, Maher, and cousin Hafez on how he should deal with Daraa, but he still wanted to sound out other people close to him. Maybe there were other ways to bring the situation under control. Maybe he was missing something or was not being given the full picture by the hard-liners. He also wanted to see where everyone stood on what just happened in Daraa—who was in favor of a tough response and who was not.

"What's your decision?" Bashar asked Manaf.

"My decision is that you throw Atef Najib in jail and sack the governor. Go down to Daraa tomorrow and make peace with the people," said Manaf. He told Bashar that families of the dead should be generously compensated and all those detained in Daraa, including the boys who had sprayed the graffiti, should be released immediately.

"What do you know about the dead?" asked Bashar.

"They were killed during the protests. They're not from powerful families, but still you should go down and be conciliatory," said Manaf.

Manaf explained that this would quickly bring the situation under control—the idea being that Bashar's gesture would mean a lot to Daraa's people, who were seen within the regime as simple and emotional tribal folk.

"These are generous and good-hearted people," said Manaf.

"Okay," said Bashar before ending the call.

Back in Daraa, events were moving fast. After the burial of the two young men killed on the first day of protests, angry youth were determined to stay on the streets to defy regime forces. They decided to head to *Sahet al-Saraya*, or Serail Square, in the northern section of the city, Al-Mahata. They wanted to organize a sit-in there in front of the provincial government palace, Baath Party headquarters, and other symbols of authority located around the square.

"To the Mahata, to the Mahata!" they shouted after the funeral. They were immediately confronted by security forces. More people were shot dead and many more were wounded or arrested.

Sheik Sayasneh, the Omari mosque's blind cleric, pleaded with protesters not to go to the government square and to stay in the city's old section, Al-Balad, so they wouldn't provoke further violence by regime forces. He told them they could have their sit-in at the mosque and make their demands from there. Surely there was enough respect for the mosque's sanctity that security forces would not breach its threshold so easily. It would offer protesters some measure of protection from the deadly force being deployed on the streets.[35]

Many accepted Sayasneh's offer and moved to the mosque. But there was a limit to his ability to control people, given that this was still a spontaneous outpouring of popular anger and frustration led by the youth, with no clear leader and objective.

"This was a people's revolution, not a revolution of the educated and the elite," said Sally Masalmeh. "There were all sorts of people among us: high school dropouts, laborers, farmers, and so on. The youth were the hardest to control."[36]

Arguments broke out between sons and fathers, who wanted to hold back their children from risking their lives on the streets.

"Why should we listen to you? You were the ones who brought us to this miserable state," sons told their fathers.[37]

"Why did you not rise against Hafez? Why did you just watch him hand power to Bashar?"

Very quickly the Omari mosque and its courtyard turned into a base for protesters. They decided to set up a field hospital there to treat those wounded in ongoing confrontations with security forces. The city's hospital was far away, and the nearby small clinics were reluctant to take in the wounded, fearing it could expose them to punishment by the regime. The only option was to set up the makeshift hospital at the mosque. Pharmacists and Daraa residents donated surgical packs, portable oxygen machines, stretchers, medicine, and other supplies.

This was an opportunity for some women who wanted to take a more active role in the uprising. Those with medical training and experience headed to the mosque courtyard to help. Sally had completed first aid and CPR training the previous summer, so she went, too, despite attempts by her parents to stop her.

"You could count the girls on one hand," said Sally. "We wanted to help in any way we could. All the taboos were starting to crumble."

There were still limits, though. All the women left at sundown, and only men spent the night at the mosque to keep the sit-in going. Foam mattresses and blankets were brought to the prayer hall. People took turns sleeping. They were starting to get more organized. They formed a media committee. They wrote their demands on cutouts of white bedsheets and hung them on the mosque's outer wall.[38]

These demands included the following:

"End the state of emergency" which had been in place since 1963.

"Release prisoners of conscience."

"Freedom of expression, freedom to protest."

"Fight corruption and provide jobs to recent graduates."

"Raise the minimum wage and salaries, and reduce taxes and improve living standards."

The revolution that Sally and other young Syrians were watching unfold across the region had finally come to Syria, at least to Daraa.

While a revolutionary spirit gripped the city's south side around the Omari mosque, there was a different mood on the opposite side of the city, where the regime was in control. At the Baath Party's local headquarters off Serail Square, the *mukhabarat* commanders dispatched by Bashar huddled with Daraa officials and tribal notables loyal to the regime. The *mukhabarat* chiefs made it clear that the mosque sit-in could no longer be tolerated. It was March 22, now three days since the protesters they called "terrorists" had taken over the mosque. The children who were detained for spraying the graffiti had been released the day before, after many had endured horrific torture.

The president, Bashar, agreed to sack Daraa's governor and review the protesters' other demands, and as such those inside the mosque should leave at once, demanded the *mukhabarat* chiefs through mediators. Protesters scoffed at what the regime cast as major concessions. They knew that the governor had no real power and was conveniently being made the scapegoat. What about the one with the real power, the security chief and Bashar's cousin, Atef Najib? What about all the people who had been killed and detained since March 18? They did not trust the regime.

One of the main mediators between the regime and protesters in the mosque was Muwafaq al-Qaddah, a Daraa native and rich businessman based in the United Arab Emirates.[39] He was a self-made man who had built his fortune starting as a traveling salesman. Qaddah was among those courted by Bashar and encouraged to invest in Syria when Bashar launched his economic liberalization. Like most other businessmen, Qaddah partnered on several projects with Bashar's cousin Rami Makhlouf. Despite his regime links, Qaddah was generally well respected and liked in Daraa. He was a local farmer's son who had gone to the Gulf and done well.

Qaddah could not say no when Bashar asked for help in ending the standoff in his hometown Daraa. He immediately flew to Damascus and headed down to Daraa. There he was told to liaise with the office of Bashar's brother, Maher, who was overseeing the crisis cell in Daraa and was monitoring the situation hour by hour. One of Maher's crony businessmen, Mohammad Hamsho, was friends with Qaddah. The two would keep in touch throughout the emergency.[40]

On the evening of March 22, Qaddah met for hours with protesters at the Omari mosque. Past midnight he thought there was a breakthrough. The protesters agreed to leave the mosque on condition that all those arrested since March 18 would be immediately released. The fate of those missing—dead, alive, or held by the regime—would also be ascertained. All other demands were subject to future discussions.

It was very late already. So Qaddah and his entourage got into their cars to head back to the crisis cell on the other side of the city to inform its leaders about the deal that they had just struck with the protesters.

As the peace delegation left the Omari mosque, the entire city was plunged into darkness. Streetlights were extinguished and power went off in all homes. Cellular phone service was also cut.

Sally was asleep. She was in bed next to her mother. Her father was still up in the living room.

Suddenly the crackle of heavy gunfire pierced the silence and darkness.

"Oh my God! Could they be storming the Omari?" said Sally as she jumped out of bed.

She ran into the living room. Her two younger brothers were already there with her father. Her mother came out from the bedroom.[41]

The mosque was a few hundred meters from their home. They could hear everything. The gunfire grew louder and more intense and sustained. It sounded like machine guns. The booms of explosions rang through the air.

Sally and her siblings started to cry. Her brothers wanted to run back to the mosque and be with their friends who were there. Her tearful mother barricaded their way and locked the front door. They would die if they stepped outside.

"Allahu akbar, people of Daraa! Help us, we are being slaughtered!" cried a

man over the mosque's loudspeaker.[42] "Persevere, my brothers—stay in your place, we will be victorious. We do not have weapons, we are peaceful."

And then, addressing the security forces: "You killers, you mercenaries."

Indeed, all the shooting was done by regime forces: not a single bullet was fired from inside the mosque. There were only cries for help and shouts of defiance.

As regime forces closed in on the mosque, they started chanting: "With our soul, with our blood, we sacrifice ourselves for you, O Bashar!"

A doctor and a medic who rushed over to the mosque in an ambulance were both shot dead by regime sharpshooters hunkered down on adjacent roofs. At least six people inside the mosque were also murdered, and many others were wounded.

Bashar's cousin Atef Najib entered the mosque after it was taken over. He wore military fatigues and carried an assault rifle.[43] He stood in the courtyard and began shooting in the air.

"You sons of bitches!" he shouted as he emptied one magazine after another.

He was surrounded by dozens of armed men, mostly in plainclothes. They were laughing, smoking cigarettes, and back-slapping one another. They looked like gangsters. Many spoke with the distinctive accent of Bashar's Alawite sect.

"We killed them," one of them announced before joining the others in a trancelike chant: "God, Syria, and Bashar!"

When the news reached Qaddah, he was stunned. He felt betrayed. He had been used as bait by regime forces. They were preparing the assault even as he was inside the mosque assuring protesters that a deal could be worked out and that their demands regarding detainees could be fulfilled.[44] Qaddah called Maher al-Assad's associate Hamsho from the crisis cell command center to express his anger.

Shortly after, Maher himself called back and asked to speak to Qaddah. He was on speakerphone. All the *mukhabarat* commanders who had overseen the storming of the mosque were sitting around and could hear Maher, too.[45]

"So, Muwafaq, I heard you shit in your pants—ha ha ha!" said Maher as he laughed uncontrollably.

The next day Bashar and Manaf spoke again by telephone.

"How can this carnage happen?" demanded Manaf. "This is unreal. I thought Muwafaq Qaddah was your emissary and was negotiating on your behalf."

Bashar said Qaddah was being played by the protesters who, he claimed, were armed and dangerous and part of a foreign conspiracy. He said he had spoken to his brother, Maher, and cousin Hafez Makhlouf before the order was given to storm the mosque.

"We had no choice but to nip this whole thing in the bud," Bashar said.

After the call this thought occurred to Manaf: "They have wasted no time in taking the Hama manual out of the drawer."

10

The Conspiracy

On March 29, 2011, one week after the bloody storming of Daraa's Omari mosque, Michel Samaha, a Lebanese ex-minister and diehard Bashar loyalist, arrived in Paris.

Bashar trusted the heavyset, bespectacled, and bald Samaha completely. He dispatched him to assure the French that what happened in Daraa was no more than an isolated local incident involving a group of agitators and fanatics who had illegally taken up arms and barricaded themselves inside the mosque, necessitating intervention by authorities. It was the normal procedure followed by any sovereign state, including France.

The truth was that the assault on the mosque was a cold-blooded murder of six unarmed protesters and a doctor and medic who tried to aid the wounded. Then the *mukhabarat* planted assault rifles, grenades, bullets, and bundles of Syrian banknotes inside the mosque, filmed these alleged finds and broadcast the footage on Syrian state television.[1] Protesters were cast as members of an armed gang who had killed the ambulance crew. According to Manaf, a whole story was fabricated about protest organizers being paid agents working for Israel, the West, and hostile regional governments and liaising with old enemies like the Muslim Brotherhood and Islamist extremists. The regime told Syrians it was a conspiracy while asserting to French officials that it was a simple law-and-order issue.

"The president [Bashar] will make a very important speech. He will announce major reforms. He sent me to assure you that everything will be okay," Samaha told Claude Guéant, the French president's point man for dealing with Bashar.[2]

Samaha was part of Bashar's team that was interacting with the French since the onset of the rapprochement in 2007. He accompanied Bashar and Asma on at least three trips to Paris, including the one in December 2010, just before protests began to sweep through the Arab world.

France, the United States, and other Western countries were at first taken by surprise. They had hardly had time to assess the fast-moving events and their policy implications as pro-Western strongmen were pushed aside by the revolting masses in Tunisia and then Egypt. Later, France and its allies raced to intervene in Libya. Armed with a UN Security Council resolution authorizing the use of force, on March 19, 2011, France was the first to bomb Gaddafi's troops as they tried to advance on the rebellious city of Benghazi.[3] Then the United States, Britain, and others followed suit. In justifying the actions of the United States and its allies in Libya, US president Obama said, "We cannot stand idly by when a tyrant tells his people that there will be no mercy."[4]

As Paris, Washington, and other Western capitals grappled with Libya, Syria now seemed like yet another place where they would have to make difficult decisions.

The day after the brazen mosque killings, many angry Daraa residents took to the streets. Women of all ages turned out in droves. Sally and her girlfriends wore jeans and wrapped keffiyehs, traditional male headdresses, around their heads, leaving only their eyes exposed. Security forces were taken aback when women intervened and freed dozens of men who had been rounded up and put on buses.

"Do not touch our boys!" shouted one woman as she boarded a bus and told the detained men to get out.

In Damascus, Manaf sensed that Bashar was lost and uncertain of what to do to bring the situation under control after the mosque assault. He seemed torn between the idea that the Daraa protests were a conspiracy warranting violence to reassert regime authority and the fact that the uprising was a popular one with genuine demands and grievances requiring him, perhaps, to be more conciliatory and accommodating.[5]

His brother, Maher, his cousins the Makhloufs, and *mukhabarat* hard-liners had pushed for maximum force from the start. They believed that shooting and killing some people would make others think twice before taking to the streets to protest; fear of the dreaded regime would be maintained. But there were those around Bashar, like Manaf, who felt that violence would only provoke more bloodshed and would complicate the situation further. Even on the night of the storming of the Daraa mosque, Bashar was wrestling with those two conflicting approaches. Or maybe he thought he could do both—a carrot *and* a stick.[6] Bashar sacked Daraa's governor in an attempt to appease protesters, but when they asked for the release of all detainees and were answered with the storming of the mosque, it only unleashed more anger and violence.

The day after the bloodshed in Daraa, Bashar convened an emergency meeting of the Baath leadership. Bashar now seemed more willing to support those advocating dialogue and concessions as a way to deal with the situation. One of Bashar's advisers, Bouthaina Shaaban, held a press conference afterward to convey the meeting's results. She said that all detainees arrested since the start of protests in Daraa would be released—precisely what protesters inside the mosque had asked for minutes before they were attacked by regime forces.

Shaaban, an Assad family loyalist to the bone, said that a committee would investigate events in Daraa, salaries of government employees would be raised, new job opportunities for the youth would be created, and the performance of the central and local governments would be reassessed. Other measures to be studied: new anticorruption mechanisms, lifting the state of emergency, a draft law authorizing political parties, a new media law, amendments to the law governing land use in border provinces like Daraa, and ending the practice of arbitrary arrests.[7]

At the same time, Shaaban denied that Bashar had given shoot-to-kill orders but, without being specific, conceded that there might have been "misconduct" by some security personnel. She echoed the position of the hard-liners: what happened in Daraa was a conspiracy against Syria because of its support for resistance movements like Hezbollah, and Daraa had been chosen due to the ease of smuggling weapons and money from neighboring Jordan.

She described what was going on as a standoff between the Syrian state and people and their "enemies" who wished to undermine the country's "unity, stability, and peace." While offering what at first seemed to be major concessions, Shaaban arrogantly added insult to injury, as far as Daraa's people were concerned. Instead of calming down, the situation was inflamed.

The next day, March 25, people from all over Daraa and surrounding towns and villages converged on the city's Serail Square. Sally was among those at the protest, the largest so far. She and many others held up olive branches and banners. Protesters seemed more organized than before. It wasn't long before snipers posted on rooftops of surrounding government buildings began shooting at them.[8] Several people were killed. Sally and her friends hid in a shop for hours. Regime forces also opened fire and killed people who had taken to the streets in a town north of Daraa. In response, enraged youth knocked down a statue of Hafez in the middle of Serail Square and tore down a large billboard showing a smiling, waving Bashar. Protests in solidarity with Daraa erupted across Syria that day.

In Damascus, thousands marched through the old quarter, but they were quickly infiltrated and surrounded by security forces.[9] Some protesters managed to reach Marjeh Square. They chanted for freedom and dignity and climbed over the base of the steel column in the middle of the square, where Mazen Darwish and others had been violently attacked by regime thugs ten days earlier for demanding prisoner releases.[10]

Protests also sprang up in several large towns around Damascus. Thousands took to the streets after Friday prayers. In Douma, home to about half a million people, protesters were led by Adnan Wehbeh, a well-respected physician, longtime regime opponent, and secular figure. They occupied the town's municipal square for several hours.[11]

In the central city of Homs, protesters came out in large numbers to support Daraa and to demand the ouster of the local governor, whom they accused of corruption. Later, an angry mob broke off from the main protest and attacked the city's officers club. A guard was killed. The incident immediately brought sectarian animosities to the surface, since the guard was a member of Bashar's Alawite community and most of the protesters were Sunni. One of the largest protests was in the coastal city of Latakia, where thousands, including women and children, marched through the streets. They briefly occupied one of the main squares to hold a peaceful sit-in. But the following day—Saturday, March 26—clashes underpinned by long-simmering sectarian tensions erupted between loyalists backed by security forces and some on the protesters' side. At least a dozen people were killed in Latakia.[12]

That day Manaf spoke with Bashar by telephone.

"We give them a meter and they want two meters. We cannot just keep making concessions," griped Bashar when Manaf argued for a bold conciliatory move toward the people of Daraa, like punishing his cousin Atef Najib.[13] By then there had been about sixty deaths in Daraa alone.[14]

"So what do you propose we do right now?" said Bashar.

"Someone from Daraa came to see me and told me that as a first step we should consider all the dead martyrs and give their families money," Manaf told Bashar.

"Okay, fine, let's give them a million pounds each," said Bashar. That amount in Syrian pounds was at the time equivalent to about 20,000 US dollars. Blood money was commonly used for conflict resolution in rural and tribal parts of Syria. Bashar's office sent Manaf 57 million pounds in cash. They had counted fifty-seven "martyrs." Manaf immediately sent the money to Daraa for distribution. Many families refused to take it.

Bashar hoped that the money and a few gestures he could unveil in his upcoming parliamentary speech on March 30 would be enough to appease Daraa.

But even his supporters were expecting him to do more.

"What dragged the whole country [into this situation] were the security branches in Daraa that mercilessly killed left and right," said Yusif Abu-Roumieh, a lawmaker and Daraa tribal leader, during a parliament session ahead of Bashar's speech. "The people of Houran were waiting for his excellency the president to come down and apologize and offer his condolences." In a daring act, the tribal sheik publicly negated the official story about the protesters being part of a conspiracy.[15]

Ahead of his speech, Bashar tasked Manaf and others around him to meet with young activists as well as more traditional opposition figures like those thrown in jail around the time of the short-lived Damascus Spring a decade before. Ostensibly the purpose was to drum up ideas and solutions that could be incorporated in the speech. But it was also a useful way to identify the main protest instigators and organizers and figure out who had the most sway. Perhaps some could be convinced to cooperate with the regime to implement some of the changes Bashar was promising.

Manaf liaised with Shaaban, Bashar's political and media adviser. "When you speak about solutions, it's as if I am hearing our eternal leader [Hafez], rest his soul," Shaaban gushed when she met with Manaf at the palace.[16]

Mohammad Nasif, the longtime *mukhabarat* chief and Bashar mentor who had been recalled from retirement in 2005 and appointed presidential adviser, reached out to activists like Mazen Darwish, who were believed to have more influence on the street than the better-known political opponents.

Mazen was in solitary confinement at Branch 215 of Military Intelligence, one of the four main *mukhabarat* agencies.[17] Each agency had several branches in Damascus and across the country. Each branch was usually responsible for a geographic area down to a neighborhood or street, or had certain functions like wiretapping phone conversations, or was tasked with dealing with a specific segment of the population like doctors or known political opponents. It was common for someone to be detained, interrogated, and tortured by multiple agencies and branches. Getting cleared by one did not mean that a person was not wanted by another agency or branch.

Mazen had been arrested twice since March 16, once for organizing the protest outside the Interior Ministry and the second time for speaking out on Arab news channels about the Daraa killings, or, as the *mukhabarat* put it, spreading "fake news" in the service of "the nation's enemies."

On the evening of March 24, the door to Mazen's cell suddenly opened.[18]

"You're getting out," said the guard.

Freedom from these *mukhabarat* dungeons was like being born again. As he was about to step outside, another guard said this: "There are orders this time to release you. You may have gotten away, but we're not done with you yet. We shall meet again."

Mazen called his wife, Yara.

"Yes, darling, we know, we are at the office waiting for you," she said.

The office was filled with fellow activists. They cheered and clapped when Mazen arrived and then took turns to hug him. Less than thirty minutes later the doorbell rang. A man speaking with an Iraqi accent and dressed in an expensive suit stepped inside and asked to see Mazen.

"I am Hassan Jamaleddin. General Mohammad Nasif sends you his greetings, and he has asked to see you," said the Iraqi man as Mazen took him aside.

"Now?" said a puzzled Mazen.

"Yes, now," answered the man.

"I just came out of prison and I need to shower," protested Mazen.

"I think your shower can wait for the sake of the country," responded the man.

Mazen asked the man to give him a few minutes. He went inside and told his colleagues. Everyone thought he was being rearrested by another *mukhabarat* branch. It was decided that he should go with the man but someone would trail them to find out where he was being taken.

After a short drive Mazen found himself on the outskirts of Damascus in an area called the Assad Villages. It was past 10:00 p.m. He was outside an imposing mansion. The gate opened. Dozens of guards milled about. He was led into the house. He walked through the marble floor entryway. Crystal chandeliers hung from the ceiling. Mazen was taken to a lounge area with plush sofas. Shortly after, an imposing figure came down the stairs. He was an elderly man wearing a white traditional garment with a woolen cloak draped around his shoulders. This was Mohammad Nasif, one of the most powerful *mukhabarat* chiefs, who had served the Assad family for decades. Regime opponents imprisoned in the 1980s remembered him as a fearsome but articulate figure.

"You fools, you think there's heaven and hell. Heaven is where I am living and hell is what you're living through," he often told those he interrogated and tortured.[19]

Nasif, also known as Abu Wael, was practically part of the Assad family and a father figure to Bashar. He had mentored him when Bashar was being groomed to inherit power from Hafez. Now, at the age of seventy-five, he was still by Bashar's side as a trusted aide.

For almost fifteen minutes, Nasif lectured Mazen about how what was happening was a conspiracy by Syria's enemies in the region and by the West.[20]

"General, with all due respect," said Mazen, "this is the talk we hear on state television day and night. I do not think you summoned me here to discuss that."

Mazen and his fellow activists had already started creating a body that would attempt to unify all the protest movements that were emerging across Syria and to foster greater coordination in methods and goals. But to Nasif, he presented himself as someone who was simply in touch with some protest organizers. Mazen thought that the regime probably knew everything, but he was not going to volunteer the information.

"Please call me Uncle Abu Wael," said Nasif.

"I'll call you Uncle when I am here on a social visit," replied Mazen politely.

What followed was a lengthy discussion lasting for hours. Nasif was preoccupied with swaying Mazen and getting him to embrace Bashar's latest reform promises, while Mazen spoke about all the missed opportunities for reform, starting with the short-lived Damascus Spring between 2000 and 2001 and ending with the period between 2007 and 2010, when the regime was engaging with the West.

"But all you cared about was how to prolong and protect the regime," said Mazen. "You left people no choice but to take to the streets. They waited too long."

"This young man [Bashar] is kind, polite, open-minded, and eager to reform," said Nasif, sounding parental. "In fact, he's closer to you guys than us old-timers. We must not ignore Syria's delicate regional situation, the conspiracy, and Israel, which wants to destroy Syria."

At some point, after several cups of strong Turkish coffee, Mazen proposed a solution. The regime could give people the chance to express themselves in a public space, a square perhaps. It could be protected by the security forces so that "infiltrators and agents of foreign powers" do not shoot at people, as the regime claimed had happened in Daraa.

"'Square' equals bringing down the regime! You must completely forget this idea!" Nasif shot back, beginning to lose his poise and calm, and becoming visibly agitated and angry.[21]

It was already 4:00 a.m. Mazen had spent almost five hours with Nasif. They agreed that Mazen would come to his office in the city later that day and hand over a list of demands, but not the idea of using a public square as a forum.

The list Mazen gave him, some hours later, included about a dozen points, such as: releasing detainees, restructuring the *mukhabarat* and ending its blanket immunity, and drafting a new constitution to create an independent legislature and judiciary.

"The decision is not up to me," said Nasif. "I am simply the president's security adviser. I will take these papers tonight to the president. Expect a call from me tomorrow."

They met again the day after.

Nasif told Mazen that Bashar had agreed to repeal the emergency law, which he had already raised as a possibility in the press conference given by his adviser Shaaban. Mazen said that this step would be meaningless without also curbing the *mukhabarat*'s powers and making necessary constitutional changes.

"These things will take time but we are open to discussing them all," said Nasif as he held up the papers which had illegible scribbles in blue in the margins. "Look, here are two sentences handwritten by the president himself. He will use them in his upcoming speech." Certain words were circled and there were check marks next to some points.[22]

In the lead-up to Bashar's speech, the signals coming from the regime were hardly conciliatory.

The regime mobilized pro-Bashar rallies across the country, ramped up its campaign of lies and disinformation, and took steps to deepen polarization among Syrians.[23] Regime authorities deported a Reuters correspondent who had been reporting from Syria since 2006, alleging he was filing "fake news"; two of his colleagues were also briefly detained.[24]

From the start, the regime wanted to deny independent media access and freedom to report on events in Syria, leaving Syrian citizens with no choice but to rely on social media and YouTube videos.

On March 30, 2011, a few hundred people gathered in central Damascus outside parliament. Security force personnel, many in plainclothes, formed a ring around the crowd. Uniformed policemen were present, too. But this would not be a demonstration like those over the past twelve days. Almost everyone in the crowd held up a poster with Bashar's face. Most of the men and the few women were in their late teens and twenties. They could have been from the Baath Party's Revolutionary Youth Union, the crowds usually brought out on special occasions to show love and adoration for the president. They could also have been government employees and university students who had been told that there was a rally they must attend. There were dire consequences for disobeying such directives.[25] All that mattered, though, was how this looked on camera, given that the spectacle was being broadcast live. This was the regime of make-believe.

The moment Bashar stepped out of his black Audi in front of parliament, they went crazy.[26]

"Allah, Souriya, Bashar wa Bas!" ("God, Syria, and Bashar only!"), they shouted.

A red carpet was rolled out on the steps leading up to the entrance.

Surrounded by his security detail in black suits, Bashar stopped as he reached the top of the stairs. He looked back at the crowd and waved and smiled broadly.

A triumphant Bashar strode into the domed chamber after the speaker of parliament introduced him as "leader of the Arab world" and guardian of the "Arabs' last citadels." Every single one of the deputies jumped up from their seats to clap and repeat a deafening mantra-like chant: "With our soul, with our blood, we sacrifice ourselves for you, O Bashar!"[27] This was the same rubber-stamp parliament ordered by Hafez's men a decade earlier to change the constitution so that Bashar could inherit power from his father.

An ecstatic-looking Bashar stood at the podium and joined in the clapping.

"It's hard to say anything to that," said a beaming Bashar in response to those chanting his name.[28] He was eager to prolong the moment, wanting to make sure that those whom he believed were plotting against him saw this outpouring of total devotion and fealty, real or not.

Indeed, the next words out of Bashar's mouth were an assertion that the protests that had started in Daraa and spread elsewhere were part of a foreign conspiracy, a sinister plot against him and against Syria. It was like the conspiracy he had faced in 2005 after Hariri's assassination in Lebanon and the conspiracies confronted by Hafez in the 1970s and early '80s. "We have to admit their intelligence in choosing very advanced methods," said Bashar confidently with an undertone of derision, "but we also admit their stupidity in choosing the wrong country and people, where these types of conspiracies do not work."[29]

He offered what he said was proof of this alleged conspiracy and explained that it involved people inside Syria and in both neighboring and faraway countries. He said it was timed with the uprisings across the Arab world, but that what was happening in Syria was fundamentally different.

He then echoed the same reasoning used by his *mukhabarat* chiefs when they assured him in their reports earlier in the year that Syria was immune from the protests sweeping the region.[30] The protests in other Arab countries, he insisted, were legitimate popular expressions of dissatisfaction with old rulers who had been in place for decades and were propped up by the West. In fact, they were proof of an Arab awakening and the failure of these regimes in "taming" their people, said Bashar. He said that he was going to send "experts" to Tunisia to see what lessons, particularly regarding income inequities, could be applied in Syria.

Syria was different, said Bashar. Internally he was modernizing and opening up the economy, and externally he was challenging the dictates of neo-imperial Western powers and supporting "Arab resistance movements" like Hezbollah in Lebanon. There was no justification for a similar uprising in Syria, as far as he was concerned. The way he and the *mukhabarat* saw it, the conspiracy aimed to weaken and break up Syria in order to "remove the last obstacle in the face of the Israeli project."

Bashar omitted the fact that his family has been ruling Syria and possessing its economy and resources for four decades with the help of one of the world's cruelest police state apparatuses, and that, for the most part, Israel and the West were absolutely fine with the Assads staying in power.

Bashar promised to study all reform proposals, he assured members of his rubber-stamp parliament, but he was not going to be "hasty."

The nearly one-hour discourse was interrupted by rapturous parliamentarians standing up to read poetic verses or to pledge their allegiance and near servitude to the Assad family. One of them told him that Syria was too small for him and that he must become leader of the entire world.

At the end, a defiant Bashar said he would welcome a war to defend his regime and reminded his audience, in his usual cold-blooded demeanor, that he and his allies Iran and Hezbollah had derailed US plans to redraw the region's political map after the invasion of Iraq in 2003. The American idea at the time was that regime change in Iraq would have a "domino effect" on the rest of the Middle East, including Iran and Syria. But instead Syria and its partners went on the offensive in Iraq and Lebanon by unleashing violence, terror, and war.

"What happened was the opposite: the plans themselves turned into dominos and we struck them and they fell one by one, and this [latest] project will fall," vowed Bashar.

11

Make Peace

Manaf watched Bashar's speech in his office at the Republican Guard base high above Damascus. He was stunned as it concluded; right up until the president's appearance, he had expected Bashar to be more conciliatory, to show genuine and heartfelt regret for some 100 civilians shot dead by his forces in Daraa and elsewhere and to offer something concrete and bold to assuage the people.[1]

Before the speech, Bashar gave Manaf the impression that he would announce major concessions, but in the end Bashar went with the advice of his uncompromising brother, cousins, and *mukhabarat* chiefs. What's more, Bashar championed his imperious and bloody kinsmen. It was Bashar's cousin Atef Najib, after all, who had mishandled the situation in Daraa from the start. Another cousin, Hafez Makhlouf, dispatched the strike force that shot and killed protesters on March 18. And his brother, Maher, oversaw the storming of the Daraa mosque.

After the speech, Bashar's longtime mentor, Mohammad Nasif, called Mazen.

"I know you're not happy, but nothing has changed, and when you see the president tomorrow he'll explain everything to you," said Nasif.

"There's no need," replied Mazen, who felt duped and manipulated by the regime. "The president just declared war and war is not my profession and I can't be part of it."

Many Syrians were angered by Bashar's provocative words and what they saw as his disrespectful tone and posture in the face of a grave situation.

He did not even hold a minute of silence to honor all those who had been killed since March 18.

Two days after the speech, protests engulfed many parts of the country. In the town of Douma, near Damascus, the Assad family's response was swift and bloody.

Security officials in Douma had gathered local council members the night before (March 31, 2011), warning them that they intended to be merciless toward any protests. "This Friday is not going to be like the previous Friday, we are warning you," the council members were told.[2] The town is a mere ten miles from Damascus and off the main highway to Aleppo. The *mukhabarat* viewed protests in Douma as a direct threat to Bashar.

On April 1, many people defied the ban and headed to the town's main square, already occupied by security forces. After people were chased away, most went home and only a few protesters remained on the streets. Then green buses started arriving on the edge of the square. Inside was a mix of soldiers, *mukhabarat* agents, and pro-regime thugs. Most were in civilian clothes. Some had guns, while others carried sticks, swords, and chains.[3] Among them were about 300 men belonging to Manaf's Republican Guard unit.[4] The newly arrived forces fanned out into the streets, attacking everyone they encountered, cursing and shouting expletives. People inside their homes heard the insults.[5] This was a conservative and tightly knit community where honor was deeply valued.

"We have come to teach you a lesson," shouted the thugs spitefully unleashed on the city. "Come out and face us if you're men."

Regime forces stormed the city council building and ransacked offices.

"Can I please ask what unit you belong to," a parliament member from Douma asked a young soldier.

"I serve Bashar al-Assad. To hell with you and parliament...Half of you are traitors," sneered the soldier.

Angered by what they saw as an unprovoked attack on their city by the regime, hundreds of Douma youth took to the streets. Clashes escalated and soon the situation was out of control. Some officers in Manaf's unit, particularly Sunnis, were upset over how Douma's residents, Sunnis like them, were taunted and demeaned.

One of them called Manaf and explained to him what had happened. Manaf then called Bashar.[6]

"Let me go to Douma and calm people down," he implored. Manaf knew some influential community leaders there and hoped he could help defuse the situation.

"Okay, give me fifteen minutes and I'll get back to you," said Bashar.

Bashar called back shortly thereafter and told Manaf not to worry; his cousin Hafez was handling the situation.

A bit later Manaf's assistant, Ali Taher, walked into the office. "Sir, the situation in Douma is under control, our guys are coming back," he said.

Manaf's soldiers arrived at the base at about 11:00 p.m. Many were ashen-faced and barely spoke.[7]

Manaf tried to give a pep talk. "You did your best," he said. "It's a tough situation, but we have to differentiate between saboteurs and those with legitimate demands."

The most senior officer in the group stayed on as the others left. "Sir, something very horrible happened today," said the officer. "Colonel Hafez [Makhlouf] and his men pushed everyone aside and began shooting directly at people in Douma, they killed twelve and wounded forty-four."[8]

Manaf was speechless. The family was doubling down on violence.

As in Daraa, their thinking was that Douma's people had to be terrorized so that they and others would think twice about protesting, especially after Bashar had laid out the contours of the alleged conspiracy in his speech and vowed to defeat it.

That night, a television station owned by Maher al-Assad's protégés broadcast lies about what had happened in Douma, saying that people were killed by alleged armed gangs and that cell phone footage of the dead had been fabricated.[9] It claimed that people had faked their wounds with red paint—a variation on the story of the guns and cash in the Daraa mosque.

Just before the killings in Douma, Manaf had been in contact with community leaders in Daraa and there was talk of them coming to Damascus to meet with Bashar. Manaf told them that Bashar might go as far as arresting his cousin Atef Najib and putting him on trial.

Two of Daraa's most influential clerics, Mohammad Abazeid and Ahmad al-Sayasneh, then visited Manaf.

"You're absolutely right, I agree with you on everything," Manaf told them. "But you need to calm people down—please, this is our country and we cannot just let it go up in flames. Draft your specific demands, he [Bashar] understands the situation.[10]

"And by the way, the president is ready to create 50,000 new jobs in Daraa, provided you end the protests," Manaf added.

"We have no power over the people—we cannot stop them. I also think people want freedom more than jobs," said Sayasneh.[11]

"Think about it and get back to me in forty-eight hours," said Manaf.

Now blood had been spilled elsewhere, not just Daraa.

Manaf became convinced that Bashar's brother, cousins, and *mukhabarat* chiefs were intentionally escalating the situation and arousing people's anger in order to justify a total crackdown on protests. Maybe they were not giving Bashar the full picture, maybe they were providing him with misleading information in order to sustain the conspiracy theory.

Bashar was effectively trapped in the palace and relying on their reports. By meeting with community leaders from Daraa and Douma, Manaf hoped that he could relay an accurate, unfiltered picture to his friend. He also thought that Bashar should meet with these leaders himself. Maybe, if he heard strong and frank language from them, he would appreciate the gravity of the situation and realize that using violence was making things worse.

If sincere dialogue and engagement succeeded in calming the situation, then Manaf could emerge as a hero within the regime. The Tlasses had loyally stood with the Assads every step of the way. His father, Mustafa, killed to defend the regime, starting with the crushing of protests in 1963–64 and then the bigger challenges in the 1970s and early '80s.

But those were different circumstances, Manaf thought. The way he saw it, Islamist extremists were a real factor back then, but now these were average Syrians from all backgrounds, with legitimate grievances and demands. Now, unlike then, there were uprisings all over the Arab world and regimes were crumbling. Syria was in the glare of Arab and Western media. And then there was social media—people could get the message out themselves. These times were drastically different. He was a military officer and had thus far been steadfast in his loyalty, but he could not see himself being part of the decision to kill people. This was 2011, and he was not his father. There was still a chance to salvage the situation—still an opportunity to make peace.

After the April 1 killings in Douma, Manaf sensed that Bashar was stepping back a bit, realizing that perhaps it was a mistake to rely too much on people like his cousin Hafez.

More than 150,000 people filled the streets of Douma for the mass funeral of those killed on April 1. They called them martyrs. A massive funeral tent was erected next to the city's grand mosque. People came from all over Damascus and beyond to offer their condolences, among them Syrians of all backgrounds and religious affiliations.[12] There were Sunni clerics, Christians, famous actors, and the daughter of Sultan Pasha al-Atrash, an icon of the Arab struggle for independence from colonial powers after the First World War. The Atrashes were royalty among the Druze minority concentrated in southern Syria next to Daraa and in the Damascus suburbs.

Muntaha al-Atrash spoke at the tent. She wore no veil. Her address to a gathering of men in conservative Douma exposed regime lies about the protesters being Islamist extremists. She and others urged unity, called for restraint, and pleaded with people not to resort to arms and revenge but instead to keep protests peaceful.

Bashar decided to send his chief of protocol at the palace to offer his condolences and apologies for what happened. The official, Moheyldin al-Meselmani, came with a group of prominent Damascene clerics in a convoy of ten presidential sedans.

"Get out!" shouted a man as Meselmani and his delegation stepped into the tent. "Get out! You kill people and then you come to offer your condolences—get out!" Others joined in. Meselmani was forced to leave.[13]

Even Bashar's brother, Maher, who had taken a tough line from the start, might have realized that what happened in Douma was a horrible mistake. He tried to be conciliatory in his own way.

One of Maher's protégés, Ammar Saati, president of the national student union, summoned members of the Douma city council to his office in Damascus. He handed each one of them a gift, a brand new smart phone.

"General Maher personally sends you his regards, and rest assured—those who committed mistakes will be punished," said Saati.[14]

Late on the night of Sunday, April 3, Manaf met with some of Douma's protest leaders. They included the physician Adnan Wehbeh, a calm and articulate man who was among those trying their best from the start to avert friction between protesters and the security forces. Also present was a civil engineer called Nizar al-Smadi, who was more of a hard-liner advocating confrontation.

In the first meeting, which lasted more than six hours, Manaf mostly listened to the Douma delegation. The next day they met again and spoke about a possible solution. It was agreed that Manaf would go to Douma first and do a *sulha*, a peacemaking and reconciliation meeting popular in tribal and rural parts of Syria. It usually involved the party in the wrong admitting guilt and offering an agreed-upon recompense to the aggrieved party. Then everybody would shake hands, hug, and share a meal. After the *sulha*, Manaf said, a meeting would be organized with Bashar so that the people of Douma could officially present him with their demands.

"Fantastic idea, yes—go, but be careful," Bashar told Manaf when he sought to get his consent the following day.[15]

On Wednesday, April 6, Manaf arrived at the farm in Douma where the *sulha* was to be held. Before rapid urbanization and population growth, the countryside around Damascus known as the Ghouta was largely a collection of farms and orchards. In addition to its natural beauty, the area was the main source of meat, milk, and fresh produce for the capital's residents. Despite the growth of towns like Douma and others, the Ghouta retained aspects of its rural past.

The farm belonged to a wealthy local. A villa stood in the middle of the sprawling plot. Several hundred people were seated on plastic lawn chairs arranged in front of the house.[16] All around them were plum, apricot, and other fruit trees.

It was a breezy and sunny day.

Lots of local men with hunting rifles and pistols milled around. As in most rural areas of the Levant, guns were symbols of manhood, honor, and pride, usually brought out for weddings and grand celebrations, funerals, and whenever the community felt threatened or under assault.

Manaf came unarmed. He was the guest of honor. He looked around and saw Mohammad Hamsho, a businessman and member of parliament who was one of Maher al-Assad's cronies. They sent Hamsho to watch him and report back, Manaf thought.

There was a mix of opinions among the gathered Doumanis (Douma natives). There were those suspicious of dialogue, who wanted retribution for the killings by Hafez Makhlouf and his men. They were in the majority.

Others, like Wehbeh and even Smadi, believed Manaf was truthful and sincere, and they spoke favorably of him to others. Some in Douma were loyal to the regime and opposed the protests from the start. They wanted to end the standoff with Bashar's cousin and the powerful *mukhabarat*.

At first Manaf offered his condolences for the dead, or martyrs as Doumanis called them, and then he spoke about the Arab Spring and people's legitimate demands but also said they had to appreciate Syria's special situation as a country technically at war with Israel.

"We are a country with a cause: resistance to Israel," said Manaf.[17]

"Enough! What does Palestine and the resistance have to do with what we have come here to discuss?" demanded an angry voice in the crowd. Many concurred.

"These are martyrs. What happened was absolutely unforgivable. We want to change the whole system," spoke out Khaled Taffour, a young and charismatic mosque imam and cleric, who was among those adopting a combative posture.

Maher's man Hamsho was among those filming the exchange with their cell phones. Everyone was told to put away their phones before going any further.

"I have come to tell you in the name of the president that your dead are martyrs and we are sorry," Manaf said.[18]

There was silence then many people nodded in agreement. One of the protest leaders gave a thumbs-up.

Manaf then said something that would put him on a dangerous collision course with Bashar's family and the *mukhabarat*.

"And yes, one of my guys told me that he saw Hafez Makhlouf himself shooting at the protesters," said Manaf.[19]

"Then now we know with whom to settle our score," shouted an angry man.

"I promise you that you will have justice, but you must be patient," said Manaf.

A discussion followed about compensation to the families of the dead and a possible meeting with Bashar during which they could speak their mind.

"The president is ready to implement all reforms," Manaf told them.

Manaf proposed that as a show of goodwill ahead of the meeting with Bashar it would be helpful if there were no more protests in Douma, but if these protests were inevitable then they should be very organized and controlled. No chanting for the downfall of the regime and slogans like *"He who kills his people is a traitor,"* Manaf told them.[20]

A tough-looking man with a handlebar mustache just like the characters of *Bab al-Hara*, a popular Syrian television period drama, stared angrily at Manaf.

"But we want freedom!" growled the man, who was a well-liked protest organizer called Abu al-Fawz.

"Yes, boss, you'll have freedom," said Manaf, trying to lighten up the mood.

Others, like Smadi and Wehbeh, spoke about the lack of trust. They said nobody believed that Bashar and his regime were prepared to make real changes and concessions, given the bloody response from day one.

"Let's give him [Bashar] a chance—he's a human being like you," argued Manaf.

To overcome the impasse over Manf's proposal that protests cease or scale back, it was agreed that Manaf would discuss it further with the Douma delegation he had been meeting with.

There were no hugs or handshakes, but everyone was treated to lunch paid for by Bashar's office. Trays of roasted lamb on heaps of rice were brought out from the house.

A few people, including Abu al-Fawz, refused to eat. "We do not need you or your food," he grumbled as he walked away.

Manaf returned to Damascus and called Bashar.

"Things went very well. Douma does not want to rebel or protest, but we promised to implement their demands," an overoptimistic Manaf reported.[21]

"Bravo!" replied Bashar. "You're working harder than the entire leadership combined."

"You probably received Hamsho's report and video," said Manaf at the end.

"Don't worry about Hamsho—he's a nobody," said Bashar dismissively.

They agreed that the next step would be for Bashar to meet the Douma delegation after assessing their ability to control protesters on April 8, which was the following Friday.

By then all the big protests were happening on the first day of the weekend in Syria, Friday. All across Syria, activists who were starting to coordinate more closely among themselves came up with names for each of the Fridays. They wanted to have a unified message. That Friday was going to be "Friday of Perseverance."

Protests erupted across Syria, from Deir Ezzour in the east to Latakia in the west, and from Daraa in the south to predominantly Kurdish areas in the northeast.[22] Even in Douma, people came out despite Manaf's peacemaking mission, albeit in smaller numbers than the previous week. This underscored the difficulty of controlling a popular uprising that, so far, lacked clear leadership and was still trying to coalesce in the face of the regime's deadly crackdown. It was hard to hold back the enraged youth who wanted to confront the security forces. It was also hard to reconcile the different agendas and motivations. There were those willing to engage the regime and those who were completely against it.

The leader of the Muslim Brotherhood, a group with a long-running and bloody vendetta with a regime that considered it a terrorist organization, had weighed in from Istanbul the week before to announce that Bashar lacked "the will and ability to reform."[23] Activists like Mazen Darwish and others were for increasing the momentum of street protests following their bitter letdown after Bashar's speech.

More people were shot dead that Friday, especially in Daraa, as security forces used lethal force to break up the protests. In Douma, telephone and Internet connections were cut and one person was killed by security forces. Manaf deemed the fewer number of protesters and the single casualty in Douma a relative success compared to the previous week, when twelve people were killed.

He met with the Douma delegation the next day to discuss their upcoming audience with Bashar. As they arrived, Manaf was wrapping up a meeting with Khaled Meshaal, the leader of the Palestinian militant group Hamas, who was based in Damascus at the time. Meshaal was worried about the situation, especially regime reports about the involvement of Palestinian refugees residing in Syria in some of the violent confrontations with security forces in the western city of Latakia. To Israel, Meshaal was a "terrorist," but at the time he was admired by many Arabs as a charismatic "resistance leader." It would later become hard for him to reconcile his association with the Assad regime and his image as a freedom fighter.

Manaf urged Meshaal to say a word to the Douma delegation and encourage them to give dialogue with the regime a chance. Meshaal said he did not want to interfere in Syria's internal affairs.

"You are in my office. Nobody will know," said Manaf.

Meshaal agreed.[24]

At that very moment, Manaf received a call on his cell phone from a number that he did not recognize.

"Hello, who's this?" asked Manaf.

"I am Mohammad Hamsho," said the caller.

"Who is Mohammad Hamsho?" said Manaf playfully at first.

"Come on, Manaf. I am Mohammad Hamsho. I was with you in Douma three days ago," said Hamsho. "You must immediately kick out the Douma delegation that's in your office now."

"Who do you think you're calling?" asked Manaf in a harsher tone.

"General Manaf, is not that you?" said a flummoxed Hamsho.

"That's worse — you know who I am and you're giving me orders," said Manaf.

"Well, I meant to say that General Maher [al-Assad] sends you his regards and tells you to kick them out," said Hamsho.

"Listen, Mohammad, Maher is your general not mine — let him speak with Bashar al-Assad and have Bashar al-Assad call me. That's my chain of command," said Manaf.

"Well, well, you're a big shot now," said Hamsho.

"Bigger than you think," said Manaf.

Hamsho passed the phone to Khaled Qaddour, another one of Maher's acolytes.[25]

"The general [Maher] sends you his best regards. We are just worried that you have set the bar too high and the delegation you're meeting with will ask the president for things he won't be able to deliver," said Qaddour in a polite and conciliatory tone.

"Listen, I have my way and you have your way and we will see which is the right way," said Manaf at the end of the conversation.

Manaf then had to contend with the Douma delegation in his office. They were upset about the continued use of deadly force by the security forces.

"How can you ask me to tell people not to protest?" the opposition leader Wehbeh challenged Manaf.

Manaf assured him things would change after their meeting with Bashar, which was set for the following day, April 10.

After they left, Manaf called Bashar's chief of protocol Meselmani to prepare for the meeting. Meselmani informed him that the *mukhabarat* had already given him the list of Douma representatives who were supposed to meet with the president. All were regime loyalists.

"This is useless. These people will just clap for him," said Manaf.[26]

Meselmani concurred.

They agreed to keep the influential opposition figures and activists that Manaf was meeting with and just add a few names from the *mukhabarat* list.

On April 10, Bashar met with the Douma delegation. He offered his condolences and told them that all those killed in Douma were martyrs and their families would be compensated. He promised to investigate the killings and punish the perpetrators. He would release all Douma residents detained since the start of the protests (about 200), and the wounded would be treated at the government's expense. He spoke about political reforms that he planned to undertake. All sounded good. He was gentle, attentive, and conciliatory. He said he would meet with them again in one week.[27]

That week Bashar also met with a delegation from Daraa for the first time. Again, the *mukhabarat* wanted to exclude those connected with the protests and have Bashar meet only loyalists and regime supporters. In the end, it was fifteen from the side of the protesters and forty-five from the regime side.[28] The most vocal figure on the protesters' side was the cleric Sayasneh, who spoke about the slaughter of dozens of unarmed protesters, the storming of the mosque, the arrest of hundreds, and the heavy security presence on Daraa streets. The meeting lasted several hours. Bashar listened attentively but gave the impression that he was learning about all these things for the first time.[29]

"Really?" Bashar exclaimed several times. "Unbelievable!"

Someone in the delegation told him about the regime's fake news broadcast on state television and the fabrications about weapons seized in Daraa.

"They're still broadcasting that stuff?" said Bashar. "I do not watch TV."[30]

Sayasneh told him that many in Daraa were upset that he did not console them in his speech to parliament and instead spoke about the conspiracy.

"My speech was intended for the outside world," Bashar replied.[31]

He assured them he would address all their grievances, including dismantling security and army checkpoints inside Daraa. As for his offending cousin Atef Najib, Bashar told them that he was removing him from his post but that he could not put him on trial because nobody had pressed formal charges against him.[32] What the delegation did not know was that he had briefly detained Najib.[33]

After the meeting, Syrian state television spoke to Sayasneh, who expressed his gratitude to the president and praised his "open heart" — precisely the kind of public relations boost the regime had hoped for.[34]

Shortly after Sayasneh had returned to Daraa, Najib called him.

"When will Daraa's youth stop their childishness?" demanded Najib in a mocking tone.[35]

"What childishness? The situation is calming down," said Saysneh.

"Do not worry, they'll be taught a lesson soon," said Najib menacingly.

As for Douma's activists and opposition figures, Bashar's other cousin, Hafez, ordered their arrest one day before their second meeting.[36]

They were severely tortured.

"How could this happen?" an enraged Manaf asked Bashar.

"There was a misunderstanding," Bashar replied calmly.

"Okay, free them from prison and meet with them," insisted Manaf.

"The problem," said Bashar, "is that they were beaten very badly. They are in no shape to see me. But we have freed them now."

12

You're Too Soft

It was mid-spring 2011. The death toll was mounting as Bashar sent his soldiers and tanks to quash rebellious communities, but protesters were not giving up. Bashar's wife, Asma, was in her office in Damascus, in the foothills of Mount Qasioun, within walking distance from the private residence in the Malki neighborhood where she and Bashar and their three children lived.

The office was in an area where relatively modern and upscale Malki met Muhajreen, a more traditional district with remnants of late-Ottoman-era architecture. An old, disused tramway line cut through the main cobblestone avenue. In the narrow alleyways, potted plants dangled from balconies of homes sandwiched next to one another. A series of old and new steps connected the parallel streets built into Qasioun's flank.

Asma was meeting with the chief executive officer of her NGO umbrella group, the Syria Trust for Development.[1] She urged Omar Abdelaziz Hallaj to press ahead with the Trust's projects despite the protests and deadly violence spreading across many parts of Syria. Damascus and its suburbs were boiling, too. In Muhajreen, where Asma sat, young Damascenes fired up by revolution plotted weekly protests and came up with catchy slogans against Bashar, whom they called their "undesirable neighbor,"[2] something Asma may or may not have known.

Regardless, Asma was determined to go about her business as if everything was normal. She had often boasted privately about the stoicism, fortitude, and work ethic instilled in her while growing up in Britain. She expected others to emulate her.

Asma told Hallaj that this was the perfect time to push the organization's agendas, given the president's reform plans. And reform was all that everyone was talking about day and night—so what better moment could there be, she explained to Hallaj.[3] She told him that the president was personally interested in input from the Trust on how laws could be changed to restructure provincial and local administrations to give them more power, especially when it came to development and spending while also fostering accountability and transparency. Asma told Hallaj that he'd have a chance to lay out these proposals in a one-on-one with Bashar. Hallaj, a graduate of the University of Texas who previously worked on urban development and heritage conservation in other parts of the Middle East, was typical of the talent Asma surrounded herself with.

"I totally agree with you the time is right," he told Asma, "but if I push my guys to work on reform, they need to know they're protected."[4]

"What do you mean?" replied Asma, sounding a bit puzzled. "If your team is working on reform, nobody is going to harm them."

"But that's not what's happening on the streets. People who are asking for reform are being arrested," said Hallaj.

"Well," said Asma, "the street is one thing and working on reform is another."

What Hallaj did not tell Asma was that among the Trust's nearly 250 staffers were people who secretly took part in anti-regime demonstrations. Most employees, of course, attended the pro-Bashar rallies mobilized by the regime and, as was the case with many government workers, those contracted by the Trust to provide security, construction, and engineering services were also deployed to violently subdue protests. The regime called it "crowd control."

As far as Asma and Bashar were concerned, all Syrians should embrace reform—provided it was within the parameters and at the pace proposed by Bashar. They believed that protesting against the regime on the streets was not an expression of a desire for reform and change but, rather, was knowingly or unknowingly participating in a conspiracy against Syria, as outlined by Bashar in his speech at the end of March 2011.

From Asma's point of view, fantastic things had already started happening before protests began. There was great buzz from the December

2010 Paris trip. The Trust was taking on bigger and more ambitious projects. The partnership with France's Louvre to renovate Syria's museums was going to be launched later in 2011. Construction was underway on a futuristic-looking and energy-efficient building in the heart of Damascus for Massar, her children's learning and discovery center. The space, inspired by the damask rose, was designed by the international Danish architectural firm Henning Larsen and located on one of the capital's most prized pieces of real estate—the old fairgrounds across from the Four Seasons Hotel.[5]

"A shell structure allowing a playful and dazzling scenography of light into the interior spaces—like light filtering between rose petals...The center of the rose forms a large communal orientation space. This is where people meet, share knowledge, and develop new ideas together—a cross pollination of knowledge." This was how Henning Larsen described the project, due to be completed in 2013.[6]

There might be delays, but the project was going to be finished as the situation calmed down, Asma told Hallaj. The construction site was already being used on the weekends by the *mukhabarat* as an assembly point for forces bused out to protesting areas for "crowd control."

Asma had as much of a stake in the regime as Bashar and his clan. She saw herself as a warrior and survivor. Her enemies better not be fooled by her silk dresses and radiant smile.

By then, Asma's touch was everywhere, both at home and in shaping Syria's image abroad.

She completely remodeled the Assad family residence in Malki where Bashar and his siblings grew up, did the same for an old presidential mansion, and fixed up the Assads' summer home in Latakia with the help of a famous British landscape architect.[7] She spent a few million US dollars on abstract sculptures.[8] In March 2011, as protests were kicking off and turning violent, *Vogue* magazine had a whole spread on her titled "Asma al-Assad: A Rose in the Desert."[9] The main photo was of her wrapped in a red-wine-colored pashmina and standing on top of Mount Qasioun at twilight, with Damascus visible below. Joan Juliet Buck, the writer who flew in for the piece right after Asma's return from Paris, spent time with her and Bashar and the children at home playing and eating fondue and later singing carols at the annual Christmas concert of the children's choir they supported.

"This is how you fight extremism—through art," Bashar told Buck during the concert. "This is the diversity you want to see in the Middle East."[10]

The article depicted them as the modern and tolerant Middle East power couple who nurtured and protected minorities like Christians. Bashar also made sure that he repeated to Buck what he often told foreigners: he had studied eye surgery because "it's very precise...and there is very little blood."

The article was the idea of one of Asma's aides at the Trust, a friend from her London days.[11] He approached the New York public relations firm Brown Lloyd James, which already represented several high-profile clients in the Middle East. The firm's principal, Peter Brown, was friends with *Vogue* editor-in-chief Anna Wintour.

Two months after the article came out and as the regime's crackdown became bloodier, Brown's firm sent another Asma aide a memorandum with advice on "crisis communications."[12]

The firm claimed that the US government "wants the leadership in Syria to survive," despite the strongly worded condemnation of the violence by President Obama in April and the executive order he signed at the end of that month imposing sanctions on Bashar's brother, Maher, his cousin Atef Najib, and *mukhabarat* chief Ali Mamlouk. It said that these were warning shots to prod Bashar to stop killing protesters and implement credible reforms. But the firm said the window was closing fast, as US media coverage was intensifying and officials like Senator John Kerry were beginning to reassess their positions.

Brown Lloyd James recommended drastic changes in the way the regime was articulating its reform agenda. The reform program needed "a face or brand," Bashar must communicate more often with more "finely tuned messaging," Asma must "get in the game" and do "listening tours," and a reform "echo chamber" must be developed, especially in foreign media, focusing on Bashar's desire to conduct reform in "a non-chaotic and rational way."

"Refocusing the perception of outsiders and Syrians on reform will provide political cover to the generally sympathetic US government, and will delegitimize critics at home and abroad," concluded the firm.[13]

The PR firm was very close to the mark in its portrayal of the prevailing thinking and mood among officials in Western capitals, at least in the first few weeks of protests in Syria.

France's ambassador to Syria, Éric Chevallier, was one of these officials. Syria was Chevallier's first posting, in 2009; he was a medical doctor by training and had until then worked mostly in international humanitarian assistance with the French government, as well as various NGOs and UN agencies. He accepted the Syria mission at the urging of his longtime mentor and current boss, foreign minister Bernard Kouchner, also a physician turned politician.[14] The forty-nine-year-old Chevallier combined French charm and boyish good looks with a businesslike, practical approach to diplomacy.

To veteran French diplomats with long experience in the Middle East, Chevallier was the new kid on the block. From their perspective, he was impressionable and too eager to cozy up to Bashar and members of his inner circle, including the Tlasses.

Chevallier was interviewed for *Vogue*'s March 2011 piece on Asma. "I hope they'll make the right choices for the country and the region," he told the writer about Bashar and Asma in December 2010.[15]

While Chevallier appeared to his detractors like an enthusiastic promoter of the Assad couple, he believed he was simply advancing his country's policies in Syria. France was among the first in the West to bet on rehabilitating the Syrian regime and Bashar, with strong encouragement from Qatar's superrich ruling family. The Americans, the British, and others started to reengage with Bashar after France had already made overtures, sending Sarkozy to visit Damascus in 2008 and frequently hosting Bashar and Asma in Paris. Some thought that the French had moved too fast, but France believed it had a national-interest stake in trying to steer Bashar in the right direction.

"There were two ways for them to lead the country: stick to his father's regional alliances and family policies, or try to move forward toward a more open society, stable foreign policy, and being part of the solution in the region instead of being the problem," argued Chevallier.[16]

The day after the fall of French ally Zine al-Abidine Ben Ali in Tunisia, Chevallier sent a cable to Paris from Damascus. "Could we have a rose revolution in Damascus?" he wrote in the subject line, alluding to the damask rose. Chevallier reported that many Syrians were transfixed by what was happening in Tunisia, but it was too early to predict whether the country was going down a similar path.

He saw many similarities between the two countries: a youthful population hungry for freedom, sick of corruption, and eager for a share in the economic gains monopolized by regime cronies.[17] But there was also a major difference: Syria had a much more formidable and deep-rooted police state. In Tunisia, significant elements of the military and police abandoned Ben Ali, precipitating his departure. Furthermore, Syria, unlike Tunisia, had a more complex social fabric and a deep alliance with Iran and its Hezbollah militia.

"It's important to watch what happens" in Syria, Chevallier concluded his dispatch.

Later, when protests started in Syria, Chevallier reported to Paris that "people were indeed demonstrating for dignity and freedom."[18]

Chevallier and other Western diplomats in Damascus believed that this was the perfect opportunity for Bashar to make the right choices and implement real and bold reform. He did not have to go like Ben Ali, Gaddafi, and Mubarak; he could be the one to buck the trend and emerge as the people's champion, the French thought at first.

Even after the regime's deadly response to demonstrators in Daraa, Chevallier and other diplomats held out such a possibility. Chevallier lobbied several regime figures to convince Bashar to punish his cousin Atef Najib for the actions taken in Daraa.

"Tell the Syrian people you have arrested Atef Najib," Chevallier told one regime official. "Put this guy on Syrian state TV with a clear message: This is not the way we want to treat our people, it was a mistake. This will totally be the turning point if you do that. You will be supported by everybody."[19]

Indeed, Najib was detained for a few days but then let go after his mother called her sister, Bashar's mother, to plead for her son's immediate release.[20]

The tone of Chevallier's cables began to change in late April 2011, as the killing of protesters persisted and spread beyond Daraa.

"This will be very tough, bloody, and long," he warned Paris.[21]

Chevallier believed that the clock was ticking for Bashar, and all the steps the Syrian president had taken so far were in the wrong direction.

The clock was ticking back in Paris, too. In exactly one year, April 2012, there would be a presidential election, and Sarkozy was running for a second term. The campaign had started and his socialist opponents were already hounding him about what they saw as his inconsistent approach toward the Arab Spring uprisings: he was rushing to bomb Gaddafi in Libya but hardly saying anything about Bashar, whom he had feted at the Élysée Palace four months before. Sarkozy finally spoke out at the end of April 2011, calling the situation "unacceptable."[22]

In the interim, the Americans and Europeans were hoping that their allies in the region, Qatar and Turkey, could convince Bashar to stop the violence and take dramatic steps toward reform. At first, the coverage of the uprising in Syria by the Qatari-owned Al Jazeera—the Arab world's most popular news channel—was not as intense as it was for other countries. The channel also went out of its way to air the regime's point of view and perspective. The Qataris and Turks sent several senior emissaries to Bashar. One proposal was to rein in the *mukhabarat* and security forces and at the same time prepare to hold the first multiparty elections in Syria. They promised to back him as the lead candidate because they believed that he was still popular among many Syrians. Bashar listened attentively and seemed willing to follow the advice, but his actions were ultimately anything but conciliatory.[23]

A month into the uprising, it was clear that any overtures of reform were going to be on Bashar's terms while hard-liners in his family and *mukhabarat* ratcheted up the violence against protesting areas.

"Look, we do not want to meet with people who have high expectations and unreasonable demands. We do not want to embarrass ourselves by making promises we won't be able to deliver," Bashar told Manaf after members of the Douma delegation were arrested and tortured for several days.[24]

Adnan Wehbeh, the respected doctor and protest organizer, returned to Douma bandaged and with bruises on his face and body.

"Serves you right to believe the Tlasses, they are part of the regime. How can you trust them?" many in Douma admonished Wehbeh.[25]

Still, Bashar met with delegation after delegation from most rebellious towns and cities to hear their grievances. The majority were vetted by the *mukhabarat* before they saw him and were usually dominated by regime loyalists. Manaf kept passing on to Bashar's office names of more-credible figures with sway over protesters and urged that they be included in these delegations. Manaf found out that many of the people he recommended were instead arrested by the *mukhabarat*. Community leaders from the towns of Kisweh and Moadhamiya near Damascus and the town of Talbiseh near Homs were later tortured to death in detention.[26]

In mid-April, as protests were being met with increasing violence, Bashar named a new prime minister and government and issued several decrees, including one ending the state of emergency and another outlining the conditions and rules for protesting.

Bashar and Manaf met at the palace shortly thereafter. Bashar looked stressed but a bit more upbeat than before.[27]

"We made incredible concessions, but they [the protesters] are not stopping," Bashar told Manaf with some exasperation.

Manaf argued that Bashar should have nominated a more independent figure for prime minister in order to show people that things were indeed changing, rather than selecting the classic Baath Party functionary as he had done.

"The [party's] regional command selected him," Bashar said.

"Come on," Manaf pushed back, "the country is entering a dark tunnel and you tell me the regional command chose him." Manaf was a leader in this same party and knew that its structures were simply fronts for the real power—Bashar, the family, and *mukhabarat*. "I thought the whole point here was to make real reforms," continued Manaf. "People are expecting more."

"No, the party will decide these things," insisted Bashar.

Manaf detected duplicity when Bashar began to talk about all the delegations he was meeting with.

"We have to hear people's demands. They have to feel that I am close to them," said Bashar.

"But at the end people have big expectations," said Manaf.

"I am telling everyone there is a state and institutions and that everything has to be done in accordance with the law and what's permissible under the law," retorted Bashar.

The family-based regime that had ruled Syria for more than forty years with fear and terror, spurned every opportunity for genuine reform over the years, and killed protesters the moment they took to the streets, was now seeking to refashion itself on its own terms and wanted Syrians and the world to buy into it. Ultimately, though, this was a family and regime interested in one thing only: survival at any cost.

Mazen Darwish, the lawyer and activist, felt it was a mistake to have engaged with Mohammad Nasif.[28] It exposed him and his colleagues. But what choice did he have? They released him from prison and then dragged him to meet Nasif. The regime wanted to manipulate and co-opt him and his fellow activists—use them to lend credibility to its reform promises. And now when they refused to play the game they all became wanted by the *mukhabarat*, which labeled them "enemies of the leader and nation." Some were in hiding already. Many used pseudonyms. Mazen spread rumors of discord among activists and circulated that he had broken ranks when his role as messenger between them and the regime ended.

Going forward, Mazen's involvement in organizing and supporting the protest movement had to be kept secret. One effort that had started from almost day one of the protests in March 2011 was gathering momentum and had to be sustained despite the risks. He and his colleagues were expanding the network of what they called the Local Coordination Committees (LCCs), or *tansiqiyat* in Arabic. These were dozens of groups of grassroots activists spread out across the country, in city neighborhoods, towns, and villages—a mosaic of ethnic, religious, and class backgrounds. The goal was to collaborate through social media on organizing protests and adopting unified messages, both on the streets and in interactions with television stations and journalists around the region and world. They shared tips on how to harness tools like Facebook and YouTube to achieve their goals, and discussed measures and tactics to protect themselves.

Representatives of these committees, which included Syrians living overseas, held regular Skype conference calls. Many were young Syrians comfortable with technology and committed to truthfulness, accuracy, and nonviolence. They were the citizen journalists that the world was relying on to know what was happening as the regime spun its lies and false narratives and blocked or restricted access by traditional media. One of their jobs was to document atrocities and violations committed by regime forces at first and then later by all parties.

Notwithstanding personal rivalries and ideological divisions which emerged very early on among activists, they all more or less strove for one thing: finding a way to merge various protests springing up in different neighborhoods, towns, and villages into one large protest and occupy a major square in Damascus or another big city. There would be unity and strength in numbers. All the world would be watching, and the regime would perhaps think twice about killing everyone in the square, the activists reasoned.

People would stay in the square until Bashar resigned or fled. It would be just like Egypt's Tahrir Square in Cairo. Syrians still longed for an outcome like that in Egypt and Tunisia, even though the polarization, violence, and bloodshed in the streets indicated that things could be headed toward a Libya scenario—rebels taking up arms to fight the regime.

Among those yearning for a Tahrir Square in the heart of Damascus was the painter Khaled al-Khani. He had his long-standing grudge against the regime that killed his father, but he was absolutely committed to keeping protests peaceful and unarmed, no matter the provocations by the regime. Khaled often joked to his friends that he was a coward because the slightest sound of gunfire scared him. They knew perfectly well that his fear was a result of the trauma of having lived through the Hama massacre as a seven-year-old boy.

Khaled was among those arguing strongly against any engagement with the regime or giving any credence to Bashar's reform promises, which he believed were lies.

"Believe me," Khaled told his friends, "you'll get nothing through dialogue and politics. This regime is ready to destroy the country rather than dismantle its police state."[29]

In the back of his mind was his own father's experience. Hikmat al-Khani was among those in his native city of Hama who opposed the insurgency waged in the late 1970s by Islamist militants linked to the Muslim Brotherhood. But at the same time Hikmat felt that real changes needed to take place in the way the country was governed by Hafez and his regime. He and his best friend, Omar Shishakli, met with regime representatives and received promises of reform, including from Manaf's father, Mustafa. Shishakli was later abducted by the *mukhabarat* in 1980.[30] His mutilated body was dumped on the street.[31]

Khaled was among those in Damascus who were starting to head out to Douma every weekend to protest. The crowds on the streets and the town's tightly knit community fostered solidarity and even a feeling of protection, despite the deadly violence deployed by the regime there. This solidarity was missing so far in the capital, where fear and mistrust reigned. Khaled and others believed that large protests in Douma and several towns in the capital's eastern suburbs could be merged with protests that were starting to spring up in neighborhoods on the edges of Damascus. Protesters from all these areas could converge on Abbaseen Square, a large traffic roundabout and a major crossroads on the city's east side paved with black basalt cobblestone. This would become the place where hundreds of thousands, and even a million people, would gather until the regime was toppled.

On his first trip to Douma, Khaled met Adnan Wehbeh, the physician and local protest leader who was tortured after meeting Bashar with Manaf's help. They bonded immediately. Khaled saw Wehbeh as a wise and influential figure in the protest movement who, like him, was committed to peaceful struggle against the regime.

"Forget it, it's impossible," Khaled told Wehbeh on April 15, 2011, just before the first major attempt to get to the square was made that day. "The whole area around Abbaseen is carpeted with forces. They are ready to shoot."[32] Many protesters still wanted to try.

Some 40,000 people from Douma and surrounding towns marched

about ten miles toward Damascus. The moment those in front reached the fringes of the square, regime forces unleashed a barrage of gunfire. Many were wounded and dozens were arrested. Those in the back fled if they could.[33]

There was another attempt a week later, on Good Friday, ahead of Easter Sunday. Protesters saw the day as an opportunity to show unity among Christians and Muslims, proving that their uprising was for all Syrians regardless of their religion. It was agreed that this time there would be two big marches from the eastern suburbs toward Abbaseen Square. One would come from the northeast and another from the east via an office tower and commercial complex. In Douma, tens of thousands flooded the main avenue. Khaled was with them, chanting and clapping.[34]

"The people want to topple the regime," they shouted. "Leave! Leave!" they chanted, addressing Bashar.

"No reform with blood!" read placards carried by protesters.[35]

Those coming from other towns closer to Damascus arrived first. One protester carried a placard with a cross and crescent to signify Christian-Muslim unity. They were in front of the office complex when regime gunmen posted on the building's rooftop opened fire at them. Bullets rained from everywhere.[36]

"Car, car, car!" screamed one man frantically, pleading for help to rush his friend to the hospital. The anguished man was on the ground with his friend in the middle of the street after everyone else had abandoned them and scattered for cover amid the crackle of machine-gun fire. His friend was motionless and slumped in a pool of blood with a big hole in the back of his head.

That day, April 22, 2011, was the bloodiest day since the start of the uprising in March. At least 110 protesters were killed by regime forces throughout Syria.[37] It was the same day on which Bashar issued decrees regarding the state of emergency and right to protest, as if Bashar were signing these hollow laws with the blood of all these victims.

It was a grim week; just days before the regime killed protesters in Damascus to prevent them from occupying a square, deadly force was deliberately used to squash a brief, peaceful sit-in in the center of Homs.

On April 18, 2011, tens of thousands took to the streets for the funerals of protesters killed by security forces. The funerals spawned fresh protests. People decided to occupy one of the city's main squares, New Clock Tower Square. They sang the national anthem and tied a large Syrian flag to the white clock tower's base. More people joined.[38] Many called on Bashar to give up power. At one point there were almost 100,000 people in the square. The mood was both defiant and joyous. By nightfall most left, but thousands decided to stay. They were going to camp in the square and demonstrate against the regime day and night.

Manaf sent two of his men to Homs to try to calm protesters and convince them to get off the streets before the regime had the chance to respond with force.[39] He knew that the Assads intended to shoot everyone in the Homs square to prevent a prolonged sit-in. Maher al-Assad and Hafez Makhlouf had given the order to the Homs operations commander, General Ali Younes, who was also deputy head of the *mukhabarat*'s Military Intelligence Directorate.[40]

Manaf kept in touch with his envoys by phone from Damascus. Both men had contacts inside the *mukhabarat* and could act as mediators between both sides, he hoped.

The situation in Homs and the surrounding countryside was explosive when Manaf's emissaries arrived. They first went to Manaf's hometown, Al-Rastan, fifteen miles north of Homs city. Thousands of protesters had taken to the streets and smashed the statue of Hafez al-Assad at the town's southern entrance, a massive white stone idol that stood on a thirty-two-foot pedestal; it had been proudly commissioned and unveiled by Mustafa Tlass in the mid-1980s, not long after Hafez's Hama massacre.

Protesters managed to separate the head, which rolled down the hill, where a mob trampled on it while deliriously shouting curses. They kept hammering what remained of the statue until it came tumbling down.[41] One person was seriously injured when a piece of the statue fell on him; he was rushed to the hospital in Homs, where he was arrested and taken to the army hospital instead. A large mob besieged the hospital and would not leave. Manaf defused the situation by getting the hospital to release the man while his envoys tried to pave the way for Manaf to meet with townspeople.

Even though many Syrians called Al-Rastan "the second Qurdaha," comparing it to the Assads' loyal hometown, most townspeople despised Mustafa Tlass and his sons. One of those who brought down Hafez's statue was Nazem Tlass, a distant relative. He was proud of it.[42]

"Al-Rastan had to put up with tyranny and injustice, just like the rest of Syria—there was no exception," said an army officer from the town who sided with protesters.[43]

Indeed, the dynamics in Al-Rastan were no different from those in any rural and predominantly Sunni area like the Aleppo countryside, Daraa, and Deir Ezzour.

There were a few natives who held senior positions in the party, army, and government, but they were always subordinate to the Alawites who had the real power, especially Assad clan members and the *mukhabarat*. Mustafa had been Hafez's lifetime companion, but he was most certainly second to him. Even at the Ministry of Defense, which Mustafa headed for more than three decades, the real decision maker was his office manager, Issam Kheirbek, an Alawite general and nephew of Bashar's mentor, Mohammad Nasif. These sectarian cleavages and imbalances were accentuated on the ground. Many in Al-Rastan and wider Homs province were angered that most local government jobs went mainly to Alawites.

The town's fortunes began to improve when Bashar took over, which many credited to his relationship with Manaf. Al-Rastan's quota of those accepted at the Homs officers' academy went up to almost fifty per year, and a modern hospital that had been under construction for decades was finally completed.[44]

"We are the ones who secure the Assad family's pact with Syria's Sunnis," Manaf would often say privately.[45]

It was precisely this oppressive patronage, closer to a bondage system, that people in Al-Rastan wanted to overturn when they toppled Hafez's statue. More than four decades of bottled-up resentment and anger was finally unleashed and, for many, there was no going back.

Just like in Daraa, it was usually the elders who were afraid of the wrath of the regime and more amenable to dialogue, while the youth wanted to press ahead with their revolution and emancipation. Manaf's envoys witnessed this firsthand when they entered Al-Rastan the day the statue was brought down.

"The whole time, we felt we were ten steps behind as developments raced ahead. Things were much bigger than us and our ability to solve them," one of the men recalled.[46]

The next day, as news of the large sit-in at New Clock Tower Square spread around the countryside, many people in Al-Rastan and nearby towns flocked to Homs city. Manaf told his envoys to follow.

It was a scary scene when they arrived around midnight. Thousands of soldiers, security forces, and regime thugs were encircling the square and hunkering down on the roofs of surrounding buildings. The regime also mobilized more than 500 mostly Alawite students from the Baath University in Homs to assist in clearing the square.

Protesters were told to disperse or face dire consequences. The commander of Homs operations, Ali Younes, ordered local Sunni clerics to pressure protesters to leave. Some left, others refused. A few thousand were determined to stay in the square no matter what. After midnight, Younes received an order from Bashar's brother, Maher: clear the square now.[47]

Soldiers closed in on protesters and aimed their weapons. Those on rooftops did the same. One of Manaf's envoys grabbed a bullhorn that was in the hand of an officer at the scene and stood in the middle of the square between protesters and soldiers. He told soldiers that they could not shoot at their brothers. Protesters started cheering for a moment, thinking that the army was going to disobey orders, as had happened in Tunisia.[48]

Then, at about 2:00 a.m. on April 19, 2011, all hell broke loose. The crackle of gunfire echoed through Homs for more than an hour. Even now there are no precise figures for the number of people killed at New Clock Tower Square, or those who were detained or went missing afterward. Once the smoke cleared, big shovels and trucks were brought to the square to clear out the bodies of the dead and the anti-Bashar banners they had carried before they were killed. The debris was towed away and fire engines hosed the square to make sure that all looked clean in the morning.

Manaf's peace envoys were caught in the crossfire. One, Abu Rasul, went missing for three days, turning up later in the Homs military hospital, where he was detained with horrific injuries. His partner eventually located him.

"It was a slaughterhouse," the man remembered. "People were between life and death. Everyone was shackled to their beds. Doctors and nurses were hitting them with chains, iron rods, and chairs, especially those from Al-Rastan. A nurse ripped someone's leg with her hands. When I found Abu Rasul his rib cage was broken, his head was swollen, his teeth were smashed, and part of his leg was missing. He was almost dead."[49]

When Bashar began to deploy army units in parts of Syria to control the early protests, Manaf thought this could be a positive development, and he encouraged Bashar to do so. Perhaps the army could act as a buffer between the protesters on one side and the *mukhabarat* forces and pro-regime thugs on the other, similar to what had happened in Egypt. Of course, Manaf knew the structure of the army and the limits of its power. His father, Mustafa, practically built the army alongside Hafez and the other Baathist officers when they grabbed power in 1963.

The idea of the army playing a more independent and moderating role and Bashar moving away from the hard-liners was wishful thinking, if not delusion. It was soon clear that the army's early intervention, especially in places that had a history of sectarian animosities and tense local social dynamics, made matters worse and fueled more violence.

At the end of April 2011, Bashar ordered the army to carry out military operations in several of the cities and towns that had risen up against him—Baniyas, Daraa, Douma, and Homs, among others.[50] The bloodiest was in Daraa, where the first two protesters had been killed by his forces a month prior.

It was April 25, 2011, just after the muezzin at the Omari mosque next to Sally's home called for dawn prayers.[51] She heard the rumbling of engines on the streets. She looked from the balcony and saw tanks, armored vehicles, and army trucks.

"Tanks!" she called to her mother when she rushed back inside.

"That's it, we are going to be another Hama," shuddered her mother, referring to the siege of that city in 1982 by Hafez's forces and the massacre of its inhabitants.

Power and all telephone communications were cut off as the army entered old Daraa, or Al-Balad. Soldiers set up checkpoints on street corners and intersections, and snipers hunkered down on rooftops. A total curfew was imposed. All shops were closed. Anyone venturing on the street was shot dead. In just the first nine days of the siege, an estimated 200 people were killed, almost all by sniper fire.[52] Many died from their injuries because they could not be taken to hospitals or no emergency aid was available. Some families buried their dead in the backyards of their homes.

Like all those under siege, Sally and her family survived on provisions that Syrians usually stored in their pantries, such as pickled vegetables, lentils, and rice.

Several surrounding towns and villages erupted in anger and tried to march to Daraa city to lift the siege. They were met with deadly force. On April 29, at least sixty-two people were killed trying to defy the siege.[53]

At the end of April, the army and security forces stormed the Omari mosque, which had become a stronghold for protesters after the assault in March. Daraa residents had reclaimed the mosque and turned its courtyard into a square for protesting, renaming it "Dignity Square." Sally was among those involved in organizing protests there.

During the second assault in April, some of the men who had barricaded themselves at the mosque took up small arms to defend themselves. This was the perfect pretext for the army to go in. Some in Daraa said there were people among the protesters working secretly with the *mukhabarat* and that it was they who facilitated the procurement of weapons and urged confrontation with the army.[54] Making arms available to protesters was a deliberate and systematic tactic by the regime. Manaf documented several such instances with dates, names, and places.[55]

As the army pressed on with its campaign in Daraa, necessities like baby formula ran out. A group of Syrian actors and other public figures posted a statement on Facebook pleading with authorities to allow milk, food, medicine, and emergency care into Daraa. They were mocked and labeled traitors by regime officials and loyalists.[56] Fruit and vegetable vendors from a Palestinian refugee camp south of Daraa were shot at by the army after they smuggled in two pickup trucks carrying fresh produce.[57]

In early May, soldiers accompanied by *mukhabarat* officers raided almost every home in Daraa, arresting hundreds of young men. They were also looking for two refrigerator trucks in which Daraa residents had stored bodies of their dead for burial later.[58] Sally's teenage brothers were among those who escaped to farmland near the city as news of the sweeps spread.

When the army reached the family's apartment they kicked open the front door.

"Where are the gunmen? Where are the terrorists? Who among you was protesting?" they shouted.

Sally's heart sank. She had cell phones in her pockets. One of them had a Jordanian number. Since they were so close to Jordan, they could get cell phone reception from there and it was a way to communicate with the outside world after Syrian service was severed. By then Sally was one of Daraa's leading young activists. She was deeply involved in the Daraa Coordination Committee. She helped organize the weekly protests, filmed them, posted videos on social media, and liaised with other rebellious areas around Syria. Men and women were working side by side.

To protect her identity, she used pseudonyms like "Free Girl" and "Samar al-Hourani."

"We have nothing to do with the protests," Sally's mother said, addressing the officer calmly. "Search the house if you like."

They went into the bedrooms, rummaging through drawers and knocking over a closet until Sally's aunt, who lived in the apartment downstairs, offered the officers breakfast in her home. Sally's cousin, the only young man who was around, offered them cigarettes, too. They did not arrest him.[59]

Elsewhere they pocketed money and gold that they found while searching bedrooms. Very few families were left unscathed by their visits.

By mid-May 2011, military operations expanded to many towns that had dared to demonstrate against the regime, widening the circle of bloodshed and retribution, sharpening sectarian discord, and pushing people on the streets toward militancy. One other consequence of these operations: they exposed and deepened fissures within the army.

In the town of Dael, located on the strategic highway and army supply line between Daraa and Damascus, there were deadly clashes between an army unit and *mukhabarat* agents after a group of soldiers tried to rescue protesters who were being shot at by the latter.[60] Later, army tanks and more soldiers under *mukhabarat* supervision arrived to teach the town a lesson.

Manaf witnessed firsthand the consequences of plunging the army into the bloody crackdown against protesters. In late April, units of his Republican Guard alongside the *mukhabarat* led several assaults on Douma to crush the protest movement and detain all those connected to it. This was the same town where Manaf had tried to make peace after Bashar's cousin the *mukhabarat* commander Hafez Makhlouf killed protesters.

Nearly half of Manaf's unit, roughly 1,600 men, were deployed alongside other forces to take part in the late-April Douma assault. They were ordered to disperse protesters on the streets by shooting directly at them. The orders were not only coming from the *mukhabarat* but also from Manaf's fellow commanders in the Republican Guard.[61] Most of the Alawites who dominated the Republican Guard obeyed the kill orders but some Sunnis were unwilling, Douma being overwhelmingly Sunni.[62] Those who disobeyed orders were executed on the spot.

"Sir, I no longer want to go to Douma, please do not send me there. I am seeing things against my conscience and principles," Iyad Khalouf, a twenty-eight-year-old first lieutenant in Manaf's brigade, told him in May. Khalouf was one of the brightest and most promising junior officers in Manaf's unit. He was a Sunni from Rankous, a town on the outskirts of Damascus.

"Be patient," said Manaf, "the president [Bashar] said things would change soon. If they do not, then I promise I won't send you to Douma.[63]

Days later Khalouf committed suicide at the base by shooting himself in the head.

Manaf had no say as to whether his men could be deployed in Douma or not. The overall commander of the Republican Guard, Manaf's fellow brigade commanders, and even his own deputy appeared to be wholeheartedly embracing the military option. Manaf was the only one among the top officers who seemed reluctant and argued for another approach. He was branded an "appeaser."

Bashar's brother, Maher, and cousins the Makhloufs warned Manaf to watch what he was saying about them or else they were going to clip his tongue (a common expression in the Arab world signifying a threat or warning to one's vocal critics).[64] Manaf's enemies also ordered senior aides at the palace to stop dealing with him on anything related to the political reform track. Manaf's only protection was his family's special status in the regime and his father's history with Hafez, things that Bashar still seemed to value.

Then came preparations in late May for a military assault on Manaf's hometown, Al-Rastan. After the smashing of Hafez's statue, the town had kept up its protests though they were met with deadly violence by security forces. Toward the end of April, almost 10,000 people had taken to the streets after an army officer was killed during the Daraa military operation and was brought back to his hometown for burial. People blocked the highway with burning tires. The army was ordered to intervene and about twenty-three people among the protesters were killed. At night, the local branches of the Baath Party and *mukhabarat* as well as all police stations were set on fire.[65]

Now the regime was determined to subdue Al-Rastan and teach it a lesson. Manaf called Bashar and asked to see him.[66]

Bashar told him to meet him at Bassel's old office in Qasioun and not at the palace. Manaf figured that Bashar did not want others, especially his brother, Maher, to know that he was still taking Manaf's advice.

"Al-Rastan is mine, I can solve it," said Manaf, clearly understating the severity of the situation in his hometown. "All they want is for the state to consider those who died martyrs and for their families to be compensated. They want the wounded to be treated at the government's expense. They also want us to release detainees." His plan might have pleased a few pro-regime town elders but it certainly would not have satisfied the demands of protesters on the ground.

But Bashar relented regardless. He picked up the telephone and called General Abdul-Fatah Qudsiyeh, commander of the *mukhabarat*'s Military Intelligence Directorate, to inform him of the change of plans.

Manaf was told to liaise with Qudsiyeh's deputy, Ali Younes, the man who killed protesters in Homs on the orders of Bashar's brother and cousin. It was agreed that a delegation from Al-Rastan would meet Younes to discuss the settlement's terms.

The delegation went to see Younes the next day, but he refused to meet them and told them to give him their demands in writing.

The day after, there were more protests in Al-Rastan, the largest ever.

Just after, Eyad Makhlouf, an army officer and the youngest of the

Makhloufs, visited Manaf at home.[67] "Dad and Rami send you their regards," said Eyad, "and they want me to tell you that you're too nice; your solutions don't work, you don't know how to deal with people."

He asked him to stay out of Al-Rastan.

"I spoke to the president and he told me Al-Rastan was mine," said Manaf.

"It's not. Speak to him again if you want," said Eyad.

That night and the following morning Manaf called Bashar multiple times. Bashar never answered. He normally returned his calls within minutes.

On May 29, a major military operation was launched in Al-Rastan and three adjacent towns north of Homs city. Tanks and artillery shelled the towns and snipers shot anyone on the streets. At the end of the five-day operation, at least seventy-five people were killed.[68]

The orders to strike Manaf's hometown came via his nemesis, Hafez Makhlouf, the man Manaf had wanted Bashar to punish for killing protesters.[69]

A few days later, one of Manaf's cousins from Al-Rastan, a first lieutenant in the army called Abdul-Razzaq Tlass, appeared on the Al Jazeera news channel to announce his defection and urge others to follow suit. He had been stationed in Daraa.

"You joined the army not to protect the Assad family. You are an honorable officer, stay honorable—but if you are not honorable, then stay with the Assad family," Abdul-Razzaq said, addressing fellow army officers and barely concealing his anger.[70]

There had been army desertions since the start of the military operations in April, but this was among the first public and televised defections.[71]

Within days, one of Manaf's fellow generals in the Republican Guard was sent by Bashar to see him. Manaf had stopped calling Bashar after the assault on Al-Rastan.

"Why aren't you calling him?" said General Bassam Al-Hassan.

"He's a liar," said Manaf.

"Call him," insisted Al-Hassan.

"Bassam, he has been lying to me from the start," said Manaf.

"How?" asked Al-Hassan.

Manaf explained what happened with Al-Rastan and all his previous peacemaking efforts in Douma and how he had been sabotaged, undermined, and threatened by Maher and the Makhloufs. Manaf concluded that Bashar was pretending he was interested in peaceful solutions while giving hard-liners the green light to crush the protests by any means.

"Go see him tomorrow—it's important," said Al-Hassan.

The next day Manaf met Bashar at the presidential palace.[72]

They discussed everything that had happened since the first day protesters were killed in Daraa and how Bashar's brother and cousins poured fuel on the fires.

"Let's stage a coup," said Manaf at one point.

"Against whom?" said Bashar with a mix of bemusement and slight alarm.

"I will personally arrest Maher [Assad], Hafez [Makhlouf], and the others, but you have to be on board with this," said Manaf in a serious tone.

Bashar started laughing.

"I am your friend and I have advised you all along not to choose the military solution," said Manaf soberly.

"You know what's your problem, Manaf?" said Bashar. "Your problem is that you're too soft."

There was an impenetrable silence for almost a minute.

"I am too soft," replied Manaf with a hint of indignation, "but I will put in front of you two things that you no longer can ignore: poverty and sectarianism. These are now out in the open."

Bashar remained quiet.

"Okay," continued Manaf, "if you think I am too soft, I will step aside and sit in my office and not get involved in anything."

"Yes, that would be best for now," said Bashar, sounding almost relieved.

He then told Manaf that their homeland was facing a conspiracy just like the one their fathers confronted and crushed in the 1970s and early '80s. The enemies were the same, he said. Now, like then, there was no room for compromise.

13

The Hama Manual

There had been soldiers in khaki green in Hama as far back as Khaled al-Khani could remember.

He was barely four years old in 1979 when Hafez al-Assad stepped up the pressure on his hometown. It was common that year to see troops in jeeps and pickup trucks with machine guns racing down Corniche al-Asi—the riverside promenade with lush parks and giant wooden waterwheels, or *norias*, used for millennia to scoop water from the deeply carved Orontes River up into aqueducts for irrigation. There was no telling when the heavy footsteps of soldiers would echo through the narrow cobblestone alleyways on their way to arrest people from their homes, shops, and schools.[1] Thousands were sent to the *mukhabarat*'s torture dungeons and then eastward to the infamous Tadmor desert prison, described as the "kingdom of death and madness" by a poet held there for five years.[2]

The dragnets in Hama often provoked angry protests and general strikes, which then led to more repression by regime forces. While fear and violent confrontation gripped Hama that year, Khaled and his siblings were somewhat shielded from it despite the political activism of their father, Hikmat al-Khani, an eye doctor and community leader. Soldiers at checkpoints demanding IDs and searching vehicles were often smiley and playful with little Khaled, a cute and chubby boy with blond hair and blue eyes.

Still, a military atmosphere had dominated Hama since the early 1970s. Even in the games children like Khaled played at school and in the alleyways near their homes, they pretended they were soldiers chasing and shooting the bad guys.

Like many well-to-do Hama families, the Khanis lived in a traditional stone house in one of the neighborhoods along the Orontes. Theirs was Baroudiyeh, named after the gunpowder workshops that flourished there during Ottoman rule. (The Baroudis were the family that made the gunpowder, or *baroud* in Arabic.)[3] Many homes belonged to the Azms, members of a prominent landowning family that governed Hama, Damascus, and other cities in the Levant on behalf of the Ottomans. One of them was a beautiful red-tile-roof villa with a terrace and garden on the riverbank. Next to Baroudiyeh was Hama's gem, the Kilaniyeh, consisting of a series of mansions, Sufi monasteries, and souks. Many edifices, with their oriental-style balconies and oriel windows, overhung the water, evoking Venice and its palazzos.[4]

Khaled's family lived on a cobblestone alley inside Baroudiyeh. They had a two-story home built around an interior courtyard with a marble water fountain in the middle and fruit trees all around. The fragrance from bitter oranges, loquats, and plums hung in the air.[5] The family's private quarters and bedrooms were on the top floor. Depending on the season, guests were received in the courtyard or in the drawing room on the ground floor. The kitchen and the room where Khaled's aunt lived was on the same level.

Khaled's father—Dr. Hikmat, as everyone called him—was an esteemed and well-liked figure who was politically minded and cared deeply about the welfare of his city and community.[6] Growing up in Hama, he was one of those who dared climb on the giant waterwheels as they turned in order to dive from the top into the river. Like other young men, he rode horses and learned how to shoot. These were the skills that young children were supposed to acquire, according to the Prophet Mohammad. On special occasions like the main Muslim *eids*, or holidays, most Hama boys wore the traditional local dress of embroidered caftans and puffy pants. At the same time, Hikmat pursued a Western-style education, wore elegant three-piece suits, and embraced modernity, critical thinking, and open debate.

Hama was a city steeped in history—inhabited for more than 7,000 years, according to a Danish archaeological expedition in the 1930s. It came under Aramaean, Assyrian, Hellenic, Roman, Byzantine, and Muslim rule. Like the rest of the Levant, Hama was part of the Ottoman Empire for four centuries until the start of the French mandate in the early twentieth century. During the tumultuous years that followed Syria's independence in 1946, Hama was a place trying to come to grips with the impact of the upheaval on its social fabric and its fiercely protected way of life and traditions. It was the embodiment of Syria's contrasts and cross-currents, even in its layout.

The Orontes cuts the city diagonally. The southwest is called the Souk. It is the city's commercial center and the part facing west toward the sea and south toward the capital Damascus, about 140 miles away. In Souk you saw people in Western dress. The opposite side of the riverbank, the northeast, is the Hader. That's where sheep and horses were sold and Bedouins in tribal dress came for leather goods and textiles.

Hama was regarded as the epicenter of feudalism and the landed elite, but it was also the home of the 1950s peasant revolt. For some Syrians, Hama was always an insular place — a bastion of conservative Sunni Islam and xenophobia. At the same time, the small city also had a well-integrated Christian community and an animated political life, even during the early years of Hafez's rule.

Above all else, it was a city that never reconciled itself to the Baathist coup in 1963 and Hafez's subsequent power grab. It had always been seen by the regime as a symbol of contempt and defiance to its rule. Pragmatic Damascus formed a pact with Hafez. There was fierce opposition in Aleppo, but it was ultimately contained and crushed. Only Hama remained a thorn in Hafez's side — but not for long.

In the fall of 1979, discussions at the *madafeh* of Hikmat al-Khani were graver and more urgent than usual. The *madafeh* was a Hama tradition that involved prominent community figures hosting gatherings to speak about issues of the day in family-owned neighborhood halls. (Similar customs existed in most other Middle Eastern countries under different names.) Among the regulars at the Khani *madafeh* was Omar al-Shishakli, president of the Arab Ophthalmological Association and the Hama Medical Association.[7] Shishakli, a nephew of the army general who ruled Syria for a few years in the early 1950s, was a mentor and friend of Dr. Khani. That fall, talk centered on how the Assad regime's increased repression and its strategy of collective punishment risked sharpening sectarian animosities and fueling radicalization in places like Hama. Shishakli and Khani were among those who regularly voiced these concerns face to face with regime representatives such as the local governor and the defense minister, Mustafa Tlass. There were several attempts at dialogue and engagement with the regime, led mostly by Shishakli.

The message was simple: if you want Hama not to protest and go on strike, then ease the pressure and pull out the army and security forces from the city.[8]

Hama natives were also angered by the fact that most public-sector jobs in the city and province went to Baath Party members and regime loyalists. Shishkali and Khani were among signatories of a statement presented to Hafez, listing the city's grievances.[9]

Hafez was already enmeshed in the civil war in neighboring Lebanon, and he faced challenges on two fronts at home — attacks by Islamist insurgents backed by his rival Baathist regime in Iraq and rising discontent by a large cross section of the population over economic mismanagement, corruption, and an increasingly authoritarian rule.

The insurgents were part of the *Tali'a al-Muqatila*, or Fighting Vanguard, a militant splinter group of the Muslim Brotherhood party which first emerged in Hama when Baathists took power in 1963. In the 1970s the group's attacks became blatantly sectarian, targeting members of Hafez's Alawite minority, which dominated the countryside and mountains west of the overwhelmingly Sunni Hama city.

The Muslim Brotherhood was divided over the Vanguard's campaign, and a wing of the party advocated dialogue with Hafez to convince him to implement real reforms and ease his grip on public life, and to that end it cooperated with the likes of Hikmat al-Khani and Shishakli. But it was precisely such nonviolent collaboration that Hafez felt jeopardized his authority.

So Hafez's overriding strategy was to wage military campaigns against entire cities and towns like Aleppo and Hama from which Brotherhood leaders hailed, under the guise of combatting terrorism.[10] There were mass arrests, summary executions, and unspeakable torture in prisons of anyone suspected of having even the remotest link to the Brotherhood; this guilt by association extended to family members, friends, and acquaintances. All too often, many people met a tragic demise due to their name, birthplace, or look, or simply because of mistaken identity.

By late 1979, concern over the repercussions of Hafez's approach were widespread, shared even by some senior members of his Baath Party. A brief period of conciliation and engagement followed. Regime representatives held discussions about reform with intellectuals and political opponents, some prisoners were released, and demands of striking workers, most notably at oilfields in the northeast, were met.[11]

These proved to be tactical moves by Hafez, buying him some time to prepare to strike his opponents. At the Baath Party congress at the end of 1979 Hafez signaled his real intentions. He spoke of treason and conspiracies. "The masses," said Assad, employing his code for loyalists, "were ready to shed blood to defend this homeland."[12]

At the end of February 1980, doctors, engineers, lawyers, teachers, and other professionals went on strike and issued statements demanding the release of political prisoners and freedom of expression. In early March of that year, labor strikes and demonstrations calling for an end to the regime swept Aleppo, Baniyas, Hama, Homs, and Latakia, among others.[13] The military operations that Hafez ordered in response against rebellious areas resulted in the deaths of hundreds and the arrest of thousands.

Tanks and regime forces and militias occupied Hama. Protesters were shot dead and a curfew was imposed. Anyone who defied the curfew was killed.[14]

Hafez's first targets in the spring of 1980 were not Islamists but secular political opponents, human rights defenders, and champions of peaceful resistance to his regime, who he believed posed the gravest threat to his legitimacy and hold on power. Professional associations were disbanded and many of their leaders and prominent members were imprisoned or executed.[15]

Omar al-Shishakli was summoned for talks with Mustafa Tlass, the interior minister, and the governor of Hama. He was told that they wanted to discuss de-escalation in Hama. Shishakli was one of the most influential figures in the Hama protest movement and had previously dialogued with regime officials and acted as mediator between them and the city's Islamists. But the invitation to come for negotiations was a trick. Shishakli was tortured to death by the *mukhabarat* and his mutilated body was tossed on the street. Several other professionals and prominent figures in the Hama protests were killed the same way.[16]

Shishakli's monstrous murder had a chilling effect on Khaled's father, Hikmat. He told his wife that he believed it was only a matter of time before they came for him, too.

Hafez's intent was to eliminate or terrorize all those who were struggling against his regime by peaceful means like civil disobedience, labor strikes, and protests. It worked.

The confrontation was then largely between the regime and Islamists. Hafez effectively used his war with the Islamists in the early 1980s to bludgeon the Syrian people into fear and total submission over several stages.

At least 2,000 people were killed and 8,000 were detained in a blistering military operation against several rebellious neighborhoods in Aleppo in the spring and summer of 1980.[17] That same year, a decree condemning to death anyone associated with the Muslim Brotherhood silenced moderate elements in the party and pushed it closer to the extremists leading the anti-regime insurgency.[18] Now Hafez used the pretext of combatting terrorism to finish off remaining opposition to his rule.

Aleppo was subdued after the 1980 operation, but Hama remained a problem for Hafez.

In the spring of 1981, Islamist militants attacked a security checkpoint in an Alawite village on Hama's outskirts. In retaliation, regime forces and militias sealed off several neighborhoods in Hama and imposed a curfew. They went door to door rounding up teenage boys and men of all ages. Many were executed on the spot. At least 350 were killed over three days.[19]

Less than a year later, Hama was turned into a byword for the horrors that the Assad family was ready to inflict on those who dared to challenge its rule.

The night of February 2, 1982, was bitterly cold. The Khanis were asleep while the crackle of gunfire that they had grown accustomed to hearing in

Hama over the preceding few years grew louder and closer.[20] As explosions started to cut through the gunfire, the family awoke. Little Khaled had been sleeping with his aunt Fatima, who was closer to him than was his mother. His parents and siblings came down from their rooms and huddled with them. The ground floor was reckoned to be safer.

Outside, regime forces attacked a secret weapons cache for Fighting Vanguard militants in the neighborhood, provoking fierce clashes between the two sides. Since the spring 1981 assault on the city, Hafez and his lieutenants, including Mustafa, had been making plans for a major operation in Hama. This was their moment.[21]

Having flushed out the militants inside Hama, regime forces retreated momentarily to the outer perimeter where for weeks they had been bringing reinforcements and preparing to create a cordon to seal the city and its inhabitants from the surrounding countryside. Troops massed at an air base just west of the city and in the south around the soccer stadium, where the *mukhabarat* had one of its main local branches. Hafez tasked Mustafa and the army's chief of staff, Hikmat al-Shihabi, with overall responsibility for the operation.[22] Both were Sunni.

The actual commanders on the ground were mainly Hafez's kinsmen and members of his own Alawite minority, people he could count on to mobilize and incite their men in the assault on the rebellious Sunni city. They included his brother Rifaat, who led a mainly Alawite paramilitary force that was at the forefront of the fight against regime opponents. There was also his cousin Adnan al-Assad, who headed another mainly Alawite militia, and the commanders of the Special Forces and the army's Third Division, both Alawites. In addition, thousands of mostly Alawite Baath Party youth, who had undergone advanced military training, were brought to Hama.

"This has to be complete eradication...and through effective revolutionary methods, all traces of this gang [Muslim Brotherhood] must be eradicated," Hafez told about 8,000 of these young party militants at a ceremony after they had completed special training over the summer and fall in 1981 in preparation for the big attack on Hama.[23]

By then many were eager for vengeance against Sunnis in general, whom they held equally responsible for the assassination of Alawites by Vanguard extremists.

On the other side, with most advocates of peaceful opposition to Hafez's rule dead, in prison, on the run, or too afraid to speak out, the initiative in places like Hama now belonged to the zealots among the Vanguard and Muslim Brotherhood.

Vanguard fighters numbering a few hundred in Hama hoped to trigger a citywide revolt which they believed would spread to other major cities and topple the regime; this was a plot the Brotherhood and the Vanguard had been considering for a while. Some in the Brotherhood had misgivings about the timing, but they were sidelined by hard-liners.[24] The Brotherhood and Vanguard decision to rise in Hama would ultimately prove to be suicidal, leading them and the whole city into the regime's trap, with devastating consequences. In fact, most Sunnis in Hama and across Syria opposed the fundamentalism and militancy espoused by the Vanguard.

Nearly 2,000 people responded to the Vanguard leader's call to arms in Hama. Many civilians did so not because they shared the group's ideology but more out of a desire to defend their city, homes, and honor after regime forces had laid siege to Hama and cut off power and communications. Assault rifles, machine guns, rocket-propelled grenade launchers, and ammunition were distributed by Vanguard commanders. As the regime launched its operation against Hama, Vanguard fighters rounded up dozens of Baathists in the city, who were mostly government employees or people they accused of having been informants for the regime. They were executed in makeshift Islamic trials.[25]

Hafez's forces then began closing in on the city. First were the special forces, army soldiers, and crack units of Rifaat's paramilitary force. Their tanks and artillery mercilessly shelled ancient neighborhoods like Baroudiyeh.[26] The rooms on the ground floor of the Khani home were by then packed with dozens of neighbors, mostly women and children, who had rushed there for shelter in what they believed was a more secure house with thick walls.[27]

Khaled, his mother and siblings, and others hid in the bedroom of Khaled's aunt because it was the largest. As the shelling grew more intense, children screamed and cried—a soundtrack of fear and horror. Added to the cacophony were the voices of terrified mothers reciting verses of the Quran that, they believed, invoked divine powers and provided protection from the bombing.

"Exalted is He in whose hand is the realm of all things, and to Him you will be returned," intoned the women.[28] Some repeated the verses from memory, while others clung with shaking hands to pocketbook Qurans.

There was also shouting in the courtyard outside.

Peeking through the parted curtain of the room's window, Khaled saw a number of wounded people being brought into the courtyard. His father had converted the space into a field hospital. Although he was an eye doctor by training, he was doing his best to treat gunshot and shrapnel wounds. There were fighters and civilians; men, women, and children. Blood covered the floor. One woman shrieked in pain as she was pinned down by her relatives while Khaled's father tried to remove a bullet that had struck the lower part of her body.

Shortly thereafter a shell struck the top floor of the Khani home, causing heavy damage and sending dust and debris down to the ground floor. For a while everyone, especially the children, struggled to breathe.

Tanks and rocket launchers on the opposite side of the river were pounding Baroudiyeh and adjacent neighborhoods. Many buildings were on fire; smoke enveloped the area.[29]

Khaled's father decided they had to leave the house because it did not have a cellar that could protect them. They moved to their neighbors' home and put covers and blankets on the floor of the house's cramped underground vault, which was used to store bulk olives, pickled eggplants, and dried chickpeas. Khaled and his mother and siblings stayed in this basement for three days and barely saw Hikmat, who was busy treating the wounded all over Baroudiyeh.

Then word spread that regime forces had swept through and occupied most neighborhoods on the city's Souk side, on the opposite bank of the Orontes. It was only a matter of time before they crossed the river to their side. Already regime snipers posted on higher elevations on the other side were picking off anyone they spotted on the wider and more exposed streets in Baroudiyeh and adjacent neighborhoods of the Hader section.[30]

Most families decided to move northward to another neighborhood called Amiryeh, figuring it might be spared the regime's onslaught since there were no fighters there. To get there, it was necessary to run or crawl in some parts of the road to avoid being seen by snipers. Hikmat al-Khani told his wife, Nawal, who was three months pregnant, and his six children to join families fleeing Baroudiyeh. His eldest sister, Fatima, and sick brother, Mahmoud, could not make it, and he had to figure out another way to get them out. He wanted his family to go ahead first and promised to join them the next day.[31]

Hikmat and his sister Fatima decided to accompany Nawal and the children to the edge of the neighborhood, where they had to crawl to get to Amiryeh. It was February 8, 1982, a freezing cold day. As they walked upward, Khaled saw many neighborhood men he knew on street corners or in front of their homes, with rifles slung over their shoulders. Some men warmed their hands over small fires flickering inside tin canisters. They had decided to stay and defend Baroudiyeh. He recognized Muwafaq, the tailor, and ran toward him. Muwafaq sat on a bamboo chair on the street. He wore a thick wool Bedouin coat and had an assault rifle next to him.

"Hi!" said Khaled. "When is my suit going to be ready?"

Muwafaq laughed. He hugged Khaled and kissed him on the cheek.

"It will be ready when we finish with this business. Now go run, catch up with your family," said Muwafaq with a smile.[32]

As Khaled's family reached the end of Baroudiyeh, where they were going to be separated from his father and aunt, he started crying. He did not want to leave.

"Go with your mother, my love — we will join you very soon," said Hikmat.

"No!" said Khaled as he clutched his aunt's coat. "This is my mother."

Hikmat tried for a while to cajole his son to go with his mother and siblings, but he would not budge. Lingering in this area was becoming dangerous. Bodies were strewn on the street in front of shops and buildings. Most had been killed by snipers.

Hikmat slapped Khaled: "Go with your mother — now!"

A tearful Khaled trailed behind his mother, brothers, and sisters, as well as other families, as they prepared to crawl across a wide street to Amiryeh.

That was the last time he ever saw his father.

*　　*　　*

Khaled and his mother and siblings made it to the other side. The first stop for them and other Baroudiyeh families was a building with a large basement off the main street. They were turned away; there was no room, and the priority was for Amiryeh residents.

They kept walking. They knocked on several doors but nobody answered. Most people were hiding in their cellars.

They finally reached the home of Hikmat al-Khani's cousin Adnan. It was at the end of Amiryeh, not far from the Al-Manakh mosque. Adnan told them that he had no cellar but that the building across the street, which was still under construction and belonged to his friends from the Orabi family, had a spacious basement. Adnan's brother Alaeddin, who was sixteen years old, volunteered to accompany them there.

It was a miserable and dank place, completely bare, that smelled of cement; the floor was not even tiled yet. It was dark except for two or three tiny windows that only allowed thin slivers of light. Each family staked out a section. People were crammed next to each other. There was no food or water. Alaeddin ran back to his house and brought back a large jar of olives and some water. His brother Adnan and his family also joined them in the basement. The next day it was impossible for anyone to leave the place. The sound of explosions was spine-chilling.[33]

Women began reading from the Quran again for comfort and protection. One specific verse titled "Ya-Seen," would forever be associated in Khaled's memory with the horrors he and other Hamwis (Hama natives) lived through during the assault.

Soon the only food available was the dwindling supply of olives in the jar and candy that some women had in their handbags. Khaled and other children traded olives and candy with each other.

There was no toilet. Children started urinating and defecating in their clothes. Adults turned a corner of the cellar into a toilet of sorts. The stench became unbearable.

These were the conditions for almost a week.

By mid-February, less than two weeks after the start of the assault, regime forces had completely subdued any resistance from Islamist fighters and civilians who had taken up arms to defend the city. It was then, however, that regime soldiers and militiamen began committing the worst atrocities in what they called their "cleansing" operations.[34]

Girls of all ages were raped repeatedly; many bled to death. Mass executions were committed in the cellars where families hid, as well as in schools, markets, and the cemetery, among other sites. Children and babies were not spared. In several instances, people were herded into mosques, shot dead, and then these buildings were dynamited. In some cases, people were set on fire or hacked to death. A porcelain factory and the city's technical college, south of the city, became notorious temporary holding centers for thousands of male detainees of all ages. Many were severely tortured and killed there. Others were taken to the airbase.[35]

Entire neighborhoods, shops, factories, banks, and government institutions were looted. The priority was cash and gold. Industrial equipment, home furnishings, appliances, and anything of value the troops could find was loaded into trucks, and then many of these homes and businesses were set on fire. And since the mop-up operations were ongoing and Hama was still cordoned off, the looted goods were first gathered in the city's industrial zone and in farmland before they were transported later outside Hama, mostly to Alawite towns and villages west of the city.[36]

Then regime forces reached the basement where the Khanis were hiding. They opened the door and began shooting over people's heads.[37] As soldiers outside seemed to deliberate what to do with the families inside the basement, some adults told everyone to begin chanting for Hafez as a way of convincing the soldiers they were all loyalists and therefore should be spared.

"*Bil rouh bil damm nafdeek ya Hafez!*" ("With our soul, with our blood, we sacrifice ourselves for you, O Hafez!"), chanted the terrified, starving, and filthy families huddled in the basement. The children chimed in as well.

"*Ya allah halak halak, khaleh Hafez yoqoud mahalak!*" ("God, your time is up, let Hafez sit in your place!"), they chanted with even more vigor.

This had little impact on the soldiers. Someone in the basement sitting next to the stairs leading to the door overheard the soldiers saying they were going to blow up the building with everyone inside it. Adnan, the cousin of Khaled's father, volunteered to go out to convince them there were only women, children, and elderly men in the basement. He was arrested and severely beaten. Then they stormed in and told all the men to get out. Adnan's sixteen-year-old brother Alaeddin was among those taken to the porcelain factory and technical college.[38]

A bit later, the women and children who remained in the basement were ordered out. They were told to line up against the building's wall. Everyone thought they were going to be executed. Many were in tears, while others were muttering the *shahada*: "There's only one God and Mohammad is his prophet."

At that moment, some of the elderly and feisty women begged the commanding officer to let them go. "We are like your mother and grand-mother!" they told him repeatedly.

He relented on condition that they keep walking north, out of the city, and never turn back. More than a week since their separation, Khaled and his mother and siblings had no word on the whereabouts of his father, aunt, and uncle. They were conflicted about leaving, but the only choice was to stay with the pack of women and children they were with.

Bodies littered the street as they walked away from Amiryeh. They reached the Omar bin Khatab mosque. It was destroyed except for one section of the building. They encountered more carnage next to the mosque. There was a man who seemed to have been crushed to death by a tank and the body of a woman with missing hands, likely cut off by a soldier to remove her gold bracelets. Another man had been split in half.[39]

Suddenly they were surrounded by soldiers and ordered to lie down on the ground. The soldiers taunted them. The women and children were then made to crawl as the soldiers laughed and fired shots next to them. They were then herded to the only part of the mosque that remained standing. It was an annex that housed a large ablution room. Crammed inside were more terrified-looking women and children from all over the city's Hader section. The floor was littered with stale and mold-covered bread. It was a Hama tradition to leave bread at the mosque for poor people. They were starving and began devouring the old bread. A soldier who took pity on them brought yogurt from a vandalized grocery store so they could eat it with the rotting bread. He poured it on pieces of cardboard boxes. After the women and children had eaten, they fell asleep on the cold tiled floor.

The next day the officer in charge of the area around the mosque agreed to let them leave, but he wanted to make a short speech first.

"My sisters, if you have a father, husband, brother, and any other male relative, you must forget about them—nobody is going to get out alive. Just walk north and follow the road to Aleppo," he said.[40]

Khaled and his mother and siblings trekked with the other women and children for a few miles until they got to a field where people from surrounding villages had come in their cars to rescue relatives escaping Hama. Some began to sob uncontrollably at the sight of the women and children. A man rushed over to Khaled's mother.

"You are Hajj Taha's daughter, right?" he said frantically.

"Yes," said Khaled's mother, who was on the verge of collapsing.

"Okay, I will take you home," he reassured her.

They all got into his pickup truck. The children piled into the back and his mother sat in front.

He took them to Kfar Nboudeh, his mother's hometown in the northern Hama countryside.

A month later, at the start of spring, Khaled's mother found out that her husband, Hikmat, was among those taken to the porcelain factory. He was tortured to death and as a final punishment his eyeballs were plucked out.[41]

Khaled's aunt Fatima was lost for weeks. They finally found her in a village in the northern countryside. She was among a group of other escapees. Khaled's sick uncle, Mahmoud, died during the siege because his family could not get him to the hospital.

The whereabouts of sixteen-year-old Alaeddin and two other cousins remain unknown to this day. Adnan was among the lucky ones who was later released.[42]

Mohammad Farouk Tayfour, a Muslim Brotherhood leader who had advocated a truce with Hafez in 1979, lost thirty members of his family, including his ninety-three-year-old great uncle, when Hafez's forces rampaged through their neighborhood of Tawafra along the Orontes.[43] He was abroad during the massacre.

The final installment of Hafez's wrath came in early March, when entire neighborhoods like Baroudiyeh and Kilaniyeh, Hama's gem, were razed with bulldozers. Many neighborhoods on both sides of the river were also partially leveled. Dozens of historic mosques and several churches were dynamited. The destruction of the churches was blamed on Islamists.[44]

Hafez's name was sprayed everywhere. "Hafez, our leader forever!" There was also graffiti like this: "There's no God but the homeland and there's no prophet but the Baath." (A phrase considered blasphemous by any practicing Muslim and meant to inflict maximum hurt to Hama's people.)[45]

Toward the end of 1982, Khaled's mother gave birth to a baby boy. He was named Hikmat after his late father.

14

Yalla Erhal Ya, Bashar!
(Come On, Bashar, Leave!)

Spring was nearing its end in 2011 when thousands flooded Hama's Aleppo Way. It was the old road to the northern city, the route taken by those escaping death in 1982. This time, the masses moved in the opposite direction, south toward Asi Square in Hama's center. They waved olive branches and palm fronds and held signs calling for the Assad regime's downfall.

A long red, white, and black Syrian flag extending for almost a quarter mile was held aloft. It was emblazoned with these phrases: "Hama does not want the army to enter." "No to sectarianism." "The people want to topple the regime."[1]

The crowds marched past the Afamia al-Cham hotel and local Baath Party headquarters, imposing structures erected on the ruins of one of a dozen neighborhoods razed by Hafez after the 1982 massacre.[2]

The scene of defiant protesters brought tears to the eyes of many Hamwis, especially those with memories of 1982, when at least 10,000 perished and thousands still remained missing.[3] The wounded city was having a cathartic moment: speaking out in great numbers against the regime that had terrorized it three decades earlier.

Khaled al-Khani, his mother, six siblings including baby Hikmat, and Aunt Fatima were among those who had returned to Hama in the fall of 1982. Their home and neighborhood was gone; they lived in a relative's house for a few years. Not only did they have to grieve in silence, but local regime officials made all those who returned, including the Khanis, participate in boisterous pro-Hafez rallies that were supposed to celebrate his victory over the Islamists. Children whose fathers had been executed by the regime grew up singing the glories of Hafez.

The humiliation had no limit. For years, few dared pray at the mosques left standing. Almost eighty-eight mosques and five churches had been destroyed by the regime.[4] Before they were reconstructed years later, the sites of several demolished mosques became soccer fields for children like Khaled.[5] Most of Khaled's classmates in primary school had no fathers.

For years after the massacre *mukhabarat* officers extorted money, gold, and jewelry from women for proof that their husbands, sons, and fathers were alive, or for any scrap of news about them.[6] Many of these men were rotting in the hellish desert prison in Palmyra, or Tadmor in Arabic. They were executed in group hangings held in the prison's courtyard or ravaged by diseases that spread among inmates; the bodies were often dumped in mass graves.[7] The death sentences issued by the prison's military tribunal all bore Mustafa Tlass's stamp of approval.

Over the years, Hafez started releasing some Hama male prisoners on Muslim holidays. Hafez wanted to be the magnanimous sultan. The prisoners hardly posed a risk. Most had been crushed by torture and malnutrition—they were shadows of their former selves and unrecognizable to their families. They arrived home on buses from Tadmor and were usually released at Hama's southern entrance. Khaled never forgot the sight of frantic and tearful mothers and wives boarding one bus after another searching for loved ones and shouting out their names.[8]

Khaled would also never forget what had happened to him in high school.[9] A Baath committee came to interview students to join the party. Hama families wanted their children to enroll, both out of fear and also expectation that membership would improve their chance of college admission, as was and remains the case. The sight of Baathist officials in suits was intimidating; even a uniformed traffic policeman terrified many traumatized Hamwis, who also grappled with extreme poverty after the massacre.

"Youth comrade Khaled al-Khani, sir!" said Khaled as he performed a brusque military salute to the officials. This was the customary Baath greeting.

"What's your father's name?" asked one of the officials.

"Hikmat al-Khani, sir," said Khaled.

"What does your father do?" said the official.

"He's dead, sir," said Khaled.

"When and how?" said the official.

"He died during the events, he was killed by the army," said Khaled.

"What!" shouted the man.

All six got up, removed their jackets and took turns slapping and punching Khaled. He was knocked to the floor and screamed as he was being kicked. The principal rescued him.

"I am so sorry, gentlemen. Leave it to me, I am going to teach this scoundrel a lesson," said the principal as he escorted Khaled out of the room and hid him in his office.

Khaled was supposed to say that Islamist terrorists had killed his father. He was supposed to forget those who witnessed his father being captured by regime forces and taken with thousands of other men to the porcelain factory where he was tortured and gruesomely executed. Hamwis had to live with the regime's lies even in the privacy of their homes. To cope, many massacre survivors became convinced that Hafez was the nation's strict yet benevolent father who punished Hama only because he was left with no other choice.

"Childhood was a continuous horror movie," Khaled wrote years later in his diary after he reconstructed what had happened to his father, family, and city by interviewing dozens of relatives and witnesses.[10]

The uncontestable truth was that the regime had meticulously planned the assault on Hama in 1982, completely subdued a few hundred Islamist fighters in about ten days, then vengefully massacred thousands of civilians, raped women, looted homes, and razed neighborhoods, and then at the end wanted victims to believe that "terrorists" had done it to them. It was a scenario repeating itself in 2011 from the moment protesters were killed in the southern city of Daraa and in Douma near Damascus. Regime forces and Bashar's own cousin Hafez Makhlouf shot protesters dead, but the regime wanted the world to believe that the culprits were infiltrators linked to a foreign conspiracy.

"False allegations and distortion of reality" and "fake pretenses," Bashar told Barbara Walters when she interviewed him in Damascus later in 2011.[11]

✡   ✡   ✡

The large protests that gripped Hama in the waning days of spring 2011 were not only from a brutalized city finally speaking out but also from many regime opponents, like Mazen Darwish and Khaled al-Khani, who were desperate to keep the protests peaceful and prevent the country from plunging into extremism and war. It was an attempt to stop the Hama 1982 scenario from repeating itself in almost every rebellious city, town, and village across Syria.

By early June 2011, more than 1,100 had been killed and thousands arrested in attacks on demonstrators as well as in military operations in places like Baniyas, Daraa, Douma, and Homs, among others.[12] There were already signs that the regime's actions were fueling militancy in communities coming under attack and emboldening those pushing for armed confrontation.

A killing in Jisr al-Shughour—a predominantly Sunni town north of Hama where nearly 200 civilians had been killed by Hafez's forces in the spring of 1980—morphed into armed clashes between, on the one hand, Sunni residents and some Sunni army soldiers and, on the other, the mostly Alawite *mukhabarat*. Armed townspeople and soldiers who had defected to their side besieged a local unit of the *mukhabarat's* Military Intelligence Directorate and eventually stormed it and then executed all those inside, many of them Alawites. Reinforcements were sent to the town, and ultimately Bashar's forces prevailed as many residents fled to neighboring Turkey.[13] The regime said that armed groups killed 120 soldiers in what it called a massacre and claimed that townspeople had asked for the army's help.[14] The regime took foreign diplomats and journalists to the area—an ideal opportunity to buttress its narrative of foreign conspiracy and Islamist extremists.[15]

Then thousands took to the streets of Hama in early June 2011 to say enough death, no more massacres like Hama 1982. As they tried to traverse the river from Hama's Hader section to Asi Square, they were met with deadly force by regime snipers and gunmen on the street as well as those posted on the rooftop of the local Baath Party headquarters building.[16] More than sixty were killed, most wounds were in the chest and head. Nearly the entire city was on strike for days.[17] Regime forces withdrew to the city's outskirts, fearing the population's wrath. Larger protests followed in mid-June, culminating in the occupation of Asi Square.

As thousands poured into the square, large loudspeakers mounted on the back of a truck blared a moving song by an activist from southern Syria that had become the anthem of Syria's revolt.[18] "The youth, oh mother, heard freedom was at the gate, and they went out to chant for it... They struck us, oh mother, with live bullets..."

Protesters stayed in the square day and night. In solidarity, restaurant owners distributed free food.[19] The numbers on the street grew day by day. It became a carnival-like atmosphere. They danced the local Hamwi version of *dabkeh*, a traditional Levantine line dance. People were fired up by folksy anti-regime chants performed by a local activist and revolutionary singer nicknamed "the Qashoush."

"We want to remove Bashar with our strong will because Syria wants freedom! Syria wants...," shouted Qashoush with a raspy voice and rhythmic cadence.[20]

"Freedom!" erupted the crowd.

"*Souriya badda...*" ("Syria wants..."), repeated Qashoush.

"*Hurriyeh!*" ("Freedom!"), the crowd answered fervently.

Protesters declared the city theirs. They set up citizen patrols and checkpoints to protect protesters and warn of any incursion by regime forces. At first, few of those assuming security functions had weapons. It was mostly batons and sticks. Hama's Asi Square became the equivalent of Cairo's Tahrir Square. Similar attempts in Damascus and Homs in April were snuffed out by Bashar with bullets and blood.

At the palace in Damascus, Bashar was stressed out about the growing protests in Hama and the occupation of Asi Square.[21]

Manaf, sidelined by Bashar for being too soft, had nonetheless remained in his position as Republican Guard general and continued to interact with those around Bashar.

"The president is very disturbed by what's happening in Hama—why don't you speak with your contacts and see how we can calm things down," a fellow Republican Guard commander urged Manaf.[22]

There was little he could do, regardless of his differences with Bashar over the use of force. For protesters in Hama and elsewhere, who were now demanding Bashar's departure more fervently than before, the Tlasses were symbols of the regime they loathed.

Manaf was told that the Hama protesters were being joined by people from all over central and northern Syria: Aleppo, Homs, and his native Al-Rastan. Bashar had hoped that the sweeping military campaigns—starting with Daraa in late April—would have quelled the protests. As concessions, he had pardoned prisoners and tasked a committee led by his vice president, Farouq al-Sharaa, to prepare for a conference with opposition figures to discuss his proposed reforms.[23] But few if any of them had sway over the street protests.

Before his mood was soured by the takeover of Hama's Asi Square by protesters, Bashar had been in good spirits. He had resumed his tennis routine and was sleeping well at night and spending more time with his wife and children. He thought his tanks and soldiers had squelched the uprising and he was also emboldened by assurances he received from his two most important allies, Iran and its proxy, the Lebanese militia Hezbollah. They were going to defend him—no matter what. They just needed him to remain strong and steadfast.[24]

"Imagine what would happen if millions of...Arabs and Muslims... gather at the border with occupied Palestine at the same time and we want to cross the fence. What would Israel do? What would Obama do?" said Hezbollah chief Hassan Nasrallah the previous month (May 2011), threatening to harm Israel if the United States were to go after Bashar.[25]

Nasrallah spoke after Hezbollah and the Syrian regime had encouraged and assisted Palestinian activists and protesters in both Lebanon and Syria to approach the high-security border with Israel to mark the anniversary of what Arabs call the *nakba*, or catastrophe—the founding of the state of Israel in 1948. In Syria, protesters breached the fence and crossed to the Golan Heights, prompting Israeli soldiers to shoot at them. At the Lebanese border at least ten were killed, and another four in Syria.[26] The incident in Syria was unprecedented; the Israeli-Syrian border was the calmest front in the Arab-Israeli war.

The violence achieved several purposes for Bashar, Hezbollah, and Iran. First, the attention it generated deflected from Bashar's bloody campaign against protesters who derided him for using the army and tanks against them while not daring to do anything similar to Israel, which the regime claimed to be the eternal enemy. More important for Bashar and his allies, it was a message to the Americans and Europeans: expect regional mayhem if you pressure the regime and back the protesters.

Nasrallah said that the incident "terrified" Israel, which he claimed was conspiring to oust Bashar to undermine his "axis of resistance" alliance with Hezbollah and Iran.

It was far from the truth. Israel had over the years come to greatly value and appreciate the predictability of the Syrian regime when it came to the Golan Heights, despite Bashar's alliance with Hezbollah and Iran. In fact, days before the border breach, Bashar's cousin Rami Makhlouf suggested that any attempt to get rid of Bashar would be detrimental to Israel's security. "If there is no stability here, there's no way there will be stability in Israel," Rami told the *New York Times*.[27] "Don't let us suffer, don't put a lot of pressure on the president, don't push Syria to do anything it is not happy to do."

In addition to exploiting the highly charged issue of Israel's security and its very existence, Bashar and his allies could also count on emerging discord among regional and world powers over how to deal with the cataclysm called the Arab Spring.

The United States and its allies, the same countries that had embraced Bashar starting in 2007 and had held out hope that he could stop the killing and institute real change a few months into the uprising in 2011, were now adopting a more confrontational and threatening posture toward his regime.

Britain, France, and the United States believed that only pressure could restrain Bashar's devastating force against protesting communities. They tried to gather support for a UN Security Council resolution against the Syrian regime, but Russia, a Security Council member and traditional ally of Syria, signaled that it would veto the resolution.[28] The Chinese, who were averse to Western powers interfering in what they saw as the internal affairs of sovereign states, were also likely to side with the Russians. Moscow was already feeling betrayed on Libya. A UN resolution passed earlier in the year in relation to Libya was used by Western powers as cover for massive military support for armed opposition groups seeking to topple Gaddafi, something outside the mandate to protect civilians, according to Russia.

Bashar also found solace in the many fissures among regional powers.

At the start of the Arab Spring, ultraconservative and politically cautious Saudi Arabia watched the revolts with alarm, while the Al Jazeera news channel owned by its neighbor Qatar played a decisive role in mobilizing the masses. The Saudis sheltered Tunisia's strongman, Zine al-Abidine Ben Ali, and his wife when they fled their country in the face of street protests, and they looked on with horror as another longtime protégé, Hosni Mubarak, was cast aside in Egypt even as Qatar keenly sought to shape the aftermath in both countries by supporting the Muslim Brotherhood, a pan-Islamic movement. Qatar's emir Hamad bin Khalifa al-Thani told Western leaders that these were enlightened Islamists who believed in democracy, and that giving them a stake in political life was the antidote to the kind of Al-Qaeda-like extremism that obsessed the West.

While Saudi monarchs blamed Bashar for killing their man Hariri in Lebanon in 2005 and were perfectly content to see the Assad family toppled and replaced with friendlier, more-pliant leaders, the whole spirit of the Arab Spring was anathema to them. What if their own repressed subjects took to the streets and demanded the same freedoms and rights? That's what people were singing for day and night across the border in Yemen. Saudi Arabia also fretted about its archnemesis Iran, claiming it was behind events in nearby Bahrain, where protests led mainly by the long-oppressed Shiite population besieged the Saudi ruling family's fellow royals. The Saudis sent troops to crush Bahrain's budding protests.

Saudi Arabia was already anxious about Iran's expanding role in Iraq, where Obama planned to withdraw US troops and thereby leave the strategic and oil-rich country in Iran's clutches, as far as the Saudis were concerned. Israel had many of the same worries as Saudi Arabia, especially concerning Iran and the situation in Egypt.

But by late spring 2011, Qatar's emir, Hamad, believed in his great power to influence and conceive outcomes in all countries touched by the Arab Spring—and Syria would be no exception. Qatar was hardly a beacon of democracy and human rights—a small sheikhdom whose natural gas fortune is controlled by a ruling clan that has little tolerance for criticism and dissent at home — but the country's maverick emir saw in the Arab Spring a tremendous opportunity. For years Hamad, who had deposed his own father in the mid-1990s, had been on a quest to turn Qatar into a hefty regional player and upstage his larger and more established neighbor, Saudi Arabia. Hamad was going to ride the Arab Spring wave and benefit from it — not fight it like his fellow autocrats.

In Libya, Qatar joined the Western-led coalition to topple Gaddafi, supplying cash and planeloads of weapons to anti-Gaddafi forces and sending its own commandos.[29]

Hamad began to turn against Bashar after having invested billions to prop him up and passionately advocated for reengagement with him following Hariri's murder in 2005.[30] The emir had tried for several months into the Syrian uprising to convince Bashar to make bold political reforms and even forge a reconciliation with the Muslim Brotherhood, which Hafez had decimated in the 1980s. Shortly after Bashar's bloody crackdown on protesters in March 2011, the emir sent his son the crown prince to Damascus. At one point during his meeting with Bashar, Prince Tamim went to the window and pointed to a slum visible from the presidential palace. "Do you see this area?" he asked. "We are ready to help you turn it into the most prestigious neighborhood in Damascus…but please don't let the situation explode any further."[31]

Bashar assured Tamim that things were not as bad as they were being portrayed in the media, but soon thereafter he launched the military operations of April and May against protesting areas. By June, Qatar had lost patience with Bashar, and the emir told one visitor that he was determined to do everything possible to remove the Assads from power, including gathering international support for a Libya-style intervention in Syria, if need be.[32]

The emir's ally, Turkey's Islamist strongman Recep Tayyip Erdogan, also sent top officials to urge Bashar to exercise restraint on the streets — but to no avail.[33] Like the emir, Erdogan saw the Arab Spring as a unique chance to boost his country's standing in a region it regarded as its backyard. Turkey also had a big stake in Syria, with which it was bound by blood ties, a shared border, and trade.

As these countries plotted their next moves in Syria, Bashar was nonetheless feeling buoyant and confident; Iran vowed never to abandon him and Russia shielded him at the United Nations. In early June 2011, Bashar wanted to send a message to his enemies that he was Syria's master and intended to remain so. He received Lebanese leader Walid Jumblatt, who came to see him after meeting Qatar's emir.[34] The shrewd and pragmatic Jumblatt had had his ups and downs with the Assads ever since he accused Hafez of assassinating his father during the Lebanese civil war in the 1970s.

Jumblatt and an associate arrived at the official People's Palace on the Mezzeh plateau. Bashar was waiting in one of the more intimate reception rooms in what was otherwise a cavernous marble fortress. He looked rested and refreshed.

"Do you want press?" Bashar asked after greeting his guests.

"Yes, sure, yes," responded Jumblatt nervously.

They sat on damask cushions on carved wooden sofas as a photographer snapped photos.[35] Bashar wanted to show that he was not isolated and was receiving guests regularly.

"Did you notice that there were no longer any billboards of my father in Damascus?" asked Bashar with a smile after exchanging some pleasantries.[36]

"Yes, you're right," said Jumblatt, not quite knowing what to make of the remark.

But of course it was Bashar's way of saying: I am paramount leader now. "What's on your mind?" he inquired.

"You want me to speak frankly and in confidence," said Jumblatt.

"Yes, speak, do not worry," Bashar assured him.

"What's the story of Hamza al-Khatib?" asked Jumblatt.

The round-faced thirteen-year-old boy was among those who had been arrested in Daraa by regime forces at the end of April. He died from severe torture by the *mukhabarat*, and his mutilated body was handed over to his family a month later. His penis had been cut off.[37]

Hamza became a symbol of the regime's brutality around the world.

"We did not torture him," insisted Bashar. "I met his parents and told them that his body was bloated because he was starting to decompose."

"But did you kill him?" asked Jumblatt cautiously.

Bashar went on, rather breezily, to explain the shortcomings of his security forces and their lack of training in dealing with protesters on the streets and those taken into custody. The regime's story was that Hamza had died in street clashes and then his body remained at the morgue in Damascus for a month.

Eager to change the subject, Bashar told Jumblatt how some of the delegations he had been meeting with included a group of actors and directors who were worried about his personal safety. Bashar claimed that they told him they were hearing rumors that he was not in control of the situation—something no Syrian would ever dare say to the regime head, and Bashar knew that Jumblatt knew this. It was a roundabout way for Bashar to make a point. "I told them, 'Do not worry—I am in full control but I need people to fear me,'" said Bashar.[38]

"But people must love you, not fear you, Mr. President," said Jumblatt.

Bashar, however, knew perfectly well that in his regime the love, adoration, and support of most Syrians—the majority of people and not just the committed and diehard loyalists—was as fictitious as Syria's presidential referendums and popular rallies. Fear was the only real thing. The so-called gray majority, which was in the middle and had not yet decided to join the protesters, must once more fear him and his regime. The fear barrier breached by the courageous protesters and activists had to be reinstated.

"It's either us or them—we are going to fight until the end," Bashar's longtime mentor and adviser Mohammad Nasif told Jumblatt, who dropped in to see him after his meeting with Bashar. The massive protests sweeping Hama in June 2011 only affirmed to hardened old-timers like Nasif that what they were dealing with was no different from what Hafez had faced three decades before.

It was a rejection of any compromise or real political solution as advocated by the United States and its Arab and European allies.[39] It was a pivotal moment for Bashar; Iran and Russia were telling him, "Don't worry, you can count on us to help you crush the protests and confront these outside powers," yet he still needed to make sure that everyone in his regime was on board for the battle.

By then there was no doubt in Manaf's mind that his childhood friend had in fact been the one leading regime hard-liners from the start, not the other way around.[40] But there was one impediment Bashar faced, at least initially, in proceeding full throttle with his plans to crush the protests. Not everyone inside the regime was ready to embrace the fight-until-the-end game plan. Manaf was not alone in seeing matters differently and advocating for a less bloody approach. Manaf perceived nuances and differences of opinion even inside the *mukhabarat*. Cracks, dissent, and vulnerabilities within the regime were starting to become evident to Bashar, too. Army desertions and the first few televised public defections by junior officers like Manaf's cousin did not help the cause. In Jisr al-Shughour, soldiers aided townspeople in the bloody attack on the *mukhabarat* contingent there.

Most troubling of all, though, was the internal feud that played out between his minister of defense, Ali Habib, and Jamil Hassan, who headed the Air Force Intelligence Directorate, one of the four *mukhabarat* agencies.[41] Habib believed that it was a mistake to mobilize tanks and soldiers to quell the protests, while Hassan, considered a regime fanatic, wanted to use any and all means to obliterate protesters. Hassan had been a first lieutenant in Hafez's forces when Hama was massacred in 1982, and he yearned for similar solutions under Bashar.[42] The standoff between Habib and Hassan came to a head in mid-June 2011, when hundreds of thousands of protesters occupied Hama's main square.[43]

Habib started ignoring instructions by Hassan and Bashar's cousin Hafez Makhlouf to issue formal orders to mobilize army units or provide military resources like tanks, artillery, and heavy weaponry for operations against Hama and other protest towns and cities. Habib was a major general and a decorated veteran of the Syrian military, but at the end he served at the whim of the Assad and Makhlouf families and powerful *mukhabarat* chiefs, even though some were technically lower in rank.

Habib often delayed implementing orders coming from *mukhabarat* chiefs and at one point checked himself into the hospital for forty-eight hours, pretending he had a medical emergency in order to avoid the orders. When Hassan called him at the hospital, Habib said, "It's not my business, do what you want."[44]

There was also a rare challenge to the *mukhabarat* from one of Habib's subordinates.

Hassan called the commander of military police, Abdelaziz al-Shallal, and asked him to dispatch one of his units for the assault that Hassan and others were preparing on Hama.

"I don't take orders from you, I report to the defense minister," said Shallal bluntly.

"Okay, we will settle this later," replied Hassan menacingly.

It was not only Habib; Manaf felt that there was reticence by several senior regime figures to fully embrace the solutions of the Assad family and the hard-liners. They included Bashar's vice president, Farouq al-Sharaa, military adviser and former defense minister Hassan Turkmani, and to some lesser extent the head of the *mukhabarat*'s Military Intelligence Directorate, Abdul-Fatah Qudsiyeh. Manaf also sensed doubt on the part of Bashar's brother-in-law Assef Shawkat, who held the formal position of deputy defense minister. He was demoted and sidelined by Bashar in 2008 but then asked to help when the uprising started. His wife, Bashar's sister Bushra, returned from the United Arab Emirates.

Still, nobody dared voice or share their concerns openly. Everyone believed that they were being watched. Extreme caution and self-preservation became the absolute priority for Manaf and all top regime officials, notwithstanding their misgivings. "People started having double personalities to protect themselves," said Manaf. "It was hard to figure out the truth. You could not tell who was with you and who was out to entrap you."

Bashar was leading the hard-liners and wanted to decimate the protests, but he had to proceed cautiously, given the internal discord. He had to appear as if he were taking a middle-of-the-road position and catering to both camps in his regime: the bloodthirsty hard-liners and those favoring less violent solutions and accommodation. This was amply reflected in a carefully staged appearance at the University of Damascus. Bashar told students that the majority of protesters were people with "legitimate demands," and he even spoke of the need to heal the wounds and reverse the injustices of what he called "the dark period" of the 1980s, when his father crushed opponents and committed the Hama massacre.[45] He spoke about reconciliation and dialogue.

At the same time, Bashar spoke of traitors, criminals, and Islamist extremists among the protesters, whom he accused of allegedly shooting at the protests to foment strife. In a forewarning that also seemed like a veiled threat, Bashar mused about the number of alleged fugitive criminals wanted by the regime, which he put at 64,000 and then said, "I was shocked by the number…a real army. Imagine the extent of harm they could cause if even just a few thousand decide to bear arms and become saboteurs."

In another nod to hard-liners, Bashar used what would become a characteristic medical/clinical analogy when he likened his opponents to "multiplying germs." "We can't completely eradicate them [the germs], but we can work on strengthening the immunity of our bodies," he said.

Of course, nowhere in Bashar's speech was there any mention of the fact that he himself had just pardoned more than a thousand battle-hardened and radicalized prisoners as part of a broader amnesty. With the help of his *mukhabarat*, many had previously gone to Iraq after the US-led invasion to join Sunni insurgent groups, including Al-Qaeda's affiliate.[46] Upon their return to Syria, many were rounded up and imprisoned so that Bashar could show the Obama administration that he was fighting terrorism. Among the released prisoners were several Hama natives that Khaled al-Khani knew personally and had learned over the years that they had become members of Al-Qaeda's branch in Iraq.[47] Fresh from prison, they joined protesters in Hama in the summer of 2011 and were among the first to advocate bearing arms in the name of protecting civilians from the regime.

To Manaf, Bashar's actions were a deliberate effort to poison the protest movement and validate early lies that fundamentalists and extremists were its driving force. Manaf also witnessed something more sinister. The *mukhabarat* was making weapons, mainly assault rifles, available to elements of the protesters through infiltrators and agents. Leading this effort were people like Rafic Shehadeh, who commanded the powerful Unit 293 of the Military Intelligence Directorate and was eager to outdo his direct boss, Qudsiyeh.[48] The emergence of weapons among protesters meant the regime could claim that it faced an armed insurrection requiring military intervention.

In tandem with this, Bashar hunted all articulate, moderate, and secular protest activists in much the same way that Hafez had gone after the professionals and non-Islamist opponents first, people like Khaled's father, Dr. Khani, and Omar al-Shishakli.

In late spring 2011, Khaled was on the run from the *mukhabarat*. His neighbors warned him through coded messages not to go to his apartment or art studio. He hid in Damascus and then Hama. The memories of Hama and what had happened to his father and Shishakli had already traumatized Khaled for life. He could not live through such horror a second time. He wanted the regime to fall and was ready to do everything to achieve that, but the regime's increased viciousness petrified him. Violence was not his domain. After Bashar issued the amnesty, Khaled left Syria for Germany under the pretext of participating in an arts festival there. His visa was for two weeks. After four days in Germany he went to France, even as protests in his hometown Hama swelled. "Bashar is going to fall within a week, and I am returning to Syria," he told friends in Paris.

Back in Damascus, Manaf could no longer bear Bashar's lies, logorrheic discourse, and his "philosophical and theoretical musings," as Manaf described them, but self-preservation required that he maintain a connection to his childhood friend.[49] Bashar and the shared history of the Assads and Tlasses were his only protection in the face of threats from Bashar's brother, Maher, and cousins the Makhloufs. Maher was already calling Manaf "the mutinous brigadier general."

Manaf, who had been brigadier general for eight years, was passed over in the round of military promotions approved by Bashar in the summer of 2011. It was both a snub and a warning to Manaf.

Still, Manaf and the Tlasses had to demonstrate to Bashar that they were not abandoning the regime — despite their grave concerns over his actions including in their hometown, Al-Rastan. Both Manaf and his father worried about the repercussions for them from the mounting defections by junior officers in their family and hometown, and so they tried to show Bashar that they were doing their utmost to stop this.

One thing was certain: Manaf and his father were drawing a big distinction between Bashar and regime founder Hafez. Their allegiance to Hafez was and would remain absolute.

Both Tlasses, father and son, eagerly supported Bashar's ascension to power, because this was Hafez's wish. But over the years they saw Bashar's shortcomings and the influence accumulated by his brother and cousins and allies such as Hezbollah and Iran. Hafez would have never allowed it, the Tlasses believed. Their dissatisfaction also stemmed from the fact that the others had gained the power due to families like theirs, which Bashar often called the "old guard." The Tlasses' concerns over Bashar's leadership came into sharper focus at the start of the uprising. Their feeling was that Hafez would have never let the situation deteriorate so badly or let hard-liners hijack management of the crisis facing the regime. Paradoxically, there were still those among the hard-liners who viewed Bashar as too soft compared to Hafez, whose response, they thought, would have been swifter and more lethal.

Even as her husband's loyalty to his old friend wavered, Manaf's wife, Thala, tried to maintain a line to Bashar. She hoped that it would shield her husband from his enemies inside the regime.

They e-mailed and sometimes talked by phone, and in June Thala broached a subject dear to Bashar's heart: using the media to alter facts about his bloody crackdown. Thala suggested that his media and political adviser, Bouthaina Shaaban, and Ibrahim Daraji, an articulate and young international law professor, be interviewed by a French-language website called *INFOSyrie*. She said that questions could be e-mailed to them in advance.[50] The website was established by a French far-right, neo-Nazi figure who had founded a public relations firm funded by the Tlasses in the 1990s and awarded a contract by the regime.[51] The website claimed that it wanted to "re-inform" the francophone public about events in Syria."[52] Bashar welcomed Thala's suggestion.

But even as they sent signals of their allegiance, Manaf and Thala realized that the confrontation between the regime and its opponents was going to be bloody and prolonged. Regional and global powers were staking their positions, and the Tlasses would have to choose sides if they wished to remain in Syria. The United States and Europe were already indicating they would not just stand by while Bashar continued to slaughter protesters. Manaf was aware that Qatar had started facilitating the defection of army officers by offering safe passage for them and their families out of Syria, as well as protection and financial support once they were out.[53] There were already whispers about defection plans by officers and soldiers in Manaf's own Republican Guard unit.

Manaf and Thala decided to meet secretly with their friend, the French ambassador Éric Chevallier, for the first time since the start of the uprising in March 2011. Chevallier was told to go to an office on the second floor of a building in central Damascus, and he was then taken to another floor, higher up, where Manaf and Thala were waiting for him.[54]

Manaf recounted to Chevallier his efforts to avert the use of force and initiate dialogue with protesters, especially in suburban Damascus, with what he thought was the blessing and support of Bashar, and how he had been undermined by hard-liners every step of the way, and then felt betrayed by Bashar. "Bashar fooled me," Manaf told Chevallier. "I am no longer involved in anything—I am out."[55]

He did not tell Chevallier that he wanted to defect, but the diplomat sensed that abandoning the regime was very much on Manaf's mind. Talk of rifts at the palace was real after all, thought Chevalier.

Days later, Bashar and Asma showed up at the Jala'a stadium in Mezzeh, near Manaf's home. They were dressed casually in jeans and light jackets. The regime had come up with the idea of sending what it said was the largest Syrian flag ever made to Aleppo, a city that had seen few protests so far; it was presented as a spontaneous youth initiative on Facebook.

A few dozen young men and women gathered on the stadium's turf.[56] "Abu Hafez, Abu Hafez, Abu Hafez!" they shouted and pumped their fists in the air as they saw Bashar and Asma arrive. They raced to hug and kiss Bashar. He smiled nervously as he was mobbed and was then handed a little girl to hold.[57]

"Make way, guys," shouted one of the organizers.

Then Bashar and Asma got on their knees with the others and began rolling the giant flag so that it could be sent to Aleppo, as cameramen snapped photos.[58]

"One, two, three—Bashar, you're my life," loyalists chanted. "Bashar, you're after God."

The following day, on July 1, 2011, several hundred thousand people gathered in Hama's Asi Square for what was described as the largest protest since the start of the revolt in March. Some estimated the crowd to be as big as half a million.[59]

Activists decided to call that day of protests in Hama and across Syria the "Friday of *Erhal.*" Across the Middle East, *Erhal* ("Leave") became a rallying cry among protesters who were challenging their autocratic rulers and ordering them to step down from power—to leave. Hama's revolutionary singer Qashoush rocked the city with his new chant *"Yalla Erhal Ya, Bashar!"* ("Come on, Bashar, Leave!").

"Bashar, despicable one, the blood of martyrs is not cheap, pack your stuff in a plastic bag...Come on, Bashar, leave!" chanted Qashoush as he stood on a makeshift stage next to Asi Square's clock tower.[60]

"Yalla erhal ya, Bashar!" repeated the crowd with zeal.

People carried balloons and waved flags. There was Syria's current red, white, and black flag as well as the old green, white, and black one that predated the Baath coup in 1963. There were also Turkish flags to show appreciation for Erdogan's warning to Bashar to not repeat what his father did in Hama in 1982.

That day, protesting Hamwis declared their city liberated from the regime. Some went as far as to curse Hafez's soul.

Bashar's response came a few days later. The city was besieged by regime forces that included army soldiers, *mukhabarat* units, and the pro-regime thugs known as *shabiha*. The defense minister, Habib, wanted nothing to do with the operation. The pro-Bashar forces amassed on the city's outskirts began raiding neighborhoods and arresting dozens of male children and adults. At least sixteen were killed within forty-eight hours.[61] Protesters could see tanks and heavy weapons being brought to the city, but they were determined to hold on to their square, their patch of liberty and freedom of expression. So they blocked all roads leading to the central Asi Square with large dumpsters, concrete blocks, and flaming tires. Some of the more militant elements among the protesters, especially those newly released from prison by Bashar, spoke of the need to take up arms to defend Hama against an imminent massacre.

Meanwhile in Damascus, the French ambassador Chevallier met with fellow Western diplomats, including US ambassador Robert Ford, for lunch at the Italian embassy.[62] Chevallier and Ford argued it was crucial to go to Hama. They wanted to use the freedom of movement they had as diplomats to assess the situation for themselves. Syria's foreign ministry had informed all diplomats that they must get permission for travel outside the capital; it wanted to restrict them to fact-finding trips that the ministry itself organized for them. Chevallier and Ford, however, felt that it was important to show solidarity with the large number of protesters in Hama who were coming under assault by the regime.

Chevallier and Ford went separately to Hama. They liaised with opposition activists in the city who found a way to get them in despite the large presence of regime forces, mainly on the southern and western sides.[63]

On the night of July 7, 2011, Chevallier, a physician by training, made it to the Fida al-Hourani hospital where many of the casualties had been taken. He was cheered by staff and patients. In the emergency ward, he met two teenagers who had suffered multiple gunshot wounds. As he came out of the hospital he was met with more cheers and applause.

"Vive la France!" shouted a crowd that had gathered outside.

People on motorbikes insisted on escorting his car to the Afamia al-Cham Hotel, across the river. He passed through Asi Square, where protesters were determined to stay to defy the regime forces closing in on them. They set tires on fire and put other obstacles on the roads leading to the square to try to impede these forces. The protesters removed them briefly to let Chevallier's car through.[64]

The next day, heartened and feeling protected by the two ambassadors' presence, people gathered once more in large numbers in Asi Square. Many welcomed the Western visitors with roses. Chevallier left but Ford stayed on a bit longer and was mobbed by cheering crowds.[65]

"Tell Ford he has twenty-four hours to apologize to the Syrian people because he breached diplomatic norms — otherwise I am storming the US embassy," Mohammad Jaber, who was working for Bashar's brother, Maher, told prominent Damascene businessman Emad Ghreiwati, whose brother headed the Syrian American Business Council.[66]

No apology was forthcoming. Jaber and busloads of his men and regime loyalists, including some women, besieged both the American and French embassies. By then Jaber was starting to organize his *shabiha* thugs into what was called Popular Committees. They gathered with posters of a smiling Bashar dressed in military uniform and flags of Syria and the Lebanese militia Hezbollah. One placard read: "To whom it may concern, Syria is the resistance capital."[67]

The US embassy is within walking distance from Bashar's residence, and the French embassy is not far either. This was the capital's most secure area, bristling with armed agents protecting the perimeter of Bashar's compound. Nobody interfered when Jaber's men scaled the US embassy's wall and attempted also to smash their way into the French embassy. They were turned back by guards at both sites, with those at the French embassy firing shots in the air. The exterior of both embassies was vandalized.[68] "Fuk off Amrica," they scrawled in red on the US embassy wall.

The ambassadors' visit to Hama bought protesters an almost twenty-day reprieve. On July 29, 2011, hundreds of thousands amassed in the city center. Large banners covered the facades of government buildings around the square. The banners bore slogans addressed to Bashar: "Game Over" and "Leave, Syria is more beautiful without you!"

Two days later, Bashar ordered the army to crush the protests and reclaim control of the rebellious city. By then Bashar had removed his uncooperative and reticent defense minister, Ali Habib, and put him under house arrest.[69] Tanks and armored vehicles thundered into Hama's city center from all directions. A few of the protesters who had taken up arms in the weeks before tried to resist. Others raided armories of neighborhood police stations and took weapons to try to defend their city.[70] But they were no match for tanks and antiaircraft guns. Several hundred people, the majority civilians, were killed.[71] Within five days, Bashar retook the city that had been passionately chanting for his ouster.

"There's no God but Bashar," his forces sprayed on the walls of the city his father had massacred three decades earlier.[72]

15

Don't Stay with the Butcher

Bashar al-Assad waved to the crowds as he briskly came down the marble stairs of the Assad Library and made his way toward a stage set up in Umayyad Square in the heart of Damascus. He wore gray slacks, an open-neck light-blue shirt, and a navy blazer.[1] Almost a dozen bodyguards trailed him.

On stage, a chorus of youth supporters dressed in winter jackets in the colors of the Syrian flag applauded and swayed to a song composed for Bashar. Being wrapped in the Syrian flag meant you were not a traitor but a true patriot who embraced Bashar, was the regime's message. A cheerleader jumped up and down while another, in camouflage pants, pumped his fist in the air.

"*Menhebak, menhebak, menhebak...*" ("We love you, we love you, we love you..."), roared the giant loudspeakers.

Thousands of loyalists filled the square waving flags, holding up posters of Bashar, and chanting his name. They became hysterical the moment he appeared onstage.

"For your eyes, Assad, we're *shabiha* forever!" they repeated feverishly, proudly associating themselves with the thugs mobilized by the regime to assist the army and security forces in their bloody crackdown on protesters. Barricades manned by dozens of guards separated the crowd from Bashar, who looked ecstatic, confident, and even brazen. Appearing beloved was the perfect riposte to his enemies.

It was early January 2012, nearly ten months since the start of anti-regime protests. Each attempt by Bashar's opponents to rally in a similar way in a major square was met with lethal force. In April 2011, protesters were hunted and killed by regime snipers as they tried to reach Abbaseen Square in Damascus. That same month, regime soldiers and *shabiha*, including loyalist college students, attacked a sit-in at Clock Tower Square in Homs where more than 100,000 people had gathered at one point. Dozens were killed or wounded in the assault.[2] The opposition's occupation of Asi Square in Hama lasted weeks and attracted close to one million people on several occasions, but it ended with a military operation against the city in late July 2011. Hundreds were killed.

Now Bashar and his family and security services were orchestrating pro-regime rallies in the same squares that they were violently thwarting their opponents from holding. It was a defiant response to international efforts underway for several months to pressure the regime and force Bashar to leave power.

"For the sake of the Syrian people, the time has come for President Assad to step aside," said Obama in August 2011, as he praised the courage of peaceful protesters in the face of "ferocious brutality at the hands of their government."[3]

Obama also imposed sweeping sanctions against the regime, including restrictions on its ability to sell oil and oil products, one of its main sources of hard currency. After Obama spoke, leaders of France, Germany, and the United Kingdom said that Bashar had "lost all legitimacy," while the European Union passed its own sanctions against the regime.[4] That month there was already talk of the possibility of referring the Syrian regime to the International Criminal Court for "widespread...systematic attacks against the civilian population."[5]

In the fall of 2011, the Syrian National Council, an opposition body made up mostly of figures living in exile, was unveiled in the Turkish city of Istanbul. Burhan Ghalyoun, the affable Paris-based professor who used to lecture about political reform during the brief Damascus Spring in Bashar's first year in power, was chosen to head the opposition council.[6] This was the body that was meant to rule Syria on an interim basis upon Bashar's exit from power.

For the Assads, though, the battle for survival was just beginning.

Bashar was confident that his allies Iran and the Lebanese Shiite militia, Hezbollah, would do everything to defend him. They had signaled to

Obama early on that any move against Bashar could trigger retaliation against Israel and Western interests in the region.

"We are related to different problems [in the Middle East]. If they isolate Syria, Syria will collapse and it's going to be domino effect, everybody will suffer, so they don't have interest to isolate Syria," Bashar reminded the West when he spoke to Barbara Walters, a month before his boisterous Damascus rally at the start of 2012.[7]

Bashar also counted on the regime's constant ally Russia, which was enraged over how Western powers had used an earlier UN Security Council resolution meant for the protection of civilians in Libya as cover for regime change in that country. On October 4, 2011, Russia vetoed the first proposed Security Council resolution concerning Syria since the start of protests. Russia was joined by China.[8] The resolution had simply called on the regime to end its military offensives against protesting communities and spoke of the need for a political solution to the crisis.

Bashar derived added comfort from the fact that despite Obama's tough words and calls for Bashar to relinquish power, the US president had made it clear early on that the US would not intervene militarily in Syria to oust Bashar or act without a UN mandate. Obama's priority was to get remaining US troops out of Iraq, not plunge into another regime-change endeavor in neighboring Syria.

It became amply evident to Bashar, after he crushed the protests in Hama in the summer of 2011, that there would be no NATO military intervention in Syria against his regime, as there had been in Libya. NATO's secretary general "completely" ruled out intervention in Syria.[9] No Western powers rushed to save Hama or any other Syrian town the way they had rescued the Libyan city of Benghazi from being overrun by Gaddafi's troops. The visit by the French and US ambassadors to Hama when it was under the control of protesters might have given the city a reprieve for a few weeks, but ultimately Bashar assaulted Hama and neither NATO nor France and the United States intervened to stop him.

"The fact is we failed to protect them. But was it so easy? Did we have a magic bullet at that time? Military intervention at that moment without Security Council resolution? Not so easy," said France's ambassador Chevallier afterward.[10]

What happened in Hama in the summer of 2011 was just the start of a string of dashed expectations and bitter disappointments for Bashar's opponents. This sense of letdown and betrayal stemmed from the world-view of most people in Syria and the Middle East. For many, when the ambassadors of France and the United States, two powers that regarded themselves as defenders of universal liberty and human rights, visited protesters in Hama, then it should have automatically led to protection. And when the president of a superpower like the United States said Bashar had to step down, then that was going to become fact.

In contrast, Bashar and his allies quickly realized the limitations of any Western action against the regime. Bashar regarded his impunity as a given, rooted in the region and his family's place in its history but also in the wayward and unsteady attention of those who wished to stop him.

Bashar and his allies concluded that time was on their side.

Beginning in the summer of 2011, their priorities were surviving international sanctions, closing ranks, minimizing the impact of army defections, and, most important, eliminating all those organizing peaceful resistance to the regime. Like his father before him, it was absolutely vital for Bashar to shift the narrative from one about a brutal clan and regime killing protesters and political activists to that of a state battling armed insurgents and gangs linked to a foreign conspiracy.

"We forge ahead with firm and steady steps where there's no room for defeatists, cowards, opportunists, ignorance, and backwardness," Bashar told the crowd at the regime-organized rally in January 2012.[11] "I am confident about the future…We shall be victorious over the conspiracy without any doubt," he continued as loyalists, who looked entranced, snapped photos of him with their smartphones.

Standing in the first row not far from the stage was Bashar's wife, Asma, and two of their children, nine-year-old daughter Zein and seven-year-old son Karim. Asma smiled and looked adoringly at her husband. She was dressed in a black wool hat and a sleeveless beige winter jacket over black sweater and leggings. The children were bundled up in winter jackets. Karim wore a baseball cap in the colors of the Syrian flag with "Syria" emblazoned on it, and Zein waved a Syrian flag.

Not far behind Asma and the children, Bashar's friend Manaf watched the spectacle.[12] Observing Bashar at the rally, Manaf thought his friend was deluding himself, or worse. At that moment, Bashar's quest to save the regime appeared to Manaf like a mission impossible that would end in ruin for the Assads and those associated with them, as well as the whole country.

But just as for Bashar, survival was Manaf's priority, too.

Manaf knew that being outside the Assad family's war consensus was becoming an untenable and perilous position. He saw the defense minister, Ali Habib, removed from his position by Bashar and put under house arrest for refusing orders to attack protesters in Hama.[13] The vice president, Farouq al-Sharaa, who had been advocating dialogue and meaningful political reforms, was sidelined and later imprisoned at his home in Damascus when there was talk of him taking over Bashar's duties as president and leading a transitional government.[14] Sharaa's decades of loyalty to Hafez and then Bashar afterward counted for little in the end.

Manaf was sidelined, too, but officially he was still a general in the Republican Guard. He could be asked to take part in military operations against opposition areas. Refusing to do so was a dereliction of duty. Manaf believed that his standoff with Maher al-Assad and the Makhloufs heightened the dangers that he and his family faced.

"You have failed in your duties; you must understand that this is an assault on all of us, a big conspiracy," Bashar reprimanded about seventy Baath Party officials, including Manaf, that he had summoned to the palace for an urgent meeting, a few weeks before his splashy Damascus rally at the start of 2012.[15]

Bashar's brother Maher stared angrily at the gathered partisans as Bashar spoke sternly about mobilizing party militias to defend the regime and the lessons learned from his father's bloody era. At the meeting, Manaf felt like a plagued person, hardly anyone greeted him; they wanted to keep a certain distance from him.

The pressure on Manaf to definitively take sides was also coming from outside Syria. He was among several senior army officers who started receiving calls and messages on their private cell phones telling them to defect. "Don't stay with the butcher dictator," said one message from an American number.[16]

At the end of 2011, Manaf received a call from a man speaking Arabic with an Egyptian accent and identifying himself as someone from the office of Navi Pillay, the UN High Commissioner for Human Rights. "You're using violence against protesters. That's unacceptable...," said the man before Manaf hung up.[17]

By then Manaf and his family believed that the United States and its Western allies were done with Bashar.

"The Syrian people will win their battle and France will continue to do everything to assist them," declared France's foreign minister, Alain Juppé. "The noose is tightening around this completely 'autistic' regime, which continues its bloody crackdown."[18]

The way the Tlasses saw it, abandoning the Assads would put them in a strong position to play a leading role post-Bashar. In December 2011, Manaf took the first steps toward a break with the family. He sent this message to the US State Department through a friend who visited Damascus that month: "I am against the killing of protesters and have nothing to do with it."[19]

Around Christmas 2011, Manaf's wife and children traveled to Paris under the pretext of visiting their relatives for the holidays.[20]

His wife, Thala, contacted the French ambassador to Syria, Éric Chevallier, who was in Paris at the time and whom the Tlasses considered a friend. By then France was deliberating whether to keep its embassy open after pro-Bashar mobs attacked the French consulate in Latakia and the French chancery in Aleppo. The United States had recalled Robert Ford after the regime ratcheted its incitement against him, and pro-Bashar thugs attacked his motorcade when he visited an opposition figure in Damascus.[21] Embassies of several Arab countries which had called on Bashar to step down were also attacked.

Thala and Chevallier agreed to meet at a café on the Place Saint-Sulpice, not far from her apartment. "Manaf wants to get out," Thala told Chevallier after they settled into a booth in the back of the café. "He's no longer with the regime."[22] Waiters in white shirts and black bow ties and vests raced around with trays of drinks. Outside, Christmas shoppers perused the festive vitrines of the boutiques on the nearby Rue du Four. "It will be difficult for him to do it on his own—can you help?" continued Thala as Chevallier listened attentively.[23]

She spoke of threats to their lives and expressed worry for the safety of the couple's two youngest children, Hamza and Mounzer.[24] She said that the children's bodyguard, who was normally assigned by the palace, had been changed after Manaf broke ranks with Bashar and his brother and cousins. The new bodyguard was then killed.[25] Whether the bodyguard's death posed a real or imagined threat to the children, the truth was that few understood as well as the Tlasses the vengeful and mafia-like mind-set of the Assads and Makhloufs. The change of bodyguards might have been a message or veiled threat from the Assads—a reminder that they controlled every detail of the Tlasses' lives, including their children's safety and welfare. But the bodyguard's death could have also been linked to an emerging insurgency against the regime, which began to target anyone seen as connected to the ruling families. For some in the communities coming under vicious regime assault, the Tlasses looked as complicit in their suffering as the Assads.

Chevallier told Thala that he fully supported and welcomed Manaf's decision but that he had to first talk with his superiors.[26]

For months, Chevallier had been passing messages at every opportunity to figures within the regime, urging them to do the right thing and defect. The Americans, French, and their regional and Western allies were all betting that a weakening of Bashar's regime from within through defections, coupled with pressure from rebellious towns and cities, could bring down Bashar or force him to leave the country. As far as these outside powers were concerned, change was happening across the Middle East despite the bloodshed and turmoil—and Syria was no exception.

When Thala met Chevallier at the end of 2011, Libya had formed its first interim government following Gaddafi's gruesome killing,[27] Egypt was in the midst of its first post-Mubarak elections,[28] and Yemen's longtime dictator, Ali Abdallah Saleh, had agreed to resign as part of a deal brokered by Gulf Arab states.[29]

After his meeting with Thala, Chevallier was immersed in discussions at the French Foreign Ministry and with his country's secret service. He spoke positively about the prospect of Manaf's defection, but even so, he delivered a sober assessment of Manaf's real power and significance within the regime.[30] While the Tlasses had aided the Assads every step of the way in constructing and protecting their more than four-decade rule over

Syria, Chevallier knew that Manaf and the Tlasses had been eclipsed before the uprising by others, especially Bashar's maternal cousins the Makhloufs. The Tlasses were no longer in the "nucleus" or "heart" of the regime, explained Chevallier. Manaf had a reputation for being a general who liked to socialize and have a good time rather than plunge himself into the cutthroat power plays of Bashar's inner circle. Chevallier's point was that Manaf's defection would in no way trigger the regime's collapse.

Still, the defection of someone like Manaf could deal Bashar and his regime an immense psychological and symbolic blow. This was his childhood friend, after all. Manaf's defection to France would give Paris added influence over the transitional government that would be put in place after Bashar's hoped-for demise. Manaf could represent the interests of the Syrian army in that body. Chevallier stressed that Manaf was a part of the solution—but not an alternative to Bashar.

Weighing on the French decision to help Manaf get out was intense lobbying by his Paris-based sister, Nahed, a wealthy socialite with extensive contacts inside France's political and business establishment all the way up to the presidency.

In a separate meeting with Chevallier at the end of 2011, Nahed vowed to do everything to bring her family, including her father, Mustafa Tlass, to France. She declared to Chevallier and other French officials that the Tlasses were making a definitive break with the Assads and were backing the opposition.[31]

On the first day of 2012, Thala sent Bashar an e-mail wishing him, Asma, and their children a happy new year and victory over all his enemies "from the smallest to the biggest."[32] In a prior e-mail, Thala had cursed Arab countries for suspending Syria's membership in the Arab League. In another exchange she asked Bashar to call her, and she apologized if she was causing him "a headache from all the back and forth."

"I would never get a headache because of you, don't say that again, you are supposed to know me well by now and know how much respect I have for both of you," Bashar wrote back, referring to her and Manaf.[33]

Maintaining a direct line to Bashar, pretending nothing had changed in the relationship, and praising some of Bashar's moves offered protection and cover for the Tlasses as they plotted their exit. "Incredible!!!!!!" and

"Masterstroke!!!!!!!" Thala wrote to Bashar in reaction to a speech he gave one day before his triumphant appearance in Umayyad Square in early January 2012.[34] Manaf characterized all these contacts as a last-ditch attempt to influence Bashar and get him to stop the butchery.[35]

Manaf was haunted by the brutal killing of Ghayath Matar, a twenty-six-year-old protest leader from Daraya, a town on the edge of Damascus known for its tart, jewel-like grapes and wood craftsmen. Matar, a tailor by profession, was nicknamed "Little Gandhi" because he and his friends handed out flowers and bottles of water to the soldiers sent to assault them. He was part of a group called the Daraya Youth—bright and creative men and women committed to peaceful resistance.

"He had an innocent face and infectious smile," said Manaf, who had met Matar when he received a delegation from Daraya in his office at the start of the uprising.[36]

In early September 2011, Matar and a group of like-minded Daraya activists were entrapped and arrested by the mukhabarat. Days later, the mukhabarat's Air Force Intelligence Directorate called Matar's family and told them to collect his body from the morgue; he had died after barbaric torture. His wife was pregnant with their first child.[37]

"It was an unbearable dose of hatred, spite, and violence," said Mazen Darwish, as tears rolled down his face.

Matar had been part of the Local Coordination Committees (LCCs), the civil and peaceful anti-regime grassroots movement founded by Mazen and his colleagues. Among those captured with Matar was Yahya al-Shurbaji, another Daraya native and one of Mazen's best friends; his whereabouts were unknown.

"There are few people as ethical, smart, and spiritual as him," said Mazen about Shurbaji, who like him had been involved in reform initiatives as early as 2001. Before his arrest, Shurbaji confronted and chased out Islamist militants who had moved into Daraya farms to set up training camps in the name of fighting the regime. They were some of the militants released from prison by Bashar.[38]

Advocates of peaceful resistance, not the gunmen or Islamist fanatics, posed the gravest threat to Assad family rule. As they had for his father in

1980, they became Bashar's priority in 2011. After the bloody summer 2011 assault on protesters in Hama, Bashar's terror organs (*mukhabarat* branches) systematically went after prominent symbols of Mazen's LCCs and everyone collaborating with them and sharing their vision and methods.

These largely autonomous and cell-like structures kept multiplying as, early on, the uprising gained momentum. In big cities like Damascus where the regime was omnipresent, it was common for members of one *tansiqiya*, or coordination unit, not to know the real identity of members of another unit—for security reasons. These groups established themselves online, especially on Facebook and YouTube, which were becoming indispensable platforms for announcements and news and videos about local protest activities and regime crimes. The committees also liaised with each other online. The regime sought to identify, infiltrate, and disrupt the activist networks operating throughout the country. The objective was to unmask and apprehend key figures and sow fear in the hearts of sympathizers as well as the general public.

In the summer and fall of 2011, there were repeated attempts to unify activists on the ground, mainly by bringing together the secularists and those with Islamist leanings. Talks had to be kept secret and mostly online in order to avoid being targeted by the regime. Activist leaders held Skype conference calls. What they did not know at the time was that among them were people secretly working for the *mukhabarat*. These agents were often the ones arguing the hardest for armed resistance.[39]

Around that time, the regime sent teams of security and military officers to Tehran for training on cyberwarfare and surveillance. Iran had developed extensive know-how in the wake of its own crackdown on protests that had erupted in the aftermath of the June 2009 presidential elections, or what became known as the Green Movement.

"The Iranians were responsible for the arrest of many activists early on," said a Syrian officer who had taken part in the Iran training but later defected.[40]

The Syrian regime also obtained, via Iraq, an ally of both Damascus and Tehran, advanced internet filtering devices made by the California-based Blue Coat Systems which the regime used to block and restrict web content. Syria was subject to US sanctions, but Iraq was not.[41]

Fearing arrest by the regime, Mazen Darwish stopped making media appearances and instead worked clandestinely to support the LCCs. His lawyer friend, Razan Zeitouneh, was on the run because she topped the regime's most-wanted list. Her colleagues spread rumors that she had fled to Britain.[42] Many LCC leaders and members were in hiding or abroad after the assassination or arrest of several fellow activists.

Torturing protesters and returning their mutilated corpses to their families was a way for the regime to illustrate the heavy price of opposition. In Daraa, where the first regime killings had ignited the revolution, a civil engineer and leading protest organizer named Maan Odat was executed by a *mukhabarat* officer after being wounded when regime forces fired at a funeral turned impromptu protest. Maan could have been treated for his injuries, but instead the officer immediately took out his pistol and shot him in the mouth.[43]

Toward the end of 2011, Mashaal Tammo, a highly respected opposition leader of Kurdish origin who was working with Mazen and other youth activists, was killed by gunmen who stormed his house.[44] The previous month Tammo had survived an attempt that he blamed on the regime. A visibly shaken Mazen was among those who went up to Qamishli (northeastern Syria) to attend the funeral.[45]

On the same day of Tammo's killing, regime henchmen beat up Riad Seif at a demonstration in Damascus.[46] Seif had been the leading figure in the Damascus Spring during Bashar's first decade in power and was imprisoned for almost eight years between 2000 and 2010. Like Tammo, Seif was one of the leaders whom Mazen and his activist colleagues were eager to collaborate with in order to bolster the political credentials of their budding and youthful coordination committees.

With the methodical elimination of protest leaders and the death toll from Bashar's crackdown surpassing 5,000 at the end of 2011,[47] some of the once-peaceful activists started to support armed resistance. Money and guns trickled in, mainly via Qatar, Turkey, and groups with Islamist agendas. Those insisting on maintaining the peaceful character of the uprising were being taken out of the scene.

By the end of 2011, Bashar and his regime were a step closer to the fulfillment of the claims they had made at the uprising's onset: There were no peaceful protesters and activists, only armed groups and terrorists waging an insurrection against the state.

The year ended with twin car bombs exploding just before Christmas outside the Damascus headquarters of the General Intelligence Director-ate. Nearly all of the fifty people killed in the blasts were civilians.[48]

The attack coincided with the arrival of a group of Arab League moni-tors who had been allowed into the country after weeks of obstruction by Bashar and his regime. They were supposed to verify the implementation of a peace plan that the regime had finally agreed to and that called for, among other things, the withdrawal of the army and security forces from rebellious communities and the end of violence against protesters. The regime made sure to take the monitors to the scene of the car bombs, which it instantly blamed on Al-Qaeda.

An Iranian media adviser to the regime informed Bashar's office that it was a mistake to blame Al-Qaeda and that the United States and Syrian opposition and their Western and regional backers should be made the culprits instead.[49]

"This was the gift of Burhan Ghalyoun and his friends to Syria," claimed one of the country's most senior religious clerics the next day, dur-ing an official funeral for the victims at the Umayyad Mosque in Damas-cus.[50] It was a blatant lie, but all that mattered for the regime and its allies was vilifying the opposition and linking it to terrorism. Ghalyoun was the ally of Mazen and other secular and independent-minded activists.

For Mazen and fellow activists clinging against all odds to peaceful resistance, the explosions were an ominous event capping a year that had started with joy and hope and ended with anguish, grief, and fear.

On New Year's Eve 2011, Mazen needed to feel there was still hope for a peaceful revolution against the regime. He and his friend Razan slipped into Barzeh, a neighborhood on Damascus's fringes where lively protests were held almost nightly.

Barzeh was plunged in darkness after the regime started cutting the power supply to rebellious areas. The place had an almost medieval feel, yet the mood was exhilarating. Resourceful organizers had strung lights over the main square, powered by a small private generator.[51] Some people held flares. The setting could not have been more different from the massive and carefully choreographed pro-Bashar rally held in central Damascus a few days later.

Mazen and Razan joined hundreds in applauding and swaying to a rhythmic chant that affirmed Barzeh's solidarity with other rebellious neighborhoods and towns: Daraya, Douma, Hama, Midan, and others.[52]

"Barzeh is with you till death!" the protesters repeated in a call-out to each area.

A young man standing nearby flashed a sign that read: "Happy New Year Freedom!"

Mazen and Razan looked happy and, at least momentarily, in their element.

16

Blood on My Hands

A few days after Bashar's rally in Damascus in January 2012, Manaf was at his Republican Guard barracks in Al-Hameh in the arid hills above the capital. The sprawling compound, a short distance from the presidential palace, had nearly 6,000 officers and soldiers, as well as 120 tanks in addition to rocket launchers and other heavy weapons—a fraction of the arsenal protecting Bashar.[1]

Manaf's deputy, Issam Zahreddine—a tall, burly, and gruff-looking man with graying hair and thick beard—came to see him.[2] "The president called me and ordered us to go to Baba Amr," said Zahreddine, referring to a neighborhood in Homs city that had become a hotbed of resistance to the regime.

Manaf's heart sank. This news was like a punch in the gut.

"This is not our responsibility," said Manaf, trying to remain composed. "The Republican Guard protects the president, the palace, and Damascus."

"But I promised the president I would cleanse Baba Amr for him," retorted Zahreddine, who relished the opportunity to upstage Manaf and position himself as a faithful servant of the Assad family.

"Issam, beware," said Manaf. "There are a lot of civilians in there."

At that moment, Manaf understood that the decision to bypass him and dispatch his unit to Homs despite his own reservations was a message from Bashar: My patience is running out, we are at war, and you have to do your part. Manaf was more determined than ever to get out. He was anxiously waiting to hear back from the French after his wife's meeting with the ambassador in Paris.

Zahreddine was later promoted to the rank of major general and would earn the nickname "lion of the Republican Guard" for his unflinching loyalty to Bashar.[3]

By early 2012, Homs was one of the main battlegrounds in escalating street warfare pitting regime forces and loyalists against army defectors as well as private citizens who took up arms to defend themselves and their neighborhoods from the military. Entire neighborhoods like Baba Amr slipped out of regime control.

The situation in Homs, a city of about one million north of Damascus, showed how relentless bloodshed on the part of the regime was starting to tear Syria's social fabric, fuel militancy, and polarize people along religious lines. The majority in Homs were Sunni Muslim, but there was also a sizable Christian and Alawite community, with the latter having grown further after 1970, when families flocked from the countryside as one of their own, Hafez al-Assad, rose to power.

Old animosities and grievances were rekindled in Homs from the very start of the uprising. Tensions flared after the death of an Alawite policeman during the first protest in Homs in March 2011, and for months afterward the army and *mukhabarat*, aided by *shabiha*, or thugs, from the city's mainly Alawite sections, shot and killed protesters from mainly Sunni neighborhoods.[4] Funerals of those killed in the protests were not spared, either, resulting in more deaths. Rebellious neighborhoods were raided, and suspected activists and protesters were swept up by the dozens each time. Some were tortured to death, others disappeared forever.

By the summer of 2011, regime forces had killed nearly 600 civilians in Homs province, mostly in the city.[5] There was no precise figure of those killed in the assault on protesters who briefly occupied New Clock Tower Square.

The city began to witness a series of reprisal attacks, kidnappings, and assassinations involving Alawites and Sunnis. Youth in several rebellious Sunni neighborhoods, especially working-class areas like Baba Amr known for gun ownership before the uprising, took up arms and set up local checkpoints to protect themselves. They were later joined by army defectors, including Manaf's relative Abdul-Razzaq, and called themselves rebels or the Free Syrian Army. Few Alawite citizens ventured to Sunni neighborhoods and vice versa. Many Christians, concentrated in the city's mostly Sunni center but also present in Alawite neighborhoods, sympathized with the protesters at first but then felt squeezed by both sides as violence spiraled. The regime ratcheted up its targeting of predominantly Sunni neighborhoods, using tanks, artillery, and other heavy weapons, further fueling the cycle of bloodshed and revenge and provoking guerilla-style attacks by the rebels.

Opposition neighborhoods were cut off from one another and encircled by checkpoints.[6] Still, many people inside these neighborhoods just wanted to protest and not be drawn into a military confrontation with the regime or a war with the Alawites. Whenever there was a lull in clashes and regime bombing, thousands of residents gathered day and night inside their neighborhoods to protest and celebrate their liberation, however precarious, from the regime. People chanted, played musical instruments, and performed group dances in what sometimes looked like a big party or a thrilling rave. In November 2011, no day went by without protests inside several Homs neighborhoods.[7] The mood darkened in December, though, when, in the span of one day, nearly fifty civilians were killed in tit-for-tat Alawite–Sunni violence.[8]

Bit by bit, the uprising that had brought out the best in Syrians and projected their aspirations and yearnings was vanishing as pain, vengefulness, and war took over. It was yet another page from the playbook of Hafez as well as all the despots who clung desperately to power at the start of the Arab Spring: civil war is acceptable and even desirable to defend the leader.

Along with the regime's brutality, struggles over leadership and ideology among Bashar's opponents, fueled by the competing agendas of regional powers like Qatar, Saudi Arabia, Turkey, and others, had an equally poisonous and destructive impact on people's quest for liberation from the Assads. It was a contest for the revolution's heart and soul and Syria's shape and direction after the Assads.

The sources of friction among Bashar's opponents included money and access to funds, the role and place of Islam, the stance toward the country's minorities (particularly Bashar's Alawite community), and deepening schisms between urban and rural communities as well as between those committed to peaceful resistance and those embracing armed rebellion.

More fundamentally, this was a generational struggle. Youthful and idealistic activists like Mazen Darwish sparred with a cadre of older opposition leaders, who to the young seemed like a by-product of the very regime they wanted to topple—plagued by the same closedmindedness, selfishness, and tyrannical ways.

These clashing dynamics were on display in Homs when Mazen secretly visited the city in late 2011.[9]

Tensions flared among activists when armed men from Baba Amr started coming to an adjacent, largely bourgeois neighborhood called Insha'at to offer protection from regime attacks on protesters. Some Insha'at activists associated with Mazen felt that this marred the peacefulness of their cause. Mazen also learned that Muslim clerics in several rebellious Homs neighborhoods were handing out monthly salaries, food, and other assistance to families of protesters detained by the regime. "At a time when people like us were distributing slogans, they were giving out money and food," said Mazen.

Money, arms, and regional agendas worked to co-opt or sideline those like Mazen who were insisting on a peaceful struggle against the regime. The group with the deepest pockets was the Muslim Brotherhood. The organization had been shattered after Hafez's massacre in Hama in 1982, and many Syrians believed that its leaders had abandoned the city to its tragic fate. Its exiled chiefs saw the Arab Spring and Syria's revolution in 2011 as a historic chance for a comeback and, more important, for power. Still, the group seemed sensitive to the stigma associated with its name inside Syria and went out of its way to be collaborative and build partnerships across the spectrum of Syrian opposition, and it even conceded a visible leadership role in the first Syrian National Council in which Mazen's Local Coordination Committees (LCCs) were represented. Brotherhood representatives inside Syria enthusiastically reached out to Mazen, seeking cooperation.[10]

But on the side, Brotherhood-affiliated charities channeled generous aid to rebellious communities, especially in cities like Homs, in order to buy loyalty and a following. Funds came from Qatar and Turkey, two countries embracing the Brotherhood region-wide and shaping political transitions in Egypt, Libya, and Tunisia to favor the movement.

The Brotherhood and its patrons were among the first to support militarization in Syria under the pretext of protecting civilians. "We had doubts from the start that civil protests could compel Bashar to abandon power," said Brotherhood leader Mohammad Farouk Tayfour.[11]

In the fall of 2011, a former Muslim Brotherhood member who held Swedish citizenship organized the first shipment of arms from Libya, in coordination with the Qataris and Turks. "The Americans were monitoring the whole operation but pretended they were not seeing," said someone with firsthand knowledge of the shipments.[12] This was a reflection of both Obama's eagerness to maintain a certain distance from the Syria file and also the West's inability to keep up with developments on the ground.

No one could stop Libyan rebel militias backed by NATO and the West from pillaging huge arms depots scattered across the vast desert country. At one facility, trailer trucks waited to load crates of rockets, missiles, ammunition, and other armaments.[13]

In addition to helping funnel Libyan weapons to Syria, Qatar and Turkey also facilitated the travel of allied Libyan militia leaders to northern Syria to assist emerging local armed factions there.[14] A Qatari national who had previously spent time with the Taliban in Afghanistan was instrumental in raising donations from wealthy Gulf Arabs and channeling assistance to budding anti-regime militias in Syria.[15] He contacted Mazen's LCC colleagues and flew several of them to Qatar.[16] He echoed the argument that his government and Turkey were making to their Western allies: peaceful protests are futile in the face of Bashar's killing machine; only guns will topple him.

"The regime's barbarism and people's rage were channeled into a violent jihadist agenda," said Mazen. "We were mocked as 'the flowers-and-water-bottles folks.'... We were effectively being told, 'You mobilized the street but your role is finished.'"[17] Arguing that bearing arms played into Bashar's hands was portrayed as naïve or even worse, as complicity with the regime.

Qatar's Al Jazeera news channel, initially seen by Mazen as an indispensable ally in the struggle against the regime, started giving more airtime to Islamists and those aligned with its owner's agenda and its push to arm Syrian rebels.

"At the time we hardly grasped the impact of competing regional interests on our revolution," said Mazen.

Saudi Arabia, which saw itself as a regional powerhouse and leader of Muslims worldwide, was certainly not going to sit back and allow what it considered a small and pesky upstart like Qatar to dictate the course of events in Syria and the region.

In the Saudi camp were countries like Jordan and the United Arab Emirates. Officially they were all part of the same Western and regional alliance against the Assad regime that also included Qatar and Turkey, but at the same time the Saudis and their allies went out of their way to undermine the Qataris in Syria. The Saudis saw the main Syrian opposition body, the National Council, as being in Qatar's clutches. With vast sums of money and other inducements, they worked hard to win over council members.[18]

On the media front, Saudi Arabia's answer to Al Jazeera was its Dubai-based news channel, Al Arabiya, which ramped up its Syria coverage. Several Saudi-connected religious channels also started broadcasting highly incendiary and sectarian rhetoric aimed mainly at Bashar's Shiite allies Iran and Hezbollah as well as elements of the Syrian opposition perceived to be under Qatari control.[19]

A Syrian-born Sunni cleric living in Saudi Arabia named Adnan al-Arour became a sensation on these channels and gained a huge following inside Syria because of his fiery and populist style.[20] He assailed one opposition leader allied to Mazen as a drunk and nonbeliever and told protesters in Homs to bang on pots all night in order to topple the regime. Bashar himself could not have come up with a better caricature of the Islamist fanatics whom he claimed dominated the protest movement. The same telegenic cleric also became a conduit for donations from Saudis and other Gulf Arabs to support armed groups fighting Bashar. An entire room in his house was stacked with cash, gold, and other valuables amassed from donors.[21]

One way that Mazen and his colleagues thought they could make an impact in rebellious communities was to help set up a series of field hospitals where doctors, surgeons, and other health workers sympathetic to the uprising could offer their services on a volunteer basis. It was no longer just about treating gunshot wounds; the regime was using tanks, rockets, and heavier weapons against opposition areas. Taking a wounded person who was a protester or who came from a known opposition area to a government clinic or hospital often meant arrest or even death.

Mazen and his colleague Razan convinced the French ambassador, Éric Chevallier, to help them. In the fall of 2011, Chevallier used his diplomatic status to bring nearly a ton of medical supplies into Syria.[22] He stored them at the embassy and then passed them along in batches to activist networks linked to Mazen and Razan. Antibiotics, painkillers, surgical kits, syringes, needles, and other medical supplies were stuffed into garbage bags and dropped off in installments by Chevallier on his way back from a soccer field near Damascus where he and his staff and guards played each week.

"This is going to multi-confessional networks of human rights defenders and political activists, not radicals. It's proof that we are not only talking about supporting these people but also acting," Chevallier told his puzzled and concerned superiors in Paris when they questioned his shipment request.[23]

Still, this was a drop in the bucket compared to the funding and support given by Qatar and Saudi, which increasingly meant that they set the agenda and tone on the ground.

Soon heated arguments broke out between activists over what to call the main weekly protests held each Friday. People like Mazen wanted names and slogans evoking patriotism and inclusiveness, while Islamists pushed for ones with religious connotations. Mazen's coordination committees were labeled "elitist and anti-Islamic," while he was called a "secular Alawite."[24]

These fractures were a gift to the regime and its allies, who amplified them with provocations and lies. Bashar realized he could use the same modern media tools embraced by youthful protesters to discredit his opponents, reshape the narrative, and sow fear and confusion.

For loyalists and opponents of all hues, images and videos became weapons, and social media platforms and TV channels turned into battlegrounds.

Starting in the fall of 2011, videos of pro-Bashar soldiers and thugs torturing protesters began to appear on YouTube. Some were posted by the torturers themselves, proud of what they were doing. In one video, a man identified as a protester is kicked, trampled on, hit with a stick, and told to kneel in front of a framed photo of Bashar.[25] "Traitor, you want freedom? Who is your God, you animal?" demands his torturer, dressed in military fatigues. It was fodder for people's rage and their readiness to embrace armed rebellion against Bashar.

For Bashar's supporters, Al Arabiya, Al Jazeera, and Western media were all lying, while truth and facts were carried only by Syrian state media and Lebanese, Iranian, Iraqi, and Russian channels spreading the regime narrative.

"Do not watch Al Jazeera and Al Arabiya, it's all fake news and fake protests," Bashar's mother, Aniseh, warned a visitor in late 2011.[26]

The eighty-one-year-old Assad family matron unquestioningly believed what pro-regime media was saying at the time, namely that the protests were all fake and that channels like Al Jazeera had re-created models of Syrian cities along with their landmarks in the Qatari capital, Doha, used actors and extras as pretend protesters, and then broadcast the scenes as events in Syria. Aniseh was confident and defiant. She assured her visitor: "We're going to overcome the crisis the same way we defeated it in the 1980s under the eternal leader."[27]

Manaf, meanwhile, watched how the determination of Bashar and his family to survive and crush the challenge to their rule increased further after Hafez's longtime ally Gaddafi was brutally lynched by a mob that had cornered him in his hometown.

Bashar and Asma then sought to project resolve and strength by maintaining routines and pursuing personal interests as if all was normal. To Manaf, they looked tone-deaf and disconnected from reality as the regime was beset by mounting internal and external pressures.

Asma walked her children to school, kept office hours at her Syria Trust, and shopped online. She browsed for a fondue set on Amazon,[28] ordered designer lamps and custom-made furniture and accessories,[29] and perused the latest creations by the maker of luxurious and flamboyant footwear, Christian Louboutin,[30] who bought a mansion in Aleppo before the uprising and considered Asma a friend and muse. To get around international sanctions, her purchases were facilitated by friends and associates living abroad and often shipped to a front company in Dubai for onward delivery to Syria.[31]

"If we are strong together, we will overcome this together...I Love you...," Asma wrote to Bashar in December 2011.[32]

Bashar played tennis,[33] did his best to share meals and spend time with Asma and their children, and bought songs on iTunes through an account with someone else's name and address.[34]

Toward the end of 2011, Bashar had agreed to allow Arab League monitors into the country as part of a proposed peace deal to end attacks on protesters and military campaigns against rebellious areas, to release prisoners, and to pave the way to a political transition.[35] In fact, it was only a maneuver to ease international and regional pressure and buy time to prepare for a big offensive in Homs.

Around the same time, Bashar dispatched his brother-in-law Assef Shawkat to Homs to negotiate a truce with rebellious communities.[36] Manaf considered Assef an ally and sensed that, like him, he was unhappy with the way things were being handled. Both believed that the brutality and excessive force deployed from the start to deal with protesters was progressively pushing the country toward disaster.

Like Manaf's previous peacemaking initiatives, which had also been approved by Bashar, Assef's Homs mission was doomed from the start. Bashar, his brother, and cousins were absolutely not interested in compromise; negotiations were just a show and a stall tactic.[37]

While in Homs, Assef met with local opposition activists and leaders and even tried to offer some concessions as a sign of goodwill, but all his efforts were sabotaged by the hard-liners empowered by Bashar. When one activist told him to halt the bombing of the Baba Amr neighborhood and, at least, to evacuate severely wounded people, Assef had little choice but to say, "I do not have the authority."[38]

In mid-January 2012, Qatar's emir called for the deployment of foreign troops in Syria to end the killing,[39] and later that month Qatar led an Arab League initiative calling on Bashar to step down and transfer his powers to his vice president.[40] The emir was hoping to convince Bashar to give up power in return for asylum for himself and his family in Qatar and a promise that he wouldn't face charges at the International Criminal Court.

A few weeks earlier, the emir's daughter Al-Mayassa al-Thani had tried to sway Asma, whom she had known well before the uprising. The US-educated and outgoing Al-Mayassa oversaw Qatar's world-class museums with a multibillion-dollar budget. She spent hundreds of millions on works by Paul Cézanne, Damien Hirst, Mark Rothko, and Andy Warhol.[41]

"How can I help you?" Al-Mayassa wrote to Asma in mid-December. "I can't imagine you agree with what is going on."[42]

"My Dear Mayassa, I don't have a problem with frankness and honesty, in fact to me it's like oxygen, I need it to survive. Life is not fair, my friend, but ultimately there is a reality we all need to deal with!!! Take care, aaa," responded Asma, signing the note as Asma Akhras al-Assad (AAA).[43]

After her father's announcement, Al-Mayassa sent Asma another e-mail with a more concrete offer: Qatar was ready to grant her, Bashar, and the children asylum. "I only pray that you will convince the president to take this as an opportunity to exit without having to face charges," she wrote.[44]

Al-Mayassa never heard back from Asma.

Bashar's own response came four days later in the form of a blistering military assault on the Homs neighborhood of Baba Amr, which had become a stronghold for regime opponents, including army defectors, as well as an emblem of resistance to the Assads.

The offensive commenced on February 3, 2012, precisely on the thirtieth anniversary of the Hama massacre. In addition to the Republican Guard contingent under the command of Manaf's deputy, Zahreddine, the forces attacking Baba Amr included units of the Fourth Division, which was under the de facto leadership of Bashar's brother, Maher.[45]

"Thirty years after his father massacred tens of thousands of innocent Syrian men, women, and children in Hama, Bashar al-Assad has demonstrated a similar disdain for human life and dignity," said Obama the following day, February 4, while also assuring Syrians that America won't leave them to Bashar's "killing machine."[46] "We will help because we stand for principles that include universal rights for all people and just political and economic reform," he assured them. "The suffering citizens of Syria must know: we are with you, and the Assad regime must come to an end."

These proved to be hollow assurances, almost immediately.

Later that same day, Bashar received a boost of international support when Russia and China vetoed a Security Council resolution demanding that his regime "cease all violence and protect its population," and withdraw its forces from towns and cities.[47]

As Obama condemned Bashar and promised not to abandon Syrians, Bashar's forces tightened the siege of Baba Amr; nobody could leave, and food, medicine, and other essentials were not allowed in. The densely populated neighborhood of cinder-block apartment buildings and old houses was then pummeled day and night with heavy artillery, rockets, and mortar shells until rebels withdrew at the end of the month and regime forces triumphantly went in.

"It's absolutely sickening," Marie Colvin, an American reporter with the *Sunday Times*, described the assault on Baba Amr to the BBC on February 21, 2012.[48] She was one of a handful of journalists smuggled in by rebels to report from inside. She said that she counted fourteen shells fall on the neighborhood in the span of thirty seconds and watched a baby die of shrapnel wounds because of a lack of medical supplies at the makeshift local field hospital.

The following day, Colvin and French photographer Remi Ochlik were killed in a rocket attack by Bashar's forces on a house in the neighborhood that was serving as a media center, said witnesses.[49] Photographer Paul Conroy and French reporter Edith Bouvier were injured in the same attack. A Homs-based *mukhabarat* commander later said targeting the reporters was "justifiable" because they had been smuggled into Baba Amr from Lebanon and had embedded themselves "with the terrorists."[50]

A wounded civilian from Baba Amr who escaped on February 24, 2012, described to Human Rights Watch the intensity of the shelling. "On February 23, I was in my house when the whole building shook as if an earthquake had happened," he said. "I looked outside the building and saw that a rocket went through the building adjacent to mine, completely demolishing the roof.

"Seconds later, another rocket hit the same building, destroying the second floor, and a few seconds later, a third rocket destroyed the first and ground floor. In three to four minutes the building had fully collapsed. I directly went outside to see if anyone survived. I pulled one woman but she had no legs. Her legs were cut off."[51]

Ahmed al-Hamid, a native of Baba Amr and physician who helped set up the local field hospital, was among those fleeing as Bashar's forces closed in on the neighborhood.[52] His parents remained behind. His sister, who lived in another part of Homs, pleaded with regime forces to allow her into the neighborhood on February 26, 2011, so she could take food to her parents and other family members trapped inside. They let her in, but on her way out she was shot in the neck by a sniper and later died. Her father heard about it and went to look for her. He was kidnapped, tortured, and killed by pro-Bashar militiamen.

As the military campaign was underway in Baba Amr, Bashar's brother, Maher, and his cousins the Makhloufs did not let up their pressure on Manaf; they were determined to draw him in and implicate him in the Homs carnage. Telling the world that, contrary to growing rumors, the Tlasses, natives of Homs province, had not abandoned the Assads would give the regime and Bashar a boost. One of Manaf's aides walked in and told him to get on the internal army radio network for an update from inside Baba Amr by Zahreddine. He was told that Bashar, the defense minister, and the chief of staff were all listening in on the call.[53]

Manaf told his aide to leave the room, but he did not get on the call. He did not want to give the impression that he was involved in the military assault against Baba Amr or supportive of it. "They wanted me to have blood on my hands, too," Manaf thought.

In total, close to 800 people, the majority of them civilians, were estimated to have been killed in the February 2012 assault on Baba Amr and other parts of Homs.[54] Witnesses said more people were summarily executed in early March during mopping-up operations as pro-Bashar Alawite militiamen from Homs and elsewhere went on a rampage, looting and burning homes.[55] It was a scene cut straight from the Hama massacre, three decades earlier.

"God, Syria, Bashar, and the [Republican] Guard," Manaf's deputy Zahreddin and his men chanted as they triumphantly paraded through the devastated streets of Baba Amr after it fell into their hands.[56]

17

We Have to Win!

On June 21, 2012, Hassan Merhi al-Hamadah, an air force colonel, flew his Russian-made MiG-21 fighter jet from Al-Khalkhalah airbase in southern Syria and crossed the nearby border with Jordan.[1] He told the Jordanians that he was defecting and asked for asylum. They allowed him to land in Al-Mafraq on their side of the border. He and his copilot got out of the plane, tore off their Syrian army insignias, and fell to the ground to pray and thank God for their safe passage. They were now part of the so-called Free Syrian Army, which said it was fighting for the people, not Bashar and his family.

The regime called Hamadah "a deserter and traitor to his homeland and military honor." The day of his defection, about 125 people, nearly half of them from the army and security forces, were killed in fighting across the country. It was one of the bloodiest days since the start of the uprising in March 2011.[2]

The following day, Manaf was alone at home in the Mezzeh district of Damascus. It was the start of summer, and the squat cactus trees across from Manaf's villa and other elegant residences were already laden with yellow and orange prickly pears, a fruit beloved by Damascenes. The cactus fields, separating the upscale quarter from a slum where people of humbler means still lived, were a reminder of Mezzeh's past as farmland on the city's fringe.

Manaf's wife, Thala, and their two young boys, Hamza and Mounzer, had gone to Beirut, where the eldest son, Mustafa, attended college. Their daughter, Lamia, was at university in Montreal.

Manaf switched between news channels. Al Arabiya and Al Jazeera were still talking about the air force colonel's defection and its significance.

"We have long called for members of the Syrian armed forces and members of the Syrian regime to defect and abandon their positions rather than be complicit in the regime's atrocities," said a Pentagon spokesman.[3] A defected *mukhabarat* officer told Al Jazeera it was proof that the regime and the army were crumbling, and he urged all officers to defect as soon as possible because time was running out, as he put it.[4]

Manaf's phone rang. It was his friend and fellow Republican Guard general, Talal Makhlouf, who came from the same family as Bashar's maternal cousins (but more distantly related) and was a career military man, unlike other Makhloufs such as the *mukhabarat* chief Hafez and business tycoon Rami.[5]

"I have to see you, I have a message for you," said Talal.

"Okay, I am home," said Manaf. "Come by."

Talal, stocky and clean-shaven, arrived shortly after. He was three years older than Manaf, but they were friends from their days at the military academy in Homs. Like Manaf, Talal had been part of the cadre of rising army officers around Bassel al-Assad, Bashar's eldest brother and heir to the Assad family's rule before he was killed in the 1994 car crash. Manaf offered his guest cardamom-flavored black tea.

"You must go see him tomorrow," said Talal referring to Bashar as he sipped his tea, "but on condition there be no recrimination. Let bygones be bygones."[6]

"What does he want?" said Manaf.

"I do not know," responded Talal.

"Talal, tell me — what does he want?" insisted Manaf.

"He probably wants you to go on a mission to Qatar, Saudi Arabia, and Turkey to ask them to stop arming the rebels," said Talal.

"Why me?" said Manaf, barely concealing his shock. "Let him send [Vice President] Farouq al-Sharaa, [Foreign Minister] Walid al-Moallem, or the defense minister."

"You are more effective, and people will listen to you," said Talal calmly.

"Really!" Manaf cried out. "Well, if I am more effective and people listen to me, why didn't he take my advice and allow me to advance my peaceful solution?"

"Go," said Talal, "go see him for your sake."

"What do you mean?" snapped Manaf.

"Please go, I beg you," implored Talal. "I am your friend and I am advising you to go for your sake. Think about it and give me your answer quickly. You must go see him, it's imperative."

"Okay, I'll think about it," responded Manaf.

What Talal did not know was that Manaf's wife had gone to Beirut to secretly meet with French operatives and receive final instructions for their escape from Syria.[7] The French had finally agreed to help Manaf get out, but it was not only about him; his wife, children, father, and in-laws all had to leave, too, and as soon as possible. No member of his immediate family could stay behind; in the eyes of the regime, all would be complicit in his defection.

There was already media speculation that the Tlasses were abandoning the Assads after his brother, Firas, and his wife, Rania, and their children left earlier in 2012 for Dubai, like many wealthy Damascenes, as international sanctions took effect and the conflict deepened.[8] Firas posted a denial of his defection on his Facebook page, but talk persisted after the family patriarch, Mustafa Tlass, visited Paris in the spring of 2012 for what he said was a routine medical checkup.[9]

At the same time, hard-liners around Bashar, especially his brother and cousins, were ratcheting up pressure on Manaf to join "cleansing operations" that were still underway in Homs following the bloody attack on Baba Amr—or "liberation from terrorists," as the regime put it. Bashar's kinsmen wanted him to prove his loyalty and publicly dispel the defection rumors.[10]

"It's not a choice between defeat or victory. We have to win," said Bashar when he made a defiant televised appearance in Baba Amr around the first anniversary of the uprising, in March 2012.[11]

Manaf was convinced that his refusal to take part in the Homs military operation, coupled with talk of his family's rift with the Assads, would sooner or later cost him his life. Either he had to become a killer like Bashar or be killed. He believed that the first warning shot from his enemies had come right after the Baba Amr assault, when a series of road-side bombs exploded inside his base in Damascus, wounding several of his soldiers.[12] The bombs were planted on an internal road between his office and main gate.

His line to Bashar wasn't going to offer protection for much longer, Manaf thought. It was Bashar himself, after all, who was overseeing the scorched-earth campaign against rebellious towns and cities.

While Bashar presided over the whole campaign, implementation and enforcement was the responsibility of what Manaf began to call "the trinity of hard-liners": Bashar's brother, Maher, his cousin Hafez Makhlouf, and Jamil Hassan, who headed the *mukhabarat*'s Air Force Intelligence Directorate.[13] Hassan became de facto defense minister after Bashar removed Ali Habib and appointed Dawood Rajha, the chairman of the army's joint chiefs of staff, as a figurehead defense minister in his place. Hassan, a ruthless and bloodthirsty regime veteran, mobilized forces and army equipment and resources as he, Hafez, and Maher saw fit. These men often got together at night to eat dinner and plot the next day's killing.[14]

The troops increasingly resembled bands of killers rather than a conventional force.[15] Those dispatched to rebellious communities were usually a mishmash of forces drawn from various army units and *mukhabarat* departments, as well as pro-Bashar thugs and militiamen. It was hard to distinguish who was who as they all wore the same military fatigues.

Officially, they were all called the Syrian army, but the reality was that the actual Syrian army was plagued by desertion, plummeting morale, and deep mistrust and suspicion. Pooling forces from across the army, *mukhabarat*, and militias and bringing them together under the army's banner countered that. It ensured that people obeyed orders and watched one another for any hesitation or treason. Most of those sent on "cleansing missions" were Bashar loyalists who had no qualms about committing massacres in his name.

On paper, decisions on how to deal with what the regime was calling the *azmeh*, or "crisis," had to be made by a committee of military, security, and *mukhabarat* chiefs as well as ministers and other government officials. It was called the Crisis Cell and its members included the defense minister and his deputy, Assef Shawkat, Bashar's brother-in-law. The reality, however, was that the small circle of hard-liners under Bashar were calling the shots in close coordination with representatives of Iran and its main regional proxy, the Lebanese militia Hezbollah.[16] Orders often went directly from this circle to field commanders, thus bypassing the Crisis Cell. Iran and Hezbollah weighed in on key decisions, since both had direct lines to Bashar and his tight circle.

Iran had significantly augmented the number of its advisers and operatives inside Syria and was already involved in providing training, weapons, communications, and Internet surveillance equipment as well as all forms of support to Syrian regime forces. In 2012 it was routine for Syrian commercial flights from Tehran to Damascus to transport crates of weapons and ammunition. "Iranian depots were wide open for the regime," said a Syrian army officer sent to Iran for training.[17]

As Iran and Hezbollah witnessed the unraveling of the Syrian army from the inside, they worked on assembling more irregular forces and sectarian militias in Syria and they drew contingency plans for direct military intervention, if necessary, to save Bashar. "We are tens of thousands of well-equipped and trained mujahedeen fighters in Lebanon ready for martyrdom...We are a force...that will surprise every enemy," boasted Hezbollah chief Nasrallah.[18]

Even with Iran and Hezbollah firmly behind him, it was still vital, domestically and internationally, for Bashar to keep up appearances that he was the president of a sovereign state with functioning institutions and laws.

In early 2012, as Bashar punished pro-opposition neighborhoods in Homs, the regime held a referendum on a new constitution that eased the ruling Baath Party's monopoly on political life and allowed multi-candidate presidential elections, at least on paper.[19] He wanted to show the world that he was in fact both "fighting terrorism" and "initiating reforms," but on his own terms.

Ten days before the referendum, a dozen armed men decked with ammunition vests raided the office of activist and human rights lawyer Mazen Darwish. Mazen came out of his room to see assault rifles pointed at fifteen of his team members, including his wife, Yara.[20] He had just been on a Skype conference call with fellow activists to discuss the launch of a new online publication titled *We've Come Out for Freedom*.

"What's going on!" cried Mazen. "Who are you?"

"We're from the security forces—isn't it obvious?" said one of the gunmen.

"It's not—what if you are terrorists? Show me your IDs," insisted Mazen.

"We're from the security forces and we're here to search the office," said the same armed man.

"Do you have a warrant?" demanded Mazen. "The president repealed the emergency law. You can't just barge into private property without a warrant."

"We received a tip about an imminent bomb attack on a kindergarten in the area, so we didn't have time to get a warrant," said the man.

"Well, you better hurry up and search the office before the bomb goes off," said Mazen sarcastically.

A few hours later, Mazen and his team were all handcuffed and led down to the street. There were more gunmen in a convoy of vehicles that included a pickup truck with a machine gun mounted to its back. The entire neighborhood had been cordoned off. The central bank building and the Laïque, the exclusive school that Bashar and Manaf had attended, were nearby. Some neighbors and shopkeepers gathered on the opposite side of the street to watch as the manacled activists waited for regime buses to take them to prison.

Mazen found out that the arresting force was from the *mukhabarat*'s Air Force Intelligence Directorate, headed by the dreaded Jamil Hassan, responsible for some of the most heinous crimes committed against protesters since March 2011.

Mazen and his team were taken to the Mezzeh Airbase, where men and women were separated and Mazen was held apart, blindfolded, handcuffed, and thrown onto the floor of the hallway outside the prison cells. His captors put a blanket over his head.

He was like that for almost three days before his first interrogation with an officer. The following day he was taken to what appeared, from the glimpses he managed, to be a big office. A voice instructed his guards to take off his handcuffs but keep him blindfolded. Mazen would later find out from his interrogators that he was in the presence of the notorious Jamil Hassan himself.[21]

"You're Mazen?" Hassan quipped.

"Yes," said Mazen.

"Let's see now," mused Hassan, "what don't you like about Bashar al-Assad?"

"There's really nothing personal between us," replied Mazen, "but I don't like presidents who are turned into Gods and eternal leaders. I want a president who is a government functionary serving a limited term and whose powers are kept in check."

"What are you working on?" demanded Hassan.

"Freedom of press and expression and documentation," said Mazen.

"What are you documenting? You want to take us to The Hague!" site of the International Criminal Court, shrieked Hassan.

"Why The Hague?" Mazen said calmly. "I am documenting for the transitional justice program here in Syria. It's nothing new, I have been working on it since 2005 and you know that."

"But aren't you also corresponding with entities outside Syria?" persisted Hassan.

"No," said Mazen.

"You think you're the leader of a popular revolution, Che Guevara," Hassan mocked. "You want to topple the regime."

"Leader no, Guevara no, topple the regime, as in 'change and reform,' yes. This is something I speak and write about openly. I am for change, but you know I am absolutely against bearing arms and fighting—you know my position," said Mazen.

"We'll see about that," said Hassan threateningly.

Before his arrest, Mazen had turned down an offer to leave Syria, at least momentarily, from Éric Chevallier. Chevallier was providing many activists and regime opponents, who feared arrest or worse, with laissez-passer papers permitting them to enter France, given the exceptional circumstances.[22] This type of document is similar to that given to French citizens who lose their passports, and the prospect of obtaining one was a big deal for those anxious to flee Syria.

Mazen and his colleague Razan Zeitouneh had a heated argument as they tried to convince one another to accept Chevallier's offer.[23]

"Leave, please! We actually need you more outside Syria," said Razan, referring to the role Mazen could play while abroad in rallying financial and political support for their cash-strapped Local Coordination Committees.

"You're the one who should leave," responded Mazen. "You're in hiding anyway."

A month after Mazen's arrest, Chevallier left Damascus as France and allies Britain, the Gulf Arab states, and Turkey shut their embassies and recalled their diplomats.[24] Like the other ambassadors who left Damascus, including America's Robert Ford,[25] Chevallier would remain his country's envoy for Syria but would now operate from abroad.

By early summer 2012—as Bashar's forces committed unspeakable horrors while his allies sat on his war council and as America's Gulf Arab allies dumped arms and cash and fueled militancy on the opposition side—the United States and its Western allies were putting their weight behind a six-point plan to be implemented by former UN secretary-general Kofi Annan in his capacity as a joint United Nations–Arab League envoy to Syria.

The plan called for a ceasefire by all parties and mainly committed the regime to work on a political process to meet the "legitimate aspirations" of its people, facilitate the delivery of humanitarian aid, release detainees and political activists, respect the right to protest, and allow free access to the media.[26]

In tandem, the United States and its Western allies said they were doing everything they could, short of direct military intervention, to weaken Bashar and his regime. They openly encouraged defections in the army, security forces, and government. They doubled down on economic sanctions, throwing the net wider to include all those associated with the Assad family and regime. The assets of Bashar's wife, mother, sister, and sister-in-law were frozen, and they were all banned from travel to European Union member states or even from shopping online with European firms.[27] The Group of Friends of the Syrian People, composed of more than sixty countries, was created to serve as a conduit for supporting the opposition. These countries recognized the Syrian National Council as a "legitimate representative" of the Syrian people.[28] On top of that, the United States and its Western allies gave the nod, albeit covertly, to regional countries like Qatar, Saudi Arabia, and Turkey to boost the arming and funding of the Free Syrian Army factions fighting Bashar.[29]

The United States and its Western allies wanted to put sufficient pressure on Bashar through sanctions, defections, and the armed opposition building up on the ground so he would capitulate and agree to some sort of a political settlement, including his departure from the country.

This strategy assumed that the regime derived its strength from the army, government, and other institutions found in normal states, when in fact the underpinnings of this regime were the family and clan, more than two million Alawites, the *mukhabarat* system, the Hezbollah militia in Lebanon, and Iran. Tens of thousands of soldiers and officers, a prime minister, and other government officials ultimately defected, but all were peripheral to the regime. They were not part of its nerve center.

As the pressure increased on Bashar in the spring and summer of 2012, he hit back harder and more indiscriminately and viciously. He knew that nobody was going to intervene to stop him.

"This is a much more complicated situation," reasoned President Obama in early March 2012. "The notion that the way to solve every one of these problems is to deploy our military, that hasn't been true in the past and it won't be true now. We've got to think through what we do through the lens of what's going to be effective, but also what's critical for US security interests."[30]

With fresh support from regional countries in the spring and summer of 2012, groups under the banner of the Free Syrian Army (FSA) significantly increased the scale, intensity, and effectiveness of their guerilla assaults on regime forces, especially on the outskirts of Damascus, in Homs city and surrounding areas, and the provinces of Aleppo, Hama, and Idlib, farther north.

In response, the regime mobilized heavier weapons, including helicopter gunships and some air assets, and committed gruesome massacres against civilians in several areas where the FSA had support and sanctuary.

This had a chilling impact on the conflict dynamics, making it look increasingly like a civil war between the mostly Sunni rebels and their supporters, on one side, and on the other, the Alawite-dominated regime and its core minority constituencies.

The regime's increased bloodiness undermined the credibility of the main opposition body, the Syrian National Council, already beset by infighting, schisms, and the conflicting agendas of regional states. For average Syrians in areas under attack, what good was a council recognized by more than sixty countries if it could not rally international support to protect them and stop the massacres? Why are not the Friends of the Syrian People saving them from the carnage?

On the last Friday of May 2012, regime forces stationed in Al-Houla, a cluster of towns northwest of Homs, opened fire on an anti-regime protest. Almost all residents were Sunni. This provoked an attack by rebels on regime positions and checkpoints in the area. Clashes followed, and then the regime began shelling the area with mortars and artillery. Several civilians were killed, and when rebels appeared to have been repulsed, pro-Bashar militias from surrounding Alawite and Shiite towns came in and went on a rampage, executing people and looting property. More than a hundred people were killed, most of them from two families known for supporting the opposition.[31] It was a grim scenario that repeated itself in several other towns and villages.

Images of Houla residents shrouding their dead in white, according to Islamic tradition, and holding a mass burial reverberated across the world. Manaf and Thala could not sleep that night.

Thala called Asma in the morning.[32]

"Why this massacre in Houla?" demanded Thala. "Why did this happen? Lots of people were killed."

"What massacre?" Asma shot back. "What are you talking about? I have heard nothing. More importantly, where is your husband, why is not he taking part in the battles against terrorists?"

*   *   *

On June 20, 2012, almost a month after the Houla massacre, Asma headed to the Al-Fayha sports complex in Damascus to spend time with youth from the country's Paralympics team. It was a chance to make a public display of the regime's compassion and show that she was going about her business as normal. To Syrians buckling under her husband's bombs, she looked cruel and evil.

Asma wore bell-bottom jeans, a fashionable belt with a big buckle, high heels, and a navy T-shirt emblazoned with this slogan in white Arabic calligraphy: "You're beautiful, my country!" She casually walked into an indoor court where she greeted the children with smiles, handshakes, and kisses. Portraits of Bashar and Hafez loomed above.[33] She played badminton with two boys and cheered others as they dribbled and shot basketballs into nets. Nearby, cameramen filmed Asma and the children.

Two days later, Thala returned from Beirut, where she had met French secret service agents to discuss the plan to get Manaf and the family out of Damascus. Their two youngest children, Hamza and Mounzer, flew from Beirut to a summer camp in Switzerland, something they have done each year. The eldest son, Mustafa, stayed in Beirut for now in order not to arouse suspicion.

Manaf worried that he was endangering his wife, but she was the one who insisted on being central to the operation every step of the way. They had talked about it endlessly during many sleepless nights. She was convinced that it was the only way to protect her husband and children; they had to make the leap, there was no looking back.

"Everything is okay and I gave them the name of the man and they'll call him," Thala scribbled on a piece of paper as she and Manaf sat next to each other in their living room. "The departure will be within a week."[34]

They assumed that the house was bugged and that all their phone conversations and e-mails were monitored. There were three *mukhabarat* cars watching the house—two were on their street and one was on the Mezzeh Highway near the Jala'a Stadium.

The man Thala referred to was the intermediary between her husband

and the smugglers tasked by the French to get him out of Syria. All communications between Manaf and the smugglers had to be through the intermediary. He was a former army officer who had served under Manaf's father before becoming a teacher of Arabic literature and poetry. He had remained loyal to the family.

The French instructed them to choose someone Manaf could trust but who was not a member of the family or particularly close to him.

"Someone will call you. This person is a source of security to me. Go see him and then let me know what he says," Manaf told the intermediary without giving more details.[35]

Thala stayed in Damascus for three days. One night they hosted friends for dinner, and on a second night they went out to dinner at a restaurant in Damascus. They wanted to give the impression that everything was normal. Thala left again for Beirut on June 25.

The next day, Talal Makhlouf called Manaf again. He wanted to know when he was going to see Bashar.[36]

"Have you spoken to him?" asked Talal. "How did it go?"

"Not yet, but I will soon," responded Manaf. The window was closing. He had to leave. It was now or never.

The following day, June 27, the intermediary came to see Manaf at home.

"I met Abu Alaa and we have to see him tomorrow," he said. Abu Alaa was the smuggler connected to the French. He wanted to finalize plans with Manaf in person.

The next morning, Thursday, June 28, the intermediary waited for Manaf in an alleyway next to a cemetery. Manaf put on jeans, a T-shirt, and sneakers, pretending he was going for a morning walk. The cemetery was about ten minutes away on foot. About a thousand British soldiers were buried in the Damascus Commonwealth War Cemetery, an immaculately maintained grassy plot with rows of tombstones and large cypress trees on the perimeter. Nearly half of the soldiers had perished in a cholera and influenza epidemic that struck Damascus in October 1918.[37] They were part of a contingent that entered the Syrian capital as liberators after defeating the Ottoman Turks. The British were supporting Arab tribesmen in a revolt against the Ottoman Empire, which was unraveling in the waning days of World War I. The two victorious European colonial powers, Britain and France, were staking their claims to Ottoman dominions, and by capturing Damascus the British hoped to beat the French and install a loyal Arab king to rule over much of the Levant. One of the masterminds of this plan was a British officer by the name of T. E. Lawrence, better known as Lawrence of Arabia. He, along with British generals and the future King Faisal, were among those who marched into Damascus that fall. Eventually Britain lost Syria to France in the carve-out that ensued.

"Good morning, let's go," said Manaf as he jumped into the intermediary's car parked next to the cemetery's outer wall.[38]

They made their way through alleyways and got on the Al-Motahalik al-Janoubi, the flyover that ringed Damascus. This was the only spot where it seemed the *mukhabarat* had not posted people to watch Manaf, or so he thought.

The car sped east and then swung up north. Fifteen minutes later they were in front of Hameesh Hospital in Barzeh on the city's northeast side.

"Okay, come back to the same spot in thirty minutes," said Manaf as he got out.

The moment was tense for him, but residents of the capital were still going about their daily routines. There was traffic on the streets. A crowd of people lined up at a nearby bakery to buy packs of pita bread, one of the staples still subsidized by the regime.

Manaf crossed the street. He spotted a bearded man in his thirties pacing on the sidewalk and asked him, "Are you Abu Alaa?"

"Yes! How did you know? You must be Abu Nizar," said the man, referring to Manaf by an adopted pseudonym.

"Yes, I am," said Manaf.

"We have to leave this Sunday because my cover has been blown," said Abu Alaa.

Abu Alaa, a native of Homs, was up until then a liaison between rebels in the city and surrounding countryside and the *mukhabarat*. Sometimes he interacted with the most senior figures in the *mukhabarat*, people like Ali Mamlouk and the ruthless Bashar loyalist Jamil Hassan. Abu Alaa passed messages between the rebels and regime. Sometimes they needed to work out temporary ceasefires or exchange detainees and bodies. Abu Alaa was the go-to fixer for these arrangements. People like him were indispensable in every war. Abu Alaa also worked for the rebels to ferry people, weapons, cash, journalists, and just about anything they needed across the porous border between the Homs countryside and Lebanon. He tried to evade the *mukhabarat*'s surveillance, but he'd just been summoned by them to explain why he had made a call to the city of Tripoli in Lebanon. He was convinced it was a trap and that he was going to be arrested, so he planned to skip the appointment and instead smuggle Manaf and remain on the rebel side in Homs for good.

"I cannot leave Sunday," said Manaf, "it's impossible."

"Why?" asked Abu Alaa nervously.

"It's just not possible," said Manaf, not wanting to explain further.

Manaf had booked a seat for his father on Monday on the flight to Cyprus. The family had a summer vacation home on the eastern Mediterranean island, just across Syria's coast. The elder Tlass spent almost every summer there, especially after his wife, Lamia, passed away in 2006. His departure was perfectly normal. But the problem was that there were only two flights a week from Damascus, Monday and Thursday. Manaf was not going to risk exposing his father to detention by the regime if he left a day earlier on Sunday. They both had to leave on the same day.

"Monday is not going to work," said Abu Alaa.

"Okay," said Manaf, "I am not going, then."

A tense silence followed as they strolled along the busy road. Speeding by were ubiquitous boxy yellow taxi cars made in Iran and buses blowing out black smoke. This was one of the busiest thoroughfares in Damascus. The working-class district of Barzeh and nearby Qaboun were among the first areas in the capital to protest against Bashar.

"I guess I have no choice," Abu Alaa said finally. "I'll take a chance, I won't go see the *mukhabarat* on Sunday."

"Meet me further up the road across from Ibn al-Nafees Hospital on Monday at 1:00 p.m. sharp," added Abu Alaa. "But it has to be Monday or never."

He shook Abu Alaa's hand and crossed the street. The intermediary was already there waiting in his blue Lada. Manaf was in a race against time.

That day an Iranian television station aired an interview with Bashar. He did his best to maintain his usual cold, detached facade, but there was also an undertone of menace. Bashar called his opponents "a mix of criminals," "mercenaries," and "illiterates." He assured his Iranian patrons that he was not budging, no matter the pressure from the West and its Arab allies, and that he remained firmly anchored in Iran's so-called axis of resistance. He said that the West was going to think twice before intervening in Syria because it knew that this could provoke a major "earthquake" in the region—another one of his favorite analogies.[39]

The next day, Friday, June 29, a pro-regime businessman whom Manaf called Abu Ali came to see him. Abu Ali was Alawite, from the same sect as Bashar, and had close dealings with Bashar's maternal cousins the Makhloufs, including Rami, the businessman, and Hafez, the security chief. He was also on good terms with the Tlasses. Mustafa Tlass had often lunched with Abu Ali.

"Abu Mustafa [that is, Manaf], you must go see the Makhloufs," Abu Ali told Manaf as they sipped coffee.[40]

Now, thought Manaf, they were sending him Abu Ali after Talal Makhlouf had failed to bring him around.

"Go see them," pleaded Abu Ali, "I kiss your hand."

"Okay, organize dinner with Abu Rami," said Manaf, coolly referring to Bashar's maternal uncle, Mohammad Makhlouf.

"I'll call Hafez [Makhlouf] now," said Abu Ali.

Abu Ali pulled a cell phone from his pocket and called Hafez Makhlouf, a man who had undermined Manaf's conciliatory moves toward protesters every step of the way—the same man who personally killed and tortured protesters.

"I am at the general's home, and he wants to come over for dinner," said Abu Ali, who then gestured with his other hand toward Manaf to ask him when he wanted to do it.

"Tuesday is good," said Manaf.

It was one day after Manaf's planned exit.

18

Exiting

It is not possible for us to host him in Russia—we have too many of them already," joked Sergei Lavrov, Russia's foreign minister, with his counterparts from Western and Middle Eastern countries during a pause from their talks on June 30, 2012, at the Palais des Nations, the United Nations headquarters in Geneva.[1]

They were talking about where Bashar might go after stepping down and handing his powers to a transitional government. They mused whether it would be just Bashar and his wife and children, or the entire Assad family and their henchmen, too. Was it fifty, or more like 200 people in the regime?[2]

"I know Europe is difficult, but I am sure we can find a country in South America or Africa to take him," said a European foreign minister as the top diplomats stood with their coffee cups in the hallway outside the conference room.[3] Through the large panoramic windows, Lake Geneva glistened beneath a clear sky as the Mont Blanc summit loomed in the distance.

It was a world away from the mayhem of Syria. Civilian deaths since the start of the uprising in March 2011 were approaching 13,000. The number of refugees in neighboring countries neared 120,000, triple what it had been in March 2012 when some countries spoke about the need to establish safe havens for civilians inside Syria.

Foreign ministers from the five permanent members of the UN Security Council—Britain, China, France, Russia, and the United States—had flown to Geneva to discuss a solution. They were joined by their counterparts from Iraq, Kuwait, Qatar, and Turkey, each with their own stake in Syria. Representatives of the European Union and Arab League also attended.

Iran and Saudi Arabia, two key regional players who were on opposite sides of the escalating war in Syria, were notably absent from the talks.

There were hours of deliberations and discussions throughout the day. The neatly dressed and famously wily Lavrov kept stepping out of the room to take calls from his boss at the Kremlin, Vladimir Putin.[4] The equally experienced Laurent Fabius, who just became foreign minister in the new government of French president François Hollande, sensed that the Russians were starting to envision the possibility of Bashar being swept aside soon. So far, the Russians were uncompromising in their defense of the Syrian regime and had even delivered attack helicopters to Bashar days before the Geneva meeting.[5] Still, Fabius believed that Russia had come to the meeting with the sole objective of extracting maximum concessions and protecting Russian interests in Syria in the proposed settlement they were trying to forge that day. He felt Lavrov's hardball tactics during the talks, as well as the Kremlin's telephonic interjections, all served that purpose.

The Russians were already reassured by the United States and its Western allies before the meeting that nothing would happen to Russia's naval base in Tartous on Syria's west coast if Bashar were to leave.[6]

Later that day, the foreign ministers gathered in an austere auditorium to hear the UN Syria envoy, Kofi Annan, read a statement outlining their agreement. The event was broadcast live by Arab and Syrian channels; many anxious Syrians tuned in, so did Bashar and Manaf in Damascus.[7]

A concerned but calm-looking Annan said that members of the Syria Action Group—the ad hoc grouping of the countries gathered on that day—had agreed on a road map for ending the conflict.[8] It called on both the regime and the rebels to abide by an immediate ceasefire and urged Bashar to release detainees, especially those arrested for taking part in peaceful protests; to permit international journalists to work in the country; and to give humanitarian agencies access to opposition-held areas. Both the Assad regime and the opposition would then form a transitional or interim government with full executive powers, which technically meant taking away Bashar's formal authority as president. This interim body would then draft a new constitution and hold new elections.[9]

"The transitional governing body could include members of the present government and the opposition and other groups and should be formed on the basis of mutual consent," stressed Annan.[10]

But it was these two words, *mutual* and *consent*, which summed up the plan's fatal flaw. There was no explicit mention of the post of president or of Bashar in the statement, or any reference to him leaving power. His executive powers were simply expected to be transferred to a new transitional body made up of members of his current government and the opposition. It was those two words that Lavrov insisted on inserting in the final communiqué after taking one last call from the Kremlin during the off-camera talks.[11]

Annan envisioned Bashar's international backer Russia, and to a lesser extent China, convincing him to embrace the plan. The Americans and their allies who supported the opposition were expected to bring them to the negotiating table.

As Annan spoke, Lavrov was busy taking notes. He sat in the front row one seat over from Hillary Clinton, then the US secretary of state. Britain's then foreign minister William Hague sat between them.[12]

"The Action Group has pledged action and they are sending a message of determination and hope, but today's words must not become tomorrow's disappointments," said a somber Annan, foreshadowing the sharp disagreements among world and regional powers. "The hard work starts now, we must work together to implement what has been agreed, we cannot do this alone."[13]

No sooner had Annan concluded his remarks than the rifts were out in the open.

Lavrov held a press conference in the same building and went out of his way to stress that there was nothing in the plan about Bashar leaving power. "There is no attempt to impose any kind of a transition process," he told reporters. "There are no prior conditions…and no attempt to exclude" anyone.[14]

Down the hall from where Lavrov spoke Clinton also met with reporters, but she had a completely different take on the agreement. "What we have done here is to strip away the fiction that he and those with blood on their hands can stay in power. The plan calls for the Assad regime to give way to a new transitional governing body that will have full governance powers. Now, in deciding to accept the minor textual changes, we and our partners made absolutely clear to Russia and China that it is now incumbent upon them to show Assad the writing on the wall...He needs to hear loudly and clearly that his days are numbered."[15]

Clinton said that she was traveling to Paris the following week for a meeting with the Syrian opposition and their European and Arab backers. The Paris meeting was timed to coincide with Manaf's bombshell defection. What stronger indication that Bashar's end was near than a member of his own inner circle jumping ship, the thinking went.

Fabius told reporters in Geneva that the pillars of Bashar's regime were going to be tried for war crimes. It was intended as an ultimatum to Bashar: Leave now or face trial.[16]

The next day, Sunday, July 1, Manaf was in his office at the base.[17] It was early in the evening and he was planning to sleep there. He had already told his aide Ali that he was going to have dinner with the Makhloufs on Tuesday. Ali, a member of Bashar's Alawite community, seemed happy that his boss was finally making peace with the powerful Makhloufs and ultimately with the *ma'alem el-kbeer*, or the big boss — Bashar.

"Great! It's all good by the will of Allah," said Ali.

Over the prior ten days, Manaf had quietly and slowly removed, then burned, all important documents from his office. There was hardly anything left. He'd take one last look tonight.

He did not want to leave anything behind that could be used against him or those who had been in contact with him over the years.

On one wall in the office were photographs of him with the Assads. There was one from the early 1990s of a boyish and handsome Manaf with Bashar, both in military uniform. There was a similar one with Bassel, the one who was supposed to have been president.

A framed photo on his desk showed him with Hafez months before "the eternal leader" died in June 2000. It was taken during a visit by Hafez to his friend, the elder Tlass, while Mustafa convalesced at the hospital after heart surgery. Hafez had a big smile but already looked very frail. Manaf, dressed casually in a short-sleeve shirt and slacks, looked happy, too, with his right arm wrapped around Hafez.

Manaf woke up at about 7:00 a.m. the next day, Monday, July 2, tense but determined. He washed his face and got dressed. He pulled out a copy of the Quran from the bookshelf. Religion had never been a big part of his life, but occasionally he did pray and fast during Ramadan, the Muslim holy month. He read a few verses to put himself at ease.

Shortly before midday he left the base. He decided to borrow a black armored sedan that belonged to one of his guards rather than take his own SUV. It was seen as perfectly normal for someone in his position, a commander in the Republican Guard, to want to break the routine and use different cars for security reasons. In addition, taking a different car at the last minute protected him from any tracking devices that may have been put in his SUV.

He went home to Mezzeh. He quickly changed into a pair of jeans, casual shirt, and sneakers. He had prepared three plastic bags to take with him. One contained two pistols, an Italian-made Beretta and an Austrian-made Glock, both 9-millimeter in caliber and capable of firing twelve shots.[18] Another larger bag had two slim, lightweight bulletproof vests. In the third bag were about a dozen spinach pies, made by his favorite bakery shop in Damascus. In his pocket was a cheap Nokia phone in which he had put the SIM card of his own private number. There was just enough power in it to last until he met up with Abu Alaa, the smuggler.

Manaf grabbed the bags, closed the door, and walked over to the car parked in his driveway. He turned the engine on, backed out, and drove to Mezzeh Highway in the direction of Barzeh, arriving fifteen minutes before his rendezvous with Abu Alaa. He parked the car in an alleyway near a bakery and walked down toward the main road. He sat on a park bench next to the Ibn al-Nafees Hospital. He waited. Abu Alaa did not show up at 1:00 p.m. as they had agreed. Then all of a sudden two men in a black car drove by and stared at him. They were for sure *mukhabarat*, he thought. He could tell. His heart sank.

Minutes later Abu Alaa pulled up. He was in a Nissan sedan with a damaged fender.

"I am sorry, get in—quickly!" said Abu Alaa as Manaf jumped into the seat next to him.

"What happened?" said Manaf.

"I had an accident on my way. I paid the guy 5,000 lira on the spot," said Abu Alaa nervously.

"I am glad you're okay," said Manaf. "Let's just go up to my car, I want to grab something."

They went up to the alleyway where Manaf had left his car. He quickly got the three bags and hopped back into Abu Alaa's car.

Abu Alaa then drove down toward Abbaseen Square, which protesters had tried to occupy early on only to be shot and killed each time by the regime.

Abu Alaa parked behind a yellow Buick on a side street off the square.

"Okay, get out — we have to change cars," said Abu Alaa.

Manaf grabbed his bags and jumped into the back seat of the Buick. Abu Alaa got in front next to the driver.

"Abu Mohammad, this is Abu Nizar," said Abu Alaa, introducing them to each other.

"I am honored," said the driver with a smile.

"Me too. God bless you," said Manaf, who was still assuming the pseudonym Abu Nizar.

It was past 2:00 p.m. as the car moved northeast toward the highway to Homs city, about 100 miles away. They joined the buses, minivans, and cars leaving Damascus. They drove past the October War Panorama Museum, a white, castle-like structure built with the help of North Korea to commemorate Hafez al-Assad's "victory" in the 1973 Arab–Israeli war, which in reality had ended in defeat for Egypt, Syria, and other Arab states.[19] It was the epitome of the lies on which the Assad regime was founded with the help of the Tlasses and others. A massive Stalinist mural inside the museum depicted Hafez being feted by the people, with Mustafa Tlass dressed in military uniform by his side. Outside, Hafez stared down from a large mural.

As Damascus disappeared behind them, Manaf reflected on the past and what had brought him to this dramatic moment of having to run away just to save his life. He consoled himself with the thought that his exit was necessary but temporary. All the signs were that Bashar's regime was on the brink of collapse. Manaf would come back. He believed that he had no blood on his hands. He reckoned his refusal to take part in the killing of Bashar's opponents would give him the moral authority and right to be part of whatever new system emerged from the ashes.[20]

They sped down the highway past the towns of Harasta and Douma, where Manaf had worked hard at the start of the uprising to negotiate a

305

compromise between protesters and Bashar, only to see these efforts undermined by regime hard-liners.

One month earlier, on June 3, 2012, Adnan Wehbeh, the Douma-based physician and peaceful protest leader that Manaf had met with many times, was shot dead inside his clinic.[21]

These towns were battle zones now. The driver stepped hard on the gas pedal.

The road rose up and soon they were skirting past the ancient Christian town of Maaloula, nestled in the Qalamoun Mountains, one of the few places on earth where people still spoke Aramaic, the language of Jesus Christ.

"You look familiar," said the driver all of a sudden, addressing Manaf.

"Maybe you are confusing me with someone else," responded Manaf.

"Okay, drop it," Abu Alaa snapped at the driver.

It was silent again in the car.

About thirty minutes later they approached the town of Deir Attiyeh. On a hill overlooking the highway stood an oversize statue of Hafez with his right arm raised up as if he were saluting all those passing by.

"If you are whom I think you are, then your friend is finished—God bless you!" exclaimed the driver, Abu Mohammad.

A few miles from Homs, the car pulled into the parking lot of a bakery and sweets shop beside the highway. Manaf and Abu Alaa hurriedly bid the taxi driver goodbye and jumped into a pickup truck that was waiting for them. In it were armed men—probably smugglers turned rebel fighters, Manaf reckoned. They drove off the highway and got on rugged back roads that snaked through farmland to reach the town of Al-Qusair, south of Homs and close to the Lebanese border, which had long had a reputation, even before the uprising, for being a hub of smuggling between Lebanon and Syria. It was a crucial link in the opposition's supply line from Lebanon to Homs and beyond.

In Qusair, Manaf stayed for a few hours in the home of a local rebel leader and smuggling boss—a short, wiry man called Mustafa. They waited for the all-clear to head to the border. Smugglers like Mustafa had long-standing arrangements with border patrol officers in Lebanon and Syria who allowed them to move people and goods back and forth in return for money or other forms of compensation.

Later Manaf was taken closer to the border. Mustafa led him and Abu Alaa to a house under construction with a swimming pool, really just a hole in the ground filled with water. The pool was not tiled yet. There were fighters smoking and lounging by the pool, including a man who lost an arm. Manaf just greeted them with the customary *salam alaykoum* but otherwise kept to himself and said little. There was a doctor there, visibly nervous, who like Manaf was being smuggled out.[22] Anyone who provided medical services to opposition communities topped the regime's most-wanted list.

At about 8:00 p.m. the signal came for them to go to the border, which was barely discernible. There's no fence along the porous border, which runs through farmland, canals, and villages. In some places, the Syrian border guard is no more than a lone young conscript with a rifle sitting on a plastic lawn chair next to the canal.

Manaf and the others ran for a few yards across the border into Lebanon. There they got on motorbikes. They soon arrived at a Lebanese army checkpoint where a sedan with tinted windows was waiting for Manaf. He hugged Abu Alaa and Mustafa and gave them his two pistols and bulletproof vests as gifts. Manaf's trajectory from the border to a safe house in Beirut had been arranged by General Wissam al-Hassan, a powerful Lebanese security chief who had his own score to settle with Bashar over the murder of his former patron, Rafic Hariri.[23]

By 11:00 p.m. that night the Syrian regime had discovered Manaf's escape, and Hezbollah operatives were looking for him in and around Beirut.[24] The French secret service managed, however, to get Manaf out by sea to nearby Cyprus and then onward to France.[25] Thala and his son Mustafa flew out from Beirut airport and were reunited with him in Paris, where the other children and the family patriarch, Mustafa Tlass, had arrived, too.

For days afterward, Manaf sat with French intelligence officers for long debriefings.

There was no immediate public reaction from Bashar, but Manaf's home was raided and several of his aides, including his driver, were arrested.[26]

Meanwhile France, the United States, and their allies were betting that the defection of Manaf and others in Bashar's circle, coupled with rebel offensives in both the capital, Damascus, and the largest city and economic hub, Aleppo in the north, could exert sufficient pressure on the regime and trigger one of two scenarios: Bashar agreeing to leave power in exchange for immunity from trial, or elements of his regime staging a coup.

Manaf's exit was only one part of a bigger secret plan the French and their allies had been working on that summer.

Four days after Manaf's escape, foreign ministers from more than 100 nations, nearly half the countries on the planet (as French officials boasted) gathered in Paris on July 6, 2012, for a conference of the Group of Friends of the Syrian People.

"Bashar al-Assad has to leave; a transitional government must be formed. This is in everyone's interest," said French president Hollande, addressing officials gathered at a convention center on the Seine's left bank, a few blocks from the Eiffel Tower.[27]

The Syrian opposition wanted immediate action by those professing friendship to the Syrian people, not more words and threats, to end the slaughter. "We are facing a regime that's out of the ordinary, it's more like a gang," pleaded veteran opposition leader Riad Seif, who had fled Syria after he was attacked by regime thugs earlier in 2012.[28]

In her speech at the conference, Hillary Clinton said that there was "a steady, inexorable march toward ending the regime" and called on China and Russia, both absent from the meeting, to support a Security Council resolution to implement the Geneva communiqué, or what became known as the Annan plan.[29]

Later that day Fabius, the French foreign minister, held a press conference to officially announce Manaf's defection, calling it a "hard blow" for Bashar.[30] "This regime must fall and liberty must reappear in that beautiful country," he said.

Away from the conference and the glare of TV cameras, the French quietly worked with their US and Middle Eastern allies to bring the whole plan to fruition. This was the plan that was going to spell the demise of the house of the Assads, a clan whose inner workings Fabius knew very well from his time as prime minister in the 1980s and which he often likened to an international terrorist organization.[31] Thirty years ago, a 37-year-old Fabius had been bitterly opposed to French reengagement with

Hafez al-Assad; for him it was yielding to the terrorism that he and other officials accused the Syrian regime of committing against France, both on its soil and abroad, most notably in Lebanon. For Fabius and others who shared his thinking it was coddling the *barbaric state.*[32]

Now France was assisting in the end of the Assads' reign of terror, as Fabius saw it.

A central element of the plan, which was supposed to play out right after Manaf's bombshell defection, involved top Syrian army and security generals, especially from Bashar's Alawite sect, breaking with the Assad family and siding with the rebels.

As Fabius later explained, "the certitude we acquired fairly quickly was that...if we did not want a collapse of the [Syrian] regime, perhaps as happened in Iraq with dramatic consequences after the US intervention, then we had to find a solution that blended the moderate resistance with elements of the regime who were not heavily compromised, but still elements of the regime, including the military."[33]

Fabius believed that Manaf's defection would shake the regime and that Manaf would be someone very palatable to the Russians, given their long history and friendship with his father, Mustafa Tlass. Still, he and other French officials were not convinced, at least privately, that Manaf was the leader to replace Bashar. They saw him as "a component" of what they called a future "collective leadership."[34] In this leadership council, which would rule the country until elections were organized, there were other figures representing regime constituencies, most notably Bashar's Alawite sect.

One of the names circulated early on among all the powers actively working to push Bashar aside was that of his brother-in-law Assef Shawkat.[35] Although Assef's star had dimmed three years before the 2011 uprising, the sixty-two-year-old general remained the consummate regime insider and one of the few figures viewed by Bashar and his brother and cousins as a real threat to their grip on power. Like regime founder Hafez al-Assad, Assef was a self-made man from a humble background who had clawed his way to the top with cutthroat determination and ambition. His family hailed from the coastal province of Tartous, part of the regime's stronghold in western Syria. The Assads and Makhloufs were from adjacent Latakia.

Before he was demoted by Bashar in 2008, Assef had handled the most delicate and top-secret files for the regime in his capacity as *mukhabarat* chief. He was involved in the oil deal Bashar had with Saddam before the 2003 US invasion, as well as the supply of arms to Lebanon's Hezbollah militia, infiltration of radical Sunni Islamists and their recruitment for regime missions, and contacts with Western intelligence agencies under the guise of counterterrorism cooperation. Assef was a black box of Assad family secrets.[36]

Over the years, the charismatic and ruthless Assef had built a loyal following in his Alawite community and in the ranks of the military and *mukhabarat*, something that kept him under the watchful eyes of Bashar and Maher. Even after he was blamed for major security breaches in 2007 and 2008 and was demoted to deputy defense minister, he retained his military rank and, of course, his place in the family as Bushra's husband.

He was back in the spotlight at the start of the uprising in 2011 as Bashar and his kinsmen mobilized to crush the protests and the challenge to their family's rule. Assef was part of the special Crisis Cell that included army and *mukhabarat* chiefs as well as key government ministers. It quickly became evident to Assef, though, that all major decisions were being made by a tighter circle around Bashar, including Maher and the Makhloufs. These men's orders were to show no mercy to protesters and to shoot to kill in order to scare people off the streets, and they sabotaged Assef's de-escalation attempts.

Manaf considered Assef a friend and an ally, and they met frequently. While they shared criticism of Maher, the Makhloufs, and the uncompromising loyalists around Bashar, they were also extremely cautious of one another. Manaf sensed Assef's frustration with the situation and Bashar's strategy, but there was never any frank talk about defection or a palace coup. Everyone in the regime kept their cards close to the vest. They often spoke in code; it was hard to discern plans and motives.[37]

What Manaf did not know at the time was that Assef had secretly reached out, mainly through trusted businessmen, to several foreign intelligence services including the CIA as early as the summer of 2011 to tell them he opposed the scorched earth campaign led by Bashar and his brother and cousins and that he had an alternative plan to resolve the conflict.[38] That same summer a senior Turkish official met with Bashar to urge elections and a new government that would keep Bashar president but bring in an Islamist Sunni prime minister and Assef Shawkat as defense minister. It was then that Bashar and his brother began to fret over Assef's loyalty and set out to blunt all his moves.

"So now you're unemployed, like me," joked Manaf with Assef after the failure of his Homs mission and as Bashar readied to attack the city in early 2012.[39]

Assef was not going to give up easily. He had faced off with Maher before. Assef defied Maher by negotiating a truce with some rebels near Damascus. The Assad brothers were alarmed by the fact that some leaders in the Crisis Cell seemed to be taking Assef's side. It was the kind of rift that Bashar could not afford to have as pressure on his regime mounted at home and abroad. In late May 2012, before Manaf's escape, Assef had survived an attempt by his regime rivals to kill him by poisoning his takeout lunch.[40]

Assef then stepped up his secret contacts with several of the countries that were lined up against Bashar.[41] He wanted to know what they were ready to offer him if he were to turn on Bashar. He was someone with a long and bloody history both inside and outside Syria in the service of the Assad family. He was a member of the dreaded clan that Syrians had risen up against. Assef had been under US sanctions since 2006, and fresh sanctions and asset freezes were imposed on him and his family after the uprising in 2011.

But working to Assef's advantage were years of relations with regional and Western intelligence agencies. He regarded Phillipe Rondot, a retired senior French intelligence officer with whom he had extensive dealings, as a dear friend.[42] Assef and his wife, Bushra, and their children often vacationed in France.

Before Manaf's defection, Assef sent a secret message to the French declaring his intention to break with Bashar. They looked into ways to assist him, but then it was too late.[43]

What Assef and the French and their allies did not know was that Bashar and Iran were also secretly plotting their next dramatic chess move.

On July 15, 2012, ten days after the announcement of Manaf's defection and one day after France commemorated the storming of the Bastille, thousands of rebels from around Damascus raided the capital. Aided by sympathizers and collaborators on the inside, they christened their operation "Damascus Volcano."[44]

Fighting was concentrated mainly in neighborhoods on the city's south side, but rebels managed to cut off key highways, including the one to the airport. In the meantime, Assef got into a huge argument with his longtime nemesis, Maher, over whom was to blame for the stunning breach of the capital's defenses. Assef was at his Damascus villa with his wife and children when Maher called him.[45]

Maher was so angry that his screaming could be heard by Assef's children, who sat nearby.

"Pack up, we are going to Moscow!" a visibly shaken and upset Assef told his wife, Bushra, afterward. He then called Bashar to ask permission to take a break with his family for a week in Moscow.

"Postpone it. This is absolutely not the right time," Bashar told him.[46]

Over the next two days fighting inched closer to the city center. There was an exchange of gunfire near parliament and the central bank, close to Bashar's residence. Rumors spread that Bashar and his family had left Damascus and flown to Latakia on the coast.

"We're coming for you!" vowed one rebel on Al Jazeera, addressing Bashar.[47]

On July 18, the regime convened a Crisis Cell meeting at the headquarters of the National Security Bureau, a bunker-like cinder-block structure nestled among residential buildings in the Rawda neighborhood, near Bashar's home. Embassies were all around. This was one of the capital's most secure zones.

Several of the *mukhabarat* chiefs who were part of the Crisis Cell and were supposed to be there, given the gravity of the situation, did not show up that morning.[48] Before midday, Syrian state television announced that Assef, along with the defense minister, Dawood Rajha, and Hassan Turkmani, a top general and presidential adviser, had all been killed in a "terrorist explosion" while they were meeting.[49] Hardly anyone in the neighborhood had heard the blast or seen smoke from its aftermath. The TV announcement was made with highly uncharacteristic speed, efficiency, and even serenity, considering that this was supposed to be a strike directly to the regime's heart. Everything seemed preplanned. The army issued a statement vowing to avenge "the martyrs," and the new defense minister spoke on TV. Later that same day, the interior minister, Mohammad al-Shaar, who had been at the same meeting but was only lightly wounded in one arm, was seen laughing and cracking jokes at the hospital where he was taken.[50]

At least four different rebel groups claimed they had carried out the attack.

After Assef's death, a relaxed-looking Bashar was shown swearing in the new defense minister at the presidential palace in Damascus. Bashar skipped the military funeral held for Assef and the two other top generals and sent instead his vice president, Farouq al-Sharaa, who had been under house arrest ever since Arab states called on Bashar to step down and transfer his powers to Sharaa seven months earlier.[51] Sharaa was let out just for the funeral—a show of cold-bloodedness and vengefulness that rivaled the plot of any Hollywood gangster film. What better way to forewarn Sharaa about the perils of defection than to have him officiate the funeral of Assef and the others.

Bashar also skipped Assef's burial ceremony in his hometown in western Syria, where throngs of regime loyalists massed and chanted Bashar's name.[52]

In tandem with these dramatic developments, regime artillery positioned on Mount Qasioun, helicopter gunships, and tanks unleashed their fury on neighborhoods overrun by rebels. Most of the rebels were armed only with assault rifles. Their most sophisticated weapon was probably a rocket-propelled grenade (RPG) launcher. Thousands of Damascenes fled to Lebanon.[53]

Older residents said that the last time the capital had been shelled this viciously and indiscriminately was by the French during the waning days of their mandate over Syria in 1945.

In Paris, Manaf was thunderstruck at the news of Assef's death.

He did not have the slightest doubt that it was an inside job executed with Bashar's full knowledge and approval because of concerns over Assef's loyalty.[54]

A French official with whom Assef had communicated his desire to defect agreed. "Assef was killed by people in the heart of the regime because they thought he was being prepared as an alternative for Bashar."[55]

19

No Role for You

It was late July 2012, the start of Ramadan, the Muslim month of fasting from dawn to dusk. Manaf Tlass was in Mecca in Saudi Arabia. An unstitched piece of white cloth was wrapped around his body like a Roman toga: it was what all Muslim men must wear while on pilgrimage to the holy city.[1] It was Manaf's first time in Mecca; he was performing a lesser pilgrimage known as *umrah*. (The more important pilgrimage *hajj* is required by all able-bodied Muslims at least once in their lifetimes.) Manaf was not particularly religious, but he wanted to project a symbolic break with the past and a cleansing of sins to an opposition constituency that was increasingly under the sway of Islamists, particularly inside Syria.

The temperature had eased from a sweltering 110 degrees Fahrenheit as night fell. A bearded cleric at Manaf's side explained the rituals of *umrah* as they were trailed by an entourage of uniformed soldiers, security officers, and minders in traditional Saudi dress. They crossed the gleaming marble esplanade of the Grand Mosque toward the Kaaba, the cubelike monument that is Islam's holiest site, illuminated by giant stadium floodlights.

Saudi Arabia was the first stop for Manaf on a tour that would also take him to Qatar and Turkey.[2] All three regional states were deeply enmeshed in the effort to topple Bashar al-Assad. Saudi kings had always exercised a paternalistic role over countries of the Levant, including Syria. The kingdom's financial largesse was at times vital for both Hafez and Bashar, but it was also part of a relationship that was marred by periods of estrangement because of the Assads' alliance with Saudi archenemy Shiite-led Iran and the Assad's embrace of its agenda in the region. In 2006,

Bashar castigated the kingdom's Sunni rulers, calling them "half men" for opposing his ally and Iran's proxy, Hezbollah, in its war with Israel that year, an insult they never forgave. Still, there were extensive kinship ties between Saudi and Syrian families. One of the many wives of King Abdullah was the sister of the wife of Bashar's uncle Rifaat. Osama Bin Laden's mother was Syrian, too. Manaf's brother-in-law, the arms dealer Akram Ojjeh, held Saudi citizenship.

In the 1980s, Saudi Arabia gave refuge to survivors of Hafez's massacre in Hama, including figures in the Muslim Brotherhood and their families. While Saudis were not hosting those fleeing the carnage three decades later, they were nonetheless eager to take the lead in shaping the military and political battle against Bashar and what came after. The Ministry of Foreign Affairs and its seasoned but ailing chief, Saud al-Faisal, was often the one articulating the kingdom's position in official meetings.

But by the summer of 2012 it was another prince, the newly appointed spy chief, Bandar bin Sultan, who was driving the kingdom's efforts in Syria, albeit from behind the scenes.[3] Bandar was the longtime former Saudi ambassador to Washington and veteran of US–Saudi covert operations, including in Afghanistan. He was a figure in the Iran-Contra scandal. A stop in Saudi Arabia was imperative for anyone seeking a leadership role in the post-Bashar Syria that could emerge from the war's wreckage.

"Bashar must go, these are the [Saudi] king's orders," Bandar told Manaf when they met in the coastal city of Jeddah near Mecca.[4]

Later, Manaf read a televised statement to the Syrian people broadcast by the Saudi-owned channel Al Arabiya. He was clean-shaven and slightly tanned, with strands of his long salt-and-pepper hair falling on his forehead. His shirt was open at the neck. It was a look he always cultivated— the insider with a rebellious streak.[5]

Reading from a piece of paper, barely looking at the camera, and speaking haltingly and with poor Arabic diction, Manaf sought to convey anger with the regime for confronting the uprising with bullets, tanks, and warplanes; he also maintained some distance from the opposition, both armed rebels and politicians. His underlying message was that there were "noble" people like him within the regime, army, and Bashar's Alawite community, and that a way should be found to reach out to them to avert plunging deeper into civil war and to preserve the country's social fabric and institutions. "I call for doing the impossible to protect Syria's unity and start rebuilding a new Syria not based on revenge, exclusion, and self-ishness. Our duty as Syrians today is to comfort one another and deny the regime and others the chance to fuel conflict between us."

Manaf said his intentions were purely patriotic—but convincing Syrians that someone whose family was at the heart of the Assad regime and entangled in its crimes was now the nation's savior and an alternative to Bashar was going to be a long shot, especially with a sober, nuanced message. It was by no means the resounding and definitive split with the regime that many in the Syrian opposition as well as their backers, including the Saudis, were hoping to hear from Manaf.

"I came out to express my rage at the events taking place in my country and did not announce I was with the regime or the opposition," he said later.[6]

Bit by bit, Manaf was consumed by frustration, disillusionment, and anger as he tried to overcome the past and struggle with his own demons and limitations.

"Manaf, there's no Syrian de Gaulle," Éric Chevallier told him bluntly when he arrived in Paris.[7] "You are not de Gaulle; it cannot be you alone. I am sorry—I know you, I know who you are. I think you can be part of the solution, but do not tell me you can be the only one—you have to deal with the others."

Manaf boasted that there were many senior Alawite officers who trusted him and were prepared to defect from the regime—provided that the leadership proposed as an alternative to Bashar was not going to tear down the state and seek retribution from Alawites and others associated with the Assads.[8] This was certainly the most desirable outcome for France, the United States, and other Western countries backing the rebellion.

There were, however, serious doubts whether Manaf could deliver, especially after Bashar and his allies closed ranks within both the regime and the Alawite community following the spectacular assassination of

Assef Shawkat and other military and security leaders two weeks after Manaf's departure.

Moreover, the question was whether Manaf, the son of a man who considered himself a pillar of the Assad family regime, was capable and ready to be just a team member in an already fragmented opposition body that was suspicious of his motives, rejected him because of his past, and saw him as potential competition. He also had to wrestle with crosscurrents within his own family. His wife, Thala, pleaded with him to retreat from the scene and not get involved in the conflict.[9] She yearned for privacy for their family and feared for Manaf's life. French secret service agents were assigned to protect him and his family as they settled into their new life in Paris.

Mustafa Tlass moved in with his Parisian socialite daughter, Nahed, in her apartment in the French capital's affluent Sixteenth Arrondissement.[10] The eighty-year-old general was deeply saddened by the turn of events and Bashar's choices.[11] He might also have regretted Hafez's decision to make Bashar his successor and his own role in the process, but he was loyal to Hafez's legacy in every other way. Mustafa decided that the best thing to do was to withdraw and remain silent. There were calls by some Syrians in Paris to put him on trial for his complicity in the regime's crimes, especially in the 1970s and '80s,[12] but he was immune for the time being.

Notwithstanding the ups and downs in France's relations with Syria, over the decades the Tlasses had rendered important services to the French state, which had a long tradition of standing by what it viewed as its "third world" allies and clients.[13] One call from the French ambassador to Mustafa was all it took to chase away rioters who besieged the French embassy in Damascus in 2006 over the Prophet Mohammad cartoons, republished by the French weekly *Charlie Hebdo* after running in a Danish paper.[14] The cartoons, which included one depicting Mohammad as a terrorist, were reprinted by several European papers, sparking a violent reaction across the Muslim world, where many people found them deeply offensive and blasphemous.[15] In Syria, the Danish and Norwegian embassies were burnt to the ground, but the French mission remained untouched, thanks to Mustafa Tlass's intervention.

It was not only his family's history with the Assads that Manaf had to contend with but also his elder brother's political ambitions and rivalry. After moving to Dubai in March 2012, Firas Tlass, one of Syria's oligarchs who for decades profited from his family's privileged position, sought to cast himself as an active supporter of the uprising and build a following for himself, including on social media.

"Firas Tlass, an opposition leader—what a joke!" was Manaf's reaction.[16] Similarly, Firas, who had been largely kept in the dark about Manaf's plans, was lukewarm about any future leadership role for his brother. "I am not promoting anyone," he said after Manaf's exit. "The country [Syria] deserves better than just a repackaging of the regime."[17]

Bashar himself kept quiet for weeks after Manaf's defection. He deemed it beneath him to address it and did not want to give the impression that he paid any mind to his friend's exit. So instead, the first reaction came from Bahjat Suleiman, one of Bashar's ex-mentors and a former *mukhabarat* chief who was at the time ambassador to Jordan. His son was married to the sister of Manaf's wife. Suleiman called Manaf a "deserter" and "traitor" and alleged that he had defected because Bashar did not appoint him defense minister in the new government formed in June 2012. He said it was better for Syria to be rid of "microbes and parasites" like him.[18]

Bashar finally spoke at the end of August 2012 but did not mention by name Manaf or others who defected that summer. He said he had been fully aware or at least had had strong suspicions that certain people— "the cowardly, weak, and corrupt"—planned to flee. "This is a positive process, a self-cleansing process for the state and homeland," said Bashar in an interview. "It was conveyed to us that several persons were about to flee Syria. What did we do? We said, 'Let's facilitate [his departure], let him go... There was an inclination to stop them, but we said no, stopping them would not be correct. The exit of these people was the right thing.'"[19]

Bashar's statement only made matters worse for Manaf, fueling the perception that perhaps he had left Syria with Bashar's knowledge and blessing. There were suggestions that the Tlasses had worked out a deal with Bashar or that Bashar had allowed the Tlasses to slip out of Syria because he felt it was the least he could do for them in return for decades of service and devotion to the Assads. There were some who even believed

318

that Manaf's defection was staged and that he was secretly still loyal to Bashar and was on a mission to infiltrate and co-opt the opposition. Many people he considered friends and acquaintances kept their distance, just to be safe. A family friend who also left Syria told Manaf, "Before anything, you should redeem yourself. You should publicly ask the Syrian people for forgiveness for your family's history and role in the regime."[20] Manaf was deeply hurt because he had personally pleaded with Bashar a few years earlier to spare this friend's husband from arrest by the *mukhabarat*.

Those who cast themselves as revolutionaries and regime opponents did not want to be seen associating with Manaf, at least publicly. A member of the circle of artists and creative types whom he used to hang out with at bars in Damascus and whom he again encountered abroad did not want to be photographed with him at an opposition gathering in Paris.[21] A veteran regime opponent told Manaf: "My advice to the Tlass family is to get out of the scene and politics. It's impossible for you to have a role after the role you played with Bashar and Hafez. There's no place for the Assads, Makhloufs, and Tlasses in Syria's future."[22]

Manaf sought council from all his contacts in Paris, including Burhan Ghalyoun, who had recently stepped down from leadership of the main Western-backed opposition body but remained influential. Ghalyoun urged Manaf to work on encouraging Alawite officers in Bashar's military and security apparatus to defect and join the opposition. He advised that Manaf should return to liberated areas of Syria and show rebels that he was truly on their side. "They have to feel you're with them, not sitting comfortably in a mansion in Paris while they fight," Ghalyoun argued.[23]

Manaf refused flat-out, not wanting to be under the command of another officer, as surely he would be if he joined the rebels. "I am the general who defied Bashar al-Assad!" Manaf told Ghalyoun.[24]

One opposition leader said Manaf's biggest problem was his belief that he was the most qualified to lead the opposition, at least the military wing of it, despite serious doubts about his capabilities. Manaf, he said, "was preoccupied with why people were not contacting him and his place in the revolution and military council. He was like a pretty girl waiting for suitors."[25]

*   *   *

The opposition was hardly a cohesive body when Manaf left Syria. It was riven by leadership and ideological struggles fueled by the competing agendas of its regional and international backers.

The Free Syrian Army (FSA), for example, despite its central role in the opposition, was a collection of ragtag and loosely linked rebel groups, army defectors, and civilians who took up arms. They had little means initially, but exhibited immense courage and determination in driving out regime forces from their neighborhoods and hometowns.

Many of the defectors who initially fled to Turkey were restricted to camps near the border with their families. Sometimes entire villages fled, fearing harsh reprisals for being associated with defectors. Defected soldiers often moved back and forth—they fought inside Syria and then returned to Turkey for breaks to see their families.

Quickly there were disagreements over who was going to lead the fledgling FSA: defectors or civilians who had taken up arms. There were rifts among the defectors, too.[26] There was great mistrust and fear of infiltration, especially after the FSA's founder, an army colonel who was one of the first defectors, was abducted by the regime when he went back to Syria from Turkey. Backed by Qatar and Turkey, the Muslim Brotherhood sought to control the FSA by providing arms and aid to those factions more aligned with its agenda.

By the time Manaf came out in the summer of 2012, Saudi Arabia was actively working to counter the influence of Qatar and Turkey on the ground. Western states like France and the United States, which wanted their regional allies to collaborate rather than undermine one another, pushed for revamping the FSA to give greater say to professional and nonsectarian army officers. For a short while, it seemed that all the regional players were rallying behind a joint leadership for military councils emerging across rebel-held areas in Syria.

The French encouraged Manaf to participate in the efforts underway. Intelligence officers and diplomats from Britain, Germany, and the United States came to Paris to meet with Manaf. He traveled to Jordan, where he met with a hundred recently defected officers in the presence of the Jordanian intelligence services. Almost all were Sunnis like him.[27] He talked about the dangers of going too far in embracing Islamist currents in the opposition and told them that Alawite, Christian, and Druze fellow officers were their brothers. An officer whose son was among protesters shot dead in Daraa in the early months of the uprising said that it was hard to forgive Alawites because they had become killers for Bashar.

In Daraa itself, army defections had spiked dramatically, and defectors were carrying out hit-and-run attacks on regime forces; the regime responded by executing those it caught trying to defect and bombing rebellious communities indiscriminately. Every week, thousands trekked for miles to reach the Jordanian border. Families carried meager belongings in plastic sacks or duffle bags. Some children showed up without their parents. Most went to a desert refugee camp in Jordan.

Manaf remained frustrated because Western and Arab officials seemed uninterested whenever he told them that he was in contact with some 120 senior officers from Bashar's Alawite sect who were ready to defect immediately but needed certain guarantees.[28]

As regime atrocities deepened sectarian hatred, many in the opposition pressured their regional backers to keep figures like Manaf out of any leadership position. There was a widespread narrative that Western countries including France wanted to rehabilitate and repackage regime insiders like the Tlasses, or worse, bring in an Alawite like the late Assef Shawkat as an alternative to Bashar. "The Tlasses were absolutely hated in rebel communities," said one member of the rebel leadership council. "When the Syrians told the Qataris his dad was a killer, they said keep him out. The French were the only ones trying to market him. The FSA was already fractured and plagued with many problems. We did not need to add to the mix another problem called Manaf Tlass."[29]

Manaf was convinced that his enemies and rivals were waging a smear campaign against him. A deluge of articles, especially in Western media, focused on the background and wealth of his family and its long association with the Assads, suggesting he was frivolous and superficial, a member of the jet-setting elite. The photo that often accompanied these articles showed him chomping on a cigar. A German newspaper called him the "Syrian Alain Delon," after the 1960s French movie star and sex symbol.[30]

One of the few Syrian opposition figures championing Manaf was Michel Kilo. Kilo traveled to Moscow from Paris to meet with Russia's foreign minister, Sergei Lavrov, days after Manaf's defection. He called on Russia to abandon Bashar and said that a national unity government made up of elements of the regime and opposition could lead the country instead and someone like Manaf "with no blood on his hands" could be at the helm for a transitional period.[31] The French and their allies thought that this could comfort the Russians, given their warm ties and extensive dealings with the Tlass family patriarch, Mustafa, during his long tenure as defense minister.

Russia's master, President Vladimir Putin, however was in no mood for compromise with the West.

Putin was just starting to plan his grand Syria gambit; he was on a quest to avenge what he saw as US-led efforts to interfere in his reelection throughout 2012,[32] and his ambitions no less than to rewrite the post–Soviet Union and Berlin Wall global order. At the start of his third presidential term in the spring of 2012, Putin increasingly viewed the conflict in Syria and the tumultuous events in the broader Middle East as a unique opportunity to challenge America and project Russian might. Moreover, the idea of citizens in the Middle East rising up to defy longtime despots with the West's encouragement and support was something that posed a grave threat to his own grip on power, especially given the recent history of the United States backing protest movements and political dissidents in Russia as well as former Soviet republics.[33] It was almost inevitable that Putin would use the leverage he had in Syria as part of a broader offensive to combat this perceived threat from the Arab Spring and its potential ripple effects.

In a major foreign policy address delivered on July 9, 2012, Putin assailed what he called "the export of bomb-and-missile diplomacy and intervention in internal conflicts" by the West in the Middle East and North Africa, and he said that Russian diplomats had to adopt a new ethos and be "more active" in influencing situations. It was no longer acceptable to just be "passive observers and follow developments."[34] "I am sure that many of you still have the tragic events in Libya before your eyes," he said. "We cannot allow a repeat of such scenarios in other countries — in Syria, for example."[35]

Muammar Gaddafi had had extensive dealings with the former Soviet Union, and just before the Arab Spring turmoil Putin clinched arms, energy, and infrastructure deals in Libya worth billions of dollars.[36] The

Libyan dictator's stunning and brutal demise and the consequent loss of many of these contracts, coupled with Putin's determination to roll back the wave of regime change sweeping the Middle East, altered his calculus.

In Syria, Hafez had worked to maintain close relations with the Soviets. He built his army with their weapons and advisers, but he was never fully Moscow's client.[37] When the Soviet Union collapsed the Russians largely withdrew from the geopolitical contest in the Middle East, but now Putin wanted to make a comeback—through the Syrian gate. The Russians had a deep and nuanced understanding of Syria; they knew Bashar was no Hafez. The father had made his power while the son inherited it. Bashar was someone who desperately needed Putin—not the other way around.

After agreeing to Annan's six-point plan in Geneva at the end of June 2012, in mid-July Russia and China once more vetoed a UN Security Council resolution that could at least have given teeth and an enforcement mechanism to this plan, which called on the regime to pull back troops and heavy weapons from populated areas, and on both rebels and the regime to abide by a ceasefire.[38] It would have also extended the mandate of a small UN team in Damascus to observe compliance. It was the third veto by Russia and China regarding Syria since March 2011. Annan resigned shortly after.[39]

As Putin prepared to wade deeper into Syria, Bashar's principal patron, Iran, was already in battle mode. Iran geared up to provide Bashar with billions of dollars in financial assistance and loans to help the Syrians weather international sanctions and to replenish the regime's fast-emptying coffers. Iran also stepped up delivery of weapons and ammunition to Syria by air via Iraq, and, along with its Lebanese proxy, Hezbollah, it began mobilizing sectarian militias to shore up the collapsing Syrian army.[40]

Qasem Soleimani, the head of Iran's overseas covert operations, was in Damascus on the day that Bashar's brother-in-law Assef and his associates were killed in mid-July 2012. Soleimani helped orchestrate the regime's vicious response to rebel attacks inside Damascus and to the threats of a palace coup by Assef and others.[41] After meeting with Bashar the following month, the personal representative of Iran's supreme leader Ayatollah Ali Khamenei, Saeed Jalili, said, "What's happening in Syria is not an internal matter but a struggle between the axis of resistance on one hand and the enemies of this axis in the region and world on the other.[42] Iran won't allow under any circumstances the breakup of the axis of resistance, of which Syria is a fundamental part."

Alarmed by Iran's deepening involvement in Bashar's defense, and frustrated by what they saw as the absence of American leadership and Obama's reticence toward the fast-moving events in Syria, Gulf Arab states led by Qatar and Saudi Arabia lobbied the United States and their European allies to allow them to significantly increase arms supplies and other forms of support to Syrian rebel groups fighting the regime. The Saudis were already frustrated with Obama over the withdrawal of US forces from Iraq at the end of 2011, which they considered a win for Iran, given its influence over the Iraqi government and its support for militias there, too. France's foreign minister, Laurent Fabius, recalled that "there was tremendous pressure by the [Syrian] resistance and Arab allies that we help them to create a favorable situation" in the war against the regime.[43]

So when attempts to precipitate a collapse of the regime through defections and the Damascus offensive failed, regime opponents and their outside backers shifted their attention to Aleppo, Syria's business and industrial center.

Except for scattered protests in poor, working-class neighborhoods that were brutally confronted by regime thugs, Aleppo remained mostly quiet during the first year of the uprising. Loyalist merchants and business owners who were eager to protect their interests and prevent Aleppo from being swept up in the revolutionary fervor paid thugs from two notorious clans, the Berris and Hamidis, to make sure no one dared to rise up.[44] Things changed in early 2012 with the influx of families from Homs fleeing regime attacks there. University students organized large and animated protests. Some of the neighborhood protests also started to get larger and bolder, but the response from the thugs and *mukhabarat* was savage. Protesters were often attacked with truncheons, knives, and swords.[45]

Meanwhile, swathes of the countryside in Aleppo and the adjacent province of Idlib were already in the hands of rebel factions that included

Islamists and Free Syrian Army groups. As the regime was busy dealing with the rebel incursion in Damascus in mid-July 2012, rebels from the countryside around Aleppo overran several military and security positions east and south of the city center. Many of these fighters had until recently worked in factories owned by the city's prominent families. An Aleppan businessman close to Bashar described it this way: "They got weapons and saw a chance to challenge their masters. This is human nature."[46]

The schism between city and countryside was deep in Aleppo. Rebels were welcomed as liberators in several working-class neighborhoods like Salahuddin, where many of the inhabitants hailed from the countryside or were related to the fighters. Rebels took over police stations in several neighborhoods and rounded up those suspected of having been regime collaborators and informants. Several members of the Berri clan, accused of being pro-regime thugs, were captured, tortured, and then lined up against a school wall and executed by rebels in a hail of bullets lasting almost a full minute as a crowd of spectators cheered *"Allahu akbar!"* —"God is greatest!"[47]

In response Bashar dispatched large military reinforcements to Aleppo, but instead of dislodging the rebels, the fighting engulfed the entire city, including its architectural gem—the ancient quarter with its maze of vaulted souks, historic mosques, and stone homes at the foot of the famed citadel. Regime forces ransacked and burned most of the shops in the old souks, while rebels looted the factories on the city's edges.[48] The city would settle into four years of grinding, almost primordial warfare, with the regime holding the traditionally more prosperous west side of the city and the airport, and rebels controlling the poorer east side connected to the countryside and their main supply line from Turkey.

The momentum that Bashar's opponents had that summer from defections by military and civilian regime figures, as well as territorial gains by rebels inside Syria, started to dissipate. Still, the opposition was certainly in no mood for compromise with Bashar, especially as regime atrocities increased. It believed that victory over the regime on the battleground was near and inevitable.

The reality, however, was far more complex. By the summer of 2012, what had begun as a people's struggle for liberation from their oppressor was becoming a multilayered conflict that more and more drew in outside powers and their agendas.

While rebels seemed sure they were going to topple the regime, some of their backers, particularly the United States, were no longer so confident. Bashar and his allies behind him demonstrated in no uncertain terms how far they were prepared to go to defend Damascus and hang on to power. Aircraft and heavy artillery were deployed; Alawites and other minorities were armed; massacres were committed in rebellious communities and Bashar's own brother-in-law Assef Shawkat was eliminated by the regime after his loyalty became suspect. According to Obama, Bashar "doubled down in violence on his own people."[49] There was also another development that the world had to contend with: indications in the summer of 2012 that Bashar and his inner circle were weighing the possibility of deploying chemical weapons in battle.

Manaf's ex-colleague, Republican Guard commander Bassam al-Hassan, was one of Bashar's main advisers on weapons procurement and his point man in dealing with the Scientific Studies and Research Center, which operates all the sites producing nonconventional arms like chemical weapons.[50] Syria had for a long time possessed stockpiles of chemical weapons including mustard gas, nerve agents such as sarin and VX, and blister agents, and had developed the means of delivering them with rockets and missiles.

In the summer of 2012, the United States started receiving intelligence that the regime was moving chemical weapons from some of its sites but said that it was unclear whether this was done to transport them to more-secure locations or to actually use them. "We have been very clear to the Assad regime," said President Obama, "but also to other players on the ground, that a red line for us is we start seeing a whole bunch of chemical weapons moving around or being utilized. That would change my calculus. That would change my equation."[51] He went even further, warning of "enormous consequences."

At precisely the same moment that Obama spoke in mid-August 2012, Bashar began deploying a crude but horrific weapon against civilian populations in rebellious communities. In addition to intensifying airstrikes by the regime's fleet of Russian-made MiG jets, empty oil barrels loaded with

TNT and packed with pieces of steel rods and shrapnel were tossed from helicopters. These so-called barrel bombs were capable of bringing down buildings and tearing the flesh of anyone caught in their path. They were among the weapons used to attack at least ten bakeries and breadlines in Aleppo city and the surrounding countryside in August 2012 alone, killing at least 100 people and maiming dozens.[52]

That month US Secretary of State Hillary Clinton met with her Turkish counterpart to discuss the possibility of establishing a no-fly zone at least in northern Syria, which would encompass Aleppo and Idlib provinces, where the overstretched regime was increasingly resorting to helicopters and warplanes.[53] This was a concrete way to protect civilians in opposition areas and would also send a forceful and unequivocal message by the United States and its allies in the face of Bashar's crimes and Russia's intransigence. Moreover, it could have given Bashar's opponents the space they needed to demonstrate their ability to govern themselves without being preoccupied day and night with bombs raining from the sky. Turkey, a member of NATO and host to a major US airbase nearby, said it would do everything possible to make the no-fly zone work. The French were also keen, signaling that they would be ready to participate in its enforcement over parts of Syria.

Nevertheless, a no-fly zone in Syria was "not on the front burner" was the response from Washington through Defense Secretary Leon Panetta. He said that the United States could successfully enforce such a zone but it would require a "major, major policy decision."[54]

Laurent Fabius, France's foreign minister, said his government was informed by Washington that such an undertaking required a "significant military commitment." The French were told that one of the obstacles to implementing a no-fly zone was the need to work out "de-confliction" arrangements with Russia, meaning avoiding the possibility of military confrontation with Moscow while the coalition operated in parts of Syria's airspace.[55] That made little sense, because at the time Russia's involvement and presence was limited to the weapons it supplied the regime and its military advisers in western Syria, where it had a small naval base on the Mediterranean to repair and refuel ships.

Fabius and other French officials believed that Obama's unenthusiastic reaction to the no-fly zone idea that summer had more to do with the fact the US president was deep in campaign mode ahead of the November 2012 elections.[56] For Obama, intervening in Syria, even in a limited way, was a slippery slope toward another protracted and costly Middle Eastern adventure like the US invasion of Iraq.

Instead of immediate and resolute action by the West to stem the mounting carnage and stream of refugees fleeing Syria, the United States and its European allies stuck with an already bankrupt and failed UN process to deal with the crisis, a decision that bought Bashar and his allies ample time and made the situation on the ground catastrophic and infinitely more complex.

The regime's grisly message came in the closing days of summer 2012.

After the rebels' foiled attempt to bring the battle to Bashar in Damascus, there was a particularly gruesome assault on the opposition stronghold of Daraya, next to the capital, that bore all the hallmarks of the take-no-prisoners and kill-them-all solutions inflicted on Hama in 1982 and favored by regime fanatics.

Forces led by Maher al-Assad's Fourth Division, which was among the army units equipped with the latest Russian-made tanks, helicopter gunships, and rocket launchers, pummeled Daraya nonstop, forcing rebels inside to abandon their resistance and withdraw to the outskirts. In the mop-up operations that ensued and in which Alawite militiamen also participated, mass executions were carried out of civilians who hid in their homes, cellars, and even in the town's cemetery.[57] The focus was on males of all ages. About 500 people, most of them civilians, were killed in the bombardment and executions that followed.[58]

There was then a concerted effort by the regime to make sure Daraya stood out as a cautionary tale to opponents and Syrians at large, the so-far neutral majority that Bashar often referred to in his interviews and discourse.

The assailants filmed themselves rounding up men for executions. "Shall I liquidate them for you!" shouted a man in military uniform and a baseball cap and speaking with a distinctly Alawite coastal accent as he and another armed man in military fatigues made six Daraya men in civilian clothes lay facedown on the ground. Their hands were cuffed behind their backs.[59]

A correspondent from Addounia TV, the station owned by Maher's cronies, was brought in to portray the carnage as the work of "terrorists" and mock those who had protested for freedom. With her camera in tow, Micheline Azar flitted between the dead bodies of men, women, and children who were shot in the head by regime snipers as they attempted to flee Daraya.[60]

Azar interviewed a dazed and wounded woman in the cemetery about her husband and male children from whom she said she had been separated as they were escaping to Damascus. Azar also spoke to a small girl covered in the blood of her dead mother, who lay in the back of a motorbike rickshaw. A small boy who appeared to be the girl's brother was still alive and propped up against his mother's body. A younger child next to them was motionless with what looked like a gunshot wound in his head.[61]

"This is first and foremost a war of wills...Everybody wishes the job is finished in weeks, days, or hours. This talk is illogical. We are waging a global and regional war and we need time to conclude it," Bashar told Addounia days later, never once mentioning the Daraya butchery.[62]

20

Holy War: At Your Service, O Bashar!

South of central Damascus and just off the airport road lies the town of Seyda Zeinab, named after Zeinab bint Ali, a granddaughter of the Prophet Mohammad. A shimmering, golden-domed mausoleum and mosque stands on the spot where Zeinab is believed to be buried.

In the year AD 680, Zeinab's brother Hussein and his supporters revolted against the Damascus-based Muslim caliph Yazid, whom they saw as usurper of the title after his father's death. They believed that Hussein, a direct descendant of Mohammad, was the rightful caliph.[1] They also argued that Yazid's Umayyad dynasty, with its dictatorial rule and obsession with worldly pleasures, had strayed from the true path of Islam preached by Mohammad.

Still, Hussein and his partisans were very much in the minority, so that same year they set out from Medina (in modern-day Saudi Arabia) to Kufa (in modern-day Iraq) to rally support for their cause. Hussein's sister Zeinab and her husband and children joined the caravan. On the way, they were ambushed by Yazid's army in the desert near Karbala in Iraq and ordered to surrender. Hussein's small contingent was no match for the army, but they were determined to hold their ground even as they were slaughtered one by one.

At one point in the epic of Karbala, as retold by Shiite clerics and scholars, one of Zeinab's other siblings, Abu Fadhel al-Abbas, a handsome and brave knight, was attacked while he fetched water for his besieged companions.[2] Al-Abbas was riddled with arrows, shot through the eye, and lost both arms. but still managed to hold onto a pouch of water for his brother with his teeth. His brother, Hussein, was ultimately beheaded. Hussein's severed head and the women were brought to Damascus as trophies for Yazid. Some Shiites believe that Zeinab was paraded through Damascus without a veil or perhaps even naked.

The bloody events marked the definitive split in Islam between Shiites and Sunnis. Since then, Shiites have seen themselves as the underdogs who sided with the Prophet Mohammad's massacred progeny against the tyrannical Sunni rulers representing the majority. Shrines like the one for Zeinab in Damascus and those of her brothers Al-Hussein and Al-Abbas in Karbala became sacred pilgrimage sites and potent symbols for a faith shaped by persecution and victimhood over the centuries.

The tragic yet heroic Karbala narrative rallied Shiite Iranians in what they called the *Defa Moghadas* (Sacred Defense) during their long war with Iraq in the 1980s. Iraqi leader Saddam Hussein, a Sunni backed by Sunni Saudi Arabia and its Western allies, was a perfect Yazid-like figure. The narrative also inspired Hezbollah's ideological and Iran-trained Lebanese Shiite fighters during their battle to liberate southern Lebanon from Israeli occupation.[3]

The story of Karbala had even more resonance later in Iraq, the saga's original setting, where it spurred Shiite youth to join Iran-backed militias to fight Sunni insurgents who could not reconcile themselves to Saddam's fall and the ascendancy of Shiites after the US-led invasion in 2003. Iraq's Shiites believed that they faced the descendants of the killers of *Al al-Bayt*—the House of Mohammad.[4] The destruction of a Shiite shrine in Samarra, north of Baghdad, in 2006 by Sunni militants linked to Al-Qaeda was the touchstone for the worst Sunni–Shiite bloodletting in the country.

Now Bashar and his Lebanese and Iranian allies borrowed from the same historic narrative to cast themselves as the righteous party of Hussein fighting the Sunni extremists, or *takfiris*—fanatics ready to excommunicate and kill Shiites and other minorities in the Levant such as the Christians. All the rebels without exception were branded by Bashar as *takfiris* backed, he claimed, by the "Great Satan" America, Israel, and their tools in the region, wealthy Gulf Arab Sunni states. The mission in Syria would also be another *Defa Moghadas* (Sacred Defense) for Hezbollah and Iran. It took a good deal of work for this narrative to be fully consummated but, once it was adopted, its repercussions would go far beyond Syria and the defense of Bashar for many years to come.

In the spring of 2013, several banners fluttered at the entrance of a pilgrims' hotel in Seyda Zeinab. There was the yellow flag of Hezbollah (Party of God) with its green logo showing the name in stylized calligraphy with an arm rising up and clutching an assault rifle. Next to it were the Syrian flag and the banners of the Syrian army and a new militia created by the Syrian *mukhabarat* called Liwa Abu Fadhel al-Abbas ("the Brigade of Abu Fadhel al-Abbas"), after the valiant brother of the revered Hussein.

In the hotel lobby there was a massive poster of Bashar in military fatigues and aviator sunglasses. Plastic flowers were pasted all around it and also a small portrait of a dour Hafez hanging on the wall next to it. Across from father and son was a framed painting of the twelve infallible imams sacred to Shiites, including Hussein and his father, Ali. For Alawites, members of the Shiite-linked sect to which the Assads belonged, Ali was a godlike figure. Even their name, Alawites, means the followers of Ali in Arabic.

Many Shiites continued to frown upon what they saw as heretical Alawite beliefs, even after Hafez had obtained a *fatwa* (edict) from a popular and influential Lebanese cleric in the 1970s declaring Alawites a subsect of Shiite Islam. However, now they were all Shiite brothers under Iran's umbrella, fighting their common historical enemies.

Before 2011, hundreds of thousands of Shiites from Lebanon, Iran, Iraq, and elsewhere used to converge on Zeinab's mausoleum to pray and weep while recollecting the Karbala saga. Since 2011 there had been hardly any pilgrims and most hotels were filled with families displaced by war.

This particular hotel had been turned into a command and recruitment center for the Liwa Abu Fadhel al-Abbas militia. It housed the office of the commander, Maher Jatta, or Abu Ajeeb al-Wahesh ("the Monster"), as his men called him admiringly. The tattooed thirty-year-old street vendor turned *mukhabarat* agent was until recently responsible for the Seyda Zeinab Popular Committee, one of many local militias hastily formed by the regime and its allies as army defections multiplied and the threats to Bashar's seat of power, Damascus, became more serious.[5]

"The guys in the Popular Committees just wanted to steal and they did not pray," said Jatta, his bushy black beard neatly trimmed. Jatta's military uniform bore patches on the arms and front pocket reserved for members of a special-ops unit of the *mukhabarat*'s Air Force Intelligence Directorate headed by the infamous Jamil Hassan.

Jatta called Hassan "my boss" and described him as an ultra-secular man contemptuous of religion and "all the fantasies" associated with it, but during internal discussions in the fall of 2012 about alternatives to the Popular Committees, Hassan grudgingly went along with the idea of launching a militia that evoked the narrative of Karbala and Zeinab's plight in order to attract Shiite men to fight on Bashar's side.[6]

"We need a symbol to rally Shiites from all over the world, not just Syria. We need to fight with ideology, not like before," explained Jatta, who is himself a Syrian Shiite but was admittedly not very religious before 2011. He described his own transformation from hustler to devout Shiite. The new decor was meant to attest to that.

A framed photograph of Iran's supreme leader, Ali Khamenei, with his signature thick white beard, eyeglasses, and black turban, was on the wall next to his desk. Across from the desk on an opposite wall were photographs of Hezbollah's Nasrallah and Iraq's Moqtada al-Sadr, both populist clerics with a huge following.

A large poster of Bashar and Maher in military fatigues was on the wall behind the desk in what had previously been the hotel manager's office.

"We sacrifice our soul and blood for you, Bashar," was tattooed on Jatta's left hand, just beneath the knuckles. Dying for Bashar was now blended with Zeinab's defense. "We're going to fight until the last drop of blood for our lady Zeinab," Jatta vowed.

"At your service, O Zeinab!"

Thousands of volunteer fighters were preparing to come to Seyda Zeinab from all over to defend the shrine, said Jatta. His Liwa Abu Fadhel al-Abbas militia already had a Facebook page on which it posted regular updates on threats to Zeinab's shrine, like the mortar shell that exploded in the plaza around it recently and the alleged text messages he said he had received from *takfiris* (by which he meant Sunni rebels) in adjacent towns vowing to "demolish the shrine and turn it into an ice-skating rink."

Hezbollah chief Nasrallah, one of Bashar's main allies and defenders, also chimed in that same spring with cataclysmic forewarnings: "Destroying or blowing up this shrine would have extremely grave consequences. Things would get out of everyone's control."[7]

What Nasrallah did not say was that already, months before, battle-hardened Iraqi militiamen from groups trained and funded by Iran to attack the US military when it maintained a major presence in Iraq were flocking to Syria to join the fight alongside Bashar. The *mukhabarat*'s Liwa Abu Fadhel al-Abbas militia was a catalyst and promoter of this influx. The battle mobilization order came from the *veli-faqih* ("guardian jurist"), Iran's supreme leader.[8]

The *veli-faqih* had to be obeyed by his followers because he was supposed to be ruling on behalf of the last Shiite imam, who was currently in a state of occultation but would return at the end of times to save the world.

A holy war narrative began to morph—beyond just protecting Zeinab's Damascus shrine.

In the Shiite holy city of Karbala in Iraq and not far from the shrine of Zeinab's brother Hussein, one bookshop could barely keep up with the brisk demand for books and maps about an end-of-times battle involving a dozen different armies that Shiites believe will take place in Iraq and Syria—a battle presaging their hidden Imam's return to save humanity.

Iraqi Shiite clerics allied to Iran spoke about it in their sermons. The battle to defend the Shiite faith in Iraq and the growing civil war in Syria were one and the same, they kept saying. The pitch was that *yes they were fighting with Bashar, but this was much bigger than Bashar, this was potentially apocalyptic.* Their hidden Imam and savior intended for them to join this battle.

For many Iraqi Shiites, events in Iraq itself, coupled with the more than a dozen global and regional powers immersing themselves in the Syrian conflict, seemed like a fulfillment of the prophecy.

In Iraq, Obama's decision to withdraw the last remaining US troops at the end of 2011 in order to fulfill his campaign promise brought out into the open a simmering power struggle among Iraq's many ethnic and sectarian groups. It was made worse in the context of the Arab Spring revolts, what was happening across the border in Syria, and the broader sectarian-driven proxy wars between Iran and Saudi Arabia. Iraq's Shiite prime minister, Nouri al-Maliki, an increasingly autocratic and paranoid figure who refused to forge a meaningful reconciliation with Sunnis from the Saddam era, was politically dependent on Iran, but he also needed American troops to keep all his enemies and rivals at bay.

In the end, the interests of Obama and Iran seemed to overlap: Obama was anxious to leave Iraq, and Iran wanted US troops out at any cost so it and its so-called axis of resistance partners could declare victory over the Americans.

With US troops out, Maliki feared that regional Sunni states like Qatar, Saudi Arabia, and Turkey were conspiring against him through their Sunni protégés in Iraq in the same way that they were backing Bashar's opponents in Syria.[9] Maliki therefore moved closer to the Iranians and Bashar.

Equally, Sunnis in Iraq, and by extension their regional allies, felt that the Americans were handing over the country to Iran. Sunnis from Iraqi tribal areas bordering Syria felt betrayed and abandoned after they had partnered with America to drive out Al-Qaeda militants from their areas a few years earlier in what had become known as the Awakening.

Maliki struck first, going after Sunni members of his government, including the vice president, for allegedly plotting to topple him with the backing of regional powers. This plunged the country into a deep political crisis, triggered protests and civil disobedience and calls for autonomy across many Sunni areas, and pushed violence back to levels not seen since the sectarian strife of 2005–2007.[10] The discord reenergized both Al-Qaeda's local franchise (the Islamic State of Iraq) and Iran's Shiite militias. Average Iraqis looked to these entities for protection as their already fragile state became more divided and dysfunctional.

By then, many of the protagonists needed a holy war.

Bashar needed the *earthquake* with which he had always threatened the West each time he felt they were working to get rid of him. Iran wanted to trounce its archenemy, Saudi Arabia, and solidify its presence and reach from Tehran to the Mediterranean shores; Syria became ground zero for the war against those who wanted to stand in Iran's way.

Al-Qaeda had its own holy war narrative, but, more important, the group saw events in Iraq and Syria as a tremendous opportunity for a comeback. And so did the leaders of Al-Qaeda's Iraqi franchise, many of them former Saddam loyalists who had never gotten over his demise, notwithstanding their supposed transformation into pious jihadists.

America's regional allies (Qatar, Saudi Arabia, and Turkey) also did not mind a holy war as long as it remained confined to Iraq and Syria and ultimately served their own agendas and achieved their respective goals.

Jabhat al-Nusra, or the Nusra Front, was formally launched in January 2012 as the Syrian affiliate of what was still known at the time as the Islamic State of Iraq. Nusra was led by Ahmad al-Sharaa, a Daraa native in his thirties who went by the nom de guerre Abu Mohammad al-Jolani. He was among those sent by the Syrian regime to Iraq to wage jihad at the start of the US-led invasion in 2003. He and the other volunteers were welcomed at the Syrian embassy in Baghdad.[11] Later Jolani was arrested and then returned to Syria, where he collaborated with the Syrian *mukhabarat* to channel fighters to Iraq to fuel the insurgency and undermine US postinvasion efforts to stabilize the country.

Starting in the summer of 2011 as Syria was in the throes of the popular uprising against Bashar, Jolani slipped across the border to Iraq to discuss the establishment of a Syrian wing with Abu Bakr al-Baghdadi, head of the Islamic State of Iraq. All the cells and networks that had been in place when Bashar and his *mukhabarat* were facilitating the transfer of foreign fighters to Iraq via Syria during the previous decade were reactivated and became the "building blocks" (as one analyst put it) for establishing the Syrian franchise throughout 2011.[12] Most of the early recruits were the Islamists and jihadists freed from prison by Bashar in May 2011. Foreign fighters came later. Between December 2011 and December 2012, Nusra claimed responsibility for at least forty suicide bomb attacks in major cities that targeted mostly the *mukhabarat* and regime forces that were killing Syrians.[13]

"I literally flew—the sky was red," said one resident of an eastern Damascus neighborhood who was home on October 9, 2012, when massive twin explosions hit a nearby outpost for the *mukhabarat*'s Air Force Intelligence Directorate, killing more than 100.[14]

Still, many in the opposition were uneasy about what they regarded as an ominous development. First, these attacks often killed civilians, too, and second, the terror and sectarian mayhem they had long associated with Iraq was spreading to Syria. Some in the opposition blamed the *mukhabarat* for being behind the attacks in an effort to muddy the waters and taint regime opponents by linking them to terror, something Bashar had set out to do from the onset of protests in the spring of 2011. It was not farfetched to believe that the notorious *mukhabarat* was carrying out these bombings, but Nusra was real and most of the attacks were theirs. Some of Bashar's opponents were in a state of denial about a problem that had begun to plague their ranks. The truth was that all the conditions were there to favor the rise of Nusra and other extremist groups.

Nusra filled a leadership void in the ranks of the opposition as Bashar killed or imprisoned peaceful protest leaders, people like Mazen Darwish and many others, and crushed any hope for a moderate and inclusive opposition to establish itself in areas liberated from his regime. Nusra tapped into the rage and vengefulness that consumed Syrians after each atrocity committed by Bashar. It also played on a growing feeling among many average Sunnis in Syria: only Nusra's religious fanatics, who were also Sunnis, could protect them from the ideology-driven Shiite fighters dispatched by Iran to defend Bashar. Many believed their only succor was God and Nusra.

Paradoxically, both Bashar and Nusra were greatly aided by the opposition's internal divisions and a deepening rift between their two main regional backers, Qatar and Saudi Arabia, as well as a schizophrenic US approach in dealing with the grim developments in Syria and the wider region.

As Bashar's warplanes rained bombs on civilians in opposition-held areas, Hillary Clinton wanted serious consideration to be given to the idea of a no-fly zone, and she discussed it with British, French, and German allies in the summer of 2012. Former CIA director David Petraeus, meanwhile, sketched a plan to vet, arm, and train Syrian rebels. Defense Secretary Leon Panetta was increasingly frustrated with the gridlock over Syria.

"Petraeus and I argued that there was a big difference between Qatar and Saudi Arabia dumping weapons into the country and the United States responsibly training and equipping a non-extremist rebel force," said Clinton. "And getting control of that mess was a big part of our plan's rationale."[15]

Obama wanted to hold off. In the endeavor to end the Syrian tragedy and affect change, the Americans seemed to have one foot in and the other out. Obama was horrified by Bashar's atrocities and called for his resignation, but at the same time he signaled that this was not America's problem.

By then, the Saudis had a team in Turkey whose sole job was to lure rebel factions away from Qatar with cash and supplies of weapons. Sunni clerics from Gulf Arab states flew to the Syrian–Turkish border with suitcases of cash to back their favorite rebel factions.[16] Factions adopted Islamic-sounding names in order to increase their chances of securing this support. Some of these clerics were taken inside Syria so they could be filmed and photographed with members of their adopted rebel faction. This material was used to raise more funds.

To counter rising Islamist militancy and sectarian fearmongering, a new opposition body was unveiled in the Qatari capital, Doha, in November 2012, after long deliberations involving US envoy Robert Ford, France's Éric Chevallier, and others.[17] It was hoped the National Coalition of Syrian Revolutionary and Opposition Forces would be broader and more representative of Syria's sectarian and ethnic demographics, and that it would be unified and capable of controlling the plethora of armed groups fighting the regime, while also creating credible alternative local government structures in liberated areas.

Moaz al-Khatib, a respected, well-liked, and moderate Damascene Sunni preacher, who had left Syria a few months earlier, was appointed president of this new coalition. He had no prior political experience. Symbolically, his deputies were an unveiled woman, Suhair al-Atassi, and a secular veteran regime opponent, Riad Seif.

It was hoped that Khatib's Islamist background put him in a better position than others to secure acceptance for the coalition from many of the Islamist rebels gaining strength on the ground, the idea being that a large block of moderate Islamists would sideline and neutralize extremists linked to Al-Qaeda. Khatib himself believed that, with the right support and resources, he could even convince certain Nusra Front elements to distance themselves from Al-Qaeda.[18]

Within days, most Arab states, as well as Britain, France, and Turkey, recognized the coalition as the sole legitimate representative of the Syrian people. Qatar's emir went a step further by orchestrating the handover of Syria's seat in the Arab League to the opposition and inaugurating their new embassy in his capital, Doha,[19] where futuristic skyscrapers and stadiums rose from the desert sands as part of a spending spree of more than US$200 billion in preparation for hosting the 2022 World Cup.[20]

"We consider them a legitimate representative of the aspirations of the Syrian people, [but] we're not yet prepared to recognize them as some sort of government in exile," the ever-so-cautious Obama said in Washington just after his reelection for a second term.[21]

It was not long before the new Syrian opposition body was mired in the Qatari–Saudi feud.[22] A Syrian businessman brought in by Qatar to be the coalition's budget controller and de facto leader co-opted his colleagues with money.[23] The Saudis and their allies then pushed hard to expand the opposition body by installing their own people in order to dilute the sway of Qatar and Turkey.[24]

Similar discord and dueling agendas plagued the effort to reorganize the rebel groups and bring them under the control of the political leadership. The Saudis, with the Emiratis and Jordanians on their side and their Western allies behind them, pressured the Qataris and Turks to divide the battleground into five fronts. The Saudis wanted the central and southern zones, which included Damascus.[25] This was supposed to sideline the militant Islamists but it actually had the reverse effect.

During a meeting in the Jordanian capital, Amman, a defected army officer turned rebel commander objected to this plan, arguing that it would lead to further fragmentation rather than unity.[26] Retorted Prince Salman bin Sultan, the brother of Saudi spy chief Prince Bandar, "You will fight like that and if you're not interested, 'to my shoe'"—an expression offensive to Arabs.

"The plan is going forward whether you like it or not," added the prince.[27]

Meanwhile, the head of the opposition's political body, the moderate cleric Moaz al-Khatib, resigned in the spring of 2013 after some of his colleagues called him a "traitor" for making overtures to Bashar's backers, Iran and Russia, and proposing contact with the Assad regime to discuss humanitarian relief for civilians.[28] The Saudis eventually installed their own man at the helm, but in the end both the political and military opposition bodies proved ineffectual and hollow structures as their backers worked at cross-purposes.

To counter the Saudi moves, both Qatar and Turkey significantly upped their financial and military support for a constellation of Islamist groups allied to Al-Qaeda's Nusra Front,[29] branded as extremists by the United States and its Western allies; Nusra got the official "terrorist organization" designation from Washington. These groups, though, were the most effectual on the battleground and garnered support among populations in opposition areas that were coming under brutal assault from Bashar. The Islamists seemed like the only ones doing something concrete while Obama was objecting to the supply of heavy weapons that could better deal with the regime's tanks and warplanes even as Iran and its militias got increasingly involved on Bashar's side. These Islamists also started taking the leadership role in running people's daily affairs in the liberated zones.

The United States and its European allies, including Britain and France, were mainly providing so-called nonlethal aid to the opposition's revamped military leadership. This aid included things like vehicles, computers, bulletproof vests, and night-vision goggles. To average Syrians, the Western approach to defeating Bashar seemed cynical if not complicit with the regime that was murdering them day after day.

"The idea was not to give them the means to win the battle; it was to give them the means to be more structured in order to show the regime that there was no military victory possible and a need to go to the negotiating table," said one Western official, describing Washington's strategy at the end of 2012.[30] The premise was that Bashar would rush to negotiate his exit if he saw an organized rebel force.

The dissonance in America's Syria strategy was turning surreal.

Obama wanted to maintain his distance but the United States was still eager to control what its regional allies Qatar, Saudi Arabia, and Turkey were funneling to rebels in Syria. In Turkey, where Qatari cargo planes laden with weapons purchased from Eastern Europe and elsewhere landed regularly, CIA operatives took on the role of inspectors and advisers who "were sort of looking the other way," because America was not supposed to be involved in arming the Syrian rebels, as per Obama's official policy.[31]

CIA officers often met with members of Qatar's special forces and Turkey's intelligence services at a secret maximum-security location on the outskirts of the Turkish capital, Ankara, that became known as "the farm."[32] It was an old military base consisting of a block structure and some trailer homes at the foot of a mountain nestled amid trees and guarded by dogs.

"There were red lines: no snipers, no antitank and no antiaircraft weapons," according to one person present at the meetings.[33] There was fear that these more sophisticated weapons could fall into the wrong hands. Still, the Qataris and Turks sometimes passed on these prohibited weapons and even a small shipment of Chinese-made shoulder-fired missiles capable of downing the regime's warplanes. "This is top secret — the Americans do not know about it," they often told the Syrians when the Americans were not in the room.[34]

Between the fall of 2012 and spring 2013, Obama refused to consider the no-fly zone even as Bashar was massacring Syrian civilians in ever-greater numbers. He also rejected the proposal to bring the rebels under more Western control and scrutiny as America's regional allies competed for their loyalty with cash and weapons. Obama did authorize "nonlethal" aid to rebels and hundreds of millions of dollars in assistance to the refugees fleeing the war, things like food, water, blankets, and medical services. There were more than 700,000 refugees in neighboring countries by the end of 2012,[35] while the death toll surpassed 60,000.[36]

At the same time, the holy war narrative was amplified and began to spread beyond Iraq and Syria.

France's foreign minister, Laurent Fabius, called the American policy a "macabre fool's bargain," and he explained, "The sentiment given was that he [Obama] was doing a lot to help the Syrian resistance, but in reality he did not do much. He never wanted to get involved in the process."[37]

✻   ✻   ✻

Weighing on Obama's decisions was what was happening in Iraq and the countries touched by the Arab Spring.

Libya was sliding into anarchy. The United States and its Western allies imposed a no-fly zone there and helped rebels defeat Gaddafi but largely took a back seat when it came to helping a new state emerge from the ashes of conflict and four decades of tyranny. Tribal and clan-based militias refused to disarm, there was violent retribution against those accused of having been loyal to Gaddafi, rifts between the country's different regions deepened, especially east versus west, and Islamist extremists were gaining strength. Fueling these fights was the race between the Qataris and other Gulf states, such as the Saudi-allied Emiratis, to control post-Gaddafi Libya.

On the anniversary of 9/11 in 2012, Islamist militants launched an attack on the US mission in Benghazi, Libya's second-largest city. The US ambassador, J. Christopher Stevens, and three other Americans were killed.[38] One of the triggers for the assault was a crude and amateurish movie trailer insulting the Prophet Mohammad that was produced and promoted by right-wing Christian evangelicals in the United States and Egyptian-American Christians opposed to the new Islamist-led and democratically elected government in Egypt.[39]

In Egypt itself, opponents of the first post-Mubarak president, Mohammad Morsi, seized on a controversy over the drafting of a new constitution to mobilize a march on the presidential palace in December 2012. Morsi and the leadership of his Muslim Brotherhood party were accused of wanting to impose Islamic law on the country.

Protesters besieged the palace in Heliopolis on Cairo's east side, covering its walls with subversive graffiti and chanting against Morsi. Some scaled the perimeter as Morsi was rushed to safety.[40] Months of protests and turmoil followed. Morsi, who was strongly supported by Qatar and Turkey, was eventually ousted in a military coup in the summer of 2013 by army generals and former regime figures backed by Saudi Arabia and the United Arab Emirates.[41]

In the spring of 2013, as Iran's ideologically driven Shiite militiamen flocked to Syria to defend Bashar, a leadership struggle between Al-Qaeda's Iraqi and Syrian affiliates reached a breaking point. The Nusra

342

Front sought to align itself more with the Syrian rebels and their Syria-focused agenda and assure them it had no transnational jihadist agenda, at least for now, while Al-Baghdadi in Iraq moved to bring what he regarded as a renegade group back under his firm control.[42]

In April 2013, he announced that he was abolishing the Nusra Front and that from then on there was only one Al-Qaeda-affiliated entity in both Iraq and Syria—the Islamic State in Iraq and Al-Sham, or ISIS. Bilad al-Sham (sometimes spelled "al-Cham") is the name usually given to the area encompassing the Levant: Israel, Jordan, Lebanon, the Palestinian territories, and Syria. Baghdadi's Levantine and pan-Arab aspirations were no different from those long espoused by the Baathist regimes in both Iraq and Syria. Syria was the "pulsing heart of Arabism," according to Assad regime dogma. The Baath Party manifesto speaks of "Arabs as being one nation with the natural right to live in one state."

While he was at it, Baghdadi warned Syrians against replacing Bashar with democracy, as had happened in Iraq when the Americans invaded and toppled Saddam, or as in Egypt, Libya, and Tunisia, where revolts swept aside dictators there, too.

"Look at their condition and what has become of them, and beware that you be stung from the hole which the Muslims in those countries have been stung," Baghdadi said as he made the case for Islamic rule. It was short of declaring a caliphate.[43] (In its most basic sense, the caliphate refers to the entities that came to be after the Prophet Mohammad's death and ruled over the Arabian peninsula and, later, parts of Asia, Africa. and Europe in the name of Islam. The term evokes the grandeur and power of the *ummah*, the Muslim nation, before it broke into nation states. The Ottoman Empire considered itself a caliphate.)

Notwithstanding his motives, Baghdadi's warnings about democracy and his use of Iraq and the countries of the Arab Spring as cautionary tales could have come right out of the mouth of Bashar—and they did. "They are soap bubbles, just like the [Arab] Spring is a soap bubble that will burst," said Bashar mockingly about calls for him to leave power.[44]

He spoke in early 2013 to a packed auditorium of regime officials and loyalists at the Dar al-Assad for Culture and Arts, also known as the

Damascus Opera House. "What's certain is that the majority of the people we are facing now are terrorists who espouse Al-Qaeda's ideology," said Bashar, dressed in a charcoal suit, white shirt, and thickly knotted tie.[45] "Yes, ladies and gentlemen, it's not only opposition versus loyalists and an army versus gangs and killers—we are now in a state of war in every sense of the word, we are confronting a vicious external aggression."[46]

Bashar stood on a stage in front of a massive collage of portraits of civilians and soldiers killed since the start of the conflict, done in the colors and pattern of the Syrian flag—the work of a savvy new media team.

It was in this same venue that, in May 2008, Bashar and Asma watched *Richard III: An Arab Tragedy*. In this version of Shakespeare's *Richard III*, an army general in an unspecified Arab state murders his way to the crown.[47]

Bashar was even caught smiling at one of the play's lines about public support for this fictional usurper: "We have done an Internet survey of the entire population, and 99 percent of them want you to become king. The other 1 percent don't have Internet."

Less than five years later, Bashar was the solo performer on the same stage.

21

The Clan's Knights and Soothsayers

It was early 2013 and John Kerry, who took over as US secretary of state from Hillary Clinton, was in the hills north of Rome meeting with representatives of the Syrian opposition and Arab and Western foreign ministers supporting their cause.

The setting was an elegant Renaissance-era villa surrounded by placid gardens that had been commissioned by the Medicis and were later appropriated by fascist leader Benito Mussolini.[1] This was Kerry's first major Syria gathering since his appointment, but he was no stranger to the country.

In his previous role as chairman of the Senate Foreign Relations Committee, Kerry tried to convince Bashar in 2009, a year into the Obama presidency, to make different choices, as the Americans liked to say at the time: break away from Iran and its proxy, Hezbollah, and stop exploiting terrorism and terrorists, including those linked to Al-Qaeda.

Like most Western leaders, Kerry was naturally charmed by Bashar and his British-born wife, Asma. Even if, four years later, Kerry had a better understanding of the Assad clan's brutal nature, he still had to stick to his boss's objectives in Syria, namely to make sure that the United States stayed at reasonable arm's length from another messy conflict in the Middle East and thus avoid a second Iraq.

During the Rome meeting, Kerry spoke of the urgency of the situation and "concrete steps" that needed to be taken in Syria.[2] "We are determined to find a way forward to a better day that we know awaits Syria, a day that will not come as long as Assad is in power," said Kerry, who also promised $60 million in US aid to scattered rebel communities coming

345

under daily bombardment by Bashar. The money was supposed to help them better communicate with one another and boost their local regime-free governance bodies, but no solution was offered on how to stop the planes raining down bombs on these communities day after day.

The way forward seemed more of the same on that afternoon in February 2013, two years after Bashar had smashed peaceful protests and declared war on his people and all those who tried to help them. The opposing camp was, for sure, more resolute. Iran rallied sectarian militias to defend Bashar and Russian president Putin plotted how to further his own agenda by exploiting Bashar's desperation to survive and America's seeming disinterest and weakness.

The thrust of the US plan, meanwhile, was to continue backing UN-led efforts to broker a political solution—a process that already seemed dead in the water. At the same time, the United States tried to convince Russia to abandon support for Bashar as it hoped that military pressure from Syrian rebels could compel him to negotiate his exit from power.

As Kerry spoke about a way forward, the man who was supposed to help orchestrate that much-hoped-for political settlement was ready to quit.

Veteran conflict mediator Lakhdar Brahimi, who had taken over the role of UN–Arab League Syria envoy after Annan's resignation in the summer of 2012, was considering giving up, like his predecessor, after barely six months on the job.[3]

The white-haired and bespectacled seventy-nine-year-old Brahimi was a former Algerian diplomat and had long been a front-row witness to the tyranny, war, and agony that has roiled the Middle East, including his native Algeria—from the ruins of the Ottoman Empire and colonialism to the Cold War and rise of political Islam. He was involved in Algeria's war of independence against the French between 1954 and 1964, which killed more than a million people; a few decades later Algeria plunged into civil war.

In the late 1980s, Brahimi helped negotiate an end to the fifteen-year Lebanese civil war in which Bashar's father was a key player. He headed the UN mission in Afghanistan between 2001 and 2004. In 2004, he took on the daunting task of mediating among Iraq's sectarian and ethnic groups to form the first government that succeeded the US-led occupation authority installed after the toppling of Saddam.[4]

But to Brahimi, Syria was nothing like these other conflicts. He likened it more to the Spanish Civil War of the 1930s. Germany's Hitler and Italy's Mussolini backed their fellow fascists in Spain, the Nationalists, with arms and soldiers. The Soviets under Stalin helped the left-wing Republicans with the tacit support of Britain and France, who were not fully committed to the fight. The United States was officially neutral, but American citizens joined thousands of volunteers flocking to Spain to fight with the Republicans.

In Syria, the array of actors involved was even more dizzying, and "the interests of the Syrian people were forgotten when outside forces came," thought Brahimi.[5]

Brahimi was already caught in the Qatar-Saudi feud, two US allies who were supposed to be working together to affect a solution in Syria. Bashar, meanwhile, accused Brahimi of "egregious bias,"[6] and Russia backed Brahimi's mission as long as it did not involve Bashar leaving power.

"Assad is not going anywhere," announced Russia's foreign minister, Lavrov.[7] He even suggested that the United States and its allies were secretly thankful for all the Russian vetoes at the Security Council in relation to Syria: "No one has any appetite for intervention. Behind the scenes, I have a feeling they [Britain, France, and the United States] are praying that Russia and China go on blocking intervention."[8] Lavrov believed that it was only a matter of time before the United States came around to accept Russia's position on Syria.

Indeed, Obama had already signaled his uneasiness with arming Syrian rebels. "We have seen extremist elements insinuate themselves into the opposition," he said, "and one of the things that we have to be on guard about...is that we're not indirectly putting arms in the hands of folks who would do Americans harm, or do Israelis harm."[9]

Israel was one of the least visible but more crucial actors in the Syrian tragedy. It had a direct stake in the outcome, given that Syria was a neighbor. Israel preferred to deal with the adversary it already knew, the Assad family, not some unknown antagonist. Israel, however, was alarmed when Iran and Hezbollah significantly increased their military presence inside Syria to save Bashar. In response, Israel began launching in early 2013 air-strikes on targets associated with this presence.[10]

Still, the statements coming from Moscow and Washington around that period gave succor to Bashar. Russia was saying no departure and no to Western intervention, and America was speaking about Islamist terror-ists and threats to Israel's security. Bashar reckoned that he remained indispensable for these world powers, no matter the atrocities and war crimes attributed to him, but he was nonetheless furious with Brahimi for daring to suggest that he give up power.

They had met on the day before Christmas in 2012.

Bashar received Brahimi and his team in a large reception room at the People's Palace on the Mezzeh plateau, overlooking Damascus and the rebel-controlled suburbs beyond.[11] On that day, as was the case on most days, the suburbs were engulfed in plumes of smoke from near-constant regime bombardment by warplanes as well as heavy artillery positioned near the presidential palace.

Brahimi already knew Bashar; they had met a few times when he worked on Iraq. He had also had dealings with Hafez, whom he first met in Damascus in September 1970, shortly before Hafez's coup against his Baathist comrades.[12]

After greetings and pleasantries, Brahimi and Bashar sat on two arm-chairs in the front of the room. On Bashar's side were diehard Assad fam-ily loyalists such as Foreign Minister Walid al-Moallem and political adviser Bouthaina Shaaban.[13]

A massive wooden coffee table separated them from Brahimi's team. All windows in the room had honey-colored curtains that were tied back. On the wall behind Bashar and Brahimi were three large antique-looking wooden shutters inlaid with mother-of-pearl motifs, a touch of old Damascus.[14]

Bashar was in great shape — relaxed, rested, and confident. He wore a nicely cut navy blue wool suit. He was calm and well informed about the situation.[15] At that point, the reports that he and his inner circle were getting from field commanders came almost hourly. Bashar sat with his long white hands clasped in front of him as Brahimi spoke.

The trilingual (Arabic, English, and French) diplomat came across as someone genteel, self-effacing, warm, and very funny at times.

"You know, Mr. President, change is indispensable. Speaking as an Algerian, we had ten years of civil war. I hope you can avoid that in Syria. We can't govern our countries the way we governed them in the 1950s and 1960s. Times have changed—it has to be different," said Brahimi, measuring every word and speaking calmly and deferentially.[16]

"Yes, of course," said Bashar, pausing before adding, with a faint smile: "But if we're speaking about democracy, then I have the right like every Syrian citizen to run for office if I choose to. There's no reason to prevent me, and if people want me, I stay, and if they don't, I go."

"Be the kingmaker instead of the king," said Brahimi.

"Why not?" said Bashar with a smirk as he fixed his blue eyes on Brahimi. "Really, I have not decided yet whether I want to run or not, and if I do, the people will decide if I stay or not," he insisted.

He had already held power for a dozen years. The constitution, which had just been adopted in a regime-orchestrated referendum in February 2012, while blistering military campaigns against protesting towns and cities were in full throttle, allowed Bashar to run in presidential elections in both 2014 and 2021 for seven-year terms each time; he could rule until at least 2028.

"The situation is improving you know," Bashar told Brahimi with a smile.[17]

"The only solution is chemical: we must exterminate them all, they and their families and children, all—these people do not deserve to live," said Mohammad Jaber, an Alawite businessman and militia leader working for the Assad family, speaking about regime opponents in the privacy of his suite at a Damascus hotel in early spring 2013.[18]

Days later, the regime fired a rocket carrying a chemical agent, accidentally killing some of its own soldiers as it tried to thwart rebel groups, including the Al-Qaeda-linked Nusra Front, from encircling the section of Aleppo controlled by Bashar. The rebels wanted to sever the regime's supply lines from Damascus to Aleppo.[19]

This had not been the first instance of suspected chemical weapons use. Three months before (December 2012) opposition activists reported that six people were killed in a poison-gas attack on a section of central Homs controlled by rebels but besieged by regime forces.[20] It happened just after Obama's second warning to Bashar against deploying chemical weapons; the first one (the famous "redline") had been in August 2012.

"If you make the tragic mistake of using these weapons," said Obama in December 2012 addressing Bashar, "there will be consequences, and you will be held accountable."[21]

Hillary Clinton also weighed in on the same day: "We are certainly planning to take action if that eventuality were to occur."[22]

Citing information from multiple sources, US officials said that the regime was already mixing chemicals to produce sarin, a poison gas that effectively hijacks a person's nervous system. High exposure can lead to death, mainly by suffocation due to uncontrollable secretions in the lungs.

"The intelligence that we have causes serious concerns that this is being considered," said Leon Panetta a few days later.[23]

Russia's Lavrov said that these were "rumors" and "nothing of the kind is being planned or might be planned." He said that Russia had received from Bashar "very firm assurances that this is not going to be used under any circumstances."[24]

Either Lavrov was lying, or Bashar was lying to Lavrov. Jaber, who worked for the Assads and had business dealings with the Russians, not only admitted the use of chemical weapons, he bragged about it.

Russia shielded Bashar again in the spring of 2013 from accusations of chemical weapons use and sided with him at the United Nations.

The Syrian regime's UN representative, Bashar al-Jaafari, said that it was "armed terrorist groups" who had fired the rocket on an army position in the village of Khan al-Assal near Aleppo, killing at least twenty-five, and he demanded that the UN carry out an immediate investigation.[25]

Britain and France informed the UN that they suspected the regime had used chemical weapons not only in the Aleppo countryside but also in several locations around Damascus, including Adra, Daraya, and the eastern suburbs.[26] Just as in western Aleppo, the regime was desperate to keep rebels around Damascus from advancing toward the capital.

For months after these chemical weapons incidents in early 2013, the Assad regime lied, stalled, and muddied the waters on the world stage, a game it has been perfecting for decades, and took maximum advantage of the rift in the Security Council and the United Nations' notoriously protracted deliberations and procedures.

This bought time for the Assad family and its loyal henchmen to do everything that needed to be done on the ground inside Syria to ensure their survival including deploy chemical weapons again, but with far more dreadful results.

"We are General Maher's people!" boasted Jaber, the militia leader and businessman, referring to Bashar's brother, Maher.[27] He wanted the world to know that he was part of a group of Assad family associates who planned to massacre, gas, starve, and torture all those who rose up against the regime. He dared Obama to stop them.

By the spring of 2013, Jaber was working out of a top-floor suite at a hotel in central Damascus after sending his wife and children to Moscow for safety. A heavyset man in his mid-fifties, Jaber lounged in his suite wearing a T-shirt and sweatpants. He was clean-shaven and his hair was dyed jet black and slicked down with copious amounts of gel. Freshly squeezed orange juice and a massive dish of fruit were on the table in front of him. A retinue of beefy, bearded bodyguards stood outside, next to the hotel elevator.

The Assads could always count on men like Mohammad Jaber and his brother, Ayman, who was married to a daughter of one of Bashar's cousins. The Jabers were involved in the regime's operation to help Saddam smuggle oil from Iraq in defiance of UN sanctions, a few years before the US-led invasion in 2003, which netted hundreds of millions of dollars for the Assads and their relatives.[28] In reward for their services, the Jabers became shareholders in the business cartel created by Bashar and his cousin Rami Makhlouf and were allowed to venture into the steel and iron sector. They were also involved in founding the Addounia TV channel, alongside other cronies of Maher al-Assad. The Jaber brothers' garish mansions on the hills above the Mediterranean coast and flashy mob-like lifestyle were the talk of their hometown of Latakia in western Syria.[29]

As war and international sanctions besieged Bashar and his regime, diehard loyalists like the Jabers and others stepped up to confront the challenges alongside the Assads and Makhloufs. For Alawites like the Jabers, it was self-preservation and a belief that their destiny was tied to the regime's survival—but it was also opportunity. The war was a chance to profit and elevate their status as old-time regime families like the Tlasses broke with the Assads.

"People like Firas [Tlass] have been living off the bounty of this country and then they fled...All the Damascene businessmen turned out to be traitors," said Jaber as he peeled an apple and took a bite from it.[30]

Like the Assads and Makhloufs, the Jabers were on the US and European sanctions list, but through offshore schemes, as well as allies and front companies in countries like Iraq and Lebanon, the pro-Bashar businessmen worked to evade sanctions and ensure that the regime got everything it needed to sustain its killing machine.

A crucial product was fuel, which the regime had to have to run everything from tanks and warplanes to power plants and factories. Syria's own oil production, limited to begin with and concentrated in the east near Iraq, had almost ground to a halt because of the war, so the regime had to supply most of its needs from outside. The Jabers organized oil shipments by land and sea, mainly from Iran and Iraq. They also mobilized their own armed convoys to deliver the oil within Syria—for handsome fees.

The burly and bearlike Mohammad Jaber, or Abu Jaafar as his men addressed him, often led the perilous missions. A few times he flew to Baghdad and the southern oil city of Basra with suitcases of $100 bills to buy oil for the regime and then accompanied convoys of tanker trucks by land through insurgent territory.[31] Al-Qaeda-linked fighters were concentrated in the desert between Iraq and Syria, but Jaber was able to work out deals with some of them; they refrained from targeting his convoys in return for cash or other favors from the regime.[32]

In addition to sanctions evasion, there was another important role that men like Jaber played in helping the Assads survive the existential threat they faced: they were instrumental in rallying Alawites around the regime.

When protests broke out in early 2011, Jaber quickly mobilized thugs, or *shabiha* as they became commonly known. Jaber led a pack of them in April 2011 when they descended on a Turkish coastal city to disrupt one of the first opposition conferences and physically assaulted those arriving to attend it.[33] Jaber also organized and led attacks on the French and US embassies in Damascus after envoys of the two countries visited protesters in Hama in July 2011.[34]

As the standoff escalated and began to morph into an armed struggle, and while the Syrian army was hobbled by defections and desertions, Jaber was among the Alawite bosses who actively recruited men from their sect to join militias defending the regime. Recruits received a monthly stipend, an assault rifle, a military uniform, and an ammunition vest, among other items. There were promises of compensation to their families in case they were "martyred."

The Jabers' sprawling steel plant on the coast, between the cities of Jableh and Latakia, became a base for militiamen and a staging ground for assaults on pro-opposition areas. The plant was also one of the sites churning out the barrel bombs that Bashar rained on these areas.[35]

Financial incentives were certainly a draw for many impoverished Alawites to join these militias, but there was a more fundamental and visceral motivation. Many Alawites, members of a minority sect, believed that by defending the regime they were fighting first and foremost to preserve their very existence. According to this view, a win by the opposition, dominated by members of Syria's Sunni majority, would spell their end — their annihilation. Alawites felt that their relative advances and privileges under the Assad family, compared to the misery and marginalization they had suffered previously, were well worth fighting for.

Even though only a few Alawites enjoyed the magnificent wealth of the Assads, Jabers, and Makhloufs, and most actually struggled to make a living, many still felt that they were the rulers of Syria and not just a minority seen as uncouth and heretical by the Sunni majority.

Indeed, Alawites dominated the sprawling civil service bureaucracy, the omnipresent *mukhabarat* system, and the army's top officer ranks. Some Alawites turned these positions into vehicles for extortion, bribe-taking, and business rackets of all sorts. It was sufficient for an Alawite living in predominantly Sunni Damascus or Homs to speak with the distinctive accent of Syria's coastal region to be feared and treated with deference.

Consequently, Alawites believed that the fall of the Assads would equal their doom. It was an idea subtly and often not so subtly perpetuated by the regime from the moment protests erupted in 2011. Then the regime did not have to do much after it deliberately killed and imprisoned those in the opposition advocating unarmed resistance and sectarian coexistence. This cleared the way for the empowerment of militants and extremists on both sides of the conflict.

All Alawites who dared suggest there might be options for their community other than the Assads and war were silenced. Among them was a medical doctor and longtime regime opponent called Abdelaziz al-Khayer, a dissenter in his community who hailed from the same town as the Assads. In the 1980s Khayer, a communist, was on the run and lived underground because Hafez was hunting anyone who threatened his power. Khayer was captured in 1992 and remained in prison until 2005.[36] Some have called Khayer Syria's Nelson Mandela.

At the start of the protests in 2011, Khayer was part of an opposition group that didn't call for the overthrow of Bashar, rejected armed struggle, and worked from inside Syria.[37] Khayer and his colleagues were even regarded by other opposition groups as "traitors" and "regime stooges."

Khayer and his stepson and another colleague were kidnapped by the *mukhabarat* in September 2012 as they left the regime-controlled airport in Damascus. They were part of a delegation that had returned from meetings in China and Russia, where they tried to secure support for an opposition conference they planned to hold inside Damascus. Nothing happened to the others in the delegation. The fate of Khayer has been unknown ever since.[38]

Taking Khayer and other like-minded Alawites out of the picture meant that those in the community pushing for a scorched-earth campaign of massacres and chemical-weapon attacks against regime opponents had the upper hand. For these people, even Bashar was not tough enough in the face of what they saw as a repeat of the events of the 1970s and early '80s that culminated in the Hama massacre of 1982.

"If the president [Bashar] listened to us, we would not have gotten to this stage—our president was the one who embroiled us in all of this. If he had struck with an iron fist a year ago it would have been over by now," lamented Jaber in the spring of 2013.[39] "If Hafez al-Assad, God rest his soul, were still alive, none of this would have been allowed to happen."

The 1982 massacre was forever framed in the minds of many Alawites as a necessary evil to deter Sunnis from ever mounting another challenge to the regime. The same mind-set was at work under Bashar, but the consequences were far more devastating.

"We just surrounded them and slaughtered about 250," bragged Brigadier General Jamal Younes, a heavyset man with graying hair and moustache. Younes was Alawite and in charge of an army unit commanded by Bashar's brother, Maher. He was speaking about an assault in the summer of 2012 on a village in the Hama countryside that harbored army defectors and opposition activists.[40]

It was one of a string of massacres committed by the regime in 2012 and 2013 in the Damascus suburbs, the Hama countryside, Homs city, and the western coastal region. They all followed a similar scenario, more or less. Army units that possessed the heavy weapons but lacked the necessary manpower surrounded rebellious communities and bombarded them nonstop until they had quashed any armed resistance on the inside. They were accompanied by Alawite militiamen and *mukhabarat* members, who were primarily responsible for going in afterward to do the mop-up operations, or what the regime called "cleansing"; this involved executing civilians and then looting and burning homes.

When finished, these forces usually sprayed graffiti like this one on the walls of the ransacked villages and towns: "Assad or nobody; Assad or we burn the country."

General Younes was particularly proud of his partnerships with Mohammad Jaber and his men, the militia of Bashar's cousin Rami Makhlouf, and a bloodthirsty Alawite *mukhabarat* colonel called Suheil al-Hassan, who went by the nom de guerre "the Tiger."[41] These were the Assad clan's knights.

"I always tell Sunnis: Bashar al-Assad is your protector because he's the only one [inside the regime] holding us back and preventing us from doing everything we want," said Younes as he sat across from Mohammad Jaber in the latter's office in the Latakia steel plant where militiamen gathered in the courtyard ahead of a fresh assault on Hama villages.[42]

Next to Jaber were shelves stacked with mementos, including a large framed photograph of himself in military uniform standing shoulder to shoulder with a beaming Bashar at the palace in Damascus.

While Bashar greatly appreciated what men like Jaber were doing to defend the regime and was fully aware that the only reliable fighting forces he possessed were the militiamen from his Alawite sect and those brought into the country by his Shiite allies, Iran and Hezbollah, publicly he still needed to project the image of a president for all Syrians, regardless of their religion or sect.

Bashar had to act like the commander of a national army fighting to save Syria from a "global conspiracy" and "terrorists."

More crucially, Bashar needed to claim deniability: he had to maintain a certain distance from the bestial killers and torturers he empowered and mobilized to save his regime. So, in tandem, a whole different team worked on Bashar's image as the sovereign and legitimate leader, and also the narrative of Bashar as the savior of Syria and even humanity from the scourge of terrorism. These image makers were the Assad clan's soothsayers.

Bashar's new communications director, Luna al-Chebel, an attractive and articulate former news presenter with the Qatar-owned Al Jazeera channel, worked on *the president* brand.

"The media conspiracy is 80 to 90 percent of the conspiracy against Syria," proclaimed Chebel one month into the protests in 2011, labeling Arab and Western journalists covering the popular uprising as "enemies of the people" and declaring that most American reporters were "undercover spies."[43]

Under Chebel, the presidency had for the first time its official Facebook page and Instagram, Twitter, and YouTube accounts. Press releases, interviews, and presidential decrees, as well as videos and photos of the official activities of Bashar and his wife, Asma, were disseminated on these platforms. Everything seemed sharper and more thought through than before. On Instagram, photographs of Bashar and Asma were mixed with photos of Syrian athletes, beauty queens, accomplished Syrians such as writers and filmmakers, soldiers fighting on the front, and volunteers painting a school allegedly damaged by "the terrorists."[44] Occasionally there was a spontaneous shot of Bashar typing on his laptop or walking up the stairs to his office with a briefcase.[45]

Asma's image also transformed by early 2013. She was slowly becoming the nation's first mother, often appearing with her hair pulled back, minimal makeup, simple attire, and flat shoes as she consoled the wives and mothers of the "army's martyrs." Gone were the stiletto shoes and stylish hairdos of the previous year.

"What a classy PONYTAIL for the most elegant lady in the world," her hairdresser and fashion consultant, Milad Hannoun, known for his over-the-top and glamorous makeovers, wrote in a caption of a photo of Asma hugging a child that he posted on his Instagram account.[46] He often called her his "idol" and "soul mate." As war and sanctions engulfed the Assads, Hannoun traveled to Dubai, Paris, and New York to shop for Asma, albeit for her new deconstructed and simple look.[47] He was not on the EU or US sanctions list.

Asma's team of young, tech-savvy, and Westernized assistants at the Syria Trust pitched in to help with the new media strategy and campaign. Many of their colleagues had either joined the opposition or left the country as the Assads chose to face protesters with bullets and tanks.

On March 21, 2013—Mother's Day as well as the first day of spring—Asma met at the presidential palace in Damascus with a group of women described as the mothers of martyrs of the Syrian army. It was the answer to regime opponents marking the second anniversary of their revolution.

The video of Asma and the women was aired on state television and shared online via social media.[48] It was in essence a slickly produced recruitment video to help shore up the gutted and demoralized army with this underlying message: Here are mothers from all of Syria's regions who sacrificed their sons and husbands; where are the rest of you, where are the men to rise up and defend the motherland, to defend our honor? Where are the knights? It was an appeal to chivalry and manhood, a resonant theme in Middle Eastern societies.

In the video, women pass one by one through large double doors and walk along a red carpet reserved for guests of honor toward Asma, who gives them long and sometimes tearful hugs. She wears a no-frills top and skirt, low-heel pumps, no jewelry, and light makeup. She crouches to greet an elderly mother in a wheelchair.

"I have four sons and I adore them, but I have consecrated them to this homeland…Let them all die. I am not sad, but may God end this crisis," says a woman wearing a white veil that exposes some of her hair.[49]

The women gather in a large marble hall beneath a sign lettered in beautiful Arabic calligraphy: "With your soul we protect the jasmine." (For Syrians, Damascus was the city of jasmine and in regime propaganda Asma was the Lady of Jasmine.)

"Every mother who has a son protecting this country is a great mother and every mother of a martyr who has sacrificed the most valuable thing in her life is an even greater mother," Asma tells the women. "I know there are mothers who have sent sons and grandsons to protect this country, and I know some of you have packed the clothes of your own grandsons on their way to join the army…With every heartbeat of worry and fear for them, there's another beat of determination, defiance, strength, power," she adds, pausing after each one of these last four words.[50]

Although her lines and delivery were well-rehearsed and polished, with no hint of spontaneity, still she spoke with the kind of emotion, passion, and force absent from most of Bashar's discourse and public appearances. She was trying to connect to her audience in ways he rarely did. Asma made sure to be photographed with each mother alone. The mothers were then treated to a lunch buffet. Asma herself served them lamb and rice and other Syrian specialties.

A key figure in the regime's revamped media strategy was Khaled Mahjoub, a businessman friend of Bashar. He was a high school friend of Bassel al-Assad and Manaf Tlass, and then when Bassel died he was in the circle of friends and acquaintances that Bashar inherited from his brother.

During Bashar's mentoring and grooming period in the 1990s, Mahjoub was often seen at social gatherings with the president-in-the-making. Many summers, Mahjoub joined Manaf, Bashar, and Bashar's brother-in-law Assef Shawkat in Latakia.[51] They often met to play cards at the Cote D'Azur, a staid state-owned beach resort from the early years of Hafez's rule that resembled a Soviet sanatorium but was popular with regime elites. This was before Bashar's flamboyant cousin and business partner, Rami Makhlouf, built a modern resort down the coast.

As the regime turned the 2011 uprising into war, Mahjoub, a natural-ized US citizen and fluent English speaker, chose to remain by Bashar's side. The fifty-seven-year-old wore horn-rimmed eyeglasses, was clean-shaven, and had his mostly gray hair slicked back. He often puffed on a big cigar. He could have been a Wall Street banker from the go-go 1980s.

Mahjoub was given a delicate mission by the palace: work with the *mukhabarat* to actively influence how the Syrian conflict was being portrayed in Western media and raise the alarm about the perils of US and European sup-port for rebels in conjunction with their Qatari, Saudi, and Turkish allies.[52]

Mahjoub argued that the actions of these countries in Syria were a pre-lude to another 9/11 — the idea being that the United States was repeat-ing in Syria what it had done when it partnered with the Saudis to fund and arm the mujahedeen in their fight against the Soviets in Afghanistan, only to spawn Al-Qaeda and Bin Laden years later.

"The US and the West will start to realize that more than 90 percent of the armed opposition are Salafist Wahhabi jihadists made by petrodollars — the same type of terror that hit the US on September 11. They are going to shift and deal with the regime in order not to have a failing state in Syria next to a failed state called Iraq," said Mahjoub confi-dently in the spring of 2013 over coffee at the Masa Mall, a shopping cen-ter not far from Bashar's private residence.[53]

"God blessed Syria, because the opposition is more stupid than the regime," he added with a broad smile.

Mahjoub had already arranged for two veteran Middle East reporters, the BBC's Jeremy Bowen and the *Independent*'s Robert Fisk, to meet with alleged foreign fighters being held by the *mukhabarat*'s Air Force Intelligence Director-ate at the Mezzeh Airbase.[54] This was the same entity, headed by the ruthless Jamil Hassan, that was torturing and killing protesters and activists. The air-base was where Mazen Darwish and his colleagues were first taken when Hassan's men raided his office in Damascus ten months earlier.

Bowen was allowed to interview six purported jihadists, including an elderly Algerian-French man who told him that he came from the French city of Marseilles because he could no longer bear to see dead Syrian children on TV.[55] Mahjoub, for his part, claimed that he was a "civil activist" taking on this mission on his own and that Bashar had nothing to do with it.[56]

In collaboration with the *mukhabarat*, Mahjoub operated a company that bypassed the bureaucratic channels to obtain visas for Western journalists and facilitated their reporting inside Syria—for big fees.[57]

"Everything worked out amazingly with ABC—the explosion happened while they were here and the footage they took at the scene was spectacular!" said Mahjoub's assistant with enthusiasm.[58] One of the reports filed by ABC News anchor and correspondent Terry Moran during a February 2013 visit to Damascus was from the flaming wreckage of a blast in downtown Damascus that was claimed by the Nusra Front and that killed some fifty people, including many children.[59] It was one of a series of deadly explosions in the capital that day.

The twin goal of the regime's media campaign was to alert Westerners to the consequences of their governments' backing of the opposition and rebels, who were painted as Islamist terrorists and fanatics, while also reinforcing a long-standing regime narrative: Bashar the secular and tolerant Arab leader, who was the protector of minorities, especially Christians.

Among those who were instrumental in promoting this idea were people like Ahmad Badreddine Hassoun, a Sunni cleric appointed by Bashar as grand mufti, the country's highest Muslim religious authority.

In his caftan and oversize white turban, and with his warmth and smile, Hassoun was meant to represent, at least to the Western journalists and delegations he regularly met in Damascus, the Sufi and moderate brand of Islam espoused by Bashar and the supposedly righteous Sunnis who supported him. Many of the delegations included white supremacists and European radical-right political figures.[60]

Only a few years earlier, in October 2011, Hassoun had threatened America, Europe, and Israel with suicide bombers if the West ever intervened in Syria.[61] "The sons and daughters of Lebanon and Syria will set off to be martyrs on the land of Europe and Palestine, and I say it to all of Europe and...America: martyrs in your midst are ready," shouted Hassoun as he waved his index finger threateningly during a speech to a Christian-led Lebanese interfaith delegation visiting Aleppo.

Hassoun's twenty-one-year-old son had been shot dead a few days earlier by what he later described as Syrian assailants allegedly paid by Saudi Arabia and Turkey because of his pro-Bashar stance.[62]

Hassoun's Christian alter ego was a pro-regime Lebanese-Palestinian Carmelite nun called Mother Agnes Mariam, who confessed that she had been an itinerant pot-smoking hippie before she found God in 1971.[63] The sixty-year-old nun always wore a brown habit, a white wimple, and a dark veil. A large cross dangled from her neck. She has lived in Syria since 1994 at a desert monastery between Homs and Damascus dedicated to Saint James the Mutilated, who was believed to have been beheaded for his faith in the fifth century.

As early as 2011, the nun brought Western journalists to Syria and traveled abroad in 2012 to talk about alleged beheadings being committed by forces linked to the rebels. Mother Agnes was affiliated with the Voltaire Network, a website that describes itself as an alternative media outlet, which is managed by a Damascus-based French conspiracy theorist named Thierry Meyssan.[64] Mother Agnes's role only got bigger.

Starting in 2013, many Western reporters were admitted by the regime for short visits. Most came by land via the Beirut–Damascus road, which remained the main lifeline for the regime and Syrians living under its control in the capital and surrounding areas.

Reporters moved mainly within Damascus and sometimes in parts of Homs and the western coastal region, mostly accompanied by Mahjoub's team or other regime-designated minders and always under the *mukhabarat's* watchful eyes.

In addition to being fed the regime's narrative, reporters and visiting Western delegations had a chance to marvel at how, despite the war, life continued as normal inside Damascus — at least on the surface.

Westerners got to see clean streets, well-tended parks, busy markets, and people going to work and school. Life seemed uninterrupted, despite the security checkpoints all over the city, the regime warplanes buzzing overhead on their way to drop bombs on opposition-held areas, the thunderous sound of regime artillery firing from Mount Qasioun, and the plumes of black smoke billowing in the distance.[65]

A highlight for visiting reporters and Western delegations hosted by the regime was a trip to the traditional Souk al-Hamidiyeh in the city's old quarter, brimming with shoppers, vendors, and colors amid the wafting scents of spices and handmade soaps. All along the souk's main vaulted passageway, shops displayed lingerie, glittery evening gowns on plastic mannequins, leather goods, blankets, stacks of towels, and every clothing and household item imaginable. More sellers hawked their wares in the middle of the passageway.[66]

North of the souks, civil servants on lunch break crowded the cafeterias and sandwich shops around parliament and other government buildings.

"Thank you, Russia; Thank you, China," read graffiti emblazoned on the marble column of a building to show the gratitude of Bashar loyalists to both countries for vetoing numerous Security Council resolutions condemning the regime.[67]

A flier plastered on an adjacent wall announced "musical performances and sumptuous dinners" at special prices on the rooftop terrace of a downtown hotel. Near the Four Seasons Hotel, where United Nations humanitarian agencies had begun to set up shop, a sushi restaurant served sashimi and California rolls made with fish trucked in from Lebanon daily.

While the regime sought to use Western media to influence public opinion in the West, its message to Arabic-speaking audiences was sharpened and broadened. In addition to its own TV channels in Syria and those of allies Hezbollah and Iran, a new channel was created in Beirut to rival Al Jazeera and promote the agenda and perspective of the regime and its allies in a slick and more professional way.

Al Mayadeen launched in mid-2012 under the direction of two former Al Jazeera anchors at a cost of about $30 million, of which $25 million came supposedly from Bashar's cousin Rami and the rest from Iran.[68] The station denied it, saying its owners were Arab businessmen, including Syrians, but refused to reveal their identities.

The regime's messaging became much more strategic and coordinated.

In early summer 2013, Bashar met at his cozy private office with the correspondent of *Frankfurter Allgemeine Zeitung*, one of Germany's most prestigious dailies. He declared that all rebels were "terrorists" and that there were no such thing as "good" and "bad" fighters.

Bashar warned Europe against arming the rebels. "If the Europeans supply weapons, Europe's backyard would become a terrorist haven, and Europe would pay a price for this. Terrorism would mean chaos here... The second effect would be the direct export of terrorism to Europe," he said as he rattled off the virtues of his regime, a haven of "secularism" and "tolerance" for Christians and minorities now besieged by "terrorists."[69]

At precisely the same moment that Bashar's interview came out, his friend Khaled Mahjoub organized a tearful and emotional encounter between Tunisian mothers of alleged jihadists captured by the regime and the mothers of martyrs of Syrian soldiers, like those whom Asma had met at the palace.

The setting was the grand Umayyad Mosque, held up by the regime as a symbol of tolerance and coexistence because it was built on the ruins of a Christian basilica, vestiges of which remained. Guests of honor included the regime's mufti, Hassoun.

"Europe today is having a new Pakistan on your border," warned Mahjoub in an interview with Lyse Doucet, the chief correspondent of the BBC, which reaches more than a quarter-billion people around the world.[70]

A Tunisian mother told Doucet that her son "wouldn't kill anyone." And under the auspices of the regime and Mahjoub's initiative, Tunisian and Syrian lawyers were collaborating to make sure Tunisians held by the regime were accorded "fair trials," reported Doucet.

Nowhere in Doucet's heartfelt television piece was a clear explanation of the circumstances and dates of arrest of these Tunisians. What Doucet did not know[71] was that the Syrian *mukhabarat* had, early on, rounded up dozens of Tunisian male citizens who had been residing and working in Damascus for years before the uprising. Many were tortured and made to confess that they were jihadists.[72]

Members of a delegation of European far-right politicians who were being hosted by the regime that same week also spoke to Doucet.

"If they come back to our country, they will fight jihad not in Syria anymore but on European soil," Filip Dewinter from Vlaams Belang, a Belgian right-wing political party, told Doucet. "This is a very, very big threat for all European countries."[73]

Around the same time, Bashar's friend Mahjoub played a central role in spreading the "sex jihad" story, a lie spun by pro-Bashar media outlets and later picked up by some Western ones—essentially that a group of Tunisian girls had allegedly gone to Syria and returned home pregnant or infected with the AIDS virus after having had sex with jihadists there.[74]

The lie had all the elements of the massive Russian disinformation campaign that would target the US presidential elections three years later.[75]

During their short stays in Damascus, few of the reporters and Western visitors met with anti-Bashar activists from all religious and economic backgrounds still determined to work clandestinely and at great risk to themselves and their families to help opposition areas being besieged and bombed by the regime. Few of the visitors were exposed to these scenes and stories:

- *mukhabarat* henchmen bundling a suspected regime opponent into the trunk of a vehicle in a busy Damascus market as shopkeepers and passersby watched silently
- a grandmother from a rebellious town displaced in Damascus and trying to care for her grandchildren and daughters-in-law after her husband and male sons had all been arrested by the regime
- young men hiding in their homes because they did not want to be drafted into the army
- and a barbershop owner next to Bashar's residence sobbing uncontrollably when he recalled his nephew, who had been arrested by the *mukhabarat* and returned as a cold corpse to his parents because of something he had written on Facebook[76]

And for sure, few if any knew what was happening inside the *mukhabarat*'s torture chambers and dungeons, which were nestled in residential neighborhoods, on busy commercial streets, and even next to the presidential palace.

Two months after their detention at the Mezzeh Airbase, where they witnessed prisoners forced to get on their knees and make animal sounds, roll in their own urine and feces, and endure torture until they wrote demeaning confessions, Mazen Darwish and many of his fellow activists were transferred in the spring of 2012 to an underground prison run by Maher al-Assad's army division.[77] It was more of a hastily built dungeon divided into a few cells. The Assads were running out of space to put all the people being swept up by their *mukhabarat*.

The dungeon was accessed through a large metal door and stairs. There was one small opening in the ceiling, through which the guards above could check on the prisoners. Mazen and dozens of others were crammed into a cell measuring about five by three meters (sixteen by ten feet). Among them were teenage boys as young as fourteen. The feeling everyone had was that they had been thrown into this hole in the ground and would be forgotten forever.

Prisoners were blindfolded, had their hands tied behind their backs, and were ordered to kneel against the walls. Soldiers then descended on them with batons, cables, metal chains, and stun guns. Some soldiers carried a new torture instrument that they had fashioned and named "The Lakhdar Brahimi" after the UN–Arab League envoy had pleaded with Bashar several times to release opposition prisoners. It was a long piece of green PVC pipe with metal screws attached to one end to cause maximum pain and injury. Brahimi's first name Lakhdar meant "green" in Arabic (akhdar).

As jailers struck people, they shouted "You want freedom, right?" and "Brahimi wants us to free you."[78]

In addition to torture, soldiers emptied buckets of garbage and sewage water down on the bloodied prisoners through the opening in the ceiling. Mazen endured this for almost six months. He tried to cope by organizing discussion sessions in whispers about Syria's history and future. Others tried to give lessons to detainees who were illiterate.

With one of the studs of his jeans Mazen wrote down the names of at least 105 prisoners on a piece of paper he hid inside his jacket's lining when he was arrested. Two of his colleagues wrote more names on ripped strips of clothing, using their own blood.[79] They thought that getting the names out was perhaps a way to hold Bashar accountable for those kidnapped and held incommunicado by the mukhabarat.

In the fall of 2012, toward the end of Mazen's stay at the Fourth Division dungeon, a fellow detainee started hemorrhaging after a particularly bad torture session. Soldiers wanted to take him to the Mezzeh Military Hospital, known as the 601. Mazen and the others were horrified—they had heard from new arrivals at the dungeon that many of those taken to the 601 ended up dying. Bodies of those killed under torture were also piling up at the 601.

Since the start of the uprising, the hospital, which was within walking distance from the People's Palace where Bashar met Brahimi, had been divided into two sections—one for soldiers and another for the *mukhabarat*'s prisoners.

An activist who was taken to the 601 saw patients chained to their beds by their ankles. The wards were filthy and smelled of feces and vomit most of the time. Surgery often meant death, nothing was disinfected, and no anesthesia was administered.[80]

Torture usually happened around meal-time, and at night guards with nicknames like Ezrael, the biblical name for the Angel of Death, and Abu Shakoosh ("the one with the hammer") got very drunk and dragged patients from their beds and out to a hallway where they tortured them to death. Sometimes bodies were left in the hallway or dumped in the toilet until they were collected by other prisoners enslaved by the guards.

All bodies were eventually taken to a hangar in the hospital's parking lot, where they were tagged with number cards and photographed before being dumped in mass graves.[81]

Mazen and more than a hundred others went on a hunger strike to prevent their fellow prisoner from being taken to the 601, and they demanded that a doctor be brought to the dungeon instead. A doctor came and treated the man, but the next day at dawn soldiers stormed in and took Mazen upstairs. They forced his head and legs into a car tire, a common torture technique in Syria known as the *dulab* ("tire"), and beat him until he nearly passed out. They tossed him inside a small toilet, a hole in the ground, and left him there for almost twenty-four hours.[82]

The next day, Mazen was back in the custody of Jamil Hassan's Air Force Intelligence Directorate. This time they took him to their branch in central Damascus, not far from the old quarter's Bab Touma, or Saint Thomas Gate. A nearby street was named after the poet and writer Gibran Khalil Gibran. On the outside, the building looked like any government building or police station. Jamil Hassan's office was on one of the top floors.

The prison was two floors deep underground. There were more than forty individual and two group cells. Mazen was taken down the stairs and along a green-tiled passageway and then led into a tiny cell that was supposed to be for solitary confinement. But there were already five people there. They were running out of room. The ceiling was a wire mesh, above which rats scurried back and forth nonstop. Mazen got the customary torture session that all new arrivals were subjected to and then a jailer came to see him two days later.

"You are the lawyer, right?" said the man.

Mazen said nothing.

"Anyway, happy holiday, and his excellency the general [Jamil Hassan] has sent you a special gift. Please come with us," said the man as he opened the cell door. It was late October 2012 and it was the first day of the Muslim holiday of Eid al-Adha, Feast of the Sacrifice. For a split second Mazen was comforted.

He was then led out to the hallway. There were already seven guards standing there with batons, chains, and steel rods. One of them immediately punched him in the face, knocking him down on the floor. All seven attacked him. He was unconscious minutes later. He woke up in the bathroom with the shower running over him. Blood was coming out of his mouth and nose.

"Boss, this guy is awake," he heard a man say.

"Take him back to his cell," a voice answered gruffly from outside. Mazen was dragged by his feet and shoved into his cell. The others made room for him. They used clothing items to stop the bleeding.

Mazen was taken out the next day and tortured the same way. He lost all his nails. On the fourth day he woke in a room under the stairs. He was on top of a motionless body. It was a dead person. Mazen wanted to scream but it seemed like he had lost his voice.[83]

22

Macabre Coronation

It was the summer of 2014, thousands of guests gathered in a vast auditorium at the presidential palace in Damascus.[1] They were seated in clusters according to their profession or designation; actors sat together and so did members of the clergy, ministers, mothers of martyrs, and so on.

The speaker of the rubber-stamp parliament was called to the stage, where a podium had been set up. There were Syrian flags on each side. Two soldiers from the Republican Guard in their full military regalia marched in, one carried an ancient handwritten copy of the Muslim holy book, the Quran, and the other a copy of the constitution adopted by the regime two years before. They placed them next to the podium.

Outside at the palace's main entrance, a Republican Guard officer opened the door of a black sedan with tinted windows. Bashar al-Assad stepped out onto red carpet. The presidential guard of honor stood motionless beneath the searing July sun while a band played the national anthem. To the sound of grandiose military marches, Bashar walked toward the palace entrance past formations that were supposed to represent various branches of the armed forces.

As the music turned more imperial, two honor guards opened a massive double door and Bashar strode down the red carpet laid out in dramatic contrast to an all-white marble hallway. When he entered the auditorium, the audience stood up and applauded for nearly two minutes.

Every detail of the ceremony to install Bashar as president for another seven years, from his triumphant entry down to the music and the stage color and height, was meant to replicate the grand inauguration ceremony of Russian president Vladimir Putin at the Kremlin in 2012.[2]

Bashar's aching and lifelong desire to be taken seriously as a strong leader was on full display. He was already a huge fan of Putin and drew parallels between the Russian leader's confrontation with the West and his own dealings with Western powers since inheriting power from Hafez in 2000. Putin's first presidential term had begun that same year, precisely a month before Hafez's death.

According to the narrative eagerly embraced by Bashar and articulated at nearly every opportunity, both he and Putin were leaders who rejected a unipolar superpower system and were intent on standing up to the hegemony and arrogance of the United States and restoring the global balance that had prevailed under the former Soviet Union. And the part that Bashar loved the most was seeing himself and Putin as smooth and ruthless operators with nerves of steel, ready to do anything to attain their goals. Bashar thought it was only fitting for him to have an inauguration ceremony exactly like Putin's.

After taking the oath of office, Bashar spoke for more than an hour, addressing his supporters as "honorable Syrians" who prevailed over "dishonorable" protesters.

"Years have gone by since some chanted for freedom, but you turned out to be the free ones in the age of enslavement, you were the masters in the age of mercenaries...They drowned in illusion, and you made reality," said Bashar.[3]

Bashar's underlying message was precisely the same as that delivered twelve days earlier by Abu Bakr al-Baghdadi: The righteous were those who stood with the leader—and the damned were those opposing him.

"Obey me in what I obey Allah through you," declared Baghdadi, dressed in black robes and turban, after he stepped out of a vehicle with tinted windows and made a spectacular entry, just like Bashar's, into the marble-columned prayer hall of the Al-Nouri mosque in the Iraqi city of Mosul to deliver a sermon.[4]

Just like Bashar's inauguration ceremony, Baghdadi's appearance and discourse was filmed by multiple cameras from different angles. The two men seemed to be moving in lockstep. The previous month, June 2014, Baghdadi's shura (consultative) council of the mujahedeen elected him caliph, commander of a self-declared Islamic State that extended from Aleppo in Syria to Baghdad's edges, and soon beyond, they hoped.[5] That same month Bashar's war council engineered his reelection.[6] Both men praised the supposedly democratic processes that had anointed them leaders.

Even Baghdadi's capture of Mosul and bloody rampage through Iraq that same month was tied to a fateful decision made by Bashar sixteen months before.

Baghdadi and a band of a few thousand fighters from his terror group had marched on Mosul from the Syrian border area west of the city.[7] It was a vast desert frontier region encompassing the Syrian provinces of Deir Ezzour, Hasakeh, and Raqqa that Bashar decided to abandon to Islamist extremists in early 2013 as rebel forces backed by the United States and its allies increased pressure on him in Aleppo and Damascus.

"I wanted reinforcements but they refused," said the Syrian officer in charge of Hasakeh's Ya'arubiya border crossing, nearly seventy miles west of Mosul, about his call to Damascus at the end of February 2013 to ask for help in defending his post after it was attacked by rebels, including elements of the Nusra Front.[8] Syria's Nusra was at the time still part of Baghdadi's Iraq Al-Qaeda franchise before splitting from it two months later.

The Syrian officer told his commanders in Damascus that he was confident he could hang on to his position, and he proposed to engage the assailants until additional forces were dispatched. The order from Damascus was unequivocal: Leave now.[9] The Syrian regime even arranged with its allies in Baghdad to remove the Syrian officers and soldiers from Ya'arubiya.

Forty-eight hours later, Raqqa province and its administrative seat also called Raqqa were surrendered in a similar manner.[10]

This was the same border region through which Bashar had sent foreign fighters to fuel Iraq's insurgency and bog down the United States after it toppled Saddam in 2003.

It was under Saddam's brutal Baathist rule that Baghdadi had grown up into the Sunni fundamentalist that he became. He was detained for ten months by US troops early on in their occupation of Iraq before rising up in the ranks of Al-Qaeda's Iraqi franchise, which eventually brought together many former operatives in Saddam's security and military apparatuses.[11] They were all cut from the same cloth as Bashar's *mukhabarat* agents, something that greatly facilitated cooperation between the two sides after Saddam's fall.

Like Saddam's Iraq and the Assads' Syria, the Islamic State decreed that everyone had to submit to the ruler or face dire consequences. The Islamic State's decision to blow up border posts between Iraq and Syria in the summer of 2014 and herald the end of the 1916 Franco-British Sykes-Picot Agreement would have made every Baathist proud.[12] Baathists in both Iraq and Syria saw the accord, which had carved out nation-states in the Levant and Arabian Peninsula after World War I, as a curse and conspiracy by colonial powers to divide and control Arabs and create Israel.

The fact that the Islamic State was effectively birthed from the womb of the terror regimes of Iraq and Syria hardly mattered, as truths and nuances were buried under a deluge of news, images, and videos of the apocalyptic army of black-clad militants and their barbaric crimes.

It could not have been a more perfect backdrop for Bashar's July 2014 inauguration speech, branding all his opponents "terrorists" and "degenerates," without exception.

"The ugly faces were revealed after the mask of freedom and revolution was removed," Bashar charged.[13]

He told countries that backed his opponents to brace themselves for terror attacks on their soil.

"Isn't what we see today in…all the countries plagued by the fraudulent [Arab] Spring…tangible and concrete proof of the credibility of what we have been warning about over and over again," he said. "Soon we'll see regional and Western countries that supported terrorism also paying a heavy price."[14]

The audience was cheering Bashar's coronation and what he gloatingly described as "the official death of…the Arab Spring."

As promised by Bashar, the first attack would happen six months later in France, the same country that had suffered from terrorism in the 1980s when it was in the camp challenging Hafez in Lebanon.

Belarus's Alexander Lukashenko, Myanmar's Thein Sein, North Korea's Kim Jong-un, Russia's Vladimir Putin, South Africa's Jacob Zuma, and

Venezuela's Nicolas Maduro were among the leaders who cabled Bashar to congratulate him[15] on what was by every measure a farcical and sham election organized by his *mukhabarat*.

There was also a letter from Richard Black, a Virginia state senator, characterizing the elections as a "sweeping victory" and noting the "Syrians who flooded to the ballot boxes."[16] This same state legislator, who regularly appeared in Russian state-owned media, had sent a letter to Bashar the previous month praising the Syrian army for its "heroic rescue of Christians," including thirteen nuns kidnapped by the Nusra Front in 2013.[17]

Residents of the ancient Christian town where the nuns had been abducted, however, said that the army had done nothing to stop militants from overrunning the town. Some of the nuns and their families were thankful to the Nusra Front for removing them from the monastery because the Syrian army had started shelling it viciously and indiscriminately after the militants' entry. The nuns were released in a complex deal involving a prisoner swap and ransom money.[18]

As for the elections held in early June 2014, by then the death toll had surpassed 200,000 and the number of refugees—just those registered by the United Nations in neighboring countries—was about three million. Millions more were displaced inside Syria.[19]

In the lead-up to the elections, Bashar's face was everywhere in Damascus. Loyalist businessmen competed to erect the biggest and flashiest Bashar billboards along with the catchiest slogans.[20]

"Yes to the leader of resistance and perseverance," read a banner strung across a main road by a car dealership owner. It showed Bashar flanked by his brothers, Maher and Bassel, all in military uniforms.

"We're all with you!" screamed large billboards of Bashar plastered on the facade of every government building.

Two candidates, a former minister and a member of parliament, were vetted by the *mukhabarat* to run as token candidates against Bashar and give the impression of reform and seriousness in implementing the new constitution adopted in 2012. Until then the Assad family's fig leaf of legitimacy had been referendums, held every seven years since 1970, in which father and then son were the only candidates.

"The man is popular. I did not expect him to have all this popularity, but the man is very popular," one of Bashar's presumed challengers declared before the elections.[21]

On election day, workers at polling stations stuffed ballots on behalf of absent family members and friends, while civil servants and families displaced by the fighting and living in temporary shelters in Damascus were brought in government buses to polling stations and ordered to vote for Bashar.

In the Zahera Jadida neighborhood, public school teachers chanted and danced for Bashar as an official with a bullhorn instructed those lining up to vote to mark the empty white circle under Bashar's photo and name on the ballot paper, which also had the photos and names of the two other candidates.[22]

In Midan, a district that had been a hotbed of protests against Bashar, *mukhabarat* agents posed as election workers and manned voting kiosks set up inside the neighborhood's alleyways.[23] Silent and grim-faced residents lined up to vote fearing retribution if they boycotted.

In Lebanon, at the time home to more than one million Syrian refugees and where the regime had an embassy and where its ally Hezbollah was more powerful than the dysfunctional Lebanese government, tens of thousands clogged the road to the embassy to vote after rumors circulated that not doing so could preclude them from ever returning to Syria or obtaining official documents like passports.[24] It was a spectacle that the regime's propaganda machine celebrated with gusto.

Bashar was declared the winner with 88.7 percent of the votes.[25]

How was Bashar's regime, which was sustained by lies, propaganda, fear, brute force, and terror, any different from Al-Baghdadi's self-styled and media-savvy caliphate with its legions of loyalists and supporters? In fact, they were two faces of the same coin.

But by the summer of 2014 Bashar had become a secondary preoccupation to the world, including those who had rallied to support his opponents and tried to push him out of power, like the United States and its European allies.

The Islamic State (the rebranded ISIS) pressed on with its rampage to capture more territory in Iraq and Syria, slaughtering and enslaving minorities like Yazidis and later beheading Western hostages. The ghouls of ISIS dominated the headlines.

As the ISIS monster got bigger and scarier, the more tolerable and even acceptable Bashar and his regime—and for that matter, all other oppressive rulers around the Middle East—became, no matter the crimes they committed against their people.

In fact, Bashar and his allies were more than happy to facilitate the growth and expansion of this menace. They hardly put up a fight as they relinquished to the terror group airbases, military facilities, and entire towns and regions deemed peripheral.

Senior army officers often flew out of these remote posts, leaving behind unfortunate conscripts to face their grim fate at the hands of ISIS. Regime cronies and businessmen had no problem dealing with ISIS, especially after the group captured oil installations in the east. They purchased fuel from the terror group and sold food in areas under its control.[26]

Bashar and Al-Baghdadi commenced preparation for their macabre coronations more than a year before that summer of 2014.

After ISIS broke away from Al-Qaeda in the spring of 2013 and declared itself an independent terror group in competition with Al-Qaeda's Syria affiliate, Nusra, the first people it began killing were army defectors and members of the moderate rebel factions favored by the United States and its Western allies, providing the greatest service to Bashar.

"Iran was doing all the thinking and planning for Bashar. Iran's intelligence services possess lethal capabilities; they have certainly maintained tactical alliances with elements of Al-Qaeda and ISIS," said an Iraqi politician close to Bashar and the Iranians.[27]

Indeed, the rise of ISIS and the fact that it was waging war on all rebel factions allowed Bashar and Iran to concentrate on defending and reclaiming areas deemed vital and strategic, like the city of Homs and the suburbs of Damascus.

By the summer of 2013, rebels and their supporters were hemmed in and besieged in a few Homs neighborhoods, including the old quarter. The Iran-planned operations usually followed a pattern.[28] The regime's war planes and heavy artillery viciously bombed opposition areas, and then Iran's Shiite fighters, led by its Lebanese proxy Hezbollah, who were pumped up before the battle on the idea that they we were confronting the enemies of their faith and descendants of the killers of Imam Hussein and his companions in AD 680, went in to do the close-quarter combat.

After most civilians and rebels fled and the area was subdued, the *mukhabarat* and pro-Bashar Alawite militiamen did their "cleansing."

They executed or captured anyone left behind and then looted homes and businesses and set them on fire. A *mukhabarat* officer's war booty from the town of Qusair near Homs, which was captured in a Hezbollah-led offensive in June 2013, included a farm tractor, a cow, and pickup trucks laden with furniture, refrigerators, TV sets, and other household items.

"Assad or nobody; Assad or we burn the country," was scrawled on the walls of Qusair, not far from graffiti sprayed by Hezbollah fighters paying tribute to their revered Zeinab.[29]

For months after being recaptured from the opposition, many Homs neighborhoods were subjected to vulture-like looting sweeps by Bashar's militiamen with the intent of making sure nobody ever returned to these areas.[30] In one neighborhood, all that was left after the dismantling of kitchen sinks, doors, windows, and tiles were the memories of former inhabitants—photo albums and books strewn on the streets.

At the same time, Bashar and his allies were merciless in confronting threats to an essential corridor of territory extending from the capital Damascus to the western coastal region via Homs.

In early May 2013, Bashar's militiamen executed at least 300 civilians, including those killed with meat cleavers when Alawite henchmen went on a rampage in and around Baniyas, a largely Sunni city on the vital coastal highway to the regime stronghold of Latakia.[31] All visible opposition to the regime in the area had been crushed in the first few weeks of the uprising in 2011, but there remained clandestine resistance involving army deserters.

After the Baniyas massacre, several Sunni clerics in the region, called for jihad in Syria to defend their Sunni coreligionists (in this context jihad means an obligation to defend fellow Muslims, not holy war as commonly construed).[32]

Having the opposition painted with the same brush as Sunni fanatics was precisely what Bashar, Iran, and Russia wanted, especially after the White House announced—around the same time as the jihad call—that it had concluded that the Assad regime had crossed the chemical weapons redline set by Obama, and as such the US president was now officially authorizing what was still called "nonlethal aid" to moderate rebels under the umbrella of the so-called Supreme Military Council and still with a view to "achieving a negotiated political settlement" in Syria.[33]

In parallel with this announcement, the CIA began a covert operation code-named Timber Sycamore to vet, train, and arm Syrian rebels.

To most regime opponents, Obama's response to the atrocities of Bashar and his backers seemed too little too late, tone-deaf, impotent, and even downright collusive with their enemy.

People wanted vengeance and the tragic consequences played out at the start of August 2013 in remote mountain villages in Latakia province along the Turkish border.

An ISIS leader called Abu Ayman al-Iraqi was instrumental in inciting both foreign jihadists and Syrian fighters, including those with groups deemed moderate by the United States and its Western allies, to take part in a rampage on a string of Alawite villages in the area.

Abu Ayman spoke about just retribution for Bashar's carnage in Bani-yas four months earlier.[34] At least 190 civilians were killed, including 57 women and 18 children.[35] One Alawite woman was shot dead by an ISIS commander because she was too beautiful and a quarrel was about to break out among his fighters over who was going to have her, so he decided to kill her instead.[36] Some 200 women and children were taken hostage.

Months before, Alawite civilians had begged regime authorities to boost defenses around their villages, but their pleas were in vain. The regime kept a tiny and ill-equipped army contingent in the area and stood back when the massacre and abductions played out.[37]

A few days after the massacre, the commander of the Supreme Military Council endorsed by Obama showed up in a rebel town from where the assault was launched to meet with his men and dismissed reports of atrocities.[38] These were Obama's "moderate rebels," howled pro-Bashar media.

That summer other rebel commanders were determined to take the fight to Bashar in Damascus.

On August 7, 2013, on the first day of the Eid al-Fitr holiday marking the end of the Muslim holy month of Ramadan, rebels in the city of Douma fired a barrage of rockets and mortar shells on the Damascus neighborhood where Bashar and his family lived. They claimed to have hit Bashar's convoy as he made his way from his home to a nearby mosque for traditional Eid prayers.[39] Explosions shattered windows in the upscale Malki neighborhood as streets near the Assad residence emptied and ambulance sirens wailed. Bashar was unharmed.

"We targeted the convoy of the leader of the Nusairi gang," declared Douma-based rebel commander Zahran Alloush on Qatar's Al Jazeera, using a derogatory term to describe Bashar's Alawite sect. "May we celebrate Eid in the coming years in a country cleansed from the filth of the Nusairi scoundrels."[40]

Alloush was among the militants released from prison by Bashar during the first weeks of the uprising. He was from Douma, the same city where Bashar's cousin Hafez Makhlouf shot and killed protesters a week into the uprising and where Manaf Tlass tried to mediate between locals and Bashar, only to see his efforts sabotaged by his enemies at the palace.

As peaceful protesters were silenced, Alloush formed a group called the Army of Islam, which initially received generous support from Qatar and was then bankrolled by Saudi Arabia after it squeezed out its smaller Gulf rival from leadership of the campaign to topple Bashar.

While the United States officially kept its distance from men like Alloush, he actually coordinated with rebel groups backed by a covert command center in neighboring Jordan staffed by CIA agents and their Saudi counterparts, among others.[41]

Precisely two weeks after the audacious attack on the perimeter of Bashar's residence, the regime decided to launch what it called a "preemptive operation" against the Sunni-dominated and opposition-controlled eastern suburbs of Damascus. Alawite army officers said they had intelligence that rebels tied to the Jordan command center were planning a major offensive in Damascus and as such the regime needed to act first.[42]

The real motivation was probably this: Alawite loyalists clamored for revenge after the attack on their villages; soldiers and militiamen wondered why they should fight for the regime in Damascus when their mothers and wives back home in the coastal region were under threat.[43]

Bashar could not wait to turn Obama's redline warning into a mockery.

✳   ✳   ✳

The regime's operation kicked off in the predawn hours of Wednesday, August 21, 2013, when large rockets laden with sarin hit Zamalka. It was one of the towns of the Eastern Ghouta, an expanse of territory east of Damascus controlled by various rebel groups—mostly local men who had taken up arms after the regime's deadly crackdown on protests. There were still around two million civilians in these "liberated" areas, and residents tried to attend to their normal affairs despite the regime's siege and daily bombardment.[44]

When the rockets hit Zamalka and surrounding areas, people were asleep in their homes. They hardly heard them, because, unlike conventional rockets carrying incendiary warheads, these rockets triggered no explosions.

"I saw people dead in their beds, and those who tried to escape from their homes collapsed at the front door or on the stairs—it was as if someone just pressed a button and people froze in their place," said one of the rescuers. [45]

Smaller-caliber sarin-bearing rockets struck a few hours later, just before dawn, Moadhamiya, another rebel-controlled town southwest of the city that the regime had been desperately trying to subdue and recapture.[46]

The Twitter and Facebook feeds of journalists covering Syria were flooded with YouTube videos filmed and uploaded by citizen journalists inside the rebel zones. There were images of lifeless and pale-looking children still twitching with spasms and foaming at the mouth or being washed with water and injected with atropine amid the horror-filled screams of adults around them.[47]

Later, rows of children were wrapped in white shrouds and readied for burial, according to Islamic tradition.[48] More than 1,400 people were killed, almost one third of them children.

It was impossible to reach the areas affected by the attacks, initially because their perimeter was under siege by regime forces and then also because the regime began bombing these same areas nonstop but now with conventional weapons.[49]

Launching chemical attacks the day after UN inspectors had arrived in Damascus to investigate earlier incidents gave Bashar perfect deniability. "Fake news!" screamed the regime. "The images and dialogue are all fabricated and maybe also prerecorded... The Syrian forces are conducting an operation in Ghouta... but with full respect to civilians and residential areas... These people are actors paid to do this silly stuff," declared Bashar's minister of information, Omran al-Zoubi, defiantly.[50]

Meanwhile, the regime stepped up its bombing of the areas it just gassed, ignoring calls by world powers to cease hostilities and give access to UN inspectors, who were already in Damascus, to investigate the opposition's accusations.

"We are pressing ahead with our cleansing operation until we get rid of the last gunman," said an army officer on the edge of the Ghouta as plumes of black smoke and explosions engulfed the area.[51]

For five continuous days, the UN chemical weapons inspection team sat at the Four Seasons as the regime rained bombs and missiles on people it had just gassed.[52]

In the same luxury hotel also lived and worked teams representing the UN's various humanitarian agencies. Many had been there since the start of the year, after their agencies signed an agreement with the regime's government, a UN member, to be able to access opposition-held areas from Damascus. Every request made since the start of the year to provide humanitarian aid to the areas that were just gassed had been rejected by the regime.

The hotel's banquet halls were converted into work spaces for the UN teams. Amenities like a gym, a pool, an outdoor café, and an Italian restaurant functioned normally.[53]

"We hear the situation is very dire," said a hotel-based UN official about one of the gassed areas, located a mere eight miles away.[54]

On the sixth day after the attack, the regime stopped its bombardment of the suburbs and allowed UN inspectors in to collect samples to confirm the use of chemical weapons. No medical aid was permitted, even though there were thousands of people who were still suffering from the effects of the attack and local hospitals could not cope.

Ascertaining chemical-weapons use took precedence over saving lives.

"With their gas masks they looked like aliens swooping in to take their samples," said a resident of the Eastern Ghouta who was present when the team arrived in their white SUVs marked "UN."[55]

As inspectors went in to gather samples, Bashar met with a Russian reporter in Damascus, denying he was involved in the attack and saying that he counted on Russia to back him against any attempt by the United States and its allies to use the UN investigation results against him.[56]

Bashar's media office sent out from its Twitter account a barrage of nearly eighty tweets with quotes from the interview.[57]

In what looked like a dress rehearsal for Russia's cyberwarfare campaign to disrupt and influence the 2016 US elections, legions of social media trolls promoted lies and fake news stories in order to negate and bury the truth that was emerging about the attack. In tandem, young hackers with names like "The Pro" and "The Shadow" from the Syrian Electronic Army (SEA),[58] an outfit personally nurtured and supported by Bashar, took the *New York Times* website offline for twenty hours.[59] The SEA's servers were based in Russia. Others believed it was an Iranian proxy.[60]

The group had emerged in May 2011 with tactics like inundating Obama's official Facebook page with pro-Bashar messages, but by 2013 its methods were more sophisticated, suggesting that it was benefiting from more-powerful cyberwarfare expertise and support. Already a few months before the chemical-weapons attack, the SEA had hacked the websites and Twitter accounts of major news organizations like the Associated Press and the *Washington Post*.[61]

On August 30, 2013, the tenth day after the chemical-weapons attack, US secretary of state John Kerry laid out the proof against Bashar[62] and forcefully made the case for action as six US warships mobilized in the eastern Mediterranean near Syria, ready to strike regime targets with a barrage of Tomahawk missiles.[63]

Mindful of the weapons of mass destruction (WMD) debacle associated with the invasion of Iraq in 2003,[64] Kerry said that the intelligence regarding the Syrian chemical-weapons attack had been "reviewed and re-reviewed" multiple times.

Three days before the actual attack, regime chemical weapons personnel had been monitored on the ground as they made their preparations. Syrian regime elements close to the areas attacked were notified ahead of time and instructed to take precautions like putting on gas masks. The launch sites and impact points of the rockets carrying sarin were known with great precision. The rockets were fired from regime-controlled areas and struck opposition-controlled or contested areas.[65] The intercepted communications of one senior regime official in the aftermath confirmed the regime's responsibility for the attack.

"It matters that nearly a hundred years ago, in direct response to the utter horror and inhumanity of World War I," said Kerry, "that the civilized world agreed that chemical weapons should never be used again. It matters because if we choose to live in a world where a thug and murderer like Bashar al-Assad can gas thousands of his own people with impunity, even after the United States and our allies said no, and then the world does nothing about it, there will be no end to…the dangers that will flow from those others who believe that they can do as they will."[66]

France, too, concluded there was no shred of doubt that the Syrian regime had ordered and carried out the chemical-weapons attacks.[67] Paris wanted to go ahead with military strikes against the regime even after British lawmakers voted against their country's participation in such a mission.

The French believed that the Americans shared with them the imperative of responding to this particular regime atrocity, but it was hardly going to be like the US invasion of Iraq.[68] Instead, this was going to be a series of missile strikes on set targets, intended more than anything else to send a message of resolve by Western democracies against the use of such weapons.

"I repeat: We're not considering any open-ended commitment. We're not considering any boots-on-the-ground approach," said Obama on the same day Kerry spoke. "What we will do is consider options that meet the narrow concern around chemical weapons."[69]

The goal was not to topple Bashar but weaken him significantly and boost the fortunes of the opposition camp. The French were on the same page. "The idea was not to destroy Bashar, not at all," said French foreign minister Laurent Fabius. "The idea was to choose targets in a manner that would bring him to the negotiating table."[70]

This was the same fixed idea that had underpinned the Western approach to the situation in Syria from the start—the notion that Bashar and his patron Iran, along with its proxy, Hezbollah, were just going to capitulate and make major concessions on the negotiating table if sufficient pressure was applied on the regime on the ground.

Still another French official said he had high expectations that the strikes could alter the equation this time and cause the regime to crumble from within. As military action was being considered, some senior regime figures sent secret messages to the French side saying they were sickened by Bashar's actions and wanted to defect and collaborate.[71]

On the same day that Obama and Kerry made their public statements, Obama called French president François Hollande and told him he needed another twenty-four hours to be ready.[72] The French assumed that the second call was going to be a discussion about the targets and the joint operation's zero hour.

In the afternoon of Saturday, August 31, 2013, Hollande was in the Élysée Palace's *salon doré*, an imperial bedroom converted into a presidential office. Surrounded by gilded panels and carvings, he sat behind a beautifully sculpted desk in the style of Louis XV covered with files that overflowed onto an adjacent table. This was the last weekend before the *rentrée scolaire*, the official start of the new school year, and he had barely taken a break all year.[73]

One of Hollande's closest advisers, Paul Jean-Ortiz, had just spoken with US national security advisor Susan Rice, to prepare for the conference call with Obama during which the two leaders were supposed to make a final decision on launching military strikes to punish Bashar and his regime for the horrific August 21 attacks near Damascus.

The French were in a state of total mobilization. After speaking to Obama the day before, Hollande was planning to give the order to his military that same Saturday or the following day at the latest.[74] The UN inspectors were expected to be out of Syria by then.

Rafale fighter jets taking off from French bases in Djibouti in the Horn of Africa and Abu Dhabi in the Persian Gulf were supposed to fire five Scalp missiles at preselected targets inside Syria.[75] These were most likely the airbases, radar installations, and communications hubs that enabled the Syrian regime to keep up its indiscriminate bombardment of civilians in opposition areas throughout the country. Hitting these targets would also disable or significantly diminish the regime's ability to respond to the strikes.

The French strikes were scheduled for predawn Damascus time. The green light from the French president would come the night before at 9:00

p.m. Damascus time. He would have one final chance to call it off five hours later, at 2:00 a.m. Strike time was two hours after that, at 4:00 a.m.[76]

The French also had a communications strategy in place, already-drafted statements, mapped-out possible scenarios, and a clear idea of the next steps to be taken. They wanted to act as quickly as possible because they were concerned that, if they waited much longer, their targets would lose their value and Bashar would have more time to prepare his defenses. They certainly wanted to do it before a G20 summit hosted by Putin in Saint Petersburg five days later on September 5.

Hollande was already bracing for Putin's reaction. He knew the Russian leader had called Germany's Angela Merkel to tell her the chemical-weapons attack was somehow arranged by the United States and was "part of an American-led conspiracy to justify action against Bashar."[77]

"It was as if we were back to the foreign policy of the Soviet Union... just like a Cold War scenario," Hollande commented.[78]

There was one scenario, though, that the French had not anticipated.

Obama called Hollande on Saturday, August 31, to inform him he needed more time. He told Hollande that the British parliament vote was a new element that had to be considered. He said that the fact that any action taken would lack a UN Security Council mandate was something that needed to be thought through carefully.[79] Obama also let Hollande know that he wanted to get the US Congress involved in the decision, and this was going to require more time.

"Obama told us there would be a delay, but President Hollande and I interpreted the conversation to mean that military action was off the table," Fabius said.[80] "We could not act on our own — not because we did not have the means but because the operation was already planned as a joint intervention."

The French leader's instincts were right. The day before he spoke to Hollande, it seemed Obama had for the most part made up his mind and wanted to call off the strikes altogether, and thus the delay was just a retreat tactic.

Obama took a long walk on the South Lawn with his chief of staff, Denis McDonough, who was the aide most opposed to military action. Obama told him that this could be a trap by the Assad regime and that

Bashar could put civilians at military installations and use them as human shields.[81] There was also the likelihood that Bashar and his allies could emerge more defiant and ruthless from the aftermath of the strikes.

"Official ambiguity reigned for a few days," said Fabius, describing the period that followed Obama's second phone conversation with Hollande.[82]

On the ground in Damascus, there was fear and apprehension behind the regime's facade of defiance as the prospect of intervention seemed real and credible, at least for a few days.[83] As the threat loomed, entire units of the army and *mukhabarat* moved into schools inside residential neighborhoods like the Satee al-Hosari middle school for girls in Abu Rummaneh. The nearby Damascus Community School, the American school, was already a military installation, and more soldiers and equipment moved in.[84]

Apartments that were vacant because their owners had fled the conflict were opened and occupied by senior army and *mukhabarat* officers. In Kfar Sousseh, home to several *mukhabarat* branches, antiaircraft guns and rocket launchers were positioned outside residential buildings.

Meanwhile the *mukhabarat* organized stunts like escorting loyalists up to Mount Qasioun to erect tents out in the open and announce to journalists that these volunteers planned to sleep there, hoping the message would dissuade the United States and its allies from bombing military installations on the mountain.[85] The mountain chain was planted with missile launchers and heavy artillery guns that the regime used to bomb civilians and rebels alike in the suburbs.

At around the same time, the *mukhabarat* started moving groups of prisoners from its dungeons to military and security installations. A large group of prisoners was moved to the Mezzeh Air Base and a nearby base belonging to the Fourth Division.[86]

Bashar's electronic army, meanwhile, attacked the US Marines' recruitment website.

"Obama is a traitor who wants to put your lives in danger to rescue Al-Qaeda insurgents," read a message posted by SEA and linked to the Marines website. It said it was a message from "your brothers in the Syrian army, who have been fighting Al-Qaeda for the last three years."[87]

Bashar, meanwhile, said rhetorically about French parliamentarians supporting action by their president against him to boost the opposition, or the "terrorists" as he called them: "Will they support those who perpetrated the September 11 attacks in New York, or those who bombed the metro [in 2004] in Spain? How can France fight terrorism in Mali and support it in Syria?"[88]

Bashar vowed mayhem if the United States and France conducted airstrikes against his regime. "Once the barrel explodes, everyone loses control," he said. "What is certain is the spread of chaos, wars, and extremism in all its forms everywhere."[89]

He left the possibility of future chemical-weapons attacks hanging. He said he could not confirm or deny that he possessed such weapons, but if he did, the decision to use them was "centralized"—meaning it was his.[90]

Even Bashar's eldest son, Hafez, who was eleven at the time, appeared to chime in. "12 hours we waited...48 hours they said, we're waiting...I just want them to attack sooo much, because I want them to make this huge mistake of beginning something they don't know the end of it," read a widely shared Facebook post from an account in Hafez's name.[91]

Some in the regime, however, seemed genuinely concerned that the ruling clan might have finally overplayed its hand by using chemical weapons on such a large scale and that dire consequences awaited everyone. Deputy foreign minister Faisal al-Mekdad appealed to Kerry personally and called for dialogue with members of Congress.[92]

As for the people, they stocked up on food and bread and braced themselves for a long confrontation.[93] Regime opponents in Damascus wanted the United States and its allies to strike Bashar. The feeling of many, especially after the horrific chemical-weapons attack, was that they were being held hostage by a psychopath and yearned to be freed.

Of course, loyalists like business owners and members of minority groups, especially Christians, worried that Western airstrikes could provoke the regime's collapse and an onslaught of rebels from the suburbs, whom they saw as barbarians and extremists.[94]

As Obama vacillated while, technically, still waiting for a vote in Congress, and Kerry made passionate pronouncements for days about the need to punish Bashar, the Russians plotted their next moves.

Russia's foreign minister, Sergei Lavrov, announced that he had received what he called a credible fifty-page report by Mother Agnes, the supposedly peace-loving nun who was also one of the Syrian regime's main propagandists and a *mukhabarat* collaborator. The report's central assertion was an outrageous lie: rebels transported Alawite children kidnapped in the Latakia mountains to the Damascus suburbs and used them to stage a chemical-weapons attack.[95] The executioner was now the victim.

On September 5, 2013, the drama shifted to the suburbs of Saint Petersburg, where Putin was hosting a summit for the G20, a forum for the world's top economic powers.

The setting was a monumental eighteenth-century palace commissioned by Peter the Great. Syria was not formally on the agenda but was on everyone's mind. After an elaborate opening ceremony and a dinner for heads of state, Obama proposed that the group issue a statement condemning Bashar for his use of chemical weapons and calling for a unified and strong international response.

Putin argued that there was no proof that Bashar was responsible. Other leaders around the vast, oval-shaped dining table then took turns weighing in on the matter.[96] In the presence of countries like Argentina, Brazil, China, India, and South Africa, that either supported Bashar or shared Russia's worldview, Obama's motion failed to win a majority.

During an exchange between foreign ministers at the same summit, France's Fabius went through all the evidence that he said implicated Bashar personally in the chemical-weapons attack. Russia's Lavrov gestured with his hand to pause the conversation. He looked Fabius and the others directly in the eyes and smiled.

"You have made your arguments and I have made mine," said Lavrov calmly. "We could continue like this for a while, but Laurent, do you see that glass of fruit juice in front of you on the table? You see it orange [it was], but you know what, I see it blue. You can give me all the arguments in the world but I will continue to say it's blue."[97]

So it did not really matter to the Russians whether Bashar used chemical weapons or not. Something much bigger was at play. Putin believed that he was leading the charge to transform the world order. Russia could no longer be ignored. The West could not impose its agenda and worldview on Russia. Putin wanted to erase memories of the humiliation and weakness after the collapse of the Soviet Union. As far as he was concerned, Obama had flinched over enforcing his redline in Syria and now was his chance to showcase the strong, new Russia.

Bashar idolized Putin. For Bashar, Putin was the embodiment of what he always yearned to be: the tough and uncompromising leader who showed no hint of weakness. Someone who outsmarted his enemies and maintained his power and furthered his agenda with cutthroat resolve.

"Russia is defending its legitimate interests in the region," pronounced Bashar after the chemical-weapons attack. He said that the United States thought that "Russia was perpetually destroyed," but now it was back to stop the US from interfering in other countries' affairs.[98] "Russia itself has suffered and continues to suffer from such interference," declared Bashar in what he described as a message to the Russian public.

It was the perfect match, as far as Bashar was concerned. Putin wanted glory and power, while he and his family just wanted to survive.

After the G20 summit, Bashar dispatched his foreign minister, Walid al-Moallem, to Moscow at the urgent request of the Russians. The portly Damascene and veteran diplomat relished the image that regime loyalists projected of him as a fox whose deliberately slow manner of speech and sarcastic tone was enough to win any argument.

On September 9, 2013, just hours after Kerry said that a punitive strike against Bashar could be averted if he surrendered "every single bit" of his arsenal of chemical weapons, and Lavrov countered that Russia would work with the Syrians on such an initiative,[99] a grim-faced Moallem appeared from Moscow to make a televised statement.

"Our commitment to the Russian initiative has the goal of ending our possession of chemical arms," said Moallem.[100]

The way Putin saw it, Obama now owed him because he had helped him find a way out of his redline predicament, and as for Bashar, Putin had saved his neck and thus further opened the way for Russia to play the most dominant role in shaping events in Syria.

At the end of September 2013, a UN Security Council that for more than two and a half years could not agree on condemning Bashar's slaughter of Syrians, passed a unanimous resolution to force him to hand over his chemical weapons and destroy his capabilities to make them.[101]

Bashar and his allies pressed on with a campaign to strangle rebellious communities across the country, ultimately killing people in far greater numbers and in more brutal ways. Civilians were starved into submission and pummeled with barrel bombs and airstrikes on their homes, hospitals, markets, and schools. Chlorine substituted for sarin, at least while Obama was still around.

"We won't allow them to be nourished to kill us," said an Alawite militiaman and Bashar loyalist enforcing a total siege imposed on Moad-hamiya, one of the towns gassed two months earlier.[102] He was given orders to shoot to kill anyone trying to leave or enter.

The militiaman, who said he was a law student, stood at his sniper nest of cement blocks and sandbags on a building rooftop. Empty bullet cas-ings littered the floor. The rebel-controlled town center was a bleak and jagged landscape of destroyed apartment buildings and dense clusters of one-story homes pummeled nonstop by Maher al-Assad's forces stationed on a nearby mountain.

Inside the siege perimeter, residents of a town famed for its olive trees were reduced to eating whatever greens they could forage.

No single event in the history of the Syrian conflict helped Islamist extremists justify their terror and message of hate more than the chemical-weapons attack and the way the international community handled its after-math. It became a potent and resonant recruitment tool. So far, it had been mostly foreign members of Nusra, Al-Qaeda's Syria affiliate, who were ready to take on suicide bombing missions; now Syrians, too, would be con-vinced to join the "martyrdom-seekers."

Bitterness and disillusionment also gripped the most ardent secularists.

"Why does the West insist on dealing with our dead and injured as if they were less valuable than a Westerner—and as if our casualties don't even deserve respect and compassion?" blogged Mazen Darwish's friend and colleague Razan Zeitouneh in mid-October 2013 from the Eastern Ghouta, where she was hiding from the regime and where she had wit-nessed the aftermath of the chemical-weapons attack.[103] "Syrians won't forget that the international community forced the regime to dismantle its chemical weapons, yet couldn't force it to break the siege on a city where children are dying from hunger on a daily basis."

At the start of 2014, the UN-mediated talks in Geneva between representatives of the regime and opposition were supposed to be one of the achievements that flowed from the US-Russian collaboration on destroying Bashar's chemical weapons. Positions, however, remained more entrenched than ever.

Saudi Arabia, which by then exercised the most sway over the Syrian opposition, did everything to keep Bashar's patron Iran out of the talks, even though UN envoy, Lakhdar Brahimi, thought that Iran's presence was essential. The indirect talks were formally just between the two Syrian sides, but representatives of all the major states with stakes in the conflict were in Geneva, too. Publicly, the opposition delegation declared that it was only there to negotiate Bashar's exit, while the regime insisted that the talks should be about combatting terrorism.

In closed-door sessions with Brahimi, the opposition seemed more willing to at least get the process rolling—but not Bashar's delegation. "I am not authorized to agree to any agenda or sign any paper. I am here to discuss terrorism and terrorism only," the regime's UN representative, Bashar al-Jaafari, told Brahimi.[104]

The talks failed and Brahimi resigned, and then the world's attention shifted elsewhere. A wave of popular protests in Ukraine ousted the Russian-backed president. Putin sent forces to the country's Russian-speaking east and annexed Crimea, which he called "reunification." Obama and the European Union imposed sanctions against Russia and Putin's inner circle, and continued to call for a diplomatic solution to the crisis. War followed in Eastern Ukraine. For Putin, the rebels and separatists of Ukraine were "patriots"—as opposed to the "terrorist" rebels in Syria.

France's foreign minister, Fabius, was convinced that Putin's bold actions in Ukraine were the result of careful observation of how Obama responded to Bashar's use of chemical weapons in Syria. The United States can talk tough—tell Bashar he must leave power and draw redlines barring chemical-weapons use—but ultimately it was unprepared to take action to back its threats. Putin concluded that from then on he could get away with a lot, thought Fabius.[105] The world was changing.

23

A Game of Nations

It was the first weekend in October 2014, and fall was invading the Jardin du Luxembourg near Manaf Tlass's Parisian apartment.

Pathways were carpeted with dry brown leaves, and what was left on the trees was colored in spectacular hues of gold and red. Joggers circled the park. Elderly men played *pétanque*, a game of *boules*, on a gravel patch while seemingly content and happy families strolled past statues and busts of queens, saints, and ancient Greek gods.

Manaf sat in a café at one of the park's entrances, smoking a cigar and sipping espresso. Tourists at a nearby table forked bites of delicate pastries and savored hot chocolate in porcelain cups.

"Syrians are being slaughtered on the altar of international agendas," said Manaf as he launched into a sort of monologue.[1] "The regime is a third-tier player," he continued. "Bashar is just a figurehead. He handed everything over to the Iranians, who are now negotiating directly with the Russians and others.

"Syria needs real leaders. Bashar, Maher, and Rami are kids. They are like kids who inherited a toy from dad and destroyed the toy rather than share it with others. As for the opposition, I am not even going to waste my breath on them. A game of nations is now deciding Syria's fate."

Manaf was turning fifty-two in one month. He still wanted to be seen as the rebellious insider. He was unshaven and wore jeans, sneakers, and a windbreaker. It had been more than two years since he left Syria.

Bashar had reached out to Manaf over the summer, right after his reelection charade, with a concrete offer. The emissary was a Syrian businessman who was a common friend of theirs.

"Abu Mustafa, it's time to return to the homeland. The president wants you to come back. He's willing to offer you any position you want," said the businessman who traveled to Paris to meet with Manaf.[2] "He [Bashar] loves you and has nothing against you."

"If I wanted a position, I would have stayed in Syria. Nothing has changed since I left. It's the same killing and destruction—why should I go back? Tell him no thank you," said Manaf.[3]

This thought went through Manaf's head but he did not share it with the businessman: "Yeah, sure, *this is a very loving regime*; he [Bashar] killed his own brother-in-law [Assef Shawkat] and he did not care. I do not think he [Bashar] would care much about me."

The businessman called Manaf later to tell him that Bashar was disappointed by his answer. Manaf concluded that Bashar still saw him as a threat and bringing him back to Syria was one way to control him, if not eliminate him altogether.

By then Manaf's life had settled into a sort of routine. Over the past year he discretely traveled to Jordan and Turkey, where the CIA ran joint-operations centers alongside representatives of its Western and Arab allies to vet, train, and arm Syrian rebels as well as plan and approve offensives against the regime.[4] Manaf was among many who offered advice.

The setup exemplified Obama's arms-length approach in dealing with Syria from the start. The CIA program was supposed to be covert because, officially, the United States was only providing "nonlethal" aid to the rebels, meaning things like vehicles, bulletproof vests, and night-vision goggles.

To many Syrians, including Manaf, the program was more about controlling what the rebels were getting from Qatar, Saudi Arabia, and Turkey than providing them with the means to win battles against Bashar and his allies.

"Iran and Russia were helping Bashar in broad daylight and the American program was secret, meaning they could dump us at any moment," said a defected army officer who knew Manaf well and headed a group that was receiving assistance through the joint-operations centers.[5]

When not flying to Jordan or Turkey, Manaf often met in Paris for lunch or coffee with opposition figures who were more willing to embrace him. Sometimes they invited him to their functions and meetings.

By 2014, new Syrian opposition groupings were emerging that were closer to Russia and more amenable to the idea of compromise with Bashar to end the bloodshed. They favored a gradualist approach to reform and transition that did not entail Bashar's immediate abdication. These groups had names like "the Moscow platform" and "Cairo platform" and included Syrians like a former deputy prime minister, a former foreign ministry spokesman, the ex-wife of the son of a former *mukhabarat* chief, a popular actor, and others who saw the opposition that emerged at the start of the revolution as too rigid in their positions and beholden to Islamists.[6]

At least once a week, Manaf went over to his sister Nahed's apartment to have lunch with his father, Mustafa Tlass, who was still alert but had lost weight and looked frail. Manaf often picked up a baguette, a bottle of red wine, or his father's favorite Greek appetizers, and walked for more than one hour from his apartment in Saint-Germain on the left bank of the Seine to his sister's place on the opposite side of the river, close to the Bois de Boulogne park. Sometimes they played poker.

Occasionally he took his dad out to his favorite restaurant, where the old general and once-legendary sex maniac made sure he kissed every waitress twice on the cheeks before they sat down at their table.[7]

"We packed a small bag, we thought we were coming for a month and that the regime would fall and we would return to Syria," Mustafa's longtime caregiver would often tell people in Paris. He too had to leave Syria when the Tlasses departed in 2012.[8]

Manaf's wife, Thala, pursued advanced studies in art history and was more than ever determined to protect her husband and family from what she called the "bubbling cauldron" of Syria.[9]

But Manaf could not get Syria out of his head or the idea that he was destined to be Syria's savior.

By the fall of 2014, Manaf was banking on a deal between Russia and the United States over Syria that could culminate in him being anointed as the compromise figure to replace Bashar: a son of the regime, an insider, and an army general, but not a killer, and at the same time a reform-friendly figure but not a radical, an Islamist, or an extremist.

Manaf hoped that the dispute over Ukraine and Russia's annexation of Crimea, and the subsequent sanctions imposed on Moscow by the United States and its European allies, did not preclude these powers from collaborating to solve other pressing world crises like the war in Syria and the spread of the Islamic State.[10] Their collective involvement in negotiations with Iran to freeze its nuclear program in return for sanctions relief was proof it was possible, reasoned Manaf.

"Manaf thinks he's going to come at the moment chosen by the superpowers. This idea that the world's intelligence services are saving him for later has really gotten into his head," said a defected Syrian officer who was regularly in touch with him.[11]

Manaf had a foot in each camp. The previous year (2013) he had traveled to Berlin, Brussels, and London where he met with diplomats and intelligence and security officials in these European capitals that were backing the opposition and those fighting to oust Bashar from power.[12]

"We can't repeat the Iraq experience of dismantling the army and state," Manaf told them referring to what followed the US-led invasion of the country in 2003. "We must build bridges between the two warring sides [regime and opposition]."[13]

Manaf later flew to Russia, a country doing everything it could to keep Bashar in power.

"Russia can play a big role to help the Syrian people emerge from their hardship. It can put pressure at least on one side, and if there's a true will we can get there. With the help of Russia and America, we can overcome this situation," Manaf declared from Moscow after meeting Russia's foreign minister Sergei Lavrov.[14]

Manaf then returned to Paris where he met with CIA officers working on Syria. Manaf told them that they must maintain channels of communication with army officers inside Syria, who were still on the regime side but supposedly had patriotic motives like him and were not beholden to the Assad family. He argued that the United States should facilitate contacts between Alawite officers on the regime side and Sunni army defectors with the opposition and that he, Manaf, was best positioned to assist with that.[15]

This idea took on new urgency after the regime's chemical-weapons attacks in suburban Damascus in the summer of 2013. Manaf received funding from a London-based Syrian businessman and support from the British government to organize meetings between Syrian officers who stood on opposite sides of the brutal war.

Manaf assembled a team and rented a villa in the Turkish capital Ankara which became the venue for these secret talks.[16] Some Alawite officers, who were retired but held powerful positions in their clans, managed to get out to Lebanon and then flew to Turkey for these meetings. There were a few emotional encounters.

"There was an Alawite colonel who lost two of his brothers in the war and a Sunni colonel with the FSA [Free Syrian Army] who also had a dead brother. They hugged and said they were willing to overcome their personal grudges for the sake of Syria," recalled Manaf.

It was possible that Bashar was aware of these meetings and considered them a useful indirect channel to the opposition and their Western backers as well as his old friend Manaf, even though Manaf denied this.

Manaf later received support from the United States, via the CIA, to continue these meetings but then the whole effort stalled.[17]

"The Americans met directly with a group of Alawite officers but the problem was that there was a different dynamic on the ground. My project was fragile and it clashed with bigger and more violent projects," said Manaf.

Underscoring how messy and complex the situation had become by the fall of 2014, the United States was on the same side as Iran and its Shiite allies and proxies in Iraq in combatting the Islamic State after it captured Mosul. In Syria, Washington was collaborating with Kurdish militiamen who had ties to Bashar and Iran.

In their battle against the Islamic State, the Americans were starting to partner with the Syrian affiliate of a Kurdish separatist guerrilla movement, the Kurdistan Workers' Party (Partiya Karkarane Kurdistan or PKK), which had been fighting the Turkish state for decades and was designated a terrorist organization by Washington.[18]

The Syrian regime had long-standing ties with the PKK from the days of Hafez, who also hosted their leader, but when the regime wanted to curry favor with Turkey and the West it turned against the PKK. At the start of the uprising in 2011, though, Bashar released PKK-linked figures from prison, and later he and Iran worked out an arrangement with the PKK that allowed its Syrian affiliate, known as the YPG (Yekineyen Parastina Gel), to administer northeast Syria in return for letting the regime maintain a security and military foothold there and receive the area's oil.[19]

One of the first things the YPG did was to crack down on its rivals and all those who took part in peaceful protests against Bashar.[20] The Kurdish militiamen had big ambitions, and they wanted to survive too.

To shield themselves from their enemies, which included Turkey, Syrian rebels, and the Islamic State, and to gain more autonomy from Bashar, the Kurdish militiamen formed an alliance with the Americans to fight the Islamic State.[21] American volunteers joined the Kurds after the Islamic State beheaded American journalists and aid workers.

As Obama's top priority became fighting the Islamic State in both Iraq and Syria, he and members of his administration, especially Secretary of State Kerry, continued to repeat like a mantra that there was no military solution in Syria, only a political one.[22] They said that America's support for the moderate rebel groups fighting Bashar was only intended to bring him to the negotiating table. The world watched these same moderates get crushed bit by bit by Bashar and the Islamic State, and hobbled by warlords in their midst and the competition between their regional backers Qatar and Saudi Arabia, two US allies.

By the fall of 2014 and following months of bloody battles against Syrian rebels opposing it, the Islamic State was largely in control of the eastern half of Syria along the border with Iraq. In addition to Iraqis and Syrians, there were more than 12,000 foreign fighters in the ranks of the Islamic State, most of them from Europe and North Africa.[23]

The Islamic State's rival, the Al-Qaeda-linked Nusra Front, meanwhile was relegated to the western half of Syria, where in many places it shared territory with an array of Syrian rebel groups. Many of Nusra's members were Syrian, but there were foreigners, too.

While Nusra was labeled a terrorist organization by the United States, and those groups receiving support from Washington were banned from dealing with it, the struggle between Qatar and Saudi Arabia over control of the Syrian opposition played to Nusra's advantage.[24] Tensions between the two neighbors had reached a boiling point in 2013, and in an attempt to defuse them Qatar's emir agreed to abdicate the throne to his son.[25]

Saudi grievances were many and they included: Qatar's outsize role in the region in the wake of the Arab Spring, its backing of the Muslim Brotherhood and Islamists who had briefly taken power in Egypt, and its quest to compete with and upstage Saudi Arabia in places like Syria. The United States was also furious with Qatar over the delivery of a small batch of antiaircraft weapons to Syrian rebels despite a US interdiction on doing so.[26]

While Saudi Arabia sought to control both the political and armed wings of the Syrian opposition, Qatar, along with its ally Turkey, were not going to give up so easily. The duo upped their support to Islamist rebel groups allied to the Nusra Front.[27]

Later, Nusra and its Islamist allies led a raid on an arms depot near the Turkish border belonging to the main rebel body supported by the United States and its Western allies. They looted tons of weapons, ammunition, military gear, and vehicles. The incident had a chilling effect on US efforts to support rebels fighting Bashar.[28]

By the fall of 2014, the United States and its coalition partners were bombing Islamic State positions in largely desert eastern Syria while Bashar and his allies were left to concentrate all of their firepower on rebel-held towns and neighborhoods in the country's western half—home to the major cities, including Damascus, that mattered the most to Bashar.

Bashar and his patrons Iran and Russia claimed that they, too, were fighting terrorists, given the Nusra Front's presence in these areas. Russia supplied the weapons and Iran most of the manpower, including tens of thousands of ideologically driven Shiite militiamen from Afghanistan, Iraq, Lebanon, Pakistan, Yemen, and elsewhere.[29]

Under the pretext of fighting terror, Bashar's helicopters rained bombs on civilians in opposition areas. Some of the bombs were filled with chlorine, even though he had signed the convention prohibiting the use of the substance as a weapon at the same time that he agreed to give up his chemical arms in the Russian-brokered deal in the fall of 2013.[30] Chlorine gas inhalation burns the lungs and causes death, depending on levels of exposure.

Rebel commanders begged their American backers to provide them with a limited batch of antiaircraft weapons, just to act as a sort deterrence against the airborne attacks that were killing the most people.

"Send minders with us to Syria, we will fire the missiles and then give you back the launchers, make them operable only through fingerprint detection, find a solution, help us!" pleaded one commander.[31]

Even the French, who had been the most eager to help the Syrian rebels from the start and who had discreetly provided them with some weapons starting in late 2012 before the lifting of the EU arms embargo, had no choice but to accept the restrictions.

One French official offered his government's brutal reasoning: "By not giving them the antiaircraft missiles we could be blamed for not doing the right thing, but we were not proactively involved; on the other hand, if we gave it to them and it got in the wrong hands and a civilian aircraft came down, then we were going to be held responsible."[32]

Bashar relished the fact that his jets and helicopters were unhindered as they slaughtered civilians in Syria's western half at precisely the same time that US jets were flying over eastern Syria, also unhindered, to bomb the Islamic State. Officials in his regime offered coordination with the Americans, through the Russians.[33]

On the ground, Bashar could count on direct and extensive collaboration with United Nations humanitarian agencies to enable him to use access to food and medicine as another weapon to punish those who defied him and reward those who submitted to his rule.

Valerie Amos, the UN's top relief official, had declared the situation in Syria by early 2013 an "L3" (level three)[34]—a humanitarian disaster that required the highest level and fastest mobilization, on par with the aftermath of an earthquake or a tsunami.

Instead of working out on-the-spot humanitarian pauses and ceasefires with all the combatants in order to allow relief to flow immediately to the worst-impacted battle zones, as required by such an extreme emergency proto-col, UN aid officials sat for several months negotiating a framework agreement with Bashar's representatives to govern every facet of their presence and activi-ties in the country.[35] They had to go through this process every six months.

"We were negotiating with them sometimes over single words in the document," said one UN aid official who served several stints in Damas-cus but later spoke of the disgust and shame she and many others in the organization felt over the Syria mission.[36]

Regime-controlled areas across the country became home to several million Syrians displaced from opposition-held zones, besieged and bombed day and night by Bashar. These people were hardly regime supporters, but many had few other options. UN agencies could only provide aid to these people through regime entities and officially approved local NGOs that were often connected to Assad family members and regime cronies.[37]

To access opposition-held areas, UN agencies had to send a letter or fax to the Ministry of Foreign Affairs explaining the reason for the request, detailing the contents of every aid truck and box and providing names and ID copies of every single person who was going to be on the aid convoy. The ministry would then turn around and forward all the infor-mation to the mukhabarat, which was responsible for the most horrific atroc-ities against regime opponents from the moment protests began in 2011. The mukhabarat had the final say.[38]

Approval hardly ever came, and on the rare occasion it did, the regime nitpicked with UN agencies over what items were going to be permitted—for instance, no to surgical kits to treat war-inflicted injuries but yes to toilet paper and personal hygiene kits. Even if approval was granted, the regime often derailed the convoys by claiming that there were military operations underway and that it was unsafe to proceed.

"There were requests that remained pending for more than two years," said the UN official. "This was deliberate punishment. The [Syrian] gov-ernment's attitude was that if these people were living in rebel-held areas then to hell with them. Those wounded in war had a right to treatment. The most basic rules of war were broken."[39]

Even after the aid was dispatched toward opposition-held areas, which the UN termed "cross-line" operations, there was no guarantee that regime militias and forces besieging certain communities would not block entry or remove items from the convoy.[40] In early 2014, regime soldiers used their combat knives to slash open UN food ration parcels and remove pita bread packets intended for a community south of Damascus where almost thirty people already perished from hunger and some were reduced to eating cats to survive.[41]

After the 2013 Ghouta chemical-weapons attack, UN food rations, largely paid for by the countries opposing the regime, became one of the main gives by Bashar in the capitulation offers he made to opposition communities under the pretext of "national reconciliation." The terms were simple: You surrender, you eat. All males in these areas were also expected to "regularize their status" with the *mukhabarat*, which often meant being drafted into the army or sent to prison.[42]

In the winter of 2014 and in tandem with the first UN-mediated encounter between the regime and opposition in Geneva, the various world powers involved in the conflict agreed on a deal to allow food and medical aid into the old quarter of Homs, where nearly 6,000 people, half of them civilians, had been under siege by the regime for more than 600 days.[43]

The regime bombed from the sky and forces led by Hezbollah militiamen and elements of Iran's Islamic Revolutionary Guard Corps closed in on the ground.

By then many of the Homs city rebels were part of an Islamist coalition allied tactically on the ground with Al-Qaeda's affiliate, the Nusra Front, and backed by Qatar and Turkey. Nusra often carried out car bombings in the Alawite-dominated and regime-controlled sections of Homs in an attempt to relieve pressure on those besieged in the old quarter. The casualties were always civilian.[44]

The regime first claimed that there were no civilians, only combatants, left in central Homs but then wanted the United Nations to evacuate only certain categories of civilians and rejected the supply of food and medicine. Many rebels wanted to make a last stand and felt that nobody had the right to drive them and the civilians out of their homes and city, even though all odds were stacked up against them.[45]

Finally, a tit-for-tat compromise (evacuation for food) was hammered out by Yacoub El Hillo, head of the UN humanitarian mission in Syria. The fifty-year-old Sudanese was a veteran of UN relief operations in Africa and the Middle East.[46]

On the first day, almost a hundred civilians came out in buses escorted by UN vehicles. Women with malnourished infants and old men, many with missing teeth, thick beards, and torn and soiled winter clothes, stepped out of the buses. They looked as if they had been living in caves for years.[47] Some were so weak that they had to be carried on stretchers or put in wheelchairs.

The following day, regime militiamen in coordination with Homs-based *mukhabarat* chiefs[48] fired mortar shells on a UN aid convoy after it crossed to the rebel side; eleven people were killed, mostly hungry and sick civilians that had gathered around the trucks.

When the operation resumed, more people, including men, wanted to leave old Homs. The regime said that they were all presumed to be combatants or that they were wanted by the *mukhabarat* until proven otherwise. The UN communicated this to those desperate to leave and they agreed to this condition,[49] perhaps thinking that the involvement of representatives of the world body could offer them a measure of protection from the regime.

The first stop for the evacuees was a former banquet hall on the front-line. Hordes of regime militiamen and *mukhabarat* agents gathered all around. Graffiti was sprayed on the outer wall: "Assad or nobody; Assad or we burn the country."[50]

As people got off the UN-escorted buses, regime forces began to curse and threaten to kill the men, while aid workers tried to shield them. They punched, slapped, and hit with the butts of their rifles a few of the civilians before one UN official protested loudly.[51]

At one point, the *mukhabarat* abducted about a dozen male evacuees from inside the banquet hall and herded them back into one of their own small buses before another UN official realized what had happened and rescued them.[52]

Hundreds of men and their families were then taken to a school where they were supposed to be vetted by the regime.[53] For several nights, UN aid workers came to the school to prevent abduction by the *mukhabarat* and the militias.

A few were released from the school in return for signing a pledge to be loyal to the state and never again bear arms.[54] It did not matter if they were never armed in the first place. They also had to pledge to vote for Bashar and attend mass-support rallies for him when asked to do so.[55]

The freed men were then made to take part in a release ceremony at a local high school theater presided over by the Bashar-appointed Homs governor and the UN's El Hillo, who sat onstage.[56] In the first row sat *mukhabarat* chiefs like Abdul-Kareem Salloum, an army general from Bashar's hometown, who headed a Homs *mukhabarat* branch where hundreds of opposition activists, including women, had been tortured and sexually assaulted and in some instances executed since 2011.[57]

El Hillo lauded the teamwork between the UN aid agencies and the governor and other regime officials, and congratulated the freed men on being given the chance by Bashar's government to return to their normal lives.[58] The governor lectured them about the "conspiracy" that their country had allegedly been battling since 2011 and before.

Shortly thereafter, many of those escorted out of the besieged old quarter by the UN and handed over to the regime started disappearing, even those who had signed the pledges. Their families said that they were either taken to *mukhabarat* branches or drafted into the army. Others simply vanished.[59]

"The UN is not the protector of Syrians in Syria—they are under the protection of the state," said El Hillo, who worked from a suite at the Four Seasons luxury hotel in Damascus. Behind him was a framed photograph of himself handing his credentials to the regime's foreign minister beneath a portrait of Bashar.[60]

El Hillo described his work in Homs as a "successful experiment" that should be replicated elsewhere. "If I were to recommend it, I would, but obviously this is a Syrian–Syrian matter," he said.[61]

In May 2014, El Hillo was invited once more by the regime to Homs, this time to monitor the complete and final evacuation of those who had remained in old Homs, mostly combatants and a few civilians.[62]

A deal brokered between regime patron Iran and rebel backers Qatar and Turkey called for their transfer to other rebel-held areas farther north in return for freeing an Iranian woman and seventy Alawite and Shiite Syrian civilians held by rebels.[63]

401

It was a hugely symbolic and strategic victory for Bashar, even though he was getting back an empty and destroyed city. What mattered was that Homs, a city his opponents once called "the revolution's capital," was again under his control.

The scale of destruction was epic, with entire streets and buildings reduced to mountains of rubble. "Assad or nobody; Assad or we burn the country" was sprayed in big bold letters on a wall along a street where Bashar's militiamen and soldiers had looted every single apartment and then set many of them on fire.[64]

Going forward, Homs 2014 became more or less the model that Bashar and his allies applied in a string of other rebellious areas, including east Aleppo and those around Damascus, like Daraya, Madaya, and Zabadani.

The formula was straightforward: starve and bomb whoever was left there under the watchful eyes of the world and the UN humanitarian agencies sitting in Damascus until both fighters and civilians either sur- rendered or agreed to leave their homes and move out to Idlib province in the north, which was increasingly under the control of Nusra and other Islamists.

Meanwhile, in areas under regime control, relief provided by UN aid agencies flowed smoothly and abundantly. There it was in Bashar's interest to demonstrate to destitute families fleeing rebel-held areas that they would get food and other forms of aid from the UN if they again submit- ted to his authority.

The aid also helped cushion the impact of price inflation and shrink- ing purchasing power on the constituencies whose loyalty Bashar needed in order to continue the war: Alawites and minorities, as well as soldiers and militiamen and their families. The UN agencies hardly ever distrib- uted the aid themselves. It went to government entities and NGOs desig- nated by the regime.

At least until the end of 2015, one UN aid worker said that the regime almost never provided detailed recipient lists, meaning that the United Nations did not know who was the final beneficiary of the aid.[65]

On top of that, Assad family members and cronies signed deals with

UN agencies. At least two UN agencies partnered with Asma al-Assad's Syria Trust in contracts worth millions of dollars.

UNICEF, which was supposed to defend the rights of children in the world, paid Rami Makhlouf's charity, Jamiyet Al-Bustan Al-Khayriyeh (The Orchard Charity Foundation), almost $270,000 on one occasion.[66] This charity had a militia operating under the same name and committing horrendous war crimes to defend Bashar.[67] As early as the fall of 2012, Rami and other regime cronies had been awarded multimillion-dollar contracts by various UN agencies to supply them with goods and commodities they needed for their aid packages.[68]

In addition, the wife of the regime's deputy foreign minister Faisal al-Mekdad worked for a full year in the office of the UN's El Hillo, its most senior representative in the country. She handled a dossier related to human rights violations in Syria.[69]

Billions of dollars were earmarked for the United Nations' Syria aid effort over the years, yet at almost every opportunity senior UN officials, including the secretary general, pleaded that they needed more money—because otherwise people were going to starve.[70]

24

Abu Ali Putin

There were hardly any young men left in the town of Masyaf and the surrounding villages hugging the mountains that descend toward the Mediterranean coast, the heartland of Bashar's Alawite sect.

Most of the women wore black to mourn a husband, son, or other male relative killed fighting for Bashar. Before the war, a bread van that went around the villages in the morning used to play sweet and dreamy songs by the Lebanese diva Fairuz; now it announced the names of the dead men, or the martyrs as they were called, and blared sorrowful verses of the Quran while it made its deliveries.[1]

Beyond the regime's propaganda and the Alawites' facade of defiance and absolute loyalty, there was grief and anguish in almost every home and a feeling among many families that their loved ones were expendable fodder in the Assads' war of survival.[2]

In the summer of 2014, many Alawites were enraged when senior officers and commanders flew out of an airbase near Raqqa, leaving behind hundreds of soldiers to face approaching Islamic State militants.[3] They were captured, paraded in their underwear, and then executed. The lucky ones escaped in the desert and some made it home eventually, while others were lost forever.[4]

The scenario of officers flying out and leaving soldiers behind repeated itself when the Islamic State captured the ancient city of Palmyra in the spring of 2015.

It was as if the regime wanted the Islamic State to expand in order to scare the world, and so having a few thousand conscripts and militiamen killed in the process hardly mattered.

"Young men from poor families are dying for nothing!" said the son of a retired Alawite army officer about the legions of men from his sect who joined regime militias for money or because of scaremongering.[5]

The pitch from the regime businessmen turned militia leaders and warlords, like the Jaber brothers, was simple: We need to fight them in Aleppo, Damascus, and Homs — otherwise these savages will be at the doorsteps of our homes on the coast.[6] These were the same *takfiris* (Sunni fanatics) that massacred Alawites in the 13th century and hunted us down in the 1970s and '80s, continued the pitch.

It was not only the Islamic State menace coming from the desert in the east; by the spring of 2015 an Islamist coalition that included the Nusra Front was making significant advances in the provinces of Hama and Idlib in northwestern Syria on the edges of the Alawite homeland.

These battle-hardened fighters had more-sophisticated weapons and skills, and they were destroying the regime's tanks and armored vehicles, and shooting down the occasional regime jet taking off from the Hama airbase.[7] They were also vowing to march on Qurdaha, the Assads' hometown.

So even if many average Alawites were fed up and angry with the Assads at that point, they had few other options than to keep fighting and sacrificing for the regime. Their fate was intertwined with that of Bashar, for better or worse.[8]

Murals and monuments for the "martyrs" were erected in nearly every town and village square. Rows of photographs of dead soldiers and militiamen in defiant postures and often brandishing their weapons were assembled like pagan offerings around large posters of Bashar and Hafez.

The Assads wove themselves into their sect's occult religious beliefs. Inside the white-domed shrine of an Alawite miracle maker, tucked in an apple orchard in the mountains above the coastal city of Jableh, were large framed portraits of Bashar and Hafez next to the holy man's tomb.[9] Another frame had a collage of dozens of passport-size photos, all of them men killed fighting for the regime since 2011.

Still, there was a limit in the reservoir of Alawite men to fight for Bashar. Many families lost several sons and were sending the remaining ones abroad, especially to neighboring Lebanon. The parents' thinking was that if they themselves died in Syria then at least one son would survive to preserve the family line.

Other minorities, like the Christians and Druze, went to greater extremes to protect their children from being drafted by Bashar. Even though many saw Bashar as the lesser of two evils, they still felt that what was going on was largely a fight between Bashar's Alawite sect and the Sunni majority.

By the spring of 2015, more than 30,000 Druze men in southern Syria were wanted for military service. These men were either smuggled through the mountains to neighboring Lebanon, also home to a sizable Druze community, or hid in their homes under the protection of armed town elders ready to block any attempts by the regime to round up conscripts.[10]

Since the regime was in a state of war and needed all the men it could muster, the duration of the compulsory military service, which previously had been eighteen months, became indefinite in almost all cases. Bashar also called up reservists; all men up to the age of forty-two now could be drafted even if they had completed their military service. Those not complying were caught on the streets and at checkpoints.[11]

Syrians were not the only ones trying to escape the Assad family's burner. In the southern Lebanon town of Bint Jbeil, controlled by the Hezbollah militia and christened its "resistance capital," one father compelled his teenage son to move to Dearborn in the US state of Michigan, home to a sizable Lebanese Shiite community with dual citizenship, after the boy—who was not even eighteen—wanted to go to Syria to fight on the side of the Assad regime.[12] The son wished to prevent the desecration of Zeinab's shrine, the justification put forward by the pro-Bashar camp.

Like Bashar's militia leaders, Hezbollah recruiters touted the idea that Shiite men had to take the fight to the *takfiris* (all Syrian rebels were labeled Sunni fanatics) and not wait for them to come to their villages and homes in Lebanon.

Farther north from Bint Jbeil in a village above the coastal city of Tyre, Bassam Saleh mourned his twenty-seven-year-old son Raed, a Hezbollah fighter presumed dead in the Aleppo countryside in February 2015 though his body was never found.

"My son and many other resistance fighters had noble intentions, but they were exploited for a specific agenda," he said. "Today Hezbollah is defending Iran's agenda, it's very clear—it serves Iran and benefits from Iran."[13] By then Hezbollah was sending teenagers in its youth movement, the Mahdi Scouts, to fight for Bashar. One of them who had worked in Raed's car repair shop was also killed in 2015 in the Damascus suburbs.[14]

As for Iraqi Shiites, the majority among the militiamen sent by Iran to Syria, by 2015 many were opting to stay on their home turf to fight an increasingly barbaric and vicious Islamic State or flee the region altogether.

In March 2015, Bashar invited half a dozen Russian print and television reporters to the palace for an interview.

"Russian presence in different parts of the world including the Eastern Mediterranean and Syrian port of Tartous," pontificated Bashar, "is extremely important to create a balance that the world lost after the breakup of the Soviet Union more than twenty years ago. We most certainly welcome any expansion of the Russian presence in the Eastern Mediterranean, specifically on Syrian shores."[15]

Two months before Bashar spoke, one of the most senior advisers to Iran's supreme leader, Ali Khamenei, had held extensive talks with Putin and Russian officials.[16]

Later, in the summer, Putin conducted more talks with Khamenei's adviser as well as Qasem Soleimani, the head of the elite Quds Force of the Islamic Revolutionary Guard Corps, who was leading Iran's campaign in Syria.[17]

In tandem, Bashar announced in a speech at the palace in Damascus that he did not have enough men to defend and hold all areas in Syria and as such had to prioritize which ones were more strategic and vital than others.[18]

Two months later, on September 30, 2015, Putin gathered members of his government at his countryside house outside Moscow to announce that he had received an official request from Bashar to intervene militarily in Syria to fight terrorism.[19]

Russia's strikes over the following week, which included a spectacular display of cruise missiles fired from warships in the Caspian Sea, did not target the Nusra Front nor the Islamic State but instead the rebel groups that were being backed by the United States and its allies.[20]

Around the same time, Russia began establishing a permanent airbase next to the Bassel al-Assad International Airport in the Assads' home province of Latakia,[21] and Russian jets tag-teamed with Bashar's Russian-supplied jets to bomb hospitals, schools, and all the infrastructure that sustained civilians in opposition-held areas across Syria.

"It was absolutely terrifying. Sometimes you had five or six jets bombing us at the same time," said Ali Othman, an army defector, who was fighting with a US-backed rebel faction and living with his family in the mountains north of Latakia city along the Turkish border.[22] His baby girl, Nahla, had been born in a Médecins Sans Frontières–supported maternity hospital the day before it was bombed by the Russians.[23] The family fled to Turkey. Putin's direct entry into the war also coincided with a spike in the use of banned weapons like cluster bombs.[24]

Syria became a field for Putin to showcase and test Russia's arms systems and latest-model fighter jets while boosting his standing and prestige, and challenging America in the Middle East.

"You know, in Syria we give the name Abu Ali to the tough and brave man," Bashar's minister of information told Russia Today.[25] Vladimir Putin was now "Abu Ali Putin" for diehard Bashar loyalists. He was elevated to the pantheon of their greats: Bashar, Bassel, Hafez, and Maher al-Assad; Hassan Nasrallah and Ali Khamenei.

It was not only Bashar and his supporters who were enamored of Putin; the monarchs and autocrats of the Middle East, including traditional US allies and some of those who until recently had been calling for Bashar's ouster, trekked to Moscow one by one in the summer and fall of 2015 to meet the new sheriff in town. From the start they had never liked the idea of the Arab masses rising up to demand freedom, and Putin was someone who truly understood them.

"I want to express our tremendous gratitude to the Russian leadership and people for the help they are providing Syria," gushed Bashar as he met with Putin at the Kremlin in October 2015 during his only known trip outside Syria since the December 2010 Paris trip, a few months before the start of protests.[26]

Bashar grinned nervously.[27] His tics, which were usually under control when he delivered his scripted speeches and gave his Western media interviews in Damascus, were slightly noticeable once more. He could barely contain himself as he walked a little behind a swaggering Putin into one of the Kremlin's chambers for a working dinner with the Russian leader and his ministers.[28]

As Russia decimated opposition enclaves in Syria, Obama and his secretary of state, Kerry, issued protests and condemnations, but otherwise America did little to stop the Russians, Bashar, and the Iranians.

"September 2015 was a huge turning point—we knew we were sold out to the Russians by the Americans," said a defected Syrian army officer working with the US at the time.[29] "It was one of two things: either the Americans gave the Russians the green light to strike whomever they wanted, or the Americans were too afraid to get into any confrontation with the Russians."

Putin went out of his way to suggest that he and Obama were in synch on Syria despite outward differences. He launched his bombing campaign as he met with Obama at the United Nations in New York,[30] his generals coordinated with their American counterparts to make sure that Russian jets did not bump into American ones over Syrian skies, and his foreign minister Lavrov huddled with Kerry to work on convening talks between Bashar's regime and the opposition in Geneva;[31] Russians spoke of the Kerry–Lavrov "bromance."[32]

As Syrians were slaughtered in ever greater numbers after the Russian intervention or began to flee the country in droves, Kerry spoke of a negotiated political settlement with the regime.

Around that time, Obama notched what would be touted as one of his presidency's main achievements: a nuclear deal with Bashar's patron Iran.[33]

By then Obama had, for all intents and purposes, washed his hands of the moderate Syrian rebels whom he called "farmers, dentists, and folks" who did not stand a chance against the ruthlessness of Bashar and the barbarity of the Islamist extremists.[34]

Obama, however, still wanted these same Syrians to stop fighting Bashar and turn their guns on the Islamic State instead. To that end, Obama authorized the Pentagon to fly rebels to the US airbase in Qatar for weeks of training and vetting which included an inspection of their beard length and a quiz on the nature of their Islamic faith.[35] "Those that join our program are forbidden from fighting the regime," a US general told one Syrian rebel commander who was being interviewed to join the Pentagon-led effort.[36]

Obama seemed to have made a simple cost–benefit analysis: Syria was of little strategic import to the US compared with oil-rich Iraq, and there was more to gain by collaborating with Iran and Russia on fighting the Islamic State and reaching an accord on Iran's nuclear program than by confronting them in Syria over their protégé, Bashar.

Moreover, fear that the mayhem of Iraq and Syria was spilling over to the West trumped all other concerns, especially after twenty-two people were killed in Paris in January 2015 in an attack on an editorial meeting at the satirical weekly *Charlie Hebdo* and a hostage-taking rampage at a kosher food market.

The French-born assailants said that they did it for Al-Qaeda in the Arabian Peninsula and for the Islamic State. One of them had previously been jailed after he was arrested trying to catch a flight to Damascus in 2005.[37] He wanted to join the foreign jihadists whom Bashar's *mukhabarat* were assisting at the time to cross over to Iraq to fight the "infidel" Americans and their allies.

In Paris, Manaf Tlass saw the Russian intervention, nine months after the *Charlie Hebdo* attack, as the best chance to save Syria, which he likened to a maiden being raped by world powers. More important, he saw it as his ticket to return to Syria as the savior, given the sense of betrayal he felt toward the West; the way he saw it, they pushed him to break with Bashar and then hardly gave him a chance to lead.

"Russia is a great power. It has history in Syria. It helped build the Syrian army before it was taken over by the Assad family. I hope you can help us bring back this army," Manaf told Russia's deputy foreign minister Mikhail Bogdanov during a meeting at the Russian embassy in Paris days after Putin entered the war in Syria in the fall of 2015.[38]

"Our priorities are the military institution, the Syrian state, and keeping Syria unified," the bespectacled and Arabic-speaking Bogdanov assured Manaf.[39] "We want to bring back honorable patriots like you to the army. We are not attached to Bashar al-Assad."

Manaf told Bogdanov that he was secretly in touch with army officers still inside Syria, including members of Bashar's Alawite sect, and that they were all enthusiastic about Russia's involvement. They believed that Russia would push back Iran and its proxy, Hezbollah, who had practically swallowed the Syrian state as the price for saving Bashar, explained Manaf.

At that moment, the idea began germinating in Manaf's head that the Americans and Russians would get together to reconstitute the army by combining those supposedly still-honorable and patriotic officers and soldiers on Bashar's side (those without blood on their hands) with the moderate rebels and defectors.

This new army would fight the Islamic State and then turn its attention to extremists on all sides, both anti- and pro-Bashar. Iran and its militias would be told to leave Syria. As part of a political settlement, a new military council—headed by Manaf—would rule Syria on an interim basis and create the right conditions in which to draft a new constitution and hold elections.

If Russia and the United States hammer out a deal, then Bashar has no choice but to accept his eventual exit, Manaf told those he saw after his meeting at the Russian embassy.

Manaf dismissed as a sideshow the talks between the regime and the opposition that Kerry and Lavrov were so keen on convening in Geneva as soon as possible. The real plan was the military council, he confided to the interlocutors with whom he often met at the Au Vieux Colombier café, across from his apartment near Saint-Sulpice church.[40]

As Manaf plotted his return to Syria, hundreds of thousands of Syrians were plotting their exit at any cost after Putin's dramatic moves.

Even Sally Masalmeh, the girl from the southern city of Daraa who was eighteen when she defied family and tradition to seize a role in the revolution against the Assad regime, was by the fall of 2015 ready to give up, at least for now. What's to be done if the two superpowers, America and Russia, want Bashar to stay, Sally and others like her wondered.

After she and her parents and most of her siblings had fled to neighboring Jordan in 2013, Sally returned at the start of 2014 to what was known by then as the liberated zone of Daraa province, which included half of Daraa city, most of the countryside to the east and west, and part of the border area. The idea was that civilians like Sally could contribute to running the day-to-day affairs of this zone while the fighters, including two of her brothers, would free the rest of the province from the regime.

"You're out of your mind. What do you think—you're going to liberate Syria?" demanded her family and friends in Jordan when she told them she was returning to Daraa.[41]

She was the only woman in a bus of some thirty male fighters that dropped them at the Jordan–Syria border. By then the Jordanians were only allowing fighters back and forth as they continued to host a command center dominated by American, Emirati, and Saudi operatives that supported the Syrian rebels affiliated to what became known as the Southern Front. Sally managed to secure an exception through a rebel commander.

At the border they climbed up an earth berm, navigated their way through a trench, and climbed back up another mound to get to the Syrian side. In normal times, the journey from the border to Daraa city took fifteen minutes. Now it was a one-hour drive through fields and back roads, with the car's headlights turned off to avoid detection by the regime's planes.

Sally barely recognized her city, which was plunged in near-total darkness; many homes had been demolished or reduced to bare-bone structures by the regime's relentless bombing. Even the beloved Omari mosque, which had become a rallying point for protesters in 2011, was gone, its minaret destroyed and much of the remaining edifice heavily damaged.[42] Daraa was now a divided city, with the regime controlling the northern half and rebels the rest.

Sally's neighborhood and family home with its rosebushes and lemon trees were part of the front line now and off-limits.

Sally stayed with her brother Shaker and his wife at an absent relative's house in the liberated section. Her youngest brother, Fadi, was a fighter in one of the city's main rebel groups headed by a defected army officer. Fadi was barely twenty but seemed much older than his age, Sally thought. She tried to convince him to quit fighting and contribute in other ways to the cause, which they still called the revolution. They argued and shouted at each other, but he was not going to change his mind.

Fadi had watched his best friend die from a sniper bullet at the end of 2012. In the liberated zone, makeshift screens were erected across most of the streets fronting the regime-controlled part in order to block the view of snipers there. It was a precarious existence.

Every few days, the regime's Russian-made jets raided the rebel zone. Mechanisms were developed to warn people to take cover, although these proved futile as barrel bombs were dropped from helicopters directly onto residential buildings. There was no particular reason for using them except to kill civilians and remind people of the high cost of living outside Bashar's control. The macabre scene repeated itself almost daily: bodies pulled from underneath the wreckage and the lucky survivors emerging dazed, bloodied, and completely covered in dust.[43]

Still, the liberated zone had its own local government council, a military council that brought together all rebel factions, and civil defense and relief and medical aid committees among other structures. During the time that Sally had spent in Jordan in 2013, she went to Turkey for training seminars on institution building and management sponsored by international donors. She now wanted to teach others in Daraa how to prepare budgets and financial reports, increasing accountability and transparency and streamlining operations to boost efficiency.

She barely slept three to four hours a night, so busy was she working on documentation of the regime's brutality, speaking to the media, organizing activities for children traumatized by war, and helping distribute aid across the liberated zone.

Sally felt empowered to affect change, to make a difference, to challenge and take initiative—values not only discouraged throughout more than four decades of Assad family rule but also punishable by prison or worse.

What the police state nurtured in people was fear, paranoia, mistrust, and the acceptance of corruption and bribery as an inescapable fact of life. The idea was that the system was rotten and the only way to get ahead was to cheat and lie. It was hard to break free from this legacy in one, two, or even ten years. Maybe it was going to take an entire generation.

For sure there were many, especially young people like Sally, who truly believed they were in the midst of a revolution against the old system and all its ills, and who were passionate, sincere, and honest about everything they did. Yet it was also hard for people not to revert to what they had been taught all their lives.

The reality that Sally began to confront in 2014 was bleak. Many rebel commanders were now greedy warlords competing for local control as well as the weapons and funds they received from their foreign backers, whose whims only escalated with each passing day. A Southern Front commander was told by the United Arab Emirates that it would not support him unless he moved his wife and children to the UAE from Qatar, his previous benefactor.[44]

413

Rebel leaders sought to dominate the local government body, which was supposed to be an independent civilian structure. They demanded their percentage from the humanitarian and medical aid coming through the border.[45] Nothing was for free. They had no qualms sacrificing the common good to settle their own scores. These divisions often created the perfect opportunities for Al-Qaeda's Nusra Front and other extremists to assert themselves.

One time, Sally was with her brother Shaker visiting an aid center outside Daraa city when they were stopped at a Nusra checkpoint. The gunmen, mostly Daraa natives, were all masked.[46] "Why are you dressed indecently?" one of them said to Sally while looking away.

She wore a hijab, long sleeves, and jeans but not the black head-to-toe covering.

"I am free to dress any way I want," she told him defiantly. "Go liberate us from Bashar al-Assad, stop the bombardment, and provide people with a decent life instead of picking on me."

The gunman asked Shaker to get out of the car and took him aside. He lectured him on how he should be ashamed for allowing his sister to appear like that in public. Shaker promised she would cover up. It was a lie to defuse the situation.

November 2014 brought unbearable loss. Sally's youngest brother, Fadi, was killed when he rushed in with other fighters from Daraa city to help fellow rebels in a nearby town who had come under attack by regime forces.

A bullet hit him in the back and he probably bled to death.[47] It took a while for his comrades to retrieve his body from the battlefield. They brought him to Sally so she could say goodbye.

They lay him down on the floor. He looked serene and even smiling. She touched his face. It was cold.

"He's still a baby, no!" she shouted, and then sobbed uncontrollably.

Sally went back to work a week a later, but nothing was ever the same.

There was some joy, though, in the spring of 2015. Malek al-Jawabra, a young man and neighbor who had a crush on her and whom she had sort of been dating for six months already, proposed to her. He was two years older than her and had been studying law before the war. He participated

414

in the first protests in Daraa but never bore arms. He was now volunteering to teach English and math to children in the liberated zone.

The engagement ceremony was truncated, discreet. Malek's parents were able to sneak over from the regime side, but Sally's parents could not come from Jordan. Sally wore a red dress and Malek a suit. They exchanged rings, and sweets were served to the few guests in attendance.

Later in 2015, just before Putin's direct military intervention in Syria, rebels came under tremendous pressure from civilians in Daraa city to launch an operation to drive the regime out from the rest of the city.[48] People were sick of the status quo, of being culled bit by bit by the regime's barrel bombs while rebel commanders were consumed by their internal struggles and quest to enrich themselves.

Rebels drew up the plans and got them approved by their backers at the operations center in Jordan. They even had a name for their campaign: Southern Storm. Many civilians left the city, moving to farms on the outskirts while the fighting was underway. They were willing to endure anything for the chance to rid their city from the killer regime once and for all.

Rebels had driven the regime out of the official border post with Jordan and the historic town of Bosra, and it seemed they could do the same in Daraa.

It took months for the battle to even begin and there were several false starts, too, as rebel commanders squabbled over which faction was going to control the city after its full liberation. There were also high tensions over the participation of Islamist groups. The rebels could exclude the Nusra Front, as the Americans were demanding, but not another Islamist group whose members were city natives.[49] Some rebel commanders were also diverting ammunition and funds they were receiving from their backers away from the battle.

The operation finally got underway in the summer of 2015, but the rebels were decimated by the fierce regime response, which they had grossly underestimated. Iranian and Hezbollah commanders were in charge of the counteroffensive, which operated from the Army's Ninth Division base in As Sanamayn, north of Daraa city.[50]

Making matters worse was a decision by one of the rebel commanders, a carpenter turned warlord, to open a new front west of the city on the border of Suwayda, the Druze-dominated province. He was able to capture a regime base and then he besieged an airbase, but the regime responded by mobilizing Druze militiamen, raising the specter of a war between the Druze and Sunni Muslims from Daraa.

The whole operation was halted in July after close to 800 people were killed on the rebel side.[51] The regime pressed on with its barrel-bomb campaign more savagely than before. One of Sally's closest colleagues, a twenty-nine-year-old activist and citizen journalist called Tareq Khodr, was cut to pieces by a barrel bomb in mid-August.[52] More friends and colleagues were killed the same way in an attack the following day, August 16, 2015, on a food market in the city's liberated zone.

Sally and Malek had planned their exit from Daraa the same day. They had decided to join the stream of refugees heading to Europe that summer, Germany specifically. Sally's eldest brother, Mohammad, was there already with his family, and it looked like the Germans were going to take in all Syrian asylum seekers.

Tears of goodbye were mixed with those of mourning for their dead friends.

Jordan was hardly allowing anyone through from Syria, not even through the informal border crossings. So Sally and Malek and others fleeing Daraa that summer had to travel for more than 600 miles (1,000 kilometers) through the desert—much of it Islamic State territory—to reach the Turkish border in the north.

Their smugglers collaborated with and bribed both regime *mukhabarat* officers and Islamic State militants to allow people through.[53] The regime and the Islamic State were not only sharing the profits from people trafficking in this desolate and barren expanse of territory along the Iraqi border; also, as Sally and Malek saw, dozens of fuel tankers were crossing from the Islamic State side to the regime side.

The Islamic State also seemed happy to do the *mukhabarat*'s dirty work.[54] Sally and Malek were interned with hundreds of others at an Islamic State camp in Al-Mayadin in Deir Ezzour province, where they were interrogated for days to determine whether they were protest leaders, army defectors, or members of the Free Syrian Army (FSA)—all were the opponents that bothered Bashar the most.

It was like being in one of the regime's *mukhabarat* branches, the exact same terror. In fact the Islamic State had created its own secret police modeled after that of the Baathist regimes of Iraq and Syria.[55]

Four men in Malek's group were taken away and executed after they were charged with having been FSA members.[56] It was Malek and Sally's most harrowing experience in their two-week ordeal across Syria. Malek was so traumatized that he barely spoke during the journey from Deir Ezzour to Aleppo after they were let go by the Islamic State. From there they were smuggled into Turkey.

The day they arrived, everyone was talking about Aylan al-Kurdi, the three-year-old Syrian boy whose body washed up on a beach in southwestern Turkey after the rubber boat he was in with his family capsized while they were trying to reach the Greek island of Kos. His mother and brother died, too. Only the father survived.[57] Close to 4,000 people perished in the Mediterranean that year as they tried to escape to Europe from conflict zones in Africa and the Middle East.[58] Many were Syrians.

Sally cried all night, thinking she had made a mistake and certain that death awaited her and Malek. They stayed with a friend in Istanbul for three weeks, debating what to do next. Then they decided to take a chance and made their way to Turkey's western coast. Three times their raft was turned back by the Turkish coast guard as they tried to reach the Greek island of Lesbos from Assos in Turkey.[59] They succeeded on the fourth try from the Turkish city of Izmir.

Because of the deluge of people arriving at its shores, Greece stopped enforcing the European Union regulation that mandated the processing of asylum seekers at their first port of entry. Sally and Malek traveled to Athens and then onward to Macedonia and Serbia.[60]

The problem was Hungary, which was not letting people through and wanted to turn them back to where they came from per the EU regulation. Europe was split that summer between countries like Hungary that wanted to build walls and fences to keep refugees and migrants out, and countries like Germany that wanted to have quotas for EU member states to take them in.[61]

Hungary's ultranationalist prime minister Viktor Orban said that the mostly Muslim refugees were anathema to a European identity "rooted in Christianity."[62]

Sally, Malek, and their companions, who included a friend's brother and his family and two resourceful young men from Aleppo they had met along the way, maneuvered through the chaos and desperation at the Keleti train station in Budapest, where thousands of refugees had been converging.[63] They managed to get to the Austrian border. It was raining when they reached Vienna, where they hugged each other and cried. From there they took a train to Munich. German police waited on the platform for the new arrivals.[64]

As for Mazen Darwish, the human rights lawyer and free speech advocate who had dreamed of toppling the regime with peaceful protests, he too fled Syria a few weeks later in the fall of 2015 as Putin doubled down on saving Bashar and strangling the Arab Spring.

After being held incommunicado and tortured almost to death for more than eight months in the *mukhabarat*'s prisons and dungeons, Mazen had to sign a charge sheet accusing him of "promoting terrorist acts."[65]

One of the more absurd allegations against Mazen was that he had traveled to Washington in 2009 and met with John Kerry, when he was still senator, to conspire against Syria. Mazen was banned from leaving Syria, but he and four other activists did meet with Kerry in Damascus for about half an hour, a day after the US official's dinner with Bashar in early 2009 and with the regime's full knowledge.

Mazen was told he would have to await his trial at either Adra or Saydnaya prisons near Damascus; the latter was a certain death sentence, where a military tribunal routinely ordered summary executions for most of the protesters and political prisoners sent there.

"Congratulations!" erupted Mazen's inmates and hugged him when they found out he was being sent to Adra.

Activists called Adra the "Four Seasons" of Bashar's prisons; with cash and bribes to guards, prisoners could get decent food delivered from restaurants, Internet access, liquor, and whatever else their hearts desired as well as regular visits.[66]

From behind a barred window, Mazen saw his mother and his wife, Yara, who along with other women in Mazen's group had been released four months after their arrest at the office in February 2012. Mazen had not seen his wife or mother for more than a year. They barely recognized him. He looked pale and had lost nearly half of his body weight.

There were tears and laughter but also grim news. Nearly two dozen of Mazen's closest friends and colleagues had been either tortured to death by the regime or were missing in the maw of Bashar's detention system. Yara worked tirelessly to get Mazen out, taking up his case with UN officials, ambassadors, and anyone with possible influence.

Six months into his stay at the Adra prison, Mazen was formally accused of "having too much popularity among other prisoners, who treat him with respect and deference and even call him *ustaz*" (meaning "teacher" or "learned one" in Arabic), so he was kept in near isolation.[67]

At the end of 2014 they transferred him to Hama prison, which had a reputation of being under the sway of Islamists. He feared that maybe they wanted to get him killed in prison and then blame it on extremists, as happened with his colleague Nizar Rastanawi in Saydnaya prison in 2008.

Mazen was assigned to what was called the terrorism wing, which had about 800 people.[68] He was pleasantly surprised, though. Many of the Hama-area protest organizers and peaceful activists he had collaborated with at the start of the uprising were being held there, too. One of them was the man the prisoners nominated as their chief. There were only a handful of prisoners deemed extremist or militant—since Bashar had intentionally freed most of them at the start of the uprising in 2011.

Mazen was given a hero's welcome: they carried him on their shoulders and started singing and clapping, a prison version of a Damascene traditional ceremonial sword dance called the "Arada."

Then came the ordeal of being taken every few weeks to Damascus to make appearances in front of a judge at the counterterrorism court—but only to have his trial postponed each time.

Two days before each trial date, he was shackled and taken to Homs prison and from there to a special transit section at Adra and then to Damascus. It was the same sequence but in reverse for the return trip to Hama.

Bashar issued a blanket pardon in 2014 for certain categories of prisoners and technically Mazen was covered. He still had to go through the formality of a trial, though, so to prevent him from being released, the *mukhabarat* instructed the judges to keep postponing his trial indefinitely.

At the fifteenth postponement, in May 2015, Mazen cracked in court.

There was a fourteen-year-old boy who was also being held in Hama on terrorism charges and had come to court with Mazen that day to make an appearance in his own case. They were all standing up. Mazen put his hands on the boy's shoulders and moved with him a bit closer to the judge's bench.

"Look at this terrorist!" he shouted. "Do you not think that Bin Laden, Zarqawi, and Baghdadi would laugh at you if you told them he was a terrorist? What can I do if you are a regime that's terrorized by a pen? Just as it's clear that I am not a terrorist, it's also clear that you are not a judge and do not have a say over anything."[69]

There was total silence in the courtroom for a while. Then Mazen turned to the security officers behind him and said, "Tell your bosses to send my sentence to the judge and let's get it over with!"

He was hauled along with two of his colleagues to Branch 285 of the *mukhabarat*'s General Intelligence Directorate in central Damascus. Bashar's trusted *mukhabarat* chief, Ali Mamlouk, had an office in the same building.[70]

Mazen and the others were all stripped naked and tortured while they hung from the ceiling or were made to put their head, neck, and legs into a car tire. His torturers made them drink their own urine, and during the first few days they did not let them fall asleep.[71] Every few minutes they came in and poured buckets of freezing water over them. This went on for forty-five days.

While he was at Branch 285, Mazen was awarded the UNESCO/ Guillermo Cano World Press Freedom Prize.[72] The previous year Salman Rushdie had shared his PEN Pinter prize with Mazen.[73] The UN Human Rights Council Working Group on Arbitrary Detention had also issued a detailed report about the unlawful imprisonment of Mazen and two of his colleagues.[74]

Later in 2015, Bashar pardoned about two hundred prisoners, includ-

ing Mazen—all peaceful protesters brutally tortured and branded as
"terrorists." Like his father in the 1990s, Bashar was being magnanimous
for the holiday of Eid al-Fitr, state media told Syrians.[75]

After another stint at Hama prison and then another short stay at
Branch 285, Mazen was freed on August 10, 2015, but he was barred
from leaving the country and ordered to appear in court yet again.[76]

The day he was freed and while he was still in his prison clothes—
shorts, a torn T-shirt, and flip-flops—the minister of justice asked to
see him.

Mazen looked and felt like a shipwreck survivor, who just made it to
shore.

Najm al-Ahmad was a lawyer like him and they knew one another, but
obviously they had followed starkly different paths. A haggard-looking
Mazen was taken to Al-Ahmad's office, which was at the historic Palace of
Justice near the old souks. The counterterrorism court was in the same
building.

An elderly gentleman in an expensive suit was sitting on a leather chair
in Al-Ahmad's large, wood-paneled office at that moment. He was from
the presidential palace.[77]

"Where have you been?" said Al-Ahmad, sounding genuinely surprised. "I signed your release more than a month ago."

"I was running a quick errand at Branch 285," said Mazen sarcastically.

The minister and the palace gentleman grew visibly tense. Someone
came in with a tray of teacups.

"You know your arrest was a mistake—you're one of our honorable
patriots whom we're all proud of. The whole thing was a mistake and it
evolved in a bad way," said Al-Ahmad in a somewhat sincere and even
compassionate tone. "But now the homeland is above all else and we must
work hand in hand because the knife is over all of our necks. Daesh [ISIS]
wants to slaughter us all. You're Alawite, they're going to slaughter you
first. Even before me. Even if you are opposition, we must all work
together now."

"Doctor Najm please, you see my condition," beseeched Mazen, "let's
have this conversation another day."

"Let me order you another tea," persisted Al-Ahmad. "You know something? All these years you were in prison nobody asked about you— all your contacts with international organizations and human rights groups but none of them asked about you or even said a word about you.

"Only two people asked about you. Your brother, and he does not really count because he's your next of kin. So technically only one person was asking about you the whole time—his excellency President Bashar al-Assad. Believe me, Mazen, no month passed without him calling me directly to inquire about you and your case and trial."

On the wall behind the minister and above his chair and head was a framed portrait of Bashar in a suit, looking contemplative.

There was a long silence in the room.

"Your excellency," replied Mazen and then paused, trying his best to tame the rage he felt at that moment, "so you mean to tell me that the president and the minister of justice were talking about my case every month, really? I thought all along that you were the ones detaining me and trying me for terrorism...but it turned out I was totally mistaken and I had been kidnapped by Daesh, and the Syrian state was worried about me and was doing everything to free me."

The meeting ended, and shortly after his release Mazen started getting visits from one of Maher al-Assad's aides as well as a businessman close to Mamlouk, the *mukhabarat* chief. It was the same message relayed by the minister: "We must unite against Daesh and we must work together to save the homeland. You have been talking about transitional justice and reconciliation since 2005. Now we have a reconciliation ministry. Come work with us."[78]

Maher then sent word to Mazen that he wanted to meet him. Mazen managed to postpone it once but then the pressure became intense.

Mazen and his wife, Yara, decided to flee Syria. He had no passport because the regime refused to issue him one, plus he was banned from travel. They were able to raise $10,000 and used it to bribe a senior regime officer at one of the border posts with Lebanon.[79] The German embassy in Beirut issued him a special travel document and a visa. They flew to Berlin.

25

Daesh or Bashar?

It was Easter 2016, and spring had returned to Damascus. A convoy of sedans and SUVs accompanied by *mukhabarat* officers pulled up at the entrance of an Ottoman-era mansion in the Muhajreen neighborhood on the footsteps of Mount Qasioun.

A thirty-member French delegation that included conservative lawmakers, far right personalities, and Christian association representatives stepped out of the vehicles.[1] They stood in front of a charming stone mansion with arched windows, white wooden shutters, and an expansive and well-groomed garden all around.

They walked up double stairs leading to the main entrance on the second floor where Bashar, smiling and dressed in a smart navy-blue suit and tie, waited for them.

The more than century-old Nazim Pasha mansion had undergone a multimillion-dollar remodeling overseen by Bashar's wife, Asma.[2] The marble and wood-paneled interior mixed modern with traditional— inlaid mother-of-pearl Damascene furniture, abstract art, stylish light fixtures, and simple flower arrangements.

The mansion, used by the Assad couple to receive foreign delegations and journalists,[3] was supposed to reflect their aesthetic of understated elegance and also convey intimacy and Levantine charm. The family was striving once more to make the world forget its atrocities and crimes, a trick it has been perfecting for nearly five decades.

The Easter 2016 visit by the French delegation coincided with the

Russian-led recapture of Palmyra,[4] the ancient city that Bashar had abandoned and allowed the Islamic State to occupy for almost one year, during which IS blew up temples, carried out executions in its amphitheater, ransacked its museum, and beheaded Syria's most prominent antiquities scholar.

Valerie Boyer was one of the lawmakers in the delegation that was received by Bashar. She would later become the spokesperson for François Fillon, a French presidential election candidate who wanted to reengage with both Bashar and Putin.

"Would you rather talk to Daesh [ISIS] or Bashar al-Assad?" said Boyer indignantly when asked by a French news channel about making contact with the man responsible for killing hundreds of thousands and displacing millions.[5]

"Today," she continued, "we have a common enemy [with Bashar]—terrorism...We have to be pragmatic and move forward...We are destabilized, we are in a dramatic situation...Let's lift the Russian embargo and negotiate with those fighting Daesh—the Syrian army."

This had been the fourth visit by French officials to Damascus since the January 2015 *Charlie Hebdo* attack;[6] all were organized by the regime in collaboration with allies in France.

For months after that attack, Bashar promised the French and other Europeans more terror on their soil and described France as "the spearhead" of the campaign against him and vowed that it would pay for its "mistake" in Syria.[7]

"First France, second the UK—not the US this time," Bashar told celebrated French broadcaster David Pujadas in an interview at the mansion. "Obama acknowledged that the moderate opposition is illusive—he said that it is fantasy."

Bashar signaled that he had information about upcoming terror plots in France but that he would not share it unless the country ceased its support for the opposition and renounced its calls for him to leave power,[8] a proposition rejected by Hollande.

By May 2015, France estimated about 1,700 of its nationals were fighting in both Iraq and Syria with Sunni extremist groups like the Islamic State and the Nusra Front out of a total of about 30,000 foreigners, a quarter of them from Western Europe.[9] This was separate from the tens of thousands of Shiite foreign fighters on Bashar's side.[10]

On November 13, 2015, at the start of the weekend, Paris was rocked by a bombing and shooting rampage at the Bataclan concert hall and a number of cafés and restaurants that left 130 dead and close to 400 wounded—the deadliest day in the country's history since the end of World War II.[11]

"It's an act of war—an act of absolute barbarity," a somber Hollande told the French people as he announced the deployment of soldiers on the streets of Paris.[12]

This was like no other war France and the West would face.

Six of the ten attackers were French citizens of North African descent. Many returned to Europe from Syria tracing the same sea and land route taken by hundreds of thousands of refugees including Sally Masalmeh and her husband Malek.

The mastermind and recruiter for the Paris attacks was a Belgian of Moroccan origin turned Islamic State commander. He answered to the Islamic State's spokesman and chief of external operations, Abu Muhammad al-Adnani, who was obsessed with striking Europe, especially France.[13] In an audio recording the year before, Adnani had called on Muslims to kill Europeans—"especially the spiteful and filthy French."[14]

It mirrored the rage that Bashar and his henchmen felt toward France for being the "spearhead" in supporting Syrians who sought to liberate themselves from the regime.[15]

As it so happened, the Syrian regime was hosting multiple French delegations in Damascus at precisely the same moment as the November 2015 attacks in Paris.

A previously announced meeting of foreign ministers from several countries led by the United States and Russia to discuss Syria was also taking place in Vienna. France was expected to be among those voicing the hardest and most uncompromising position toward Bashar at that meeting.[16]

"We warned about what's going to happen in Europe…and we said, 'Don't mess with the fault line in Syria.' It's going to be like an earthquake that will reverberate around the world, and unfortunately the European officials didn't pay attention to what we said—they didn't learn from what happened at the beginning of this year, from *Charlie Hebdo*," crowed

Bashar the day after the November attacks, as he stood at the entrance of the Nazim Pasha mansion speaking to French reporters.[17]

Europe was terrorized and practically on its knees.

All eyes were on Russia, the rising power inside Syria and Bashar's new indispensable patron after Iran.

The Europeans had joined the US-led coalition that was bombing the Islamic State in Iraq and Syria, but now they needed to show their fearful citizens that they were doing everything possible to eradicate this threat—even if it meant partnering with the devil.

Hollande rushed to Moscow two weeks after the November 2015 Paris attacks to meet Putin and make the case for a grand international coalition to fight the Islamic State and other extremists. For Hollande, another crucial part of the solution was a new transitional government in Syria that would adopt a new constitution and hold elections.

"And it goes without saying that Assad does not have any role to play in the future of his country," Hollande told reporters as Putin stood by his side at the Kremlin.[18]

"I feel that President Assad's army and he himself are our natural allies in the fight against terrorism," retorted Putin,[19] even though he knew that the army he was referring to hardly existed and that the most effective force on the ground on the regime side was made up of Iran's Shiite militias, including Hezbollah and others.

None of these details mattered to Putin. Something far bigger was at stake.

Europe, which had tried to isolate him and had passed sanctions against Russia after his annexation of Crimea and military intervention in eastern Ukraine in early 2014, was now coming to him for help in confronting the terror menace. He went from pariah to protector.

For the longest time the United States had been the dominant power broker in the Middle East, but now was Russia's chance to change that. A new world order was emerging.

"Let's deal with the devil: we should work with Vladimir Putin and Bashar al-Assad in Syria," urged London mayor Boris Johnson, who later became the United Kingdom's foreign secretary.[20]

After the November 2015 Paris attacks, Putin, Bashar, and their allies were practically given license by the UN Security Council to crush all opposition to the Assad regime. A resolution was passed unanimously in December 2015 calling for a ceasefire in Syria but excluding the Islamic State, the Nusra Front, and unspecified "other terrorist groups," which was interpreted by Bashar and his allies to mean everyone living in opposition areas, both civilians and combatants.[21]

Between 2016 and 2018, the world mostly watched as the Iranian-Russian-Syrian regime coalition bombed homes, hospitals, markets, and schools in opposition areas because "other terrorist groups" were there. In addition to the regime's favorite barrel bombs and chlorine bombs, other weapons deployed by this coalition included at least thirteen types of internationally banned cluster bombs and incendiary munitions which ignited hard-to-extinguish fires and caused horrible burns.[22]

By February 2016, the death toll since March 2011 approached half a million, the majority of them civilians killed by the Syrian regime, not the Islamic State, the Nusra Front, or any other group.[23] The number of those seeking refuge abroad touched five million. By mid-2016 almost one million people were under siege, mainly by Bashar's and Iran's militias, and they were deprived of food, medicine, and every other basic human necessity.[24]

The world looked on as babies were pulled from underneath the rubble of residential buildings in east Aleppo after being bombed by Bashar and the Russians, or were starved to death in the besieged suburbs of Damascus by the militias of Bashar and Iran.[25]

UN secretary-general Ban Ki-moon voiced the same "grave concern" that he had been expressing since March 2011,[26] while John Kerry was "outraged" by every atrocity committed by Bashar and his allies.[27]

In Geneva, where the regime was supposed to be holding peace talks with the opposition per the December 2015 UN Security Council resolution, Bashar's delegation, which included a notorious *mukhabarat* officer, spent months wasting time on things like the agenda for the talks and its own vision for a political solution—a sprinkling of opposition figures in a new government under Bashar.[28]

The protection of Christians and other minorities was a crucial frame for Putin's actions in Syria, and it resonated with many people in the region and beyond.

"Middle East Christians [are] experiencing a real genocide...Any fight against terrorism is moral—we can even call it a holy fight," said a senior cleric in Russia's powerful Orthodox Church on the day that Putin launched his military campaign in Syria.[29]

The Russian church moved in lockstep with Putin's foray into Syria, seeing it as a historic opportunity to rebuild and strengthen its presence in the region. The Imperial Orthodox Palestine Society, an organization founded during tsarist times to tend to the needs of Russian pilgrims in the holy lands, provided massive quantities of humanitarian assistance to the Syrian regime and built a school in Damascus.[30] The society also sought to restore its properties in Jerusalem and expand its activities throughout the Levant.

" 'Russian Palestine' today is an essential instrument for consolidating Russia's positions," said Russian foreign minister Lavrov, a member of the society, who often labeled as "hypocritical" those calling on Bashar to leave power.[31]

Many in the Levant began speaking of a grand coalition of minorities including Alawites, Christians, and Shiites among others taking shape under the patronage of Iran and Russia.

As media outlets broadcast the trail of destruction left by marauding fanatics sweeping through Christian towns and villages in Syria, and as countries like Lebanon with a significant Christian population were rocked by attacks and bombings attributed to Sunni extremists, Bashar, Putin, and Hezbollah chief Nasrallah looked like the heroes waging this new "holy fight." There was some dissent, but it was eventually drowned out.

"The Syrian regime and Daesh [ISIS] are identical in their criminality and thirst for blood—they are from the same school...Don't make us choose between Daesh and Bashar," pleaded a Christian Lebanese lawmaker.[32]

But already the influential and powerful patriarchs of nearly all Christian denominations in the Middle East, who had the Vatican's ear, were tacitly or explicitly for Bashar.

"I know President Assad and the Syrian government, and they protect Christians in Syria," said Ignatius Joseph III Younan, Patriarch of Antioch for the Syriac Catholic Church, sitting in business class on a flight from Beirut to Rome for a meeting with Pope Francis about Syria.[33]

Bashar and his media portrayed the pope as being on their side in "the fight against terrorism" after his strong opposition to any military action that would have punished the regime for killing hundreds of civilians with chemical weapons in August 2013.[34]

Bashar also pointed to the fact that the pope never withdrew his envoy to Damascus, who lived and worked within walking distance from the Assad residence. Bashar's media office relished the chance to tweet photos of his meeting at the Nazim Pasha mansion with the papal nuncio, Cardinal Mario Zenari, who smiled as Bashar examined a letter from the pope.[35]

The truth was that Syrian Christian youth actively took part in the early peaceful protests against the regime, but they too were killed or jailed, or they fled the country during the ensuing crackdown.[36]

At the same time, though, many Syrian church leaders, like Gregorius III Laham, patriarch of the Melkite Greek Catholic Church, staunchly defended Bashar throughout, even calling him once "a progressive from a British-Syrian milieu."[37] Others, like Greek Orthodox bishop Luca al-Khoury, collaborated with the *mukhabarat* and actively recruited Christian youth for pro-Bashar militias.[38]

A month after the November 2015 Paris attacks, around Christmas, Bashar and Asma, wearing a festive red scarf, showed up unexpectedly at the Our Lady of Damascus church. They laughed, chatted, and took selfies with adoring congregants. Video clips of their appearance were shared widely on social media.[39] The message was that Christianity would cease to exist in Syria if the Assads were to be swept aside.

The chants of "Muslims and Christians, we want freedom!" by Damascene youth from both faiths during an impromptu nighttime demonstration outside that same church in March 2012 were now a distant memory.[40]

Bit by bit, Bashar recast himself at home and abroad from butcher of his people to protector of Christians and minorities and savior from the horrors of Muslim extremists.

"The relations that bind our two countries are not only political but also sentimental," Bashar's friend Hala Chawi, a Christian Damascene businesswoman, told French parliamentarians during a meeting inside the Palais Bourbon, France's capitol building.[41] Her son George Chawi had been sanctioned by the European Union at the start of the uprising for his role in the Syrian Electronic Army, but she was not and could travel freely.[42]

In his renewed outreach to France, Bashar could count on decades of cooperation with the country's intelligence services, which included many people opposed to Hollande's line in Syria. There were also long-standing ties with politicians ranging from neo-Nazis and extreme-right figures to members of Hollande's own socialist party as well as wealthy, influential, and mostly Christian French citizens of Lebanese and Syrian origins.[43]

As France reeled from one deadly attack after another linked to the Islamic State, the goal of the delegations' visits to Syria was not only to burnish Bashar's image and break his isolation but also to use French lawmakers and other figures to pressure their government to reverse its line on Bashar and ease or lift sanctions on him and his cronies in return for information on terrorists and their plots.

Two conservative French lawmakers with ties to Putin lobbied the hardest for this in the halls of power,[44] while SOS Chrétiens d'Orient and Coordination Chrétiens d'Orient en Danger, two organizations founded in 2013 to raise the alarm about what they called the "extermination" of Christians in the Middle East, raised funds from the public for humanitarian aid and missions to persecuted communities in the Levant and organized trips to Syria for French citizens.[45]

SOS Chrétiens, which has links to pro-Bashar Lebanese Christian leaders as well as French intelligence and far-right figures, worked directly with Bashar's aides and the *mukhabarat* to organize these trips.[46]

The itinerary usually included a meeting with Bashar's mufti, Hassoun, to present the "moderate face of Islam" espoused by the regime—as opposed to the "fanatics" of the Islamic State and the French government–backed Syrian opposition—and then a chat at the Ministry of Foreign Affairs about the secular nature of the regime and its leader Bashar. There was also a visit to Maaloula, the ancient Christian town briefly captured by Al-Qaeda's affiliate, the Nusra Front, in the fall of 2013.[47]

Of course, in the narrative presented to French visitors there was no room for facts like these: the regime did little to prevent the fall of Maaloula because its residents had refused to join pro-regime militias; most of the damage to Maaloula's churches and monasteries was caused by indiscriminate shelling by regime forces; and Bashar himself released hundreds of militants from prison at the start of protests in 2011 and later intentionally ceded entire cities, regions, and bases close to the Iraqi border to ISIS.

With every fresh deadly attack in France and Europe in the spring and summer of 2016[48] — suicide bombers at the Brussels airport and metro, and a militant in a truck mowing down Bastille Day revelers on the seaside promenade in Nice in southern France — the more voices came out calling for collaboration with Bashar and Russia and speaking of the West's mistake in backing Bashar's opponents.

The narrative of Bashar the ally against Islamist terrorists and protector of Christians spread to all those Western countries that initially embraced the opposition but were now confronting terror, an influx of refugees, and rising xenophobia and populism.

"It is unconscionable that the international community refuse to talk to the secular leader of a nation," wrote Andrew Ashdown, an Anglican priest who led a British delegation to Syria that met with Bashar in the fall of 2016.[49]

Among those feted in Damascus by Bashar's regime that year were members of the European Solidarity Front for Syria, a group of neo-Nazi and neo-fascist youth organizations and figures from Belgium, Greece, Italy, Poland, and Serbia, among others, that held pro-Bashar rallies throughout Europe. The group's logo featured a map of Europe in black set against a Syrian flag.[50]

Paradoxically, Bashar could also count on plenty of support from the left and far left, including prominent figures in Britain associated with organizations like the Stop War Coalition, which was formed in 2001 in response to the US-led war on terror and the invasion of Iraq.

One of the coalition's cofounders, George Galloway, a former Labor Party parliamentarian, had his own show on Russia Today, which often hosted people parroting the Syrian regime's lies and conspiracy theories.[51]

In the United States, too, the tide began to shift in favor of Bashar and his allies as early as 2014, when Washington began liaising with the regime, albeit at arm's length, so that it would not get in the way of its military operations against the Islamic State in Syria. The regime bragged about these contacts and portrayed them as a sort of reengagement with the Americans. While it accommodated the United States in its anti-ISIS campaign, the regime stepped up its bombardment of civilians in opposition-held areas. This gave the impression that there was a sort of division of labor and that Bashar had the green light from Washington to strike the enemies whom he cared most about while Americans focused on the Islamic State.

Far-right websites like *Breitbart*, whose executive chairman Steve Bannon would later become Donald Trump's chief strategist, and *InfoWars* (founded by US conspiracy theorist Alex Jones) lauded Bashar, the supposed defender of Christians and warrior against terror.[52]

It was not just the fanatical fringe helping Bashar's cause.

A former journalist named Nir Rosen, working with the Center for Humanitarian Dialogue, a Geneva-based conflict resolution group, began actively promoting the idea that the United States had to abandon calls for Bashar to leave power. He said the focus should be instead on local ceasefire agreements between rebels and the regime whereby opposition-held enclaves would be allowed to run their own affairs as both sides united to fight the Islamic State and other extremists.

"It's a race against time," argued Rosen, "because soon there will be no partners to negotiate with on the opposition side" — that is, because all were supposedly going to join either the Islamic State or the Nusra Front.[53]

In the summer of 2014, Rosen boasted about his access to the regime's most notorious *mukhabarat* chiefs and his regular meetings with them in Damascus. He spoke of his ongoing efforts to lobby Obama administration officials to embrace his proposal and give up on the idea of Bashar's departure.

Rosen divided these officials into friends and foes depending on their stance on the Bashar issue.[54] Enemies included Secretary of State John Kerry, National Security Advisor Susan Rice, and US ambassador to the UN, Samantha Power. Friends included Robert Malley, a senior adviser to Obama on the Middle East and the anti–Islamic State campaign, and a former National Security Council director named Steven Simon, who remained influential.[55]

In the spring of 2015, Simon traveled to Damascus to meet with Bashar to press him to embrace the idea of the localized ceasefires and urge him to stop dropping barrel bombs on opposition-held areas and focus instead on fighting the Islamic State.[56]

The meeting was arranged by Khaled al-Ahmad, a businessman friend of Bashar. Al-Ahmad had previously met with Simon and Robert Ford, the US Syria envoy. Al-Ahmad was also among the Bashar cronies whom Rosen was regularly meeting and corresponding with as early as 2011 in order to share information about the opposition and assure them that the United States and its European allies were incapable of referring Bashar's atrocities against protesters to the International Criminal Court.

"I think this is all bullshit. These guys can do nothing and the international community (meaning America and Europe) can do nothing. See you all soon," Rosen wrote in an email in October 2011 to al-Ahmad, George Chawi from the Syrian Electronic Army, and Lebanese Bashar loyalist Michel Samaha, later accused of involvement in a Syrian *mukhabarat* plot to carry out bombings in Lebanon.[57]

Ford left the foreign service in 2014 amid frustration, and at times open dissent at the US State Department, with Obama's policies in Syria.[58]

The Islamic State's attacks in Europe, starting in early 2015, and Russia's entry into the war that year on the regime's side completely reversed Bashar's fortunes.

As for the localized ceasefires Rosen was promoting, opposition-held areas were bombed and starved into submission in the name of fighting terrorism, and any ceasefire agreements with those that remained were largely on the terms of Bashar and his backers, Iran and Russia.

In August 2016, the United Nations expressed "extreme concern" over demographic changes being engineered in towns surrendering to the regime, such as Daraya, near Damascus.[59]

"You are sad and upset, but we are actually happy that Daraya reverted to the homeland's bosom and we are also pleased that you're upset," answered Bashar from inside a destroyed and deserted Daraya as he chuckled and mocked the town's peaceful protesters and activists whom he had killed or jailed in 2011 as "revolutionaries for hire."[60]

That same summer of 2016, Republican presidential candidate Donald Trump heaped praise on Putin and said "it would be great to get along with him," even as Russia, Iran, and the Syrian regime intensified their bloody campaign to retake the rebel-held eastern section of Aleppo.[61]

Russia led the aerial bombardment, while Iran's officers and volunteers as well as the Hezbollah militia from Lebanon and Shiite fighters from Afghanistan, Iraq, and elsewhere led the combat on the ground.

The area, roughly the size of Manhattan,[62] remained by late 2016 home to more than 200,000 civilians and about 8,000 fighters, of whom about 900 were affiliated with the Nusra Front.[63] For the regime and its allies, everyone was a terrorist and deserved to die.

The world stood by as Bashar and his allies closed in on those left in east Aleppo, striking homes, hospitals, and clinics with air-to-surface missiles, bunker-busting bombs, cluster munitions, barrel bombs, chlorine bombs, and incendiary weapons. More than 3,500 civilians were killed between June and December 2016, and medical facilities were attacked more than seventy times.[64]

Aleppo burned, but back in Damascus Asma al-Assad was busy solidifying her position as first lady.

Earlier that year Bashar's mother Aniseh passed away at the age of eighty-six. She had eagerly backed her sons Bashar and Maher and her nephews the Makhloufs in all their bloody actions to preserve the Assad clan's grip on Syria. For her it was also about the legacy of her husband, Hafez, father and builder of modern Syria, as she and loyalists regarded him.

After the assassination of her son-in-law, Assef Shawkat, on the orders of her sons, as Manaf Tlass and Western officials believed, Aniseh spent most of her time in Dubai with her daughter, Bushra.

"She married a leader and birthed a leader," a TV station tied to her son Maher eulogized, showing archival footage of Aniseh and Hafez on foreign visits.[65]

"She shunned camera lights and showy public appearances."

As women and children in east Aleppo buckled under the regime's brutal assault, Asma invited a reporter from a Russian state-owned TV station to spend a week with her. The result was a documentary titled "Asma al-Assad: Between War and Peace," which included an interview billed as her first in years.[66]

In simple attire, with her hair tied back in a ponytail and driving her own SUV, she is shown traveling outside Damascus and even braving a stretch of road that skirted past territory allegedly controlled by "terrorists."[67]

She cries at the bedside of a soldier disabled by war. She then visits a rehab center for soldiers who had lost limbs. "We are receiving a new batch" of prosthetics, Asma assures a young soldier who had lost both legs.[68]

At her private office in Damascus she receives the families of dead soldiers, or the martyrs, as they were called.

"We are ready to sacrifice everything for you and Bashar al-Assad, I swear to God," a mother who says she has lost two young sons fighting for Bashar tells Asma. "This is a gift for Bashar al-Assad," the mother continues as she hands Asma a framed photograph of her two dead sons. They are in their late teens or early twenties at most. Both wear military fatigues and pose with their assault rifles.[69]

Asma is shown as the comforter of a nation traumatized by war waged by outside powers and somehow unconnected to the Assads' actions and their determination to survive at any cost. Asma's aides are shown following up on a flood of requests from families displaced by war or coping with the loss or disability of soldier relatives. These requests are written on scraps of paper and handed to Asma during visits to these families.

"I don't like formalities. If it's a sad story, you cry; if it's a happy story, you laugh," says Asma about her meetings with soldiers and their families as she sits down with the Russian reporter for an interview at the Nazim Pasha mansion that she has redecorated.

"I love this place because it's right in the heart of the city," she tells the reporter as they stroll in the garden.[70]

There are some of the usual talking points from her first interviews with Western media after she married Bashar, but in general she wants to project an image of resilience and toughness, of a leader's wife doing her part in wartime.

"Being first lady was never part of my career plan... You may remember also that at some stage I was the desert rose, the elegant first lady bringing reform... What's important is that I remain humble and true to who I really am," Asma tells the Russian reporter, casting the West as whimsical and treacherous.[71]

As for her husband, Asma says he has remained an attentive and caring father despite all the burdens of war. "He's very calm, very thoughtful, always polite... easy to talk to... He takes his role as father very seriously, he's a very giving man," says Asma.[72]

Meanwhile some of the war's most searing images were coming out of Aleppo, which Asma's *very giving* husband wanted to retake at any cost.

Civil defense rescuers known as the White Helmets pulled a baby out from the rubble of his home; he was the only survivor in his family.[73]

There was a man completely submerged under the wreckage except for his bloodied and dust-covered head.

A group of men cradled newborns in their arms and transported them to safety; the infants had been rescued from a hospital coming under aerial bombardment.[74]

A teenage boy sobbed inconsolably over his dead little brother in a body bag at the morgue.[75]

Then there was a boy named Omran Daqneesh, rescued from the rubble of his home, sitting stunned on an orange ambulance seat, wiping blood from his cheek and staring at the camera.[76]

"A lot of this is because of Hillary Clinton, because what's happened is, by fighting Assad, who turned out to be a lot tougher than she thought, and now she's going to say, oh, he loves Assad, she's—he's just much tougher and much smarter than her and Obama," said Trump when asked, during the last debate before Election Day, about Aleppo and what he would do about it if elected.[77]

For months Trump and his surrogates had asserted that, if elected, Clinton would invade Syria and side with the allegedly Islamic State–linked "terrorist opposition" against Bashar and his allies, supposedly the only ones fighting terrorism.[78]

Electing Clinton would open "the floodgates" of "diseased," "fanatical," and "rapist" Muslim refugees to the United States, claimed one Trump cheerleader, a Lebanese-born Christian.[79]

All these lies and hysterical statements were also spread by the Russian-sponsored fake news that inundated social media, especially Facebook, around the same time.[80]

Later that fall, after Trump's stunning election win, German chancellor Angela Merkel spoke at her own party's conference, calling the indiscriminate bombardment of civilians in Aleppo a "disgrace" and expressing shock that there were not more protests in Germany and across Europe against the crimes being committed. "Something is not right," she said.[81]

As far as most Europeans were concerned, though, the war was now on their streets and not just in far-off Aleppo. In Brussels, army trucks packed with soldiers crossed quaint cobblestone squares like the Place du Grand Sablon. "The European continent is on fire," exclaimed graffiti in central Amsterdam.[82]

In Paris, the sight of armed soldiers patrolling the streets was now a fact of daily life. The slightest suspicion could cause an entire city block to be cordoned off for hours by assault-rifle-carrying police officers. This was also a city in mourning.

Makeshift remembrance shrines sprang up outside the bars, restaurants, and other venues attacked on November 13, 2015. People left flower bouquets and teddy bears and lit candles. In a small park across from the Bataclan concert hall, where the most people were killed, a man arranged flowers around a marble plaque with names of the victims, who included several of North African origin just like the attackers. Nearby, a lone girl sat on a bench in the drizzle and stared ahead.[83]

A mile or so to the west, passersby seemed hardly moved by the sight of a few dozen Bashar opponents and a handful of French sympathizers on the footsteps of the opera house known as the Palais Garnier protesting the savage campaign in Aleppo. Busts of Beethoven, Mozart, Rossini, and other composers tucked in niches high up in the columned facade looked down on the protesters as they played mournful Syrian revolutionary songs from 2011 and held up banners denouncing Bashar and Putin.[84]

"Syria's democratic future is without Bashar, without Daesh!" read one. "Putin = War Criminal," said another.

By then, though, the peaceful beginnings of the Syrian uprising and the regime's subsequent brutality and atrocities were a fading memory as the focus in most people's minds was on the present threats from the Islamic State and refugees fleeing to Europe.

These were key issues in France's heated presidential election primaries in the fall of 2016. The candidate of the extreme right, Marine Le Pen, argued for collaboration with Bashar and the Russians, and so did the conservative front-runner, François Fillon, a former prime minister.[85]

Away from the Bataclan and the Palais Garnier, on the opposite bank of the Seine, Manaf Tlass walked through the Jardin du Luxembourg. He had just turned fifty-four, his hair was grayer, and he had a few more wrinkles on his face.

It was a sunny but cold morning. Joggers and police officers armed with submachine guns passed by, and a group of elderly men and women did *tai chi* moves across from a bronze monument honoring the painter Eugène Delacroix—the artist's bust was surrounded by the angels of time and glory and Apollo in dramatic poses.

The dome of the Pantheon rose up in the distance on the hill of the Quartier Latin beyond the park's iron fence.

"World powers are taking turns raping Syria—damn them all!" said Manaf bitterly. "The West gave us the impression they cared about the blood that was being spilled, they said the regime's days were numbered when I left Syria…Look at them now, rushing to take photographs with Bashar," he added, referring to the Western delegations that flocked to Damascus.[86]

At least 200 defected officers had gone back to Syria with the help of the Russians, he said. "They lost hope. They went back to live in subjection again just to survive. I can't judge them—maybe some were blackmailed after their relatives were arrested by the regime. Maybe they were demeaned outside Syria," he said.

"I can't return. He [Bashar] sentenced me to death. He wants me to beg for forgiveness."

In early 2015, the regime's special counterterrorism court issued a death sentence against Manaf, but it was not final and he could appeal it if he chose to.[87] All he had to do was ask Bashar to pardon him.[88]

"I have been stabbed in the back!" said Manaf angrily as the conversation turned to the Americans.[89]

His outburst was typical of his severe mood swings around that period. One day he was on top of the world, speaking of his imminent return to Damascus and being courted by world powers as Syria's last hope. The next day, everything looked bleak and dark, and these same powers were fooling him and the innocent Syrian people. One day Bashar was finished, a hollow figurehead president flailing in the wind, and the next Bashar was still capable of getting him in Paris and harming him and his family if he divulged Assad family secrets or was too critical of the regime.

Of course, it did not help that Manaf was sidelined and jobless, living off his savings and waiting for something that, by then, neither he nor the majority of Syrians had any say over.

This time, though, his rage was all-consuming. It was frightening.

Manaf explained that he had been secretly working with the CIA for more than a year on furthering the idea of a Syrian military council composed of both army officers still with the regime and moderate rebel forces.

Manaf would return to Damascus under the protection of America and Russia, and Bashar would stay on in his position but largely with ceremonial powers, and the military council would stabilize the country and prepare for elections.

A newly reconstituted army under the military council would confront extremists, including the Nusra Front, which had embedded itself among opposition forces, as well as Hezbollah and the Iran-backed militias dominating the regime side. Manaf would be at the helm of this council.[90] (Hafez al-Assad also established a transitional military council immediately after his 1970 coup.)

It was the perfect plan, in fact it was the only remaining hope for Syria and Syrians, Manaf and a coterie of his allies and advisers often repeated.

"The Americans even told me that I would meet with Putin, the Americans were liaising with the Russians, this would have been the natural and logical next step," said Manaf.[91]

This sounded like a Syrian variation on what had happened in Libya around 2014 after that country was plunged into warfare between the militias that fought Gaddafi and was then plagued by extremists, including the Islamic State. There Khalifa Haftar, a former general and Gaddafi companion who had lived in exile in suburban Washington, DC, and collaborated with the CIA for years,[92] was backed by Egypt, the United Arab Emirates, and later Russia in his battle against what he and his outside supporters considered an Islamist-dominated government in the country's west, in the capital, Tripoli.[93]

In Syria, too, Russia and the United States looked as if they were in harmony even as Moscow bombed American-backed rebels inside the country.

The two major powers convened meetings in Vienna bringing together all countries involved, including Iran and Turkey, and eventually shepherding a resolution through the Security Council outlining a road map for a political settlement, and they helped restart peace talks in Geneva in early 2016.[94]

The Americans also—to the delight of the Russians—softened their position on Bashar: he did not have to leave right away.[95] He could remain through the transition. Manaf believed that Russia and the United States were together capable of imposing this solution and neutralizing all potential spoilers inside the regime and around the region.

Manaf said the CIA supported and funded efforts by him and his team in reaching out to various rebel factions to get them to embrace the idea of a ruling military council in Syria that would bring together those deemed honest and patriotic on both sides, regime and opposition.

Manaf's team included two defected Syrian army lieutenant colonels loyal to him and a former movie set assistant in Syria turned opposition activist in exile,[96] who penned flattering articles and Facebook posts about Manaf and his vision for "the salvation and liberation of our nation and people."[97]

· Starting in early 2015, Manaf's team traveled to southern Turkey and opposition-controlled sections of northern Syria across the border where they met with rebel commanders to secure buy-in for Manaf and his project, which they touted as having the blessing of the United States and other major powers.

More than three dozen rebel commanders, including one who headed a large faction backed by Turkey, signed handwritten preliminary agreements to support Manaf and his project and pledged to work with him to "topple Bashar al-Assad and the ruling gang," keep Syria unified, and protect Syria's minorities among other goals.

All rebel commanders vowed to surrender their weapons upon the establishment of the military council and new army. Some said that they expected to be paid salaries in return for endorsing Manaf and his project.[98]

There was hardly any mention of justice and accountability for war crimes committed by all sides, especially the regime.

These agreements, along with notes and observations by Manaf's team, were recorded in a black soft-cover Moleskin reporter notebook that was kept by Manaf.

Similar written pledges of support for Manaf were secured in 2016 by his relative Zeid Tlass, [99] a defected Syrian air force colonel.

At the same time, Manaf continued to reach out to Alawite officers inside Syria.

"If there's a solution for Syria, we are with you—but you have to hurry," those officers still on Bashar's side told Manaf.[100]

Then, just before the US presidential elections, the Americans pulled the plug on Manaf's whole plan, paving the way for Iran and Russia to retake east Aleppo for Bashar and to bolster Bashar's position as the figurehead leader, according to Manaf.[101]

"I began to sense that they [CIA] were abandoning the project, funding stopped and obstacles started to emerge," said Manaf. "Something much bigger than me was happening and I did not fully grasp it."

In a deal brokered mainly between Russia and Turkey (representing armed groups), east Aleppo surrendered just before Christmas 2016. Even then Bashar continued his practice of humiliating those whom he dominated; there were also summary executions by his militias.[102]

Thousands of families with battered suitcases and plastic bags—some carrying their pets and birdcages—marched silently in the rain as regime forces in pickup trucks sped past them flashing victory signs.[103]

Enforced disappearance, army conscription, or death was the fate of the young opposition activists and medics who ended up in regime custody. Among the captured was Alaa al-Shawaf, a twenty-something telecom engineer who had volunteered as a paramedic in east Aleppo. He was subsequently tortured to death by the *mukhabarat*.[104]

Bashar was not just going to be content to see the West, which he believed conspired against him, look away begrudgingly and queasily (voicing the occasional indignation) as he committed his atrocities because they deemed him the lesser of two evils and were more worried about ISIS than what he, Bashar, did to his people.

On the contrary, he wanted to revel in what he regarded as his victory over the West. Bashar demanded and expected full and total vindication. It was the Assad family way throughout a bloody reign approaching half a century.

"We say before and after the birth of Jesus Christ...before and after the fall of the Soviet Union...we will now say before and after the liberation of Aleppo in relation not only to the situation in Syria and the region but the whole world," said a buoyant and content-looking Bashar in a video message recorded at the entrance of the Nazim Pasha mansion.[105]

26

Dictators Strike Back — but Hope Endures

In February 2017, Amnesty International revealed that the Assad regime had executed up to 13,000 people at its Saydnaya prison between September 2011 and December 2015.[1] Most of the dead were opposition activists and protesters captured and tortured by the *mukhabarat* and then referred to a military tribunal at Saydnaya. Mass hangings took place in the prison's basement, usually on Mondays and Wednesdays, in what was described as an extermination policy — another page that Bashar tore out of his father's sinister playbook.

The same military tribunals had hanged thousands of Hafez's suspected opponents at Tadmor prison in the 1980s and '90s.[2] The sentences were often signed on Hafez's behalf by his defense minister, Mustafa Tlass.

Among those executed at Saydnaya was Mazen Darwish's friend and fellow opposition activist Bassel Khartabil, a computer wizard who was instrumental in helping overcome restrictions introduced by the regime so that news of the early protests and Bashar's deadly crackdown could reach the world via the Internet.[3]

Khartabil was arrested exactly one month after the raid on Mazen's office in February 2012.[4] The two friends overlapped at Adra prison, where Mazen witnessed Khartabil's marriage while in detention to his fiancée, the love of his life, Noura.[5] Shortly after Mazen's release from prison in the summer of 2015 Khartabil was transferred from Adra to Saydnaya, where he was hanged.

"You can forge anything these days," said Bashar when asked about the Amnesty report by American journalist Michael Isikoff, during an interview in one of the smartly decorated reception rooms of the Nazim Pasha mansion.[6]

"We are living in a fake news era," added Bashar. He dismissed as "photo-shop" a photograph handed to him by the reporter of the emaciated and brutalized corpses of *mukhabarat* prisoners that piled up in a hangar at the 601 military hospital in Damascus.[7]

The election of Donald Trump was "promising," Bashar told Isikoff, because the new US president's priority was "to fight terrorism,"[8] not support those Syrians still struggling to rid themselves of nearly five decades of Assad family rule — a regime that terrorized its people, sponsored terrorism abroad, and outlasted eight US presidents, starting with Nixon.

Here, instead, was a US president who promoted propaganda and lies and dismissed truths and facts, whose actions and words demeaned and threatened opponents, someone who had no problem polarizing and dividing his people in order to secure his position and rule — just like the Assads.

Here was a US president for whom family and absolute loyalty were the first and foremost considerations and for whom wealth, raw power, self-aggrandizement, and vanity mattered more than anything else.

The oath that President Trump took to defend democratic values seemed to mean very little, especially when viewed in the context of such statements as these: for weeks before his election victory Trump warned that his supporters might take up arms if he did not win,[9] and two years into office he said that financial markets would plunge into chaos if he were ever to be impeached.[10]

Many asked if Trump was normalizing and empowering autocracy around the world, some even compared his leadership style to that of a Middle Eastern dictator.[11]

As the consequences of Trump's election consumed America and the world, Bashar and his regime — with the support of his patrons Iran and Russia (not to mention the de facto blessing of the US and many European governments) — began to rewrite history. Like the reality-show host turned US president, Bashar constructed his own reality using social media platforms like Facebook and Twitter. These were the exact same tools that empowered many of Syria's youth to express themselves creatively and openly when they took to the streets in 2011 and chanted for *hurriyeh*, or freedom, but were then shot dead month after month.

Some Syrian youth were tortured to death for simply posting words of protest on Facebook or viewing anti-Bashar pages. Now these same outlets were awash with photos, words, and videos of Bashar, Asma, and their children.

The eldest, Hafez, turned sixteen and was as tall as his father. The daughter, Zein, and the other son, Karim, were in their early teens. On Christmas 2016, they were shown with their parents visiting orphans at a Christian monastery near Damascus.[12] In February 2017, they posed with their parents and cousin Bassel, the son of Bashar's sister Bushra and the late Assef Shawkat, during a visit to the Assad hometown of Qurdaha in western Syria.

The publication of these photos was an attempt to dispel talk of a family rift and Bashar's role in Assef's death, even all these years later. They all looked happy, relaxed, and rosy-cheeked in their winter clothes with the mountains behind them.[13]

In summer 2017, Bashar, Asma, and their children were shown seated on the floor of a wounded soldier's home in the Hama countryside; a caring, loving, and patriotic family—like any presidential family in Europe—that did not abandon its people and country through six years of war.[14]

"In Syria, history is being written by the righteous, in blood," a defiant and somewhat jubilant Asma lectures a group of mothers from Aleppo in a video posted earlier on a Facebook page dedicated to her and her every utterance and appearance.[15]

Later that year, sixteen-year-old Hafez traveled to Brazil for an international math competition, where he told a local newspaper that most people were "blind" about the true nature of his father. "I know what kind of man my father is," Bashar's eldest son said. "As president people say a lot of things [about Bashar]...this isn't reality."[16]

In Damascus, his mother feted the sixteenth anniversary of her Syria Trust for Development and, like Bashar, spoke of the "treason," "ignorance," and "extremism" of those who rose up in the spring of 2011.[17]

Seven years later, the whole world seemed to have been turned upside down. The world looked for leadership from the strongmen of China and Russia, two nations that through their actions in Syria wanted to enshrine a new standard: Interfering to stop a regime from massacring its own people was meddling in the internal affairs of a sovereign state.

Meanwhile, fear gripped Europe and the United States turned inward, managing its own scandals and controversies while turning its back on the world's problems — or making them worse.

As for those leaders who once wanted to unseat Bashar, Turkey's increasingly authoritarian Recep Tayyip Erdogan launched a sweeping crackdown on his opponents, on journalists, and on free speech itself, and in the summer of 2016 he pivoted toward Russia and Putin after he accused the West of conspiring with generals in his army and an exiled cleric to overthrow him.[18]

Saudi Arabia, which did everything to control and co-opt Syria's main opposition bodies, gradually walked away from them and eventually said that it had no problem whatsoever with Bashar staying in power, as long as Bashar's protector was Putin and not Iran's Khamenei.[19]

The kingdom had other priorities: the thirty-something crown prince, Mohammad bin Salman (known as MBS), needed to woo the West and remove all obstacles to inheriting the throne from his father, just like the youthful and supposedly reform-minded heir Bashar twenty years before him.

Like the Assads over the decades, the Saudi royals hunted down their critics at home and abroad and in even more barbaric fashion sometimes, as happened with Saudi journalist and author Jamal Khashoggi later in 2018.[20]

As for Saudi Arabia's proxy wars with Iran, the focus shifted from Syria to Yemen, where children died from bombs, starvation, and disease in a country that also once joyously embraced the Arab Spring and chanted for freedom.[21]

Qatar, the wealthy emirate that championed the Arab Spring to further its agendas, pivoted toward both Iran and Turkey to stave off a trade and diplomatic boycott led by Saudi Arabia and also Egypt,[22] now ruled by a ruthless army general who banned free speech and tortured detainees in the name of fighting terrorism but was admired by Trump and feted by the leaders of Britain, France, and Germany.[23]

Britain, which had vigorously supported Bashar's opponents, reeled from one terror attack after another in 2017 in the heart of London and in the northern city of Manchester, while it wrestled with the looming consequences of its impending exit from the European Union.[24]

In France, where the Assads outlasted six presidents since Georges Pompidou, Emmanuel Macron, the boyish and charismatic president who took over in 2017, said that his country was no longer demanding Bashar's departure from power "out of pragmatism," even though it still considered him a war criminal who had to answer for his crimes.[25] Macron said that France's priority was to eradicate extremism and that it was up to Syrians to decide who was going to lead them.

In Germany, where Angela Merkel had called the decision to take in one million refugees in 2015 one of her nation's "crowning achieve- ments,"[26] a far-right nationalist party called the Alternative for Germany (in German, *Alternative für Deutschland* or AfD) scored significant wins in parliamentary elections held in the fall of 2017 on a platform of expelling Syrian and other refugees, who were blamed for crime and terror acts like the truck attack on a Christmas market in Berlin the year before.[27]

AfD lawmakers later traveled to Damascus to meet with Bashar's mufti, Hassoun, and other regime officials and to prove to their anti- immigrant constituency and Germans at large that the country was suffi- ciently safe to repatriate Syrians.[28]

The AfD delegation's regime-planned itinerary mirrored that of Dem- ocratic US congresswoman Tulsi Gabbard and former congressman and presidential candidate Dennis Kucinich, but the Americans had the bonus of meeting with Bashar, the purportedly secular leader and protector of Christians whom Gabbard said should be America's ally in the fight against "radical Islam."[29]

In the summer of 2017, as Trump banned Syrians and others from majority-Muslim countries from entering the United States and pressed ahead with his plans to build a wall along the Mexico border, white supremacists gathered at a rally in Charlottesville, Virginia. Some shouted, "Assad is the man, brother!" and vowed to "barrel bomb" their opponents in the United States just like Bashar did in Syria. One of them wore a black T-shirt with the caption "Bashar's Barrel Delivery."[30] Later a counterprotester was plowed down and killed by a driver who idolized Adolf Hitler.

Manaf Tlass greeted Trump's election with cautious optimism. He thought that perhaps the new American president—who admired Putin's strength, lavished him with praise, and dismissed allegations of having colluded with him to undermine his opponent, Hillary Clinton—was best suited to work with the Russians in Syria to revive the military council solution.

And naturally Manaf thought that there was still no better candidate than himself to lead this council, which would rule Syria on an interim basis and slowly ease Bashar out.

Only weeks before this sudden burst of optimism, Manaf had been consumed by anger, regret, and depression. He wondered whether he and his family had made the right decision to flee Syria and break with the Assads. He spoke of feeling trapped in a life largely dictated by who his father was and his family's history with the Assads.

"For forty years I have been trying to get out of this shit but I have not been able to!" he shouted as he walked one night down the busy Rue de Rennes next to his home.

Maybe he could have become a movie director, as he always dreamed, instead of an army general. He often sought respite from dwelling on his situation by going to the movies alone. Paris was a cinephile's paradise.[31]

Still, Manaf and his family were rather fortunate, considering the tragedies that befell many Syrians, who often lost everything.

The Tlasses got out alive, were living under the protection of the French state, and were able to preserve some of the wealth they had amassed under the Assads. And notwithstanding his bouts of despair, Manaf was still hoping to return to Syria, to the presidential palace no less.

Under Trump, Manaf's chances could not be better. Tough army generals and regime insiders across the Middle East were all being embraced by the West, enthusiastically or begrudgingly, as the best antidote to the region's dalliance with democracy and freedom at the start of the Arab Spring, which, as far as many were concerned, was what had spawned terror, wars, and a massive refugee crisis.

"The military council is our last hope to prevent the breakup of Syria and to separate all the belligerents from one another—otherwise we're headed toward a system of mandates by different world powers across Syria," said Manaf in the winter of 2017 as he strolled on the Boulevard Saint-Germain, past designer boutiques and famous outdoor cafés.[32]

"The Russians, Turks, and Iranians are formulating solutions to present to Trump," added Manaf.

By then, Putin was working with the Iranian and Turkish leaders to launch his peace plan in Syria that would, of course, guarantee everyone's respective interests. The Turks now cared less if Bashar remained in power as long as self-rule was denied to Syrian Kurds across the border.

The Iranians, meanwhile, wanted to reap dividends from seven years of shedding blood and treasure to save Bashar, which translated into wedding themselves to the regime's political, military, and economic power structure, something only Bashar and the Assads could guarantee.

As for Putin, he wanted the world, especially the West, to recognize him as the man who had saved humanity from the scourge of "Islamic terror."

The West had to get on its knees and admit that it had made a huge mistake in trying to weaken Russia after the fall of the Soviet Union, and of course keeping Russian military bases in Syria for many more years to come was one concrete way of projecting the might of the new Russia.

Incredibly, Trump assisted Putin in attaining these goals while regularly praising the Russian president's moves in Syria.[33]

Manaf and his Syrian allies had wasted no time in reaching out to Trump, through the Russian door. A month before Trump's election win, one of Manaf's friends and supporters, and a protégé of the Russians, Randa Kassis, met for lunch with Trump's son Don Jr. at the Ritz Carlton in Paris.[34] The crux of her message was that Moscow and Washington had to work together in Syria to save it from Islamist radicals and that Bashar's departure from power was not essential, at least not right away.

"But Bashar, Maher, and Rami won't give up so easily—they amassed a huge war chest and will fight until the end," said Manaf as he settled at a table at an outdoor café across from the Saint-Germain food market.[35]

"Iran, too—they have been investing in Bashar for more than fifteen years."

"Bashar al-Assad assassinated!" shouted a man cycling past the café.

"That's Ali, the guy I buy my newspapers from. He tells me this every time he sees me," explained Manaf with a pained smile.[36]

Bashar did not die. Instead, he emerged stronger and more defiant and vengeful as Russia led a campaign that eliminated opposition enclaves in Syria one by one and bolstered the regime's position at home and abroad. The war crimes that accompanied this effort and the additional thousands of civilians killed or displaced hardly seemed to matter.

On April 4, 2017, almost three years after the Organization for the Prohibition of Chemical Weapons (OPCW) announced that it had shipped and destroyed Syria's chemical weapons and won the Nobel Prize for it, and as the world did little to stop the regime's use of chlorine-filled munitions after that initial announcement, Bashar's warplanes attacked the opposition-held town of Khan Sheikhoun in Idlib province with the nerve agent sarin, killing at least ninety people, including thirty children.[37]

Enraged and pained by the murder of children and also eager to show that he was tougher than Obama, Trump ordered cruise missile strikes against the airfield in Homs province from which the Syrian planes had taken off, but the Russians alerted the regime to evacuate the airbase beforehand.[38]

A week later, Russia vetoed a Security Council resolution condemning the Khan Sheikhoun incident,[39] even as the regime's warplanes were again taking off from the same Homs airfield.[40] The world moved on, once more.

"I want us to understand — we are not living in an isolated epoch but one which is connected to preceding periods decades ago," a defiant Bashar said in a speech in Damascus in the summer of that year, alluding to a sort of continuum between his atrocities and those committed by Hafez.[41]

"It's true, we lost our best young people as well as infrastructure that cost us a lot of money and hard work, but in return we won a healthier and more homogenous society," he added. In other words, Bashar believed that the systematic elimination of all those who challenged his rule, or what he and his regime called the "cleansing campaign," was bearing fruit.

Then, after six years of trying to help the Syrian rebel cause, first through regional allies and then directly albeit covertly, hesitantly, and with deeply conflicting motives and goals, Washington pulled the plug on the whole effort — much to the delight of Bashar and his Iranian and Russian patrons.

In the summer of 2017, Trump formally ended the CIA-led program to arm and train rebels fighting Bashar,[42] and then he joined Russia in announcing ceasefires in the remaining opposition areas, which reverted to the regime one after another in horrendous bombing campaigns and surrender deals.[43]

Later, a joint OPCW-UN panel investigating the use of chemical weapons in Syria concluded that the Assad regime was responsible for the Khan Sheikhoun sarin attack,[44] a finding dismissed and ridiculed as a "joke" by Russia.[45]

It was as if the world was telling Bashar and his patrons: *we are with you in your quest to reassert regime authority over all of Syria but please do not be too bloody and if you must, then please do not use chemical weapons again.*

That same summer of 2017, Mustafa Tlass, the man who had accompanied Hafez from scrappy cadet to paramount ruler and who had killed in order to defend and protect the house of Assad, passed away.

The last images of him showed a frail but happy old man in a colorful woolen sweater playing with one of his great-grandchildren in the cozy living room of his daughter Nahed's Parisian apartment.[46]

The Tlasses thought of burying the family patriarch in his hometown of Al-Rastan, as he would have liked. Bashar still respected the elder Tlass and believed that the family's decision to leave Syria had been mainly Manaf's. It was the same way that Manaf still considered Hafez "sacred" despite his split with Bashar.

In the end, the Tlasses concluded that it was "too problematic," as Manaf put it, to bury his father in Syria — reaching Al-Rastan would have to be facilitated by Bashar, plus many of the rebels inside Al-Rastan despised the Tlasses.[47]

Mustafa Tlass was buried in Paris instead.

From a cottage in a town outside Paris surrounded by forests, Khaled al-Khani, the painter who had lost his father and childhood home during the 1982 Hama massacre ordered by Hafez and approved by Mustafa Tlass as defense minister, watched history more or less repeat itself.[48]

In every area reverting to regime control, residents had to chant for Bashar, thank the army for liberating them, and tell TV cameras that it was the terrorists and not Bashar and his allies who dropped bombs on them, killed their children, starved them into submission, and looted and burned their homes — exactly what Khaled and his family and the others who returned to Hama after the 1982 massacre had had to endure.

Like those under Hafez, Syrians under Bashar once more had no choice but to live with the regime's lies as the Assad's reign of fear and terror was reinstated with more vigor.

In the first four months of 2018, almost 2,500 civilians were killed in the Eastern Ghouta near Damascus,[49] the same area Bashar had gassed with impunity in 2013.

The world looked on as the Russians and Iranians helped Bashar retake the area. Putin raved about having tested more than 200 weapons in Syria,[50] including air-dropped incendiary munitions that burned their victims in Ghouta alive[51] while Iran supplied Bashar with artillery shells filled with chlorine-like substances that, on at least six occasions, poisoned Ghouta's people to death.[52]

A bomb filled with similar chemicals was dropped from an aircraft in early April 2018, killing almost fifty people. The United States and its allies responded with airstrikes against the regime's chemical weapons facilities, but it hardly mattered as Bashar and his patrons entered Ghouta triumphantly while cowed and terrified civilians chanted for Bashar and Putin.[53]

"Everyone is exhausted and fearful," said a man in Damascus. "We must surrender to the fact that there's nothing we can do if the entire world wants Bashar to stay."[54]

Not everyone though was willing to surrender and keep silent. Bashar could declare victory, but for many Syrians nothing would ever be the same because they themselves were not the same.

One major difference from Hafez's era and the 1980s was that, after the 2011 revolt, hundreds of thousands of Syrians forever set themselves free from deception, indignity, and fear — they were unchained from five decades of Assad family rule.

There was no turning back for these Syrians. They spoke out in every way—art, film, public advocacy, politics, theater, and words—and silencing them all would be impossible. They were like birds who were roaming the world and hoped one day to return home.

After a period of depression and major health complications, Khaled was recovering, painting more furiously, and expressing himself in ways he had never done before. His friends, now scattered all over the world, came to visit.[55] They shared tastes and memories of home as Khaled cooked dishes like *mloukhiyeh* (a stew of greens with chicken and rice) and *makloubeh* (layers of rice, eggplant, and beef) in his kitchen in the French countryside.

Like many Syrians, Khaled wanted justice for all the crimes committed by the Assad family. He made a public appeal on Facebook to Syrians to come forward and join him as codefendants or witnesses in a case brought by a Swiss-based legal advocacy group against Bashar's exiled uncle, Rifaat, for his role in the 1982 Hama massacre and other war crimes.[56]

The group Trial International submitted significant evidence to the Swiss attorney general, but there had been barely any advance in the case.[57] Publicizing the lawsuit could spur Switzerland to take the case more seriously, especially after Rifaat's assets in Britain, France, and Spain were frozen and charges of tax fraud and embezzlement were brought against him in France in early 2017.[58]

But making the case for justice and convincing the world that they had as much of a stake as Syrians, if not more, in seeing Bashar tried and punished for his war crimes was not going to be so easy.

"The Americans, Russians, and Iranians can liberate Mosul, Raqqa, and Deir Ezzour and declare victory over the Islamic State, but without justice and accountability, a change in the political system, and coming to terms with the legacy of the past fifty years, count six months or one to two years and you will have something worse than Islamic State," said Mazen Darwish, sitting in the Berlin apartment he shared with his wife and associate, Yara Bader.[59]

"If they want to repatriate refugees and stop the exodus of new ones there must be justice and guarantees for people to return. Can we go back if the same organs, regime, and people remain in place? The same police state with the same sectarian, gang-like, and mafia mind-set? People—and myself included—won't return unless there's change. Going back would be like committing suicide."

The ashtray in front of him was already overflowing as he smoked cigarettes and sipped bitter Turkish coffee. In the living room there were reminders of the Damascus he sorely missed. On the walls were small framed photographs of scenes from old Damascus. A little girl standing in the sun at the entrance of a traditional Damascene house with an arched entrance built of black and white stones. Elderly men playing backgammon at an outdoor coffee shop.

Next to the window was a cluster of potted plants, including a small one bearing shiny lemons, evoking the citrus trees that Damascenes were fond of growing in the courtyards of old homes.

Mazen and Yara had arrived in Berlin on November 9, 2015, on the anniversary of the day the wall fell in 1989.

For months, Mazen obsessed that his stay in Germany was temporary and that he had to return soon to advocate for the release of his friends and fellow activists who remained in Bashar's prisons.

He got little sleep at night, and even when he did it was fitful. Sometimes he trembled so violently in his sleep that his wife had to wake him up. For a while he had trouble being in crowded places and was uncomfortable looking people in the eye. Once he was smoking next to the window when a chopper flew by at a low altitude. His immediate reflex was to jump away and cower behind the sofa.

In early winter 2016, he made the mistake of agreeing to an interview with a German news channel that was filmed inside the main prison complex operated by the State Security Service, or Stasi, of the defunct German Democratic Republic (GDR).

After reunification, the detention facilities located in what was once a restricted zone of Berlin's Hohenschönhausen district became a memorial and reminder of the horrors of the past. Everything was kept intact—the high wall, barbed-wire fence, and watchtowers that ringed the sprawling compound, the filthy and peeling wallpaper of the interrogation rooms where confessions were extracted, the prisoner uniforms and toilet pails.[60]

While the GDR's crimes paled in comparison to those of the Assads, and the Stasi's prison complex looked like a holiday retreat compared with the *mukhabarat*'s dungeons, Mazen had flashbacks and could barely breathe at one point, especially in an underground section called the "U-Boot," or submarine.[61]

To get there, he had to go down a flight of stairs, beneath which was what Germans called a "crawling cell"—exactly like the one in which Mazen had once found himself, lying over a lifeless body after he passed out from torture. The crypt-like underground prison consisted of rows of sixty damp solitary-confinement cells behind gray steel doors with small openings.

After that experience, Mazen was finally convinced he needed therapy.

His situation improved, but as for so many traumatized Syrians it was going to take him years to come to grips with what he had been through. One way of healing was perhaps going back to doing what he was most passionate about.

Toward the end of 2016, he received a grant from his Danish NGO partner to relaunch the Syrian Center for Media and Freedom of Expression in Berlin, almost five years after the *mukhabarat* raided the office in Damascus and hauled him and his team to prison.

The following year and around the sixth anniversary of what he and many Syrians still called the revolution, Mazen and a small team, including Yara, moved into an office on one of Berlin's many colorful streets.

Their focus was Mazen's advocacy for accountability and justice, but they broadened their work to include supporting and training independent Syrian journalists and combating hate speech.

One of the first things Mazen did was to plaster an empty wall with photographs of his missing colleagues Razan Zeitouneh, Khalil Maatouq, and others.[62] (Razan, her husband, and two of their colleagues were kidnapped at the end of 2013 in Douma, when it was still under rebel control.)

Later, in a groundbreaking move that could potentially shatter nearly half a century of Assad regime impunity, seven Syrian plaintiffs joined forces with Mazen's center, his fellow Syrian human rights lawyer and former prisoner Anwar al-Buni, and the Berlin-based European Center for Constitutional and Human Rights to file a complaint in March 2017 with the German Federal Public Prosecutor against several *mukhabarat* chiefs and officers. (Germany is one of the few countries that applies the principle of universal jurisdiction.)

Two months later, the federal prosecutor in Karlsruhe — a city in southwest Germany where more than 1,000 Jews perished in Nazi purges between 1933 and 1945 — heard the testimony of Mazen, Anwar, and a dozen or so Syrian witnesses and survivors of torture.[63] The next step was for Germany's chief federal prosecutor to issue arrest warrants for the defendants.

Additional cases against the *mukhabarat* were filed later that year, and the federal prosecutor was also given high resolution images and metadata of the photographs taken by the defected Syrian military photographer code-named Caesar. This was the first time this had happened since the world was horrified at the start of 2014 by the gruesome photographs of thousands of corpses of those tortured, starved, and mutilated at *mukhabarat* prisons between 2011 and 2013.[64]

Syria was not a signatory to the treaty that established the International Criminal Court dealing with war crimes and crimes against humanity, and referral to the ICC by the UN Security Council was not an option, either, as long as China and Russia shielded Bashar.

A UN commission had been investigating war crimes in Syria since August 2011, and a French judge was appointed by the secretary general in 2017 to head a team to collect and preserve the evidence[65] — testimonies of more than 5,200 witnesses and victims; photographs, videos, medical and forensic reports, satellite imagery, and even a list of suspected war criminals[66] believed to include Bashar and key members of his family and regime. But no action could be taken, so the only path forward left for Mazen and his colleagues was to explore other avenues to justice and build cases against the regime in European courts in the hope that this could exert sufficient pressure on those blocking a Security Council referral to change their minds.

The road to justice, though, was filled with many challenges and perils.

In the summer of 2017, a Spanish judge rejected a case brought by a Syrian woman with Spanish citizenship under the principle of universal jurisdiction against regime *mukhabarat* chiefs for the arrest, torture, and execution of her brother. She had found his picture among the tens of thousands of images smuggled out by Caesar.[67]

These legal setbacks came amid a major shift in mood in Europe and around the world as many leaders increasingly viewed the situation in Syria as simply a civil war that had to end with a political settlement and compromise by all sides so that the focus could continue to be on combating Islamist extremists and stemming the flow of refugees—the twin menaces and priorities for the European continent.

The attitude seemed to be that if Bashar, a man once labeled a war criminal by some Western leaders, remaining in power and facing no prosecution for his atrocities was somehow going to keep terrorists and refugees at bay, then the tradeoff was acceptable.

"It does not matter who's the victim and who's the executioner. Today what's important is for Syrians to find a way to live with each other," Lilianne Ploumen, the Dutch minister for foreign trade and development cooperation, told Mazen during a meeting in the spring of 2016.[68]

Mazen then argued to Germany's embattled chancellor, Angela Merkel, that Europe had to stop viewing the situation in Syria through the binary of either Bashar or Islamic State/refugees, and that it was time for an overhaul in strategy to give priority to justice and the country's democratic, independent, and nonviolent forces.

They were both laureates of the Roosevelt Foundation's prestigious Four Freedoms Awards, based on a historic speech by Franklin D. Roosevelt in 1941.[69]

"I can't do more for Syria...My advice to you is to see Putin," Merkel told Mazen.

Putin's solution was for Syrians to forget what Bashar had done to them and work with him and his regime to draft a new constitution and hold elections—in which Bashar, of course, could run.[70]

"There won't be peace if you want to put the justice and accountability file on the table. You must choose: accountability or peace," Staffan de Mistura, the UN Syria envoy tasked with mediating between the regime and opposition (effectively under the auspices of the Russians), told Mazen during a meeting in Geneva.[71]

De Mistura was the man Putin hoped would put the stamp of approval on his peace plan. He eventually quit.[72]

Later, Mazen started receiving threatening messages on his cell phone from regime loyalists.

"You think you're secure in Germany? We can reach you wherever you are and crush you under our feet...Just wait—we're going to make an example out of you for the whole world," one of them read.[73]

In June 2018, Germany's federal prosecutor issued an arrest warrant for Jamil Hassan, the director of the *mukhabarat*'s Air Force Intelligence Directorate and one of Bashar's main inner-circle henchmen.[74] He had personally interrogated Mazen, mocked his work as a human rights lawyer, and ordered his torture. It was a big step forward for justice.

But then that same month came a particularly brazen message from Bashar, Hassan, and other suspected regime war criminals: *We killed you, tortured you, gassed you, displaced you, destroyed your lives, and now we are admitting to the whole world we did it, but you'll never be able to get us.*

In the summer of 2018, the *mukhabarat* and the army began issuing official death notices for thousands of activists and protesters tortured to death in dungeons and prisons or hanged by military tribunals.[75]

Among them were nearly two dozen of Mazen's best friends, including fellow activists from the town of Daraya near Damascus who had handed out roses and bottles of water to the forces that Bashar sent to assault them in the spring and summer of 2011.

Those calling for Bashar's ouster by peaceful means had to die, but Bashar was perfectly happy to work out surrender and repatriation deals with those who bore arms against him, as he did that same summer with Russia's help and the blessing of his neighbors Jordan and Israel.

The regime reclaimed areas in southern Syria that included the city of Daraa, where Bashar had killed the first protesters in March 2011. Bashar's forces planted flags in the exact same spot across from Israel where Hafez had once celebrated his false victory over the Jewish state.[76]

Hafez won "the liberation war" and Bashar won "the cleansing war," announced the state broadcaster verbatim from Damascus.

The Israelis, who played a pivotal behind-the-scenes role in Syria, liaised with both Trump and Putin and let it be known that they were fine with Bashar as long as he kept his allies Iran and Hezbollah away from the southern border.[77]

That summer, Putin also launched a plan to rebuild Syria and repatriate

Syrians in Europe and countries like Lebanon and Turkey, but he wanted the West to foot the bill and deal with Bashar as the legitimate leader of his country.

Bashar would also get to choose who could return—and how, and when—to devastated and destroyed towns and cities like Daraa, Daraya, Homs, and others, according to the Russian plan.[78]

This applied to the Tlasses' hometown of Al-Rastan, which was among the first to take up arms against Bashar and sought to rid itself of what many of its residents regarded as the stigma of the Assad-Tlass partnership. The town surrendered that same summer in a deal brokered by the Russian army.

Those that rejected the deal moved to the last rebel-held enclaves in northern Syria while the ones that stayed had no choice but to plead with the Tlasses to use their influence with the Russians to prevent Bashar's forces from entering the town because they feared arrest or death. Nahed Tlass managed to get them a six-month reprieve.

"Do not worry, the six months can be extended. I am ready to vouch for the Russians for sixty years, not just six months," Nahed told some of the townspeople she spoke to by telephone from Paris.[79]

Manaf largely stayed out of the negotiations.[80]

Less than six months later, Al-Rastan high school students chanted "For your eyes, Bashar!" as desperate and hungry townspeople gathered to receive food rations distributed by Russian and Syrian regime soldiers.[81] The regime did return to Al-Rastan, the same town that had smashed Hafez's statue in the first few weeks of the uprising against the Assads.

As Bashar set out to reinstate the facade of his government and state institutions, his first priority was to rebuild his army. But few wanted to serve, including those who voiced their admiration and support for him. Instead, young men wanted for compulsory military service continued to flee to Lebanon or farther afield.[82]

Can the Assads' kingdom of lies, fear, and terror ever truly reassert itself? It was one of many unanswered questions as 2018 came to a close.

Bashar could declare victory—but at what price and under what conditions? He could lean on his longtime patron Iran to push back at the dictates and agendas of his other patron, Russia—but for how long?

Many Iranians, though, began to wonder why their government was backing a war criminal and mass murderer,[83] and maybe Russians would at some point wonder the same.

Even Bashar's own Alawite community still wanted him to account for the tens of thousands killed or missing in defense of the Assads,[84] while warlords and militia leaders who helped save his regime were not willing to just quietly fade into the background.[85]

"Intra-Alawite discord is what Bashar fears the most," said Manaf.[86]

Despite all the vulnerabilities, 2018 ended with Bashar never more confident in his own staying power and the longevity of his family's reign, which was nearing the half-century mark.

Trump announced he was withdrawing about two thousand US soldiers from eastern Syria because the Islamic State was supposedly defeated, leaving Putin as the country's uncontested power broker.[87]

There were no signs that Putin was going to abandon Bashar as the region's other brutal autocrats, who also survived the Arab Spring, rushed to embrace Bashar again.[88]

Trump even spoke of the possibility that his Saudi allies would help Bashar and the Russians rebuild Syria.[89]

Manaf still hoped for a turnaround in his fortunes somehow, even if it seemed far-fetched.

"I would go back to Syria. I want salvation for my country," he said sitting on a bench in a sun-drenched Place Saint-Sulpice. "But on condition that neither security nor military power is in his [Bashar's] hands. I have no problem to be with him [Bashar] if he abides by these conditions and submits to the will of the people."[90]

The people, though, still had a problem with Bashar.

The fight to end the Assad family's rule was hardly over yet for people like Mazen, Khaled, the Daraa activist Sally Masalmeh, and hundreds of thousands of other Syrians.

Their quest for liberty, freedom, and dignity was no different from the long and painful struggles of the past century: the civil rights movement in the United States, the dismantling of apartheid in South Africa, or the overthrow of despots in Eastern Europe.

"They are trying to bury us, but they do not know we're the seeds of a revolution," wrote Sally on her Facebook page as she watched the regime retake what she and others had called the liberated zone of Daraa.[91]

Sally and her husband, Malek, had settled in the Baltic Sea island of Rügen, which had been part of the former East Germany before reunification. It was a world away from Daraa and Syria in every sense.

This was a landscape of windswept pebble beaches, shoreline dunes, dramatic white chalk cliffs, inland forests, and a series of brackish water lagoons that the Germans called *Bodden*.[92]

Except for a brief summer, it was a desolate and cold place draped in snow most of the winter. Sally and Malek settled in the island's main town, Bergen. Under their asylum arrangements, they received a housing allowance and a monthly stipend in return for studying the German language and civics and then finding work, all part of the so-called integration process for refugees.

They moved into a small apartment in a *Plattenbau* with a balcony overlooking an empty field on the edge of the old cobblestone-paved town center. (*Plattenbauten* are boxy East German–era public housing buildings made of prefabricated brown-and-sand-colored concrete slabs.)

They livened up the whitewashed interior with a red carpet, a framed poster of Van Gogh's "Sunflowers," colorful curtains, and little mementos from home like worry beads and a small hookah.[93]

They immersed themselves in their German language courses. Malek began to work, while Sally prepared to go to college.

"My body is here, but my soul is still in Syria," said Sally as she wiped away her tears.

In the evening, a neighbor, another refugee from the province of Idlib, came over with his oud. He picked out a melody as Sally sang a popular revolutionary song from her native Houran region, while Malek listened quietly.

"*I walk with pride on your rose petal-covered streets / I carve your name on my eyelids, to Houran, to Houran,*" sang Sally. "*My people, your deliverance is near / Your defiance has mesmerized the world / Bashar, shoot your guns, to Houran, to Houran / We are up to the challenge / The revolution started here and I won't settle for anything less than your death sentence, Bashar.*"[94]

Note on Characters

first met Bashar's friend and companion Manaf Tlass in October 2014, more than two years after his defection. We stayed in touch and met again a few times in early 2016 and in the summer of that same year. I was in Paris from October 2016 until January 2017, a period during which many of my interviews with Manaf took place, either in the apartment I was renting or at his favorite spot, outdoors in the Luxembourg Gardens. Manaf's dialogues with Bashar, recounted here by me, are based on Manaf's memories and recollections, but everything he told me was verified and cross-checked with others — relatives, friends, acquaintances, former regime associates, and others he had interacted with inside and outside Syria. I conducted many long interviews with these sources — corroborating Manaf's version of events — over different periods in France, Germany, Jordan, Lebanon, Qatar, Turkey, and the United Kingdom. Many of those with whom I spoke were not particularly sympathetic to Manaf and his family, and some even held the Tlasses to be just as responsible as the Assads for the misfortune of Syria and its people.

By agreeing to talk to me, after much hesitation and many abrupt changes of heart, and despite strong opposition by his wife, Thala, Manaf may have been motivated by a desire to be better understood by those Syrians who still see him, his father, and his family as being complicit in the Assads' crimes over the decades. Notwithstanding Manaf's agenda, leadership aspirations, and pretensions, as well as the circumstances that drove him and his family to break with the Assads, I am absolutely certain about one thing: his choice not to take part in the killing of protesters at the start of the uprising in 2011 and during the regime's subsequent military operations was motivated by genuine moral concerns. It's worth noting

461

that the portrayals and scenes that take place after Manaf's exit from Syria in the summer of 2012 were informed by my reporting for the *Wall Street Journal* and my own conversations and experiences, in addition to eyewitness accounts from inside Syria.

I first met Khaled al-Khani in Paris in the fall of 2014. There was a lot of pain during many of our conversations but also passion, warmth, generosity, humor, brutal honesty, and delicious Hama dishes cooked by Khaled. I first spoke to Sally Masalmeh over Skype in the fall of 2015; I was in Jordan and she and her husband Malek were in a camp for Syrian asylum seekers in Germany. We met in early 2017 and then again in the summer of 2017 when I visited them on the island of Rügen in the Baltic Sea. Both times they insisted, as is the custom in their native Houran region, that I stay with them in their small apartment, filled with memories of their native Daraa and their *thawra*, or revolution.

Finally, my first meeting with Mazen Darwish was in Berlin in the winter of 2016–17, a little over a year after he and his wife, Yara Bader, left Syria. Both graciously received me in their apartment and patiently put up with hours of interviews and questions. There were more meetings in the summer of 2017 and winter of 2018. These were Mazen's first in-depth reflections and conversations about his time in prison, his interactions with the Assad regime, and the new Syria that he and his friends and colleagues dreamt of and strove so patiently and courageously to forge at the start of the Arab Spring. "If the regime considers this a conspiracy, then yes, I am a proud co-conspirator," he often told me. He paid a heavy price for his efforts—and some of his best friends paid an even heavier price—but he has remained committed to peaceful resistance and is now one of the lead lawyers in the cases being heard in European courts against members of the Assad family and their henchmen.

I tried several times to interview Bashar al-Assad when I was reporting from inside Syria. After the damning portrait sketched by my sources, I thought the opposing perspective would better contribute to the journalistic record. My formal requests, which had to be faxed to the Ministry of Information and the presidential palace, were ignored at first. Then, finally, one day I received a call from someone in Bashar's office telling me that they were sending a car to bring me to the palace in order to discuss my many pending requests. I was met by a young and articulate member of the Assads' savvy media team who basically offered this deal: to increase my chances of securing a one-on-one with the president I should consider writing about the "amazing" work of Bashar's wife, Asma, which has been uninterrupted by war, as the aide put it. "For sure it would be interesting to know more about the first lady's work," was my answer. Later, any chance of interviewing Bashar evaporated when I dared to report the facts about his sham presidential elections in 2014—piercing that lie annoyed his image makers more than anything else that I had written about the regime's massacres and atrocities. "You offended God," one Syrian friend told me.

Acknowledgments

Several women in different countries were crucial in all stages of creating this book—from initial idea and proposal to research and writing and final production. I am grateful to all of them. I am also grateful to Manaf Tlass, Mazen Darwish, Khaled al-Khani, Sally Masalmeh, and the more than fifty people—most of them Syrians scattered all over the world—for agreeing to participate in many interviews and re-interviews.

I have to thank Caroline Ayoub for her early collaboration and unwavering support throughout. Her courage and commitment to coexistence and a new Syria were inspirational. "Syrians speak ten languages now, nothing can stop them," she told me in 2019. Thanks to Lina Sinjab for introducing me to Caroline and reminding me what I should be looking for to better understand Syria.

In Damascus, I am indebted to all the Syrians who helped me in every way do my work and stay safe while I was based there as a reporter for almost two years. I know I can't mention your names for security reasons but I am absolutely certain that sooner or later you'll "come out to the sun, light, and freedom," as the Fairuz song promises. I owe so much to my Damascus-based research assistant, who took immense personal risks by agreeing to work with me after I was expelled by the regime.

In Lebanon, I am thankful to Malek Mrowa for helping me secure an interview that was vital for some of the depictions of the early years of the Assad children.

In Turkey, I am especially thankful to Isam al-Rayyes, as well as the contributions and insights of Suhair al-Atassi, Mohammad Munir al-Faqir, Khaled Khoja, Riad Seif, Diab Serriya, Oubai Shahbandar,

Mohammad Farouk Tayfour, and many others. I also need to thank Fadi Ahmad for all his assistance in the Syrian-Turkish border zone.

In Qatar, sheiks Moaz al-Khatib and Ahmed al-Sayasneh shed light on key moments of the Syrian struggle for dignity and freedom.

In Jordan, Suha Ma'ayeh and Wajd Dehne provided invaluable assistance.

In Paris, I am immensely grateful to Joseph Bahout, Michel Duclos, and Isabelle Hausser for their contributions, insights, and all their generous assistance in securing key interviews. I need to thank Éric Chevallier for taking the time during a family holiday as well as a diplomatic crisis situation in Qatar to shine light on so many crucial moments of this narrative with honesty and above all humanity. I will forever treasure the hours spent with Burhan Ghalyoun talking Syria, past and present, as well as the prescient insights of Ghassan Salamé on the Assads, Arab Spring, and curse of the Middle East's "neo-patrimonial" regimes. Many thanks also for the contributions of Ammar Abd Rabbo, Khattar Abou-Diab, Shadi Abufakher, Ayman al-Aswad, Laurent Fabius, Michel Kilo, Noureddin Labbad, Georges Malbrunot, Haitham al-Manaa, Bernard Pêcheur, Bilal Zaiter, and others who wished to remain anonymous. And thanks to Tammam al-Omar for the powerful book cover.

In Berlin, I learned a lot from Anwar al-Bunni and Joumana Seif about life for the hundreds of thousands of Syrians who sought refuge in Germany and the courageous quest by some of them to hold the Assad family accountable for its crimes. Ayham Majid-Agha graciously hosted me at his home to speak about the Syrian spirit and character, and Manuela Zahradnik made it possible for me to sit in on a German-language class for Syrian refugees.

In London, I must thank Rana Kabbani and Damian Quinn for pointing me in the right direction and helping me secure key interviews.

Before the book, I had the privilege of working at the *Wall Street Journal* with a talented and incredibly devoted team of editors and reporters on covering Syria and the Arab Spring, one of the most consequential stories of our time. I am indebted to my former editor Bill Spindle for his fortitude and unflinching support during some of the darkest hours. I will also

Acknowledgments

never forget the colleagues who put their hearts and souls into telling Syria's story: the great Nour Alak (aka Jimmy), Nour Malas, Rima Abushakra, Rudeynah Baalbaky, Dana Ballout, Maria Abi-Habib, Raja Abdulrahim, Carole Alfarah, Farnaz Fassihi, Joe Parkinson, Ayla Albayrak, and many others across the region and the world, including Jill Kirschenbaum and Sarah Slobin.

At the *Journal*, I owe special thanks to Sam Enriquez for his patience and empathy while editing my stories from Syria and for pushing me to write this book.

I am lucky to be published by Reagan Arthur, who believed in the book's importance. I am equally fortunate to have collaborated with Little, Brown's talented executive editor Vanessa Mobley; her profound empathy, thoughtful edits, and sure-handed guidance made all the difference. Thanks also to Ira Boudah, Sareena Kamath, Lena Little, Mario Pulice, and many others at Little, Brown.

I am also deeply grateful to Michael Noon (aka Abu Phin) at Little, Brown's managing editorial department and his colleagues, especially Michael Fleming and Melissa Mathlin, for all their heroic efforts.

I can't imagine this book ever coming to life without my amazing literary agent, Christy Fletcher; her guidance and support through every aspect of the process were indispensable. I must also thank Sarah Fuentes at Fletcher & Co. for commenting on and editing an early draft.

Finally, I need to thank all my friends for their encouragement and support, including but not limited to the following: Nisar for pushing me to just sit down and write, Uffe and Silvan for hosting me in Berlin, Nayla for hosting me in New York and surrounding me with her love, Zina for hearing me out and offering very sound advice, Nadim and Claude for the wonderful breaks from writing, Laurent for the Paris breaks, and Frank for the hiking trips.

Of course nothing would have been possible without the unconditional love and support of my family in the United States.

Notes

Introduction

1. United Nations Secretary-General, "Note to Correspondents: Transcript of Press Stakeout by United Nations Special Envoy for Syria, Mr. Staffan de Mistura," United Nations official website, April 22, 2016, https://www.un.org/sg/en/content/sg/note-correspondents/2016 -04-22/note-correspondents-transcript-press-stakeout-united.
2. Marc Bennetts, "Putin: Syria War Is Priceless for Testing Our New Weapons," (London) *Times*, June 8, 2018, www.thetimes.co.uk/article/putin-syria-war-is-priceless-for-testing -our-new-weapons-qkz3qsdqw.
3. Amnesty International, "Human Slaughterhouse: Mass Hangings and Extermination at Saydnaya Prison," February 7, 2017, www.amnesty.org/download/Documents/MDE2454 152017ENGLISH.PDF.
4. Garance le Caisne, "They Were Torturing to Kill: Inside Syria's Death Machine," *The Guardian*, October 1, 2015, www.theguardian.com/world/2015/oct/01/they-were-torturing-to -kill-inside-syrias-death-machine-caesar.
5. Phillip Connor, "Most Displaced Syrians Are in the Middle East, and About a Million Are in Europe," Pew Research Center, January 29, 2018, www.pewresearch.org/fact-tank/ 2018/01/29/where-displaced-syrians-have-resettled/.
6. Étienne de La Boétie, *Discours de la Servitude Volontaire*, originally published as *Le Contr'un* (*The Against-One*) in Paris in 1576 (Paris: Gaillmard, 2016).
7. Marjorie Miller and John Daniszewski, "Mourners Say Goodbye to Syria's 'Lion,'" *Los Angeles Times*, June 14, 2000, http://articles.latimes.com/2000/jun/14/news/mn-40864.
8. Michel Duclos, in discussion with the author, November 2016.

Chapter 1 You're Next, Doctor

1. "The Biggest Syrian Flag Flutters from Highest Pole," *DP News*, July 7, 2010, accessed February 7, 2016, www.dp-news.com/pages/detail.aspx?articleid=45921. The flag was the idea of Rami Makhlouf, Bashar al-Assad's cousin and Syria's most powerful businessman.
2. Manaf Tlass, in discussion with the author, January 2016.
3. Ibid., October 2014.
4. Ibid.
5. Michel Kilo, in discussion with the author, October 2014. "Mr. Michel, do you know what we'll do if, God forbid, people in Syria take to the streets and demand the regime's downfall?" a *mukhabarat* general quizzed Kilo, a sixty-year-old former communist and literary figure who translated the works of German philosophers. He was among those jailed in the early 1980s during Hafez's reign and a second time in 2006 under Bashar. "You'll

crush the protests," responded Kilo. "Actually, nothing will be left standing in Syria, not even a stone on top of another—nothing!" said the general.

6. Jay Solomon and Bill Spindle, "Syria Strongman: Time for 'Reform,'" *Wall Street Journal*, January 31, 2011.

7. "Excerpts from Mrs. Al-Assad's Statements," President Bashar al-Assad official website, accessed February 8, 2017, www.presidentassad.net/index.php?option=com_content&vie w=category&layout=blog&id=165&Itemid=487.

8. Omar Abdelaziz Hallaj (former chief executive officer, Syria Trust for Development), in discussion with the author, September 2014.

9. Friend of Assad and Tlass families, in discussion with the author, November 2016.

10. Manaf Tlass, October 2014.

11. Ibid.

12. Human Rights Watch, *Egypt-Inspired Protests across Middle East Meet Violent Clampdown*, February 8, 2011, accessed February 18, 2017, www.hrw.org/news/2011/02/08/egypt-inspired -protests-across-middle-east-meet-violent-clampdown.

13. Shadi Abufakher, in discussion with the author, July 2017.

14. Facebook page for "Toward Popular Mobilization in Syria, Day of Rage February 5, 2011," accessed February 18, 2016. www.facebook.com/syriarageday25.2.2011/.

15. Mazen Darwish, in discussion with the author, December 2016.

16. "Imad Nasab Recounts Details of What Happened in Hariqa," *Zaman Al Wsl* sourced to *Al-Watan* newspaper, February 22, 2011, accessed February 18, 2017, www.zamanalwsl .net/news/18452.html.

17. Moaz al-Khatib, in discussion with the author, July 2017.

18. "Muammar Gaddafi's Full Speech," YouTube video, 1:15:15, posted by "Web7269," September 19, 2012, www.youtube.com/watch?v=pfCNfMUgbU4.

19. Kareem Fahim and David Kirkpatrick, "Qaddafi's Grip on the Capital Tightens as Revolt Grows," *New York Times*, February 22, 2011, www.nytimes.com/2011/02/23/world/ africa/23libya.html?pagewanted=all&_r=0.

20. "Muammar Gaddafi's Full Speech."

21. Ayham Majid-Agha, in discussion with the author, July 2017. Majid-Agha and others present that day said the *mukhabarat* mobilized large buses and even a delivery van belonging to Ghrawi, a nearby fancy chocolates boutique, to block access to the Libyan embassy.

22. "Syrians Protest Ghaddafi at Madfaa Square Damascus Feb. 24, 2011," YouTube video, 4:08, posted by "Syrian Heart," February 24, 2011, www.youtube.com/watch?v=dhXzZLhQTYk.

23. Gaelle Raphael, "Al-Shabbi's 'The Will To Life,'" *Jadaliyya.com*, May 1, 2011, http://www .jadaliyya.com/Details/23935/Al-Shabbi%60s-The-Will-to-Life.

24. Khaled al-Khani, in discussion with the author, October 2014.

25. Ibid.

26. Amnesty International, *Report from Amnesty International to the Government of the Syrian Arab Republic*, November 1, 1983, accessed January 25, 2018, www.amnesty.org/en/documents/ mde24/004/1983/en/.

27. Hama countryside Christian, in discussion with the author, April 2018.

28. Darwish, July 2017.

29. Human Rights Watch, *Group Denial: Repression of Kurdish Political and Cultural Rights in Syria*, November 2009, accessed February 18, 2017, www.hrw.org/sites/default/files/reports/ syria1109webwcover_0.pdf.

30. Human Rights Watch, *Syria: Investigate Security Force Shooting of Kurds*, March 26, 2010, accessed February 18, 2017 www.hrw.org/news/2010/03/26/syria-investigate-security -force-shooting-kurds.

31. Darwish, December 2016. Mazen was summoned to the *mukhabarat* in February 2011. He was quizzed about the timing and date of any possible protests.

32. Souad Jarous, "Assad Issues General Amnesty to Prisoners…Political Prisoners Not Included," *Asharq Al-Awsat*, March 8, 2011, http://archive.aawsat.com/details.asp?section=4&issueno=11788&article=611520#.WKh5txhh2T9.

33. Darwish, December 2016.

34. Ibid.

35. "Protest at Ministry of Interior, March 16, 2011," YouTube video, 1:03, posted by "Zaina Erhaim," April 1, 2011, www.youtube.com/watch?v=iMi67_IzU-E.

36. Manaf Tlass, October 2016.

37. Tlass family friend who was regularly invited to the mountain house, in discussion with the author, December 2015.

38. Manaf Tlass, October 2014.

39. Ayman al-Aswad, in discussion with the author, November 2016.

40. Manaf Tlass, October 2014.

Chapter 2 Embracing the Clouds

1. The military academy was founded by the French in 1921 and was based in Damascus until it moved to Homs in 1932. Until 1945, its recruits were from both Lebanon and Syria.

2. Nadine Méouchy, in discussion with the author, March 2018.

3. It was common at the time for well-to-do families in the big Levantine cities like Aleppo, Beirut and Damascus to have a live-in Alawite maid. It was a class-minded society, and Alawites were relegated to the lower rung.

4. Mustafa Tlass, *Mira'at Hayati: Al-Aqed Al-Awal 1948–1958, Al-Nidhal* [*My Life's Mirror: The First Decade 1948–1958, The Struggle*] (Damascus: Dar Tlass, 2006), 157. Author's translation.

5. Ibid., 47.

6. Ibid., 175.

7. The founders were Michel Aflaq, a Greek Orthodox Christian and Salaheddin Bitar, a Sunni Muslim.

8. Tlass, *Mira'at Hayati: Al-Aqed Al-Awal 1948–1958*, 277. Author's translation.

9. Mustafa Tlass, interview by Ghassan Charbel, *Al-Wasat Magazine*, June 19, 2000, 438.

10. Tlass, *Mira'at Hayati: Al-Aqed Al-Awal 1948–1958*, 283. Author's translation.

11. Ibid., 285.

12. Ibid., 290.

13. Ben Fenton, "Macmillan Backed Syria Assassination Plot," *The Guardian*, September 27, 2003, www.theguardian.com/politics/2003/sep/27/uk.syria1.

14. Tlass, *Mira'at Hayati: Al-Aqed Al-Awal 1948–1958*, 655. Author's translation.

15. General CIA Records, "Activities of the Communist Party in Aleppo and Northern Syria," January 19, 1949, declassified February 2, 1999, accessed January 25, 2018, www.cia.gov/library/readingroom/document/cia-rdp82-00457r002200580009-9.

16. Patrick Seale, *Asad: The Struggle for the Middle East* (Berkeley: University of California Press, 1990), 55. The Makhloufs were members of the Syrian Social Nationalist Party which advocated Levantine unity.

17. Ibid., 54.

18. Ibid., 58.

19. "Syria Welcomes Gamal Abdul Nasser—*Al-Ayyam*, 26 February 1958," *Syrian History* website, accessed May 16, 2017, http://syrianhistory.com/en/photos/6242.

20. Burhan Ghalyoun, in discussion with the author, November 2016.

Notes

21. Nasser's man in the Southern Region (Syria) was Abdul-Hamid al-Sarraj, who was appointed interior minister. Many believe Sarraj's bloody and terroristic methods laid the foundations for the police state later presided over by the Assad family.

22. Hafez al-Assad was assigned to a crop dusting unit, according to Mustafa Tlass's memoirs.

23. Seale, *Asad*, 69.

24. Hanna Batatu, *The Old Social Classes and the Revolutionary Movements of Iraq* (London: Saqi Books, 2004), 801.

25. Mustafa Tlass, *Mira'at Hayati: Al-Aqed Al-Thani 1958–1968, Al-Thawra* [*My Life's Mirror: The Second Decade 1958–1968, The Revolution*] (Damascus: Dar Tlass, 2006), 139. Author's translation.

26. Hazem Saghieh, *Al-Baath Al-Souri Tareekh Moujaz* [*The Syrian Baath: A Brief History*] (Beirut: Dar al-Saqi, 2012), 36. Author's translation.

27. Tlass, *Mira'at Hayati: Al-Aqed Al-Thani 1958–1968*, 303. Author's translation.

28. Seale, *Asad*, 77.

29. Tlass, *Mira'at Hayati: Al-Aqed Al-Thani 1958–1968*, 414. Author's translation.

30. "A Decree Suspending Civil Rights of Those That Betrayed the People's Cause," *Al-Baath* (Damascus, Syria), March 24, 1963.

31. Tlass, *Mira'at Hayati: Al-Aqed Al-Thani 1958–1968*, 423. Author's translation.

32. Seale, *Asad*, 82.

33. Farouq al-Sharaa, *Al-Riwaya al-Mafqouda* [*The Missing Story*] (Beirut: Arab Center For Research and Policy Studies, 2015), 34. Author's translation.

34. Tlass, *Mira'at Hayati: Al-Aqed Al-Thani 1958–1968*, 433. Author's translation.

35. Ibid.

36. Saghieh, *Al-Baath Al-Souri Tareekh Moujaz*, 42. Author's translation.

37. Tlass, *Mira'at Hayati: Al-Aqed Al-Thani 1958–1968*, 467. Author's translation.

38. Raphael Lefèvre, *Ashes of Hama: The Muslim Brotherhood in Syria* (London: Hurst & Company, 2013), 100.

39. Tlass, *Mira'at Hayati: Al-Aqed Al-Thani 1958–1968*, 480. Author's translation.

40. Ibid., 485.

41. Ibid., 488.

42. Seale, *Asad*, 102.

43. Tlass, *Mira'at Hayati: Al-Aqed Al-Thani 1958–1968*, 631. Author's translation.

44. Saghieh, *Al-Baath Al-Souri*, 49. Author's translation.

45. In official Arab media, Israel's 1967 land gains were portrayed as the *naksa*, or setback.

46. Tlass, *Mira'at Hayati: Al-Aqed Al-Thani 1958–1968*, 840. Author's translation.

47. Ibid., 842.

48. "The Syrian Baath Party as Seen by Abu-Saleh, Part 8," Al Jazeera Arabic website, last accessed November 7, 2018, www.aljazeera.net/p rograms/centurywitness/2005/1/10/ حزب-البعث-السوري-كما-يراه-أبو-صالح-ح9.

49. Mustafa Tlass, *Mira'at Hayati: Al-Aqed Al-Thaleth 1968–1978, Al-Zilzal* [*My Life's Mirror: The Third Decade 1968–1978, The Earthquake*] (Damascus: Dar Tlass, 2006), 54. Author's translation.

50. Mustafa Tlass, interview with RT (*Russia Today*), YouTube video, 26:06, posted by "RT Arabic," July 13, 2009, www.youtube.com/watch?v=CKmlE_xOkdM.

51. General CIA Records, *Intelligence Memorandum: Communist Economic and Military Aid to Syria*, July 1, 1972, declassified January 18, 2011, accessed January 26 2018, www.cia.gov/library/ readingroom/document/cia-rdp85t00875r001700030111-4.

52. Abdul-Halim Khaddam, in discussion with the author, November 2016.

53. Al-Sharaa, *Al-Riwaya al-Mafqouda*, 41. Author's translation.

54. The World Bank, *Syrian Arab Republic Development Prospects and Policies: Report of a 1977 World Bank Mission*, Vol. II—The Main Report, 4, accessed May 17, 2017, http://documents .worldbank.org/curated/en/569411468120843337/pdf/multi-page.pdf.

55. Tlass, *Mira'at Hayati: Al-Aqed Al-Thaleth 1968–1978*, 444. Author's translation.

56. Ibid., 445.

57. "Gaddafi Makes a Declaration in Damascus," Al-Baath (Damascus, Syria), November 18, 1970.

Chapter 3 Embracing the Clouds

1. This was the flag adopted by the Federation of Arab Republics, an attempted but never consummated union of Egypt, Libya, and Syria in the early 1970s.

2. "The President Leader Kisses the Cherished Flag and Raises It to Flutter High in the Sky of Quneitra," *Al-Baath* (Damascus, Syria), June 27, 1974.

3. Manaf Tlass, in discussion with the author, October 2016.

4. "Three Hundred Journalists were in Quneitra," *Al-Baath* (Damascus, Syria), June 27, 1974.

5. Manaf Tlass, October 2016.

6. "Our Masses Live the Joy of Liberation," *Al-Baath* (Damascus, Syria), June 28, 1974.

7. National Security Archive, "The October War and US Policy," October 7, 2003, accessed February 21, 2017, http://nsarchive.gwu.edu/NSAEBB/NSAEBB98/#III.

8. Lakhdar Brahimi, in discussion with the author, December 2016.

9. Ghassan Salamé, in discussion with the author, November 2016.

10. "President Hafez al-Assad Complete October 6 War Speech," YouTube video, 8:31, posted by "ArbsTb," October 6, 2013. www.youtube.com/watch?v=QmbMKs7eQtg.

11. Walter Isaacson, *Kissinger: A Biography* (New York: Simon & Schuster, 1992), 544.

12. Library of Congress, Cable to General Scowcroft from Secretary Kissinger, May 22, 1974, declassified December 4, 2009, accessed January 26, 2018 www.cia.gov/library/reading room/document/loc-hak-260-2-56-9.

13. Isaacson, *Kissinger*, 566–68.

14. James F. Clarity, "US and Syrians to Reestablish Diplomatic Ties," *New York Times*, June 17, 1974, www.nytimes.com/1974/06/17/archives/us-and-syrians-to-reestablish-diplomatic -ties-nixon-and-assad.html?_r=0.

15. Salamé, November 2016.

16. "Syria My Beloved—The Original and Complete Version," YouTube video, 3:29, posted by "phmohanad," November 26, 2009, www.youtube.com/watch?v=yKli72vTPmE.

17. Burhan Ghalyoun, in discussion with the author, November 2016.

18. Ibid.

19. "The President and Prime Minister Perform Prayers at the Umayyad Mosque," *Al-Baath* (Damascus, Syria), December 1, 1970.

20. Michel Seurat, *Syrie L'État de Barbarie* [*Syria the Barbaric State*], (Paris: Presses Universitaires de France), 29.

21. Syrian Arab Republic People's Assembly, Legislative Decree 23, "Establishing the Revolutionary Youth Union," January 1, 1970, http://parliament.gov.sy/laws/Decree/00014191.tif.

22. Baath Vanguards website, accessed May 16, 2017, www.syrianpioneers.org.sy/node/5.

23. General CIA Records, *Intelligence Memorandum—Communist Economic and Military Aid to Syria*, July 1, 1972, declassified January 18, 2011, accessed January 26 2018, www.cia.gov/ library/readingroom/document/cia-rdp85t00875r001700030111-4.

24. "A Flood in Baath Country," 2003 Film by Omar Amiralay Produced by AMIP-Arte France, YouTube video, 46:14, posted by "AinOuzon," September 1, 2014, www.youtube .com/watch?v=t9a9pPZTwmc.

25. Bashar al-Assad classmate at Laïque School, in discussion with the author, October 2017.
26. Manaf Tlass, October 2014.
27. "Laïque: A History Briefing of the Institute," website of Laïque School Class of 1978, accessed May 17, 2017, www.laique78.com/ehistory.htm.
28. Former Laïque School student, in discussion with the author on condition of anonymity, January 2017.
29. Manaf Tlass, October 2016.
30. Bashar al-Assad childhood friend, in discussion with the author, October 2017. The house was owned by Rashad Pharaon, a Damascene physician who became the personal doctor of Saudi Arabia's first monarch and was given Saudi citizenship and later made health minister. Like other Levantine protégés of the Saudi royals, the Pharaons amassed a great fortune. Decades later, Pharaon's son was sought by US authorities in connection with one of the largest bank frauds in history.
31. Ibid.
32. Ibid.
33. Ibid.
34. Ibid.
35. Ibid.
36. Manaf Tlass, October 2016.
37. Rana Kabbani, in discussion with the author, March 2017.
38. Tlass family friend, in discussion with the author, December 2016.
39. Ibid.
40. Mustafa Tlass, *Mira'at Hayati: Al-Aqed Al-Thani 1958–1968, Al-Thawra* [*My Life's Mirror: The Second Decade 1958–1968, The Revolution*] (Damascus: Dar Tlass, 2006), 519. Author's translation.
41. Tlass family friend, December 2016.
42. Naomi Joy Weinberger, *Syrian Intervention in Lebanon: The 1975–1976 Civil War* (New York: Oxford University Press, 1986), 25.
43. Ibid., 15.
44. Laurent Fabius, in discussion with the author, December 2016.
45. Weinberger, *Syrian Intervention in Lebanon: The 1975–1976 Civil War*, 293.
46. Jeremy M. Sharp, *Syria: Background and US Relations*, special report for Congress, Congressional Research Service, May 1, 2008, 25.
47. Patrick Seale, *Asad: The Struggle for The Middle East* (Berkeley: University of California Press, 1990), 289.
48. Raphael Lefèvre, *Ashes of Hama: The Muslim Brotherhood in Syria* (London: Hurst & Company, 2013), 103.
49. Ibid., 97.
50. US Embassy in Damascus, "SARG Prepares Political Response to Worsening Economic Crisis," US State Department cable, June 13, 1977, released by WikiLeaks, declassified by State Department May 22, 2009, accessed May 17, 2017, https://wikileaks.org/plusd/cables/1977DAMASC03699_c.html.
51. Jonathan Randal, "Assad Acts to Restore Image Shaken by Corruption, Unrest," *Washington Post*, September 23, 1977, www.washingtonpost.com/archive/politics/1977/09/23/assad-acts-to-restore-image-shaken-by-corruption-unrest/1217b939-7a56-4fbc-999f-0baaf6a9de40/?utm_term=.58492e95225c.
52. Paul Maler (Michel Seurat), "La Société Syrienne Contre Son État" ["Syrian Society Against Its State"], *Le Monde Diplomatique*, April 1980.
53. "Martyrdom of Comrade Doctor Ibrahim Naama," *Al-Baath* (Damascus, Syria), March 19, 1978.

54. Human Rights Watch, *Human Rights in Syria, Chapter 2: The Great Repression 1976–1982*, Sepember 1990, accessed on Internet Archive, https://archive.org/stream/bub_gb_N-xjxWYW nlwC/bub_gb_N-xjxWYWnlwC_djvu.txt.

55. "Vague d'Agitation Confessionnelle en Syrie" ["Wave of Sectarian Trouble in Syria"], *Le Monde Diplomatique*, October 1979.

56. Lefèvre, *Ashes of Hama*, 107.

57. US Embassy in Damascus, "Hussein-Assad Meeting: Muslim Brotherhood and Internal Syrian Problems," US State Department cable, July 23, 1979, released by WikiLeaks, declassified by State Department March 20, 2014, accessed May 18, 2017, https:// wikileaks.org/plusd/cables/1979DAMASC04856_e.html.

58. "Vague d'Agitation Confessionnelle en Syrie."

59. Ibid.

60. US Embassy in Damascus, "Prospects for Assad's Survival," US State Department cable, September 16, 1979, released by WikiLeaks, declassified by the State Department March 20, 2014, accessed May 18, 2017, https://wikileaks.org/plusd/cables/1979DAMASC06042_e .html.

61. Manaf Tlass, October 2016.

62. Bashar al-Assad childhood friend, in discussion with the author, October 2017.

63. Ibid. Manaf Tlass also confirmed the story of Abu Subaih, who was the driver of Adnan al-Dabbagh, the interior minister at the time. Bashar was friends with Dabbagh's children and often rode with them when they were driven around by Abu Subaih. Dabbagh was married to the aunt of Bashar's future wife Asma al-Akhras.

64. "Saddam," YouTube video, 37:51, posted by "Baynetna Tube," uploaded November 20, 2012, https://www.youtube.com/watch?v=lQkBkzDdrsA.

65. Mustafa Tlass, *Mira'at Hayati: Al-Aqed Al-Rabe('ayn) 1978–1988, Al-Sumoud* [*My Life's Mirror: The Fourth Decade 1978–1988, Perseverance*] (Damascus: Dar Tlass, 2006), 450.

66. Ibid., 452.

67. US Embassy in Damascus, "Syria's Stability—Political Reporting," US State Department cable, May 23, 1979, released by WikiLeaks, declassified by State Department March 20, 2014, accessed May 18, 2017, https://wikileaks.org/plusd/cables/1979DAMASC03383_e .html.

68. The Syrian Human Rights Committee, "Rifaat al-Assad's Speech at the Seventh Regional Congress of the Arab Socialist Baath Party," accessed May 18, 2017, http://www.shrc .org/?p=7462.

69. Mohammad Farouk Tayfour, in discussion with the author, August 2017.

70. Seurat, *Syrie L'État de Barbarie*, 95–96.

71. Manaf Tlass, October 2016.

72. The American Presidency Project, "Jimmy Carter, 39th President of the United States: 1977–1981, Meeting with President Hafiz al-Asad of Syria, Remarks of the President and President Asad Prior to Their Meeting," May 9, 1977, www.presidency.ucsb.edu/ws/ ?pid=7488.

73. Human Rights Watch, *Human Rights in Syria—Chapter 2*.

74. Ibid.

75. Hafez al-Assad, "Mr. President Hafez al-Assad's Opening Remarks at the Emergency Meeting of the Confederation of Handicraftsmen Unions," March 11, 1980, President Bashar al-Assad official website, accessed May 18, 2017, www.presidentassad.net/index .php?option=com_content&view=article&id=518:11-3-1980&catid=262&Itemid=493.

76. Hafez al-Assad, "Mr. President Hafez al-Assad's Speech at the Extraordinary Fourth Congress of the Confederation of Farmer Unions," March 10, 1980, President Bashar al-Assad

official website, accessed May 18, 2017, www.presidentassad.net/index.php?option=com
_content&view=article&id=665:10-3-1980&catid=213&Itemid=476.

77. Hafez al-Assad, "Mr. President Hafez al-Assad's Speech at the Extraordinary Conference
of the National Students of Syria Union," March 17, 1980, President Bashar al-Assad official website, accessed May 18, 2017, http://www.presidentassad.net/index.php?option=com
_content&view=article&id=521:17-3-1980&catid=262&Itemid=493.

78. Manaf Tlass, October 2016.

79. Human Rights Watch, *Human Rights in Syria, Chapter 2.*

80. Amnesty International, *Report from Amnesty International to the Government of the Syrian Arab
Republic*, November 1, 1983, accessed January 25, 2018, www.amnesty.org/en/documents/
mde24/004/1983/en/.

81. Ibid.

82. Farouq al-Sharaa, *Al-Riwaya al-Mafqouda [The Missing Story]* (Beirut: Arab Center For
Research and Policy Studies, 2015), 63. Author's translation.

83. Seurat, *Syrie L'État de Barbarie*, 100.

84. Manaf Tlass, October 2016.

85. Anwar al-Buni, in discussion with the author, December 2016.

86. Manaf Tlass, October 2016.

87. Bashar al-Assad classmate at Laïque School, in discussion with the author, October 2017.

88. Manaf Tlass, October 2016.

89. Hafez al-Assad, "President Hafez al-Assad's Remarks at the Graduation Ceremony of the
Youth Knights," November 7, 1980, President Bashar al-Assad official website, accessed
May 18, 2017, www.presidentassad.net/index.php?option=com_content&view=article&id
=533:7-11-1980&catid=262&Itemid=493.

90. "From the Training of the Parachutist Knights in Syria," YouTube video, 3:33, posted by
"Fursansouria," February 1, 2012, www.youtube.com/watch?v=sOeZWIwDPwo.

91. Khaled Khoja, in discussion with the author, August 2017. Khoja, who was born the same
year as Bashar al-Assad, was a teenager when he was arrested in 1980 and again in 1981
because of the political activities of his father, a physician, and other family members.
Khaled Khoja would later become one of the leaders of the main Syrian opposition body
that emerged after the 2011 revolt against Bashar.

92. Human Rights Watch, *Human Rights in Syria, Chapter 2.*

93. Associated Press, "Bomb Explosion in Syria Kills 64 Hurts 135 in Crowded Area," *New York
Times*, November 30, 1981, www.nytimes.com/1981/11/30/world/bomb-explosion-in-syria
-kills-64-and-hurts-135-in-crowded-area.html.

94. Christian Chesnot and George Malbrunot, *Les Chemins De Damas [The Roads of Damascus]*
(Paris: Editions Robert Laffont, 2014), 22–23.

95. Human Rights Watch, *Human Rights in Syria, Chapter 2.*

96. Susanne Koelbl, "A 101 Course in Mideast Dictatorships," *Der Spiegel*, August 8, 2005,
www.spiegel.de/international/spiegel/syria-a-101-course-in-mideast-dictatorships-a
-343242.html.

97. Manaf Tlass, December 2018.

98. General CIA Records, "Monthly Warning Meeting—February 1982," February 22,
1982, declassified May 17, 2007, last accessed January 26, 2018, www.cia.gov/library/
readingroom/docs/CIA-RDP83B01027R000300040040-0.pdf.

Chapter 4 Golden Knight

1. Farouq al-Sharaa, *Al-Riwaya al-Mafqouda [The Missing Story]* (Beirut: Arab Center For
Research and Policy Studies, 2015), 101. Author's translation.

Notes

2. Manaf Tlass, in discussion with the author, October 2016.

3. Ibid.

4. Mustafa Tlass, *Mira'at Hayati: Al-Aqed Al-Rabee 1978–1988, Al-Sumoud* [*My Life's Mirror: The Fourth Decade 1978–1988, Perseverance*] (Damascus: Dar Tlass, 2006), 388. Author's translation.

5. Mustafa Tlass, *Mira'at Hayati: Al-Aqed Al-Thaleth 1968–1978, Al-Zilzal* [*My Life's Mirror: The Third Decade 1968–1978, The Earthquake*] (Damascus: Dar Tlass, 2006), 472. Author's translation.

6. Manaf Tlass, October 2016.

7. Ibid, December 2018.

8. Ibid, October 2016.

9. Ibid.

10. Al-Sharaa, *Al-Riwaya al-Mafqouda*, 108. Author's translation.

11. Manaf Tlass, October 2016.

12. Tlass, *Mira'at Hayati: Al-Aqed Al-Rabe('ayn) 1978–1988, Al-Sumoud*, 392. Author's translation.

13. Manaf Tlass, October 2016.

14. Ibid., November 2016.

15. Tlass family friend, in discussion with the author, December 2016.

16. Manaf Tlass, December 2018.

17. Ibid., October 2016

18. Ariane Chemin, "Les Diners de Madame Ojjeh" ["The Dinners of Madame Ojjeh"], *Le Monde*, October 2, 2006, www.lemonde.fr/a-la-une/article/2006/10/02/les-diners-de-madame-ojjeh_819062_3208.html.

19. Michel Abu-Najem, "Al-Wasat Speaks to Nahed Tlass Ojjeh, Who Has Caused a Political Storm in France," *Al-Wasat*, May 31, 1993, 70.

20. Michael Dobbs, "Mitterrand, Assad End Talks with Assurances on Terrorism," *Washington Post*, November 29, 1984, www.washingtonpost.com/archive/politics/1984/11/29/mitterrand-assad-end-talks-with-assurances-on-terrorism/2ea0bc1d-31d9-4333-b230-07d8d8ec8939/?utm_term=.e091849190ce.

21. Laurent Fabius, in discussion with the author, December 2016.

22. Michel Duclos, in discussion with the author, November 2016.

23. Manaf Tlass, December 2018.

24. Ronald Koven, "Prominent Enemy of Syria's Assad Is Slain in Paris," *Washington Post*, July 22, 1980, www.washingtonpost.com/archive/politics/1980/07/22/prominent-enemy-of-syrias-assad-is-slain-in-paris/03d0ff98-33a5-4c84-9fe8-a3b0b3df0851/?utm_term=.5c8dce1f5d55.

25. Raphael Lefèvre, *Ashes of Hama: The Muslim Brotherhood in Syria* (London: Hurst & Company, 2013), 113.

26. Pierre Marion, interview with *Le Nouvel Observateur* by Serge Raffy, September 12, 1986, http://referentiel.nouvelobs.com/archives_pdf/OBS1140_19860912/OBS1140_19860912_042.pdf.

27. Christian Chesnot and George Malbrunot, *Les Chemins De Damas* [*The Roads of Damascus*] (Paris: Editions Robert Laffont, 2014), 20–22.

28. Robert Fisk, *Pity the Nation: Lebanon at War*, 3rd ed. (New York: Oxford University Press, 2001), 446–47.

29. Ibid., 530.

30. Jane Mayer, "Ronald Reagan's Benghazi," *The New Yorker*, May 5, 2014, http://www.newyorker.com/news/daily-comment/ronald-reagans-benghazi.

31. Mustafa Tlass, interview with *Der Spiegel*, translated by Edna McCown, *New York Review of Books*

31, no. 18, November 22, 1984, www.nybooks.com/articles/1984/11/22/war-of-liberation-a
-talk-with-the-syrian-defense-m/.

32. US State Department, *Country Reports on Terrorism 2013*, accessed May 20, 2017, www.state
.gov/j/ct/rls/crt/2013/224829.htm.

33. Manaf Tlass, December 2018.

34. Duclos, November 2016.

35. Chesnot and Malbrunot, *Les Chemins De Damas*, 24.

36. General CIA Records, "Codel Tower's Conversation with Syrian President Assad Feb
21—Full Memcon," February 22, 1984, declassified November 19, 2010, accessed January 26, 2018, www.cia.gov/library/readingroom/document/cia-rdp90b01370r00080103
0002-8.

37. Mustafa Tlass, interview with *Der Spiegel*.

38. Tlass family friend, in discussion with the author, December 2016.

39. Manaf Tlass, August 2016.

40. Many Defense Company officers, almost all Alawite, followed Rifaat al-Assad into exile
but the majority joined a new army division (The Fourth Division) that was later commanded by Hafez al-Assad's youngest son, Maher.

41. US Embassy in Damascus, "The Syrian Muslim Brotherhood," US State Department
cable, February 26, 1985, released by WikiLeaks, classified Secret by State Department,
accessed May 18, 2017, https://wikileaks.org/plusd/cables/85DAMASCUS1314_a.html.

42. Manaf Tlass, October 2016.

43. Defected Syrian army officer from Al-Rastan, in discussion with the author, August 2017.

44. Abdul-Halim Khaddam, in discussion with the author, November 2016.

45. "Opening Ceremony of the Tenth Mediterranean Games in Latakia, Syria, 1987," YouTube video, 3:38:43, from broadcast by Syrian state television on September 11, 1987,
posted by "Sadik Awikeh," January 17, 2016, www.youtube.com/watch?v=tORIGGnMzLw.

46. "The Martyred Knight Bassel al-Assad in a Rare Clip," YouTube video, 1:59, from broadcast by Syrian state television in September 1987, posted by "Qais Sultanah," January 23,
2016, www.youtube.com/watch?v=IZ9aAe9XvXA.

47. Bassel al-Assad friend, in discussion with the author on condition of anonymity, January
2017.

48. Ibid.

49. Bashar al-Assad's high school friend, in discussion with the author, October 2017.

50. Manaf Tlass, December 2018.

51. Former regime official, in discussion with the author on condition of anonymity, March
2017.

52. Former Bassel al-Assad assistant, in discussion with the author on condition of anonymity
for fear of reprisal by the Assad family, December 2016.

53. Ibid.

54. Ibid.

55. Ammar Abd Rabbo, in discussion with the author, October 2016.

56. Dmitri Trenin, "The Mythical Alliance: Russia's Syria Policy," Carnegie Moscow Center,
February 12, 2013.

57. Andrew Rosenthal, "Mideast Tensions; Bush Says Syria Supports the Use of Force on Iraq,"
New York Times, November 24, 1990, www.nytimes.com/1990/11/24/world/mideast-tensions
-bush-says-syria-supports-the-use-of-force-on-iraq.html.

58. Human Rights Watch, *Human Rights Watch World Report 1989*, January 1990, accessed January 27, 2018, www.hrw.org/reports/1989/WR89/Syria.htm#TopOfPage.

59. World Bank Databank, data.worldbank.org, accessed on January 26, 2018, https://data .worldbank.org/indicator/FP.CPI.TOTL.ZG?locations=SY&view=chart.

60. Abdallah al-Dardari, in discussion with the author, February 2017. Dardari later became planning minister under Bashar.

61. Nadine Picaudou, "La Syrie Ne Renonce Pas à Ses Ambitions Régionales" ["Syria Is Not Renouncing Its Regional Ambitions"], *Le Monde Diplomatique*, December 1992, www .monde-diplomatique.fr/1992/12/PICAUDOU/44873.

62. Manaf Tlass, October 2016.

63. Ibid, December 2018.

64. Ibid.

65. Ibid.

66. "Mysterious Endings, Mahmoud al-Zoabi," YouTube Video, 48:49, Al Jazeera documentary, posted by "Al Jazeera Arabic," December 10, 2017, www.youtube.com/watch?v =hIftnkMarIA.

67. American Presidency Project, "William J. Clinton, 42nd President of the United States, 1993–2001 — The President's News Conference with President Hafiz al-Asad of Syria in Geneva," January 16, 1994, www.presidency.ucsb.edu/ws/?pid=50132.

68. Al-Sharaa, *Al-Riwaya al-Mafqouda*, 302.

69. Manaf Tlass, October 2016.

70. Stephen Kinzer, "Ex–East German Agent Guilty in Terror Bombing," *New York Times*, April 12, 1994, www.nytimes.com/1994/04/12/world/ex-east-german-agent-guilty-in-terror -bombing.html.

71. Al-Sharaa, *Al-Riwaya al-Mafqouda*, 303. Author's translation.

72. Manaf Tlass, October 2016.

73. "Bassel Beloved of the Millions," *Al-Baath* (Damascus, Syria), January 22, 1994.

74. "The Martyr Bassel al-Assad and the Eternal Leader's Eulogy," YouTube video, 1:23, from broadcast by Syrian state television, posted by "samidoonsyrians," May 20, 2011, www .youtube.com/watch?v=Kcij0xbPm28.

Chapter 5 *To Whom the Horses after You, Bassel?*

1. Manaf Tlass, in discussion with the author, October 2016.

2. Wafic Saïd, in discussion with the author, April 2017.

3. Bashar al-Assad friend, in discussion with the author, October 2017.

4. Maarouf family relative, in discussion with the author, February 2018.

5. Bashar al-Assad friend, October 2017.

6. *Bachar El-Assad, Le Pouvoir ou La Mort* [*Bashar al-Assad, Power or Death*], documentary film by Christophe Widemann for France 2 Channel, 120:00, December 12, 2017.

7. Manaf Tlass, October 2014.

8. "Bashar al-Assad at the Funeral of His Brother Bassel, January 1994," *Syrian History* website, accessed May 20, 2017, www.syrianhistory.com/en/photos/6307.

9. Bahjat Suleiman, "Why Is Bassel the Role Model and Bashar the Hope?" *Aleppo Economics* magazine, January 1, 1997, posted by All4Syria.info website, accessed May 20, 2017, www.all4syria.info/newcd/articles_president/althawra.html.

10. Manaf Tlass, October 2016.

11. Ibid.

12. Tlass family friend, in discussion with the author, December 2015.

13. Walid Jumblatt, in discussion with the author, November 2014.

14. Khaled Khoja, in discussion with the author, August 2017.

15. Manaf Tlass, December 2018.

16. "New Hospitals in the Provinces Named After the Nation's Deceased," *Al-Baath* (Damascus, Syria), February 1, 1994.

17. Former Bassel al-Assad assistant, in discussion with the author, December 2016.

18. Editorial, "Bashar Al-Assad: The Difficult Challenge," *Addiyar* newspaper (Beirut, Lebanon), April 22, 1995.

19. Ammar Abd Rabbo, in discussion with the author, November 2016.

20. Ibrahim Hamidi, "Two Prominent Dossiers: Lebanon and the Fight against Corruption, Major Bashar al-Assad Breaks into Politics," *Al-Wasat* magazine, May 1, 1995, 170.

21. Former regime official, in discussion with the author on condition of anonymity, March 2017.

22. Malek Mrowa, in discussion with the author, March 2017. Others said some Lebanese politicians, who were diehard Assad family loyalists, continued the practice even after the Syrian army left Lebanon in 2005. A medic at a private Beirut hospital recounted witnessing a Lebanese member of parliament kiss the hand of Bashar's father-figure mentor and adviser, Mohammad Nasif, as he lay on his deathbed in the spring of 2015.

23. Steve Coll, *The Bin Ladens: An Arabian Family in the American Century* (New York: The Penguin Press, 2008), 440.

24. Abdul-Halim Khaddam, in discussion with the author, November 2016.

25. Ibid.

26. Manaf Tlass, November 2016.

27. Former Bashar al-Assad friend, in discussion with the author, January 2017.

28. Tlass family friend, December 2015.

29. Manaf Tlass, December 2018.

30. Former Bashar al-Assad friend, January 2017.

31. Manaf Tlass, November 2016.

32. Former aide of Bassel al-Assad, in discussion with the author, December 2016.

33. Former Syrian Computer Society associate of Bashar al-Assad, in discussion with the author, January 2017.

34. Ghassan Salamé, in discussion with the author, November 2016.

35. Serge Halimi, "Memoires du President Chirac" ["President Chirac's Memoirs"], *Le Monde Diplomatique*, November 2011, www.monde-diplomatique.fr/2011/11/HALIMI/46916.

36. Ibid.

37. Bashar al-Assad, interview by Ghassan Charbel, *Al-Wasat* magazine, August 23, 1999, 395.

38. "Mohammad Bin Rashed Visits Jabal Ali Zone 1999," YouTube video, 1:33, posted by "HH Mohammad bin Rashid al-Maktoum Official Channel," January 30, 2012, www.youtube.com/watch?v=yXgaDw_xOZU. Manaf Tlass in Bashar's entourage.

39. Bassam Haddad, *Business Networks in Syria: The Political Economy of Authoritarian Resilience* (Stanford, CA: Stanford University Press, 2012), 89.

40. Tlass family friend, in discussion with the author, December 2015.

41. Ibrahim Hamidi, "When the Police Chief Knocked on the Door of the Former Prime Minister He Fired a Shot in the Air and a Second One in His Mouth," *Al-Hayat*, May 23, 2000, http://daharchives.alhayat.com/issue_archive/Hayat%20INT/2000/5/23/طرق-قائد الشرطة-باب-رئيس-الحكومة-السابق-فاطلق-رصاصة-في-الهواء-وثانية-في-فمه-لا-تمثيل-رسمياً-في-تشييع-الزعيم-وت.html.

42. Khaddam, November 2016.

43. Barbara Plett, "Attack Renews Syrian Family Feud," *BBC News* website, October 22, 1999, http://news.bbc.co.uk/2/hi/middle_east/482938.stm.

44. Manaf Tlass, November 2016.

45. Former regime official, in discussion with the author, March 2017.

46. Manaf Tlass, December 2018. On paper, Maher al-Assad was a major in the army's Fourth Division but in reality he was de facto commander of the whole unit, which when established absorbed most members of Rifaat al-Assad's paramilitary group (*Saraya al-Difaa*, The Defense Companies) after it was disbanded by Hafez al-Assad.

47. Jean-Pierre Perrin, "La Famille Assad S'Entre-Dechire" ["The Assad Family Tears Itself Apart"], *Libération*, November 29, 1999, www.liberation.fr/planete/1999/11/29/la-famille -assad-s-entre-dechire-le-gendre-du-president-syrien-blesse-par-son-beau-frere-hospita lise_288112.

Chapter 6 New King and Early Spring

1. Farouq al-Sharaa, *Al-Riwaya al-Mafqouda* [*The Missing Story*] (Beirut: Arab Center for Research and Policy Studies, 2015), 456. Author's translation.

2. Manaf Tlass, in discussion with the author, December 2018. Manaf recalled how Hafez al-Assad had concentration and memory problems during his last meeting with Bill Clinton in March 2000.

3. Al-Sharaa, *Al-Riwaya al-Mafqouda*, 457. Author's translation.

4. Ibid.

5. Abdul-Halim Khaddam, in discussion with the author, December 2016.

6. Mustafa Tlass, interview by Hiyam Ali and Ali Mahmoud Jadid from *Syriasteps* website, posted on the *Golan* website, June 11, 2010, www.jawlan.org/openions/read_article.asp?cat igory=188&source=6&link=3173.

7. Manaf Tlass, October 2014.

8. Ibid.

9. Ibid.

10. Tlass family friend, in discussion with the author, December 2017.

11. Ibid.

12. "Announcement of Hafez al-Assad's Death on Syrian Television," YouTube video, 4:41, posted by "Malath Alzoubi," June 9, 2015, www.youtube.com/watch?v=BptINo5JBmI.

13. Khaled al-Khani, in discussion with the author, October 2014.

14. "Funeral of the Eternal Leader Hafez al-Assad, Part One," YouTube video, 1:00:32, from broadcast by Tele Liban, June 2000, posted by "Tartous TV," November 20, 2011, www .youtube.com/watch?v=fG2o_c87How.

15. Malek Mrowa, in discussion with the author, March 2017.

16. Ibid.

17. Cards seen by the author.

18. "Funeral of the Eternal Leader Hafez al-Assad, Part Two," YouTube video, 1:00:36, from broadcast by Tele Liban, June 2000, posted by "Tartous TV," November 20, 2011, www .youtube.com/watch?v=z_dIIZips-g.

19. Marjorie Miller and John Daniszewski, "Mourners Say Goodbye to Syria's 'Lion,'" *Los Angeles Times*, June 14, 2000, http://articles.latimes.com/2000/jun/14/news/mn-40864.

20. Manaf Tlass, November 2016.

21. Associated Press, "French Rain Shells and Bombs on Syrians in Damascus," *Chicago Tribune*, May 31, 1945, http://archives.chicagotribune.com/1945/05/31/page/1/article/french-rain -shells-and-bombs-on-syrians-in-damascus/.

22. "Mr. President Bashar al-Assad's Speech at the People's Assembly after Taking the Oath of Office," YouTube video, 1:04:14, broadcast by Syrian Radio and Television on July 17, 2000, posted by "Syria RTV," July 10, 2013, www.youtube.com/watch?v=dsNwHs9B6RI.

23. Ibid.

24. Manaf Tlass, October 2014.

25. "Saudi Crown Prince Goes to Syria," Kuwait News Agency, July 18, 2000, accessed May 20, 2017, www.kuna.net.kw/ArticlePrintPage.aspx?id=1098103&language=ar.

26. Wafic Saïd, in discussion with the author, April 2017.

27. Philippe Quillerier-Lesieur, "Jacques Chirac a Damas" ["Jacques Chirac in Damascus"], *RFI* (Radio France Internationale website), June 13, 2000, www1.rfi.fr/actufr/articles/006/article_2803.asp.

28. Former friend of Bashar al-Assad, in discussion with the author, October 2017.

29. Ibid.

30. A friend of the Akhras family, in discussion with the author, December 2015.

31. "President Assad's Wedding," YouTube video, 1:00, posted by "Al-Naser Qadem Min Halab," December 11, 2011, www.youtube.com/watch?v=ScDeLd9ByLA.

32. Manaf Tlass, December 2018.

33. Peter Beaumont, "From Schoolgirl Emma to Asma, the Syrian Icon," *The Observer*, December 12, 2002, posted on President Bashar al-Assad official website, accessed May 20, 2017, www.presidentassad.net/index.php?option=com_content&view=article&id=881:from-school-emma-to-asma-the-observer-december-15-2002&catid=164&Itemid=477.

34. Damascus native, in discussion with the author, February 2017.

35. Lebanese political figure, in discussion with the author on condition of anonymity, April 2017.

36. Samir Kassir, *Demoqratiyat Souriya Wa Istiklal Lubnan* [*Syria's Democracy and Lebanon's Independence*] (Beirut: Annahar Publishing House, 2004), Appendix, 209.

37. Burhan Ghalyoun, in discussion with the author, November 2016.

38. Mazen Darwish, in discussion with the author, December 2016.

39. Brian Whitaker, "Syria to Free 600 Political Prisoners," *The Guardian*, November 17, 2000, www.theguardian.com/world/2000/nov/17/brianwhitaker.

40. Kassir, *Demoqratiyat Souriya Wa Istiklal Lubnan*, Appendix, 212.

41. Manaf Tlass, October 2016.

42. Six months after Bashar came to power, Assef Shawkat arrested and imprisoned Ahmed Abboud, a retired but still influential Alawite general. Abboud's daughter was married to one of the sons of Rifaat al-Assad, Bashar's banished uncle.

43. Manaf Tlass, December 2018. Besides Assef, Bashar acquired two more brothers-in-law after his marriage to Asma. Asma had two siblings, both male.

44. Ibrahim Hamidi, "In the First Official Reaction… Omran Criticizes Civil Society Advocates," *Al-Hayat*, January 1, 2001, http://daharchives.alhayat.com/issue_archive/Hayat %20INT/2001/1/30-في-اول-موقف-رسمي-و-تشديد-على-الحرية-المسؤولةآو-الخطوط-الحمر-عمران-ينتقد دعاة-المجتمع-المدني-جزء-من-استعمار-جديد.html. The Syrian regime was closely following the case of Saadeddin Ibrahim, a dual Egyptian-American citizen and sociology professor and political activist, who was jailed in Egypt in 2000 on charges of receiving funds from the European Union for his Ibn Khaldun Center for Developmental Studies.

45. "The Attack on Nabil Suleiman: Message to Syrian Intellectuals?" *Al-Wasat* magazine, February 12, 2000, 472.

46. Bashar al-Assad, Interview by Asharq al-Awsat translated by Al-Bab, *Al-Bab* website, February 6, 2001, http://al-bab.com/documents-section/interview-president-bashar-al-assad #POLITICAL.

47. Ghalyoun, November 2016.

48. "Riad Turk Challenges the Syrian Regime from Damascus," YouTube video, 1:54, posted by "freesyrianyouth," September 26, 2009, www.youtube.com/watch?v=6GIbkIHsSoI.

49. Riad Seif, in discussion with the author, August 2017.

50. Ghalyoun, November 2016.

51. Darwish, December 2016.

52. Manaf Tlass, October 2014.

53. Peter Ford, "Europe Cringes at Bush 'Crusade' against Terrorists," *Christian Science Monitor*, September 19, 2001, www.csmonitor.com/2001/0919/p12s2-woeu.html.

54. Seymour Hersh, "The Syrian Bet," *The New Yorker*, July 23, 2003, www.newyorker.com/magazine/2003/07/28/the-syrian-bet.

55. Manaf Tlass, December 2018. "Bashar essentially told the Americans 'I want to collaborate in fighting terrorism in return for safeguarding my rule,'" said Manaf.

56. Ibid., October 2014.

57. Ibid.

58. Ibid.

59. Former Syrian envoy to Iraq Noureddin Labbad, in discussion with the author, November 2016.

60. US Central Intelligence Agency, "The Procurement of Conventional Military Goods in Breach of UN Sanctions," posted on CIA website April 23, 2007, accessed May 20 2017, www.cia.gov/library/reports/general-reports-1/iraq_wmd_2004/chap2_annxJ.html.

61. "The Operation to Capture the Three Zionist Soldiers on October, 7, 2000," Hezbollah's official website, accessed May 20, 2017. https://www.moqawama.org/essaydetails.php?eid=4571&cid=161

62. Bashar al-Assad, Speech at the Arab League Summit in Beirut, March 27, 2002, President Bashar al-Assad official website, www.presidentassad.net/index.php?option=com_content&view=article&id=960:27-2002&catid=294&Itemid=469.

63. Linda Grant, "The Hate That Will Not Die," *The Guardian*, December 18, 2001, www.theguardian.com/world/2001/dec/18/september11.israel.

64. Manaf Tlass, November 2016.

65. Ibid., December 2018. Manaf witnessed the spectacle in Qurdaha. The men were from the Syrian Social Nationalist Party (SSNP), which was founded by a Lebanese Christian and is dedicated to the principle of establishing Greater Syria, an area that includes Israel, Jordan, Lebanon, Syria, and southeastern Turkey. Bashar's maternal cousins the Makhloufs are prominent and active backers of the SSNP. The party's symbol resembles a swastika in circular motion.

66. Ibid., October 2014.

67. Ghassan Salamé, in discussion with the author, November 2016.

68. Flynt Leverett, *Inheriting Syria: Bashar's Trial by Fire* (Washington, DC: Brookings Institution Press, 2005), 143.

69. Amnesty International, "Charges Filed against Syrian Official for Torture of Maher Arar Survivor of Rendition in US War on Terror," press release, September 1, 2015, www.amnestyusa.org/press-releases/charges-filed-against-syrian-official-for-torture-of-maher-arar-survivor-of-rendition-in-us-war-on-terror/.

70. Colin L. Powell, "On the Record Briefing en Route to Damascus, Syria," May 2, 2003, US Department of State Archive website, accessed May 20, 2017, https://2001-2009.state.gov/secretary/former/powell/remarks/2003/20156.htm.

71. Leverett, *Inheriting Syria*, 126–27.

72. Ibid.

73. "Syria's Mufti Calls for Martyrdom Operations Against the Invaders," *Al Jazeera Arabic* website, March 27, 2003, last accessed on December 25, 2018, https://www.aljazeera.net/news/arabic/2003/3/27/مفتي-سوريا-يدعو-لتنفيذ-عمليات-استشهادية-ضد-الغزاة.

74. Manaf Tlass, December 2018.
75. Darwish, December 2016.
76. Al-Khani, October 2014.
77. Manaf Tlass, October 2014.
78. Tlass family friend, in discussion with the author, December 2015.
79. Manaf Tlass, December 2018.
80. Tlass family friend, December 2015.
81. Manaf Tlass, October 2014.
82. Ibid.
83. Bernard Pêcheur, in discussion with the author, November 2016.
84. Ibid.
85. Beaumont, "From Schoolgirl Emma to Asma."
86. "The Assad and Chirac Families at the Élysée Palace in Paris—June 25, 2011," *Syrian History* website, accessed May 21, 2017, http://syrianhistory.com/en/photos/3684.
87. "Syrian President Meets Queen," *The Telegraph*, December 17, 2002, accessed May 21, 2017, www.telegraph.co.uk/news/1416391/Syrian-president-meets-the-Queen.html.
88. "Paris: Visite de Bachar el Assad Perturbée" ["Paris: Bashar al-Assad's Visit Disturbed"], Ina.fr video, 02:07, from original broadcast by France 2 television channel, June 26, 2001, www.ina.fr/video/CAB01027711.
89. Alan Philps, "Assad Accuses Israel of Being More Racist than the Nazis," *The Telegraph*, March 28, 2001, www.telegraph.co.uk/news/worldnews/middleeast/syria/1328194/Assad-accuses-Israel-of-being-more-racist-than-the-Nazis.html.
90. Clyde Haberman, "The World: Assad Greets the Pope; Welcome, Man of Peace. Let's Go Hate My Enemy," *New York Times*, May 13, 2001, www.nytimes.com/2001/05/13/weekinreview/the-world-assad-greets-the-pope-welcome-man-of-peace-let-s-go-hate-my-enemy.html.
91. Michel Duclos, in discussion with the author, November 2016.
92. Detlev Mehlis, "Report of the International Independent Investigation Commission Established Pursuant to Security Council Resolution 1595 (2005)," October 19, 2005, 8, United Nations official website, accessed May 21, 2017, www.un.org/news/dh/docs/mehlisreport.pdf.
93. Bashar al-Assad, Conference of the Syrian Diaspora in Damascus, October 9, 2004, posted on President Bashar-al Assad official website, last accessed May 21, 2017, www.presidentassad.net/index.php?option=com_content&view=article&id=974:9-2004&catid=296&Itemid=469.
94. Khaddam, December 2016.
95. "Hariri to Muallem in Recording: I Can No Longer Take It," *Al-Hayat*, May 7, 2015, accessed May 21, 2017, http://www.alh ayat.com/Articles/9042748/الحريري-للمعلم-في-تسجيل-لم-أعد-قادر-أ-على-التحمل.
96. Ronen Bergman, "The Hezbollah Connection," *New York Times Magazine*, February 10, 2015, www.nytimes.com/2015/02/15/magazine/the-hezbollah-connection.html?_r=0.
97. The immediate aftermath of the bombing was witnessed by the author.

Chapter 7 Hit Them Where It Hurts

1. Hassan M. Fattah, "A Leading Syrian Minister Dies, Apparently a Suicide," *New York Times*, October 13, 2005, www.nytimes.com/2005/10/13/world/middleeast/a-leading-syrian-minister-dies-apparently-a-suicide.html.
2. Abdul-Halim Khaddam, in discussion with the author, December 2016.

Notes

3. Manaf Tlass, in discussion with the author, December 2018. Tensions between Bashar and Kanaan had been mounting before Hariri's assassination, according to Manaf. "Kanaan acted like God in Lebanon and then he came back to Syria and tried to forge a place for himself in the power orbit around Bashar," said Manaf. "Bashar started to get jealous of him and wanted to clip his wings."

4. "US Recalls Ambassador to Syria," press statement by spokesman Richard Boucher, US State Department, February 15, 2005, https://2001-2009.state.gov/r/pa/prs/ps/2005/42305.htm.

5. Detlev Mehlis, "Report of the International Independent Investigation Commission Established Pursuant to Security Council Resolution 1595 (2005)," October 19, 2005, 53, United Nations official website, accessed May 21, 2017, www.un.org/news/dh/docs/mehlisreport.pdf.

6. Andrew Tabler, "How to Deal with Syria: Find Out Who Is in Charge," *Institute of Current World Affairs Letters*, October 23, 2005, accessed on May 21, 2017, www.icwa.org/wp-content/uploads/2015/08/AJT-6.pdf.

7. Susanne Koelbl, "A 101 Course in Mideast Dictatorships," *Der Spiegel*, August 8, 2005, www.spiegel.de/international/spiegel/syria-a-101-course-in-mideast-dictatorships-a-343242.html.

8. Samir Kassir, *Demoqratiyat Souriya Wa Istiklal Lubnan [Syria's Democracy and Lebanon's Independence]* (Beirut: Annahar Publishing House, 2004), 49.

9. "Seyyed Hassan Nasrallah and the First Call in the July 2006 War: The War Is Total," Archives of the Al-Manar Channel Website, posted July 18, 2013, accessed May 21, 2017, http://archive.almanar.com.lb/article.php?id=540395.

10. Manaf Tlass, November 2016.

11. "Nasrallah: Our Rockets That Hit Haifa Were Made in Syria," *Al-Akhbar* newspaper website, July 19, 2012, accessed on May 21, 2017, www.al-akhbar.com/node/98121.

12. Bashar al-Assad, speech at the opening of the Fourth Congress of the Union of Journalists, August 15, 2006, posted on President Bashar al-Assad official website, accessed May 21, 2017, www.presidentassad.net/index.php?option=com_content&view=article&id=989:15-2006&catid=298&Itemid=469.

13. Manaf Tlass, November 2016.

14. Ibid.

15. Ibid.

16. Bashar al-Assad, interview by CNN's Christiane Amanpour, CNN website, October 12, 2005, http://edition.cnn.com/2005/WORLD/meast/10/12/alassad.transcript/.

17. Manaf Tlass, December 2018.

18. Iraqi insurgent leaders and figures interviewed by the author in both Iraq and Syria between 2004 and 2013.

19. Brian Fishman, ed., *Bombers, Bank Accounts, and Bleedout: Al-Qaida's Road in and out of Iraq*, by Peter Bergen, Joseph Felter, Vahid Brown, and Jacob Shapiro, The Combating Terrorism Center at Westpoint, July 22, 2008, accessed May 21, 2017, https://ctc.usma.edu/app/uploads/2011/12/Sinjar_2_FINAL.pdf.

20. Ibid.

21. Diab Serriya, in discussion with the author, December 2017.

22. Manaf Tlass, November 2016.

23. Bashar al-Assad, "America Must Listen," interview by Spiegel, *Spiegel Online*, September 24, 2006, http://www.spiegel.de/international/spiegel/spiegel-interview-with-syrian-president-bashar-assad-america-must-listen-a-438804.html.

24. Noureddin Labbad, former Syria envoy to Iraq, in discussion with the author, November 2016.
25. Iraqi official, in discussion with the author, November 2009.
26. James A. Baker III and Lee H. Hamilton, *The Iraq Study Group Report* (New York: Vintage Books, 2006).
27. Bashar al-Assad's childhood friend, in discussion with the author, November 2017.
28. Ibid.
29. Manaf Tlass, November 2016.
30. Ibid.
31. Hiyam Ali, "Kuzbari: My Priority Is the Manufacture & Trade of Paper," *Asharq al-Awsat*, October 5, 2007, http://archive.aawsat.com/details.asp?section=6&article=440034&issu eno=10538#.WovaQTOB3yI.
32. US Embassy in Damascus, "Attacking Bashar's Money," US State Department cable, January 24, 2008, released by WikiLeaks, accessed February 20, 2018, https://wikileaks.org/plusd/cables/08DAMASCUS54_a.html.
33. Hiyam Ali, "Kuzbari: My Priority Is the Manufacture & Trade of Paper,"
34. Maarouf family member, in discussion with the author, February 2018.
35. "Women For Peace Bicycle Ride Begins in Syria," *The Jerusalem Post*, April 7, 2007, https://www.jpost.com/Middle-East/Women-For-Peace-bicycle-ride-begins-in-Syria.
36. Former Asma al-Assad aide, in discussion with the author, January 2017.
37. Omar Abdelaziz Hallaj (former chief executive officer, Syria Trust for Development), in discussion with the author, September 2014.
38. Ammar Abd Rabbo, in discussion with the author, November 2016.
39. Former Syrian foreign ministry official, in discussion with the author, March 2017.
40. Ibid.
41. Ibid.
42. Labbad, November 2016.
43. Manaf Tlass, November 2016.
44. Jeff Stein, "How the CIA Took Down Hezbollah's Top Terrorist, Imad Mughniyah," *Newsweek*, January 31, 2015, www.newsweek.com/2015/02/13/imad-mugniyah-cia-mossad-303483.html.
45. Manaf Tlass, November 2016.
46. Ibid., December 2018. According to Manaf Tlass, Iran suspected Assef Shawkat betrayed Mughniyeh and it was also angry with him for his close ties to ex-Saddam regime officials, who were based in Syria and directing an insurgency against the Americans as well as Iraq's newly empowered Shiites — Iran's allies.
47. Most media reports said General Mohammad Suleiman was killed at his beach chalet by Israeli commandos but one former French intelligence official told the author in 2016 that he believed the killing was an inside job ordered by Bashar.
48. Former Syrian official, in discussion with the author, March 2017. Asked about this in December 2018, Manaf Tlass said he was caught up in a turf war inside the Republican Guard between two powerful Alawite generals.
49. Mustafa Tlass, interview by RT (*Russia Today*), YouTube video, 26:06, posted by "RT Arabic," July 13, 2009, www.youtube.com/watch?v=CKmlE_xOkdM.
50. Syrian businessman, in discussion with the author, January 2017.
51. Western diplomat, in discussion with the author, December 2016.
52. "Syria's First Lady Wants New Conversation with West," *ABC News* website, February 6, 2007, http://abcnews.go.com/GMA/story?id=2852589.
53. Ibid.

54. Bashar al-Assad, interview by Diane Sawyer, *Good Morning America* (ABC), February 5, 2007, http://abcnews.go.com/GMA/story?id=2849435&page=1.

55. Western diplomat, in discussion with the author, December 2016.

56. Ariane Chemin, "Les Diners de Madame Ojjeh" ["The Dinners of Madame Ojjeh"], *Le Monde*, October 2, 2006, www.lemonde.fr/a-la-une/article/2006/10/02/les-diners-de-madame -ojjeh_819062_3208.html.

57. Ibid.

58. Michel Duclos, in discussion with the author, November 2016. Dumas once missed an urgent cabinet meeting because he had gone to Damascus for a long weekend with Nahed Ojjeh, according to Duclos.

59. Karl Laske, "Une Nouvelle 'Ex-Amie' Accuse Roland Dumas," ["Another 'Ex-Girlfriend' Accuses Roland Dumas'], *Libération*, June, 27, 1998, https://www.liberation.fr/societe/ 1998/06/27/une-nouvelle-ex-amie-accuse-roland-dumas_238750.

60. Chemin, "Les Diners de Madame Ojjeh."

61. Renaud Lecadre, "Firas Tlass, 'Partenaire Local' de Lafarge en Syrie" ["Firas Tlass, Lafarge's Local Partner in Syria"], *Libération*, December 14, 2017, www.liberation.fr/ france/2017/12/14/firas-tlass-partenaire-local-de-lafarge-en-syrie_1616777.

62. Ayman al-Shoufi, "Syria: Billions That Have Dried Up," *Assafir*, December 18, 2013, http://arabi.assafir.com/Article/3786.

63. Syrian businessmen, in discussion with the author, December 2017.

64. Manaf Tlass, December 2018.

65. Isabelle Hausser, in discussion with the author, November 2016.

66. "Total Signs Three Oil and Gas Agreements in Syria," Total S.A., accessed May 21, 2017, www.total.com/en/media/news/press-releases/syrie-total-signe-trois-accords-petroliers -et-gaziers.

67. Duclos, November 2016.

68. Claude Guéant, in discussion with the author, November 2016. Guéant said Sarkozy had received personal assurances from Bashar and guarantees from the Qataris and Turks that the Syrian regime would do everything to bring to an end the campaign of bombings and assassinations that had targeted the critics and opponents of the regime and Hezbollah in Lebanon.

69. Duclos, November 2016.

70. "Full Admission by the French of Syria's Pivotal Role," *Al-Watan* (Damascus, Syria), July 13, 2008.

Chapter 8 Precious Interlocutor and Unavoidable Player

1. "President Assad and His Wife Meet Members of the Syrian Community," Syrian Radio and Television website, December 12, 2010, accessed May 21, 2017, www.rtv.gov.sy/index .php?p=13&id=67142.

2. Claude Guéant, in discussion with the author, November 2016.

3. "Syria's First Lady Asma al-Assad Speech at the Paris Diplomatic Academy in 2010," YouTube video, 52:42, posted by "Antikrieg TV," September 14, 2016, www.youtube.com/ watch?v=ySlT5un6Ddg.

4. Ibid.

5. Asma al-Assad, interview by Régis Le Sommier, *Paris Match*, December, 17, 2010, www .parismatch.com/Actu/International/Asma-et-Bachar-el-Assad-deux-amoureux-a-Paris -156785.

6. Guéant, November 2016.

Notes

7. US Embassy in Damascus, "Special Reports: Wolf, Pelosi, and Issa Codels (April 2–6)," April 11, 2007, US State Department cable, released by WikiLeaks, accessed May 17, 2017, https://wikileaks.org/plusd/cables/07DAMASCUS348_a.html.

8. Manaf Tlass, in discussion with the author, October 2014.

9. Jeremy M. Sharp, *Syria: Background and US Relations*, special report for Congress, Congressional Research Service, May 1, 2008, 25–31.

10. Guéant, November 2016.

11. Eric Schmitt and Thom Shanker, "Officials Say US Killed an Iraqi in Raid in Syria," *New York Times*, October 27, 2008.

12. David Ignatius, "What Bashar al-Assad Hopes for with Barack Obama and Mideast Peace," *Washington Post*, December 24, 2008, www.washingtonpost.com/wp-dyn/content/article/2008/12/23/AR2008122301998.html.

13. US Embassy in Damascus, "Reengaging with Syria: The Middle East's Unavoidable Player," US State Department cable, January 28, 2009, released by WikiLeaks, accessed May 21, 2017, https://wikileaks.org/plusd/cables/09DAMASCUS82_a.html.

14. "Operation Cast Lead: Israel Strikes Back against Hamas Terror in Gaza," Israeli Ministry of Foreign Affairs, January 21, 2009, www.mfa.gov.il/mfa/foreignpolicy/terrorism/pages/israel_strikes_back_against_hamas_terror_infrastructure_gaza_27-dec-2008.aspx.

15. David Blair, "Israeli Contender Defies Syria on Eve of Poll," The Telegraph, February 9, 2009, https://www.telegraph.co.uk/news/worldnews/middleeast/israel/4569861/Israeli-contender-defies-Syria-on-eve-of-poll.html.

16. US Embassy in Damascus, "Kerry–Asad: Improving the US–Syria Relationship," US State Department cable, February 27, 2009, released by WikiLeaks, accessed May 21, 2017, https://wikileaks.org/plusd/cables/09DAMASCUS160_a.html.

17. Ibid.

18. US Embassy in Damascus, "Kerry–Asad: Saudis May Be Sowing the Seeds of Lebanon's Next Civil War," US State Department cable, February 27, 2009, released by WikiLeaks, accessed May 21, 2017, https://wikileaks.org/plusd/cables/09DAMASCUS159_a.html. The title of this cable could be misleading; it was Bashar who claimed that the Saudis were "sowing the seeds of Lebanon's next civil war" in his discussion with Kerry. It was a way for Bashar to deflect the pressure from Kerry over Iranian-Syrian support for Lebanon's Hezbollah militia.

19. Manaf Tlass, October 2014.

20. David Remnick, "Negotiating with the Whirlwind," *The New Yorker*, December 21 & 28, 2015, www.newyorker.com/magazine/2015/12/21/negotiating-the-whirlwind.

21. US Embassy in Damascus, "Scene Setter for Senator Specter's Dec. 29–31 Visit to Damascus," US State Department cable, December 18, 2008, released by WikiLeaks, accessed May 21, 2017, https://wikileaks.org/plusd/cables/08DAMASCUS896_a.html.

22. Manaf Tlass, October 2014.

23. Michel Duclos, in discussion with the author, November 2016.

24. US Embassy in Damascus, "Asad Discusses Iran and Gaza with CODEL Specter," US State Department cable, January 4, 2009, released by WikiLeaks, accessed May 21, 2017, https://wikileaks.org/plusd/cables/09DAMASCUS3_a.html.

25. US Embassy in Damascus, "CODEL Gregg's December 30 Meeting with President Assad," US State Department cable, January 4, 2010, released by WikiLeaks, accessed May 21, 2017, https://wikileaks.org/plusd/cables/10DAMASCUS8_a.html.

26. Khaled Yacoub Oweis, "Syria and Iran Defy Clinton in Show of Unity," Reuters, February 25, 2010, www.reuters.com/article/us-syria-iran-idUSTRE61O33X20100225.

27. Eric Chevallier, in discussion with the author, December 2016.
28. Mazen Darwish, in discussion with the author, December 2016
29. Ibid.
30. Ibid.
31. "Timeline: Iran's Post-Election Protests," *Financial Times*, June 11, 2010. www.ft.com/content/ 533d966e-755a-11df-a7e2-00144feabdc0.
32. Bashar al-Assad, interview by Alain Gresh, *Le Monde Diplomatique*, July 9, 2008.
33. Manaf Tlass, in discussion with the author, December 2018. Coppola was on his way to a film festival in Beirut but he was prevented from landing there because his private jet had parts manufactured in Israel. The ban on any dealings with Israel is vigorously enforced by Lebanon's most powerful faction, Hezbollah. So Coppola had to land in Damascus instead. Manaf helped the famous director get to Beirut by land on condition he come back to see Syria. Coppola returned to Syria. Manaf dined with Coppola, who also met with Bashar and Asma.
34. Damascene businesswoman, in discussion with the author, December 2015.
35. Khaled al-Khani, in discussion with the author, October 2014.
36. Duclos, November 2016.
37. Chevallier, December 2016.
38. Manaf Tlass, November 2016.
39. Ibid., October 2014.
40. Khalid Abu-Ismail, Ali Abdel-Gadir and Heba El-Laithy, *Poverty and Inequality in Syria (1997-2007)*, Arab Development Challenges Report Background Paper 2011/15, United Nations Development Programme, http://www.undp.org/content/dam/rbas/doc/poverty/BG_15 _Poverty%20and%20Inequality%20in%20Syria_FeB.pdf.
41. Ibid.
42. Manaf Tlass, October 2014.
43. Duclos, November 2016.
44. Darwish, December 2016.

Chapter 9 No More Fear after Today

1. Ayman al-Aswad, in discussion with the author, November 2016.
2. Ibid.
3. Ibid.
4. Ibid.
5. Mazen Darwish, in discussion with the author, December 2016.
6. Aswad, November 2016.
7. Ahmad al-Sayasneh, in discussion with the author, July 2017.
8. Ibid.
9. Darwish, December 2016.
10. Marwa Al-Ghamian, in discussion with the author, November 2014.
11. Aswad, November 2016.
12. Malek al-Jawabra, in discussion with the author, January 2017.
13. Ibid.
14. "Demonstrations Next to the Omari Mosque, Daraa," YouTube video, 13:21, posted by "Syria0syria0," March 19, 2011, www.youtube.com/watch?v=JEKOCfqoxis.
15. Al-Sayasneh, July 2017.
16. Ibid.
17. "Demonstrations Next to the Omari Mosque, Daraa."
18. Manaf Tlass, in discussion with the author, November 2016.

19. Al-Jawabra, January 2017.
20. "Unique Video, Watch the First Protest in Daraa, March 18, 2011," YouTube video, 12:06, posted by "Bayareq Houran," March 16, 2013, www.youtube.com/watch?v=rnCJ5KItKXE.
21. Al-Jawabra, January 2017.
22. "Shabiha Helicopters Land in Daraa at the Start of the Syrian Revolution, March 18, 2011," YouTube video, 5:55, posted by "Zeina Erhaim," January 16, 2012, www.youtube.com/watch?v=f425H-g8iJ0.
23. Al-Jawabra, January 2017.
24. Ibid.
25. Ibid.
26. "Daraa al-Balad, March 18, 2011, Syria's First Demonstration and the First Shooting During the Revolution," YouTube video, 5:03, posted by "The Coordination Committee of the City of Nawa," March 18, 2015, www.youtube.com/watch?v=OKvyWzFjc14.
27. Al-Jawabra, January 2017.
28. Sally Masalmeh, January 2017.
29. Ibid.
30. Al-Jawabra, January 2017.
31. Masalmeh, January 2017.
32. Manaf Tlass, in discussion with the author, October 2014.
33. Ibid.
34. "President Bashar al-Assad's Delegation to Daraa," YouTube video, 9:34, posted by "Rami Alasssad," March 24, 2011, www.youtube.com/watch?v=WCyitnKE4FA.
35. Al-Sayasneh, July 2017.
36. Masalmeh, January 2017.
37. Ibid.
38. "These Were the Demands of the People of Daraa the Night the Omari Mosque Was Stormed," YouTube video, posted by "Sari Sahhar," April 6, 2011, www.youtube.com/watch?v=0EgKmQ5n3mw.
39. Manaf Tlass, November 2016.
40. Ibid.
41. Masalmeh, January 2017.
42. "The Night of the Storming of the Omari Mosque, March 23, 2011," YouTube video, 9:21, posted by "anahourani2011," April 22, 2011, www.youtube.com/watch?v=8SSZLHu3rf0.
43. Manaf Tlass, November 2016.
44. Ibid.
45. Ibid.

Chapter 10 The Conspiracy
1. Manaf Tlass, in discussion with the author, November 2016.
2. Claude Guéant, in discussion with the author, November 2016.
3. Liz Sly, Sudarsan Raghavan, and Joby Warrick, "France Fires First Shots against Libya after Gaddafi's Forces Enter Benghazi," *Washington Post*, March 19, 2011.
4. The White House, Office of the Press Secretary, "Remarks by the President on Libya," March 19, 2011, *The Obama White House Archives*, accessed June 5, 2017, https://obamawhitehouse.archives.gov/the-press-office/2011/03/19/remarks-president-libya.
5. Manaf Tlass, November 2016.
6. Ibid.

7. "The Syrian Leadership Promises Reforms," YouTube video, 3:30, posted by "BBC News Arabic,"March 24, 2011, https://www.youtube.com/watch?v=XC9ldpVvS4w.

8. Sally Masalmeh, in discussion with the author, January 2017.

9. Shadi Abufakher, in discussion with the author, August 2017.

10. "Al-Marjeh demonstration, March 25, 2011," YouTube video, 1:38, posted by "Syrian-FreePress," March 25, 2011, www.youtube.com/watch?v=fpdekOoVYHM.

11. Ali Ezzo Rhebani, Douma city council member, in discussion with the author, November 2016.

12. Human Rights Watch, *We've Never Seen Such Horror: Crimes against Humanity by Syrian Security Forces*, June 1, 2011, www.hrw.org/report/2011/06/01/weve-never-seen-such-horror/crimes-against-humanity-syrian-security-forces.

13. Manaf Tlass, November 2016.

14. Ibid.

15. "The Request of the Deputy Abu-Roumieh from Bashar to Apologize for Events in Daraa," YouTube video, 2:28, posted by "FreeMediaSyria," April 5, 2011, www.youtube.com/watch?v=2dAUSuN32xg.

16. Manaf Tlass, October 2014.

17. Mazen Darwish, in discussion with the author, December 2016.

18. Ibid.

19. Khaled Khoja, in discussion with the author, August 2017.

20. Darwish, December 2016.

21. Ibid.

22. Ibid.

23. "Media Lying Against Syria," YouTube video, 15:13, posted by "HananNoura," April 2, 2011. https://www.youtube.com/watch?v=t2lmqzl3QM0.
    Syrian state television broadcast what it said were confessions by an Egyptian national who had been detained by the *mukhabarat* in Syria. The footage was later shared widely by regime loyalists on YouTube. The man claimed he came to Syria to stir trouble and that he was liaising with another alleged co-conspirator based in Colombia.

24. Reuters, "Syria Frees Reuters Reporter, Photographer Missing," April 1, 2011. https://www.reuters.com/article/idINIndia-56060520110401.

25. University student who took part in pro-Bashar rallies, in discussion with the author, June 2017.

26. "Bashar al-Assad's Speech in the People's Assembly after Syria's Events," YouTube video, 14:06, from an original broadcast on March 30, 2011 by Syrian state television, posted by "Bedoonta3lee9," March 30, 2011, www.youtube.com/watch?v=97iMoKAxfwQ.

27. Ibid.

28. Ibid.

29. "The Full Transcript of President Bashar al-Assad's Discourse in Front of the People's Assembly on March 30, 2011," President Bashar al-Assad official website, accessed June 5, 2017, www.presidentassad.net/index.php?option=com_content&view=article&id=1093:30&catid=303&Itemid=469.

30. Manaf Tlass, October 2014.

Chapter 11 Make Peace

1. Manaf Tlass, in discussion with the author, October 2014.

2. Ali Ezzo Rhebani, Douma city council member, in discussion with the author, November 2016.

Notes

3. Ibid.
4. Manaf Tlass, November 2016.
5. Rhebani, November 2016.
6. Manaf Tlass, November 2016.
7. Ibid.
8. Ibid.
9. "Addounia Channel's Report on What Happened in Douma 1/4/2011," YouTube video, 0:58, original broadcast on Addounia TV posted by "fatter hasan," April 1, 2011, www.youtube.com/watch?v=RUCpDewZZds.
10. Manaf Tlass, November 2016.
11. Ahmad al-Sayasneh, in discussion with the author, July 2017.
12. Rhebani, November 2016.
13. Ibid.
14. Ibid.
15. Manaf Tlass, November 2016.
16. Rhebani, November 2016.
17. Ibid.
18. Manaf Tlass, November 2016.
19. Ibid.
20. Ibid.
21. Ibid.
22. "The Syrian Revolution: The Friday of Perseverance Report 8-4-2011," YouTube video, 10:12, original broadcast by Al Arabiya news channel posted by "syriaus," April 4, 2011, www.youtube.com/watch?v=RjpRUE07A1op.
23. "Sham, Al Jazeera's first report on Friday of the Martyrs, April 1, 2011," YouTube video, original broadcast by Al Jazeera Arabic news channel posted by "ShaamNetwork S.N.N.," April 8, 2014, www.youtube.com/watch?v=oLcnxgn14Vc.
24. Manaf Tlass, October 2014.
25. Ibid.
26. Ibid.
27. Ibid.
28. Ibid.
29. Ahmad al-Sayasneh, in discussion with the author, July 2017.
30. Nizar al-Hiraki, in discussion with the author, July 2017.
31. Al-Sayasneh, July 2017.
32. Ibid.
33. Manaf Tlass, November 2016.
34. "Addounia TV—Interview with Sheik Ahmed al-Saysneh," YouTube video, 1:03, original broadcast of Addounia TV in April 2011 from Syrian state television posted by "Syrianagent2011," April 27, 2011, www.youtube.com/watch?v=1ZlZma2hXjw.
35. Al-Sayasneh, July 2017.
36. Ibid.

Chapter 12 You're Too Soft

1. Omar Abdelaziz Hallaj (former chief executive officer, Syria Trust for Development), in discussion with the author, September 2014.
2. Mohammad Munir al-Faqir, in discussion with the author, August 2017.
3. Hallaj, September 2014.

4. Ibid.
5. "Massar Children's Discovery Center," Henning Larsen, accessed June 12, 2017, www .henninglarsen.com/PdfArchive/Project_2710.pdf.
6. Ibid.
7. Adrian Blomfield, "Syria: Lord Recruited to Design Garden for Assad Family, Emails Show," *The Telegraph*, July 8, 2012, www.telegraph.co.uk/news/worldnews/middleeast/ syria/9384976/Syria-Lord-recruited-to-design-garden-for-Assad-family-emails-show.html.
8. Manaf Tlass, October 2014.
9. Joan Juliet Buck, "Asma al-Assad: A Rose in the Desert," *Vogue*, March 2011, posted on Gawker website, accessed June 12, 2017, http://gawker.com/asma-al-assad-a-rose-in-the -desert-1265002284.
10. Ibid.
11. Anonymous source, in discussion with the author, November 2016.
12. Memorandum from Brown Lloyd James to Fares Kallas, May 19, 2011, no. 2089956, WikiLeaks Syria Files, https://search.wikileaks.org/syria-files/emailid/2089956.
13. Ibid.
14. Eric Chevallier, in discussion with the author, December 2016.
15. Buck, "Asma al-Assad: A Rose in the Desert."
16. Chevallier, July 2017.
17. Ibid.
18. Ibid.
19. Ibid.
20. Manaf Tlass, November 2016.
21. Chevallier, July 2017.
22. "Sarkozy Hausse le Ton Contre le Régime Syrien" ["Sarkozy Raises His Tone against the Syrian Regime"], *L'Express*, April 26, 2011, www.lexpress.fr/actualite/politique/sarkozy -hausse-le-ton-contre-le-regime-syrien_986551.html.
23. Manaf Tlass, November 2016.
24. Ibid.
25. Ali Ezzo Rhebani, in discussion with the author, November 2016.
26. Manaf Tlass, November 2016.
27. Ibid.
28. Mazen Darwish, in discussion with the author, December 2016.
29. Khaled al-Khani, in discussion with the author, October 2014.
30. Ibid.
31. Syrian Human Rights Committee, *Atrocities Endured by Hama Residents*, December 26, 2004, www.shrc.org/?p=7185.
32. Al-Khani, October 2014.
33. Ibid.
34. Ibid.
35. "Douma 22-4-2011, Great Friday Protest, Tens of Thousands," YouTube video, 5:26, posted by "3ayeef," April 22, 2011, www.youtube.com/watch?v=ieoBrv7sVns.
36. "Zablatani Massacre after the Attempt by the Youth of Saqba and Surrounding Areas to Reach Abbaseen Square on Great Friday," YouTube video, 1:41, posted by "lion4syria," April 27, 2011, www.youtube.com/watch?v=UlGJj3E7Zc8.
37. Human Rights Watch, *We've Never Seen Such Horror: Crimes against Humanity by Syrian Security Forces*, June 1, 2011, 11, www.hrw.org/report/2011/06/01/weve-never-seen-such-horror/crimes -against-humanity-syrian-security-forces.

Notes

38. "Homs Sit-in at the New Clock: The Full Story," YouTube video, 8:00, posted by "thefreehoms," April 18, 2013, www.youtube.com/watch?v=ie580fHgxu8.
39. Manaf Tlass, November 2016.
40. Ibid.
41. "Smashing the Idol Hafez al-Assad in Al-Rastan the Syrian Revolution 2011," YouTube video, 1:32, posted by "Aboamin Amin," April 17, 2011, www.youtube.com/watch?v=pdIQ_OhUXck.
42. Germany-based defected army officer, in discussion with the author, July 2017.
43. Al-Rastan defected army officer, in discussion with the author, August 2017.
44. Ibid.
45. Ibid.
46. Germany-based defected army officer, July 2017.
47. Manaf Tlass, November 2016.
48. Germany-based defected army officer, July 2017.
49. Ibid.
50. Khaled Yacoub Oweis, "Syrian Forces Storm Town after Protest, Say Activists," Reuters, April 12, 2011, http://in.reuters.com/article/columns-us-syria-idINTRE72N2MC20110412.
51. Sally Masalmeh, in discussion with the author, January 2017.
52. Human Rights Watch, *We've Never Seen Such Horror.*
53. Ibid.
54. Sally Masalmeh and Malek al-Jawabra, in discussion with the author, January 2017.
55. Manaf Tlass, in discussion with the author, November 2016.
56. Hazem Suleiman, "Turning Artists into Traitors: Successful Soap Opera," *Al-Akhbar,* May 9, 2011, www.al-akhbar.com/node/11661.
57. Masalmeh, January 2017.
58. Masalmeh and Al-Jawabra, January 2017.
59. Masalmeh, January 2017.
60. Manaf Tlass, November 2016.
61. Human Rights Watch, *By All Means Necessary! Individual and Command Responsibility for Crimes against Humanity in Syria,"* December 15, 2011, 29, www.hrw.org/sites/default/files/reports/syria1211webwcover_0.pdf.
62. Manaf Tlass, November 2016.
63. Ibid.
64. Ibid.
65. Defected army officer, in discussion with the author, August 2017.
66. Manaf Tlass, November 2016.
67. Ibid.
68. Human Rights Watch, *We Live as in War: Crackdown on Protesters in the Governorate of Homs,* November 11, 2011, 29, www.hrw.org/sites/default/files/reports/syria1111webwcover_0.pdf.
69. Manaf Tlass, November 2016.
70. "Defection of First Lieutenant Abdul-Razzaq Mohammad Tlass," YouTube video, 4:32, from broadcast by Al Jazeera Arabic news channel posted by "mohammedhariri1," June 6, 2011, www.youtube.com/watch?v=FpYRNP8TCBI.
71. Manaf Tlass, November 2016.
72. Manaf Tlass, October 2014.

Chapter 13 The Hama Manual

1. Khaled al-Khani, in discussion with the author, October 2014.

494

Notes

2. Human Rights Watch, *Syria's Tadmor Prison: Dissent Still Hostage to a Legacy of Terror*, April 1996, www.hrw.org/reports/1996/Syria2.htm#P166_23507.

3. Al-Khani, October 2014.

4. "Watercolors of Hama in the 1930s," National Museum of Denmark website, http://en.natmus.dk/historical-knowledge/historical-knowledge-the-world/the-lands-of-the-mediterranean/the-far-east/digital-hama-a-window-on-syrias-past/watercolours-of-hama-in-the-1930s/.

5. Al-Khani, December 2016.

6. Ibid.

7. Ibid.

8. Ibid.

9. Ibid.

10. Raphael Lefèvre, *Ashes of Hama: The Muslim Brotherhood in Syria* (London: Hurst & Company, 2013), 112.

11. Human Rights Watch, *Human Rights in Syria, Chapter 2: The Great Repression 1976–1982*, September 1990, accessed on Internet Archive, https://archive.org/stream/bub_gb_N-xjxWYWnlwC/bub_gb_N-xjxWYWnlwC_djvu.txt.

12. Mustafa Tlass, *Mira'at Hayati: Al-Aqed Al-Rabe('ayn) 1978–1988, Al-Sumoud* [*My Life's Mirror: The Fourth Decade 1978–1988, Perseverance*] (Damascus: Dar Tlass, 2006), 450.

13. Human Rights Watch, *Human Rights in Syria, Chapter 2*.

14. Ibid.

15. Ibid.

16. Al-Khani, December 2016.

17. Human Rights Watch, *Human Rights in Syria, Chapter 2*.

18. Lefèvre, *Ashes of Hama*, 109.

19. Human Rights Watch, *Human Rights in Syria, Chapter 2*.

20. Al-Khani, December 2016.

21. "The Black Box: Hama 82," Al Jazeera Documentaries, 51:31, November 28, 2013, www.aljazeera.net/programs/black-box/2013/11/28/82-حماة.

22. Ibid.

23. Hafez al-Assad, "Mr. President Hafez al-Assad's Speech at Graduation Ceremony of the Third Tour of Revolutionary Youth Union Parachutists," October 1, 1980, President Bashar al-Assad official website, accessed June 26, 2017, www.presidentassad.net/index.php?option=com_content&view=article&id=673:1-10-1981&catid=214&Itemid=476.

24. Lefèvre, *Ashes of Hama*, 126.

25. Michel Seurat, *Syrie l'État de Barbarie* [*Syria the Barbaric State*] (Paris : Presses Universitaires de France), 112–13.

26. "The Black Box: Hama 82."

27. Al-Khani, December 2016.

28. "Surah Ya-Seen [36]—Al-Qur'an al-Kareem," Quran.com website, https://quran.com/36.

29. Al-Khani, December 2016.

30. Ibid.

31. Ibid.

32. Ibid.

33. Ibid.

34. Syrian Human Rights Committee, *Hama Massacre: February 1982, a Genocide and Crime against Humanity*, February 1, 2006, www.shrc.org/?p=8427.

35. Ibid.

36. Al-Khani, December 2016.

Notes

37. Ibid.
38. Ibid.
39. Ibid.
40. Ibid.
41. Ibid.
42. Ibid.
43. Mohammad Farouk Tayfour, in discussion with the author, August 2017.
44. Syrian Human Rights Committee, *Hama Massacre*.
45. "Why Am I Drawing Um Ibrahim?" YouTube video, 19:23, original broadcast by Orient News posted by "Emma Suleiman," uploaded January 31, 2012, www.youtube.com/watch?v=54EHiLzTHx8.

Chapter 14 Yalla Erhal Ya, Bashar! *(Come On, Bashar, Leave!)*

1. "Syria Top News—Syria—Hama—A Closeup of the Syrian Flag," YouTube video, 1:56, posted by "SyriaTopNews," June 18, 2011, www.youtube.com/watch?v=FiGWYf_9dRQ.
2. Human Rights Watch, *Human Rights in Syria, Chapter 2: The Great Repression 1976–1982*, September 1990, accessed on Internet Archive, https://archive.org/stream/bub_gb_N-xjxWYWnlwC/bub_gb_N-xjxWYWnlwC_djvu.txt.
3. Syrian Human Rights Committee, *Hama Massacre 1982: Legal Responsibility Requires Accountability*, July 7, 2003, www.shrc.org/?p=6742.
4. Human Rights Watch, *Human Rights in Syria, Chapter 2*.
5. Khaled al-Khani, in discussion with the author, November 2016.
6. Ibid.
7. Mustafa Khalifa, *Al-Qawqa'a: Yawmiyat Mutalasles* [*The Shell: Memoirs of a Hidden Observer*] (Beirut: Dar Al-Adab, 2016), 141–43.
8. Al-Khani, November 2016.
9. Ibid.
10. Ibid.
11. Bashar al-Assad, interview by Barbara Walters, *ABC News*, December 7, 2011, http://abcnews.go.com/International/transcript-abcs-barbara-walters-interview-syrian-president-bashar/story?id=15099152.
12. United Nations, "UN Rights Chief Urges Syria to End Assault on Its Own People," United Nations News Center website, June 9, 2011, www.un.org/apps/news/story.asp?NewsID=38665#.WVyrXTOBI8c.
13. Eric Chevallier, in discussion with the author, December 2016.
14. "Syria Crisis: Investigating Jisr al-Shughour," *BBC News* website, June 22, 2011, www.bbc.com/news/world-middle-east-13857654.
15. Chevallier, December 2016.
16. "Sniper in Hama on the Friday of the Children of Freedom, June 3," YouTube video, 3:48, posted by "FreeSyria," June 4, 2011, www.youtube.com/watch?v=vinh4IaHlO8.
17. Liam Stack, "Syrian Tanks Move In on City as Thousands Mourn Protesters' Deaths," *New York Times*, June 4, 2011, www.nytimes.com/2011/06/05/world/middleeast/05syria.html.
18. "Ugarit Hama, Dignified Scene of Friday's Protests with 'Ya Haif' Song and the Long Flag, Part 3, Hama 17 6," YouTube video, 2:08, posted by "Ugarit News—Syria," June 17, 2011, www.youtube.com/watch?v=zFKOic6gaI0.
19. Al-Khani, December 2016.
20. "Hama 10 6 2011 'Syria Wants Freedom' Song from Asi Square," YouTube video, 2:29, posted by "freesyria01," June 15, 2011, www.youtube.com/watch?v=jeqn99XTZfk.

21. Manaf Tlass, in discussion with the author, December 2016.

22. Ibid.

23. Nicholas Blanford, "Syria's Assad Offers Amnesty to Political Prisoners," *Christian Science Monitor*, May 31, 2011, www.csmonitor.com/World/Middle-East/2011/0531/Syria-s -Assad-offers-amnesty-to-political-prisoners.

24. Manaf Tlass, November 2016.

25. "Packed Hezbollah Gathering in Nabi Sheet for the Resistance and Liberation Anniversary 2011," *Moqawama* website, May 25, 2011, www.moqawama.org/essaydetails.php?eid=20819 &cid=141.

26. Ethan Bronner, "Israeli Troops Fire as Marchers Breach Borders," *New York Times*, May 15, 2011, www.nytimes.com/2011/05/16/world/middleeast/16mideast.html.

27. Anthony Shadid, "Syrian Elite to Fight Protests to 'the End,'" *New York Times*, May 10, 2011, www.nytimes.com/2011/05/11/world/middleeast/11makhlouf.html.

28. Dan Bilefsky, "New Move to Condemn Syria in UN," *New York Times*, June 8, 2011, www .nytimes.com/2011/06/09/world/middleeast/09nations.html.

29. Sam Dagher, Charles Levinson, and Margaret Coker, "Tiny Kingdom's Huge Role in Libya Draws Concern," *Wall Street Journal*, October 17, 2011, www.wsj.com/articles/SB1000 14240529702040023045766270009227646507mg=prod/accounts-wsj.

30. Wisam Kanaan and Mohammad al-Chalabi, "Syria and Qatar: A Love Story and Divorce...And 'Al-Jazeera,'" *Al-Akhbar*, July 22, 2011, www.al-akhbar.com/node/17243.

31. Moaz al-Khatib, in discussion with the author, July 2017.

32. Walid Jumblatt, in discussion with the author, November 2014.

33. Manaf Tlass, November 2016.

34. Jumblatt, November 2014.

35. "Photos of his Excellency the President in 2011," Al-Assad.de website, www.alassad.de/ أرشيف-صور-السيد-الرئيس/**2011**/حزيران-2011.

36. Jumblatt, November 2014.

37. Liam Stack, "Video of Tortured Boy's Corpse Deepens Anger in Syria," *New York Times*, May 30, 2011, www.nytimes.com/2011/05/31/world/middleeast/31syria.html.

38. Jumblatt, November 2014.

39. Ibid.

40. Manaf Tlass, October 2014.

41. Ibid.

42. "The Head of the Airforce Intelligence Directorate Speaks to Sputnik about the Crisis," Sputnik News website, November 1, 2016, https://arabic.sputniknews.com/arab_world/ سوريا-أزمة-مقابلة-مخابرات-201611011020658565.

43. Manaf Tlass, December 2016.

44. Ibid.

45. "President Bashar al-Assad's Speech at Damascus University on June 20, 2011," President Bashar al-Assad official website, www.presidentassad.net/index.php?option=com_content &view=article&id=1091:20-2011&catid=303&Itemid=469.

46. Bassel al-Junaidi, "The Story of the 'Friends of Saydnaya': The Three Most Powerful Men in Syria Today," *Al-Jumhuriya* website, October 16, 2013, http://aljumhuriya.net/19328.

47. Al-Khani, December 2016.

48. Manaf Tlass, December 2016.

49. Ibid.

50. "Thala al-Khair Promotes a French Website Funded by Her Husband Manaf to Improve the Regime's Image," Syria Insight Facebook page based on e-mail in WikiLeaks Syria Files, released in 2012, accessed July 5, 2017, www.facebook.com/syria.wiki/photos/

Notes

a.455237374495396.104844.455180471167753/466861026666364/?type=3
&theater.

51. Vincent Hugeux and Hala Kodmani, "Syrie: La Legion Française d'Assad" ["Syria: Assad's French Legion"], *L'Express*, September 13, 2012, www.lexpress.fr/actualite/monde/proche-moyen-orient/syrie-la-legion-francaise-d-assad_1160179.html.

52. InfoSyrie.fr website, accessed July 5, 2017, www.infosyrie.fr/re-information/.

53. Manaf Tlass, December 2016.

54. Chevallier, December 2016.

55. Ibid.

56. "President Assad and His Wife in a Surprise Visit to Jala'a Stadium, Part 1," YouTube video, 2:20, posted by "ZeinasoftNetwork," July 27, 2011, www.youtube.com/watch?v=L6HmDf5Otdo.

57. "President Assad and His Wife in a Surprise Visit to Jala'a Stadium, Part 2," YouTube video, 1:29, posted by "ZeinasoftNetwork," July 27, 2011, www.youtube.com/watch?v=emyGUZaPaV8.

58. "President Assad and His Wife in a Surprise Visit to Jala'a Stadium, Part JALA'A3," YouTube video, 1:56, posted by "ZeinasoftNetwork," July 27, 2011, www.youtube.com/watch?v=L4kSC0oTdcI.

59. "Hama—Asi Square Demonstration on 'Leave Friday' 1/7/2011," YouTube video, 13:51, posted by "Ayham Alkasem," February 3, 2014 www.youtube.com/watch?v=LwUrpE9zKFw.

60. "Glorious Syria Hama, A Brilliant Hamwi Celebration on 'Leave Friday,'" YouTube video, 14:31, posted by "louai alzalam," August 29, 2011, www.youtube.com/watch?v=42GDzLl6Qfs&list=PL4K0x9Q_-lmD6IeGvghIbhDbzny9GGZX2.

61. Human Rights Watch, *Syria: Shootings, Arrests Follow Hama Protest*, July 6, 2011, www.hrw.org/news/2011/07/06/syria-shootings-arrests-follow-hama-protest.

62. Chevallier, December 2016.

63. Ibid., Chevallier said his entry to Hama was facilitated by the city's police chief, who was mulling defection to the opposition side.

64. Ibid.

65. "Hama—The US Ambassador's Visit to Asi Square 8-7-2011," YouTube video, 1:32, posted by "Syrian Revolution Network," July 8, 2011, www.youtube.com/watch?v=FNIk_bRweH4.

66. Mohammad Jaber, in discussion with the author, March 2013.

67. "Gunfire at Syrians in Damascus from the French and US Embassies," YouTube video, 6:54, posted by "HananNoura," July 22, 2011, www.youtube.com/watch?v=nAJN_f0bEI8.

68. Nada Bakri, "Crowds in Syria Attack US and French Embassies," *New York Times*, July 11, 2011, www.nytimes.com/2011/07/12/world/middleeast/12syria.html.

69. Manaf Tlass, October 2014.

70. "I Was There, the Assault on Hama, August 3, 2011," YouTube video of original broadcast by Alaraby TV, 26:05, posted by "Alaraby TV," October 27, 2016, www.youtube.com/watch?v=qZejluGjEeY.

71. Nada Bakri and Anthony Shadid, "Broadcasting Hama Ruins, Syria Says It Has Ended Revolt," *New York Times*, August 5, 2011, www.nytimes.com/2011/08/06/world/middleeast/06syria.html.

72. Rania Abouzeid, "Exclusive: A Visit to Hama, the Rebel Syrian City That Refused to Die," *Time* magazine, August 11, 2011, http://content.time.com/time/world/article/0,8599,2088068,00.html.

Notes

Chapter 15 Don't Stay with the Butcher

1. "President of Syria Dr. Bashar al-Assad in Umayyad Square among His People," YouTube video, 11:33, posted by "HananNoura," January 11, 2012, www.youtube.com/watch?v=oLUpQ46bkrQ.
2. Witness, in discussion with the author, August 2017.
3. The White House, Office of the Press Secretary, "President Obama: The Future of Syria Must Be Determined by Its People, but President Bashar al-Assad Is Standing in Their Way," *The Obama White House Archives*, August 18, 2011, accessed October 19, 2017, https://obamawhitehouse.archives.gov/blog/2011/08/18/president-obama-future-syria-must-be-determined-its-people-president-bashar-al-assad.
4. "US, Europe Call for Syrian Leader al-Assad to Step Down," CNN website, August 19, 2011, http://edition.cnn.com/2011/POLITICS/08/18/us.syria/index.html.
5. United Nations, "Syrian Crackdown on Protesters May Amount to Crimes against Humanity—UN Report," United Nations website, August 18, 2011, www.un.org/apps/news/story.asp?NewsID=39325#.WekAGjOB3yI.
6. Carnegie Middle East Center, *Syria in Crisis: The Syrian National Council*, September 25, 2013, http://carnegie-mec.org/diwan/48334?lang=en.
7. Bashar al-Assad, interview by Barbara Walters, *ABC News*, December 7, 2011, http://abcnews.go.com/International/transcript-abcs-barbara-walters-interview-syrian-president-bashar/story?id=15099152.
8. Euan McKirdy, "Eight Times Russia Blocked a UN Security Council Resolution on Syria," CNN website, April 13, 2017, http://edition.cnn.com/2017/04/13/middleeast/russia-unsc-syria-resolutions/index.html.
9. Reuters, "NATO Says Will Not Intervene in Syria," October 31, 2011, www.reuters.com/article/us-syria-nato-newspro/nato-says-will-not-intervene-in-syria-idUSTRE79U52Z20111031.
10. Eric Chevallier, in discussion with the author, July 2017.
11. "President of Syria Dr. Bashar al-Assad in Umayyad Square among His People," YouTube video.
12. Manaf Tlass, in discussion with the author, August 2016.
13. Ibid.
14. Ibid.
15. Ibid., December 2018.
16. Ibid., August 2016.
17. Ibid.
18. Agence France-Presse (AFP), "Paris Rappelle son Ambassadeur en Syrie" ["Paris Recalls its Ambassador to Syria"], France 24 website, November 16, 2011, www.france24.com/fr/20111116-paris-rappelle-son-ambassadeur-syrie-damas-ministre-affaires-etrangeres-alain-juppe-attaque-consulat.
19. Manaf Tlass, August 2016.
20. Ibid.
21. Anthony Shadid, "US Ambassador to Syria Leaves Damascus Amid Threats to Safety," *New York Times*, October 24, 2011, www.nytimes.com/2011/10/25/world/middleeast/us-ambassador-to-syria-leaves-damascus-amid-threats-to-safety.html.
22. Chevallier, December 2016.
23. Ibid.
24. Ibid.
25. Manaf Tlass, December 2018.

26. Chevallier, December 2016.

27. Thom Shanker and Liam Stack, "Panetta Is First US Defense Secretary to Visit Libya," *New York Times*, December 17, 2011, www.nytimes.com/2011/12/18/world/africa/leon -panetta-defense-secretary-libya-visit.html.

28. "Egyptian Elections: Preliminary Results Update," *Jadaliyya* website, January 9, 2012, www.jadaliyya.com/pages/index/3331/egyptian-elections_preliminary-results_updated-.

29. Brian Whitaker, "Yemen's Ali Abdullah Saleh Resigns—But It Changes Little," *The Guardian*, November 24, 2011, www.theguardian.com/commentisfree/2011/nov/24/yemen-ali -abdullah-saleh-resigns.

30. Chevallier, July 2017.

31. Ibid.

32. Syria Wikileaks, "Manaf Tlass's Wife Thala Khair and Bashar al-Assad Are Best Friends and She Wishes Him Victory over His Enemies," Facebook, July 31, 2012, www.facebook .com/syr.wiki/posts/364574890277421:0.

33. Ibid.

34. Syria Wikileaks, Thala Khair-Tlass message to Bashar al-Assad on January 10, 2012, *Syrian Insight*. (Website no longer available but copies of posts have been preserved.)

35. Manaf Tlass, November 2016.

36. Ibid.

37. Darwish, July 2017.

38. Ibid.

39. Shadi Abufakher, in discussion with the author, July 2017.

40. Defected Syrian army officer who took part in Iran training, in discussion with the author, August 2017.

41. Jakub Dalek and Adam Senft, "Behind Blue Coat: Investigations of Commercial Filtering in Syria and Burma," *Citizen Lab* website, November 9, 2011. https://citizenlab.ca/2011/11/ behind-blue-coat/.

42. Darwish, July 2017.

43. Haitham al-Manaa, in discussion with the author, October 2014.

44. Anthony Shadid, "Killing of Opposition Leader in Syria Provokes Kurds," *New York Times*, October 8, 2011, www.nytimes.com/2011/10/09/world/middleeast/killing-of-opposition -leader-in-syria-provokes-kurds.html.

45. "The Lawyer Khalil Ma'atouq and the Human Rights Lawyer Mazen Darwish [at the Funeral of the] Martyr Masha'al Tammo," YouTube video, 2:57, posted by "Ahmad Khalil," January 29, 2013, www.youtube.com/watch?v=b668LDHI840.

46. Riad Seif, in discussion with the author, August 2017.

47. "As Syrian Death Toll Tops 5,000, UN Human Rights Chief Warns about Key City," *UN News* website, December 12, 2011, https://news.un.org/en/story/2011/12/398082-syrian -death-toll-tops-5000-un-human-rights-chief-warns-about-key-city.

48. Kareem Fahim, "Syria Blames Al Qaeda after Bombs Kill Dozens in Damascus," *New York Times*, December 23, 2011, www.nytimes.com/2011/12/24/world/middleeast/syria-says -suicide-bombers-attack-in-damascus.html?mcubz=1.

49. "Assad Emails: 'Blaming Al-Qaida Is Not in Our Interest'—Translation," *The Guardian* website, March 14, 2012, www.theguardian.com/world/2012/mar/14/bashar-al-assad -syria12.

50. "Saeed Ramadan al-Bouti Accuses Burhan Ghalyoun of Being behind the Bombings in Damascus," Daily Motion video taken from a broadcast by Syrian State Television, 14:05, posted by "FreeMediaSyria," December 24, 2011, www.dailymotion.com/video/xna61z.

51. Darwish, July 2017.

52. "Nighttime Protest in Barzeh on New Year's Eve in the Presence of [Activists] Razan Zeitouneh and Mazen Darwish," YouTube Video, 1:37, posted by "All For Syria," December 31, 2011, www.youtube.com/watch?v=tByALHvSMLs&t=35s.

Chapter 16 Blood on My Hands

1. Manaf Tlass, in discussion with the author, November 2016.
2. Even though sidelined by Bashar, Manaf was never formally removed from his position as commander of the 104th Brigade of the Republican Guard.
3. "The Martyred Lion of the Republican Guard Bids the Battlefields Farewell," *Al Manar* website, October 20, 2017, www.almanar.com.lb/2777399. (Zahreddine was killed in a landmine explosion in eastern Syria in October 2017.)
4. Homs residents and witnesses, in discussion with the author, June 2013.
5. Human Rights Watch, *We Live as in War: Crackdown on Protesters in the Governorate of Homs, Syria*, November 11, 2011, accessed October 30, 2018, www.hrw.org/report/2011/11/11/we-live-war/crackdown-protesters-governorate-homs-syria.
6. Witnessed by the author, June 2013.
7. "The Actress Fadwa Suleiman in the Heart of the Protests in al-Bayada, Homs," from footage broadcast by the Al-Jazeera News Channel, YouTube video, 2:47, posted by "Saka2010," November 8, 2011, www.youtube.com/watch?v=LZTIPdiQVNI.
8. Homs residents and witnesses, in discussion with the author, April 2014.
9. Mazen Darwish, in discussion with the author, July 2017.
10. Ibid.
11. Mohammad Farouk Tayfour, in discussion with the author, August 2017.
12. Defected army officer turned Syrian rebel leader, in discussion with the author, August 2017.
13. Sam Dagher, "Libyans Loot Weapons from Desert Cache," *Wall Street Journal*, October 1, 2011, www.wsj.com/articles/SB10001424052970203405504576602201905770000.
14. Defected army officer turned Syrian rebel leader, August 2017.
15. Haitham al-Manaa, in discussion with the author, October 2014. Manaa was among those who met Qatari national Abdul-Rahman al-Nuaimi.
16. Suhair al-Atassi, in discussion with the author, August 2017. Atassi was a leading Syrian opposition figure and had firsthand knowledge of the offers made by Nuaimi.
17. Darwish, July 2017.
18. Riad Seif, in discussion with the author, August 2017. Seif, a leading figure from the Damascus Spring period that followed Bashar al-Assad's ascent to power in 2000, was a senior member of the Syrian National Council and later assumed leadership posts in subsequent opposition bodies.
19. Sam Dagher, "Arab Media Clash Over Syria," *Wall Street Journal*, March 24, 2012, www.wsj.com/articles/SB10001424052970203961204577269081450598296.
20. "The Charm of Telesalafism: An Influential Rebel Preacher Who Needs to Tone Things Down," *The Economist*, October 20, 2012, www.economist.com/middle-east-and-africa/2012/10/20/the-charm-of-telesalafism.
21. Burhan Ghalyoun, in in discussion with the author, November 2016.
22. Eric Chevallier, in discussion with the author, July 2017.
23. Ibid.
24. Darwish, July 2017.
25. "They Beat Him and Ordered Him 'Kneel to Your God Bashar al-Assad,' See What He Did," YouTube video, 1:01, posted by "Aly Mossallam," September 17, 2011, www.youtube.com/watch?v=QndtTv74oy8.
26. Nephew of the friend of Aniseh Makhlouf, in discussion with the author, August 2017.

Notes

27. Ibid.
28. "Assad Emails: "Harrods and Fondue Set," *The Guardian*, March 14, 2012, www.theguardian.com/world/2012/mar/14/bashar-al-assad-syria20.
29. "Assad Emails: Bougeoirs and Chandeliers," *The Guardian*, March 14, 2012, www.theguardian.com/world/2012/mar/14/bashar-al-assad-syria25.
30. "Assad Emails: 'Fwd: Christian Louboutin Shoes Coming Shortly,'" *The Guardian*, March 14, 2012, www.theguardian.com/world/2012/mar/14/bashar-al-assad-syria24.
31. Robert Booth, Mona Mahmood, and Luke Harding, "Exclusive: Secret Assad Emails Lift Lid on Life of Leader's Inner Circle," *The Guardian*, March 14, 2012.
32. "Assad Emails: 'If We Are Strong Together,'" *The Guardian*, March 14, 2012, www.theguardian.com/world/2012/mar/14/syria-middleeast1.
33. Manaf Tlass, November 2016.
34. Michael Hann and Mathew Taylor, "Assad iTunes Emails Show Music Taste from Chris Brown to Right Said Fred," *The Guardian*, March 14, 2012, www.theguardian.com/world/2012/mar/14/assad-itunes-emails-chris-brown.
35. Karim Fahim and Hwaida Saad, "Syria Agrees to Allow Outside Observers, but Activists Remain Wary," *New York Times*, December 19, 2011, www.nytimes.com/2011/12/20/world/middleeast/syria-agrees-to-allow-arab-league-observers.html.
36. Manaf Tlass, October 2014.
37. Ibid.
38. Homs activist Mahmoud Fahed, in discussion with the author, December 2014.
39. Sheikh Hamad bin Khalifa al-Thani, interview by Bob Simon, *CBS: 60 Minutes*, January 15, 2012, www.cbsnews.com/news/emir-of-qatar-favors-arab-troops-in-syria/.
40. "Arab League Calls on Assad to Delegate Power," Al-Jazeera website, January 23, 2012, www.aljazeera.com/news/middleeast/2012/01/2012122546254111178.html.
41. Robin Pogrebin, "Qatari Riches Are Buying Art World Influence," *New York Times*, July 22, 2013, www.nytimes.com/2013/07/23/arts/design/qatar-uses-its-riches-to-buy-art-treasures.html?pagewanted=all&_r=0.
42. "Assad Emails: Asma Signs Off as 'AAA'," *The Guardian*, March 14, 2012, www.theguardian.com/world/2012/mar/14/bashar-al-assad-syria27.
43. Ibid.
44. "Assad Emails: 'I'm Sure You Have Many Places to Turn to, Including Doha,'" *The Guardian*, March 14, 2012, www.theguardian.com/world/2012/mar/14/bashar-al-assad-syria9.
45. Manaf Tlass, October 2014.
46. The White House, Office of the Press Secretary, "Statement by the President on Syria," February 4, 2012, *The Obama White House Archives*, accessed October 30, 2018, https://obamawhitehouse.archives.gov/the-press-office/2012/02/04/statement-president-syria.
47. United Nations, "Security Council Fails to Adopt Draft Resolution on Syria as Russian Federation, China Veto Text Supporting Arab League's Proposed Peace Plan," United Nations official website, February 4, 2012, accessed October 30, 2018, www.un.org/press/en/2012/sc10536.doc.htm.
48. "Journalist Marie Colvin in Homs: 'I Saw a Baby Die Today,'" *BBC News* website, February 21, 2012, www.bbc.com/news/av/world-middle-east-17120484/journalist-marie-colvin-in-homs-i-saw-a-baby-die-today.
49. Baba Amr field hospital doctor, opposition activist, and citizen journalist who were all there at the time, in discussion with the author, September 2015.
50. General Abdul-Kareem Salloum, head of the Homs branch of Military Intelligence, in discussion with the author, February 2014.

51. Human Rights Watch, *Syria: New Satellite Images Show Homs Shelling*, March 2, 2012, accessed October 30 2018, www.hrw.org/news/2012/03/02/syria-new-satellite-images-show-homs -shelling.

52. Ahmed al-Hamid, in discussion with the author, September 2015.

53. Manaf Tlass, October 2014.

54. Human Rights Watch, *Syria: New Satellite Images Show Homs Shelling*, March 2, 2012, www .hrw.org/news/2012/03/02/syria-new-satellite-images-show-homs-shelling.

55. Baba Amr residents, in discussion with the author, June 2013.

56. "Brigadier General Essam Zahreddine's Victory Poem from the Heart of Baba Amr," You-Tube video, 3:24, posted by "Maher Alassad," September 8, 2012, www.youtube.com/ watch?v=8TJeJ_pDyDc.

Chapter 17 *We Have to Win!*

1. Sam Dagher, "Syrian Pilot Defects with Jet," *Wall Street Journal*, June 22, 2012, www.wsj .com/articles/SB10001424052702304765304577480281116912796.

2. Ibid.

3. Suleiman al-Khalidi and Khaled Yacoub Oweis, "Syrian Pilot Defects to Jordan, Gets Asylum," Reuters, June 21, 2012, www.reuters.com/article/us-syria-crisis/syrian-fighter -pilot-defects-to-jordan-gets-asylum-idUSBRE85D0IS20120621?feedType=RSS &feedName=topNews&utm_source=feedburner&utm_medium=feed&utm_campaign =Feed%3A+reuters%2FtopNews+%28News+%2F+US+%2F+Top+News%29.

4. "Al-Jazeera: Afaq Ahmed on the Defection of the Pilot Hassan Hamadah," YouTube video, taken from a broadcast by the Al-Jazeera news channel, 4:35, posted by "Queen-Freedom7," June 21, 2012, www.youtube.com/watch?v=kJhj6pMr7Co.

5. Manaf Tlass, in discussion with the author, August 2016.

6. Ibid.

7. Ibid.

8. Bassel Mereb, "The Sons of Major General Mustafa Tlass, Manaf and Firas, Have Announced Their Defection from the Syrian Regime and Their Families Flee to Dubai," *Beirut Observer* website, March 11, 2012. https://www.beirutobserver.com/2012/03/2012 -03-11-14-40-43/.

9. "The Traitor Mustafa Tlass Denies His Defection and That of His Children," YouTube video, taken from a broadcast by Lebanon-based Al-Jadeed TV, 2:08, posted by "Ziyad Ayoub," March 13, 2012, www.youtube.com/watch?v=HlVer8dtRok.

10. Manaf Tlass, August 2016.

11. "Full Coverage of President Assad's Visit to the Baba Amr Neighborhood and Homs," YouTube video, taken from a broadcast by Syrian state television, 8:21, posted by "Zein-asoftNetwork," March 28, 2012, www.youtube.com/watch?v=YB89WEuQ9fk.

12. Manaf Tlass, August 2016.

13. Ibid.

14. Ibid.

15. Ibid.

16. Ibid., October 2014.

17. Defected Syrian army officer, in discussion with the author, August 2017.

18. Hassan Nasrallah, speech on December 6, 2011, transcript posted on Hezbollah's *Moqa-wama* website, www.moqawama.org/essaydetails.php?eid=22614&cid=142.

19. Reuters, "Factbox: Referendum on Syria's New Constitution," February 25, 2012, www .reuters.com/article/us-syria-constitution-idUSTRE81O0BT20120225.

20. Mazen Darwish, in discussion with the author, July 2017.

21. Ibid.

22. Eric Chevallier, in discussion with the author, July 2017.

23. Darwish, July 2017.

24. Chevallier, July 2017.

25. Elizabeth Flock, "US Closes Syrian Embassy: How Often Does the US Shutter Embassies?" *Washington Post*, February 6, 2012, www.washingtonpost.com/blogs/blogpost/post/us-syrian-embassy-closes-another-diplomatic-shut-down-as-tensions-rise/2012/02/06/gIQAAsC4tQ_blog.html?utm_term=.cb3d86e90dd6.

26. "Kofi Annan's Six-Point Plan for Syria," *Al-Jazeera English* website, March 27, 2012, www.aljazeera.com/news/middleeast/2012/03/2012327153111767387.html.

27. Crispian Balmer and Dominic Evans, "EU Slaps Sanctions on Assad's Family; Mortars Hit Homs," Reuters, March 23, 2012, www.reuters.com/article/uk-syria-eu-sanctions-idUKBRE82M0DN20120323.

28. Carnegie Middle East Center, "Group of Friends of the Syrian People: 1st Conference," Reuters, May 1, 2012, www.reuters.com/article/uk-syria-eu-sanctions-idUKBRE82M0DN20120323.

29. Karen De Young, "Saudi, Qatari Plans to Arm Syrian Rebels Risk Overtaking Cautious Approach Favored by US," *Washington Post*, March 1, 2012, www.washingtonpost.com/world/national-security/saudi-qatari-plans-to-arm-syrian-rebels-risk-overtaking-cautious-approach-favored-by-us/2012/03/01/gIQArWQflR_story.html?utm_term=.0b08adId4eI3.

30. The White House, Office of the Press Secretary, "Press Conference by the President," *The Obama White House Archives*, March 6, 2012, accessed October 30, 2018, https://obamawhitehouse.archives.gov/the-press-office/2012/03/06/press-conference-president. At the time more than 60 percent of Americans believed that Obama should not intervene in Syria, according to a Pew survey.

31. Human Rights Council, *Oral Update of the Independent International Commission of Inquiry on the Syrian Arab Republic*, HRC Twentieth Session, June 26 2012, www.ohchr.org/Documents/HRBodies/HRCouncil/RegularSession/Session20/COI_OralUpdate_A.HRC.20.CRP.I.pdf.

32. Manaf Tlass, August 2016.

33. "Mrs. Asma Al-Assad with the Paralympic Team at the Fayha," YouTube video, 6:15, posted by "SyriaAlassad27," June 21, 2012, www.youtube.com/watch?v=Mo0GQzkeeb4.

34. Manaf Tlass, in discussion with the author, August 2016.

35. Ibid.

36. Ibid.

37. Damascus Commonwealth War Cemetery, Commonwealth Graves Commission website, last accessed October 30, 2018, www.cwgc.org/find-a-cemetery/cemetery/91008/DAMASCUS%20COMMONWEALTH%20WAR%20CEMETERY.

38. Manaf Tlass, August 2016.

39. "Bashar al-Assad's interview with Iranian TV," YouTube video, taken from a broadcast by Syrian state television, 47:11, posted by "TheArabianTV," June 29, 2012, www.youtube.com/watch?v=wgu4-c7R_a0.

40. Manaf Tlass, August 2016.

Chapter 18 Exiting

1. Laurent Fabius, in discussion with the author, December 2016.

2. Ibid.

3. Ibid.
4. Ibid.
5. Miriam Elder, "Syria will Receive Attack Helicopters from Russia, Kremlin Confirms," *The Guardian*, June 28, 2012, www.theguardian.com/world/2012/jun/28/syria-receive-attack-helicopter-risussia.
6. Fabius, December 2016.
7. Manaf Tlass, in discussion with the author, August 2016.
8. "Kofi Annan Calls for Transitional Government in Syria," *BBC News* website, June 30 2012, www.bbc.com/news/av/world-middle-east-18661074/kofi-annan-calls-for-transitional-government-in-syria.
9. "Action Group for Syria Final Communiqué," United Nations website, June 30, 2012, www.un.org/News/dh/infocus/Syria/FinalCommuniqueActionGroupforSyria.pdf.
10. "Concluding Remarks by Joint Special Envoy Kofi Annan at the Meeting of Action Group on Syria—Geneva," UN News Center, June 30, 2012.
11. Fabius, December 2016.
12. "Final Declaration Read by Kofi Annan, the Joint Special Envoy of the United Nations and the League of Arab States on the Syrian Crisis," UN Web TV, June 30, 2012, last accessed October 31, 2018, http://webtv.un.org/%20http:/www.unmultimedia.org/tv/webcast/archive.html/watch/final-declaration-read-by-kofi-annan-the-joint-special-envoy-of-the-united-nations-and-the-league-of-arab-states-on-the-syrian-crisis/1714086833001/?term=&sort=date&page=3.
13. Ibid.
14. "Sergey Lavrov, Foreign Minister of the Russian Federation—Press Conference," UN Web TV, June 30, 2012, http://webtv.un.org/search/sergey-lavrov-foreign-minister-of-the-russian-federation-press-conference/1714179474001/?term=2012-06-30&lan=English&cat=Media&sort=date.
15. "Hillary Clinton, United States Secretary of State—Press Conference," UN Web TV, June 30, 2012, http://webtv.un.org/search/hillary-clinton-united-states-secretary-of-state-press-conference/1714099043001/?term=2012-06-30&lan=English&cat=Media&sort=date.
16. Fabius, December 2016.
17. Manaf Tlass, August 2016.
18. Ibid.
19. Isaac Stone Fish, "The Massive Mural That Captures Syria's Surprising Alliance with North Korea," Foreign Policy, September 10, 2013, https://foreignpolicy.com/2013/09/10/the-massive-mural-that-captures-syrias-surprising-alliance-with-north-korea/.
20. Manaf Tlass, August 2016.
21. "Assassination of Adnan Wehbeh, who Initiated the Revolution in Douma," Al-Jazeera Net, June 25, 2012, www.aljazeera.net/news/reportsandinterviews/2012/6/25-اغتيال-عدنان-وهبى-محرك-الثورة-بدوما.
22. Manaf Tlass, August 2016.
23. Ibid. Wissam al-Hassan was later killed in October 2012 in a massive car bomb blast in Beirut, which his partisans and allies blamed on the Iran-Hezbollah-Assad regime axis.
24. Ibid.
25. Ibid.
26. Ibid.
27. "Conférence des Amis du Peuple Syrien—Discours d'Ouverture de François Hollande (06.07.12)" ["Friends of the Syrian People Conference—Opening Remarks by François Hollande"], YouTube video, 13:18, posted by French Ministry of Foreign Affairs and International Development, July 11, 2012, www.youtube.com/watch?v=T15pX27l-rg.

28. "Al-Jazeera: Friends of the Syrian People Conference in Paris with Commentary—Part 2," YouTube video, taken from a broadcast by Al-Jazeera, 2:15:40, posted by "Freedomfornewsyria Forall," July 6, 2012, www.youtube.com/watch?v=6OGh7t NAXrM.

29. Hillary Rodham Clinton, "Remarks at the Friends of the Syrian People Ministerial Meeting," US Department of State Archives, Secretary of State Hillary Rodham Clinton: 2009 to 2013, July 6, 2012, https://2009-2017.state.gov/secretary/20092013clinton/rm/2012 /07/194628.htm.

30. "Syria Manaf Tlass Defection 'Hard Blow' for Assad," *BBC News* website, July 6, 2012, www.bbc.com/news/world-middle-east-18741423.

31. Fabius, December 2016.

32. *Syrie L'État de Barbarie* [*Syria the Barbaric State*] is the name of a book authored by Michel Seurat, a French sociologist and researcher with France's National Center for Scientific Research. Seurat lived and worked in Syria at varying intervals between the early 1970s and early '80s. He was later kidnapped in Beirut by Shiite militants linked to Iran and the Assad regime. He died in captivity in the mid '80s.

33. Fabius, December 2016.

34. French official speaking on condition of anonymity, in discussion with the author, July 2017.

35. Ibid.

36. Manaf Tlass, November 2016.

37. Ibid.

38. A person present at a meeting in Washington between an emissary of Assef Shawkat and the CIA, in discussion with the author, January 2019.

39. Manaf Tlass, November 2016.

40. Ibid.

41. French official speaking on condition of anonymity, July 2017.

42. Georges Malbrunot, in discussion with the author, November 2016.

43. French official speaking on condition of anonymity, in discussion with the author, July 2017.

44. Sam Dagher, Nour Malas, and Joe Lauria, "Syria Rebels Take Battle to Capital's Streets," *Wall Street Journal*, July 16, 2012, www.wsj.com/articles/SB100014240527023039337045 7530253235890254.

45. Manaf Tlass, October 2014.

46. Ibid.

47. "Fierce Clashes in the Midan Neighborhood, Live on Al-Jazeera," YouTube video, taken from a broadcast by Al-Jazeera, 10:24, posted by "MidanRevolution," July 16, 2012, www .youtube.com/watch?v=FNqml4NOLII.

48. Manaf Tlass, October 2014.

49. Sam Dagher and Nour Malas, "Bomb Strikes Syria Leader's Inner Circle," *Wall Street Journal*, July 18, 2012.

50. Doctor at the Chami Hospital in Damascus, in discussion with the author, December 2014.

51. "Solemn Funeral Ceremony for the Nation's Martyrs, the Heroes," YouTube video, taken from a broadcast by Syrian state television, 5:01, posted by "SyrianTVOfficial," July 20, 2012, www.youtube.com/watch?v=4TJTcKpuu6M.

52. "The Funeral of the Martyred General Assef Shawkat in the Village of Al-Mahdahlah in Tartous," YouTube video, 0:47, posted by "Tartous Now," July 27, 2012, www.youtube .com/watch?v=GjPOKd9la2Y.

53. Sam Dagher and Nour Malas, "Syrians Flee Capital as Regime Hits Back," *Wall Street Journal*, July 19, 2012, www.wsj.com/articles/SBI00008723963904444643045775366834299928596.
54. Manaf Tlass, October 2014.
55. French official speaking on condition of anonymity, July 2017.

Chapter 19 No Role for You
1. "Manaf Tlass Performing Umrah after the Announcement of His Defection," YouTube video, taken from a broadcast by the Al Arabiya Channel, 0:15, posted by "ksadalel," July 24, 2012, www.youtube.com/watch?v=IYOIyXtd45E.
2. Manaf Tlass, in discussion with the author, October 2014.
3. Ibid.
4. Ibid. December 2018.
5. "Full Statement by Brigadier General Manaf Tlass Officially Announcing His Defection," YouTube video, taken from a broadcast by the Al Arabiya Channel, 2:53, posted by "Sameer AlHariri," July 24, 2012, www.youtube.com/watch?v=XEmORJ5f2YI.
6. Manaf Tlass, October 2014.
7. Eric Chevallier, in discussion with the author, December 2016.
8. Ibid.
9. Manaf Tlass, October 2014.
10. Ibid.
11. Ibid.
12. "War Crimes Complaint against Syria Ex-Minister in France," *Ahram Online* reprint of a story by Agence France-Presse, March 18, 2012, http://english.ahram.org.eg/NewsContent/2/8/37052/World/Region/War-crimes-complaint-against-Syria-exminister-in-F.aspx.
13. Michel Duclos, in discussion with the author, November 2016.
14. Ibid.
15. "Prophet Mohammed Cartoons Controversy: Timeline," *The Telegraph*, May 4, 2015, https://www.telegraph.co.uk/news/worldnews/europe/france/11341599/Prophet-Muhammad-cartoons-controversy-timeline.html
16. French official who spoke on condition of anonymity, in discussion with the author, December 2016.
17. Mohammad Nassar, "Businessman Firas Tlass: 45 Officers from My Family Defected from the Regime…And My Father Is 'Sad and Silent,'" *Asharq Al-Aawsat*, July 13, 2012, http://archive.aawsat.com/details.asp?section=4&issueno=12281&article=686212#.W9mL8Kd7G0I.
18. A posting by Bahjat Suleiman on his Facebook page titled *Abu Al-Majd's Diary*, www.facebook.com/people/100003780874464/بهجت-سليمان.
19. "Syrian President Bashar Al-Assad's Interview with Addounia Channel," YouTube video, taken from a broadcast by the Addounia Channel, 1:01:56, posted by "RT Arabic," August 29, 2012, www.youtube.com/watch?v=55RLmVsFt6s.
20. Manaf Tlass, January 2016.
21. Ibid.
22. Riad Seif, in discussion with the author, August 2017.
23. Burhan Ghalyoun, in discussion with the author, November 2016.
24. Ibid.
25. Syrian opposition figure who spoke on condition of anonymity, in discussion with the author, August 2017.

26. Defected Syrian army officer turned rebel leader, in discussion with the author, August 2017.
27. Manaf Tlass, November 2016.
28. Ibid.
29. Member of Syrian rebel leadership council, in discussion with the author, August 2017.
30. Michaela Wiegel, "Syrische Deserteure: Im Salon Von 'Madame O.'" ["Syrian Deserter: In 'Madam O's' Salon"], *Frankfurter Allgemeine Zeitung*, July 15, 2012, www.faz.net/aktuell/poli tik/ausland/naher-osten/syrische-deserteure-im-salon-von-madame-o-11821152.html.
31. "Michel Kilo Says Moscow Isn't Wedded to Assad," YouTube video, taken from a broadcast by the Al-Jazeera Channel, 2:20, posted by Al-Jazeera Arabic, July 9, 2012, www.you tube.com/watch?v=w8MkgN3kR5A.
32. Phil Black, "Russia Protesters Demand Putin's Resignation," CNN website, June 12, 2012, https://edition.cnn.com/2012/06/12/world/europe/russia-protest/index.html.
33. Paul Stronski, *Russia's Fight in Syria Reflects the Kremlin's Fears at Home*, Carnegie Endowment for International Peace, September 29, 2015, http://carnegieendowment.org/2015/09/29/russia-s-fight-in-syria-reflects-kremlin-s-fears-at-home-pub-61439.
34. Presidential Executive Office (Russia), "Meeting with Russian Ambassadors and Permanent Representatives in International Organizations," The Kremlin's official website, July 9, 2012, http://en.kremlin.ru/events/president/news/15902.
35. Ibid.
36. Federica Saini Fasanotti, "Russia and Libya: A Brief History of an On-Again-Off-Again Friendship," The Brookings Institution, *Order from Chaos* Blog, September 1, 2016, www .brookings.edu/blog/order-from-chaos/2016/09/01/russia-and-libya-a-brief-history -of-an-on-again-off-again-friendship/.
37. Dmitri Trenin, *The Mythical Alliance: Russia's Syria Policy*, Carnegie Endowment for International Peace, February 12, 2013, http://carnegie.ru/2013/02/12/mythical-alliance -russia-s-syria-policy-pub-50909.
38. "Security Council Fails to Adopt Draft Resolution on Syria That Would Have Threatened Sanctions, Due to Negative Votes of China, Russian Federation," July 19, 2012, United Nations website, July 19, 2012, www.un.org/press/en/2012/sc10714.doc.htm.
39. Rick Gladstone, "Resigning as Envoy to Syria, Annan Casts Wide Blame," *New York Times*, August 2, 2012, www.nytimes.com/2012/08/03/world/middleeast/annan-resigns-as-syria -peace-envoy.html?mcubz=1.
40. Michael R. Gordon, Eric Schmitt, and Tim Arango, "Flow of Arms to Syria through Iraq Persists, to US Dismay," *New York Times*, December 1, 2012, www.nytimes.com/2012/12/02/world/middleeast/us-is-stumbling-in-effort-to-cut-syria-arms-flow.html?mtrref =undefined.
41. Manaf Tlass, October 2014.
42. "Assad: We're Determined to Cleanse Syria from Terrorists and Jalili: We Won't Permit the Toppling of the Axis of Resistance," Hezbollah's *Al-Manar* website, August 7, 2012, http://archive.almanar.com.lb/article.php?id=281691.
43. Laurent Fabius, in discussion with the author, December 2016.
44. Wallada Shabouk, Aleppo protester and activist, in discussion with the author, March 2014.
45. Ibid.
46. Mohammad Naway, former secretary general of the Aleppo Chamber of Industry, in discussion with the author, March 2014.
47. Sam Dagher, "War-Crimes Fears Raised in Syrian City," *Wall Street Journal*, July 27, 2012, www.wsj.com/articles/SB10000872396390443477104577552952050181714.
48. Aleppo residents and witnesses, in discussion with the author, March 2014.

Notes

49. Mark Landler, "Obama Threatens Force against Syria," *New York Times*, August 20, 2012, www.nytimes.com/2012/08/21/world/middleeast/obama-threatens-force-against-syria.html.

50. Manaf Tlass, October 2014.

51. The White House, Office of the Press Secretary, "Remarks by the President to the White House Press Corps," *The Obama White House Archives*, August 20, 2012, last accessed October 31, 2018, https://obamawhitehouse.archives.gov/the-press-office/2012/08/20/remarks-president-white-house-press-corps.

52. Human Rights Watch, *Syria: Government Attacking Breadlines, Civilian Deaths at Bakeries Are War Crimes*, August 30, 2012, www.hrw.org/news/2012/08/30/syria-government-attacking-bread-lines.

53. Hillary Rodham Clinton, *Hard Choices* (New York: Simon & Schuster, 2014), 462–63.

54. Luis Ramirez, "Panetta: No Plans for Syria No-Fly Zone," Voice of America, August 14, 2012, www.voanews.com/a/panetta-no-decision-on-syria-no-fly-zone/1485709.html.

55. Laurent Fabius, in discussion with the author, December 2016.

56. Ibid.

57. Yasmine Hakim, Daraya activist and witness, in discussion with the author, August 2018.

58. Janine de Giovanni, "Syria Crisis: Daraya Massacre Leaves a Ghost Town Still Counting its Dead," *The Guardian*, September 7, 2012, www.theguardian.com/world/2012/sep/07/syria-daraya-massacre-ghost-town.

59. "Al-Jazeera Documentary: Daraya, Brothers of Grapes and Blood," YouTube video, taken from a broadcast on the Al-Jazeera Channel, 27:53, posted by "The Syrian 92," October 27, 2012, www.youtube.com/watch?v=lSOaIsIuh6U&feature=plcp.

60. "Addounia Channel's Report on the Daraya Massacre 25/8/2012 Presented by Micheline Azar," YouTube video, taken from a broadcast by the Addounia Channel, 13:15, posted by "HR Monitor," September 9, 2015, www.youtube.com/watch?v=jRjbLW5uBXk.

61. Ibid.

62. "Syrian President Bashar Al-Assad's Interview with Addounia Channel," YouTube video, taken from a broadcast by the Addounia Channel, 1:01:56, posted by "RT Arabic," August 29, 2012, www.youtube.com/watch?v=55RLmVsFt6s.

Chapter 20 Holy War: At Your Service, O Bashar!

1. Yitzhak Nakash, *The Shi'is of Iraq* (Princeton, New Jersey: Princeton University Press, 1994), 141.

2. Ibid., 144–45.

3. Vali Nasr, *The Shia Revival* (New York: W. W. Norton & Company, 2006), 132–33.

4. Sam Dagher, "Iraqi Shiites Mark Holy Day under High Guard," *New York Times*, January 7, 2009, www.nytimes.com/2009/01/07/world/africa/07iht-iraq.4.19165325.html.

5. Maher Jatta, aka Abu Ajeeb al-Wahesh ("the Monster"), in discussion with the author, April 2013.

6. Ibid.

7. "Sayed Hassan Nasrallah's Speech about the Shrine and Area of Seyda Zeinab, Peace Be upon Her," YouTube video, 7:58, posted by "Saenbnews," April 30, 2013, www.youtube.com/watch?v=rW_YvH9RC3Q.

8. Sam Dagher, "Fighters, Flowing to Syria, Guard Shiites," *Wall Street Journal*, May 23, 2013, www.wsj.com/articles/SB10001424127887323463704578497021387416606.

9. Joe Parkinson and Sam Dagher, "Iraq Lashes Out at Turkey as Sunni–Shiite Rift Grows," *Wall Street Journal*, January 17, 2012, www.wsj.com/articles/SB10001424052970203735304577165140234013650.

Notes

10. Sam Dagher and Ali A. Nabhan, "Iraq Blasts Point to Spillover," *Wall Street Journal*, July 23, 2012, www.wsj.com/articles/SB10000872396390443570904577545231575003126.

11. Noureddin Labbad, former Syria envoy to Iraq, in discussion with the author, November 2016.

12. Charles Lister, *Profiling Jabhat al-Nusra*, Brookings Project on US Relations with the Islamic World, no. 24, July 2016, www.brookings.edu/wp-content/uploads/2016/07/iwr_2016 0728_profiling_nusra.pdf.

13. Bill Roggio, "Al Nusrah Front Claims Yet Another Suicide Attack in Syria," *FDD's Long War Journal* website, December 4, 2012, www.longwarjournal.org/archives/2012/12/al _nusrah_front_clai_9.php.

14. Resident of Damascus Neighborhood of Qaboun, in discussion with the author, October 2012.

15. Hillary Rodham Clinton, *Hard Choices* (New York: Simon & Schuster, 2014), 463.

16. Defected Syrian army officer turned rebel leader, in discussion with the author, August 2017.

17. Suhair al-Atassi, in discussion with the author, August 2017.

18. Moaz al-Khatib, in discussion with the author, July 2017.

19. Roula Khalaf and Abigail Fielding-Smith, "How Qatar Seized Control of the Syrian Revolution," *Financial Times*, May 17, 2013, www.ft.com/content/f2d9bbc8-bdbc-11e2-890a -00144feab7de.

20. "Qatar Spending $500m a Week on World Cup Project," Agence France-Presse dispatch published in *The Guardian*, February 8, 2017, www.theguardian.com/football/2017/feb/08/ qatar-spending-500m-a-week-on-world-cup-projects-2022.

21. The White House, Office of the Press Secretary, "President Obama Holds a Press Conference," *The Obama White House Archives*, November 14, 2012, accessed October 31, 2018, https://obamawhitehouse.archives.gov/photos-and-video/video/2012/11/14/president -obama-holds-press-conference#transcript.

22. Al-Khatib, July 2017.

23. Ibid.

24. Riad Seif, in discussion with the author, August 2017.

25. Defected Syrian army officer turned rebel commander, in discussion with the author, August 2017.

26. Ibid.

27. Ibid.

28. Al-Khatib, August 2017.

29. Defected Syrian army officer turned rebel commander, August 2017.

30. Western official involved in efforts to support political and armed wings of the Syrian opposition, in discussion with the author, July 2017.

31. Defected Syrian army officer who took part in meetings in Ankara between CIA and intelligence officials from countries supporting the rebels, in discussion with the author, August 2017.

32. Ibid.

33. Ibid.

34. Ibid.

35. "Number of Syrian Refugees in Neighboring Countries Has Tripled in Three Months— UN," *UN News* website, October 2, 2012, https://news.un.org/en/story/2012/10/422542 -number-syrian-refugees-neighbouring-countries-has-tripled-three-months-un.

36. Nick Cumming-Bruce, "More than 60,000 Have Died in Syrian Conflict, UN Says," *New York Times*, January 2, 2013, www.nytimes.com/2013/01/03/world/middleeast/syria-60000 -united-nations.html?mcubz=1.

37. Laurent Fabius, in discussion with the author, December 2016.

38. David D. Kirkpatrick, "A Deadly Mix in Benghazi," *New York Times*, December 28, 2013, www.nytimes.com/projects/2013/benghazi/index.html#/?chapt=0.
39. Ibid.
40. Charles Levinson and Sam Dagher, "Egyptians Swarm Palace in Protest," *Wall Street Journal*, December 4, 2012, www.wsj.com/articles/SB100014241278873234019045781586807600961970.
41. Elizabeth Dickinson, "UAE, Saudi Arabia Express Support for Egyptian Military's Removal of Morsi," *The National*, July 4, 2013, www.thenational.ae/world/mena/uae-saudi-arabia-express-support-for-egyptian-military-s-removal-of-morsi-1.289085.
42. Lister, *Profiling Jabhat al-Nusra*.
43. "Al-Furqan Media presents a new audio message from the Islamic State of Iraq's Shaykh Abu Bakr al-Ḥussayni al-Qurayshi al-Baghdadi: 'Announcement of the Islamic State of Iraq and al-Sham,'" *Jihadology Blog*, April 9, 2013, https://jihadology.net/2013/04/09/al-furqan-media-presents-a-new-audio-message-from-the-islamic-state-of-iraqs-shaykh-abu-bakr-al-ḥussayni-al-qurayshi-al-baghdadi-announcement-of-the-islamic-state-of-iraq-an/.
44. "President Assad's Speech at the Damascus Opera House, 6-1-2013," YouTube video, taken from a broadcast by Syrian state television, 55:41, posted by "Syria Alassad," January 8, 2013, www.youtube.com/watch?v=JoxFNmdX2JY.
45. Ibid.
46. Ibid.
47. "Watching Richard III with Bashar Al-Assad," YouTube video, 2:55, posted by "Slate," June 17, 2018, www.youtube.com/watch?v=b4rUG2bcPHI.

Chapter 21 The Clan's Knights and Soothsayers

1. "Virtual Tour Villa Madama," Italian Ministry of Foreign Affairs and International Cooperation website, www.esteri.it/mae/en/sala_stampa/archiviomultimedia/audiovisivi/ta_virtuale_villa_madama_1.html.
2. "Remarks with Foreign Minister Giulio Terzi and Syrian Opposition Council Chairman Moaz Al-Khatib," US Department of State Archives, Secretary of State John Kerry: 2013 to 2017, February 28, 2013, https://2009-2017.state.gov/secretary/remarks/2013/02/205457.htm.
3. Lakhdar Brahimi, in discussion with the author, December 2016.
4. "Profile: Lakhdar Brahimi," *BBC News* website, September 3, 2012, www.bbc.com/news/world-middle-east-19463317.
5. Brahimi, December 2016.
6. Raghida Dergham, "Damaascus Accuses Brahimi of Siding With the 'Conspirators,'" *Al Hayat*, January 11, 2013, http://www.alhayat.com/article/1575048.
7. "The West 'Prays' Russia and China Will Continue Blocking Syria Action," RT (*Russia Today*) website, December 22, 2012, www.rt.com/news/syria-intervention-chemical-lavrov-651/.
8. Ibid.
9. The White House, Office of the Press Secretary, "President Obama Holds a Press Conference," *The Obama White House Archives*, November 14, 2012, accessed November 1, 2018, https://obamawhitehouse.archives.gov/photos-and-video/video/2012/11/14/president-obama-holds-press-conference#transcript.
10. Sam Dagher, "What Iran Is Really Up To in Syria," *The Atlantic*, February 14, 2018. https://www.theatlantic.com/international/archive/2018/02/iran-hezbollah-united-front-syria/553274/.
11. Brahimi, December 2016.
12. Ibid.

13. Ibid.

14. "Syrian Peace Envoy Lakhdar Brahimi in Talks with Assad," *BBC News* website, December 24, 2012, www.bbc.com/news/world-middle-east-20835332.

15. Brahimi, December 2016.

16. Ibid.

17. Ibid.

18. Mohammad Jaber, in discussion with the author, March 2013.

19. *Aleppo Conflict Timeline—2013: Encircling the Regime in Aleppo (January–March)*, Aleppo Project website, Shattuck Center on Conflict, Negotiation, and Recovery at the Central European University's School of Public Policy, last accessed November 1, 2018, www.thealeppopro ject.com/aleppo-conflict-timeline-2013/.

20. "Eng Subtitles: Patients Explain Their Symptoms after Inhaling a Gas Sprayed by Syrian Forces in Homs," YouTube video, 7:23, posted by "ANA Press," December 23, 2102, www.youtube.com/watch?v=SrAvea8_-PU.

21. "Obama Warns Al-Assad against Chemical Weapons, Declares 'The World Is Watching,'" CNN website, December 4, 2012, https://edition.cnn.com/2012/12/03/world/meast/syria-civil-war/index.html.

22. Ibid.

23. Dana Hughes, Luis Martinez, and Alexander Marquardt, "Syria's Assad May Be Considering Using Chemical Weapons, Panetta Says," *ABC News* website, December 6, 2012, https://abcnews.go.com/Politics/syrias-assad-chemical-weapons-panetta/story?id=17893409.

24. "West Faces Dangerous Game Choosing 'Bad' vs. 'Acceptable' Terrorism—Lavrov (Exclusive)," YouTube video, 27:45, posted by "Russia Today," December 23, 2012, www.youtube.com/watch?time_continue=2&v=wXP5bhIfagU.

25. "Calls for Inquiry into Syria 'Chemical Weapon Attack,'" *BBC News*, March 20, 2013.

26. UN General Assembly Security Council, *Report of the United Nations Mission to Investigate Allegations of the Use of Chemical Weapons in the Syrian Arab Republic*, 7–8, December 13, 2013, www.securitycouncilreport.org/atf/cf/%7B65BFCF9B-6D27-4E9C-8CD3-CF6E4FF96FF9%7D/s_2013_735.pdf.

27. Jaber, March 2013.

28. Ibid.

29. Latakia residents, in discussion with the author, August 2014.

30. Jaber, March 2013.

31. Ibid.

32. Ibid.

33. Ibid.

34. Ibid.

35. Author's interviews with militiamen and visit to Jaber brothers' steel plant, August 2014.

36. Fadwa Mahmoud (Abdelaziz Al-Khayer's wife), in discussion with the author, April 2016.

37. National Coordination Body for Democratic Change was established in June 2011.

38. Mahmoud, April 2016.

39. Jaber, March 2013.

40. Brigadier General Jamal Younes, commander of the 555th Regiment of the Syrian Army's Fourth Division, in discussion with the author, August 2014.

41. Ibid.

42. Ibid.

Notes

43. "Luna Al-Chebel Attacks Al-Jazeera," YouTube video, taken from a broadcast on Syria's Addounia TV Channel, 14:59, posted by "plasmajo," April 27, 2011, www.youtube.com/watch?v=iZU9svhqQE8.

44. "Syrianpresidency: Welcome to the Official Instagram Account for the Presidency of the Syrian Arab Republic," Instagram.com, www.instagram.com/p/_ZdIWIIzVK/?taken-by=syrianpresidency.

45. Ibid., www.instagram.com/p/xmAIc4ozbg/?taken-by=syrianpresidency.

46. "Miladhannoun: Hairdresser and Makeup Artist, Damascus, Syria!" Instagram.com, www.instagram.com/p/BFnzI-AJZIr/?hl=en&taken-by=miladhannoun.

47. A friend of Milad Hannoun, in discussion with the author, May 2014.

48. "Mrs. Asma Al-Assad with the Mothers of Martyrs of the Syrian Army in Damascus," YouTube video, original video produced by Asma al-Assad's media team, 13:24, posted by "Zeinasoftnetwork," April 6. 2013, www.youtube.com/watch?v=y-eIktOiKP4.

49. Ibid.

50. Ibid.

51. Manaf Tlass, in discussion with the author, October 2014.

52. Wissam Tajo (Khaled Mahjoub's associate), in discussion with the author, January 2013.

53. Khaled Mahjoub, in discussion with the author, March 2013.

54. Jeremy Bowen, "Syrian Rebel-Held Areas Fear Attack," *BBC News* video report, December 7, 2012, www.bbc.com/news/av/world-middle-east-20649670/syrian-rebel-held-areas-fear-attack.

55. Ibid.

56. Khaled Mahjoub, "Letter from Khaled Mahjoub: Robert Fisk's Untrue Accusations about Me," *The Independent*, October 7, 2013, www.independent.co.uk/voices/letters/letter-from-khaled-mahjoub-robert-fisks-untrue-accusations-about-me-8864876.html.

57. Tajo, March 2013.

58. Ibid.

59. Terry Moran, "Damascus Blast: Crater Full of Carnage and a Child-Size Body Bag," *ABC News* website, February 21, 2013, https://abcnews.go.com/blogs/headlines/2013/02/damascus-blast-crater-full-of-carnage-and-a-child-size-body-bag/.

60. "Shaaban, Hassoun Meet Delegation from European Solidarity Front for Syria," Syrian Arab News Agency, May 3, 2106, https://sana.sy/en/?p=76315.

61. "Syria's Mufti Threatens to Respond to the West with Suicide Bombers," YouTube video, taken from a broadcast by Syrian State TV, 1:44, posted by "Russia Today Arabic," October 11, 2011, www.youtube.com/watch?v=8yRoQ6Sagtw.

62. Nir Rosen, "A Conversation with Grand Mufti Hassoun," *Al-Jazeera English*, October 3, 2011, www.aljazeera.com/indepth/features/2011/10/201110312588957185.html.

63. Ben Hubbard, "A Nun Lends a Voice of Skepticism on the Use of Poison Gas by Syria," *New York Times*, September 21, 2013, www.nytimes.com/2013/09/22/world/middleeast/seeking-credible-denial-on-poison-gas-russia-and-syria-turn-to-nun.html.

64. Father Paulo Dall'Oglio, in discussion with the author, July 2012.

65. Observations recorded by the author between November 2012 and August 2014.

66. Ibid.

67. Ibid.

68. "Médias: Une Nouvelle Chaîne Panarabe à Capitaux Syro-Iraniens" ["Media: A New Pan-Arab Channel with Syrian-Iranian Funding"], *Courrier International* reprint of an article by *L'Orient—Le Jour*, June 7, 2012, www.courrierinternational.com/article/2012/06/07/une-nouvelle-chaine-panarabe-a-capitaux-syro-iraniens.

69. "Interview with Bashar al-Assad: Europe's Backyard Would Become a Terrorist Haven," *Frankfurter Allgemeine Zeitung*, June 17, 2013, www.faz.net/aktuell/politik/ausland/naher-osten/f-a-z-interview-with-bashar-al-assad-europe-s-backyard-would-become-a-terrorist-haven-12225367-p2.html.

70. Lyse Doucet, "Syrian Angst over Foreign Rebel Fighters," *BBC News*, June 17, 2013.

71. Doucet later told the author in an email in January 2019: "I think we must have been told that they had been detained in various operations. I don't remember hearing that they had been rounded up - not from Khaled, nor from the Tunisian human rights lawyers who came to Damascus, or the mothers."

72. Mohammad Munir al-Faqir, a Syrian opposition activist who was jailed for a period with the Tunisians, in discussion with the author, November 2014. Two other Syrian activists, who did not know Faqir but overlapped with the Tunisians in prison, also confirmed that the Tunisians had been tortured by the *mukhabarat* and made to confess they were jihadists.

73. Doucet, "Syrian Angst over Foreign Rebel Fighters."

74. "The Sex Jihad Scandals in Syria," YouTube video, taken from a news broadcast by Iran's Al-Alam TV station, 3:56, posted by "ON1TW2," April 27, 2013, https://www.youtube.com/watch?v=Hd4bkUliULI.

75. Adam B. Ellick and Adam Westbrook, "Operation Infektion, Russian Disinformation: From Cold War to Kanye," *The New York Times*, November 12, 2018, https://www.nytimes.com/2018/11/12/opinion/russia-meddling-disinformation-fake-news-elections.html.

76. Observations recorded by the author between November 2012 and August 2014.

77. Mazen Darwish, in discussion with the author, July 2017.

78. Ibid.

79. Ibid.

80. Al-Faqir, August 2017. Faqir was a prominent Damascus-based opposition activist who was jailed at the start of the uprising in March 2011 for about a month. He was then detained in March 2012 and was severely tortured in various *mukhabarat* prisons and was taken twice to the 601 military hospital but was lucky to survive. He was among those freed in a prisoner swap between the regime and opposition in January 2014. He has been living in Turkey ever since.

81. These were part of the archive of more than 28,000 photos smuggled out of Syria by the military defector code-named Caesar.

82. Darwish, July 2017.

83. Ibid.

Chapter 22 Macabre Coronation

1. "Oath-Taking Ceremony for His Excellency President Bashar Al-Assad and His Speech to the Audience," YouTube video, taken from a broadcast by Syrian State Television, 1:22:33, posted by "Shaamnews 100," July 16, 2014, www.youtube.com/watch?v=7xBWSIqES6Q.

2. "Full Video: Vladimir Putin's Presidential Inauguration Ceremony in Kremlin," YouTube video, 43:32, posted by "Russia Today," May 7, 2012, www.youtube.com/watch?v=TNiWnSOsAnE.

3. "Oath-Taking Ceremony for His Excellency President Bashar Al-Assad and His Speech to the Audience."

4. Naseer Al-Ajeeli, "The Nouri Mosque…Site of Daesh's First 'Sermon,' Could It Witness the Organization's Demise?" Al Arabiya, March 8, 2017, www.alarabiya.net/ar/arab-and-world/iraq/2017/03/08؟التنظيم-نهاية-نهاية-يشهد-فهل-داعش-خطبة-أول-النور-جامع.html.

5. "ISIS Spokesman Declares Caliphate, Rebrands Group as 'Islamic State,'" *Site Intelligence Group* website, June 29, 2014, https://news.siteintelgroup.com/Jihadist-News/isis-spokesman-declares-caliphate-rebrands-group-as-islamic-state.html.

Notes

6. Sam Dagher, "Syria Elections a Forum to Celebrate Assad," *Wall Street Journal*, June 3, 2014, www.wsj.com/articles/pro-assad-voters-rally-as-syria-holds-elections-1401805 888.

7. Ned Parker, Isabel Coles, and Raheem Salman, "Special Report: How Mosul Fell—An Iraqi General Disputes Baghdad's Story," Reuters, October 14, 2014, www.reuters.com/article/us-mideast-crisis-gharawi-special-report/special-report-how-mosul-fell-an-iraqi-general-disputes-baghdads-story-idUSKCN0I30Z820141014.

8. Commander of the Ya'arubiya border crossing, in discussion with the author in Damascus, March 2013.

9. Ibid.

10. Ibid.

11. Joshua Eaton, "US Military Now Says ISIS Leader Was Held in Notorious Abu Ghraib Prison," *The Intercept*, August 25, 2016, https://theintercept.com/2016/08/25/u-s-military-now-says-isis-leader-was-held-in-notorious-abu-ghraib-prison/.

12. "Al-Hayat Media Center Presents a New Video Message from the Islamic State of Iraq and Al-Sham: 'The End of Sykes Picot,'" *Jihadology* website, June 29, 2014, https://jihadology.net/2014/06/29/al-ḥayat-media-center-presents-a-new-video-message-from-the-islamic-state-of-iraq-and-al-sham-the-end-of-sykes-picot/.

13. "Oath-Taking Ceremony for His Excellency President Bashar Al-Assad and His Speech to the Audience."

14. Ibid.

15. "President Al-Assad Receives Congratulatory Cables from Leaders of Myanmar and Abkhazia," Syrian Arab News Agency, June 11, 2014, https://sana.sy/en/?p=2994.

16. "US Senator to President Al-Assad: Presidential Elections Sweeping Victory to Syrian People," Syrian Arab News Agency, June 11, 2014, https://sana.sy/en/?p=3043.

17. Elliot Hannon, "Virginia State Senator Sends Syrian President Assad Supportive Thank You Letter," *Slate*, May 27, 2014, https://slate.com/news-and-politics/2014/05/virginia-state-senator-sends-syrias-assad-a-thank-you-letter.html.

18. Sam Dagher, "Syrian Nuns Held by Rebels for Months Released," *Wall Street Journal*, March 9, 2014, www.wsj.com/articles/no-headline-available-1394378923.

19. "More Than 191,000 People Killed in Syria with 'No End in Sight'—UN," *UN News* website, August 22, 2014, https://news.un.org/en/story/2014/08/475652-more-191000-people-killed-syria-no-end-sight-un#.Wd-faDOB3x5.

20. Sam Dagher, "Assad's Campaign for Re-Election Aims to Show Resilience," *Wall Street Journal*, May 30, 2014, www.wsj.com/articles/assads-campaign-for-reelection-aims-to-show-resilience-1401406727.

21. Hassan al-Nouri (one of the two men picked by the regime to be Bashar Al-Assad's token challengers), in discussion with the author, May 2014.

22. Sam Dagher, "Syria Elections a Forum to Celebrate Assad," *Wall Street Journal*, June 3, 2014, www.wsj.com/articles/pro-assad-voters-rally-as-syria-holds-elections-1401805888.

23. Ibid.

24. Rudeynah Baalbaky, in discussion with the author, June 2014.

25. Sam Dagher, "Syrian President Bashar al-Assad Declared Election Winner," *Wall Street Journal*, June 4, 2014, www.wsj.com/articles/syrian-president-bashar-al-assad-declared-election-winner-1401911413.

26. Pro Bashar tribal sheiks from the provinces of Deir Ezzour and Hasakeh, in discussion with the author in Damascus, August 2014.

27. Iraqi politician close to Bashar al-Assad and Iran speaking on condition of anonymity, in discussion with the author, September 2014.

Notes

28. Hezbollah field commander in Homs neighborhood of Khalidiya after its recapture from rebels, in discussion with the author, August 2013.

29. Sam Dagher, "In Qusayr, Signs of an Intensifying Holy War," *Wall Street Journal*, June 6, 2013, www.wsj.com/articles/SB100014241278873240691045785296207495721 06.

30. Sam Dagher, "Violence Spirals as Assad Gains," *Wall Street Journal*, June 11, 2013, www.wsj .com/articles/SB10001424127887324904004578536872947748426.

31. Sam Dagher, "In Syria, Signs of Civilian Massacre," *Wall Street Journal*, July 30, 2013, www .wsj.com/articles/SB10001424127887324354704578637923366819536.

32. Thomas Hegghammer and Aaron Y. Zelin, "How Syria's Civil War Became a Holy Crusade," *Foreign Affairs*, posted on the website of the Washington Institute, July 7, 2013, www .washingtoninstitute.org/policy-analysis/view/how-syrias-civil-war-became-a-holy -crusade.

33. The White House, Office of the Press Secretary, "Statement by Deputy National Security Advisor for Strategic Communications Ben Rhodes on Syrian Chemical Weapons Use," June 13, 2013, *The Obama White House Archives*, last accessed November 1, 2018. https:// obamawhitehouse.archives.gov/the-press-office/2013/06/13/statement-deputy-national -security-advisor-strategic-communications-ben-.

34. Khaled Walyo, Latakia rebel fighter who was present during speech made by Abu Ayman al-Iraqi, in discussion with the author, March 2016.

35. Human Rights Watch, *"You Can Still See Their Blood": Executions, Indiscriminate Shootings, and Hostage Taking by Opposition Forces in Latakia Countryside*, October 10, 2013, www.hrw.org/ report/2013/10/10/you-can-still-see-their-blood/executions-indiscriminate-shootings -and-hostage.

36. Walyo, March 2016.

37. Residents of Blouta, one of the Latakia countryside villages that was attacked, in discussion with the author, December 2013.

38. "Visit by General Salim Idriss to the Commander of the Suqour Al-Sahel Brigade Saeed Tarboush," YouTube video, 2:10, posted by "The Media Office of the Middle-Western Front," August 12, 2013, www.youtube.com/watch?v=RnMI4lZq3Jw.

39. "Behind the News, Details of Targeting Bashar Al-Assad's Convoy, with Sheikh Zahran Alloush and Safwat Al-Zayat," YouTube video, taken from a broadcast by the Al-Jazeera Channel, 21:29, posted by "Syrian4allNews," August 8, 2013, www.youtube.com/watch?v=c6zeb RXDwZ4.

40. Ibid.

41. Defected Syrian army officer collaborating with the CIA, in discussion with the author, August 2017.

42. Syrian army intelligence officer, in discussion with the author, August 2013.

43. Alawite Syrian army officer, in discussion with the author, December 2013.

44. Human Rights Watch, *Attacks on Ghouta, Analysis of Alleged Use of Chemical Weapons in Syria*, September 10, 2013, www.hrw.org/report/2013/09/10/attacks-ghouta/analysis-alleged-use -chemical-weapons-syria.

45. Rescuer in the aftermath of chemical-weapons attack, in discussion with the author, August 2015.

46. Human Rights Watch, *Attacks on Ghouta*.

47. Observations recorded by the author, who was in Damascus on the day of the chemical-weapons attack.

48. Ibid.

49. Ibid.

Notes

50. "Syrian Information Minister Omran Al-Zoubi Denies Using Chemical Weapons in the Ghouta," YouTube video, taken from a broadcast on Al-Mayadeen TV, 6:13, posted by "SYRPRESS," August 21, 2013, www.youtube.com/watch?v=nINsa7sIxAQ.

51. Syrian Army Officer in Eastern Damascus, in discussion with the author, August 2013.

52. Observations recorded by the author, who was in Damascus on the day of the chemical-weapons attack.

53. Ibid.

54. UN humanitarian agency official based at the Damascus Four Seasons, in discussion with the author, August 2013.

55. Eyewitness and former Ghouta resident, in discussion with the author, August 2015.

56. "Bashar Al-Assad: All Contracts Signed with Russia are Implemented," *Izvestia*, August 26, 2013, https://iz.ru/news/556048.

57. Giulia Prati, *Between Propaganda and Public Relations: An Analysis of Bashar al-Assad's Digital Communications Campaign*, Journal of International Affairs, School of International and Public Affairs at Columbia University, March 9, 2015, https://jia.sipa.columbia.edu/online-articles/between-propaganda-and-public-relations-analysis-bashar-al-assad's-digital.

58. US Department of Justice, Office of Public Affairs, "Computer Hacking Conspiracy Charges Unsealed against Members of the Syrian Electronic Army, Two Fugitives Believed to Be in Syria Added to FBI Cyber's Most Wanted," March 22, 2016, www.justice.gov/opa/pr/computer-hacking-conspiracy-charges-unsealed-against-members-syrian-electronic-army.

59. Christine Haughney and Nicole Perlroth, "Times Site Is Disrupted in Attacks by Hackers," *New York Times*, August 27, 2013, www.nytimes.com/2013/08/28/business/media/hacking-attack-is-suspected-on-times-web-site.html.

60. Shane Harris, "How Did Syria's Hacker Army Suddenly Get So Good?" *Foreign Policy*, September 4, 2013, https://foreignpolicy.com/2013/09/04/how-did-syrias-hacker-army-suddenly-get-so-good/.

61. Simone Foxman and Matt Phillips, "Markets Briefly Plunge after AP's Hacked Twitter Account Falsely Reports White House Explosions," *Quartz*, April 23, 2013, https://qz.com/77413/markets-briefly-crash-after-aps-hacked-twitter-account-falsely-reports-white-house-explosions/. "Breaking: Two Explosions in the White House and Barack Obama is injured," SEA posted in April 2013 from AP's official Twitter account with nearly two million followers. This momentarily erased nearly $136 billion in US stock market value before the fake tweet was discovered and, within minutes, countered.

62. John Kerry, "Statement on Syria," August 30, 2013, US Department of State Archive website, accessed November 1, 2018, https://2009-2017.state.gov/secretary/remarks/2013/08/213668.htm.

63. Andrea Shalal-Esa, "Sixth US Ship Now in Eastern Mediterranean 'As Precaution,'" Reuters, August 31, 2013, www.reuters.com/article/us-syria-crisis-ships/sixth-u-s-ship-now-in-eastern-mediterranean-as-precaution-idUSBRE97U0IZ20130831.

64. In the case of Iraq, Saddam Hussein produced large quantities of chemical weapons when he was fighting an eight-year war against Iran in the 1980s with Western and Arab support. When these powers turned against him after his invasion of Kuwait in 1990, Saddam was ordered to destroy his chemical weapons arsenal per a UN Security Council resolution. The United States continued to accuse Saddam of hiding some of these weapons, and in the lead up to the US-led invasion of Iraq in 2003, the George W. Bush administration claimed it had intelligence that supposedly proved Saddam was working to weaponize his chemical stockpiles and also reconstitute Iraq's nuclear program. US ally Britain went further by claiming Iraq could deploy chemical and biological weapons within 45 minutes

after the issuing of an order by Saddam to do so. After the invasion, all these claims proved to be false.

65. John Kerry, "Statement on Syria," August 30, 2013, US Department of State Archive website, accessed November 1, 2018, https://2009-2017.state.gov/secretary/remarks/2013/08/213668.htm.

66. Ibid.

67. Laurent Fabius, in discussion with the author, December 2016.

68. Ibid.

69. The White House, Office of the Press Secretary, "Remarks by President Obama and the Presidents of Estonia, Lithuania, and Latvia," August 30, 2013, *The Obama White House Archives*, last accessed November 1, 2018, https://obamawhitehouse.archives.gov/the-press-office/2013/08/30/remarks-president-obama-and-presidents-estonia-lithuania-and-latvia.

70. Fabius, December 2016.

71. French official speaking on condition of anonymity, in discussion with the author, July 2017.

72. Fabius, December 2016.

73. Gérard Davet and Fabrice Lhomme, *Un Président Ne Devrait Pas Dire Ça: Les Secrets d'un Quinquennat [A President Must Not Say That: Secrets of a Five-Year Mandate]*, (Paris: Éditions Stock, 2016), 459.

74. Ibid.

75. Ibid., 463.

76. Ibid., 459.

77. Ibid., 464.

78. Ibid.

79. Ibid., 465.

80. Fabius, December 2016.

81. Jeffrey Goldberg, "The Obama Doctrine: The US President Talks Through His Hardest Decisions about America's Role in the World," *The Atlantic*, April 2016, www.theatlantic.com/magazine/archive/2016/04/the-obama-doctrine/471525/.

82. Laurent Fabius, *37 Quai D'Orsay: Diplomatie Française 2012–2016* (Paris: Éditions Plon, 2016), 94.

83. Observations recorded by the author, who was in Damascus for several weeks after the chemical-weapons attack.

84. Ibid.

85. Ibid.

86. Mohammad Munir al-Faqir, in discussion with the author, August 2017.

87. Julian E. Barnes, "Syrian Electronic Army Hacks Marines Website," *Wall Street Journal*, September 2, 2013, https://blogs.wsj.com/washwire/2013/09/02/syrian-electronic-army-hacks-marines-website/.

88. Bashar Al-Assad, interview by Georges Malbrunot, *Le Figaro*, September 2, 2013, www.lefigaro.fr/international/2013/09/02/01003-20130902ARTFIG00569-assad-s-warning-to-france.php.

89. Ibid.

90. Ibid.

91. Haroon Siddique, "Hafez al-Assad Facebook Post: 'I Just Want Them to Attack Sooo Much,'" *The Guardian*, August 30, 2013, www.theguardian.com/world/2013/aug/30/syria-facebook-hafez-al-assad-taunts-us.

Notes

92. Sam Dagher, "Syrian Official Seeks Dialogue, Warns against US Action," *Wall Street Journal*, September 3, 2013, www.wsj.com/articles/syrian-official-seeks-dialogue-warns-against-us-action-1378234131.
93. Sam Dagher, "As Syria Debate Grows, Locals Hoard Food," *Wall Street Journal*, September 8, 2013, www.wsj.com/articles/as-syria-debate-grows-locals-hoard-food-1378668445.
94. Sam Dagher, "In Damascus, Fears of Attack, Aftermath," *Wall Street Journal*, August 28, 2013, www.wsj.com/articles/in-damascus-fears-of-attack-aftermath-1377733377.
95. "Mother Agnes Exposes 'Massacre Marketing' in Ghouta 'Gas Attacks' in Syria, 2013," Maryakub.net, September 8, 2016, www.maryakub.net/2016/09/08/mother-agnes-exposes-massacre-marketing-in-ghouta-gas-attacks-in-syria-2013/.
96. Fabius, December 2016.
97. Ibid.
98. "Bashar Al-Assad: All Contracts Signed with Russia Are Implemented," *Izvestia*, August 26, 2013, https://iz.ru/news/556048.
99. Michael R. Gordon and Steven Lee Myers, "Obama Calls Russia Offer on Syria Possible 'Breakthrough,'" *New York Times*, September 9, 2013, www.nytimes.com/2013/09/10/world/middleeast/kerry-says-syria-should-hand-over-all-chemical-arms.html.
100. Sam Dagher, "Syria Saw Initial Diplomacy as Gain," *Wall Street Journal*, September 10, 2013, www.wsj.com/articles/syria-sees-latest-diplomacy-as-victory-1378844557?tesla=y.
101. "Security Council Requires Scheduled Destruction of Syria's Chemical Weapons, Unanimously Adopting Resolution 2118 (2013)," United Nations website, September 27, 2103, www.un.org/press/en/2013/sc11135.doc.htm.
102. Sam Dagher, "Syrian Regime Chokes Off Food to Town That Was Gassed," *Wall Street Journal*, October 2, 2013, www.wsj.com/articles/syrian-regime-chokes-off-food-to-town-that-was-gassed-1380767441.
103. Razan Zeitouneh, "The West Is Wrong on Syria," *Souria Houria*, October 18, 2013, https://souriahouria.com/the-west-is-wrong-on-syria-by-razan-zaitouneh/.
104. Lakhdar Brahimi, in discussion with the author, December 2016.
105. Fabius, December 2016.

Chapter 23 A Game of Nations

1. Manaf Tlass, in discussion with the author, October 2014.
2. Manaf Tlass, August 2016.
3. Ibid.
4. Ibid.
5. Defected Syrian army officer who worked closely with the CIA, in discussion with the author, August 2017.
6. Manaf Tlass, October 2014.
7. Paris-based Tlass family acquaintance who was once with Manaf and his father at one of these lunch outings, in discussion with the author, November 2016.
8. Mustafa Tlass' caregiver, in discussion with the author, December 2018.
9. Thala al-Khair, in discussion with the author, October 2016.
10. Manaf Tlass, October 2014.
11. Defected Syrian army officer turned rebel leader from Manaf Tlass's hometown of Al-Rastan, in discussion with the author, August 2017.
12. Manaf Tlass, December 2018.
13. Ibid.

Notes

14. "Russia Today Correspondent: Lavrov Was Briefed on Tlass's Positions Regarding What Was Happening in Syria," RT (*Russia Today*), Arabic language service, March 1, 2013. https://arabic.rt.com/news/609046_طلاس_مواقف_على_اطلع_لافروف __اليوم_روسيا_مراسل/. حيال_ما_يجري_في_سورية-

15. Manaf Tlass, December 2018.

16. Ibid.

17. Ibid.

18. Julian E. Barnes and Sam Dagher, "US Airdrops Weapons and Supplies to Besieged Syrian Kurds in Kobani," *Wall Street Journal*, October 20, 2014, www.wsj.com/articles/us-airdrops-weapons-and-supplies-to-besieged-syrian-kurds-in-kobani-1413761080.

19. Damascus-based official from the Patriotic Union of Kurdistan (PUK), an Iraqi Kurdish party close to both Iran and the United States, in discussion with the author, July 2014. The PUK, whose longtime former leader Jalal Talabani had warm ties with the Assad family and at the same time was hailed as an ally by Washington, helped broker the deal between Iran's head of foreign covert operations Qasem Soleimani, PKK leader Cemil Bayik, and Bashar al-Assad and his *mukhabarat*.

20. Syrian Kurdish activists based in northeast Syria, in discussion with the author, October 2014.

21. Sam Dagher, "Kurds Fight Islamic State to Claim a Piece of Syria," *Wall Street Journal*, November 12, 2014, www.wsj.com/articles/kurds-fight-islamic-state-to-claim-a-piece-of-syria-1415843557.

22. John Kerry, interview by Kim Ghattas of *BBC News*, June 24, 2014, *US Department of State Archive* website, accessed November 2, 2018, https://2009-2017.state.gov/secretary/remarks/2014/06/228345.htm.

23. Richard Barrett, *Foreign Fighters in Syria*, Soufan Group website, June 2014, http://soufangroup.com/wp-content/uploads/2014/06/TSG-Foreign-Fighters-in-Syria.pdf.

24. Defected Syrian army officer working with both US and Gulf Arab officials on supporting the rebels, in discussion with the author, August 2017.

25. Simeon Kerr, "Qatar Emir Abdicates and Hands Power to His Son," *Financial Times*, June 25, 2013, www.ft.com/content/4051896c-dd5c-11e2-a756-00144feab7de.

26. Defected Syrian army officer working with both US and Gulf Arab officials on supporting the rebels, in discussion with the author, August 2017.

27. Ibid.

28. Peter Beaumont, "Growing Strength of Syria's Islamist Groups Undermines Hopes of Ousting Assad," *The Guardian*, December 14, 2013, www.theguardian.com/world/2013/dec/14/syria-islamist-militants-growing-strength.

29. Phillip Smyth, *The Shiite Jihad in Syria and Its Regional Effects*, Washington Institute website, February 6, 2015, www.washingtoninstitute.org/uploads/Documents/other/PhillipSmyth-ShiiteJihad02062015.pdf.

30. Anthony Deutsch, John Irish, and Michelle Nichols, "Exclusive: UN Inquiry Blames Syrian Military for Chlorine Bomb Attacks—Source," Reuters, September 16, 2016, www.reuters.com/article/us-mideast-crisis-syria-chemicalweapons/exclusive-u-n-inquiry-blames-syrian-military-for-chlorine-bomb-attacks-source-idUSKCN11MIUU.

31. Defected Syrian army officer working with both US and Gulf Arab officials on supporting the rebels, in discussion with the author, August 2017.

32. French official speaking on condition of anonymity, in discussion with the author, July 2017.

33. "Al-Moallem Confirmed Syria's Readiness to Collaborate with Any Regional and International Side Including Washington to Fight Terrorism," National News Agency, August 25, 2014, http://nna-leb.gov.lb/ar/show-news/112603/nna-leb.gov.lb/nna-leb.gov.lb/ar.

Notes

34. Lewis Sida, Lorenzo Trombetta, and Veronica Panero, *Evaluation of OCHA Response to the Syria Crisis*, United Nations Office of the Coordinator of Humanitarian Affairs, March 2016, www.unocha.org/sites/dms/Documents/OCHA%20Syria%20Evaluation%20 Report_FINAL.pdf.

35. Senior UN humanitarian official speaking on condition anonymity, in discussion with the author, September 2015.

36. Ibid.

37. Ibid.

38. Ibid.

39. Ibid.

40. Witnessed by the author throughout 2014.

41. Incident witnessed by the author in January 2014.

42. Sam Dagher, "Uneasy Truces: Syrian Regime Exploits Rebel Despair," *Wall Street Journal*, March 25, 2014, www.wsj.com/articles/uneasy-truces-syrian-regime-exploits-rebel-despair -1395803434?tesla=y.

43. Sam Dagher and Joe Lauria, "Deal Reached to Ease Siege of Homs," *Wall Street Journal*, February 6, 2014.

44. Human Rights Watch, *He Didn't Have to Die: Indiscriminate Attacks by Opposition Groups in Syria*, March 22, 2015, www.hrw.org/report/2015/03/22/he-didnt-have-die/indiscriminate -attacks-opposition-groups-syria.

45. Yacoub El Hillo, head of the UN humanitarian mission in Syria, in discussion with the author, July 2014.

46. Ibid.

47. Sam Dagher, "Syria: Tweets from Homs as First Civilians Are Evacuated," *Middle East Real Time* blog, *Wall Street Journal*, February 7, 2014, https://blogs.wsj.com/middleeast/2014/02/07/ syria-tweets-from-homs-as-first-civilians-are-evacuated/.

48. General Abdul-Kareem Salloum, head of the Homs branch of Military Intelligence, in discussion with the author, February 2014.

49. El Hillo, July 2014.

50. Sam Dagher, "Yes Graffiti Here Near Frontline in #Homs Says 'Assad or Nobody, Assad or We Burn the Country' #Syria," Twitter, February 10, 2014, https://twitter.com/sam dagher/status/432868667395940352.

51. Witnessed by the author, February 2014.

52. Ibid.

53. Sam Dagher, "Syrian Regime Loyalists Seethe Over UN Aid Operation for Rebel Area," *Wall Street Journal*, February 10, 2014, www.wsj.com/articles/no-headline-available -1392073109.

54. Homs men released by the Syrian *mukhabarat* from the school, in discussion with the author, July 2014.

55. Author was made to sign the same standard *mukhabarat* form after being briefly detained by the regime in Homs in August 2013.

56. Author witnessed release ceremony held at the Zahrawi High School theater in Homs, February 2014.

57. Violations Documentation Center in Syria, *Special Report on Branch 261 of the Mukhabarat's Military Intelligence Directorate—Homs*," March 2014, www.vdc-sy.info/index.php/ar/reports/ 1395194519#.W9wRxjOB3xt.

58. Author's notes and audio recording of the release ceremony held at the Zahrawi High School theater in Homs, February 2014.

59. Homs opposition activists and relatives of the disappeared, in discussion with the author, July 2014.
60. El Hillo, July 2014.
61. Ibid.
62. Ibid.
63. Abu Rami al-Homsi, opposition activist leader who took part in negotiations, in discussion with the author, July 2014.
64. Sam Dagher, "Sadly this photo from ruins of #Homs says it all. On wall: 'Long live Assad's #Syria - #Assad or we burn the country,'" Twitter, December 20, 2014, https://twitter.com/samdagher/status/546305492881268736.
65. UN aid worker involved in Syria relief effort, in discussion with the author, September 2015.
66. Nick Hopkins and Emma Beals, "UN Pays Tens of Millions to Assad Regime under Syria Aid Programme," *The Guardian*, August 29, 2016, www.theguardian.com/world/2016/aug/29/un-pays-tens-of-millions-to-assad-regime-syria-aid-programme-contracts.
67. Author interviewed several members of Rami Makhlouf's Jamiyet Al-Bustan militia in Homs in 2013 and 2014. Many were proud of the war crimes they were committing and justified them. One identified himself as a recruiter and coordinator who worked in Rami's office in Damascus and also took part in military assaults against opposition areas in and around Homs and throughout western Syria.
68. Syrian businessmen who took part in local tenders to supply food items and other goods to UN humanitarian agencies including the WFP, UNHCR, and UNESCO, in discussion with the author, October 2012.
69. Senior UN aid official, in discussion with the author, September 2015. A subsequent story by the *New York Times* revealed that the same regime official's wife also provided consulting services to the World Health Organization in Damascus to assess the mental health of those fleeing their homes because of the fighting: Somini Sengupta, "UN Agency Hires Wife of Top Figure in Syrian War to Assist the Displaced," *New York Times*, February 26, 2016, www.nytimes.com/2016/02/25/world/middleeast/syrian-ministers-wife-named-to-assess-mental-health-of-the-displaced.html.
70. "Record $10 Billion Pledged in Humanitarian Aid for Syria at UN Co-hosted Conference in London, *UN News* website, February 4, 2016, https://news.un.org/en/story/2016/02/521552-record-10-billion-pledged-humanitarian-aid-syria-un-co-hosted-conference-london.

Chapter 24 Abu Ali Putin

1. Author's notes from a visit to Masyaf in western Syria, August 2014. Listening to Fairuz in the morning is a sacred tradition for many Syrians. The singer, whose real name is Nouhad Haddad, and her late husband and composer Assi al-Rahbani have been honored and embraced by the Assads over the years.
2. Sam Dagher, "Syria's Mothers, Divided by War, Share Sorrow of Missing Sons," *Wall Street Journal*, December 7, 2014, www.wsj.com/articles/syrias-mothers-divided-by-war-share-sorrow-of-missing-sons-1418009581.
3. Sam Dagher, "Islamic State Militants Kill Scores of Syrian Troops," *Wall Street Journal*, August 28, 2014, www.wsj.com/articles/islamic-state-militants-kill-scores-of-syrian-troops-1409256028.
4. Alawite soldier from the Hama countryside who survived in the desert and was later rescued, in discussion with the author, August 2014.

5. Son of retired Alawite army general from the Jableh countryside in western Syria, in discussion with the author, August 2014.

6. Mohammad Jaber, in discussion with the author, August 2014.

7. Sam Dagher, "Part of Incinerated Wreckage of MiG 23 Shot Down by Islamist Rebels Aug 18 Over Rabiah Next to #Hama Airbase Syria," Twitter, September 10, 2014, https://twitter.com/samdagher/status/509668142373539841.

8. Sam Dagher, "Syria's Alawites: The People behind Assad," *Wall Street Journal*, June 25, 2015, www.wsj.com/articles/syrias-alawites-the-people-behind-assad-1435166941.

9. Author's notes from visit to the Sheikh Mohammad shrine in the village of Al-Dalyeh/ Joufeen forest area in the mountains above the city of Jableh in western Syria, August 2014.

10. Sam Dagher, "Druse under Pressure to Take Sides in Syrian War," *Wall Street Journal*, August 10, 2015, www.wsj.com/articles/druse-under-pressure-to-take-sides-in-syrian-war-1439235669.

11. Hassan Mutlaq, "The Ghost of Reserve Duty: Hama's Youth Caught between the Flames of Military Service and Displacement," *Enab Baladi*, January 18, 2015, www.enabbaladi .net/archives/26528?so=related.

12. Father of young man who wanted to fight in Syria, in discussion with the author, June 2018.

13. Bassam Saleh, in discussion with the author, September 2015.

14. Ibid.

15. Bashar al-Assad, interview by Russian media outlets, Syrian Arab News Agency, March 27, 2015, www.sana.sy/en/?p=33642.

16. "Russia: Putin Meets Iran's Ali Akbar Velayati as Ties Deepen," YouTube video, taken from a broadcast by RT (*Russia Today*), 0:46, posted by "Ruptly," January 28, 2015, www .youtube.com/watch?v=OYPh4soIuKw.

17. Mohammad Ballout, "Soleimani in Moscow for the Second Time in One Month," *Assafir*, September 15, 2015.

18. Bashar al-Assad, speech transcript, Syrian Arab News Agency, July 26, 2015, www.sana .sy/?p=245771.

19. Presidential Executive Office (Russia), "Meeting with Government Members," The Kremlin's website, September 30, 2015, http://en.kremlin.ru/events/president/transcripts /50401.

20. Sam Dagher, "Russian Airstrikes Defend Strategic Assad Regime Stronghold on Syria's Coast," *Wall Street Journal*, October 1, 2015, www.wsj.com/articles/russian-airstrikes-defend -strategic-assad-regime-stronghold-on-coast-1443743860.

21. Dion Nissenbaum, "Russia Bulks Up Force in Syria, Starts Flying Drone Missiona," *Wall Street Journal*, September 21, 2015. https://www.wsj.com/articles/russia-bulks-up-force -in-syria-starts-flying-drone-missions-1442856005.

22. Ali Othman, in discussion with the author, March 2016.

23. Médecins Sans Frontières, *Syria 2015: Documenting War-Wounded and War-Dead in MSF-Supported Medical Facilities in Syria*, February 17, 2016, www.msf.org/syria-report-documents-war -wounded-and-war-dead-msf-supported-medical-facilities-syria.

24. Human Rights Watch, *Russia/Syria: Extensive Recent Use of Cluster Munitions*, December 20, 2015, www.hrw.org/news/2015/12/20/russia-syria-extensive-recent-use-cluster-munitions.

25. "Zoabi: Syrians Adore 'Abu Ali Putin,'" RT (*Russia Today*), April 15, 2016, https://arabic .rt.com/news/819303-يا سد ارو سوري -ين وت رب زيوـث حديب/.

26. Presidential Executive Office (Russia), "Meeting with President of Syria Bashar Assad," The Kremlin's website, October 21, 2015, http://en.kremlin.ru/events/president/tran scripts/50533.

Notes

27. "Russia: Assad and Putin Sit Down for Dinner in Moscow," YouTube video, taken from a broadcast by RT (*Russia Today*), 1:05, posted by "Ruptly," October 21, 2015, www.youtube .com/watch?v=JQvoXhYDado.

28. Ibid.

29. Defected Syrian army officer working with CIA on supporting moderate rebel groups inside Syria, in discussion with the author, August 2017.

30. Michael R. Gordon and Gardiner Harris, "Obama and Putin Play Diplomatic Poker over Syria," *New York Times*, September 28, 2015, www.nytimes.com/2015/09/29/world/ middleeast/obama-and-putin-clash-at-un-over-syria-crisis.html.

31. Spencer Ackerman, "Obama Tells Pentagon to Open Channel of Communication with Russia on Syria," *The Guardian*, September 29, 2015, www.theguardian.com/us-news/2015/ sep/29/obama-pentagon-channel-communication-russia-syria.

32. "Russian FM Lavrov Shares Memories of Bromance with Ex-US State Secretary Kerry," *Sputnik News*, July 21, 2017, https://sputniknews.com/world/201707211055770026 -russia-lavrov-kerry-relations/.

33. Julian Borger, "Iran Nuclear Deal: World Powers Reach Historic Agreement to Lift Sanctions," *The Guardian*, July 14, 2015, www.theguardian.com/world/2015/jul/14/iran -nuclear-programme-world-powers-historic-deal-lift-sanctions.

34. Barack Obama, interview by Norah O'Donnell, *CBS This Morning*, June 20, 2014, www .cbsnews.com/news/obama-notion-that-syrian-opposition-could-overthrow-assad-a -fantasy/.

35. Ali Othman, ex-Syrian army soldier turned rebel fighter in the Latakia countryside, who was flown to Qatar via Turkey for the anti-ISIS training several times, in discussion with the author, March 2016.

36. Syrian rebel commander, in discussion with the author, August 2017.

37. Angelique Chrisafis, "*Charlie Hebdo* Attackers: Born, Raised, and Radicalized in Paris," *The Guardian*, January 12, 2015, www.theguardian.com/world/2015/jan/12/-sp-charlie-hebdo -attackers-kids-france-radicalised-paris.

38. Manaf Tlass, in discussion with the author, December 2016.

39. Ibid.

40. Manaf Tlass, January 2016.

41. Masalmeh, January 2017.

42. Ibid.

43. Ibid.

44. Southern Front commander, in discussion with the author, August 2017.

45. Masalmeh, January 2017.

46. Ibid.

47. Ibid.

48. Ibid.

49. Sam Dagher and Suha Ma'ayeh, "In Syria, Assad Foes Pay High Price for Failed Offensive," *Wall Street Journal*, November 13, 2015, www.wsj.com/articles/in-syria-assad-foes -pay-high-price-for-failed-offensive-1447464848.

50. Southern Front commander, in discussion with the author, August 2017.

51. Ibid.

52. Masalmeh, January 2017.

53. Sally Masalmeh and Malek al-Jawabra, in discussion with the author, January 2017.

54. Ibid.

55. Charles Lister, in discussion with the author, January 2019.

56. Al-Jawabra, August 2017.

57. Adam Withnall, "Aylan Kurdi's Story: How a Small Syrian Child Came to Be Washed Up on a Beach in Turkey," *The Independent*, September 3, 2015, www.independent.co.uk/news/world/europe/aylan-kurdi-s-story-how-a-small-syrian-child-came-to-be-washed-up-on-a-beach-in-turkey-10484588.html.

58. International Organization for Migration, *Over 3,770 Migrants Have Died Trying to Cross the Mediterranean to Europe in 2015*, December 31, 2015, www.iom.int/news/over-3770-migrants-have-died-trying-cross-mediterranean-europe-2015.

59. Masalmeh, January 2017.

60. Ibid.

61. Ian Traynor, "Migration Crisis: Hungary PM Says Europe in Grip of Madness," *The Guardian*, September 3, 2015, www.theguardian.com/world/2015/sep/03/migration-crisis-hungary-pm-victor-orban-europe-response-madness.

62. Viktor Orban, "Those Who Are Overwhelmed Cannot Offer Shelter to Anyone," English translation of letter to *Frankfurter Allgemeine Zeitung* posted on the official website of the Hungarian Government, September 3, 2015, www.kormany.hu/en/the-prime-minister/news/those-who-are-overwhelmed-cannot-offer-shelter-to-anyone.

63. Masalmeh and Al-Jawabra, January 2017.

64. Ibid.

65. Mazen Darwish, in discussion with the author, July 2017.

66. Ibid.

67. Ibid.

68. Ibid.

69. Ibid.

70. Ibid.

71. Ibid.

72. Reporters Without Borders, "Mazen Darwish Awarded UNESCO Press Freedom Prize," RWB website, May 7, 2015, https://rsf.org/en/news/mazen-darwish-awarded-unesco-press-freedom-prize.

73. PEN International, "Syrian Activist Mazen Darwish Shares PEN Pinter Award with Salman Rushdie," PEN website, October 10, 2014, https://pen-international.org/news/syrian-activist-mazen-darwish-shares-pen-pinter-award-2014-with-salman-rushdie.

74. Human Rights Council Working Group on Arbitrary Detention, "Opinions Adopted by the Working Group on Arbitrary Detention at its Sixty-Eight Session, 13–22 November 2013, No. 43/2013 (Syrian Arab Republic)," United Nations General Assembly, adopted November, 15, 2013, www.fidh.org/IMG/pdf/opinion_43_2013_syria_darwish_2_.pdf.

75. "His Excellency President Bashar al-Assad Performs Eid Prayers," General Organization of Radio and TV Syria, July 17, 2015, www.ortas.gov.sy/News/index.php?d=100349&id=179812.

76. Worldwide Movement for Human Rights, "Syria: Finally Free, Mazen Darwish Must Now Be Acquitted," FIDH website, August 10, 2015, www.fidh.org/en/region/north-africa-middle-east/syria/syria-finally-free-mazen-darwish-must-now-be-acquitted.

77. Darwish, July 2017.

78. Ibid.

79. Ibid.

Chapter 25 Daesh or Bashar?

1. Matthieu Goar, "Quand une Délégation de Politiques Français Trouve Bachar Al-Assad 'Plus Détendu" ["When a Delegation of French Politicians Finds Bashar al-Assad 'More

Notes

Relaxed'"], *Le Monde*, March 28, 2016, www.lemonde.fr/international/article/2016/03/28/quand-une-delegation-de-politiques-francais-trouve-bachar-al-assad-plus-detendu_489 1157_3210.html.

2. Manaf Tlass, in discussion with the author, November 2016.

3. Dexter Filkins, "Assad Speaks," *The New Yorker*, November 1, 2016.

4. "Valérie Boyer de Retour de Syrie," YouTube video, taken from a broadcast by France24 Channel, 6:06, posted by "Christian Scherer," March 29, 2016, www.youtube.com/watch?v=WPmZ2yuSx5k.

5. Ibid.

6. Benjamin Barthe, "Les Zones d'Ombre d'un Voyage 'Privé' à Damas" ("Shadow Zones of a 'Private' Visit to Damacus), *Le Monde*, February 26, 2015, www.lemonde.fr/international/article/2015/02/26/les-zones-d-ombre-d-un-voyage-prive-a-damas_4583575_3210.html.

7. Bashar Al-Assad, interview by David Pujadas, France 2 television channel; Bashar spoke in English and the regime's Syrian Arab News Agency published a transcript, April 21, 2015, www.sana.sy/en/?p=37034.

8. Ibid.

9. The Soufan Group, *Foreign Fighters: An Updated Assessment of the Flow of Foreign Fighters into Syria and Iraq*, December 2015, www.soufangroup.com/foreign-fighters/.

10. Phillip Smyth, "The Shiite Jihad in Syria and its Regional Effects," Washington Institute website, February 2015, www.washingtoninstitute.org/uploads/Documents/pubs/Policy Focus138-v3.pdf.

11. "What You Need to Know about Paris Attacks and the Situation in France," *Le Monde*, November 14, 2015, www.lemonde.fr/attaques-a-paris/article/2015/11/14/what-you-need-to-know-about-paris-attacks-and-the-situation-in-france_4810074_4809495.html.

12. "Attentas Terroristes à Paris: État d'Urgence Décrété—Allocution de François Hollande" ["Terrorist Attacks in Paris: A State of Emergency Decreed—François Hollande's Address"), YouTube video, 3:20, posted by "France24" official YouTube channel, November 13, 2015, www.youtube.com/watch?v=-ZW6hpeKuD4.

13. Rukmini Callimachi, "How ISIS Built the Machinery of Terror Under Europe's Gaze," *New York Times*, March 29, 2016, www.nytimes.com/2016/03/29/world/europe/isis-attacks-paris-brussels.html.

14. Duncan Gardham, "ISIL Issued Warning to 'Filthy French,'" *Politico* (Politico.EU website), November 17, 2015, https://www.politico.eu/article/paris-terrorist-attacks-isil-issued-warning-to-filthy-french/.

15. Bashar al-Assad, interview by David Pujadas.

16. Laurent Fabius, in discussion with the author, December 2016.

17. "President al-Assad to French Delegation: Terrorist Attacks on Paris Can't Be Separated from Those of Beirut and Events in Syria," Syrian Arab News Agency, November 14, 2015, https://sana.sy/en/?p=61231.

18. Presidential Executive Office (Russia), "Press Statements and Answers to Journalists' Questions Following Meeting with President of France François Hollande," The Kremlin's website, November 26, 2015, http://en.kremlin.ru/events/president/transcripts/50792.

19. Ibid.

20. Boris Johnson, "Let's Deal with the Devil: We Should Work with Vladimir Putin and Bashar al-Assad in Syria," *The Telegraph*, December 6, 2015, www.telegraph.co.uk/news/worldnews/middleeast/syria/12036184/Lets-deal-with-the-Devil-we-should-work-with-Vladimir-Putin-and-Bashar-al-Assad-in-Syria.html.

21. United Nations Security Council, "Resolution 2254 (2015) Adopted by the Security Council at its 7588th Meeting, on December 18, 2015," December 18, 2015, www.securi

tycouncilreport.org/atf/cf/%7b65BFCF9B-6D27-4E9C-8CD3-CF6E4FF96FF9%7d/
s_res_2254.pdf.

22. "Amnesty: Russia May Have Committed War Crimes by Killing Civilians in Syria,"
Associated Press dispatch reprinted in the *Guardian*, December 23, 2015, www.theguard
ian.com/world/2015/dec/23/russian-cluster-bombs-killed-hundreds-civilians-syria
-watchdog.

23. Anne Barnard, "Death Toll from War in Syria Now 470,000, Group Finds," *New York
Times*, February 11, 2016, www.nytimes.com/2016/02/12/world/middleeast/death-toll
-from-war-in-syria-now-470000-group-finds.html?_r=1.

24. "Madaya: Starvation under Siege," Syrian American Medical Society website, January 2016,
www.sams-usa.net/wp-content/uploads/2016/09/Report_Madaya_Starvation_Under
Siege.pdf.

25. Ibid.

26. Kevin Lui, "UN Secretary-General 'Alarmed' over Reports of Atrocities in Aleppo," *Time*
magazine, December 13, 2016, http://time.com/4597589/un-secretary-general-atrocities
-syria-aleppo/.

27. "Kerry 'Outraged' at Syrian Airstrike on Children's Hospital in Aleppo," *Voice of America
News*, April 28, 2016, www.voanews.com/a/un-envoy-calls-for-revitalized-cease-fire-ahead
-of-more-talks/3306256.html.

28. Sam Dagher, "Syria Defies Russia in Bid to Keep Assad," *Wall Street Journal*, April 11, 2016,
www.wsj.com/articles/syria-defies-russia-in-bid-to-keep-assad-1460332538.

29. "'War on Terror Is Sacred': Orthodox Church Praises Putin Decision on Syria Airstrikes,"
RT (*Russia Today*), September 30, 2018.

30. "Imperial Orthodox Palestine Society to Open School and Mobile Hospital in Syria,"
SANA, April 4, 2017, https://www.sana.sy/en/?p=103536.

31. Ministry of Foreign Affairs (Russia), "Foreign Minister Sergey Lavrov's Interview with the
Imperial Orthodox Palestine Society's website, Moscow, July 25, 2016," Ministry of Foreign Affairs of the Russian Federation website, July 25, 2016, www.mid.ru/en/foreign
_policy/news/-/asset_publisher/cKNonkJE02Bw/content/id/2367193.

32. "Chamoun on the Anniversary of April 26: We Won't Forget the Syrian Army's Horrors
and Its Destruction of All Sects; Sami Gemayel: We Don't Want Daesh or Bashar
al-Assad, Arabs or Iran, Just Lebanon," National News Agency (Lebanon), April 30, 2016,
http://nna-leb.gov.lb/ar/show-news/220009/.

33. Ignatius Joseph III Younan, Patriarch of Antioch for the Syriac Catholic Church, in discussion with the author, December 2014.

34. Robert Christian, "Pope Francis' One Big Mistake: Syria," *Time* magazine, March 12,
2014, http://time.com/22617/pope-francis-syria-mistake/.

35. "President Al-Assad Received Letter from Pope Francis Expressing Heartfelt Sympathy
with Syria," Syrian Arab News Agency, December 12, 2016.

36. Caroline Ayoub, in discussion with the author, July 2012. Ayoub, who was deeply involved
in early peaceful protests, worked hard, especially in the Damascus suburbs, to transcend
religious divides, keep the movement secular and nonviolent, and dispel the perception
enforced by the regime that all Christians supported Bashar al-Assad. Ayoub was detained
by the regime for one month in early 2012 and was personally interrogated and insulted by
the notorious Jamil Hassan, chief of the *mukhabarat*'s Air Force Intelligence Directorate. He
kept telling Ayoub that he was shocked that a Christian like her was siding with the "terrorist" Sunni Muslims, and that Christians, Alawites, and other minorities shared one destiny.

37. "Bila Quyoud: Gregorius III Laham, Patriarch of Antioch and All the East for Melkite
Greek Catholics," YouTube video, taken from a BBC Arabic interview by Malak Jaafar,

Notes

25:30, posted by BBC News Arabic official YouTube channel, July 25, 2014, www
.youtube.com/watch?v=hWHKqpl8Vss.

38. Sam Dagher, "Christians in Homs, Syria, Grieve on Easter as Battles Rage," *Wall Street Journal*, April 20, 2014, www.wsj.com/articles/christians-in-homs-grieve-on-easter-as-battles
-rage-1398035169.

39. "Syrian President Bashar al-Assad and First Lady Asma al-Assad Visiting Christian
Church," YouTube video, 1:28, posted by "Ivan Sidorenko," December 19, 2015, www
.youtube.com/watch?v=yp-8eAPwf8I.

40. "Abbasyeen, Damascus: Muslims and Christians, We Want Freedom," YouTube video,
0:49, posted by "Souria Yahabibati," March 3, 2013, last accessed November 5, 2018,
www.youtube.com/watch?v=oUP5tdN9IYI.

41. "Complément d'Enquête—Dictatures, Business et Diplomates de l'Ombre 07/05/15,"
YouTube video, taken from an investigation by Romain Boutilly, Florian Le Moal, Gilles
Truffaut, and Slavek Kuchalski aired May 7, 2015 on the *Complément d'Enquête* program on
the France 2 TV channel, 1:04:28, posted by "Boba Fett," May 8, 2015, last accessed
November 5, 2018, www.youtube.com/watch?v=UYRcQnxI4Xg&t=2997s.

42. Ivan Watson, "Cyberwar Explodes in Syria," CNN website, November 22, 2011, https://
edition.cnn.com/2011/11/22/world/meast/syria-cyberwar/index.html.

43. Claude Guéant, former chief of staff of Nicolas Sarkozy, in discussion with the author,
November 2016.

44. Alexander Sulzer, "Syrie: Ces Parlementaires Français Sur le Sulfureux Chemin de Damas"
["Syria: Parliamentarians on the 'Sulphurous' Road to Damascus"], *L'Express*, April 15, 2016,
www.lexpress.fr/actualite/politique/syrie-ces-parlementaires-francais-sur-le-sulfureux
-chemin-de-damas_1779321.html.

45. David Perrotin, "SOS Chrétiens d'Orient, Une Association Humanitaire Discrètement
Noyautée Par l'Extrême Droite" ["SOS Christians of the East: A Humanitarian Association Discreetly Infiltrated by the Far Right"], BuzzFeed News France, May 20, 2015,
www.buzzfeed.com/davidperrotin/sos-chretiens-dorient-une-ong-discretement-noyautee
-par-lext.

46. "Complément d'Enquête—Dictatures, Business et Diplomates de l'Ombre 07/05/15,"
YouTube video.

47. Ibid.

48. Nash Jenkins, "A Timeline of Recent Terrorist Attacks in Europe," *Time* magazine,
December 20, 2016, http://time.com/4607481/europe-terrorism-timeline-berlin-paris
-nice-brussels/.

49. Andrew Ashdown, "Report of Visit to Syria: 31 August–7 September 2016," *Andrew Ashdown's Blog*, September 14, 2016, www.andrewashdown.me.uk/2016/09/report-of-visit-to
-syria-31-august-7.html.

50. Øyvind Strømmen, "Assad's Far-Right Europe Corps?" Hate Speech International website, November 25, 2013, www.hate-speech.org/other-volunteers/.

51. "Conspiracy against Assad—George Galloway—Russia Today," YouTube video, taken
from a broadcast by RT (*Russia Today*), 12:48, posted by "GeorgeGallowayForPM," April
19, 2013, www.youtube.com/watch?v=ZNYfuE3Cwj8.

52. "Assad Makes Yuletide Visit to Christian Church in Damascus," *Breitbart*, December 21, 2015.
https://www.breitbart.com/national-security/2015/12/21/assad-makes-yuletide-visit
-christian-church-damascus/.

53. Nir Rosen, in discussion with the author in Damascus, August 2014.

54. Ibid.

55. Ibid.

56. Nour Malas and Carol E. Lee, "US Pursued Secret Contacts with Assad Regime for Years," *Wall Street Journal*, December 23, 2015, www.wsj.com/articles/u-s-pursued-secret-contacts-with-assad-regime-for-years-1450917657.

57. Nir Rosen's correspondence with Syrian regime officials was among the cache of e-mails released in 2012 by pro-Syrian-opposition hackers who broke into the server of the Syrian Ministry of Presidential affairs. These exchanges were posted on a website called Syriainsight.com and on several pro-opposition Facebook pages and were printed out and read by the author. By November 2018, though, neither the website nor the Facebook pages were accessible; images of these e-mails, however, remain visible in a search on Google. See: www.google.com/search?client=safari&rls=en&tbm=isch&q=%D8%A7%D9%84%D8%B5%D8%AD%D9%81%D9%8A+%D8%A7%D9%84%D8%A3%D9%85%D8%B1%D9%8A%D9%83%D9%8A+%D9%86%D9%8A%D8%B1+%D8%B1%D9%88%D8%B2%D9%86+%D9%88%D8%AE%D8%A7%D9%84%D8%AF+%D8%A7%D9%84%D8%A3%D8%AD%D9%85%D8%AF+%D9%85%D9%8A%D8%B4%D8%A7%D9%84+%D8%B3%D9%85%D8%A7%D8%AD%D8%A9&spell=1&sa=X&ved=0ahUKEwifvKfZpL3eAhWs4YUKHck_BbcQBQg8KAA&biw=1366&bih=595&dpr=1.Rosen told CNN on March 25, 2012, that the e-mails sent by him were authentic. See: https://edition.cnn.com/2012/03/23/world/meast/syria-al-assad-media/index.html.

58. Robin Wright, "Former Ambassador Robert Ford on the State Department Mutiny on Syria," *The New Yorker*, June 17, 2016, www.newyorker.com/news/news-desk/former-ambassador-robert-ford-on-the-state-department-mutiny-on-syria.

59. "UN Aid Chief Extremely Concerned over Evacuation of Syrian Town of Darayya, Cites Need for Compliance with Humanitarian Law," *UN News*, August 2016, https://news.un.org/en/story/2016/08/537832-un-aid-chief-extremely-concerned-over-evacuation-syrian-town-darayya-cites-need#.WgBa3617E0R.

60. "President Assad Performs Eid al-Adha Prayers in Daraya and Takes a Tour Afterwards—The Messages and Significance," YouTube video, taken from a broadcast by the Ekhbariya al-Souriya TV channel on September 12, 2016, 16:09, posted by "Kalam Siyasi," September 12, 2016, www.youtube.com/watch?v=GfA2VsiizuA.

61. Grace Guarnieri, "Vladimir Putin, Bashar al-Assad, and Everyone Donald Trump Named during the Final Hillary Clinton Debate," *Salon*, October 20, 2016, www.salon.com/2016/10/20/vladimir-putin-bashar-al-assad-and-everyone-donald-trump-named-during-the-final-hillary-clinton-debate/.

62. Human Rights Watch, *Russia/Syria: War Crimes in Month of Bombing Aleppo*, December 1, 2016, www.hrw.org/news/2016/12/01/russia-syria-war-crimes-month-bombing-aleppo.

63. Maksymilian Czuperski, Faysal Itani, Ben Nemmo, Eliot Higgins, and Emma Beals, *Breaking Aleppo*, Atlantic Council website, February 2017, www.publications.atlanticcouncil.org/breakingaleppo/wp-content/uploads/2017/02/BreakingAleppo.pdf.

64. Ibid.

65. "A Glimpse at the Life of Mrs. Aniseh Makhlouf," YouTube video, taken from a broadcast by Sama TV, 3:21, posted by "Qomhane News," February 7, 2016, www.youtube.com/watch?v=AqsZH_5su64.

66. "Asma al-Assad: Between War and Peace. Exclusive Portrait in a Documentary Film by Anna Afanasyeva," YouTube video, 37:14, posted on the official YouTube channel of Russia 24, October 23, 2016, www.youtube.com/watch?v=w7LPfrB4nGQ&t=189s.

67. Ibid.

68. Ibid.

69. Ibid.

70. Ibid.

71. Ibid.

72. Ibid.

73. Sam Dagher, "White Helmets Are White Knights for Desperate Syrians," *Wall Street Journal*, May 1, 2016, www.wsj.com/articles/white-helmets-are-white-knights-for-desperate-syrians-1462146569.

74. Ameer Alhalbi, "A Day of Hell in Aleppo," AFP website, May 2, 2016, https://correspondent.afp.com/day-hell-aleppo.

75. Karam al-Masri, "A Syrian boy is comforted as he cries next to the body of a relative who died in a reported airstrike on April 27, 2016 in the rebel-held neighborhood of al-Soukour in the northern city of Aleppo" (photo), AFP/Getty Images, www.gettyimages.fr/detail/photo-d%27actualité/syrian-boy-is-comforted-as-he-cries-next-to-the-body-photo-dactualité/525269432.

76. Malaka Gharib, "The Little Boy in Aleppo: Can One Photo End a War?" NPR website, August 19, 2016, www.npr.org/sections/goatsandsoda/2016/08/19/490679863/the-little-boy-in-aleppo-can-one-photo-end-a-war.

77. Commission on Presidential Debates, "October 19, 2016 Debate Transcript," Debates.org, October 19, 2016, www.debates.org/index.php?page=october-19-2016-debate-transcript.

78. Amy Sherman, "Donald Trump Wrongly Blames Hillary Clinton for Creation of ISIS," *Politifact*, July 20, 2016, www.politifact.com/florida/statements/2016/jul/20/donald-trump/donald-trump-wrongly-blames-hillary-clinton-creati/.

79. "Brigitte Gabriel on Radical Islamic Terrorism at 'Act for America' 2016 Conference," C-SPAN, September 6, 2016, www.c-span.org/video/?c4619356/brigitte-gabriel-radical-islamic-terrorism-act-america-2016-conference.

80. Caitlin Dickerson, "How Fake News Turned a Small Town Upside Down," *New York Times Magazine*, September 26, 2017, www.nytimes.com/2017/09/26/magazine/how-fake-news-turned-a-small-town-upside-down.html.

81. Alison Smale, "Angela Merkel Calls for Ban on Full-Face Veils in Germany," *New York Times*, December 6, 2016, www.nytimes.com/2016/12/06/world/europe/merkel-calls-for-ban-on-full-face-veils-in-germany.html?_r=0.

82. Author's notes and reporting in Amsterdam, Berlin, Brussels, and Paris in fall 2016.

83. Ibid.

84. Ibid.

85. Yohan Blavignat, "Moyen-Orient: Les Propositions de François Fillon et Alain Juppé" ["Middle East: The Propositions of François Fillon and Alain Juppé"], *Le Figaro*, November 24, 2016, www.lefigaro.fr/elections/presidentielles/primaires-droite/2016/11/24/35004-20161124ARTFIG00254-moyen-orient-les-propositions-de-francois-fillon-et-alain-juppe.php.

86. Manaf Tlass, December 2016.

87. "Terrorism Court Sentences the Defector Manaf Tlass to Death," *Syria Steps*, January 7, 2015.

88. Manaf Tlass, December 2016.

89. Ibid.

90. Ibid.

91. Ibid.

92. "Profile: Libya's Military Strongman Khalifa Haftar," *BBC News* website, September 15, 2016, www.bbc.com/news/world-africa-27492354.

93. "Libyan General Khalifa Haftar Meets Russian Minister to Seek Help," Reuters dispatch published in *The Guardian*, November 29, 2016, www.theguardian.com/world/2016/nov/29/libyan-general-khalifa-haftar-meets-russian-minister-to-seek-help.

94. Reuters, "UN Envoy Says Syria Peace Talks Still On for January 25," January 13, 2016, www.reuters.com/article/us-mideast-crisis-syria-un-idUSKCN0UR2MJ20160113.

95. Bradley Klapper and Matthew Lee, "Assad Can Stay, for Now: Kerry Accepts Russian Stance," Associated Press dispatch published in the *Military Times*, December 16, 2015, www.militarytimes.com/news/your-military/2015/12/16/assad-can-stay-for-now-kerry-accepts-russian-stance/.

96. Manaf Tlass, December 2018.

97. Syria Freedom News Network (Facebook page), "Manaf Tlass, Between the Accumulation of Rumors and the Absence of Facts," Facebook post by Ahmed Mansour, July 10, 2016, https://www.facebook.com/freenews212/posts/1125300984198616.

98. Manaf Tlass's black notebook, viewed by the author, December 2018.

99. Rebel commander who signed pledge to back Manaf Tlass, in discussion with the author, August 2017.

100. Manaf Tlass, December 2016.

101. Ibid.

102. Czuperski et al., *Breaking Aleppo*.

103. "Postponement of Evacuation of Civilians and Opposition Fighters from East Aleppo," YouTube video, taken from a broadcast on France 24, 1:48, posted by "France 24 Arabic," December 14, 2016, www.youtube.com/watch?v=RX7_HGknc7A.

104. Syrian Network for Human Rights, *Ala'a al-Shawwaf Died Due to Torture in Syrian Regime Detention Center, October 19*, October 20, 2016, http://sn4hr.org/blog/2017/10/20/alaa-al-shawwaf-died-due-torture-syrian-regime-detention-center-october-19/.

105. "Bashar al-Assad Congratulates Syrians on the 'Historic Victory' in Aleppo," YouTube video, 1:44, posted by "RT Arabic," December 15, 2016, www.youtube.com/watch?v=YLvP26aelR4.

Chapter 26 Dictators Strike Back—but Hope Endures

1. Amnesty International, *Human Slaughterhouse: Mass Hangings and Extermination at Saydnaya Prison*, February 7, 2017, www.amnesty.org/download/Documents/MDE2454152017ENGLISH.PDF.

2. Soumer Daghastani, "Inside Tadmur: The Worst Prison in the World?" *BBC News* website, June 20, 2015, www.bbc.com/news/magazine-33197612.

3. Alice Su, "How One Syrian Fought to Death for a Free Internet," *Wired* magazine, September 27, 2017, www.wired.com/story/how-one-syrian-fought-to-the-death-for-a-free-internet/.

4. Mazen Darwish, in discussion with the author, August 2017.

5. Ibid.

6. Michael Isikoff, "Exclusive: Defiant Assad Tells Yahoo News Torture Report Is 'Fake News,'" *Yahoo News*, February 10, 2017, www.yahoo.com/news/exclusive-defiant-assad-tells-yahoo-news-torture-report-is-fake-news-100042667.html?soc_src=social-sh&soc_trk=tw.

7. Ibid.

8. Michael Isikoff, "Full Interview Transcript: Syrian President Bashar al-Assad," *Yahoo News*, February 10, 2017, www.yahoo.com/news/full-interview-transcript-syrian-president-bashar-assad-194809125.html.

Notes

9. Nick Corasantini and Maggie Haberman, "Donald Trump Suggests 'Second Amendment People' Could Act against Hillary Clinton," *New York Times*, August 9, 2016, www.nytimes.com/2016/08/10/us/politics/donald-trump-hillary-clinton.html.

10. Brooke Singman, "Trump Declares 'Market Would Crash' if Democrats Impeached Him," *Fox News*, August 23, 2018, www.foxnews.com/politics/trump-declares-market-would-crash-if-democrats-impeached-him.

11. Brian Katulis, "5 Signs Trump Leads Like a Middle Eastern Dictator," *Fortune.com*, April 5, 2017, http://fortune.com/2017/04/05/donald-trump-middle-east-dictator-syria-egypt-president-sisi/.

12. Syrianpresidency (Instagram account), "On Christmas Day…President Assad and His Family Visit the Orphanage at the Saydeh Monastery in Saydnaya…#SyrianPresidency #Syria #President #Assad #Asma #BestOfTheDay #Saydnaya #Merrychristmas #Xmas #Love #Orphan #family," Instagram, December 25, 2016, www.instagram.com/p/BOcbNUnhM3L/.

13. bassel_shw (Instagram account), "Where life begins and love never ends #familycomesfirst," Instagram, February 11, 2017, www.instagram.com/p/BQYbM9lD4Cg/?hl=en&taken-by=bassel_shw.

14. Syrianpresidency (Instagram account), "The wounded [soldier] Ayham Mahmoud from the village of Deir Shmayel in the Hama countryside…received President Assad and his family…#SyrianPresidency #Syria #President #Assad #Asma #Brave #Hero #injured #Challenge #SAA #Hama #EidMubarak," Instagram, June 26, 2017, www.instagram.com/p/BV0IVc-lf_S/.

15. Asma al-Assad Syria's First Lady (Facebook page), "They have taught us that history is written by the strong, in Syria it's being written by the righteous—The first lady Asma al-Assad to the mothers of Aleppo on Mother's Day," Facebook post of a video created by the Presidency of the Syrian Arab Republic (Bashar's media office), 26:23, March 22, 2017, www.facebook.com/AsmaalAssad.FirstLady/videos/vb.187267097966022/1847656218593760/?type=2&theater.

16. "Hafez Bashar al-Assad: People Are Blind Toward My Father and I Am Not the Best," RT (*Russia Today—Arabic*) website, July 18, 2017, https://arabic.rt.com/middle_east/889201-حافظ-بشار-الأسد-من-البرازيلالناس-عميان-تجاه-والدي-أما-أنا-فلست-الأفضل/.

17. Asma al-Assad Syria's First Lady (Facebook page), "…The alternative was ignorance that brought extremism and terror…," Facebook post of a video created by the Syria Trust, 1:51, July 23, 2017, www.facebook.com/AsmaalAssad.FirstLady/videos/vb.187267097966022/2035124509846929/?type=2&theater.

18. Suzy Hansen, "Inside Turkey's Purge," *New York Times Magazine*, April 13, 2017, www.nytimes.com/2017/04/13/magazine/inside-turkeys-purge.html.

19. Karl Vick, "Crown Prince Mohammed Bin Salman Talks to *Time* about the Middle East, Saudi Arabia's Plans, and President Trump," *Time* magazine, April 5, 2018, http://time.com/5228006/mohammed-bin-salman-interview-transcript-full/.

20. Kareem Fahim, Tamer El-Ghobashy, and Louisa Loveluck, "Prosecutor Says Khashoggi Was Strangled and Dismembered, but Fate of Body Still a Mystery," *Washington Post*, October 31, 2018, www.washingtonpost.com/world/saudi-arabia-not-fully-cooperating-with-khashoggi-investigation-turkish-official-says/2018/10/31/804bfc2a-dc78-11e8-8bac-bfe01fcdc3a6_story.html?utm_term=.9e8782fe6c3a.

21. Amnesty International, *Stranglehold: Coalition and Huthi Obstacles Compound Yemen's Humanitarian Crisis*, June 22, 2018, www.amnesty.org/download/Documents/MDE3185052018ENGLISH.pdf.

22. Simeon Kerr and Ahmed Al Omran, "Qatar Restores Diplomatic Ties with Iran," *Financial Times*, August 24, 2017, www.ft.com/content/bd8f21c8-889d-11e7-bf50-e1c239b45787.

23. Judy Dempsey, "Germany Welcomes Egypt's Sisi," Carnegie Europe, June 1, 2015, http://carnegieeurope.eu/strategiceurope/60260?lang=en.

24. Chris Osuh, "Spikes in Hate Crime Came after the Manchester Bombing, London Attacks, and Brexit," *Manchester Evening News*, October 17, 2017, www.manchesterevening news.co.uk/news/greater-manchester-news/spikes-hate-crime-came-after-13773496.

25. "Macron: Bachar El-Assad Est un 'Criminel'" ["Macron: Bashar al-Assad Is a 'Criminal'"], *Le Figaro* and *AFP*, September 19, 2017, http://www.lefigaro.fr/flash-actu/2017/09/19/97001-20170919FILWWW00295-macron-bachar-el-assad-est-un-criminel.php.

26. Markus Feldenkirchen and René Pfister, "The Isolated Chancellor: What Is Driving Angela Merkel?" *Spiegel Online*, January 25, 2016, www.spiegel.de/international/germany/why-has-angela-merkel-staked-her-legacy-on-the-refugees-a-1073705.html.

27. "Killings at a Berlin Christmas Market Test Germany's Nerves," *The Economist*, December 24, 2016, www.economist.com/europe/2016/12/24/killings-at-a-berlin-christmas-market-test-germanys-nerve.

28. Rebecca Staudenmaier, "German Far-Right AfD Politicians Travel to Syria in Effort to Send Back Refugees," *Deutsche Welle*, March 6, 2018, www.dw.com/en/german-far-right-afd-politicians-travel-to-syria-in-effort-to-send-back-refugees/a-42846789.

29. Yasmeen Sarhan, "The Organization That Sent Tulsi Gabbard to Syria," *The Atlantic*, January 31, 2017, www.theatlantic.com/news/archive/2017/01/the-organization-that-sent-tulsi-gabbard-to-syria/514763/.

30. Mariam Elba, "Why White Nationalists Love Bashar Al-Assad," *The Intercept*, September 8, 2017, https://theintercept.com/2017/09/08/syria-why-white-nationalists-love-bashar-al-assad-charlottesville/.

31. Manaf Tlass, in discussion with the author, January 2017.

32. Ibid.

33. Michael Crowley, "Trump Cedes Syrian Postwar Planning to Putin," *Politico.com*, November 21, 2017. https://www.politico.com/story/2017/11/21/trump-putin-russia-syria-257407.

34. "Randa Kassis Reveals Details of Her Meeting with Donald Trump Jr.," RT (*Russia Today—Arabic*) website, November 25, 2016, https://arabic.rt.com/news/85135-رندا-قسيس-تكشف-تفاصيل-لقائها-بدونالد-ترامب-الابن/.

35. Manaf Tlass, January 2017.

36. Ibid.

37. Human Rights Watch, *Death by Chemicals: The Syrian Government's Widespread and Systematic Use of Chemical Weapons*, May 1, 2017, www.hrw.org/report/2017/05/01/death-chemicals/syrian-governments-widespread-and-systematic-use-chemical-weapons.

38. Michael Scherer, "The Trump Administration Warned Russia about the US Missile Attack on Syria," *Time* magazine, April 7, 2017, http://time.com/4730306/donald-trump-vladimir-putin-russia-missile-attack-bashar-assad/.

39. "Russia Blocks Security Council Action on Reported Use of Chemical Weapons in Syria's Khan Shaykhun," *UN News*, April 12, 2017, https://news.un.org/en/story/2017/04/555292-russia-blocks-security-council-action-reported-use-chemical-weapons-syrias-khan#.Wgsgjq2B2SM.

40. Josie Ensor, "Syrian Warplanes Take Off Once again from Air Base Bombed by US Tomahawks," *The Telegraph*, April 8, 2017, www.telegraph.co.uk/news/2017/04/08/syrian-warplanes-take-air-base-bombed-us-tomahawks/.

41. "President Assad: We Will Continue Fighting and Crushing Terrorists…," Syrian Arab News Agency, August 20, 2017, www.sana.sy/?p=610816.

42. David E. Sanger, Eric Schmitt, and Ben Hubbard, "Trump Ends Covert Aid to Syrian Rebels Trying to Topple Assad," *New York Times*, July 19, 2017, www.nytimes.com/2017/07/19/world/ middleeast/cia-arming-syrian-rebels.html.

43. "Russia Has Fooled the US Again in Syria" (editorial), *Washington Post*, January 11, 2018, www.washingtonpost.com/opinions/global-opinions/russia-has-fooled-the-us-again -in-syria/2018/01/11/a3e5879c-f6fe-11e7-a9e3-ab18ce41436a_story.html?utm_term =.c5fdc877ede2.

44. UN Human Rights Council, *Report of the Independent International Commission of Inquiry on the Syrian Arab Republic*, United Nations General Assembly, Official Document System of the United Nations, August 8, 2017, last accessed on November 6, 2018, https://documents -dds-ny.un.org/doc/UNDOC/GEN/172/341/8x/pdf/1723418.pdf?OpenElement.

45. Rick Gladstone, "In UN Showdown, Russian Veto Kills Syria Chemical Arms Panel," *New York Times*, November 16, 2017, www.nytimes.com/2017/11/16/world/middleeast/ syria-chemical-weapons-united-nations.html.

46. Nahed.t.o (Instagram account), photograph of Mustafa Tlass and his grandson in Nahed Tlass-Ojjeh's apartment was seen by the author before the Instagram account was made private, https://www.instagram.com/nahed.t.o/?hl=en.

47. Manaf Tlass, June 2017.

48. Khaled al-Khani, in discussion with the author, August 2017.

49. Violations Documentation Center (VDC) in Syria database, http://vdc-sy.net/en/. The VDC documented the death of 2,450 civilians in the Damascus suburbs during the period January 1, 2018–April 30, 2018.

50. Marc Bennetts, "Putin: Syria War Is Priceless for Testing Our New Weapons," *Times* (London), June 8, 2018, www.thetimes.co.uk/article/putin-syria-war-is-priceless-for-testing -our-new-weapons-qkz3qsdqw.

51. Human Rights Watch, *Russia Backs Syria in Unlawful Attacks on Eastern Ghouta*, March 18, 2018, www.hrw.org/news/2018/03/18/russia-backs-syria-unlawful-attacks-eastern-ghouta.

52. Rick Gladstone and Maggie Haberman, "Horrific Details on Syria Chemical Attacks Left Out, for Now, from UN Report," *New York Times*, June 20, 2018, www.nytimes .com/2018/06/20/world/middleeast/un-syria-eastern-ghouta.html.

53. Liz Sly and Louisa Loveluck, "Assad Is Defiant as US-led Strikes in Syria Show No Sign of Threatening His Hold on Power," *Washington Post*, April 14, 2018, www.washingtonpost .com/world/damascus-defiant-as-trump-orders-strikes-after-syria-chemical-attack/ 2018/04/14/5ec055a6-3f5c-11e8-955b-7d2e19b79966_story.html?utm_term=.f7e 3f2c6c457.

54. Damascus resident who spoke on condition of anonymity, in discussion with the author, December 2017.

55. Al-Khani, August 2017.

56. "Crimes en Syrie, La Justice Suisse Accusée de Lenteurs" ["Crimes in Syria, the Swiss Judiciary Is Accused of Being Slow to Respond"], Radio Télévision Suisse, September 25, 2017, www.rts.ch/play/tv/19h30/video/crimes-en-syrie-la-justice-suisse-accusee-de -lenteurs?id=8947835&fbclid=IwAR0g_kxObhmapJriNQ8CSqUIhbxRd WPRB7fq4jwfOSc3ciu5hR2JdB912II&station=a9e7621504c6959e35c3ecbe7f6bed0446cd f8da.

57. "Revelations about TRIAL International's Investigation," Trial International statement, September 25, 2017, https://trialinternational.org/latest-post/in-switzerland-proceedings -for-war-crimes-against-rifaat-al-assad/.

58. Adam Sage, "European Property Worth 691 Million Euros Seized from Assad's Uncle Rifaat," *Times* (London), March 14, 2018, www.thetimes.co.uk/article/european-property-worth-691m-seized-from-assad-s-uncle-rifaat-sx6h6w2sx.

59. Darwish, July 2017.

60. Notes from author's visit to former State Security Service (Stasi) prison in Berlin's Hohenschönhausen district, July 2017.

61. Ibid.

62. Author's notes from visit to the Syrian Center for Media and Freedom of Expression office in Berlin, July 2017.

63. Anwar al-Bunni, Mazen Darwish and Joumana Seif, in discussion with the author, July 2017.

64. "Photographs and Data from the 'Caesar-File Support Group,'" European Center for Constitutional and Human Rights, September 2017.

65. "Secretary-General Appoints Catherine Marchi-Uhel of France to Head International Impartial Independent Mechanism Investigating Serious Crimes in Syria," United Nations press release, July 3, 2017.

66. Rick Gladstone, "UN Documents Syrian War Crimes, but Prosecution Moves Slowly," *New York Times*, April 24, 2017, www.nytimes.com/2017/04/24/world/middleeast/un-syria-war-crimes.html.

67. "Spanish Court Case Tests the Challenges of Universal Jurisdiction on Syrians," Global Voices in partnership with *Syria Untold*, October 2, 2017, https://globalvoices.org/2017/10/02/spanish-court-case-tests-the-challenges-of-universal-jurisdiction-on-syrians/.

68. Darwish, August 2017.

69. Mazen Darwish, Laureate Freedom of Speech Award 2016, Roosevelt Four Freedoms, www.fourfreedoms.nl/en/laureates/year:2016/award:freedom-of-speech-award/laureates:mazen-darwish.htm.

70. Darwish, August 2017.

71. Ibid.

72. Farnaz Fassihi, "UN's Special Envoy to Syria Calling It Quits," *Wall Street Journal*, October 17, 2018, www.wsj.com/articles/u-n-s-special-envoy-to-syria-calling-it-quits-1539817930.

73. Darwish, August 2017.

74. Jörg Diehl, Christoph Reuter, and Fidelius Schmid, "Germany Takes Aim at Assad's Torture Boss," *Spiegel Online*, June 8, 2018, www.spiegel.de/international/world/senior-assad-aid-charged-with-war-crimes-a-1211923.html.

75. Sam Dagher, "A Cruel Epilogue to the Syrian Civil War," *The Atlantic*, August 15, 2018, www.theatlantic.com/international/archive/2018/08/lists-of-dead-in-syria-assad/567559/.

76. Sam Dagher, "Assad Has Made His Allies Think He's Indispensable," *The Atlantic*, July 31, 2018, www.theatlantic.com/international/archive/2018/07/assad-israel-putin-iran/566423/.

77. Noa Landau, "Analysis—Russia–Israel Deal Is Clear: Iran away from Border, Assad's Rule Accepted," *Haaretz*, July 15, 2018, www.haaretz.com/middle-east-news/syria/.premium-russia-israel-deal-iran-away-from-border-assad-s-rule-accepted-1.6269407.

78. Experts and officials who received copies of the Russian plan, in discussion with the author, July 2018.

79. "Mustafa Tlass' Daughter Defends the Displacement Agreement in the Homs Countryside and Guarantees that Only Russian Forces will Enter (Audio Recording)," *Al Jisr Satellite Television* website, May 3, 2018. http://jisrtv.com/-أخبار-الجسر/الأخبار-السورية/ابنة-مصطفى-طلاس-تدافع-عن-اتفاق-التهجير-في-ريف-حمص،-وتتعهد-بدخول-القوات-الروسية-فقط/تسجيل-صوتي.

Notes

80. Manaf Tlass, December 2018.

81. "RAW: Al-Rastan Receives Russian Humanitarian Aid Along Reopened Hama-Homs Highway," YouTube video, 1:09, posted by "Russia Today," September 11, 2017. https://www.youtube.com/watch?v=ieU8pZpAzds.

82. Sam Dagher, "Assad Is Desperate for Soldiers," *The Atlantic*, May 14, 2018, www.theatlantic.com/international/archive/2018/05/syria-assad-conscription-refugees-lebanon/560282/.

83. Ali Fathollah-Nejad, "Iranians Respond to the Regime: 'Leave Syria Alone!'" *Al Jazeera English* website, May 2, 2018, www.aljazeera.com/indepth/opinion/iranians-respond-regime-leave-syria-180501081025309.html.

84. Sam Dagher, "The Families Who Sacrificed Everything for Assad," *The Atlantic*, April 12, 2018, www.theatlantic.com/international/archive/2018/04/assad-alawite-syria/557810/.

85. "Man in the News: The Assads Clip the Nails of Their Kinsman Ayman Jaber," *Enab Baladi*, June 1, 2016, www.enabbaladi.net/archives/232365.

86. Manaf Tlass, December 2018.

87. Neil MacFarquhar and Andrew E. Kramer, "Putin Welcomes US Withdrawal from Syria as 'Correct'," *The New York Times*, December 20, 2018, https://www.nytimes.com/2018/12/20/world/europe/putin-trump-syria.html.

88. Richard Spencer, "Sudan Despot in Syria for 'Genocide Summit'," *The Times*, December 18, 2018, https://www.thetimes.co.uk/article/sudan-despot-in-syria-for-assad-genocide-summit-rzh7830wf.

89. Marc Daou, "Thaw in Relations Between Arab Leaders and Syria's Assad," *France 24*, January 4, 2019. https://www.france24.com/en/20190104-syria-bashar-al-assad-diplomacy-uae-russia-iran-arab-league-saudi-arabia.

90. Manaf Tlass, December 2018.

91. Sally Masalmeh, Facebook post, July 18, 2018.

92. Notes from author's trip to Rügen to meet Sally Masalmeh and Malek al-Jawabra, January 2017.

93. Ibid.

94. Ibid.

Index

Index

Index

Assad, Bashar (cont.)
and International Criminal Court, ICC
  (and war crime trials), 261, 281, 291,
  303, 432–33, 455
and international response to chemical-
  weapons attack, 384–85
and Iran protection of [Bashar] and
  support [for Bashar], xix, xxiv, xxvi, 6,
  101, 110–11, 122, 125–26, 137,
  151–52, 153, 159, 208, 245–46, 249,
  250, 261, 269, 271, 289, 293, 299,
  311, 323–24, 334, 335, 337, 346, 348,
  356, 374–75, 390, 391, 407, 433, 448,
  451, 458
and Iran mutual defense pact, 126
and support for Iraq insurgency, 127–28,
  253
and Iraq War, xxiv, 113, 114
and ISIS, 369–70, 373–74
Walid Jumblatt and, 249–50
John Kerry and, 149–51, 345
kidnapping threat during teen years, 48–49
and Kurds, 14–15, 164, 395
and Lebanon, 86, 88–89, 104, 110–11,
  112, 118–19, 123, 126, 143, 152, 153
and Lebanon War (2006), 124
in London, 78–79
and Makhlouf family business dealings,
  130–31, 157, 158
Nouri al-Maliki and, 335
marriage to Asma al-Akhras, 102–4
and massacres committed by generals and
  warlords empowered by him, 354–56
meeting with Lakhdar Brahimi, 348–49
meeting with Russian press/media (March
  2015), 407
and modernization of Syria, 155–56
oil deal with Saddam Hussein, 110
and ophthalmology (eye surgery) career and
  references, xix, 6, 76, 78, 134, 206
on opposition as terrorists, 343–44
in Paris, 145–46. See also Paris
and personal life before marriage, 78–79,
  89, 90–91, 102
and PKK, 395
preparation for assumption of power,
  81–94
and the press, 115–16. See also media
principles for maintaining power, 121–22

pro-regime rallies during Arab Spring
  protests, 260–61, 263–64
and Putin, 369, 387, 408. See also Putin,
  Vladimir
rebuilding of army, 458
release of Islamist militants from prison in
  early 2011, 253
and religious minorities, 13, 406
response to international advice on protest
  situation, 209
response to protests, 182–83, 210–11, 218
and Russia, 249, 250, 262, 300, 301, 323,
  379, 380, 407–8, 449, 458
and sanctions, 148, 152, 262, 263, 280,
  281, 292, 293, 351, 352, 357, 430
and Saudis, 101, 104, 314–15, 445
secure position at end of 2018, 459
selective pardoning of prisoners, 16
Assef Shawkat and, 94, 135–36, 281, 309–13
and Assef Shawkat death and its aftermath
  312–13
shyness as child and adult, 43–44, 90–91,
  111, 408
and social reform, 155–56
and social media. See media and social media
as source of destruction and war crimes
  surpassing ISIS, xix
speech to parliament on March 30, 2011,
  in response to protests, 188–92
and starving opposition areas until they
  surrender or die. See siege and starve
  campaigns
and Sunnis, 159–60
swearing in as president in 2000, 100–101
Syrian Journalists Union speech (during
  2006 Lebanon war), 124–25
Manaf Tlass and, 3–4, 115, 120, 223–24,
  263–68, 318–19, 390–91. See also Tlass,
  Manaf
Mustafa Tlass and, 7, 95–97, 138, 450. See
  also Tlass, Mustafa
Tlass family and, 114–15, 137–39
Tlass–Makhlouf rivalry and, 113, 114
Total oil partnership, 142–43
and trinity of regime hard-liners, 288–89
and Trump, 443–44
UN Security Council member state foreign
  ministers' discussions June 2012 on
  future of, 300–302

540

Index

Index

Index

chemical weapons *(cont.)*
  meetings in Turkey between Alawite officers and Manaf Tlass after attacks, 394
  Obama and, xxvi, 326, 350, 375, 380–88
Cherubim Monastery, 70
Chevallier, Éric, 153, 157–58, 207–9, 256–58, 262, 265–67, 279, 291, 292, 316, 338
China
  and Bashar's crackdown on 2011 protesters, 246
  thinking on Bashar's suppression of protests, xxvi, 445
  and Hillary Clinton call to abandon Bashar, 308
  "Thank you, China" graffiti in Damascus, 362
  and Obama motion at G20 2013 to condemn Bashar's use of chemical weapons, 386
  in Trump era, 445
  and UN meeting on Bashar's future, 300, 302–3
  veto of UN Syria resolutions, 262, 282–83, 323, 347, 362
Chirac, Jacques, 88, 91–94, 99, 101, 108, 111, 116, 118, 143, 144, 148
  and Bashar's assumption of power, 101
  and lunch with Bashar as heir, 93–94
  and decorating Bashar with Legion of Honor, 118
  and Hafez's funeral, 99
  Rafic Hariri and, 88
  and Syria's public finance system, 116
chlorine, 396–97
Christians, 372
  Abbaseen Square attempted protests 2011, 214
  Assads' narrative and public image as protectors of, 206, 360, 429–32
  and anti-Bashar activism and protests, 429
  church leaders support for Bashar, 428–29
  in Homs, 274, 275
  in Lebanon, 45–47
  and Hama massacre, 13
  Putin and, 427–32
civil liberties, 106
civil war/sectarian war in Syria after 2011, 274–75, 294, 316, 334, 349, 456
Clinton, Bill, xxiv
  breakdown of Syria–Israeli peace talks, 102

1994 Geneva meeting with Hafez al-Assad, 73–75
  and Syrian presence in Lebanon, 86–87
Clinton, Hillary, 153, 447
  on chemical weapons, 350
  at Group of Friends of the Syrian People conference, 308
  and no-fly zone discussions, 337–38
  Trump's comments on, 436
  and UN meeting on Bashar's future, 302–3
Cold War, xxiii, 23, 24
Colvin, Marie, xvii–xviii, 283
Committees for the Revival of Civil Society, 105
Conroy, Paul, 283
constitution, Syrian, 39, 95, 96, 187, 188, 289, 301, 349, 367, 372, 410, 425, 456
Coordination Chrétiens d'Orient en Danger, 430
Coppola, Francis Ford, 156
corruption, and Assad family/regime
  corruption amid claims of fighting it, xxi, 9, 46–47, 69–70, 71, 84, 86, 92–93, 97, 100, 107, 116, 125 130, 131, 154, 157–159, 160, 228, 413
  as reason for Arab Spring protests in Syria, 160, 167–68, 175, 182, 208, 413
coup d'état (1961), 26
coup d'état (1963), 27–28
coup d'état (by Hafez 1970), 7, 32–33
Crimea, 389
Crisis Cell, 288, 289, 310–12
cyberwarfare, 380, 384. *See also* Russia and disinformation

Dalila, Aref, 108
Damascus
  Arab Spring protests, 165
  and Arab Spring protests, 8–9
  2011 car bombing, 271
  Charlie Hebdo protests at French embassy, 317
  and 1963 coup, 28
  Eid al-Fitr attack on Bashar's neighborhood, 376–77
  and 2014 election, 373
  image Assad regime wanted foreign visitors to see during war, 361–64
  Libyan embassy protests, 9–12
  map, xii
  2012 massacres in suburbs of, 355

Index

Index

Hamza and Abbas mosque, Daraa, 161

Hannoun, Milad (Asma al-Assad's hairdresser and fashion consultant), 357

Hariri, Rafic, 79, 87–89, 91–94, 112, 114, 118, 127–29, 138, 143, 144, 147, 154, 188, 247, 248, 307

    aftermath of assassination, 121–24

    assassination of, xxiv, 119, 120

    and Bashar's lunch with Chirac, 93–94

    and Bashar's swearing in as president, 101

    reelection as prime minister, 104

    and first meeting with Bashar in 1995, 88

    called "agent of America and France" and enemy of Syria by Bashar, 119

Hassan, Bassam al-, 223–24, 326

Hassan, Jamil, 172, 251–52, 288, 290, 291, 297, 333, 359, 366–67, 457

Hassan, Suheil al-, 355

Hassan, Wissam al-, 307

Hassoun, Ahmad Badreddine, 360, 361, 363, 430, 446

Hatoum, Salim, 31, 32

Heinz, Teresa, 149–51

Henning Larsen architects, 205

Hezbollah, 112, 114, 118–20, 125, 135, 137, 143, 147, 149–53, 181, 189, 190, 208, 255, 258, 261, 278, 293, 332–34, 345, 356, 362, 373, 381, 399, 410, 426, 428, 433, 439, 457

    assumption of Syria's role in Lebanon, 126

    Bashar and, xix, 110–11, 122, 125–26

    and Bashar's relation with Sunnis, 159

    and Cedar Revolution, 123

    and *Defa Moghadas*, 331

    in Homs, 374–75, 399

    and Israel's role in Syrian conflict, 348

    and Lebanon War (2006), 123–25

    Maher al-Assad and, 129

    Mughniyeh assassination, 136

    Raed Saleh and, 406–7

    Saudis and, 315

    Assef Shawkat and, 310

    and Southern Storm, 415

    and recruitment of Shiites to fight in Syria, 334, 374–75, 406–7

    support for Syrian government forces, 323

    and Syrian army, 289

    and Syrian protesters in Golan Heights, 245–46

and Manaf Tlass's defection, 307

Hollande, François, 301, 308, 382–84, 424–26, 430

Homs, xvii–xviii

    Baba Amr attacks, 273–76, 281, 282–84, 287–88

    1964 demonstrations, 29, 30

    Iran-planned operations in, 374–75

    2012 and 2013 massacres, 355

    poison-gas attack on, 350

    2011 protests, 214–18, 261

    Assef Shawkat's truce mission, 281

    Tadmor prison in desert of, xx, 225, 241, 442

    UN aid for, 399–402

Homs military academy, 20, 47, 60, 82–83

Houla, Al-, 294

human rights (and abuses), xxiii, 15, 74, 91, 247, 263, 403

Human Rights Watch, 56, 283

human trafficking, 416

humanitarian agencies and aid, xx, 292, 301, 362, 379, 397–403, 414, 428, 430

Hungary, 417–18

hurriyeh, 4, 11, 161, 166, 244, 444

Hussein, Saddam, 13, 35, 71, 74, 84, 86, 112, 113, 136, 335, 336, 343, 347

    Baghdadi and, 370–71

    collapse of regime and sectarian war, 128

    and Gulf War (1990–91), xxiii, 72

    Iran–Iraq War, 331

    and Jabers, 351

    loyalists in Syria, 127

    rise to power, 49

    Assef Shawkat and, 310

    sons Qusay and Uday in Syria after US invasion of Iraq, 127

    Syrian cooperation in circumventing oil embargo, 110

    toppling of regime, 109

Hussein (king of Jordan), 33

Hussein (grandson of prophet Mohammad), 330, 331, 332, 334, 375

Idlib, 50, 293, 324–25, 327, 402, 405, 449, 460

Ignatius, David, 148

Imperial Orthodox Palestine Society, 428

Independence Uprising (Cedar Revolution), 123

Index

551

Index

Index

Index

Index

Index

Index

561

Index

Index

About the Author

SAM DAGHER has reported in the Middle East for more than fifteen years, including for the *Wall Street Journal* and the *New York Times*, and has covered the Iraq War and Arab Spring uprisings. The *Journal* nominated Dagher's work from Syria for the Pulitzer Prize.